IDAHO'S 200 Cities

The Southwest

Learning about Idaho and each of its 200 incorporated cities
– Their Past – Their Present – and Their Future

Volume 2 of 3

IDAHO'S
200 CITIES
The Southwest
Volume 2 of 3

Their Past – Their Present
– and Their Future

Edited by Hal Bunderson

A Project of
The Association of Idaho Cities

Ridenbaugh Press
Carlton, Oregon
2017

IDAHO'S 200 CITIES: THE SOUTHWEST
Copyright ©2017 by the Association of Idaho Cities
All rights reserved. No part of this book may be reproduced or transmitted in any form, by any information storage or retrieval system, without written permission from the publisher, except in case of brief quotations used in critical articles or reviews.
For more information, contact Ridenbaugh Press, P.O. Box 834, Carlton OR 97111.
Printed and bound in the United States of America.
First edition October 2017
10 9 8 7 6 5 4 3 2 1

Library of Congress Cataloging in Publication Data

Association of Idaho Cities.

History – Idaho – cities

Bibliography

1. History. 2. Idaho.

I. Association of Idaho Cities. II. Title.

ISBN-13 978-0-945648-42-0 (softbound)

For more information, or to order more copies of this book, contact:

Ridenbaugh Press
P.O. Box 834, Carlton OR 97111
Phone (503) 852-0010
www.ridenbaugh.com
stapilus@ridenbaugh.com

The Association of Idaho Cities has produced Idaho's 200 Cities for the three-fold purpose of:

- Fostering goodwill, knowledge and understanding of each of Idaho's three Regions and 200 Incorporated Cities
- Helping Idahoans, in fact and at heart, learn of our shared rich heritage
- Promoting economic development and strategic planning in Idaho and in each of its 200 incorporated cities and 44 counties

Proceeds from the sale of Idaho's 200 Cities will finance the not-for-profit purposes of The Association of Idaho Cities.

The Association of Idaho Cities thanks all of the volunteers and staff – too numerous to list – for their contributions to this work.

Table of Contents

Foreword
Preface

The Region 1
Distinctive Geographic and Geologic Features 1
American Indians 3
Early Trappers/Explorers 5
Early Christian Missionaries 7
Oregon and California Trails 8
Idaho Territory 8
Gem State 14
Federal Lands 14
Agriculture and Irrigation 17
Livestock 19
Mining 21
Forest Products 27
Loss of Economic Dominance 33
Railroads 37
Hydroelectric Dams 37
World War II   38
National Wilderness Areas 41
Institutions of Higher Learning 41
Southwestern Idaho's Entrepreneurial Legacy 42
The Region's Economic Base 43

Ada County 44
Boise 29
Eagle 60
Garden City 70
Kuna 77
Meridian 86
Star 95
Adams County 103
Council 104
New Meadows 109
Blaine County 117
Bellevue 118
Carey 125
Hailey 129
Ketchum 139
Sun Valley 145
Boise County 154
Crouch 155
Horseshoe Bend 158
Idaho City 163
Placerville 171
Camas County 177
Fairfield 178
Canyon County 185
Caldwell 186
Greenleaf 198
Melba 206
Middleton 213

Nampa 222   Parma 241
Notus 233   Wilder 250

Cassia County 256
Albion 257   Malta 279
Burley 265   Oakley 284
Declo 274

Elmore County 294
Glenns Ferry 295   Mountain Home 303

Gem County 311
Emmett 312

Gooding County 320
Bliss 321   Hagerman 335
Gooding 328   Wendell 345

Jerome County 352
Eden 353   Jerome 365
Hazelton 359

Lincoln County 374
Dietrich 375   Shoshone 385
Richfield 380

Minidoka County 392
Acequia 393   Paul 410
Heyburn 399   Rupert 417
Minidoka 405

Owyhee County 424
Grand View 425   Marsing 440
Homedale 433

Payette County 446
Fruitland 447   Payette 458
New Plymouth 453

Twin Falls County 466
Buhl 467   Hollister 494
Castleford 475   Kimberly 499
Filer 479   Murtaugh 506
Hansen 487   Twin Falls 510

Valley County 521
Cascade 522   McCall 533
Donnelly 526

Washington County 543
Cambridge 544   Weiser 552
Midvale 549

Bibliography 559

Foreword

Idaho's 200 Cities is a six-volume book project that tells the story of Idaho through the history and development of its communities. Three of the books cover history and background about the three north, southwest and east regions of the state; three additional volumes consist of trivia questions and answers.

The project was conceived in 2004 by former Idaho State Senator Hal Bunderson of Meridian who served seven terms in the Idaho Senate and chaired the Senate Local Government & Taxation Committee. During his service in the Legislature, Bunderson was a passionate advocate for local government. He believed policymakers would benefit from a resource that would help them better understand Idaho's communities and their history, opportunities and challenges.

Bunderson presented his novel idea at an Association of Idaho Cities annual conference, generously offering to volunteer his time and expenses to complete this ambitious work if AIC and the cities would do their part. The conference delegates responded with a standing ovation, and the AIC Board unanimously approved the project. Bunderson's late wife, Mary Kay, joined him in his commitment. As Executive Director of AIC, I invited four experts to form a Blue-Ribbon panel of reviewers and editors to read each pre-final draft chapter approved by Senator Bunderson and offer comment:

- Bob Fick, longtime Associated Press Correspondent and Administrative Support Manager for the Idaho Department of Labor;
- Keith Petersen, formerly Idaho State Historian and Associate Director of the Idaho State Historical Society;
- Martin Peterson, former State Budget Director, Executive Director of the Association of Idaho Cities, and Special Assistant to the President of the University of Idaho; and
- Dr. James Weatherby, former Executive Director of the Association of Idaho Cities and Director of the Public Policy Center at Boise State University.

GayDawn Oyler, AIC Administrative Assistant, was designated to manage and control the work on each of the 203 chapters and trivia. In addition to her normal workload, she monitored and managed the progress on hundreds of draft manuscripts and communication between the cities and volunteers, and between Senator Bunderson and the Blue-Ribbon Panel.

As soon as the Board approved the project, Bunderson and AIC staff set about designing the book format and structure as a template for writing the city chapters. The Blue Ribbon Panel and the AIC Board approved the format. Mayors appointed city staff and citizens to help in providing original research and writing their city's chapter using the standard chapter format. Bunderson then led the effort of compiling, editing and writing where necessary, each of the city chapters. He also wrote the regional chapters and trivia books.

Over 100 people contributed several thousand hours of research, writing, proofing and editing for this project. AIC is grateful for the excellent work of these many volunteers. The purposes of this project are five-fold.

1. Promote Economic Development: The books provide valuable information for people considering moving their residence or business to or within Idaho. In a short period of time, people can learn the essential information about a city: its population, elevation, climate, geology, amenities and attractions, economy and major industries, education, health care, transportation, and utilities and services. They can also learn about the history of each city, including the pre-incorporation years, incorporation, turning points and Vision for 2050.

2. Support Long-Term Planning: AIC encourages long-range planning by cities with input from their business leaders and citizens. Over 70 percent of Idaho residents live in incorporated cities and the vast majority of Idaho's jobs and economic activity are located in cities. Idaho's wellbeing depends in large measure on the health and vitality of its cities, which is grounded in long term land use and strategic plans adopted at the local level.

3. Encourage Statewide Unity: Technology has revolutionized the way we live. The geographic, demographic and cultural barriers of the past are losing their significance. The diverse communities of Idaho have much more in common than many people realize. Understanding our shared histories and vision helps us recognize that life is better when we work together for the common good.

4. Education: These volumes are intended to provide a fun, easy way to learn highlights of Idaho history—the warts and the roses. The trivia may also be used to add interest to school history classes, as well as parties and family reunions.

5. Vision for the Future: These volumes offer a projection of what each city may look like in 2050. Going forward, it may assist city officials and candidates for public office with a better opportunity to contemplate, articulate and communicate their vision for their city or political jurisdiction.

While special care has been taken to ensure sound research and accuracy, there may still be errors. AIC invites public comment and additional trivia (with documentation) that may be considered for subsequent editions.

Proceeds from the sale of the books, net of production and publishing costs, will finance nonprofit purposes of the Association of Idaho Cities.

This book project is affectionately dedicated to Senator Hal Bunderson and his wife, Mary Kay. Senator Bunderson's dedicated service to the State of Idaho and its communities is best reflected in these words by Henry Wadsworth Longfellow:

"The heights by great men reached and kept
Were not attained by sudden flight,
But they, while their companions slept,
Were toiling upward in the night."

Ken Harward
AIC Executive Director (1998-2014)

Idaho's Cities: The Basics

Idaho's 200 cities display a wealth of diversity that reflects the social, economic, geographic and political diversity of our state. Despite these differences, Idaho cities have much in common. All look to the Idaho Constitution and state laws governing the creation, form, powers and limitations of city governments. Similarly, all municipal corporations, regardless of population size, operate under the same laws and are referred to as "cities."

About the Association of Idaho Cities

The Association of Idaho Cities (AIC) was founded in 1947 and is a nonpartisan, nonprofit corporation owned, organized and operated by Idaho's city governments. The association's mission is to promote excellence in, and advocate for, city governance, community leadership, and services to citizens to strengthen Idaho cities. AIC provides vital training, technical assistance and advocacy for Idaho's 200 incorporated cities. The organization is governed by a Board of Directors of city elected officials representing seven geographical districts.

Cities by the Numbers

- Idaho has 200 incorporated cities.
- Cities range in population from 218,281 in Boise to a low of 3 in Warm River, a tiny resort community in Fremont County (2016 U.S. Census estimates).
- There are 1,084 elected city mayors and councilors serving their communities.
- 70% of Idahoans choose to live within cities, a percentage that has been steadily increasing over the years.
- To keep Idaho communities safe there are currently 1,300 police officers, 2,700 career fire fighters, and 7,300 volunteer fire fighters responding to emergency service calls.
- Cities are responsible for 2,600 centerline miles of streets and 267 bridges.
- Cities have invested $1 billion in wastewater treatment facilities and treat over 5.84 billion gallons of wastewater each year.
- Cities have invested $475 million in drinking water treatment and delivery facilities.
- Idaho public libraries have 4.3 million print materials in circulation and nearly 1,600 public access Internet terminals.
- Idaho cities have invested $40 million in swimming pools, $90 million in parks and playground equipment, and $35 million in ballparks, tennis courts and skate parks.
- There are over 5,000 acres of city parks and open space, and over 150 miles of developed greenbelts and pathways.

Pre-Statehood

Before Idaho achieved statehood in 1890, the Territorial Legislature granted city charters to three cities: Boise, Lewiston and Bellevue. These charters covered the form of government, powers and responsibilities, taxes and revenue, indebtedness, elections, and the city's ability to grow through annexation.

Lewiston and Boise abandoned their territorial charters in the 1960s when voters approved transitioning the cities to operate under state law.

Bellevue still retains its city charter, which has several distinctive elements relative to other Idaho cities. Members of the city governing body are called aldermen instead of councilors, and the mayor and aldermen are elected to two-year terms (elected officials in cities operating under state law generally serve four-year terms). The Legislature must approve any changes to Bellevue's charter.

Incorporation of New Cities

Any community with a population of 125 or more qualified electors can file a petition for incorporation with the County Commissioners in the County in which it is located. The petition must be signed by 60% of the qualified electors of the proposed city, and must include the name and boundaries of the proposed city. The County Commissioners then have guidelines to follow, including calculating the distance between the petitioning community and any other already incorporated cities in the area, before granting the incorporation request. If the request is granted, a copy of the Articles of Incorporation and the approval are filed with the Secretary of State's Office.

Classification of Cities, Recodification of the Municipal Code

Before 1967, Idaho law provided for three classifications of cities—first class cities, second class cities and villages—with the classifications based on population. Within these three classes of cities, the law provided for four different forms of government: mayor-council, council-manager, commission and village.

Cities in each class operated under different provisions of law concerning the structure, powers and duties of city government, and these laws were amended many times over several decades. The need to modernize and simplify municipal government laws led to a recodification of the municipal code, which was passed by the Idaho Legislature in 1967.

Under the new municipal code, all city classes were abolished and the forms of government were reduced to two: the mayor-council and council-manager. All cities, from the largest in population to the smallest, would operate under the same laws and be called "cities," (except for charter cities). The recodified municipal code was much more streamlined, considerably shorter in length and easier for people to understand.

Forms of City Government

The mayor-council form of government is established by Idaho law as the default form of city government, with a mayor and either four or six councilors. The term of office for mayors and councilors is normally four-years; however, there are occasionally two-year council terms that occur when a vacancy arises in the first two years of the four-year term.

Elections for city mayors and councilors are held in November of odd-numbered years.

At local option, cities may adopt the council-manager form of government, with a five or seven-member council and a professional city manager serving at the pleasure of the council. Currently, only the cities of Lewiston, McCall and Twin Falls operate under the council-manager form of city government.

In council-manager cities, the mayor is selected by the council from among its members at the first meeting in January following a general city election for a two-year term. The mayor's primary role is in chairing council meetings, and the mayor is entitled to vote on all matters before the council, but exercises no tie-breaking or veto power.

The city manager is responsible for overseeing the administration of the city, ensuring that city laws and policies are faithfully executed, appointing department heads, advising the council of the city's financial condition, preparing and submitting a tentative budget for the upcoming fiscal year, and other duties as prescribed by the council.

Roles and Responsibilities

In cities operating under the mayor-council form of government, the mayor is the chief executive and administrative official of the city and has the following powers and responsibilities:

- Breaking tie votes of the council;
- Serving as the presiding officer at council meetings;
- May veto ordinances passed by the council, subject to council override by a majority of the full council;
- Ensuring that city and state laws are enforced;
- Supervising city employees; and
- Performing marriage ceremonies.

The city council is the legislative governing body for the city and has the following powers and responsibilities:

- Adopting local laws (ordinances),
- Determining what services will be provided by the city and the fees for these services,
- Adopting the city budget,
- Setting the city's property tax levy, and
- Receiving financial reports from the city treasurer.

Powers of City Government

Article XII, Section 1 of the Idaho Constitution charges the Idaho Legislature with responsibility to "provide by general laws for the incorporation, organization and classification of the cities and towns, in proportion to the population, which laws may be altered, amended, or repealed by the general laws."

Most of the laws governing cities are found in Title 50 of Idaho Code, titled Municipal Corporations, which defines:

- Forms of city government;
- How to incorporate new cities and disincorporate cities that no longer need to function;
- The process for enlarging the city through annexing adjacent land;
- Roles and responsibilities of the mayor, council, and other city officials;
- How to pass local laws (ordinances);
- City budgeting and finances; and
- Use of urban renewal and tax increment financing to address urban blight and promote economic development.

Cities exercise two distinctly different types of powers: governmental powers and proprietary powers.

- **Governmental Powers:** The most prominent is the police power, which vests cities with authority to pass laws to protect the public health, safety and welfare, provided the laws do not conflict with state or federal law. The police power is derived from Article XII, Section 2 of the Idaho Constitution. Other governmental powers include the powers of taxation, eminent domain and annexation and are derived from laws enacted by the Idaho Legislature.
- **Proprietary Powers:** Cities are empowered to provide certain business-type services for the benefit of citizens and businesses in the city, such as water and sewer service, solid waste collection, street maintenance, parks, airports, etc. Cities derive their proprietary powers from laws enacted by the Idaho Legislature.

How Do Cities Relate to Other Units of Government?

In our federal system of government, the federal government is supreme and cities must comply with federal law and the United States Constitution.

The situation is similar at the state level: the Idaho Legislature and the Idaho Constitution is supreme to all local governments in Idaho and the Legislature exercises considerable control over local governments through policymaking.

Cities are unique among local governments because they are created by their citizens to provide needed services for the community, and cities exercise both governmental and proprietary powers.

In contrast, counties are created by the State of Idaho to perform a mix of state mandated and discretionary functions.

- Counties are empowered by Article XII, Section 2 of the Idaho Constitution to adopt ordinances to protect public health, safety and welfare. County ordinances only apply to the unincorporated territory of the county—cities have police power authority within city limits.
- Counties serve as an arm of the state in administering the property tax system, courts, law enforcement, jails, disaster planning and preparedness, and elections at the local level.

- Other state mandated county services include: indigent medical care, public defenders for indigent criminal defendants, juvenile corrections, planning and zoning, roads and bridges, landfills, and weed control.
- County discretionary functions include: airports, ambulance service, hospitals, parks and recreation, fairs, agricultural extension, and historical societies and museums.

Special districts—highway, cemetery, water/sewer, recreation, library, etc.—are formed by citizen petition to provide necessary and desired services in a specific geographic area and have no regulatory authority.

Cities' Roles in Economic Development

Cities are the engine of Idaho's economy and city officials work in partnership with the Idaho Department of Commerce to attract and retain businesses. The infrastructure cities provide—water, sewer, streets, and stormwater drainage—is an essential factor for businesses deciding where to locate.

Over 40 Idaho communities have urban renewal agencies, which finance infrastructure to make sites ready for new businesses, as well as revitalize deteriorating downtown areas.

An urban renewal plan is adopted by the city council that identifies the work that needs to be done in an area and the funding sources that will pay for the projects. Most urban renewal projects are financed through tax increment financing, which dedicates property tax revenue from development within the area to urban renewal projects.

One of the most powerful economic development incentives in Idaho is the Tax Reimbursement Incentive (TRI), which offers a tax credit of up to 30% on income, payroll and sales taxes for up to 15 years. The incentive is available for a broad range of industries, including aerospace, agriculture, food processing and high-tech, and it is open to existing businesses looking to expand and businesses new to Idaho.

To be eligible for the incentive, the business must:
- Create at least 20 new jobs in rural areas, or at least 50 new jobs in urban areas;
- New jobs must be full-time (30 hours or more) and pay equal to or greater than the average county wage;
- The community must provide a meaningful match, which can be met through in-kind work done by city employees or through the capital investment property tax exemption;
- The company must prove its stability and a significant economic impact to the community and state; and
- The company must provide that the incentive is a critical factor in its decision to locate or expand.

Another economic development incentive often used with the TRI is the capital investment property tax exemption. Businesses that invest a certain amount in new non-retail commercial or industrial facilities can receive a full or partial exemption of property taxes on the new facility and equipment for up to five years. The county commissioners determine the minimum level of capital investment, which must be at least $500,000.

The TRI and capital investment property tax exemption have a proven track record of success in attracting and retaining businesses.

Amy's Kitchen, the nation's leading maker of organic and non-GMO convenience food, purchased the 500,000-square foot facility in Pocatello formerly operated by Heinz. Amy's currently employs approximately 400 employees. When the project is fully staffed over 15 years, the economic impact to the state of Idaho is expected to include new capital investment of $76 million, new total wages of $342 million and new direct state tax revenue of $30 million. Amy's Kitchen received a 26% TRI credit over 15 years and a 75% property tax exemption for capital investment over five years.

Quest Aircraft expanded its existing facility in Sandpoint, adding 75,000 square feet to its production facility that builds KODIAK turboprop airplanes for backcountry and personal use. By the end of the 12-year project term, it is anticipated that there will be 187 new jobs, capital investment of $5.4 million, project wages of $75.8 million and new direct state tax revenue of $4.5 million. Quest received a 25% TRI credit over 12 years. Quest was also granted a 75% property tax exemption for its investment in buildings and structural components, and its exemption for equipment and machinery was 100% in the first two years, 75% in the third year and 50% for the fourth and fifth years.

Cities' Responsibilities in Planning and Zoning

Idahoans are fortunate to enjoy a quality of life that is envied by the rest of the country. Each year, thousands of new residents come to Idaho seeking a new way of life. This growth enhances our economy through housing construction and enlarges the local tax base; however, it also results in increased citizen demands for services and infrastructure, and can lead to development that may threaten the qualities that make our communities so special.

The growth and development of our communities is guided by the planning and land use policies of city and county governments. Under the Idaho Local Land Use Planning Act, every city and county is required to adopt a comprehensive plan, a zoning ordinance, a subdivision ordinance and area of city impact ordinances. These policies are the essential tools for growth management, allowing local officials to direct future development and protect the unique features of their community.

- Comprehensive Plan: The foundational document used to guide the growth and development of a city or county. The planning process emphasizes citizen involvement and a careful study of the social, economic, and environmental characteristics of the planning area. The result is a document that represents the community's consensus about where residential, commercial, and industrial growth should occur; ensures that public services and infrastructure are developed in the most cost-efficient way; and protects quality of life for residents.
- Zoning Ordinance: Historically zoning was used to protect residential areas from incompatible industrial uses like rendering plants. Today,

zoning is used to regulate development in floodplains and on hillsides, conserve valuable agricultural land and open space, protect drinking water sources and preserve historic neighborhoods. Zoning exists to provide a regulatory framework to implement the vision defined in the comprehensive plan. The zoning ordinance consists of two main components: the zoning map and the text of the ordinance. The zoning map shows how the city or county is divided into zoning districts. The text of the ordinance defines the zoning districts, which generally fit within the broad categories of residential, commercial, industrial and agricultural, and defines the types of land uses that are permitted, conditionally permitted and prohibited in these districts. Each zoning district also has standards for lot size, lot coverage, building height, number of stories and setbacks.

■ Subdivision Ordinance: The original purpose of subdivision regulations was to provide a simple, secure method of conveying land by requiring property to be surveyed and mapped before the owner could divide and sell the land. While subdivision regulations continue to provide a secure method of conveying land, they also ensure that land is developed consistent with the comprehensive plan and that facilities and infrastructure are constructed to serve the new development that meet minimum standards of health and safety.

■ Area of Impact Ordinance: The area of city impact is the region surrounding a city that will eventually develop and be annexed into the city. The area of city impact serves two main purposes: it defines the area for city growth and establishes the land use regulations governing the urban fringe area. The area of city impact is established by negotiation between city and county officials. These negotiations result in two ordinances: an ordinance establishing the area of city impact map; and an ordinance setting forth the comprehensive plan, zoning and subdivision regulations that will apply in the area of city impact (city, county or some combination of both). Both ordinances must be approved by the city council and the county commissioners.

The Region

This chapter profiles significant historical matters that either apply to Southwestern Idaho as a whole, multiple cities within the region or conditions and events that influenced the character, culture and heritage of Idaho and the region.

Distinctive Geographic and Geologic Features

The Southwestern Idaho region extends south from the Salmon River-the River of No Return, so called because early supply boats could only make one-way trips – for about 229 miles to the Nevada border, just under half of the 479-mile length of the state. The western half of Idaho's southern border abuts Nevada and the eastern half is shared with Utah. The region includes about two-thirds of the state's 305 mile width. Southwestern Idaho and Eastern Idaho are in the Mountain Time Zone, whereas Northern Idaho is on Pacific Time.

The region has some of the most diverse and beautifully distinctive land formations and terrain in the state. The northern and eastern parts of the region include the lower portions of the 2.5-million-acre Frank Church-River of No Return Wilderness and the rugged mountains of the Payette, Boise and Sawtooth National Forests with peaks rising to over 9,000 feet.

The upper west end of Southwestern Idaho includes the resort areas of McCall, Payette Lake, Brundage, Lake Cascade and Tamarack.

South of McCall, the forested mountains give way to a warmer and drier high-desert climate of grass and sagebrush-covered foothills that overlook Idaho's capital city of Boise and more than a dozen other Treasure Valley cities as well as several hundred thousand acres of irrigated and dry farmland and vast tracts of public lands.

The Treasure Valley was so named in 1959 by Pete Olsen of Caldwell, president of a coalition of valley chambers of commerce, who issued a proclamation declaring the nickname because, as Olsen wrote, "This valley is a virtual treasure chest of natural resources, abundant recreational and cultural opportunities, agricultural diversification (and) commercial development potential."

Two Treasure Valley counties, Ada and Canyon, have less than 3 percent of the state's landmass but over 36 percent of the state's population. National media routinely recognize the greater Boise metropolitan area as an entrepreneurial and high-technology center.

South of the Treasure Valley are the Snake River; the Snake River Birds of Prey National Conservation Area; and the Owyhee Mountains, which rise over 8,000 feet and are home to the historic Silver City mining area. This vast area encompasses millions of acres of public land, managed principally by the Bureau of Land Management, interspersed with private cattle ranches and 517,000 acres of Wilderness set aside by Congress in 2009.

These vast open areas, abutting the open high-deserts of Nevada and Oregon, provide training ranges for military personnel stationed at Mountain Home Air Force Base located on the eastern edge of this sparsely settled corner of Idaho.

On the upper northeastern side of the region are the historic mining cities of the Wood River Valley and the internationally famous Sun Valley Resort.

South of the Wood River Valley, within a 30-mile radius of Twin Falls, is the lush agricultural area of the mid-Snake River Plain called the Magic Valley. During the early 1900s the federal government and private investors built hydroelectric dams on the Snake River and other streams and complex systems of irrigation canals and ditches. Within a few years, irrigation transformed over a million acres of the sagebrush desert into an irrigated agricultural oasis – an event that happened so quickly a newspaper editor gave it the enduring name, the Magic Valley.

In Southwestern Idaho the Snake River changes its course to a northwesterly direction at Murtaugh and continues toward Idaho's most westerly point of land near Weiser before turning north to Lewiston.

Box Canyon.

Most of the 1,056-mile Snake River lies within Idaho or forms the western border of the state. There are many hydroelectric dams on the river that – along with the more than 1,000-foot-deep Snake River Aquifer that lies beneath the massive and fertile Snake River Plain – are the lifeblood of Southern Idaho's agricultural industry and many cities in the region. The Snake River drops over 9,000 feet from its starting point in western Wyoming to its confluence with the Columbia River near Kennewick, Washington. (*See Eastern Idaho, The Region, Distinctive Geographic and Geological Features – Prehistoric Lake Bonneville; and The Snake River and Snake River Aquifer.*)

Along the Snake River, stretching for over 20 miles north of Hagerman to over 40 miles southeast of the city toward Twin Falls, is an aquatic phenomenon called Thousand Springs. It is one of Idaho's more amazing Unique Natural Features. Natural springs gush from the basalt canyon walls that are as high as 600 feet above the river. At the bottom of the canyon, hundreds of underground springs percolate thousands of gallons of constant 58 degree Fahrenheit water into the river, a temperature ideal for raising trout commercially.

Several of these cold crystal springs and fisheries are units of Thousand Springs State Park. Among the individual units of the park is the 652-acre Malad Gorge Park. The Billingsley Creek unit offers fishing and horseback riding. Bird watching and the annual Thousand Springs Art Festival are at Ritter Island. Around 180,000 gallons of cold spring water tumble over waterfalls and bubble up from the crystal-clear pools at Earl M. Hardy Box Canyon Springs Nature Preserve. Niagara and Crystal Springs are at the base of the Snake River Canyon where large springs burst from the canyon walls. At Niagara Springs, water flows through the traces of state and national fish hatcheries and a beautiful public fishery near an old-growth tree-covered park.

North and east of the Magic Valley are extensive beds of volcanic basalt rock from prehistoric lava flows. These vast tracts of public lands lie in both Southwestern and Eastern Idaho and include the 750,000-acre Craters of the Moon National Monument and Preserve and Idaho's Great Rift, the source of prehistoric volcanic eruptions that produced the fertile volcanic soils and lava flows that characterize this amazing landscape. (*See Eastern Idaho, The Region, Distinctive Geographic and Geological Features – Craters of the Moon National Monument and Preserve.*)

South of the Magic Valley, the mountains of the Sawtooth National Forest rise to over 10,000 feet before dropping into the massive granite rock outcroppings of the 14,440-acre City of Rocks National Reserve near the Idaho/Utah border. The remains of a prehistoric batholith that eroded leaving massive granite rock outcroppings that resemble cathedrals, towers, domes, walls and weird shapes that rise to 600 feet high and was a rest stop for California Trail pioneers was named the "City of Rocks" by James F. Wilkens, an 1849 California Trail immigrant. These pioneers camped at the City of Rocks and marked their stay by writing on the rocks with axel grease – writings that more than 150 years of wind and storm have failed to erase.

The Sawtooth National Forest is also home to two ski resorts; Magic Mountain, about 30 miles south of Hansen, and Pomerelle,10 miles south of Albion.

While the temperatures in the mountains are cool and snow accumulations often deep, the climate on the high desert of the middle and lower Snake River Plain is generally mild. Many decades ago, over 2.5 million head of sheep grazed in Idaho's southern mountains and valleys. The Lower Snake River Plain was the place many sheepherders brought their animals for winter pastures, lambing and shearing.

American Indians

Scholar Sven Liljeblad has estimated that when Lewis and Clark passed through Idaho in 1805, the population of the principal American Indian Tribes within Idaho varied from 6,000 to 10,000. The Pend d'Oreille, or Kalispel, could have numbered about 300; the Coeur d'Alene, 700; Kutenai 200 or more; and about 3,000 Nez Perce. All were distinct tribes that existed peacefully together. Some Northern Piute could also have been living within the state's boundaries. Liljeblad estimated that there were about 3,000 Shoshone and Bannock, generally in Southwestern and Eastern Idaho.

Southwestern Idaho Tribes Shoshone, Bannock and Paiute Indians were the primary tribes that, for centuries, migrated through Southwestern Idaho. At that time, most of the non-mountainous part of the region was a sagebrush-covered plain divided by the Snake River and its tributaries. Indian bands routinely set up seasonal encampments along the river and its tributaries.

In the greater Treasure Valley, the Boise River, which flows west out of the mountains, and the Payette River, which flows south from Payette Lake to the Snake River, attracted an abundance of wild game. Until dams began to be built on the lower Snake River in the early to mid-1900s, salmon and steelhead trout filled these and other rivers each year during their annual spawning migrations. The Treasure Valley was a welcomed oasis for nomadic Indians and, later, for immigrants on the Oregon Trail.

Camas Prairie near Fairfield.

Bannock War – 1878 – Idaho's Last Indian War. In 1869 the U.S. military had largely subdued the Shoshone and Bannock Indians and assigned them to live on the Fort Hall Reservation promising to provide provisions to replace those they could no longer obtain as hunters/gathers. The federal government, however, failed to keep their treaty promises so the Indians continued their summer migrations, including those to the Camas Prairie near what is now Fairfield to hunt wild game and gather Camas lily bulbs to store for the winter.

About the same time, cattlemen were moving their herds onto the Camas Prairie to graze. Some brought hogs that foraged for food by rooting up the Camas bulbs with their snouts.

The Bannocks were incensed that the settlers were destroying their traditional food sources and the U.S. government was not fulfilling its promises. In May 1878 about 200 angry Bannock warriors left the reservation and headed northwest across the Snake River, skirmishing with the miners near Silver City, then continuing on attacking white settlements, killing settlers, taking provisions and destroying property along the way.

Over the next 16 months, a voluntary militia and the U.S. Calvary engaged these and other Indians in conflicts where the army killed or scattered the Indians or returned them to their reservations. Collectively termed the Bannock War, these conflicts comprised Idaho's last Indian War. (*See Eastern Idaho, The Region, American Indians.*)

Dawes Severalty Act. In an attempt to assimilate American Indians into the white mainstream and open reservation land for settlement, Congress passed the General Allotment Act, generally called the Dawes Severalty Act, in 1877.

Under the Act, the head of each Indian family received an allotment of 160 acres of reservation land, each single person over 18 years got 80 acres and each minor or orphaned child received 40 acres. Indians who did not want to farm could either sell or lease their land. Any land not allotted was deemed "surplus" and made available for non-Indian settlement.

This policy resulted in large-scale settlement by non-Indians on former reservation lands and created a checkerboard ownership pattern throughout the reservations. This law had a significant effect on reducing the size of Northern and Eastern Idaho reservations but, in comparison, had limited effect on the Duck Valley Reservation. (*See Today's Reservations below.*)

In 1934 Congress replaced the Dawes Severalty Act with the Indian Reorganization Act which restored the remaining surplus land into tribal trusts.

Today's Reservations. Today, there are two Indian reservations and one tribal land grant located in Northern Idaho; one reservation in Eastern Idaho; and the Duck Valley Indian Reservation in Southwestern Idaho, half of which is in Nevada. Four tribes have gaming casinos and resorts on their land – the one at Duck Valley is in process. All of the tribes are involved in natural resource conservation efforts and other economic development activities.

Statue of Marie Dorion and her two children (one child is on her back - not shown in this picture) located in Old Fort Boise, Parma.

The 2000 Census reported that the Nez Perce had a population of 1,962. Their reservation lies west and south of Lewiston and encompasses about 770,000 acres.

The Coeur d'Alene Tribe numbered 858 in the 2000 Census. Their reservation is south of the city of Coeur d'Alene and comprises about 345,000 acres.

The Kootenai Tribal land is near Bonners Ferry overlooking the Kootenai River. It comprises 12.5 acres provided to the tribe in a 1975 federal land grant as settlement of a conflict – the tribe had declared a peaceful but highly publicized war against the United States seeking just compensation. The 2000 Census reported the reservation had a population of 110.

Most members of the Shoshone and Bannock Tribes live on Eastern Idaho's Fort Hall Indian Reservation near Pocatello. The 2000 U.S. Census reported 4,019 of the reservation residents were tribal members.

Other members of the Shoshone and Paiute Tribes live on the 289,820-acre Duck Valley Reservation, which the federal government established in 1877 and enlarged in 1886. The reservation straddles the Idaho/Nevada border. About half of the reservation is in Owyhee County. Most of the reservation's population resides in Nevada.

Early Trappers/Explorers

In 1811 Wilson Price Hunt led a band of explorers and trappers – 62 men, one woman and two children – into what is now Eastern Idaho. They abandoned their horses, a decision they would later regret, and launched 15 canoes on the Snake

River seeking a water route to Fort Astoria at the mouth of the Columbia River on the Pacific coast. When they reached a place on the river west of what is now Milner Dam, they began experiencing major problems navigating the Snake River's treacherous rapids and waterfalls, losing a man and some canoes. Abandoning their remaining canoes and stashing their gear, they set out on foot, arriving at Fort Astoria on February 15, 1812. (*See Eastern Idaho, The Region, Early Trappers/Explorers.*)

In 1813 a member of the Hunt party – John Reed (sometimes Reid), then an employee of the Pacific Fur Company – led eight frontiersmen, including Pierre Dorian and his wife Marie Aiowe Dorion and their two children – also members of the Hunt expedition – back to the confluence of the Snake and Boise Rivers near what is now Parma. There they built a log house and began trapping beaver. In early 1814 Indians attacked and killed the nine men. Warned of the attack, Marie made a harrowing escape with her two young sons, who were around the ages of 8 and 6. A statue of Marie stands in Old Fort Boise Park near what is now Parma. (*See the city chapter of Parma for a more detailed account of this adventure.*)

Another member of Hunt's expedition, Donald Mackenzie, joined the North West Company and built a trading post named Fort Walla Walla several miles south of the confluence of the Snake and Columbia Rivers near what is now Wallula, Washington – not to be confused with the military "Fort Walla Walla," built 30 miles west of Wallula in 1856 and which also played a role in Idaho history.

For the next few years, Mackenzie held annual "Snake Country" rendezvous up the Snake River. In the rendezvous marketing system, fur-trading companies of the early 1800s brought food, horses, guns, iron goods, trade beads, whisky, tobacco and supplies to a prearranged location. The region's mountain men, trappers and Indians would converge at that location with their winter's harvest of furs and handiwork to barter.

Some of Mackenzie's employees were emigrants from Hawaii. In 1778 Captain James Cook discovered the Hawaiian Islands, which he named the Sandwich Islands after a financier of his voyages – John Montague, 4th Earl of Sandwich. Cook recorded the islander's expression of their name as "Owyhee." British and American traders continued that pronunciation and spelling. Mackenzie dispatched three of these Owyhee trappers to explore the mountains in what is now Southwestern Idaho to assess their beaver trapping potential.

The trio never returned and were assumed killed by Indians. As a memorial, their colleagues named the Owyhee Mountain Range and River in their honor. Today's Owyhee County comprises 4.9 million acres. Geographically, it is the largest county in Southwestern Idaho and the second largest county in the state. Idaho County in Northern Idaho is the state's largest county with 5.4 million acres.

In 1824 Peter Skene Ogden, an employee of the Hudson's Bay Company, led a successful beaver-trapping expedition to the upper Snake River country. During this trip, one of Ogden's French trappers named Portneuf lost his life to hostile Indians while working a tributary to the Snake River near what is now Pocatello. Ogden named the stream the Portneuf River after his departed colleague. The name survived and would later become the name of the river valley and eastern mountain range.

French emigrant Benjamin L.E. de Bonneville took leave from the army in 1830 to lead 110 men and 20 wagons West. The following year, he and some of his men ventured into what is now the Treasure Valley. Some people have erroneously given credit to Bonneville's French Canadians for providing the name of the city of Boise – actually established in a chain of events that were started about four years later by another French Canadian, Francois Payette. (*See Eastern Idaho, The Region, Trappers/Explorers – Bonneville.*)

In 1834 the Hudson's Bay Company established a trading post at the mouth of a river near the location where John Reid and his trappers were killed 20 years earlier. After a short time, the company placed Francois Payette in charge of the post. Because of the heavily wooded floodplain of the river flowing into the Snake River from the east, Payette named the fort and the river "Boise," the French word for wooded.

The "Boise" name Payette gave to the trading post and river also became the name of a mining district and mountain basin, another Fort Boise located about 40 miles southeast, the city of Boise, a national forest, tributaries to the Boise River, a valley and a county. Later generations would honor Francois Payette by giving his name to a river with three forks, the city of Payette, a county, two lakes near McCall, a valley and a national forest. Francois Payette is likely responsible for, or is the object of, naming more Idaho places and natural features than any other person in Idaho History.

The first overland migration of pioneers to Oregon's Willamette Valley crossed Idaho in 1841 and stopped at Francois Payette's Fort Boise. (*See Oregon and California Trails below.*)

In October 1843 Captain John C. Fremont's 39-man mapping expedition followed about the same route as the first migration and also stopped to rest at Payette's Fort Boise. Several months later, Congress printed Fremont's records and maps, which became widely used by travelers on the Oregon Trail. Fort Boise was a landmark on the maps, a welcome rest stop for Oregon Trail pioneers until it was destroyed by floods two decades later.

The U.S. Army applied the destroyed fort's name to the new military fort it built in 1863 also near the Oregon Trail about 40 miles east of the old trading post and Oregon Trail landmark. Settlers in the town that rapidly grew up around the new Fort Boise named their community Boise City.

Early Christian Missionaries

Several Christian missionaries of different denominations passed through but never stopped to establish missions in Southwestern Idaho. Those that passed through were headed to Northern Idaho, Washington or Oregon.

In 1834 Methodist missionaries Jason and Daniel Lee conducted a church service at Fort Hall, a trading post in Eastern Idaho – the first church service conducted in Idaho – and then moved on to the Willamette Valley in what was then called Oregon Country, a land claimed by both the United States and England.

Two years later, Presbyterian missionaries Henry H. and Elisa Spalding, who started a mission with the Nez Perce in Northern Idaho – now, Nez Perce National Historical Park-Spalding Site – joined a party of trappers and passed through Soda Springs, Fort Hall and Southwestern Idaho.

In 1841 Roman Catholic missionary Father Pierre De Smet was a member of the first overland migration of Oregon Pioneers. The party passed through Fort Hall before part of the group split off to California. De Smet was instrumental in establishing missions in the Northwest, including the Old Mission at Cataldo – the oldest standing building in Idaho, a National Historic Landmark and part of Idaho's Old Mission State Park. (*See Northern Idaho, The Region, Early Christian Missionaries.*)

Oregon and California Trails

In 1841 the first wagon train of 70 explorers and settlers headed to Oregon Country. The trail they blazed became part of the main Oregon Trail, which eventually included several cutoffs. In 1846 England (Canada) and the United States signed a treaty establishing the dividing line between the countries at the 49th parallel. Two years later, Congress established the Oregon Territory, which extended south to the 42nd parallel, the historic dividing line between British and Spanish and Mexican claims to the West, and included what are now Washington, Oregon, Idaho, western Montana and western Wyoming.

The main Oregon Trail generally paralleled the south side of the Snake River before crossing at Glenn's Ferry. Immigrants taking the Oregon Trail "South Alternate" did not cross the river. The main trail then proceeded northwest to what is now Boise before turning west, paralleling the south side of the Boise River to Francois Payette's old Fort Boise before re-crossing the Snake River and heading northwest to the Willamette Valley. (*See Federal Lands – Private Ownership and Preservation Laws below.*)

The California Trail cut off from the Oregon Trail at Raft River, then continued southwest through the City of Rocks and on to California.

After the discovery of gold in California in 1848, the California Trail became a virtual thoroughfare of wagon trains. By 1860 over 200,000 immigrants traveled the California Trail. More than 41,000 continued northwest on the Oregon Trail.

Idaho Territory

In 1863 one of the bills debated in Congress regarded creating Idaho Territory and had a provision, passed by the House of Representatives on February 12, 1863, that named the developing boomtown of Idaho City as the territorial capital. That bill failed and on March 4, 1863, President Abraham Lincoln signed the Organic Act, creating the Idaho Territory and appointing William H. Wallace as territorial governor. The law left it up to the territorial governor to name the temporary capital city and the Legislature to name the permanent site. (*See Territorial Capitals – Lewiston and Boise below.*)

At that time, the territory included all of what are now Idaho and western Montana and Wyoming and had four counties. The Legislature consisted of a seven-member "Council" and an 11-member House of Representatives. Indian reservations were treaty lands and not part of federal territory.

Early Lewiston

"One of the most intriguing mysteries of Idaho history is the origin and meaning of the name Idaho," wrote historian Merle W. Wells. It was one of the names proffered by promoters of the new (Colorado) territory after they found Congress would reject their first choice of Jefferson because of its opposition to naming territories after former U.S. presidents. They asserted that Idaho – a name they had apparently coined – was an Indian name meaning "Gem of the Mountains," albeit "Gem" as well as "Idaho" could not be referenced to a word or term of any Indian language. The U.S. Senate Committee on Territories was favorably disposed toward naming the territory Idaho until members of the Senate discovered at the last minute that Idaho was not an Indian word. When Congress created the territory in 1861, they chose to name it Colorado, the next prominent name under consideration.

However, the name "Idaho" did not lose its appeal and was used to name geographical locations in Colorado and the Northwest. When Idaho Territory was created in 1863, the name "Idaho" beat out "Montana" as the name of the new territory. Once named, leaders of the new Idaho Territory soon adopted the previously asserted meaning of the word, "Gem of the Mountains," and, later, applied the "Gem State" nickname as the term that ably describes Idaho's natural physical beauty and mineralization. (*See Gem State below*.)

Territorial Capitals – Lewiston and Boise Governor Wallace declared the boomtown of Lewiston the temporary territorial capital and called the first legislative session to begin December 7, 1863. Lewiston was a fresh water port that received steamers coming up the Snake River from the Columbia River and the Pacific Ocean and was the most accessible town in the territory. It was the trailhead for prospectors heading to the gold fields in Pierce, 75 miles east. (*See Northern Idaho, The Region, Gold Mining*.)

Before the session started, Wallace was elected as the territorial delegate to the U.S. Congress. He resigned as governor and on December 6, 1863, left for Washington, D.C., leaving Territorial Secretary William B. Daniels to serve as acting governor and to give the first governor's address to the Legislature. President Lincoln appointed Caleb Lyon as Wallace's successor. However, Lyon did not arrive until the next August.

Lewiston was legally on Nez Perce Reservation land – technically foreign soil. However, most Lewiston residents conducted business, including buying and selling building lots, as though they had legal ownership, essentially disregarding the Nez Perce Tribe's property rights as a sovereign nation. Hoping to avoid armed conflict with the tribe and likely anticipating federal action to reduce the size of the reservation, town residents negotiated a lease for the townsite.

On June 9, 1863, the Bureau of Indian Affairs reached agreement with about half of the Nez Perce Nation to reduce the size of the reservation, which was established under the Treaty of 1855. The Nez Perce bands that refused to sign the highly controversial treaty included those led by Chief Joseph's father and, later, Chief Joseph himself – an omission that would lead to war. (*See Northern Idaho, The Region, American Indians – Nez Perce War.*)

The 1863 treaty moved the reservation boundary to the east of Lewiston making the town legally part of Idaho Territory. However, Congress did not ratify the treaty until April 20, 1867, thus delaying the treaty's legal effective date. Most settlers disregarded that technicality and proceeded with their affairs as though the 1863 treaty was in effect.

By that time, the goldfields were playing out and most miners were moving to other gold discoveries in such places as Elk City, Florence and the Boise Basin. By the fall of 1863 Lewiston's population had declined to 414.

In contrast, the Boise Basin gold rush was reaching its peak. Over 16,000 prospectors, miners and settlers had converged on the basin and started several boomtowns. At that time, Boise Basin was second only to Portland as the most populous area in the Northwest. With

Early Boise.

political power shifting to the Boise Basin and the governor not yet in Lewiston, the 1863 Legislature deferred naming the permanent territorial capital until the next session.

The second session of the Territorial Legislature convened in Lewiston on November 14, 1864, and on December 7 passed landmark legislation, signed by Governor Lyon, that created Ada County and made the 17-month-old "Boise City" a charter city, the Ada County seat of government and Idaho's permanent territorial capital.

Even though the Legislature incorporated the town, Boise had no city government. For the incorporation to be final, the law specified that the town's citizens had to approve the charter in a city election. Most Boise City residents felt the town had too much government oversight already – territory and county – and did not need any more. In the March 21, 1865, election to approve the charter, the ballot measure failed by 24 votes. Successive elections also failed to get voter approval.

On January 11, 1866, the Legislature gave Boise a new charter, superseding the December 12, 1864, charter. This charter became effective without requiring voter approval but specified that a temporary mayor and council be appointed. However, four months later, the city leaders who were appointed still refused to take the oath of office. On January 11, 1867, the Legislature called for another election to be held in ten days. Again, the anti-charter candidates that won refused to organize the city.

By this time pragmatism was about to overrule anti-charter ideology. Legal surveys of public lands were underway. Landowners could only receive title to their lots from the city – no city, no title.

The matter was finally resolved on November 18, 1867, when Judge John Cummins called a meeting of city residents to vote on the appointment of a mayor and city council. The citizens assembled, appointed Henry E. Pickett, later a justice of the Territorial Supreme Court, as mayor and the members of the city council, organizing the city and making Boise's 1866 charter effective. Lewiston, Boise and Bellevue are the only cities chartered by the Territorial Legislature. Boise and Lewiston have since rescinded their charters.

Loss of the territorial capital to Boise outraged the citizens of Lewiston and Northern Idaho who filed suit, alleging the law was invalid because the Legislature met six weeks before its official term of office began.

Lewiston Probate Judge John G. Berry sided with the plaintiffs and issued an injunction against moving the Great Territorial Seal of Idaho (Seal) and archives from Lewiston and summoned Governor Lyon to appear in court and answer the charges.

Under the guise of a duck hunting trip, Lyon crossed the river into Washington Territory where he could not be arrested and forced to appear in court. The sheriff carried out the balance of the court order by locking the Seal and archives in the Lewiston Jail.

In Lyon's absence, newly appointed Territorial Secretary Clinton DeWitt Smith became acting governor. On March 2, 1865, Smith requested the federal troops stationed nearby to retrieve the Seal and archives and rendezvous with him outside the city.

Six weeks later, Smith entered Boise with the Seal and archives. However, that did not end the dispute. Lewiston officials appealed the matter to the territorial district judge, who sustained the ruling of the lower court.

Smith appealed the case to the newly created Idaho Territorial Supreme Court in Boise. On June 14, 1866, the Supreme Court overturned the district court, establishing Boise as Idaho's permanent territorial capital.

Change in Idaho Territorial Boundaries, 1863 to 1890, Suffrage and Statehood Between the time Congress made Idaho a territory in 1863 and a state in 1890, it modified Idaho's territorial boundaries three times. These changes reduced the size of Idaho to just over a fourth of its original size, from 325,000 square miles to 84,439 square miles of land and water area, about 54 million acres.

In 1887 Congress attempted to change Idaho's territorial boundaries a fourth time by approving a bill that split off the Panhandle from Idaho Territory, adding it to Washington Territory. At the same time, certain Nevada politicians had designs on making southern Idaho part of Nevada. Citizens of Lewiston, chagrined about their loss of the territorial capital to Boise, greeted the news with a brass band and community celebration. Four days later, however, they learned that Idaho Territorial Governor Edward A. Stevenson and Congressional Delegate Fred T. Dubois had persuaded President Grover Cleveland to pocket-veto the bill. That veto put an end to further modification of Idaho's territorial boundaries. Idaho territory was now ready to become a state.

Fred T. Dubois was one of Idaho's more colorful politicians. Illinois born, he came to Idaho Territory and served as U.S. Marshal from 1882 to 1886, an arch antagonist to any man who ran afoul of anti-polygamy laws. (*See suffrage below*.) Leonard Arrington, in his History of Idaho wrote, "...the Dubois juries convicted anyone on a polygamy charge, regardless of evidence."

Dubois was a highly regarded and gifted politician, representing Idaho for fifteen years in Washington, D.C. He is the only Idaho politician that has been elected to the U.S. Congress by two parties and served with three. He was elected as a Republican as Territorial Delegate from 1887 to 1890 and to the U.S. Senate from 1891 to 1897. He served for the Silver Republican Party in the U.S. Senate in 1901 – the Silver Republicans broke with the Republican Party which supported the Gold Standard. Before the year was out, Dubois announced that he would complete his six-year term as a Democrat. Although he tried, he was not re-elected.

Governor Edward A. Stevenson.

Governor Stevenson vetoed a bill making Eagle Rock, now Idaho Falls, the location for Idaho's land grant college in 1887. Two years later in an attempt to appease the Northern Idaho faction, the 1889 Territorial Legislature passed the "olive branch" law locating the state's land grant college, now the University of Idaho, in Moscow. (*See Federal Lands – Private Ownership and Preservation Laws – 1862 Morrill Land Grant Law below*.)

Idaho's State Constitutional Convention convened on July 4, 1889. On November 5 of that year, 12,126 or 66 percent of the 18,408 citizens voting approved the constitution. The 1890 census reported Idaho's population at 88,548.

Because of Idaho's restrictive suffrage laws in effect at the time, only a minority of the adult population were allowed to vote. Although now repealed, Idaho territorial laws that carried over into statehood withheld the basic civil rights of voting, holding public office and serving on juries from people who, if their voice and vote were not silenced, could have shifted political power from the Republican politicians then in control to the Democratic Party.

The largest body of adult citizens denied suffrage rights were women.

Suffrage rights were also denied bigamists or polygamists whose marriages were essentially marked by a formal ceremony and family structure. The law also denied suffrage to adult male members of any organization that taught the acceptability of bigamy, polygamy or celestial (eternal) marriage as a doctrinal rite and who would not sign a test oath.

The law did not extend to men involved in either informal co-habitation arrangements or extramarital affairs or multiple premarital relationships common in society, non-practicing monogamists.

Since most known or suspected polygamists and bigamists were either in prison, in court or had an arrest warrant issued because of their alleged felonious actions, they had, for all practical purposes, already lost their suffrage rights. Any additional laws denying those rights were redundant as it related to them. Therefore, the primary objective of the law was to disenfranchise monogamous men who were members of an organization that taught the acceptability of bigamy, polygamy or celestial marriage.

Under these provisions of the law, any suspected members of such an organization were, under penalties of perjury, required to take a complex test oath of over 200 words before they could exercise their civil rights. If they signed the test oath, they were essentially disavowing any relationship with the suspected organization and were allowed to vote. If they were subsequently found to be a member of the organization, they were subject to arrest and prison. Any suspected organization members that refused to sign the test oath were denied their suffrage rights.

While the law did not name any organizations, the only known organization in Idaho that fit the definition of the law was the Church of Jesus Christ of Latter-day Saints, also known as Mormons, Latter-day Saints or LDS. (*See Eastern Idaho, The Region: Pioneer Settlements.*)

Members of the Church comprised about a fourth of Idaho's population, of which only a small fraction practiced polygamy, but they were perceived by leading politicos to support the Democratic Party and to vote as a block. Republican lawmakers crafted the law so as to disenfranchise this large body of adult male Church members who would not disavow their faith.

In many local elections in Southern Idaho, the test oath resulted in a huge shift of political power away from the majority to a minority of citizens with all the potential mischief such undemocratic actions could produce. (*See Eastern Idaho, The Region, Politics, Polygamy and Civil Rights.*)

Also denied suffrage rights were people of Mongolian descent, aimed at disenfranchising Idaho's Chinese populations; American Indians who had not renounced tribal affiliation; adults under guardianship; and felons.

In November 1896 Idaho voters amended the state constitution to give women the right to vote. Idaho was the fourth territory/state to do so – behind Wyoming, 1869; Utah, 1870; and Colorado, 1893. The federal anti-polygamy Edmunds-Tucker Act of 1887 overturned Utah Territory's 1870 women's suffrage law. It was reinstated in Utah's constitution when it became a state in January, 1896. Today, Idaho's adult suffrage restrictions apply only to felons.

U.S. President Benjamin Harrison signed legislation making Idaho the 43rd state on July 3, 1890.

Gem State Idaho's "Gem State," designation is a carryover from Colorado and Idaho territorial days when the U.S. Congress erroneously believed the name "Idaho" was an Indian name – no tribal language was specified – meaning Gem of the Mountains. (*See Idaho Territory preamble above.*)

What they could not know at the time was that Idaho indeed had numerous and diverse deposits of gems as well as prodigious ore bodies of precious and industrial metals and minerals in each region of the state.

From the distinctive Spencer Opal semi-precious stone in Eastern Idaho to quartz, agate, jasper, garnet, geodes and the rare Star Garnet found only in Northern Idaho and India, Idaho has many varieties of gems, metals and minerals. Perhaps the most prominent Idaho deposit of the Star Garnet, which the Legislature named as the state gemstone in 1967, is at Emerald Creek Garnet Area, a Unique Natural Feature 10 miles north of Bovill.

Today there are numerous publications directing collectors and rockhounds to old and new gemstone locations and how to beautify the gems, stones and crystals they find. Thousands of hobbyists as well as professionals make beautiful jewelry and art objects using cut and/or polished Idaho rocks, gemstones and precious metals. Many of these pieces of art are displayed and sold at gem and county fairs held around Idaho and other states as well as in jewelry stores.

By whatever measure, from its diverse natural beauty to mineralization, Idaho is indeed worthy of its designation "Gem of the Mountains."

Federal Lands

Federal land ownership generally began between 1781 and 1802 when the original colonies ceded their Western lands between the Appalachian Mountains and the Mississippi River to the new national government.

During the 1800s as the nation moved West, it acquired practical ownership of land previously claimed by France, 1803 Louisiana Purchase; England, the Treaty of 1846 (see below); Mexico, the Treaty of 1848 (see below); and Russia, the 1867 purchase of Alaska. Hawaii was annexed into the U.S. as a territory in 1898.

In substantially all cases, Congress, backed by its modern Army, did as other nations and gave limited consideration to the land claims of the Indian tribes – implementing what many termed the nation's Manifest Destiny. The land Congress did not purchase from the Indians it took by treaty, conquest or passed law that laid claim to the land – actions that the primarily nomadic hunter/gatherer Indians were ill equipped to prevent.

The total land and water surface area of the U.S. now approaches 2.4 billion acres of which nearly 2 billion is in the 48 contiguous states, 0.4 billion in Alaska and about 4 million acres comprising the Hawaiian Islands.

Eventually the federal government would transfer ownership of all but about 30 percent of the federal land preserve to private interests and to the states. Today, most of the land under federal jurisdiction is in the 11 contiguous Western states and Alaska. About 64 percent of Idaho is federal land.

Congress transferred land ownership by passing numerous laws designed to encourage settlement, promote timber harvests and metal and mineral extraction and grants to the states to help fund public education and certain infrastructure.

One of the first methods Congress used to dispose of the nation's land was payment of debts in lieu of cash to soldiers, Bounty Land Warrants, first issued to Revolutionary War soldiers and, later, to soldiers fighting in the War of 1812. However, the federal government's principal method of disposing of the property from the nation's land and mineral preserve was to use grants or to sell at low prices to private parties including farmers, ranchers, railroad companies and miners.

The following is a summary of the more significant laws affecting transfer of federal lands to private and state ownership that may have affected Idaho as well as laws providing for federal management of the remaining land in the nation's preserve.

To encourage settlement and establish an American presence in the West, Congress passed the Preemption Act of 1841, which sanctioned squatters' rights and allowed a person to claim up to 160 acres – a quarter of a 640-acre section or one square mile – of un-surveyed federal land and, later, pay a small fee per acre to the federal government for clear title.

In 1843 non-Indian settlers in Oregon Country's Willamette Valley, mostly U.S. citizens, drafted a constitution for a provisional government that included a provision allowing settlers to claim up to 640 acres of land at no charge. Many of the early Oregon Trail immigrants, who began their overland treks in 1841, were motivated by the prospect of this free land in the lush Willamette Valley.

The Treaty of 1846 with England established the boundary between the two countries at the 49th parallel. Congress created Oregon Territory – land between the 49th parallel on the north and the 42nd parallel on the south – on August 14, 1848. The new territory included what are now Oregon, Washington, Idaho, western Montana and western Wyoming.

Mexico gave up its land claim south of the 42nd parallel when it lost the war with the U.S. and signed the February 2, 1848, Treaty of Guadalupe Hidalgo. (*See Eastern Idaho, The Region, Idaho/Utah Boundary Resolution.*)

Wildflowers near Sun Valley.

Two years later, Congress passed the Donation Land Claim Act of 1850, the forerunner of the Homestead Act. It nullified provisional land grants; created the Office of Surveyor General of Public Lands to provide deeds to property; and granted 320 acres to a white male, or a white male who was 50 percent Indian, over 18 years of age who had resided on the property on or before December 1, 1850, and, if married, an additional 320 acres were deeded to his wife – essentially grandfathering many elements of the provisional government's law. Recipients had to improve the property and live on it for four consecutive years from the time they first settled. This law influenced many marriages.

Male claimants who located on property between December 1, 1850, and December 1, 1853, received 160 acres of land – 320 acres for married couples. In 1854 Congress extended the law for two more years. Thereafter, people could purchase up to 320 acres for $1.25 an acre. Subsequently, the price was increased and the number of allowable acres decreased. Publication of these liberal land grant laws further spurred the flow of Oregon Trail immigrants headed generally to the Willamette Valley as well as other locations throughout the West.

The Homestead Act of 1862 superseded the Donation Land Claim Act and provided transfer of 160 acres to a settler, conditional on them improving the property and living on the land for five years. This act was used extensively throughout Idaho.

Early settlers claimed water rights by diverting irrigation water under the "Doctrine of Prior Appropriation – first in time - first in right." Later, water rights were administered by the laws of each state as opposed to federal law. In Idaho, these laws were codified in Idaho's Constitution which was approved by the territorial voters on November 5, 1899.

The 1862 Morrill Land Grant Act provided state grants of 30,000 acres for each member of the state's Congressional delegation – Senate and House – for the purpose of providing a source of funds for a state college that taught agriculture, engineering and military tactics. The University of Idaho is Idaho's land grant "college."

The Pacific Railways Acts of 1862, 1863 and 1864 provided massive land grants including mineral rights and issuance of government bonds to railroad companies to motivate them to build the first transcontinental railroad – which was completed at Promontory Summit, Utah, in 1869 – and many other railroad lines that would be built throughout the West. Many in Congress expected this land to be sold off in smaller parcels to promote agriculture, harvest of natural resources and building townships. This was done in many cases; however, railroads needing more cash to finance their enterprises sold much of their forested land grants in large blocks to lumber manufacturing companies and investors. (*See Forest Products below.*)

The General Mining Laws of 1866 and 1872 generally codified the self-rule methodologies prospectors and miners previously used to govern development of mining districts.

The Timber Culture Act of 1873 allowed homesteaders an additional 160 acres if they planted trees on 40 of those acres. The sponsors thought the law would have the greatest use in the settlement of the Great Plains. The law had many problems, and Congress repealed it in 1891.

The Desert Land Act of 1877 generally granted farmers ownership of up to 640 acres of arid federal land if they brought it under cultivation and irrigation within three years. This law was of limited use in Northern Idaho but in the mid-twentieth century was actively used in the arid areas of Southern Idaho.

The Timber and Stone Act of 1878 – intended to facilitate logging and mining – allowed wooded and other lands unfit for farming to be sold in parcels of 160 acres for $2.50 per acre to those who certified that they were buying the land for their own use. This law was principally used in Oregon, Washington, California and Nevada and was heavily abused. It had the practical effect of greatly expanding ownership of forested and mineral lands to large timber companies and syndicates who bought the land through nominal owners. It was repealed in 1891.

In 1905 Congress passed a livestock grazing law under which the federal government sold grazing permits on Forest Reserve land as a means of managing livestock access to public lands. In 1934 Congress passed the Taylor Grazing Act, further clarifying federal grazing law on all public lands. The 1976 Federal Land Policy Management Act and the 1978 Public Rangelands Improvement Act provided, among other things, that grazing fees were to be based on market values. Matters relating to livestock grazing on public lands continue to be controversial.

Concurrent with statehood in 1890 and under other federal laws, Idaho received federal grants of about 3.6 million acres to finance public education, the penitentiary and public buildings. Subsequent sales have reduced Idaho's Endowment Trust Lands to approximately 2.5 million surface acres and 3 million mineral acres – all managed by the Department of Lands with oversight from the State Board of Land Commissioners, a five-member board of state-wide elected officeholders chaired by the governor.

At the turn of the twentieth century, Congress passed two other laws that had limited use in Northern Idaho but played crucial roles in the reclamation of the arid lands in Southern Idaho, turning sagebrush-covered deserts into agricultural oases – the Carey Act in 1894 and the Newlands Reclamation Act in 1902. In Idaho, the Carey Act had its greatest impact in the Magic Valley. The Reclamation Act that authorized creation of the U.S. Reclamation Service – now the Bureau of Reclamation – built irrigation storage, flood control and hydroelectric dams throughout Southern Idaho. (*See Agriculture and Irrigation below*.)

Generally starting with the federal land management laws – the Taylor Grazing Act of 1934 and the Federal Land Policy and Management Act in 1976 – the national policy of retaining ownership of the nation's remaining land preserve was established. Legal challenges by "state's rights" advocates seeking management or control of federal lands within a state's borders have proven unsuccessful. (*See Mining and Forest Products – Leading Causes for Loss of Economic Dominance below*.)

Agriculture and Irrigation

Carey Act Projects – Magic Valley. Under the Carey Act, the federal government ceded each Western state up to one million acres of federal land brought under irrigation. Each state was required to create a regulatory commission, which, in Idaho, was the State Land Board. Under this law, private investors built the dams and canals, platted townsites and sold water rights. The state sold the land. The law allowed farmers to purchase parcels of up to 160 acres.

Ira B. Perrine, one of the Magic Valley's first entrepreneurs, would later initiate one of the first and largest Carey Act projects in Idaho. Perrine was inspired by his personal farming experience to initiate the project. He used irrigation on his wheat, vegetable and berry farm, fruit orchard and pasture on his Blue Lakes cattle ranch in the Snake River Canyon near Twin Falls. He transported his agricultural commodities for sale to the miners in the Wood River Valley using large freight wagons. He saw firsthand how irrigation could transform the area's rich volcanic soils into productive farms.

Perrine organized a group of investors to form the Twin Falls Land and Water Company in 1900. The company applied to the state under the Carey Act to build Milner Dam on the Snake River west of Burley in 1905. He named the dam after Stanley Milner, an officer of the bank that provided the project's initial financing. The project provided gravity flow water on the south side of the river from a 10-foot – deep canal – 80 feet wide at the bottom and 120 feet wide at the top. Certain of these investors became the namesakes of the cities founded by the company – Buhl, Kimberly, Filer and Hansen. Ultimately, this project, often called the South Side Project, would provide water to around 1,300 farms and irrigate over 244,000 acres.

To irrigate land on the north side of the river, Perrine organized another group of investors. The North Side Project pumped water into storage reservoirs that would ultimately irrigate 185,000 acres and found the cities of Eden, Jerome, Hazelton and Wendell.

Between 1905 and 1914 Idaho completed 23 Carey Act projects, irrigating 850,000 acres and attracting over $100 million of out-of-state investment along with about 50,000 people who settled in the area.

Bureau of Reclamation – Minidoka Project – Magic Valley The Bureau of Reclamation's Minidoka Project was one of the agency's most complex. The hydroelectric Minidoka Dam, located 35 miles upriver from Milner Dam, included the integration of Eastern Idaho's American Falls and Palisades Reservoirs as well as Jackson Lake in Wyoming.

Completed in 1906 the Minidoka Dam created Lake Walcott Reservoir and brought 116,000 acres under cultivation. The project created the cities of Acequia, Heyburn, Paul and Rupert as well as developed what is now Lake Walcott State Park and the Minidoka National Wildlife Refuge.

Bureau of Reclamation – Boise Project – Treasure Valley For many years, private efforts to irrigate several thousand acres of Treasure Valley bench land failed or had only limited success, often because the promoters lacked the necessary capital. Many of the projects that did become operational had other problems, which placed their long-term viability in question.

Following passage of the Reclamation Act in 1902, the Bureau of Reclamation developed its "Boise Project," which eventually included an integrated system of hydroelectric dams on the Boise and Payette River drainages with thousands of miles of canals and ditches – including the integration of existing systems and the irrigation of hundreds of thousands of arable acres – providing sustainable flows of water throughout the crop-growing season. The Army Corps of Engineers participated in some of these projects.

The Boise River drainage components included the 1908 Boise River Diversion called Barber Dam that fed the 40-mile-long New York Canal to Lake Lowell near Nampa in 1909, Arrow Rock Dam in 1915, Anderson Ranch Dam in 1950 and Lucky Peak Dam in 1955. Dams on the Payette River drainages included Black Canyon Dam in 1924, Deadwood in 1931 and Cascade in 1948.

Fighting the Jackrabbit Menace Farming on the high desert during the early years had many perils. In addition to the vagaries of the weather and insects, one of the most menacing, principally in Southwestern and in Eastern Idaho, was jackrabbits. These large hares lived in underground burrows in sagebrush areas and came out at night by the thousands to feed on range grass and farm crops.

The jackrabbit populations tended to increase and subside in cycles that lasted several years. Often when populations became excessive, the rabbits contracted tularemia and died off. Humans could also contract the dreaded disease from insect and tick bites or by handling the hares.

When the jackrabbit population surged, they threatened farmers and ranchers with economic ruin. The rabbits would devour both growing crops and stacked hay.

The settlers resorted to the best option they had – drives to capture and slaughter the jackrabbits. They built a series of two net-wire fence lines for hundreds of yards in the shape of "Vs" with pens where the fence lines converged. People would spread out across the mouth of the V and walk forward beating the sagebrush. Thousands of jackrabbits ran ahead into the fenced enclosures at the base of the V and were exterminated.

In the 1980s animal rights and other groups brought national media attention to the clubbing of jackrabbits without giving workable approaches that Western farmers could use to fight or control the hoards of crop-devouring hares. In recent decades, populations of the big hares have not increased to the epidemic proportions of the past.

Jackrabbits by the millions were killed in rabbit drives - and still were not eliminated.

Livestock

Partially attracted by high meat prices paid in the mining districts but primarily motivated by free grazing on vast tracts of public lands, ranchers brought herds of cattle to Idaho and eastern Oregon in the 1860s from such locations as Nebraska, Texas, California and western Oregon. The ranchers then formed cattle drives of their grass-fattened cattle to the stockyards at Cheyenne, Wyoming, where they were shipped to Omaha, Kansas City and Chicago. Leonard J. Arrington, in his book History of Idaho wrote, "Eastern Idaho (included significant parts of the Southwestern Idaho region as defined herein) was almost one big cattle ranch in the 1870s and early 1880s."

After the Oregon Short Line Railroad completed its line between Granger, Wyoming, and Huntington, Oregon, in 1884, creating another transcontinental railroad, sheep ranchers began bringing their flocks to Idaho. Attracted by the increasing demand for wool fiber and lamb, Scottish, Basque and other emigrants herded flocks ranging in size from 2,000 to 3,000 head. Many grazed in the mountains and wintered on the more temperate high-desert Snake River Plain. Idaho Falls, Soda Springs and St. Anthony were important lamb and wool-shipping centers in Eastern Idaho. Mountain Home and Ketchum were among the largest centers in Idaho's Southwestern region.

With cattlemen and woolgrowers competing for the same public grazing lands and limited government oversight, conflicts ensued.

The Oakley cemetery bears witness to that violence. There lie the remains of three men murdered in two separate incidents while herding sheep. The first incident involved a young black man named Gobo Fango who was out on the range herding his flock in February 1886 when two cattlemen rode up and accused him of grazing his sheep on their state-approved unmarked grazing allotment. They pistol-whipped and shot him three times, with one shot entering his back and coming out through his intestines, and then rode off to tell the sheriff in Albion that they killed him in self defense.

However, Fango did not immediately die. He crawled four and a half miles to Oakley to the people who raised and educated him. There he lived five days, gave his dying testimony and bequeathed his possessions to his adopted family and the women's organization of his church. Prosecutors charged the two men with murder. The first trial ended with a hung jury as did the retrial.

Also buried in the Oakley Cemetery are sheepherders Daniel Cummins and Don Wilson. They were shot in 1896 while herding their sheep. The trial of their accused murderer, Jackson Lee "Diamondfield Jack" Davis was one of Idaho's most famous murder trials. Davis, who worked for cattle ranchers, had previous involvement in other hazing and shooting incidents involving sheepherders.

The jury found Davis guilty and sentenced him to hang. However, before authorities carried out the sentence, two men came forward and confessed to the crime, claiming self defense. Each corroborated the other's story, and their trial ended in acquittal. Governor Frank W. Hunt pardoned Diamondfield Jack.

Cattle grazing near Council.

In 1905 Congress passed a livestock grazing law under which the federal government sold grazing permits as a means of managing access to public lands. In 1934 Congress passed the Taylor Grazing Act, further clarifying federal grazing law. (*See Federal Lands – Private Ownership and Preservation Laws above.*)

By the time the United States entered World War I in 1917, over two and a half million head of sheep were in Southwestern and Eastern Idaho. Because of market factors, today's sheep herds are a fraction of what they were in the early 1900s. However, each October Wood River Valley cities commemorate their heritage of large sheep drives with the "Trailing of the Sheep Festival." One of the events of the three-day festival is herding approximately 1,500 sheep from Bellevue through Hailey and Ketchum to Sun Valley.

While the sheep industry has declined dramatically, the cattle industry has flourished. Large herds of cattle still graze on public lands. The high desert of the lower Snake River plain is now home to large dairies and feedlot operations. The sale of dairy and meat products is now over three times the cash receipts from the sale of potatoes for which Idaho is "famous." Idaho is now the third largest dairy producer in the nation.

Sheep grazing on the Camas Prairie.

Mining

Southwestern Idaho has three prominent historic mining areas, the greater Boise Basin, the Owyhee Mountains and the Wood River Valley.

Boise Basin – Gold On August 2, 1862, a band of 11 prospectors discovered significant quantities of placer gold near what is now Idaho City.

The fortune seekers came into the basin because of a tip a co-leader, Moses Splawn, received from an Indian named Bannock Louie. Splawn met Bannock Louie a year earlier while prospecting for gold at Florence, near what is now White Bird in Northern Idaho. Bannock Louie told Splawn about a mountain basin to the southwest where he saw yellow sands in the streambeds.

In the summer of 1862 Splawn persuaded a co-leader George Grimes and over two dozen other prospectors to join him in his quest to find the mountain basin.

In June, the party reached the west bank of the Snake River across from what is now Parma and the remnants of old Fort Boise, which had been flooded and abandoned four years earlier. The river was at flood stage and about two miles wide.

Many of the prospectors became discouraged during three weeks of repeated and unsuccessful attempts to cross and moved on. Eleven of the original band persevered and finally reached the other side of the river. They traveled east on the Oregon Trail for about 50 miles, then northeast into the mountains.

On a creek known today as Grimes Creek, they dug "prospect holes" in the stream's gravels and began panning for gold. Within a short time, they panned $50 to $75 worth of the precious metal. Excited, they spread out to further explore the basin and stake their claims.

Hostile Indians attacked the group, considered trespassers on their traditional homelands, killing George Grimes on August 9. They later memorialized him by naming the creek in his honor. The remaining prospectors buried Grimes' body and promptly returned to the military Fort Walla Walla, also in Washington Territory, for more supplies and reinforcements. There they appealed to the U.S. Army for protection, enlisted a band of 40 prospectors and immediately returned to the Boise Basin to stake their claims before the inevitable gold rush could develop.

News of the discovery spread rapidly. The next year, 16,000 miners and prospectors converged on the Boise Basin, creating one of the largest U.S. gold rushes since California following the discovery of gold at Sutter's Mill, about 50 miles north of Sacramento, in 1848.

The prospectors established mining boomtowns including Idaho City, originally named West Bannock; Centerville; Pioneerville; and Placerville. Prospectors then fanned out and made other bonanza gold discoveries that led to the boomtowns of Atlanta; Rocky Bar, the town that became the Alturas County seat until the mines played out and county voters moved it to Hailey in 1882; and Warner, a gold-mining boomtown deep in the mountains over 50 miles northeast of what is now McCall.

Until railroad service reached Caldwell in 1883, significant amounts of supplies and passenger traffic came from Utah. When railroad interests completed the nation's first intercontinental railroad at Promontory Point in Utah, stagecoach and freight companies, in cooperation with the railroad, established a rail depot at the now abandoned and razed town of Kelton, Utah, on the north end of the Great Salt Lake.

For nearly two decades, freight wagons and stagecoaches traveled Kelton Road between cities in Utah and Boise. Parts of Kelton Road overlapped the Oregon Trail. The Rock Creek Store and Stage Station established in 1865 near what is now Kimberly – now the historic Rock Creek Station and Stricker Homesite owned and managed by the Idaho State Historical Society with assistance from the Friends of Stricker, Inc. – is a nostalgic reminder of those bygone stagecoach days on the Kelton Road.

To reclaim the gold, Boise Basin mining methods changed from panning to sluice boxes, diverting water over placer gold bearing soils shoveled into the sluice box; water cannon to wash mountainside soils into sluice boxes; and, finally, dredging, the damming up of streams to form a reservoir of water on which a huge portable dredge-sluice floated.

The dredge-sluice worked areas that had often been previously mined by systematically scooping up soils from the valley floor into its portable sluice leaving six- to eight-foot tailing piles of gravel behind the dredge. Dredging continued until the 1950s. Today, thousands of piles of these mine tailings lie on the valley floor north of Idaho City.

One of the historic dredges that once worked Idaho streams is in the mountains of Custer County about 50 miles west of Challis in Eastern Idaho. Volunteers dedicated to preserving the history of the Yankee Fork now manage the abandoned Yankee Fork Dredge and the ghost town of Custer, which today are part of Land of the Yankee Fork State Park that also includes the 90-mile loop called the Custer Motorway Scenic Drive, Challis Bison Jump and the old mining towns of Bonanza and Bayhorse. Today, the primary access to the historic mining area is a paved forest road north from Idaho Highway 75 at Sunbeam.

In addition to the discovery of gold, the 1863 Boise Basin gold rush was a major factor in the territorial legislature establishing Boise as Idaho's permanent capital city.

Owyhee Mountains – Silver and Gold In May 1863 prospector Michael Jordon led a band of fortune seekers into the Owyhee Mountains where they discovered placer gold at what is now Jordon Creek. Word soon got out, and about 2,500 Boise Basin miners rushed 100 miles southwest to the Owyhee Mountains. During the next year, prospectors found several ore bodies of quartz rock containing silver and gold.

Ruby City was one of the area's first boomtowns. It became the county seat of Owyhee County on December 31, 1863. Owyhee County was the first county created by the Idaho Territorial Legislature. As the Ruby City mines played out over the next few years, the miners made new discoveries about a mile south and created the boomtown of Silver City. The miners voted to move the county seat to Silver City in 1867. When those mines played out, the voters again moved the county seat about 20 miles northeast in 1934 to the railroad terminus town of Murphy, now an unincorporated hamlet of fewer than 100 people.

Mine owners employed several dozen whipsaw teams to produce lumber – a team consisted of two men operating long saws that cut logs lengthwise – to provide sawn lumber to construct buildings and timbers to shore up the mineshafts. Mine owners used mule teams to haul in scores of heavy disassembled stamp mills needed to pulverize the ore in preparation for the metal extracting processes.

The most significant dispute in the Silver City area came in 1868 over the boundary line of two adjoining mining claims. The conflict, called the Owyhee War, became a shooting battle. Governor David W. Ballard quashed the conflict when he arrived in Silver City with 95 soldiers and a cannon made of brass.

Freight wagon en route from Mackay to Ketchum.

The greater Silver City mining area was Southwestern Idaho's most productive silver mining district – a major producer of silver by most standards, but modest compared to the silver production of Northern Idaho's Silver Valley. (*See Historic Mine Production below.*)

Wood River Valley – Silver and Lead Warren Callahan, a Boise Basin gold prospector, traveled from the boomtown of Rocky Bar, 60 miles west of Boise, to the gold mines in Montana in 1864. His route took him 45 miles west of Rocky Bar through the Wood River Valley where he discovered outcroppings of galena – silver-lead ore. At that time, development of hard rock mines in remote areas was problematic. Transportation alternatives and ore-refining technology were limited and there was still potential conflict with Indians. Finding no gold, Callahan moved on.

Ten years later, Callahan returned to the Big Wood River area, but, still finding no gold, he again moved on.

By 1879 the U.S. Army had established a strong presence in the area, and technology for refining lead-silver ore had improved. In addition, expectations were high that rail service would soon be available.

At that time, large numbers of prospectors began coming into the Wood River Valley and surrounding mountains. They found numerous deposits of galena ore, often lying in veins up to two feet thick. The veins contained 40 to 60 percent lead and up to 100 ounces of silver per ton. In 1880 lead sold for a nickel a pound and silver $1.50 an ounce. The prospectors established mining towns that included Bellevue, Hailey and Ketchum, building smelters in Ketchum and other locations near the mines.

Obtaining food and other supplies to supplement the wild game bagged by the miners was problematic. Supplies were shipped long distances by freight wagon or packhorse. The goods were expensive. A mine worker who earned $3 a day had to pay $1.50 a dozen for eggs, $8 for a 100 pounds of potatoes and $7 for a hundred pounds of flour. Cats to control mice cost $5 each. Today the cities of Ketchum and Sun Valley host the historic "Wagon Days" celebration on Labor Day weekend, commemorating the bygone mining days when huge freight wagons carried ore to the smelters and supplies to the miners.

In the spring of 1880 one of the miners defied the area's conventional wisdom that the valley's elevation was too high for farming. He successfully planted a garden of mostly potatoes.

Many prospectors and miners filed homestead claims and planted wheat and other crops that grew well in the short growing season. Cattle and sheep ranchers brought in their herds to graze and sold meat and dairy products to the miners.

The Oregon Short Line Railroad (OSL) began building a line between Granger, Wyoming, and Huntington, Oregon, in 1881. Upon reaching Shoshone, Idaho, in 1882, railroad officials temporarily stopped their westward construction to build a branch line north to the Wood River Valley mines.

The OSL completed this branch line in 1883, built a train depot on the south side of Bellevue and returned to constructing its line to Huntington. (*See Railroads below.*)

In 1882 Alturas County voters moved the county seat from the mining boom town of Rocky Bar, where the gold mines were playing out, to Hailey.

Murder of Governor Frank Steunenberg – Caldwell The Coeur d'Alene Mining District, better known as the Silver Valley, still stands as one of the most productive silver mining districts in the world. Silver, lead and zinc ore discoveries in the 1880s led to the creation of numerous Silver Valley communities.

The late 1800s was marked by major conflicts between mine workers and owners. The mine workers unionized, becoming members of independently organized unions or members of the Western Federation of Miners. Mine owners responded by forming the "Mine Owners Association."

What followed was a sequence of escalating maneuvers by the union and the mine owners that led to violent confrontations in 1892 and again in 1899. Destruction of property, armed conflict and death marked both conflicts. A few years after the 1899 conflict, a union representative killed former Idaho Governor Frank Steunenberg, who had declared martial law and successfully requested federal troops to restore order. Idaho's National Guard was not called up because it was involved in the Spanish-American War and based in the Philippines. (*See Northern Idaho, The Region, Silver Valley Mines.*)

Home of Gov. Frank Steunenberg, the location of his assassination in 1905, located at Sixteenth & Dearborn in Caldwell.

Steunenberg was murdered on December 30, 1905, five years after leaving office. He died as he opened the picket gate in front of his Caldwell home, triggering a bomb set by a union operative.

With astute detective work, authorities captured Harry Orchard, an alias for Albert E. Horsley, who was living in the Treasure Valley. Orchard would later confess at the trial to conspiring with leaders of the Western Federation of Miners to murder Steunenberg.

Orchard also confessed to participating with members of the union's executive committee in the murder or attempted murder of over 20 other people who opposed union demands in Colorado, Idaho and California.

Union officials engaged the famous Chicago attorney, Clarence Darrow, to lead the defense team. W.E. Borah, later to become a U.S. senator, and James H. Hawley of Boise, later to become an Idaho governor, served as prosecutors in the case that many believed had overwhelming evidence to convict. At the end of this nationally celebrated trial, the court dismissed all charges against the union officials. However, at the next union election, union members voted the officials out of office.

The court, however, found Harry Orchard guilty of murder and sentenced him to death by hanging. The court later commuted his sentence to life in prison because of Orchard's cooperation.

A statue of Governor Steunenberg stands in a small Boise park across the street facing the Capitol.

Orchard – who died in 1954 after serving 46 years in prison, the longest term ever served by an inmate in the Idaho Penitentiary – is also recognized by placards and the barren cell in which he once lived, now part of the Old Idaho Penitentiary Museum in Boise.

Historic Mine Production and Ranking Mining is one of Idaho's three historic signature industries – forest products and agriculture being the other two. Even though Idaho has numerous deposits of semi-precious gems and minerals and is called the Gem State, its greatest mining fame comes from the prodigious quantities of precious and industrial metals extracted from its mines. (*See Idaho Territory: Preamble and Gem State above.*)

Northern Idaho's Coeur d'Alene Mining District, the Silver Valley, is recognized as the largest silver-producing mining district in the United States and is one of either three or five of the most productive districts in the world. Northern Idaho mines produced 1.2 billion troy ounces (tr. oz.) of silver as well as 16.7 billion lbs. of lead, 6.6 billion lbs. of Zinc, 415 million lbs. of copper and 2.7 million tr.oz. of gold. (*See Northern Idaho, The Region, Silver Valley Mines – Historic Mine Production and Ranking.*)

Nevada, the self-proclaimed "Silver State," has produced less silver than Idaho. Nevada's total historic silver production through 2000 is substantially less than Idaho's total silver production of 1.3 billion tr. oz. The silver production of 190 million tr. oz. from Nevada's famous Comstock Lode is also less than the over 360 million tr. oz. produced by Idaho's Sunshine Mine in the Silver Valley, which is still in operation. If the right to claim the designation "The Silver State" was based on silver yield by state, Idaho would be the champion, going away.

Southwestern Idaho has three prominent historic mining areas: the greater Boise Basin, the Wood River Valley and the Owyhee Mountain's Silver City District that includes the DeLamar, Florida Mountain and War Eagle Mines. Three other mining areas that figured prominently in Southwestern Idaho mining history were Atlanta, Rocky Bar and Warner.

Southwestern Idaho's 5.4 million tr. oz. of gold produced through 2000, makes it the largest gold producing region of the state. Northern Idaho's gold production is 2.7 million tr. oz and Eastern Idaho's is 1.7 million tr. oz. Albeit, it pales to California's historic gold production of 40 to 50 million tr. oz. and Nevada's current gold yields of over 1 million tr. oz. per year.

Total estimated historical mine production (1862-2000) in Southwestern Idaho's principal mining districts is as follows:

Placer Gold

Boise Basin	2,819,000 tr. oz
Atlanta	274,000 tr. oz.
Rocky Bar	250,000 tr. oz.
Wood River Valley	203,000 tr. oz.
Greater Silver City Dist.	1,650,000 tr. oz.
Total	5,400,000 tr. oz.

Silver

Atlanta	1,178,000 tr. oz.
Wood River Valley	21,921,000 tr. oz.
Greater Silver City Dist.	74,500,000 tr. oz.
Total	97,599,000 tr. oz.

Copper

Atlanta	33,000 lbs.
Wood River Valley	5,273,000 lbs

Lead

Atlanta	2,000 lbs
Wood River Valley	244,000 lbs

Zinc

Atlanta	1,000 lbs
Wood River Valley	227,000 lbs

In recent years, the price of precious and industrial metals has increased dramatically. This condition is causing a resurgence of mining, particularly in Northern Idaho. Ore concentrates are now shipped out of state for smelting and refining. In Eastern Idaho phosphate is still the most significant mining activity. Mining in Southwestern Idaho continues to be limited.

Forest Products

When Henry and Eliza Spalding started Idaho's first sawmill on the Clearwater River in 1836 while on their mission to the Nez Perce Indians, magnificent virgin forests that included trees hundreds of years old covered many parts of Northern Idaho. Forests of Western White Pine – Idaho's state tree, which could exceed 8 feet diameter at the base and a height of over 200 feet – were common. The largest white pine in the world now stands at 219 feet near the city of Elk River. Over the last century, most of those giants have been cut to help satisfy the lumber needs of a growing nation. Others have been ravaged by fire. (*See Great Fire of 1910 below.*) Magnificent forests still cover Northern Idaho and parts of Southwestern and Eastern Idaho, but they are generally trees of younger growth.

The first sawmills were generally started to meet local market needs, often agricultural-based settlements or mine owners needing to provide timbers to shore up mineshafts and lumber for buildings at the mines and the burgeoning boomtowns they created. Later, railroads facilitated growth in forest products companies by providing service to communities built up around sawmills and transporting lumber to distant markets.

Timberlands and Sawmills For more than a century after becoming a nation, Congress passed laws transferring ownership of public lands to private interests to pay obligations, encourage settlement, build railroads, harvest the nation's timber and mineral wealth, harness water for beneficial uses and grant land to states to fund public schools and infrastructure. (*See Federal Lands, Private Ownership and Preservation Laws above.*)

Beginning in the late 1800s railroads began extending into timber regions, selling their land grant timberlands and providing transportation services to numerous new sawmills that were harvesting timber off federal and private lands. Farmers and ranchers often purchased cleared forestlands and began agricultural operations. Towns grew up around each significant commercial venture.

In 1891 Congress passed the Forest Reserve Act that allowed the President of the United States to set aside specific areas of public forestlands "to improve and protect the forest...securing favorable conditions for water flows, and to furnish a continuous supply of timber for the use and the necessities of citizens of the United States." At that time, President Benjamin Harrison placed 13 million acres into the reserve. Succeeding presidents increased the reserve's size. In 1905 Congress placed management of the forest reserves under an agency in the U.S. Department of Agriculture, now known as the National Forest System. The U.S. Forest Service now administers 191 million acres.

By 1900 forestlands in the Great Lakes states were becoming depleted and lumbermen began looking elsewhere to set up sawmills. Railroads had received, and were receiving, massive federal land grants as an inducement to provide rail service across the country.

Although not a railroad man, Fredrick Weyerhaeuser was one of the largest ultimate beneficiaries of federal forested land grants to the railroads. Already a successful lumber industrialist, buying timberlands, companies and sawmills and harvesting the merchantable timber from Wisconsin and Minnesota forests, Weyerhaeuser set his eye on the Pacific Northwest.

Weyerhaeuser resided in St. Paul, Minnesota, and was neighbors to Jim Hill, head of the Northern Pacific Railroad. The railroad received its first federal railroad grants in 1864, which – over the next several years – would exceed 47 million acres for building railroads across the Northern United States. The two men served on each other's boards. One evening Weyerhaeuser learned that Hill had to redeem bonds and was short of cash. On January 3, 1900, Hill sold Weyerhaeuser's syndicate of investors 900,000 acres of timberland in Washington for $5.4 million.

This transaction was one of the first of many ownership transfers of railroad grant timberland to Weyerhaeuser and other lumber industrialists. Later, Weyerhaeuser would form a company to hold certain of his Idaho timberlands, some of which were sold to a predecessor of Boise Cascade Corporation – now consisting of its successors, the privately owned Boise Cascade Holdings L.L.C. and the publically traded and affiliated Boise, Inc., which in 2008 acquired Boise Cascade's Paper Group operations. Both companies are headquartered in Boise. Neither company owns timberlands.

Weyerhaeuser, along with John H. Humbird and other Midwestern sawmill owner-operators and investors, went on to purchase other large tracts of railroad grant and other timberland in Washington, Oregon and Idaho – not designated as national forest reserves – and built sawmills at optimum locations.

Historically, most of Southwestern Idaho's timber harvest came from mills in Valley, Boise and Adams Counties – with logs transported to mills either located in those counties or elsewhere. Most of the historic mills across Idaho have closed. However, those that remain continue to produce large quantities of wood products.

29

(See chart of Idaho Timber Harvest and Lumber Production, 1947 to 2010 below.)

Idaho has one pulp and paper mill, the Lewiston facility of Clearwater Paper Corporation, headquartered in Spokane, Washington, a 2008 spinoff from Potlatch Corporation. The company owns vast tracts of timberlands in Idaho. At its Lewiston facility, the company manufactures lumber, bleached paperboard, pulp and consumer tissue products. *(See Northern Idaho, the city chapters of Lewiston and Potlatch.)*

The Great Fire of 1910 For two terrifying days – August 20 and 21, 1910 – following a summer of drought and high temperatures, a cold front came through bringing fierce winds that whipped smaller fires into raging infernos with flames leaping hundreds of feet high and clouds of smoke rising high into the atmosphere. These conflagrations generated their own blowtorch winds, blowing embers great distances, jumping from tree crowns to tree crowns and igniting other fires in a hopscotch fashion, ravaging Northern Idaho and western Montana.

The fire killed 85 men, mostly firefighters; destroyed several communities in Montana and Idaho; and charred others, including much of what is now Wallace – in total burning 3 million acres. Although estimates vary widely on the equivalent board feet destroyed, historian Stephen Payne, in his book Year of the Fires: The Story of the Great Fires of 1910 said, "The Forest Service settled on a figure of six billion board feet, about twice the entire national output and that in a year of record production." The conflagration was so large some credited it with blowing ash halfway around the world. The fire, sometimes termed the Big Burn or the Big Blowup, was the largest fire in U.S. history – greatly influencing future federal forest-management policies.

Fire Aftermath – Changing Forest Management Practices The Great Fire was a catalyst that persuaded Congress to pass the Weeks Act of 1911, named for John W. Weeks of Massachusetts. The Act authorized the federal government to buy private lands within the watersheds of navigable streams and include such lands in the national forest system. While the law was initially used to buy lands in the East, it was also applied in the West. One of the major provisions of the Act was legislating emergency fire fighting funds for aggressive wildfire suppression.

In 1935 the Forest Service adopted the firefighting goal termed the "10 a.m. policy" – all newly detected forest fires were to be put out by 10 o' clock the next morning. The practice of parachuting firefighters near hard-to-reach fires – now termed Hotshot Crews – began in 1940. The familiar Smoky Bear advertising character and his slogan, "Only you can prevent forest fires" began in 1944.

These aggressive fire suppression programs had the desired effect of reducing forest fires but there were adverse consequences as well. Dr. Jay O'Laughlin, University of Idaho, Forestry and Policy Analysis, said, "Remove fire from the system and over time fuels will accumulate, making the next fire more difficult to control."

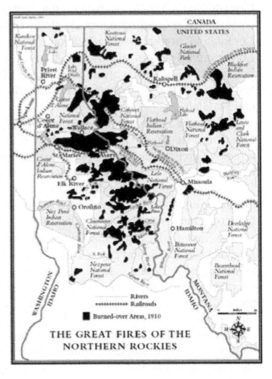

THE GREAT FIRES OF THE
NORTHERN ROCKIES

The conclusion of World War II started a nationwide housing boom. Providing lumber to build millions of homes for the families of soldiers returning from the war, many going back to school under the G.I. Bill before entering the workforce, was a federal priority. The Forest Service helped satisfy this demand by opening the national forests to increased timber harvests. In just over a decade, the timber harvest from federal lands in Idaho had more than doubled – a high level of timber harvest that would continue for over two decades – all facilitated by improved heavy tractors, equipment and trucks and the 1950s invention of the single person hand-held gasoline-engine chain saw.

At this time, the commercial practice of clear-cutting, generally defined as the removal of all stems in a specified area whether the stems were viable for merchantable timber or not, became a common but highly controversial practice of timber harvest – a practice that would continue for more than two decades. Opponents, asserting the practice was tantamount to deforestation and the destruction of natural wildlife habitat, used photos of large clear-cuts to influence public opinion in favor of their preservationist cause.

In 1965 certain federal agencies combined resources to form the National Interagency Coordination Center and National Interagency Fire Center located in Boise. There are now eight participating federal agencies. The center in Boise coordinates resources to fight fires that may occur in any of the 11 geographical areas, called Geographical Area Coordination Centers, headquartered at a city in each of 11 designated areas of the United States, including Alaska.

Beginning in the 1970s Congress passed several laws affecting the protection of the environment, ecosystems, species and riparian areas and access to federal lands for the purpose of mining and harvesting timber. (*See Mining and Forest Products – Leading Causes for Loss of Economic Dominance below.*)

By 1992 there were numerous lawsuits and court injunctions in the Pacific Northwest involving the protection of endangered species and their habitat, including future timber harvests in "old growth" forests. From that time on, as shown in the following chart, timber harvest from federal lands began to fall precipitously.

The next major change in federal forest management law came with passage of the Healthy Forest Restoration Act of 2003. Under the Act, federal agencies were required to work collaboratively with other stakeholders to reduce the risk of large destructive wild fires by thinning dense tree-stands, undergrowth and brush in forested areas; creating fire breaks; improving firefighting practices and insect control, infestations of the pine beetle have killed millions of acres of forests in the West; and requiring communities in affected areas to develop wildfire protection plans. The law also directs the courts to consider the risk of forest fires in deciding cases that could delay thinning projects. Opponents to the law generally asserted the law could lead to a return to the open commercial harvest of larger trees of the past with limited positive effect in reducing fire hazards.

Today, the Forest Service employs a mix of fire-fighting policies and tactics including prescribed burning – intentionally set fires designed to achieve specified outcomes – and natural burns low to intervene in fires started by natural causes such as lightning.

Dr. O'Laughlin said that during 2000 to 2009, the average number of acres burned each year exceeded 6 million, more than double the average of the preceding two decades.

Opponents to the federal burn practices assert they waste good timber, and, if the Forest Service employed the mixed-use methodologies used on private and state-owned forestlands,

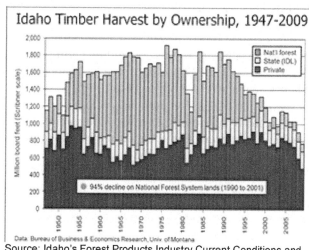

Idaho Timber Harvest by Ownership, 1947-2009

Source: Idaho's Forest Products Industry Current Conditions and 2011Forecast

forest fires could be better controlled, habitat preserved and more jobs created.

On August 7, 2007, The Idaho Statesman reported that in the heavy wildfire year of 2003 one private forestland owner of 180,000 acres experienced burns of only 100 acres, contrasted with the burn of 708,000 acres of federal forestlands in Idaho.

Forest Service managers assert their ability to fight wild fires is constrained for multiple reasons including lack of funds, road access and their priority to protect

32

homes that are increasingly being built in forested areas. In addition, Dr.
O'Laughlin said, "Forest Service management practices today are designed
primarily to modify ecological conditions rather than provide timber supplies. In
contrast to federal policies, private and state-owned forestlands are generally
managed for a mix of uses that includes timber production..."

Today, 36 percent of
Idaho's 54 million acres is
owned by private, state or
local government entities.
Federal agencies are
responsible for managing the
balance of the land – U.S.
Forest Service 39 percent,
the Bureau of Land
Management 21 percent and
other federal agencies 4
percent.

**Idaho's Lumber
Production History**

Researchers at the University
of Idaho have estimated that
Idaho's statewide lumber

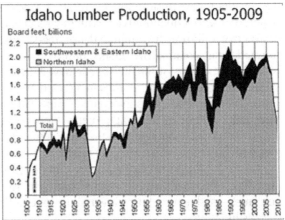

Source: Idaho's Forest Products Industry Current Conditions
and 2011 Forecast.

production grew from 1.5 million board feet (bf) in 1870 to nearly 1.2 billion in
1925 before falling to around 200 million during the Great Depression of the
1930s. Following the Depression, production rebounded as shown in the chart
below, reaching over 1.2 billion bf in 1950.

By the mid-1950s there were over 300 sawmills in Idaho. Within five decades,
all of the mills had closed except for 35. However, as shown in the chart above, the
remaining mills were producing about the same quantity as the 300 mills were
producing decades earlier. Of the 35 remaining mills, 14 each had annual
production, prior to the recent recession, generally greater than 50 million board
feet of lumber. These mills operate using state-of-the-art computer process control
systems including lasers, scanners, mechanized log and lumber handling systems
and improved saw-blade, edger and trimmer technologies that use substantially
fewer, albeit more highly skilled, workers.

As the chart illustrates, the global economic decline that began in 2007 has had
a significant adverse effect on lumber production in Idaho as it has in the industry
as a whole. However, as illustrated in previous economic cycles, production will
resume as the economy improves.

Idaho Timber Harvest by Region. As illustrated in the table below, in 2006
about 87 percent of Idaho's timber harvest came from Northern Idaho, up from 79
percent in 1979. Southwestern Idaho's share dropped from 16 percent in 1979 to 11
percent in 2006. Eastern Idaho's share fell precipitously from 8 to 1.7 percent. The
timber harvest is now cut principally from state and private forestlands.

The underlying basis for calculating timber harvest by county in the chart below is different than that used to calculate Idaho timber harvest and lumber production used in the table above – largely due to formula inconsistencies in handling the declining size of logs being milled. Dr. O'Laughlin said that many of Idaho's sawmills began to re-tool during the 1980s to handle smaller diameter logs. By 2003 nearly 60 percent of all logs processed in Idaho were less than 10 inches small-end diameter, and some mills were processing logs less than 6 inches small-end diameter.

The U.S. Census Bureau has also reported Idaho lumber production at amounts different than that shown herein. No attempt has been made to reconcile differences as the information disclosed herein is based on methodologies that are generally accepted in the industry to reasonably calculate timber and lumber harvests. The calculations do not include timber used for paper manufacturing and unprocessed logs sold to foreign countries.

Loss of Economic Dominance

The production of dimensional lumber and silver, lead and zinc ingots were Idaho's largest manufacturing businesses and dominated the economy of Northern Idaho and many cities across the state for nearly a century. In Southwestern and Eastern Idaho, these industries were less pervasive as agriculture was then dominant, but they still had a profound economic effect – placer gold mining was dominant in many communities until the mines played out.

Although totally different in operation, raw material, end product and environmental impact of processing, these two natural resource-based industries were subject to many of the same federal laws and regulations including, during recent decades, the almost total loss of access to federal lands.

The following provides leading causes for the decline in economic influence of the mining and wood products industries in Idaho as well as the nation.

Until around 1970 congressional actions toward railroad companies, settlers and natural resource-based industries were very accommodating. Motivated by a desire to connect the continent with railroad transportation, settle the West and obtain timber and minerals needed for the nation's rapidly growing economy, Congress gave railroad companies over 100 million acres of land grants, including mineral rights, that they could sell to provide cash for the construction of railroads. However, the largest numbers of federal land grants – totaling the most acreage – were to farmers, ranchers, developers and states. (*See Federal Lands – Private Ownership and Preservation Laws above.*)

The federal priority was to encourage private businesses to produce timber and minerals needed for the nation's rapidly growing economy. There was limited governmental oversight. Business practices generally focused on profitability as opposed to environmental impact and safety of workers until the 1970s.

The use of public lands for mining was, to a great extent, open to all who wished to file mining claims. Claims with proven ore bodies could become patented or deeded to the claim owner. Most of today's mining activity is on such patented land.

The use of public forests was largely unregulated until around 1905 when

President Theodore Roosevelt, often described as a conservationist who generally supported sustainable harvest and multiple-use concepts of forest management, helped create the United States Forest Service.

Beginning in 1907 Roosevelt used his executive authority to create scores of national forests, primarily in the Western states. In Idaho, he created 15 – many of which, due to changes in forest management practices and policies, have been combined or consolidated. Idaho's original national forests were the Caribou, Challis, Salmon, Clearwater, Coeur d'Alene, Pend d'Oreille, Weiser, Nez Perce, Idaho, Payette, Boise, Sawtooth, Lemhi, Targhee and Bitterroot.

U.S. Senator Weldon Heyburn from Wallace favored open use and opposed all of Roosevelt's conservation initiatives to protect and manage public lands for public recreation and commercial purposes. On the other side of the debate were the preservationists such as John Muir, founder of the Sierra Club, who wanted to maintain pristine natural environments by banning all development.

In the latter half of the twentieth century, many people across the nation became concerned about the declining quality of air in cities and industrial areas as well as ground and surface water quality, wildlife habitat and general lack of care government agencies had given to the nation's public lands, environment and worker safety. This motivated Congress to enact laws more closely in accord with preservationist ideology for the management of public lands and the commercial use of natural resources.

In 1970 Congress created the Environmental Protection Agency (EPA), the Occupational Safety and Health Administration (OSHA) and the National Institute for Occupational Safety and Health (NIOSH). A few years later, the federal Mine Safety and Health Administration (MSHA); the Federal Water Pollution Control Act, also known as the Clean Water Act (CWA); and the Endangered Species Act of 1973 (ESA), the successor to the Endangered Species Preservation Act of 1966, laws protecting specific animal species and their habitat, were also enacted.

Idaho created what is now the Department of Environmental Quality and divided Idaho's counties into seven regions, creating public health districts in each. These agencies, in cooperation with federal agencies, have legal oversight of certain environmental matters.

All federal and state agencies, and the regulations they promulgated, established minimum environmental protection and health and safety standards and practices, including those affecting worker safety and the discharge or emission of pollutants into the air as well as total maximum daily loads (TMDL), as required by the CWA, of pollutants in surface water and groundwater contamination. Compliance with these laws required major changes in the operating processes and practices of many businesses.

Certain business activities on public lands were further restricted as environmental groups used these laws to challenge the adequacy of the environmental studies and basis for approvals, aided especially by the National Environmental Policy Act of 1970 and its requirement for a "hard look" at environmental impacts of any significant action involving federal lands or resources before decisions are made.

The National Forest Management Act of 1976 required comprehensive long-range planning. Many private and federal activities became tied up in the courts with appeals and calls for incorporating new science extending project decisions for years. These lawsuits influenced federal policy and played a significant role in delaying or preventing private access to federal lands for mining and timber harvest purposes. Delays had the practical effect of stopping any business activity that had to work on a return-on-investment timetable.

Decades of aggressive fire suppression and, later, timber harvest restrictions have exacerbated deadfall build up on forest floors with the consequence of potentially more severe and exceptionally hot forest fires that destroy merchantable timber and modify wildlife habitat.

Mining and wood products were also adversely affected when Congress acted in 1964 and again in 1980 to protect 4 million acres of Idaho national forests as components of the National Wilderness Preservation System, precluding mining and timber operations as provided by the Wilderness Act of 1964. In 2009 Congress also set aside 517,000 acres of Owyhee County in Southwestern Idaho as wilderness, which has limited amounts of merchantable timber and a few mining properties.

At the time the wilderness laws were enacted, there were many relatively small parcels of private land in wilderness areas. The laws grandfathered private property rights, allowing people as well as commercial outfitters and guides to use wilderness areas for recreation, hunting and fishing. Private interests, including stock-ownership membership resorts, still own parcels of land in the wilderness. Their members and clients, many of whom are hunters, fly in on small private aircraft or helicopters to backcountry airstrips or float the rivers on rafts or ride horses into their wilderness property that often have horse stables and modern furnished cabins and lodges with small hydroelectric systems providing electricity and satellite. (*See National Wilderness Areas below.*)

Federal law changes, with attendant increased operating cost requirements to comply with the law, were only some of the reasons natural resource businesses were not successful. Competitive global market factors, competition from businesses in less or unregulated countries and cost of replacing outdated plants challenged the ability of natural resource-based businesses to achieve profitable operations, forcing many to close.

Many mines, particularly gold mines, closed because the mines simply played out, although as new metal recovery technologies became available, old mines were often re-opened and even the mine tailings were reprocessed to extract the metals that the old processes failed to remove.

With the closure of mines and sawmills, rural school districts, counties and cities that relied on their share of federal revenues from timber sales and mine production as well as local property taxes from supporting businesses sustained major losses in revenue. Congressional appropriations to make up the revenue shortfall have been inadequate.

During this time, federal agencies also began requiring owners of properties, where their industrial activity had damaged the environment, to pay the cost of cleaning up the hazardous waste called Superfund sites. The ore processing component of the mining industry was the principal activity affected by these actions. Many companies opted to go out of business, leaving the government – taxpayers – to pay the remaining clean-up costs. (*See Northern Idaho, The Region, Silver Valley Mines – Superfund and Aftermath.*)

Compared to mining, wood products businesses caused significantly less damage to the environment, albeit staying compliant with CWA regulations requires care to prevent erosion into surface waters, including that caused by road cutting and maintenance and timber harvesting. Compliance with ESA laws protecting rare plants and animals and habitat of endangered species is often problematic for timber harvesting. Although not prohibited by law, the historic practice of clear-cutting remains controversial Both mining and wood product industries were directly affected by federal health and safety laws.

By the end of the twentieth century logging and mining on federal lands had almost ceased. Albeit, the Forest Service still conducts timber harvests – generally for ecological purposes. Responding to lawsuits, courts have often blocked removing merchantable timber damaged in forest fires and pest infestations. However, in February 2011 the Forest Service released new rules intended to aid in consensus building and give the Forest

Boise National Forest.

Service more flexibility in ecosystem restoration and logging. Mining continues but generally on patented mining claims – concentrated ores are generally shipped out of state for smelting and refining.

Technological innovation has changed how mining and wood products businesses operate. These once labor-intensive businesses now have much higher productivity with significantly fewer employees, albeit the average educational requirements, skill level and wage of today's natural resource employees have increased substantially. The Idaho Department of Labor published projections of Idaho's total fourth quarter 2010 employment for natural resources businesses – mining, forestry and logging – at 3,251 and wood product manufacturing at 4,526 with average wages of $54,250 and $36,193, respectively. This compared to the state's total employment of 661,334 with an average wage of $34,332.

While lumber manufacturing remains the core business of the wood products industry, changes in the size of logs processed and new technologies and niche businesses that have emerged over the past few decades are changing the industry and, in some cases, broadening the variety of products produced from wood. In addition to expansion of small-log sawmills, there are businesses that press wood mill waste such as sawdust and chips into compressed wood pellets and logs for heating in pellet stoves and fireplaces or to be sold to paper mills. Bark is processed through large rotating screens producing various sizes of bark used as ground cover in decorative residential and commercial landscapes. Idaho businesses manufacture log homes, wood moldings, laminated beams and trusses and other specialty or niche products.

At the same time, businesses producing and selling competing products – such as steel studs and trusses, extruded plastic moldings and framing, dimensional lumber made from plastic or lumber made from wood fiber combined with resins – are slowly increasing their market shares.

Railroads

The Oregon Short Line Railroad (OSL), an affiliate of the Union Pacific Railroad, completed its line to Huntington, Oregon, just across the Snake River near Weiser on November 17, 1884. The rail link created

Fruit train near Bliss.

another transcontinental railroad and allowed the movement of passengers and freight between the commercial centers of Omaha, Nebraska, and Portland, Oregon, in the unheard of time of four and a half days.

The railroad crossed Idaho in a northwesterly direction through Pocatello, Shoshone and Caldwell before entering Oregon – stopping at Shoshone long enough to build a rail line north to the mines in the Wood River Valley. Much to the dismay of Boiseans, the more direct and shorter route bypassed Idaho's capital city. (*See Mining – Wood River Valley – Silver and Lead above.*)

Within the next several years, the OSL and other railroad companies extended branch lines to serve Idaho's expanding agricultural, timber and mining businesses and communities. On September 5, 1897, a decade and a half after railroad service reached the Treasure Valley, Nampa investors completed a branch line to Boise that not only was an economic boon to Boise but put Nampa on the map as well.

Several Southwestern Idaho cities owe their early development, economic growth and even their names to the railroad. Without the railroad, most of the economic growth in Southwestern Idaho could not have happened.

Hydroelectric dams

Swan Falls Dam Perhaps no other dam has had a greater impact on more Idaho people and businesses than Swan Falls. Built in 1900 at a cost of $250,000 and located about 14 miles southeast of Melba, the dam was built to provide power to the Trade Dollar Consolidated Mining and Milling Company about 25 miles due southwest in Silver City. It was one of the earliest and largest water rights filings on the Snake River. In the decades following, the State continued to grant other

Snake River water rights until the system was over appropriated. In 1982 the Idaho Supreme Court found in favor of Idaho Power Company, the current owner of the dam and Trade Dollar water rights. The case has resulted in perhaps the largest water rights adjudication in the nation's history. The State has spent over $90 million on its effort to determine the validity of as many as 185,000 water rights claims in Southern Idaho.

Hells Canyon Hydroelectric Dams Hells Canyon is the deepest river gorge in North America. The most significant natural resource battle of the 1950s was whether public or private entities would build hydroelectric dams on the Snake River in Hells Canyon. Advocates of public ownership proposed a federal dam which would be the second highest in the world, providing enormous storage capacity for flood control and irrigation. Southern Idaho water users feared such a dam and reservoir would limit the amount of water they needed upstream for irrigation. Idaho Power successfully advocated private ownership of the dams. With the approval of the Federal Power Commission, Idaho Power constructed three hydroelectric dams in Hells Canyon – Brownlee, Oxbow and Hells Canyon.

Brownlee, built in 1958, is 420 feet high with a reservoir surface area of 15,000 acres. Oxbow, built in 1961, is 330 feet high and backs up a reservoir with 1,150 surface acres. Hells Canyon Dam, completed in 1967, is 175 feet high with a reservoir surface area of 2,500 acres. In addition to flood control and public recreation, the dams provide electrical power to around 400,000 customers in Idaho and over 20,000 in Oregon.

World War II

Jack Simplot, Food Processing The city of Caldwell is the birthplace of the frozen French fried potato and the first large commercial food processing facility in Idaho.

It all started when Caldwell city officials entered into a public-private partnership with Jack Simplot.

In the spring of 1940 Simplot, just 31, had signed a contract on the back of an envelope to produce half a million pounds of onion powder and flakes to be delivered to Berkley, California, by that October. Up to then, Simplot had been shipping fresh onions to a California customer, who dehydrated them.

On discovering that a commercial prune dryer was used to dry onions, he ordered one for July delivery. Simplot had to work fast. He only had a short time to contract with farmers for large quantities of fresh onions and chose a suitable location near the onion-growing area of Southwestern Idaho for his onion dehydrating plant.

Caldwell city leaders learned of his enterprise and offered to give Simplot five acres if he built his plant in Caldwell. Simplot took them up on their offer and was successful beyond his wildest dreams.

The following year, months before the breakout of World War II, the U.S. Army Quartermasters Corps identified Simplot's plant as one of a few vegetable drying operations in the nation and asked him to dry potatoes. Within a year, Simplot was the leading supplier of dehydrated potatoes and onions to the military and held that status throughout World War II and the Korean War. (*See Eastern Idaho, The Region, Famous Potatoes.*)

Around 1944 Ray Dunlap, a Simplot chemist working at the Caldwell plant, invented the frozen French fried potato process. He pre-fried raw potato strips for the purpose of cooking off the water and then freezing them. He then deep fried the frozen strips again for two minutes. When done, the potato strips had a golden brown crust with a chewy center.

This patented process was the origin of the frozen French fried potato. Simplot marketed his frozen French fries to McDonalds and other large retail businesses. He sold five million pounds the first year and 10 million the next. The product is now a staple in fast food restaurants throughout the world.

After Simplot began his Caldwell food-drying businesses, he built other food processing businesses in Southwestern and Eastern Idaho as well as outside the state. He also started other agricultural businesses including livestock feedlots in Southwestern Idaho and phosphate mining and fertilizer manufacturing in Eastern Idaho.

One of Simplot's most notable investments was in Micron Technology in Boise, a high-technology business that became Idaho's largest private employer. (*See Southwestern Idaho's Entrepreneurial Legacy below.*)

Hunt Camp, Imprisonment of Citizens of Japanese Descent On December 7, 1941, the military of the Empire of Japan made an unprovoked and surprise attack on the United States naval installation and fleet at Pearl Harbor. The United States immediately broke from its isolationist policy and joined its allies in the war against the axis powers of Japan, Germany and Italy. There was great fear in the U.S. that the Japanese would follow up their successful attack with an invasion of coastal lands, facilitated by traitors and spies.

President Franklin D. Roosevelt abdicated certain of his authority and signed an unprecedented order on February 14, 1942, that gave the Army broad control over federal and state law.

General John L. Dewitt, commanding general of the Western Defense Command, issued Public Proclamation No.1 stating that all persons of Japanese ancestry living in western Washington, Oregon and California must immediately

Hunt Camp, Minidoka Relocation Center.

dispose of their property and report to authorities for transport to military internment or relocation camps yet to be built on federal land in interior states.

As with American citizens of German, Italian and other ancestry, substantially all Americans of Japanese ancestry were loyal to America, and, in fact, before the war was over, many fought and died as U.S. soldiers. The racist proclamation was a convenient policy of profiling, motivated by the mob-type hysteria many people had at that time. Years later, the federal government provided partial compensation to many of the detainees.

One of the relocation centers was Minidoka Relocation Center, a new community called Hunt. Hunt Camp, named after early 1800s explorer Wilson P. Hunt, was built on 68,000 acres of sagebrush between the cities of Jerome and Rupert.

Within a year, the barb wire fenced enclosure became a fully contained community of about 10,000 – 7,000 from coastal Washington and 3,000 from Oregon. They formed a municipal-type government with a charter and seven-member advisory council. They also had specialized committees dealing with food, health, housing, education, employment and public relations.

Hunt had over 500 barracks. The camp offered kindergarten through high school education to 2,000 students along with extensive adult and vocational programs. The interned families produced most of their own food on hundreds of acres of irrigated farmland.

Those who were physically able were encouraged to work outside the camp on neighboring farms, generally earning $16 per month. Two thousand of the detainees were working on local farms by 1944.

The last of the detainees were summarily released on October 23, 1945 – faced with rebuilding their shattered lives. The military then sold or tore down the structures, leaving a lone marker as evidence of the Hunt Camp's existence, a community so large that if it were an incorporated city during its less than four years of existence, it would have been the eighth largest city in Idaho.

Hunt Camp is now a National Historic Site operated by the National Park Service. The Jerome County Historical Society sponsors I-Farm, a public exhibit developed to preserve the area's agricultural heritage. The exhibit includes intact Hunt Camp barracks.

Mountain Home Air Force Base Following the outbreak of World War II, the U.S. Army Air Force – now the U.S. Air Force – began constructing an air base a few miles west of Mountain Home. The base opened on August 7, 1943, and soon became a training base for aviators flying B-24 Liberator Bombers.

The military designated the airfield "Mountain Home Air Force Base" on January 13, 1948. The vast tracts of surrounding public lands with varied mountainous and desert terrain coupled with the area's dry climate have proven ideal for a variety of modern military aircraft and training applications. Because of these attractive attributes and Idaho citizens' welcoming attitude, the air base continues to be an important part of the Air Forces' strategic operations and part of Southwestern Idaho's economic and social fabric.

Morrison-Knudsen Corp. (MK) Leading up to and during World War II the U.S. military had significant need for experienced heavy construction contractors. During this time, Morrison-Knudsen Corp. (MK) became one of the world's largest international heavy construction companies, bringing considerable employment and recognition to its Boise corporate headquarters.

One of the great tragedies of the war that affected MK directly occurred when World War II broke out. MK had over 1,200 employees, many from Idaho, building military facilities on Wake Island in the North Pacific. On December 23, 1941, the Empire of Japan captured the island. Most of the MK personnel were killed in battle, executed or died from inhumane treatment while imprisoned, though after U.S. forces defeated the Japanese, they found many prisoners had survived. They were treated and returned home after the war.

Sun Valley Resort All Sun Valley Resort operations closed in December 1942 due to World War II. On July 1, 1943, the military commissioned the Sun Valley Lodge as a Naval Convalescent Hospital. Averell Harriman explained, "I offered to do it. We'd have had to close it down anyway. It was the right thing to do, and it wouldn't have been possible to run this resort as a resort during the war." The last remaining bed from the time the Lodge was a hospital is on exhibit at the Blaine County Museum in Hailey.

Near the close of the war in 1945, the facility reached its patient capacity of 1,603. During the two and a half years of occupation, almost 7,000 men received medical, surgical and neuropsychological treatment for combat fatigue, now known as post-traumatic stress disorder. The Navy decommissioned the hospital in December 1945.

National Wilderness Areas

Southwestern Idaho is home to six national wilderness area units created by passage of the Omnibus Public Land Management Act on March 30, 2009. The Act created over 2 million acres of wilderness areas in nine states, including Idaho.

In Idaho, the Act established 517,000 acres of wilderness in the ruggedly beautiful, deep Owyhee Canyonlands and river gorges of Owyhee County. The six units include Big Jacks Creek, 53,000 acres; Bruneau-Jarbridge Rivers, 90,000 acres; Little Jacks Creek, 51,000 acres; North Fork Owyhee, 43,000 acres; Owyhee River, 267,000 acres; and Pole Creek, 13,000 acres.

The lower portion of the 2.4-million-acre Frank Church-River of No Return Wilderness is primarily in Northern Idaho but extends into Southwestern Idaho's Valley County and Custer and Lemhi Counties in Eastern Idaho. (*See Northern Idaho, The Region, National Wilderness Areas*)

Idaho's U.S, Senator Frank Church, who served from 1957 to 1981, is generally recognized as one of the major influencers of passage of the Wilderness Act of 1964 and establishment of a viable process for designating wilderness areas in the future. He would later co-sponsor other wilderness legislation including The Wild and Scenic Rivers Act of 1968, The Eastern Wilderness Areas Act of 1974 and The Endangered American Wilderness Act of 1978.

Institutions of Higher Learning

The region's principal institutions of higher education domiciled in Southwestern Idaho are Boise State University; Northwest Nazarene University, operated by the Church of the Nazarene in Nampa; the private College of Idaho in Caldwell; and two public community colleges, the College of Southern Idaho in

Twin Falls and the College of Western Idaho in Nampa.

Branches of other universities, colleges, technical schools and Internet-based institutions also provide degree and certificated programs.

Southwestern Idaho's Entrepreneurial Legacy

Idaho's national position as an entrepreneurial center is grounded in the success of five companies that developed in Southwestern Idaho and grew to be among the largest in the nation – Albertsons, Inc.; the J.R. Simplot Company; Micron Technology, Inc.; Morrison-Knudsen Corp.; and Boise Cascade Corporation.

Albertsons, Inc., was founded by Joe Albertson in Boise in 1939. By the end of the century its stock was publically traded, and it was one of the largest retail food and drug chains in the nation. Joe died in 1993. In 2006 the company was sold to a consortium of buyers with Supervalu, Inc., acquiring most of the properties, including the former Albertsons' headquarters in Boise. Most of the stores still bear the Albertsons name.

The 17-year-old 8th grade school dropout, Jack Simplot, started a hog feedlot operation in 1926 in Declo that would grow into the J. R. Simplot Company, a privately held company that is now one of the largest agricultural-based business conglomerates in the world.

Four entrepreneurs, Ward and Joe Parkinson, Dennis Wilson and Doug Pitman attracted start-up funding from local Boise businessmen and in 1978 started Micron Technology. With a major investment of seed money from Simplot, the company grew into one of the largest manufacturers of semiconductor chips in the world and, for several years, was Idaho's largest employer.

In 1912 27-year-old Harry W. Morrison and 50-year-old Morris H. Knudsen – experienced heavy construction workers – started Morrison-Knudsen Co. (MK) that by the mid-1900s would become one of the world's biggest heavy construction firms. In 1996 Washington Group International acquired MK and moved its headquarters to Boise.

Robert V. Hansberger is an entrepreneur of a different stripe. As president of Boise Payette Lumber Company in 1956, he engineered the merger with Cascade Lumber Company of Yakima, Washington, to form Boise Cascade Corporation. He then proceeded to fill the top management positions with graduates of the nation's prominent business schools and gave them broad operational authority to improve the profitability of the company. Within the next several decades, Boise Cascade became one of the nation's largest conglomerates. The company has since divested itself of many previously acquired businesses. Two affiliated companies – Boise Cascade Holdings, L.L.C. and Boise Inc. – continue certain of the original company's business segments and are headquartered in Boise.

The Region's Economic Base

In the mid-1900s the underlying basis of Southwestern Idaho's economy began to change. The mining industry was in decline and many sawmills closed, albeit those that remained used technological improvements to significantly increase their production with fewer employees. The loss of access to federal timberlands was devastating to some sawmill operations. Those that continued relied on timber

Treasure Valley.

harvested from private and state-owned forests that are managed for mixed use.

The agriculture industry was also changing. Technological innovation and economies of scale caused farm productivity to increase while reducing the need for farm labor, promoting farm consolidation and sharply reducing the number of family farms in Idaho. With regard to dairy and beef production, large dairy farms either developed or moved from other states to Southwestern Idaho, making Idaho now the third largest dairy-producing state in the nation.

In the 1970s Hewlett-Packard opened its Boise research and production facility, Micron Technology established its headquarters in Boise, and other high-technology businesses opened branch operations in the Treasure Valley. Hundreds of entrepreneurial high-tech startups also developed in the valley, most of them competing in the national and international marketplaces.

National news media routinely recognizes the greater Boise metropolitan area as a high-tech and entrepreneurial center and a desirable place to live.

Downtown Boise at night.

ADA COUNTY

- Boise (County Seat and State Capital)
- Eagle
- Garden City
- Kuna
- Meridian
- Star

Boise in the fall.

Boise

Statistical Data

Statistical Data
Population: 216,282 *
Elevation: 2,840 feet
Precipitation: 12 inches **
Average Snowfall: 22 inches **
County: Ada
Website: www.cityofboise.org

Temperature Range Fahrenheit: **
Spring: 34 to 71
Summer: 54 to 89
Fall: 32 to 77
Winter: 24 to 45
* U.S. Census Bureau Estimates July 2015
**Historical averages

Boise (pronounced BOY-see) is Idaho's capital and most populous city. It lies in the fertile floodplain of the Boise River on the southern edge of the Boise National Forest. Sagebrush and grass-covered foothills that move up to forested mountain peaks rising well over 7,500 feet border the city on the north and east. To the south lie vast stretches of sagebrush-covered land including the 590,000-acre Snake River Birds of Prey National Conservation Area.

The Boise River flows through the city, making it a literal oasis. This marvelous natural amenity and the black cottonwood forests that grow throughout the river's prehistoric floodplain are the basis for the city's French name of Boise, meaning "wooded" or "woods." The city's logo bears the words "Boise, The City of Trees."

More than 300,000 acres of irrigated farmland lie to the west and southwest. Interspersed in this farmland, which extends over 40 miles to the Snake River and the Oregon border, are more than a dozen rapidly growing cities.

Boise and the greater metropolitan service area called the Treasure Valley are the state's economic engine. The valley – boasting a population of nearly 600,000 – crosses the borders of five counties and extends across the Snake River into Oregon. Idaho's three largest cities – Boise, Nampa and Meridian – are located in the Treasure Valley.

Pre-Incorporation Years

When Lewis and Clark and the Corps of Discovery first entered Idaho over Lemhi Pass in 1805, the area now known as the Treasure Valley was a hunting and fishing destination for the Shoshone, Bannock and Paiute Indian Tribes. The wooded prehistoric Boise River floodplain had an abundance of wild game. Salmon and steelhead trout filled the Boise River each year during their annual spawning migrations. The Idaho Fish and Game Department still excites city anglers by periodically releasing large steelhead into the river. (*See The Region, Lewis and Clark and American Indians.*)

In 1811 explorers/fur trappers began traveling the Snake River and its tributaries, principally to trap beaver and establish trading posts. (*See The Region, Early Trappers/Explorers.*)

In 1834 after previous failures by others to develop a permanent trading post at the confluence of the Boise and Snake Rivers, the Hudson's Bay Company, a British enterprise, built a trading post near what is now Parma. A Frenchman named Francois Payette managed the remote outpost.

Payette, obviously struck by the black cottonwood and willow forests that grew on the floodplain and lined the river flowing from the east, named it the Boise River and called the outpost "Fort Boise." Settlers and governments would give permanence to the name. Decades later, Boise became the name of another fort, a city, a national forest, a valley, a county and a mountain basin that would yield 2,819,000 troy ounces (tr. oz.) of gold. (*See The Region, Mining, Boise Basin – Gold.*)

In 1841 immigrants en route to Oregon's Willamette Valley began passing through the area on a trail used by the explorers/trappers. It became the Oregon Trail, and the Hudson's Bay Company's Fort Boise was a landmark and supply station on the trail. (*See The Region, Oregon and California Trails.*)

The trail passed along the Boise River through what is now the city of Boise and generally followed the route of present-day U.S. Highway 20-26 to Fort Boise. The fort continued as a supply post until 1854 when it was abandoned after a severe flood and hostilities with the Indians escalated.

This migration of American settlers from the East increased rapidly as word spread of the fertile Willamette Valley. In 1848 the discovery of gold in California started another migration. A flood of immigrants branched off the Oregon Trail in Idaho onto the California Trail located about 150 miles southeast of Boise.

With the flood of Americans coming West, England concluded it could not hold the territory. In 1848 England and the United States negotiated a treaty establishing the boundary between the two countries at the 49th parallel, which is now most of the boundary between the U.S. and Canada.

With the nation's borders clearly established, the U.S. Congress carved up the

Western lands into territories. In 1848 the future states of Idaho, Washington and Oregon constituted the Oregon Territory. As Congress further divided the territories and created states, Idaho would undergo other boundary transformations until May 26, 1864, when Idaho Territory underwent its seventh boundary change, producing the borders that would carry into statehood. (*See The Region, Idaho Territory – Change in Idaho Territorial Boundaries 1864 to 1890.*)

On August 2, 1862, a small group of prospectors discovered gold in the Boise Basin. A skirmish ensued wherein George Grimes, the namesake of Grimes Creek, lost his life. The prospectors buried Grimes' body and withdrew to Walla Walla, in what is now Washington state. There they quickly re-supplied; recruited a much larger force of prospectors; and, in October, arrived back in the Boise Basin.

News of their gold discoveries spread. By the end of the next year, the population of the Boise Basin had swelled to 16,000. As 1864 dawned, several boomtowns were blossoming in the Basin.

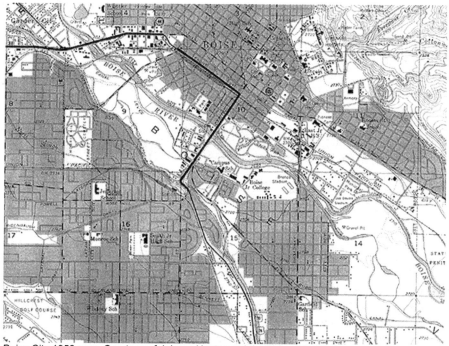

Boise City 1956 map. Courtesy of Johnny Hester and the Boise City Clerk.

Boise Basin was burgeoning, its population second only to Portland in the Pacific Northwest. Supplies of food and other goods were limited and expensive. Other than wild game, pack trains and wagons had to freight food and supplies for hundreds of miles into the gold fields. The demand for fresh food, combined with passage of the federal Homestead Act of 1862, attracted numerous settlers to the fertile irrigable land of the Boise Valley. (*See The Region, Mining, Boise Basin – Gold and Federal Land Use Laws.*)

In 1863 the U.S. Army dispatched Major Pickney Lugenbeel with a detachment of troops to establish a military post in the area. The post was to provide protection for Oregon Trail immigrants, miners and the rapidly growing farming and ranching settlements.

On July 4, 1863, Major Lugenbeel accepted the advice of local residents and selected a sagebrush-covered plateau overlooking the "wooded" river where Cottonwood Creek left the foothills. Today's Fort Boise Park, near downtown Boise, is part of the original site. He named the post Fort Boise, the same name used for the familiar but abandoned trading post located on the Oregon Trail 40 miles to the west.

The new Fort Boise was near the crossroads of the Oregon Trail, trails to the mining boomtowns in the Boise Basin and those located 100 miles southwest in the Owyhee Mountains where prospectors discovered gold in 1863 near the now historic ghost town of Silver City.

The safety provided by the garrisoned fort prompted an almost immediate platting of the new city. On July 7, 1863, three days after Lugenbeel sited the fort, several settlers and merchants in the area surveyed the new town near the fort and called it "Boise City."

On August 11, 1864, the first overland stage arrived. A census conducted that year counted 1,134 residents, including 204 women and 318 children.

United States Assay Office, Boise.

Incorporation

Eighteen months after the creation of Boise City, the Second Territorial Legislature met in Lewiston. There it passed landmark legislation that would forevermore change Boise and Idaho. On December 7, 1864, lawmakers voted to make Boise a chartered city, creating Ada County with Boise as the county seat and establishing Boise as the permanent territorial capital of Idaho. The events surrounding this landmark legislation are among the most colorful in Idaho history. (*See The Region, Idaho Territory, Territorial Capitals – Lewiston and Boise.*)

On March 4, 1863, President Abraham Lincoln signed the Organic Act creating the original Idaho Territory and appointed William H. Wallace as governor. At that time, the Idaho Territory included all of what is now Idaho, western Montana and western Wyoming.

Under the act, the governor could select the temporary location for the territorial capital and specify the time the Territorial Legislature would first convene. However, the legislature had to approve the permanent location.

On July 10, 1863, Wallace took office and designated the more easily accessible

Lewiston as the temporary capital. Technically, at that time, Lewiston was on Nez Perce Reservation land and thus not an eligible location for the capital. Lewiston did not become part of the Idaho Territory until April 20, 1867.

Following the 1860 discovery of placer gold near Pierce in the mountains 75 miles east of Lewiston, the ensuing gold rush turned Lewiston, the trailhead for the miners heading east, into a boomtown. However, by 1863 the mines were playing out. Many prospectors and miners had already moved on to the more promising discoveries in the Boise Basin and elsewhere. By the fall of 1863 Lewiston's population was 414.

Wallace's order specified the Territorial Legislature would convene its first session in Lewiston on December 7, 1863.

However, before that date arrived, Wallace campaigned for and became the territorial delegate to the U.S. Congress. He resigned as governor, and President Lincoln appointed Caleb Lyon as his replacement.

When the legislature convened, representatives of other cities were aggressively lobbying legislators to become the territorial capital. The legislature deferred action until the next session.

When the legislature reconvened on November 14, 1864, interests representing the heavily populated Boise Basin gold mining communities introduced legislation chartering the city of Boise and making it Idaho's permanent capital.

The bill passed three weeks later. One of the legislators and founders of Boise was H.C. Riggs. The name of his young daughter, Ada, became the namesake of the new county.

The Lewiston and Northern Idaho factions were outraged and filed suit, asking a judge in Lewiston to nullify the law. They asserted that the law was invalid because the Legislature met six weeks before its official term of office began, and Probate Judge John G. Berry agreed.

Berry issued an injunction against removing the Territorial Seal and artifacts from Lewiston, ruling the legislative action was invalid because the legislature acted without authority. Berry then issued a summons requiring Governor Lyon to appear in court and answer the charges.

Lyon received word of his impending arrest and, under the guise of a duck-hunting trip, crossed the river into Washington Territory.

Unable to arrest Lyon, the sheriff carried out the balance of the court order by locking the Great Territorial Seal of Idaho and the territorial archives in the Lewiston jail.

In Lyon's absence, Territorial Secretary Clinton DeWitt Smith became acting governor. Responding to Smith's request, on March 2, 1865, federal troops entered Lewiston to retrieve the seal and artifacts from the jail and rendezvous with him outside the city.

On April 14, 1865, Smith entered Boise with the seal and artifacts. However, that did not end the dispute. Lewiston officials appealed the matter to the territorial district judge who upheld the lower court order against moving the documents from Lewiston.

Smith then appealed the case to the newly created Idaho Territorial Supreme Court in Boise. On June 14, 1866, the Supreme Court overturned the district court, thus establishing Boise as the legal and permanent capital of the Idaho Territory.

Even though it was the territorial capital and the legislature had made it a chartered city, Boise had no city government. For the incorporation to be final, the law required that the town's citizens approve the charter in a city election to be held March 25, 1865. However, most of the city's residents felt that, with state and county government already in the city, they had enough government. In that election, the ballot measure failed by 24 votes.

On January 11, 1866, the legislature gave Boise a new charter'superseding the December 12, 1864, charter. This charter became effective without requiring voter approval but specified that a temporary council be appointed. The new law did not quell resistance to the formation of a city government. On May 7, 1866, the new anti-charter mayor and city council refused to organize the government. On January 11, 1867, the legislature called for another election, which was held ten days later. Again, anti-charter candidates won the election and refused to organize the city.

Surveys of public lands were beginning in 1867. In order for landowners to obtain clear title to city lots, they had to receive such title from the city – the city had to be organized. However, the mayor and one of the four city council members still refused to organize. On November 18, 1867, the matter was resolved

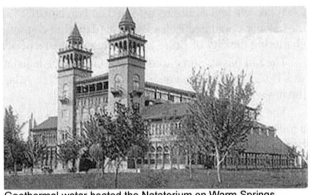

Geothermal water heated the Natatorium on Warm Springs Avenue, completed in 1892. Picture from a 1907 postcard.

when Judge John Cummins called a meeting of city residents to vote on appointment of a mayor and city council. These pragmatic citizens appointed Henry E. Pickett, later a justice of the Territorial Supreme Court, as mayor. The city government was organized, and Boise's 1866 charter became effective.

The first tasks for the new city government included better organization of the "Fire Company" and outlawing hogs running free in the city.

Turning Points

Territorial Capital The December 7, 1864, action by the Second Idaho Territorial Legislature made Boise the new territorial capital of Idaho, the seat of Ada County and a chartered city. The legislature gave Boise a new charter on January 11, 1866. This was Boise's most significant moment. That action set Boise on the path to becoming the political, economic and population center of Idaho.

Charter City Boise was the first of three chartered cities made by the Idaho

Territorial Legislature. Lewiston became a chartered city in 1881 and Belleview in 1883. Lewiston and Boise have since rescinded their charters – Boise repealed its charter in 1961. Bellevue is the only remaining chartered city in Idaho.

Unlike Lewiston and Belleview, however, Boise residents did not want to become an incorporated city with a municipal government. Breaking through the attitudinal barriers against installing a city government was a major accomplishment. However, after the city of Boise became organized, it became a model city where orderliness, efficiency and dramatic growth occurred.

U.S. Assay Office The United States Treasury constructed an assay office in Boise in 1872 – the seventh in the nation. The assay office measured the purity of gold and silver ore samples and smelted the precious metals into small ingots for shipment to the San Francisco Mint.

Selection of Boise placed the city in distinguished company and recognized Idaho's prominence in mining. (*See The Region, Mining.*)

The assay office also helped reduce counterfeiting. The August 4, 1864, edition of the Idaho Tri-Weekly Statesman reported large losses suffered by citizens from accepting "unclean gold dust at less than true value."

Today, the assay office building, one of only three National Historical Landmark buildings in Idaho, sits on a full city block on Main Street between North 2nd and North 3rd Streets, where it houses the State Historic Preservation Office.

Railroad With the completion of the Oregon Short Line Railroad's link between the railheads at Granger, Wyoming, and Huntington, Oregon, through Southern Idaho in 1884, a train could travel between Omaha and Portland in just three and a half days.

Boise Train Depot.

Unfortunately for Boise, the rail line took a direct route through Nampa, bypassing the capital city. In 1887 the Idaho Central Railway built a spur line from Nampa to Boise. The "stub," as it was then affectionately called, allowed Boise to take the next step in becoming the economic and political center of the state. On July 27, 1889, the Oregon Short Line acquired the Idaho Central Railway.

Electricity Delivery of electrical energy was another major boost for the city. However, electricity came gradually. It started with small independent or mutual hydroelectric power companies providing power to only certain parts of the city.

It began on July 4, 1887, when the Capital Electric Light, Motor and Gas Company generated electricity from a dam on the Ridenbaugh Canal near the city's south bench area. The water fed generators located 62 feet down the hillside. An 1889 contract with the City required the company to provide sufficient electricity to power 40 lights for $100 per month.

In 1895 the company operated nine generators at the site – six provided electricity for 3,500 incandescent lights, and three powered 95 carbon-arc streetlights.

Boise Gas and Light built another generating station in 1904 that used water from the Ridenbaugh-Rossi Mill Ditch and had a coal-fired steam generator for backup.

Within two years, Boise Valley Electric Railroad Company began running an electric trolley from Boise to Caldwell on the south bench. The next year, the Boise and Interurban Railroad Company built an electric rail system on a northern route along State Street to Caldwell.

In 1906 electrical power produced from Swan Falls Hydroelectric Dam, located 40 miles south of Nampa on the Snake River, began providing electrical power to Boise. The original purpose of the dam was to provide electrical power to the Silver City mines in the Owyhee Mountains. However, as mine production declined, the unused electricity was diverted to the Treasure Valley.

By 1911 the trolley and electrical power companies merged to create the Idaho Railway Light and Power Company.

The merged company played the next key role in providing transportation and electrical power in the valley. It created the Boise Valley Loop and electrical grid at a time when the excess electricity from Swan Falls powered most of the valley.

However, sources of electrical power took a major turn in 1916 when many smaller electrical companies throughout Southwestern Idaho combined to form Idaho Power Company, a private utility that would become a major force in Idaho – both as a provider of electricity and politically.

Boise Airport Boise opened its first municipal airport on land now occupied by Boise State University on April 6, 1926, following passage of the Air Mail Act of 1925, which allowed private airplanes to carry airmail. Walter T. Varney's airline began flying mail between Pasco, Washington; Boise; and Elko, Nevada. United Airlines calls the mail flights by Varney's planes, which it later acquired, the "true beginning of commercial air transportation in the United States."

The airport began moving to its present location in 1936. The military leased the air field during World War II as a training base for B-17 and B-24 heavy bomber personnel. Today, the City-owned airport has a 5,000-acre campus and new state-of-the-art aviation facilities, part of which are also used by the military. (*See Boise Today, Transportation, below.*)

Irrigation Similar to the growth of electricity, irrigation was critical to the city's growth and prosperity but took several decades to develop and culminated in the eventual consolidation of smaller systems.

The first right to divert water was issued in 1864 to irrigate land around Fort Boise and the Boise town site. Shortly thereafter, homesteaders built simple irrigation canals and ditches and diversion dams along the Boise River and its tributaries.

In 1882 engineer Arthur Foote set out to build a diversion dam on the Boise

River and a canal that would irrigate lower gradient bench land between Boise and Nampa. Financial difficulties plagued the project. After several years, Foote abandoned his dream and moved. Today, Foote's time in Boise is mainly remembered because of his wife, Mary Halleck Foote. While in Boise, she became a writer and illustrator of considerable reputation and was the subject of Wallace Stegner's Pulitzer Prize-winning book, Angel of Repose.

Several years after Foote's departure, investors picked up on his irrigation project and in 1900 opened the New York Canal, bringing 38,000 acres under cultivation.

Boise River.

The Ridenbaugh Canal evolved over much of the same period. William Morris controlled 17,000 acres on the Boise Bench. In order to complete his real estate development venture of subdividing and selling his property, he needed to provide irrigation water. Unfortunately, Morris died the following year. His nephew, William Ridenbaugh, continued the project for two years and then sold it to other investors who completed the irrigation and hydroelectric system. By 1891 the Ridenbaugh Canal provided irrigation for 22,000 acres as well as electricity to the city of Boise. In the decades that followed, the Federal Bureau of Reclamation would build dams and provide necessary financing to consolidate and develop integrated irrigation systems for the valley. (*See The Region, Federal Land Use Laws, Bureau of Reclamation – Boise Project – Treasure Valley*.)

Boise's Entrepreneurs Boise owes most of its economic success to entrepreneurs who developed their businesses into some of the largest in the world. Harry Morrison, J.R. Simplot, Joe Albertson, Bob Hansberger and the founders of Micron were among the giants who made Boise a recognized national corporate center. While many corporate ventures that started in Boise have sold or merged and their headquarters moved out of Boise and Idaho, the greater Boise metropolitan area continues to be nationally recognized as an excellent location to start and grow a business. (*See The Region, Southwestern Idaho's Entrepreneurial Legacy*.)

Boise Today

Amenities and Attractions Chief among Boise's attractions is the historic Idaho State Capitol. It stands at the north end of Capitol Boulevard and is the main focal point when driving into downtown from the south.

Downtown Boise is active and dynamic. High-rise buildings continue to change the city's skyline. New hotels; a convention center; banks; mixed commercial and condominium buildings; hospital additions; new, restored or remodeled state and local government buildings; boutique shops; and restaurants have changed downtown Boise into not only a business, financial and convention hub but also an interesting place for entertainment and excellent food.

Other high-traffic shopping locations, such as the Boise Towne Square Mall and smaller shopping centers, are located outside the downtown area.

Approximately a mile south of the State Capitol on Capitol Boulevard, elevated on the bench of the river floodplain, is the historic and stately Boise Railroad Depot. The depot is open to the public one or two days a week and is available for event reservations through the Boise Parks & Recreation Department.

A key amenity is the clear, cold Boise River that flows through the city. Each summer, thousands of people escape the warm summer days by floating down the river on inner tubes, rafts and canoes to one of the city parks on the river bank. The river is also a focal point for trout fishing, public activities and festivals.

There are extensive facilities within the city for the enjoyment of the outdoors. The city has more than 70 parks totaling 3,500 acres. Park facilities include a zoo; flower gardens; athletic fields; wildlife habitat; 25 miles of greenbelt bordering the river; locations for picnicking, outdoor musical events

Idaho Capitol Building.

and festivals; hiking in the foothills; fishing; and children's play areas and equipment. Eight golf courses are located in the city, with many more in or near other cities that dot the Treasure Valley.

Several performing arts organizations, some with proprietary facilities, offer productions annually, seasonally or throughout the year. These include the Idaho Shakespeare Festival with its outdoor amphitheater, Boise Little Theater, Ballet Idaho, Boise Master Chorale, Boise Philharmonic, Idaho Dance Theater, Opera Idaho, Boise Contemporary Theater and the Gene Harris Jazz Festival.

There are numerous museums and attractions in the city commemorating specific as well as general subjects. These include the Idaho Historical Museum, the Boise Art Museum, the Basque Museum and Cultural Center, the Idaho Black History Museum, the Idaho Military History Museum, the Museum of Mining and Geology and the Old Idaho Penitentiary Museum and adjoining Idaho Botanical Gardens. In addition, there is the Discovery Center of Idaho, the Anne Frank Human Rights Memorial, the World Sports Humanitarian Hall of Fame and the Morrison-Knudsen Nature Center.

The Peregrine Fund's World Center for Birds of Prey is located on the desert just south of the city. The primary work at the center is saving several endangered raptors from extinction. Of particular note is its success in saving the Peregrine Falcon. Today, thousands of visitors come to the center annually to observe its work and the many different raptors under study. Idaho has honored the work at the center by making the Peregrine Falcon the state raptor, and former Governor Dirk Kempthorne approved the image of the Peregrine Falcon's head for the Idaho quarter minted by the U.S. Treasury.

The 175-acre main campus of Boise State University (BSU) is located within a few blocks of downtown. It is the largest university in Idaho. The school has strong academic programs for its nearly 19,000 students and is a metropolitan research university.

For several years, BSU has had a west campus in Nampa. In 2007 voters approved creation of a community college named the College of Western Idaho at the site of the west campus.

More than a million visitors come annually to the University's main campus to enjoy the many cultural, athletic and entertainment events offered. Campus facilities include the 2,000-seat Morrison Center for the Performing Arts; the 12,000-seat Taco Bell Arena for indoor sports, cultural and entertainment events; and the 32,000-seat outdoor Bronco Stadium. In 2010 BSU announced a phased plan to increase the stadium size to 53,000 seats.

The University's perennially nationally ranked football team, the team's spectacular performance in national bowl games and its one-of-a-kind blue playing field continue to bring national recognition to the school and the city. The blue turf, first installed in 1986, represents one of the school's colors.

Idaho Anne Frank Human Rights Memorial sign.

Bronco Stadium is also the location of the uDrove Humanitarian Bowl NCAA football game held each December and broadcast nationally.

Boise has well over a hundred places of worship representing more than 50 Christian denominations along with congregations representing the Jewish, Islam,

Bahai, Buddhist and Eckankar faiths.

Prominent and historic religious structures and schools in the city include the Boise Idaho Temple of The Church of Jesus Christ of Latter-day Saints; the First United Methodist Cathedral of the Rockies; the Roman Catholic St. John's Cathedral; St. Michael's Episcopal Cathedral; and the Congregation Ahavath Beth Israel synagogue, whose building, erected in 1896, is believed to be the oldest synagogue in continuous use west of the Mississippi River.

Boise River in the fall.

Boise is home to four minor league franchises – the Boise Hawks, baseball, the ball park is in Garden City; the Idaho Steelheads, hockey; the Idaho Stampede, basketball; and the Boise Burn, arena football. In 2007 the Sports Business Journal identified 242 cities with minor league teams and ranked Boise seventh best.

Day and night downhill skiing, tubing and cross-country skiing are available 16 miles up the mountains to the north at Bogus Basin Ski Resort. The lights surrounding the ski runs at the resort illuminate the top of the mountain on winter nights.

Bogus Basin got its name for a gang of gold counterfeiters who operated in the basin during the late 1800s, coating lead to look like gold.

Boise in winter.

Six miles southeast of the city on the Boise River is the 340-foot-high Lucky Peak Dam. The dam creates the 12-mile-long and 2-mile-wide Lucky Peak

Reservoir. Immediately below the dam is Lucky Peak State Park. The reservoir is a popular fishing, boating and waterskiing destination.

One of the city's historical areas is Warm Springs Avenue on the eastern side of town. The avenue was originally a trolley line to the former Natatorium, which was heated by geothermal hot water. In 1932 because a windstorm damaged the facility beyond repair, the original Natatorium was demolished; a new swimming facility bearing the same name has taken its place.

Many prominent Boise residents built stately mansions on the avenue and took advantage of the same geothermal water that supplied the Natatorium. Many of these residences still use geothermal water for heating.

Economy and Major Employers Boise is an internationally recognized center for high-technology research, development and manufacturing. Micron Technology has 10,000 employees at its headquarters location in Boise and is the state's largest private employer. Hewlett Packard has 4,000 employees at its Boise campus. In addition, hundreds of entrepreneurial and established high-tech businesses have operations in the city and the Treasure Valley. Most of these businesses compete in the national and international marketplace.

Complementing the businesses that produce technology are hundreds of others that use technological innovation to improve their productivity and cut costs. The largest of these companies – with more than 2,000 Boise employees each – are St. Luke's Health System; Saint Alphonsus Regional Medical Center; and Albertsons, a wholly owned subsidiary of Supervalu.

In addition, Boise is the headquarters location of other large regional, national and international employers and businesses. Included in this list are the J.R. Simplot Company; Boise Cascade, LLC; Amalgamated Sugar Company; and WinCo Foods.

Other large private employers in Boise include Wal-Mart Stores, Qwest, DIRECTV, Citi Cards, Wells Fargo and U.S. Bank.

The city's major public sector employers, ranging from 1,000 to 4,000 employees each, include the Boise School District, the State of Idaho, Boise State University, the federal government and military, Ada County and the City.

Many valley residents living outside of Boise commute to the city for work. However, with the dramatic population growth in neighboring cities, employment opportunities are spreading across the Treasure Valley.

Many national publications routinely list Boise as one of the top technology centers in the nation, a place for starting a business and a desirable place to live.

Education The Boise School District serves more than 25,000 elementary and secondary students. Newsweek magazine includes the district's Boise and Timberline High Schools in its list of top high schools in the nation.

Meridian School District, the state's largest, serves several thousand students living within the western boundary of Boise. In addition, there are many charter and private schools offering primary and secondary education.

Boise State University provides most of the higher education services. Several other universities, business and professional/technical schools have facilities in the city that offer programs leading to university degrees and specialized certificates.

Health Care St. Luke's Boise Medical Center and Saint Alphonsus Regional Medical Center offer a full range of medical care. Combined, these institutions have approximately 800 beds as well as outpatient and emergency services.

The U.S. Department of Veterans Affairs operates a 46-bed hospital near Fort Boise Park with an adjacent 32-bed assisted-living and nursing home, a nine-bed substance abuse center and a cemetery in the western foothills.

Numerous health care clinics offer primary and specialized care, rehabilitation, mental health and dental services. Several nursing and assisted-living homes also operate within the city.

Transportation Surface transportation is available on several primary roads that pass through the city. Interstate 84 combines with U.S. 30 to pass through the southern part of the city. Interstate 184 connects the downtown part of the city with I-84. U.S. Highway 20-26 and Idaho Highway 44 connect Boise with cities to the west. Idaho Highways 55 and 22 connect the city with resort communities in the mountains to the north and northeast.

The Boise Airport (BOI) operates as a separate division of the City. It has 10,000-foot and 9,763-foot runways. Three million passengers use the airport each year.

The airport also has an adjoining 540-acre military base known as Gowen Field. The Idaho Air National Guard; the Army National Guard; and reserve units of the Army, Navy and Marines use the base as well as the Boise Airport runways. This military base has more than 1,500 military and civilian personnel. The National Interagency Fire Center (NIFC) is also located at the Boise Airport.

Most freight service is by truck and air. The railroad provides limited freight and no passenger service.

Utilities and Services Private companies provide electricity, telephone, water, natural gas, cable and satellite services. The City provides municipal wastewater treatment, solid waste collection and police and fire protection. The county manages solid waste disposal and provides emergency medical services.

Ada County Highway District (ACHD), a county-wide entity with an elected board, is responsible for the construction and maintenance of all local streets and roads within the county, including those within city limits.

ValleyRide is the regional public transportation authority providing bus services in Boise/Garden City and in Ada and Canyon Counties. ACHD Commuterride provides minivan transportation to specific routes and member businesses.

Vision for 2050

By 2050 Boise will be even more diverse and exciting. More architecturally pleasing high-rise buildings will dot the downtown skyline. Many of these buildings will house families and individuals who enjoy living downtown in beautiful condominiums and apartments that provide a birds-eye view of the city lights, the beautiful mountains, desert, fertile valley and spectacular sunrises and sunsets. Yet they are within short walking distance or easy commute on public transit to boutique shops, restaurants, museums, parks, plays and athletic events.

Outside the downtown area, high traffic shopping malls and commercial business campuses will continue to develop closer to where people live and shop. Well-maintained city parks and open space interspersed between quiet subdivisions of single-family and multi-family dwellings add to the vitality of the city.

Public transit will cross the city on schedules convenient for city residents, thus reducing motor vehicle traffic and pollution.

The city's recent population growth trends of one to two percent a year, with the cities outside Boise growing more rapidly, will likely continue. By 2050 Boise's population will exceed 300,000 and the population of the Treasure Valley will be over 1,000,000. Many of the people employed in Boise will continue to live in neighboring cities and commute to Boise for work.

Boise's infrastructure – including parks, libraries, rapid transit and municipal wastewater and drainage systems – will increase capacity to accommodate this growth. The cost of this growth will be born with the State more equitably sharing its growth revenues with the cities and counties that produced the growth, voter-approved local option taxes for roads and regional transit systems and an expanded use of equitable growth impact fees.

By 2050 the Boise State University student body will exceed 30,000. The university will continue to add vitality to the city as it achieves its vision of a "metropolitan research university of distinction."

Mayors

1867	Henry E. Prickett	1909	Joseph T. Pence
1868	Thomas B. Hart	1911	Harry K. Fritchman
1869	Charles Himrod	1912	Arthur Hodges
1870	Charles Hailey *	1915	Jeremiah Robinson
1872	George M. Twitchell	1916	Samuel H. Hays
1873	Thomas E. Logan	1919	Ern G. Eagleson
1875	John Lemp	1921	Eugene B. Sherman
1876	Thomas E. Logan	1925	Ern G. Eagleson
1878	Charles Himrod	1927	Herbert F. Lemp
1879	Cyrus Y. Jacobs	1927	Walter F. Hanson
1880	Charles P. Bilderback	1929	J.P. Pope
1881	James A. Pinney	1933	Ross Cady
1885	Sol Hasbruck	1933	J.J. McCue
1885	James W. Huston	1935	Byron E. Hyatt
1887	Peter J. Pefley	1936	James L. Edlefsen
1889	James A. Pinney	1939	James L. Straight
1893	Peter Sona	1941	H. Westerman Whillock
1895	Walter E. Pierce	1942	Austin A. Walker
1897	Moses Alexander	1945	Samuel S. Griffin
1899	James H. Richards	1946	H. Westerman Whillock
1901	Moses Alexander	1947	Potter P. Howard
1903	James H. Hawley	1951	Russell E. Edlefsen
1905	James A. Pinney	1956	Robert L. Day
1907	John M. Haines	1961	Eugene W. Shellworth

1966 Jay S. Amyx
1974 Richard R. Eardley
1986 Dirk Kempthrone
1993 Brent Coles

2003 Carolyn Terteling-Payne
2004 David Bieter
* Charles Hailey was elected but never took office. Himrod continued to appear in official records during Hailey's term.

Eagle City Hall.

Eagle

Statistical Data

Population: 22,502 *
Elevation: 2,550 feet
Precipitation: 12 inches **
Average Snowfall: 21 inches **
County: Ada
Website: www.cityofeagle.com

Temperature Range – Fahrenheit: **
Spring: 33 to 78
Summer: 50 to 90
Fall: 25 to 78
Winter: 22 to 55
* U.S. Census Bureau Estimates July 2015
**Historical averages

Eagle is one of Idaho's most dynamic and fastest growing cities. From a rural village with a population of 359 in 1970, it is now Idaho's 13th largest city and continues as one of the fastest growing cities in the state.

Eagle has two fabulous amenities that attract up-scale development. The city's northern terrain consists of gently rising foothills and small valleys. On the south, the city boundaries cross a prehistoric nearly two-mile-wide floodplain, including parts of the two channels of the Boise River that form the 2,400-acre Eagle Island.

The intermittent Dry Creek traverses the city, cutting across the northern foothills and emptying into the Boise River west of town.

Eagle's eastern boundary abuts the city of Boise. The cities of Meridian and Star border Eagle on the south and west, respectively.

Pre-Incorporation Years

Prior to trappers and fur traders coming into the area in the early 1800s, various tribes of American Indians hunted and fished in the lush Treasure Valley for generations.

Beginning in 1841 two branches of the Oregon Trail crossed what is now the city of Eagle. The main trail passed along the south channel of the Boise River – roughly the route of today's Chinden Boulevard. Goodale's Cutoff ran across the north end of the city – roughly following today's Hill Road – before heading in a northeasterly direction over what is now Freezeout Hill and Emmett.

In 1862 a small group of prospectors discovered gold in the Boise Basin. A skirmish ensued and George Grimes, the namesake of Grimes Creek, was killed. The small band of prospectors buried Grimes' body and withdrew back to Fort Walla Walla in what is now Washington, where they immediately replenished their provisions and recruited additional prospectors before striking out again for the Boise Basin. By October a much larger band of prospectors returned to the Boise Basin to stake their claims.

News of their gold discoveries leaked, and a gold rush ensued. By the end of 1863 some 16,000 prospectors were working in the basin. This flood of miners suppressed further Indian attacks and had a direct effect on the future of the city of Eagle.

The Interurban Trolley passes through Eagle circa 1907. Courtesy the Eagle Historical Museum.

Supplies of fresh food were limited and very expensive. Arable land made the valley the breadbasket for prospectors and miners.

One prospector, Truman C. Catlin, saw more opportunity in producing food than mining for gold. In 1863 he acquired 160 acres on the large island created by the north and south channels of the Boise River. He not only could raise food crops and livestock, but migratory salmon and steelhead trout came up the river to spawn. A large number of bald eagles also inhabited the area and fed on the fish.

The presence of the bald eagles persuaded Catlin to name his new home Eagle Island. A government survey made in 1869 also recorded the name as Eagle Island.

Polett Mace also acquired land on the island, and in 1864 Catlin and Mace built the first irrigation ditch in the area. The three-foot-wide ditch diverted enough water from the Boise River to irrigate 700 acres.

With passage of the federal Homestead Act in 1862, many more pioneers began coming into the valley to file their claims. (*See The Region, Federal Land Use Laws.*)

Over the succeeding years, a patchwork of 160-acre farms emerged and several more gravity-flow canals were constructed.

About 1877 Nova Scotia Surveyor Thomas Hugh Aikens, who later changed his name to Akins, filed a Boise River water right to his Eagle Island property.

On May 17, 1893, Aikens and his wife, Mary Conway Aikens, bought property that became a major portion of downtown Eagle. The "Aikens Addition" was on the east side of what became River Road – now Eagle Road. The property was bounded on the south by the north channel of the Boise River and on the north by Valley Road – now State Street.

Aikens campaigned to get a county bridge built across the channels of the Boise River, arguing that the road was necessary to connect the developments on Eagle Island and the northern bench with the developments south of the river.

By 1903 Aikens' efforts paid off. County voters approved a $19,784 bond to build the bridges and road, which is now Eagle Road.

The Bank of Eagle. Photo courtesy the Eagle Historical Museum.

On September 2, 1904, Aikens filed a township plat that included the Aikens property and that of retired teamster John R. Carpenter. Except for a blacksmith shop, there were no buildings on the platted land.

A high school class, including Aikens' daughter Clara, voted to name the new township "Eagle," and Clara's parents agreed.

Eagle Road became the focus of development. Within the next several years, a school was constructed, numerous business buildings built and several denominations of Christian churches took root.

Grading for the Interurban Trolley rail bed started in 1905. On August 7, 1907, the first trolley reached Eagle, connecting the city to all the other cities, towns and stops in the valley via the "Boise Valley Loop." It carried passengers, freight and farm produce. Until the trolley shut down in 1928, it played an important role in establishing Eagle as a distinct community.

After the trolley closed, the Boise and Western Railroad took over the rail freight business, and motorized vehicles became the generally accepted mode of travel.

Buildings for a bank and residence hotel added to the downtown business center. These historic buildings are still in use but for other purposes.

In 1913 food processors began what would be several decades of operation in Eagle: a meat packing plant, a cheese factory, a prune packing house and a flourmill.

Several Eagle merchants built their businesses by appealing to trolley passengers. A particular attraction was the soda fountain at the Eagle Drug Store, which later became the regionally famous Orville Jackson General Store.

The Eagle Hotel shortly after its construction. Photo courtesy of the Eagle Historical Museum.

The decade of the 1930s was eventful. Idaho opened the Eagle Island Prison Farm with 40 inmates. The Great Depression brought closure of the Bank of Eagle. The federal Works Progress Administration program built a new high school on Eagle Road. The Idaho Department of Fish and Game drilled artesian wells and opened the Eagle Island Fish Hatchery adjacent to the prison farm.

In 1941 on the eve of World War II, veteran aviator Bill Woods bought 120 acres near the intersection of Idaho Highway 55 and Floating Feather Road and built an airfield and hangars that he called "Floating Feather Airport." The Federal Civilian Pilot Training program used the field during World War II. After the war, private aircraft used it until it closed on June 8, 1988.

A fire in the downtown area destroyed or damaged several building about a year after the war

The original Eagle Drug Store, circa 1910. Photo courtesy of the Eagle Historical Museum.

ended. This inspired the citizens to form the Eagle Fire Protection District in 1947.

In 1953 in order to cut costs, the voters approved consolidating the Eagle School District into Joint School District No. 2, also called the Meridian School District. As a result, the Eagle High School building closed, and the students were bussed 10 miles southwest to Meridian High School.

Ten years later, the Eagle Library District and the Eagle Sewer District were established. The Eagle Library District began on a volunteer basis. In 1968 it became the Eagle Free Library District.

Incorporation

On February 26, 1971, in response to a citizen petition, the Ada County Commission approved Eagle as an incorporated city. The census taken a year earlier reported the population at 359, which did not include the surrounding agricultural community that looked to Eagle for shopping, church services, schools and fire protection.

The citizens sought incorporation to protect Eagle's separate identity. They were concerned that the westward growth of Boise would overtake them. In addition, the legislature had just passed the "Local Land Use Planning Act" that, among other things, sought to clarify municipal lines of authority. Eagle citizens felt the time was right to incorporate.

Turning Points

Discovery of Gold in the Boise Basin The Boise Basin gold rush of 1863 was the underlying reason homesteaders settled on Eagle Island and in the Boise River valley. Prospectors and miners were paying premium prices for fresh food and supplies. The homesteaders helped satisfy that demand.

The I.O.O.F. Hall. Photo courtesy of the Eagle Historical Museum.

Thomas and Mary Aikens The Aikens family played a pivotal role getting a county bond passed to build bridges across the two channels of the Boise River in 1903 and platting the town the following year. They were the principal early drivers promoting the infrastructure, commerce and growth that, 40 years after the Boise Basin gold rush, established Eagle as a separate community.

Establishing Eagle's Character It would take another 70 years before Eagle began to really thrive. Beginning in the 1970s several events converged to establish Eagle as a diverse yet upscale residential community.

The most prominent was construction of three large upscale residential subdivisions and a beautiful 18-hole golf course in the Eagle foothills. This successful development set the tone for future growth.

The foundation of that and future development was the formation of the Eagle Sewer District in 1963 and the subsequent establishment of the Eagle Water Company in 1972.

By 1996 the Eagle Sewer District ran out of disposal capacity and declared a building moratorium. Environmental and cost concerns restricted viable options. The problem was averted the next year because two neighboring cities agreed to cooperate. Boise has a municipal wastewater treatment facility located upriver on the south channel of the Boise River near the Boise/Eagle city boundary line. Boise agreed to accept the Eagle Sewer District effluent.

To take advantage of this arrangement, the Eagle Sewer District built a new pumping station and pipeline to the West Boise Treatment Plant and provided an on-site monitoring facility. Eagle also "de-annexed" land needed to expand Boise's treatment facility.

At about the same time the Idaho Transportation Department built the

Field of honor.

State Highway 44 Bypass south of the downtown area and widened Eagle Road – State Highway 55 – to five lanes between Eagle and Interstate 84.

These transportation infrastructure improvements had a profound effect on both commercial and residential development.

Hundreds of beautiful upscale homes were built on Eagle Island along gently curved, landscaped streets, around small lakes with many bordering a new golf course. Similarly, many new large homes were located in the foothills, others west of the city and along the channels of the Boise River.

The commercial area south and west of the original downtown filled in with a mix of multi- and single-story buildings including hotels, restaurants, offices and retail stores.

Christmas tree and gazebo.

Eagle's natural undulating foothills in the northern part of the city; Eagle Island with both channels of the Boise River on the south; and, importantly, wise city planning have established Eagle as a very desirable place to live and do business.

Eagle Today

Amenities and Attractions By careful growth management and preservation of the city's upscale character and beauty that honor its heritage, Eagle has earned recognition as a model city.

The natural beauty of the river and the foothills not only has a profound impact on residential and commercial development, but also adds greatly to other city amenities.

A paved walking and biking path – the Greenbelt – borders the north channel of the Boise River as it passes through the city. The Greenbelt will eventually connect with greenbelts adjoining cities across the valley.

The city has seven municipal parks – Heritage Park; Orval Krassen Park; Friendship Park and Tennis Court; Arboretum Park; Reid W. Merrill, Sr. Park; Community Park; and Stephen C. Guerber Park – as well as the Eagle Sports Complex.

The largest and newest park is the 15-acre Stephen C. Guerber Park, named for Eagle's long-time mayor and councilmember. Located on the north side of Hill Road, Guerber Park is a multi-purpose, regional facility with a playground, water features, a small amphitheater, pavilions and picnic tables, ball fields, a walking path and restrooms. It also displays a historic Ensign valve used from 1915 to 2002 to release water under high pressure from Arrow Rock Dam.

A new civic center now stands near the center of town just north of East State Street. Handsome public buildings including the library, U.S. Post Office and City Hall are located in the complex.

Three private 18-hole golf courses are located within the city limits with three more just outside.

There are a broad array of other outdoor sports and recreation opportunities available nearby. These attractions include fishing, hunting, hiking, water skiing, white water rafting/kayaking and horseback riding in the nearby mountains, streams and reservoirs.

Downhill skiing is available 17 miles away at Bogus Basin Ski Resort.

Eagle Island State Park is 546 acres bordered on the north and south by the channels of the Boise River. The Idaho Department of Parks and Recreation administers the park. Albeit in 2007 the city and the Parks Department reached an agreement wherein the city annexed Eagle Island State Park.

Less than 10 percent of the park is developed. A 2006 committee appointed by the governor produced a

Mountain biking.

comprehensive long-range plan for the park. When fully developed, the park will incorporate the natural amenities of the river and become a world-class, multi-use regional park.

Adjoining the park is a 32-acre fish hatchery run by the Idaho Department of Fish and Game. The committee's comprehensive plan for the park has incorporated amenities supported by Fish and Game to include kindergarten through high school student awareness, a wetland research area and an interpretative center that highlights Idaho wildlife and the salmon research performed at the hatchery.

Eagle Fun Days parade.

On the second weekend of June, the city celebrates Eagle Fun Days, a historic community festival. In addition, the city and community organizations sponsor activities generally centered on major holidays. These community events reinforce the city's heritage and provide a comfortable sense of place in a carefully restored and maintained downtown.

The city has received many awards for its accomplishments including the "Heritage Cities" award from the Idaho State Historical Society, the "Tree City USA" award from the National Arbor Day Foundation and the "Gem Communities" award from the Idaho Department of Commerce.

Economy and Major Employers The city has no dominant private employers. Most city residents commute to Boise and other areas for work.

However, in recent years large retailers such as Albertsons and Home Depot, which employ over 100 each have opened stores. In addition, several small businesses and regional offices of large organizations have moved to or expanded in the city. They include Camille Beckman Cosmetics, Tri City Meats, the regional offices of ConAgra Foods, the Idaho Potato Commission and the Rocky Mountain Section of the Professional Golf Association as well as companies involved in the construction industry such as Monroc Concrete, Wright Brothers Construction and

Evans Lumber.

The Meridian School District is the city's largest public employer.

Education The Meridian School District, the largest school district in Idaho, provides most of the elementary and secondary education to Eagle students. In the past few years, district voters have approved construction of a new 230,000-square – foot high school and 150,000-square-foot middle school. Also three elementary schools, two charter schools, an alternative high school, and several private schools provide specialized education in or near the city.

The closest institution of higher education is Boise State University, located 10 miles southeast. There are also several other higher education institutions within a 30-minute drive of the city.

Health Care There are three general medical clinics in the city. Both St. Alphonsus and St. Luke's Regional Medical Centers have major medical facilities within the city south of State Street. The St. Alphonsus Eagle Health Plaza is a 74,000-square-foot facility offering primary care, diagnostic services and outpatient surgery. St. Luke's Eagle Medical Center is a 60,000-square-foot facility with similar services. The 152-bed St. Luke's Meridian hospital is located eight miles south at the intersection of Eagle Road and Interstate 84.

Transportation Idaho Highways 44 and 55 – Eagle Road – intersect in the city.

The closest full service commercial airport is the Boise Air Terminal.

Rail service for sea/land containerized freight is available at the rail service center in Nampa.

Utilities and Services Private companies provide electricity, telephone, natural gas, cable and water. Eagle Sewer District, a public wastewater district, is responsible for the city's municipal wastewater treatment systems. The Sewer District has contracted with the City of Boise for wastewater treatment.

The Eagle Fire District provides fire and emergency medical service. It has fire stations in the commercial center of Eagle, northeast of the city near the foothills and a third in the city's west end.

The City has a joint powers agreement with the Ada County Sheriff's Office for contracted police protection.

Vision for 2050

By 2050 the city's commitment to larger lots and open spaces will continue to make Eagle a place where families will want to live, work and play.

Eagle will offer a balance of recreational opportunities including parks; ball fields; pathways along the Boise River Greenbelt; equestrian trails in the foothills; and, of course, fine golf courses.

The world-class Jack Nicklaus Golf Course will be completed in the west end of the city and will be the international headquarters of Nicklaus Associates.

Eagle Island State Park will be fully developed in accordance with its comprehensive plan as the "Central Park of the Treasure Valley."

Over the past several years, the city's population has grown on average by 12 percent – or 1,300 – annually. The city's population will continue to grow but at slower average rates. By 2050 the city will likely have between 60,000 and 65,000 residents.

Eagle's city boundaries will be set at Chinden Boulevard on the south, Boise city limits and Old Highway 55 on the east, the foothills of Gem County on the north and State Highway 16 on the west.

By 2050 Eagle will be a fully sustainable community with enough jobs that citizens will not have to commute to Boise and other cities for work. A significant number of new commercial businesses will have located in the city. More business parks and other commercial developments are in process.

Eagle will have become a frequent destination for Treasure Valley residents seeking excellent theater, music and recreational opportunities either at the city's civic and performing arts center or the performing arts venues at Eagle Island State Park.

By 2050 travel will be easier in Eagle with better access to its industry and corporate campuses. This will include the expansion and extension of Highway 16 south to Interstate 84. In addition, the Three Cities River Crossing and further improvements to Eagle Road will have greatly improved north-south traffic flow.

A public transit system – likely in the form of a light-rail trolley similar to the Boise Valley Loop that operated in the early 1900s – will be in operation. It will connect many of the cities in the Treasure Valley and high demand locations such as Boise State University and Boise International Airport.

The future for Eagle is bright. The city will continue to foster many great citizens and volunteers who care about their community.

Mayors

1971	Otis Young	1997	Rick Yzaguirre
1972	J. Marvin Adams	2002	Nancy C. Merrill
1976	Jerry Deckard	2008	Phil Bandy
1983	Carol Haley	2010	James Reynolds
1988	Steve Guerber	2016	Stan Ridgeway
1996	Charles A. Bower		

Garden City

Statistical Data

Population: 11,420 *
Elevation: 2,660 feet
Precipitation: 12 inches **
Average Snowfall: 22 inches **
County: Ada
Website:
www.gardencityidaho.govoffice.com

Temperature Range – Fahrenheit: **
Spring: 24 to 67
Summer: 45 to 85
Fall: 21 to 75
Winter: 12 to 44
* U.S. Census Bureau Estimates July 2015
**Historical averages

Garden City is a 4.2-square-mile urban enclave surrounded by the city of Boise on the north, east and south and the city of Eagle on the west. The Idaho State Capitol lies 1.6 miles east.

The foothills and mountains of the Boise National Forest outline the sky to the north and east. They provide an ever changing backdrop to the city with a clear view of the 7,582-foot-high Bogus Basin Ski Resort just 18 miles away.

The Boise River runs east to west through the city which has an elongated irregular rectangular shape six miles long and anywhere from a quarter to one and a half miles wide. U.S. Highway 20-26 called Chinden Boulevard runs through the city parallel to the south side of the river. The river and State Highway 44 form the city's northern boundary.

Pre-Incorporation Years

Garden City is located on the Boise River floodplain. Prior to the construction of the three upriver dams – Arrowrock, Anderson Ranch and Lucky Peak – spring floods were common, promoting growth of black cottonwood and willow tree forests interspersed with fields of bulrushes and grasses. Salmon and steelhead trout filled the river during their annual spawning migrations. Tribes of American Indians frequented the area during their seasonal encampments. (*See Southwestern Idaho, The Region, American Indians.*)

Explorers and trappers started coming into the area in the early 1800s. After failed attempts by other trappers to establish a trading post in the area, the British Hudson's Bay Company successfully opened a post at the confluence of the Snake River and a river flowing from the east in 1834 near what is now Parma. The French manager of the fort, Francois Payette, named the fort and the river flowing from the east "Boise," the French word for woods or wooded. (*See Southwestern Idaho, The Region, Early Trappers/Explorers.*)

In 1841 the first immigrants en route to Oregon's Willamette Valley passed through the area on what would become known as the Oregon Trail. Fort Boise was a supply station and a landmark on the trail. (*See Southwestern Idaho, The Region, Oregon and California Trails.*)

The trail ran through the Boise River floodplain, generally following the route of present-day U.S. Highway 20-26 to Fort Boise. The fort continued until 1854 when it was abandoned because of flooding and concern over hostilities with Indians.

In 1862 a group of 11 prospectors found large quantities of placer gold in the mountains of the Boise Basin. The following year, 16,000 prospectors and miners invaded the mountains, creating such boomtowns as Idaho City, Placerville, Centerville and Pioneerville.

In 1863 the U.S. Army directed Major Pickney Lugenbeel and a detachment of troops to establish a military post in the Boise River Valley. The post was to provide protection to Oregon Trail immigrants and the rapidly growing population of prospectors, miners and settlers in the Boise Basin and, a hundred miles southwest, in the Owyhee Mountains. (*See Southwestern Idaho, The Region, Mining – Boise Basin – Gold and Owyhee Mountains – Silver and Gold.*)

On July 4, 1863, Lugenbeel accepted the advice of settlers and selected a low sagebrush-covered plateau overlooking the river where Cottonwood Creek left the foothills. Fort Boise Park, located two and a half miles east of Garden City, is part of that original site. Lugenbeel named the post Fort Boise, retaining the name of the abandoned trading post landmark on the Oregon Trail 40 miles west. Three days later, area settlers platted a town next to Fort Boise and called it "Boise City." (*See Southwestern Idaho, Idaho Territory – Territorial Capitals – Lewiston and Boise.*)

When the U.S. Army established Boise Barracks in 1863, it established a "hay reserve" at what became known as "Government Island." From this reserve, the Army harvested food for its horses. Eventually, the military reduced its presence in the region, and in 1884 the Army relinquished the reserve, making it available for private ownership.

George Breidensteen bought a large parcel of Government Island land and diverted Boise River water into a canal that he built to irrigate the land. Other farmers bought smaller parcels.

In 1890 cattle rancher Thomas J. Davis, proprietor of the Bar O Ranch then operating in the Bruneau River area and owner of other land in the valley, bought over 600 acres of Government Island land that he called the GI Ranch.

Davis had a history of leasing property to Chinese immigrants who came to mine for gold but preferred gardening and selling their produce and did the same with the GI Ranch.

The Chinese farms were located on the upstream end of the property closer to Boise. They raised strawberries, onions and other produce and eventually hogs. They also started a garbage collection service. They went through Boise area neighborhoods picking up solid waste, sorting out the edible garbage and feeding it to their hogs.

Garden City circa 1920.

Incorporation

On May 22, 1949, Ada County commissioners approved incorporation of the village named Garden City, the name ostensibly derived from the village's Chinese gardens. A group of Boise businessmen promoted incorporation so they could build a small "amusement center." However, their true motives were to build gambling houses just outside the Boise city limits because the Boise City Council had just passed an ordinance banning gambling.

It was not long before numerous gambling establishments lined what is now Chinden Boulevard. The popularity of the gambling houses prompted restaurants, bars and related businesses. Residential areas that provided housing for the people working in these establishments began to develop just off Chinden Boulevard.

At the time of incorporation, the town was a peaceful garden area that covered approximately 100 acres between what are now 32nd and 37th Streets. The next year, annexations doubled the population of the village to approximately 800.

Garden City became an incorporated city in 1967 in accordance with the new law changing the legal status of incorporated villages to cities.

Turning Points

Gambling The desire of Boise developers to set up a legal gambling district outside of Boise provided a sordid start for Garden City. However, it has since become one of Idaho's leading communities.

The town's initial funding came from charging fees to the gambling houses. By 1950 the fee revenue had paid for water and sewer systems, streetlights, parks and a city hall.

In 1952 the village held a contest to rename the town's main street. Neta Danzer of Boise combined the words "Chinese" and "gardens" to form "Chinden" and received a $25 prize.

A year later, the State declared gambling illegal. The gambling establishments shut down, drying up a significant portion of the city's revenue. However, new businesses soon came, and the city began to grow again.

By 1957 further annexations increased the size of Garden City to nearly 640 acres. By the end of that decade, the village had a population of nearly 1,700.

Two of the village trustees, George Pritchard and Harold Conn, flipped a coin to determine who would be the first mayor. Pritchard won the toss. Conn became the first president of the city council.

Flood Control The new city's most significant problem was the annual spring flooding from mountain snowmelt.

In 1915 federal agencies completed the 315-foot-high Arrowrock Dam on the Boise River 13 miles east of Boise. However, it was not until 35 years later that the 456-foot-high Anderson Ranch Dam on the South Fork of the Boise River was completed, and, five years after that in 1955, the 340-foot-high Lucky Peak Dam on the Boise River was finished.

These dams not only produced hydroelectric power and water for irrigation, they substantially controlled the mountain runoff that previously posed a threat to Garden City and other farms and communities in the Boise River Valley floodplain. (*See Southwestern Idaho, Federal Land Use Laws, Bureau of Reclamation – Boise Project – Treasure Valley.*)

Chinese Origins The Chinese community that once inhabited Garden City is largely gone, but it made an important contribution to the heritage of the city. The Chinese gardens and their row-crop farming acumen are the basis of the city's name as well as that of the city's principal thoroughfare, Chinden Boulevard.

Western Idaho Fairgrounds In the heart of Garden City is Ada County's Western Idaho Fairgrounds, a 253-acre complex that includes facilities for the annual county fair and carnival, the Les Bois Horse Racing Track, the Boise Hawks Minor League Baseball Stadium, the Lady Bird Park hot air balloon launch site and ball fields.

The County acquisition of the land started decades ago with an initial purchase of 25 acres. A significant number of retail and other Garden City businesses have developed around the fairgrounds complex, further benefiting the city's economy.

City Leadership Up until the 1970s Garden City had a checkered reputation. Several sections of town had become rundown. The city experienced significant political upheaval, and there was serious division within city government.

In the 1970s significant high-end residential development began on the western side of the city and along the Boise River. These developments provided economic diversity and new leadership.

In 1994 the citizens elected a mayor with proven business and executive experience. Working with a newly elected city council, Ted E. Ellis initiated progressive and positive changes in the city's image and landscape, charting a course that has continued.

In 1995 the city formed an urban renewal agency to begin redeveloping portions of the town that had become rundown. A new multi-family apartment complex provided affordable homes in the urban renewal area.

Two years later, the Boys & Girls Club of Ada County moved into an 8,000-square-foot facility in Garden City, serving approximately 800 youth in its first year. By 2006 the club had expanded to 19,000 square feet, serving more than 2,600 youth. The Garden City Police Department has credited the club with a 30 percent reduction in juvenile crime.

In 2005 the city built a new city hall and library adjacent to the river just off Glenwood. The next year the urban renewal agency completed a major expansion of the greenbelt system along the south side of the Boise River as well as a new neighborhood park. When complete, in cooperation with the County and other cities, the greenbelt will connect Lucky Peak Reservoir on the east to Caldwell on the west.

Garden City Today

Amenities and Attractions Every resident is within easy walking distance of the abundant wildlife and recreational opportunities afforded by the clear, cold water of the wooded Boise River.

The legal boundaries between Garden City and Boise blend so smoothly that they are transparent to all but the knowledgeable observer. The multitude of amenities offered in Boise is also available to Garden City residents.

Plantation Country Club, located on the north edge of the city, is one of the longest continually operating golf courses in Idaho.

The city's greenbelt path runs almost continuously from its eastern boundary along the south side of the Boise River to the western city limits, where it meets up with the Boise City leg.

On the north side of the river is a 1.5-mile nature walking path that winds through wildlife habitat from Glenwood Street to Eagle Island.

Thousands of visitors come to the Western Idaho Fair held each August. Thousands more come to enjoy the races offered at Les Bois Horse Racing Track and the ball games at the Boise Hawks Baseball Stadium. Many business organizations use the fairground facilities for sales events and shows.

The City Hall and library complex are major attractions. When the library moved to its new location, the number of patrons increased 25 percent.

Economy and Major Employers Garden City is experiencing a renaissance of growth. Hundreds of retail businesses and specialty stores now border or are just one or two blocks off the five-lane Chinden Boulevard; State Street, or Idaho Highway 44; Glenwood Avenue; and Veterans Memorial Parkway. Many of these businesses have a valley-wide customer base.

The city's largest employer is Walmart with 550 employees. Fred Meyer and the Riverside Hotel each have around 300 employees. The city is also the headquarters of Moxie Java International, LLC, and Pro-Team, Inc.

Education The Boise and Meridian School Districts and several charter and private schools provide most of the elementary and secondary education. Garden City Community School, a new charter school serving kindergarten through eighth grade, is located outside the city.

Boise State University provides most of the higher education services. Several other universities, business and professional/technical schools have facilities nearby that offer programs leading to university degrees and specialized certificates. The Boise Bible College is located in Garden City.

Health Care Excellent health care facilities are located nearby in Boise.

St. Luke's Boise Regional Medical Center and St. Alphonsus Regional Medical Center offer a full range of medical care. Combined, these institutions have approximately 800 beds as well as outpatient and emergency services.

The federal Veterans Administration and numerous health care clinics located in Boise offer primary and specialized care and rehabilitation, mental health and dental services. Several nursing and assisted-living homes are located in Garden City.

Transportation In addition to U.S. Highway 20-26 and Idaho Highway 44 that passes through or next to the city, Interstate 84B abuts the southeastern edge of the city and connects three miles away with Interstate 84.

Commercial air service is available six miles away at Boise Municipal Airport (BOI). Railroad freight service is available in Boise.

Utilities and Services Private companies provide electricity, natural gas, cable and satellite. The City provides water, sewer and police protection. Northwest Ada Fire & Rescue provides fire protection, and Allied Services provides waste services under contract with the City.

Vision for 2050

For the past several years, Garden City's population has grown over one percent annually. Should current trends continue, by 2050 the city's population could approach 20,000.

Strategic planning is critical to protect residents' quality of life and managing growth. City and community leaders have and will continue to deal with these objectives by making improvements in city services, keeping the city's comprehensive plan updated and forming citizen committees to address important needs such as parks and waterways.

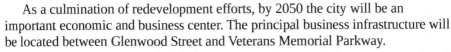

By 2050 Garden City will have taken full advantage of its principal natural amenities that include the Boise River and the city's strategic location in the heart of Ada County.

The greenbelt will link to a series of pocket parks. Plantation Island, strategically located in the center of the river, will be a major anchor park. Strolling or cycling along the greenbelt bordering the river will be a pleasurable experience.

As a culmination of redevelopment efforts, by 2050 the city will be an important economic and business center. The principal business infrastructure will be located between Glenwood Street and Veterans Memorial Parkway.

A community of artists is developing in the city, supported by ongoing cultural activities promoted by the library. This community will become a noteworthy component of the city's future identity and culture.

Garden City already is home to several of the most highly desirable residential areas in the Treasure Valley. The city will continue to seek the growth of neighborhoods where residents can live, work and play in a quality environment.

Mayors

1949 A.R. Connet *	1964 George Pritchard *
1950 Roy Titmus *	1967 George Pritchard
1953 Clifford Worley *	1975 Ray Eld
1954 Clyde Allen *	1980 Pat Westerfield
1957 Harvey Milley *	1981 Margaret Mockwitz
1958 Verna Joslin *	1986 Jay Davis
1959 William McCormack *	1994 Ted Ellis
1960 Ed Uhl *	2006 John Evans
1961 Evan Siggelkow *	* Village Chairman
1963 Joe Gowey *	

Snake River Birds of Prey National Conservation Area.

Kuna

Statistical Data

Population: 16,999 *
Elevation: 2,695 feet
Precipitation: 10 inches **
Average Snowfall: 12 inches **
County: Ada
Website: www.cityofkuna.com

Temperature Range – Fahrenheit: **
Spring: 32 to 73
Summer: 50 to 89
Fall: 29 to 78
Winter: 22 to 46
* U.S. Census Bureau Estimates July 2015
**Historical averages

Kuna is Ada County's southernmost city and one of the fastest growing in Idaho. In just two decades, Kuna has grown from a small farming community to the 16th largest city in the state.

It lies next to the Ada/Canyon County border. The vast Snake River Birds of Prey National Conservation Area (SRNCA) begins three miles south and southeast of the city. The Snake River lies 15 miles south of Kuna as it intersects the SRNCA and other high-desert public lands managed by the BLM.

Indian Creek passes through the city, a greenbelt and park border the creek. Rich farmland that grows alfalfa hay, corn, sugar beets, onions, grain and potatoes still surrounds the city. However, landowners are gradually subdividing their property to accommodate hundreds of families moving to Kuna. Most of these families come to the city because it offers more affordable housing and a quieter lifestyle within commuting distance to their employment in the Treasure Valley.

Pre-Incorporation Years

Other than nomadic American Indians of the Shoshone and Bannock Tribes that migrated through the area, little attention was given to the sagebrush-covered desert of what is now Kuna until prospectors discovered gold in the Owyhee Mountains.

In May 1863 Michael Jordon – the namesake of Jordon Valley, Oregon, and Jordon Creek – led 29 men from the Boise Basin gold fields to the Owyhee Mountains. They found large quantities of gold at Jordon Creek and started a boomtown that they named Ruby City, located about a mile north of what is now the restored ghost town of Silver City.

Basalt (lava) rock bridge. Courtesy of Ada County Historic Preservation Council. Used with permission.

In December 1863 the first Idaho Territorial Legislature meeting in Lewiston created Owyhee County with Ruby City as the county seat. In 1867 voters moved the county seat to Silver City and in 1834 to the small unincorporated town of Murphy.

In the ensuing gold rush, prospectors discovered rich silver and gold ore a few miles to the southeast at War Eagle Mountain. The new discovery caused the miners to start a new town that they called Silver City. Many Ruby City residents literally put their buildings on pole skids and pulled them by ox team to Silver City.

In the mid-1860s the Idaho Territorial Legislature granted Silver City entrepreneurs a 15-year franchise to build a toll road west to Jordon Valley and northeast to Fort Boise. Fifteen miles west of Boise, they built a stage and freight wagon stop they named Fifteen Mile Station.

First Kuna School, 1908. Courtesy of Kuna Library

In 1881 the Oregon Short Line began building a railroad from Granger, Wyoming, to Huntington, Oregon. In 1883 the railroad reached Fifteen Mile Station. There, railroad officials converted a railroad caboose into a train depot they named Kuna.

The railroad has no record as to the origin of the name Kuna, although it is the name of the basic monetary unit of Croatia and a Panamanian Indian tribe. Idaho Statesman editor Milt Kelly once called the name Kuna "the ugliest, nonsensical name that could be picked out for a railway station."

Because of Kuna's strategic location at the intersection of the wagon road between Fort Boise and Silver City as the rail stop, the small community became a hub of activity. Freight and passengers headed to Boise and Silver City transferred between the train, freight wagons and stagecoaches. By 1884 the small settlement had a post office and at least three warehouses.

In 1887 the railroad completed a branch line between Nampa and Boise. Business shifted to Nampa, thereby reducing Kuna to a railroad siding. The Kuna crossroad community immediately began drying up. Pioneer Cemetery – containing graves of the early Kuna settlers, many of whom died during a diphtheria epidemic – is about all that remains of the original settlement.

Kuna Hotel. Courtesy of Kuna Library.

About the same time, Boise entrepreneurs were in the process of planning and building irrigation diversion dams on the Boise River with canals designed to deliver gravity flow water to thousands of acres downstream. Generally undercapitalized, these efforts had limited success.

In 1902 Congress established the U.S. Reclamation Service – now Bureau of Reclamation. The Bureau of Reclamation provided federal funding and support that largely integrated or completed existing Treasure Valley irrigation systems and added a system of dams and water storage reservoirs in the higher elevations of the Boise River and its principal tributaries.

With the promise of irrigation water, homesteaders began filing their claims. However, establishing their homes and farms was arduous. Wood to build homes was scarce. Many early pioneers hauled basalt rock left by prehistoric lava flows to build their homes and animal shelters.

Kuna Savings Bank. Courtesy of Kuna Library.

The settlers' first farming task was to grub out the sagebrush that covered their land. However, once they cleared and leveled the land and planted their crops, hoards of jackrabbits moved in devouring anything green. The farmers fought the jackrabbits by organizing mass drives where they trapped the rabbits in large wire enclosures and slaughtered them.

Before the canal systems brought water to their farms, settlers hauled water for stock and human consumption in barrels from the Snake River. Later, they dug, by hand, an 18-foot-deep community well in the bed of Indian Creek. Indian Creek was dry most of the year.

In 1905 Fremont H. Teed and his wife used the Desert Land Act to file a 200-acre claim at the site of what is now Kuna. They platted the townsite and on July 21, 1905, obtained postal authority approval to re-establish the Kuna post office.

In 1907 Teed and his brother-in-law, D.R. Hubbard, filed claims on land adjacent to each other and platted it into lots designated for orchards.

In 1908 the Reclamation Service completed construction of the reservoir at Deer Flat, a deep depression in the earth's surface a few miles southwest of Nampa. They used the excavated soils to build large earthen embankments around the depression including the 73-foot-high Deer Flat Dam. The New York Canal, a diversion of Boise River water at Barber Dam in Boise, feeds the reservoir.

Water started filling the reservoir on February 22, 1909. The reservoir – named Lake Lowell for J.H. Lowell of Nampa who was a principal proponent in lobbying the Reclamation Service to come to the Treasure Valley – has 28 miles of shoreline. It not only provides irrigation water for 50,000 acres of surrounding farmland, including Kuna, but it is an excellent fishery and part of the Deer Flat National Wildlife Refuge.

By the fall of 1908 Kuna opened its first school with 14 students in a 16-by-24-foot tent. However, the tent proved inadequate for winter conditions. In January, the school moved into the Teed home. During the summer of 1910 school patrons raised $7,000 and built Kuna's first school building.

Former Kuna Mercantile as it looks today. Courtesy of The Arrowrock Group, now TAG Inc.

In November 1908 eleven of the 75 people residing in Kuna met in the school tent to organize Kuna's first Sunday school. There were three Methodists, one Episcopalian, one Baptist and one Congregationalist. They voted to name their Sunday worship the Methodist Episcopal Sunday School.

In 1909 Hubbard decided it was time to sell the lots that he and Teed had platted. He advertised in the Idaho Daily Statesman that the lots would go on sale October 4, 1909. The ad specified that there were 200 lots for sale at $100 each. Any lots not sold in advance would go on the auction block.

On October 4, Hubbard hired a train with four coaches to pick up passengers at Boise, Nampa and stops in between and bring them to Kuna for the lot sale and auction. Hubbard's promotion was successful. He sold 140 lots before the auction started, and the remainder he auctioned off.

People took considerable pride in their new community. On October 25, 1909, one family went so far as to give their newborn son, the first birth in the town, the name of Kuna Evan Havard Hodkinson.

On May 11, 1910, several farmers organized the Kuna Grange. The Grange not only promoted agriculture, but it became a cooperative. Grange members in the valley ordered needed commodities – such as coal – from their respective grange. The grange, in turn, combined the orders to make one large purchase – such as a railcar of coal – at a significant discount.

By 1910 the downtown area had a bank, a hotel and the town's first brick building – a two-story structure that still stands.

In 1911 developers platted some larger parcels of farmland into commercial orchards of smaller acreage. Avalon Orchard Tracts Company platted 713 acres that became vineyards and apple and prune orchards. Another developer platted a 240-acre parcel that became orchards with three varieties of apples.

The expanding commercial base caused the railroad to improve its Kuna facilities. In 1913 the railroad replaced the old train depot with a new facility. The old converted boxcar depot was in ill repair. Passengers seeking to keep warm while waiting at the depot for the next train would break off boxcar side and floorboards for firewood.

Kuna's first regular newspaper, the Kuna Herald, went to press on November 19, 1914.

For several years, recreation in Kuna was homemade. Street carnivals, picnics, contests and debates all contributed to the recreational pursuits of Kuna residents.

Incorporation

On September 13, 1915, Kuna became an incorporated village. At that time, the townsite covered 540 acres and had a population of 227.

Turning Points

Stagecoach and Railroad Stations Construction of the Fifteen Mile Station stagecoach stop on the toll road between Silver City and Boise in the mid-

Kuna Methodist Episcopal Church. Courtesy of Kuna Library.

1860s was the first step in establishing the future city of Kuna.

The second step came in 1883 when the railroad selected the same location for its Kuna railroad depot. The community prospered for the years 1883 to 1887 when the railroad made Kuna its transportation hub for the transfer of passengers and freight between Kuna and Boise or Silver City. However, the economy collapsed and Kuna nearly passed out of existence in 1887 when railroad interests built a rail line from Nampa to Boise. However, following the availability of irrigation water in 1909, the railroad helped bring Kuna back to life.

Irrigation The prospect of irrigation water that came in 1909 set in place a series of actions that re-established Kuna. It prompted action in 1905 by Fremont H. Teed and his wife to acquire a 200-acre parcel at the site of what is now Kuna, plat the townsite and obtain postal authority approval to re-establish the Kuna post office.

After the water arrived, irrigation gave Kuna a sustainable economy. Fertile land once covered with tall sagebrush became fields growing agricultural commodities. Hundreds of families came, transforming the land into a manmade oasis.

Roads By mid-twentieth century, railroad transportation was losing market share to motor vehicles. This trend had a significant adverse effect on Kuna's economy. As the railroad business dried up, only limited motor vehicle traffic traveled the poor roads to the small community. Kuna's 1960 and 1970 populations were 516 and 593, respectively. As recent as 1970 some stretches of road to Kuna were still dirt or gravel.

However, after completion of Interstate 84 through the Treasure Valley, people began moving to Kuna.

The Idaho Department of Transportation widened State Highway 69 to a five-lane corridor from I-84 in Meridian to Kuna and the Ada County Highway District made several additional road improvements. After completion of this eight-mile stretch of Highway 69, hundreds of families began moving to Kuna for affordable housing within commuting distance of their work.

The New Economy Over the past decade and a half, Treasure Valley cities have experienced unprecedented growth in jobs and population. This has had a profound effect on the city of Kuna. Since 1990, residential growth has been dramatic. Commercial growth is now beginning to catch up.

Many developers have acquired contiguous farmland and requested annexation of new subdivisions. The city has also

Kuna Skate Park. Courtesy of Joe Luppens.

encouraged development by embarking on a program of protective annexations to fend off annexation attempts by Meridian and Boise. In addition, the city has annexed land needed for a new sewer system.

Kuna Today

Amenities and Attractions The city has a one-third-acre downtown municipal park with a gazebo, playground, picnic tables, shelter and restroom facilities. The Kuna Library has over 43,000 books and thousands of audio and video materials.

The Indian Creek Greenbelt is a downtown park area that has a 1,500-foot path that winds through the trees along Indian Creek.

The Indian Creek BMX track, a bicycle motocross facility sanctioned by the American Bicycle Association, and skate park is located a few miles from the downtown area.

The Snake River Birds of Prey National Conservation Area includes 590,000 acres of federal, private and state land and 10,000 acres of surface water. An abundance of desert brush and grasses grow from the deep silt-loam volcanic soils.

Numerous species of small wildlife including rodents, rabbits and birds inhabit the land. A variety of fish in the nearby Snake River and reservoirs add to the diversity of wildlife. These varieties of habitat attract large numbers of falcons, eagles, hawks and owls.

The SRNCA has the densest population of breeding raptors in North America. Many raptors nest along rock outcroppings and ledges along Snake River Canyon cliffs that rise to over 300 feet above the river below. SRNCA officials have identified up to 25 species of nesting, migrating or wintering birds of prey. In total, about 260 wildlife species inhabit the area, including one of the nation's largest concentrations of badgers.

Kuna Fire Station. Courtesy of The Arrowrock Group, now TAG Inc.

Visitors, bird watchers and outdoor enthusiasts can easily access the SRNCA using the Western Heritage Historic Byway, extending south of Kuna past Swan Falls Dam. The Byway passes through diverse topography and 10 points of historical interest including old mining settlements and archaeological sites.

The World Center for Birds of Prey, famous for its conservation and recovery efforts for the Peregrine Falcon and several species of rare and endangered birds of prey, is located in south Boise, about 10 miles due southeast of Kuna.

Kuna Cave, an underground lava tube often explored by Boy Scout troops and other amateur spelunkers, is located nine miles south of town. The cave is the inspiration that led to the Kuna High School sports teams adopting the mascot name, "Kavemen."

Deer Flat National Wildlife Refuge is located eight miles west. The Refuge encompasses 10,600 acres, including the 9,000-acre Lake Lowell and about 100 islands in the Snake River. The Refuge provides habitat for wildlife including thousands of migratory and nesting ducks and geese.

The 107-foot-high hydroelectric Swan Falls Dam is located 18 miles south of Kuna. It is the oldest hydroelectric dam on the Snake River and has 1,525 acres of reservoir surface area. The dam, built in 1901, initially provided electricity for the historic mining town of Silver City. Silver City is now a restored ghost town located in the Owyhee Mountains about 40 miles southwest of Kuna.

Celebration Park, an anthropological park of Indian art dating back 12,000 years, is located about 18 miles south of Kuna.

Community events include the Kuna Community Auction in March; an art show and contest in June; Kuna Days during the first weekend in August with a parade, carnival, firehouse barbecue and fireworks; and the Christmas Night Light Parade through town. Each Saturday in the summer, there is a farmers' market.

Fraternal and service organizations include the Farmers Grange, Kiwanis, Lions and VFW. The Kuna Senior Center offers activities for seniors, including meals and transportation.

Economy and Major Employers Most of the city's workforce commutes to Boise and other nearby cities for work. Kuna School District has over 250 employees and is by far the city's largest employer.

The downtown area includes a variety of smaller retail, financial and service businesses.

Education The Kuna School District boundaries include the area surrounding the city in both Ada and Canyon Counties. The district operates a high school, middle school and six elementary schools in the city.

The closest institution of higher learning is Northwest Nazarene University in Nampa. Boise State University, in cooperation with the Kuna School District, offers certain freshman college and professional/technical night courses.

Swan Falls Dam. Courtesy of Mike Williams.

Health Care The city is located within a half hour's drive from several regional and specialized hospitals. The closest major hospital is St Luke's Regional Medical Center - Meridian. Doctors, dentists and a rehabilitation clinic have offices in Kuna.

Transportation State Highway 69 goes directly into the city, which is about eight miles from Interstate 84. Kuna is 15 miles from the Boise Municipal Airport.

Utilities and Services Private companies provide electricity, natural gas, telephone, cable, satellite and wireless services. The local irrigation district provides water for farmland located in the city with many subdivisions receiving irrigation through pressurized systems.

The City provides water and sewer services as well as fire protection and EMS services. The County Sheriff's Office provides police protection under contract with the city.

Vision for 2050

Since 1990 Kuna's population has grown over six fold. For the next several decades, managing growth and building needed infrastructure and services will be major issues for the city.

It is not unrealistic that by 2050 the city's incorporated and area of impact boundaries will extend in all directions to exceed 12,000 acres and 80,000 people.

Within five years, a large superstore will locate in the city. This anchor store will attract a wide variety of smaller retail stores and other commercial businesses.

Within the next four decades, there will be major commercial developments between Locust Grove and Five Mile. The city will have annexed 4,000 acres south of the railroad tracks wherein developers will have constructed upper-end homes along with parks and other neighborhood amenities. By that time, transportation agencies will have built a needed railroad overpass paid by agency funds and impact fees.

Snake River Canyon Overlook. Courtesy of Western Heritage Historic Byway web page at ITD.

The city will have a more educated workforce that, in turn, will bring higher paying jobs. These employees will work for a mix of businesses, many of which will use telecommunication technology to allow employees to reduce commute time and costs by working more out of their homes. These residents will want and receive adequate parks, golf course and extended greenbelt pathways.

City and community leaders will work together to see that growth pays for growth and identify and deliver the municipal, recreational and cultural facilities and attractions needed to maintain the hometown feel of Kuna and enhance the quality of life.

Mayors

1915 A.H. Christenson *	1922 Franklin B. Fiss *
1919 Victor Carlson *	1931 B.J. Leonard *

1933 H Bernard Matthews *	1976 Duane Yamamoto
1935 H.C. Sims *	1980 Maxine Kramer
1939 H. Bernard Matthews *	1982 Robert G. Faddis
1959 Norman E. Covert *	1984 Willard G. Nelson
1961 J.M. Smith *	2004 O. Dean Obray
1964 Lawrence Hayes *	2007 J. Scott Dowdy
1967 Lawrence Hayes	2012 W. Greg Nelson
1968 Mary Pride	2016 Joe Stear
1972 Charles Bird	* Village Chairman

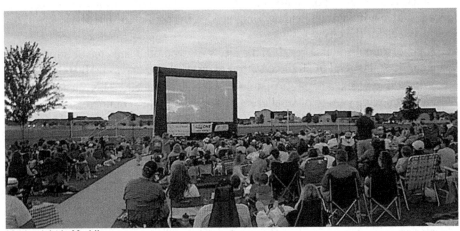

Movie night in Meridian.

Meridian

Statistical Data

Population: 87,743 *
Elevation: 2,600 feet
Precipitation: 12 inches **
Average Snowfall: 22 inches **
County: Ada
Website: www.meridiancity.org
Temperature Range – Fahrenheit: **

Spring: 32 to 73
Summer: 50 to 89
Fall: 29 to 78
Winter: 22 to 46
* U.S. Census Bureau Estimates July 2015
**Historical averages

Meridian became Idaho's third largest city in 2005. Its population is over 26 times larger than it was in 1970 when it had a population of 2,616 and was ranked 30th. Thousands of farmland acres and open space still surround the community. However, the city's agricultural origins are rapidly giving way to urban growth.

This growth placed pressure on city infrastructure and schools. Careful planning and management by city and school officials and the willingness of school patrons to pass bonds for new schools allowed for orderly growth. The city and the greater Treasure Valley surrounding it continue to receive national recognition as among the best places in the nation to live.

Meridian is midway between the downtowns of Idaho's two largest cities – Boise and Nampa. In the past, a large percentage of the city's workforce commuted outside the city for work. However, this is changing. From 2000 to 2010, the city's job creation doubled with several new commercial developments and business campuses.

Pre-Incorporation Years

Around 1811 the first trappers and explorers came into the Treasure Valley seeking beaver pelts and trading opportunities with Indians. At that time, the Shoshone and Bannock Indian Tribes were the principal occupants of the valley. (*See The Region, American Indians.*)

The British Hudson's Bay Company built a trading post about 32 miles northwest of what is now Meridian near Parma in 1834. The French-Canadian Francois Payette managed the trading post, which was on a heavily wooded flood plain at the confluence of a river flowing from the east and the Snake River. He named the post Fort Boise and the river Boise, the French term for wooded. The old fort stood until destroyed by flood in 1854. (*See The Region, Early Trappers/Explorers.*)

The first overland party of explorers and immigrants traveling to Oregon passed through the Treasure Valley in 1841. Two years later, Captain John C. Fremont, a topographical engineer, led a surveying expedition that stopped at Fort Boise, which he made a landmark on his map to Oregon. Immigrants used Fremont's maps extensively in establishing the Oregon Trail. (*See The Region, Oregon and California Trails.*)

The southern portion of the Oregon Trail that passed through the Treasure Valley ran through northern Meridian near what is now U.S. Highway 20-26.

An event occurred in 1862 near today's Idaho City that directly impacted the founding of Meridian. Prospectors discovered gold in the Boise Basin. In the following year, 16,000 prospectors and miners flooded to the mountains of the Boise Basin. Leonard J. Arrington in his book, History of Idaho, stated that "within a year of its founding, Idaho City...had 6,167 people...[it] was now the largest city in the Northwest, even greater than Portland." (*See The Region, Mining, Boise Basin – Gold; and Idaho Territory.*)

The gold rush prompted an immediate demand for food and supplies. Initially, freighters hauled supplies for hundreds of miles on pack trains and wagons. Passage of the 1862 Homestead Act allowed a citizen to convert 160 acres of public land to private ownership if he or she improved and lived on the claim for five years. Many homesteaders came into the Treasure Valley, staked their claims on the fertile irrigable land and began producing crops and livestock for sale to the miners. (*See The Region, Federal Lands – Private Ownership and Preservation Laws.*)

On July 4, 1863, U.S. Army Major Pickney Lugenbeel arrived with a detachment of troops to construct a military fort in the area and provide protection to the miners, settlers and Oregon Trail immigrants. Lugenbeel selected a location on a sagebrush-covered foothill several blocks north of the site of the present-day State Capitol Building. He gave the military outpost the name "Fort Boise," the same name as the destroyed fort shown on the Oregon Trail maps. Three days later, settlers and merchants surveyed a town next to the new fort and named it "Boise City."

The Idaho Territorial Legislature convened in Lewiston on December 7, 1864, and passed a law creating Ada County and incorporating the 17-month-old Boise City, making it the county seat and Idaho's permanent territorial capital. (*See The Region, Idaho Territory – Territorial Capitals – Lewiston and Boise.*)

At that time, what is now Meridian was an arid but fertile land covered by native grasses and sagebrush. Meridian's first settlers filed homestead claims along Five Mile Creek, where they could divert seasonal irrigation water for crops.

However, reclaiming large sagebrush-covered acreages on the higher elevations near what is now Meridian required diverting Boise River water at even higher elevations several miles upriver near Boise. Private attempts to build these diversion dams and irrigation canals were generally undercapitalized and ownership of the projects changed hands multiple times.

The Oregon Short Line Railroad completed its rail line between Granger, Wyoming, and Huntington, Oregon, in 1884. Completion of the rail line created a new transcontinental railroad connecting the commercial centers of Omaha, Nebraska, and Portland, Oregon. Following a more direct route to Huntington, the rail line bypassed Idaho's capital city and the future city of Meridian and went through Caldwell. At that time, Nampa was a rail stop for trains to take on water. (*See The Region, Railroads.*)

A year later, school patrons built a one-room schoolhouse for children of all ages. This facility was the beginning of the community's public education system.

Railroad entrepreneurs built a branch line from Nampa to Boise in 1887. The future city of Meridian

Early Meridian.

became a mail drop on the line named Hunter after the railroad superintendent, John Hunter.

The railroad was a boon to the emerging community. The mail drop gave the town its first identity as well as rail access to distant markets. The railroad and the prospect of irrigation encouraged more homesteaders to file claims around what is now Meridian. Dairy products, livestock and fruit became leading farm commodities.

Nampa-Meridian and Settlers Irrigation Districts are the principal irrigation districts serving the greater Meridian area. The predecessor to the Nampa-Meridian District began in 1877 and was completed in 1891, delivering water through a 500-mile canal system that included the Ridenbaugh Canal. The predecessor to Settlers was started in 1884 by local homesteaders with a plan to divert Boise River water near what is now Ann Morrison Park and ultimately include a 20-mile main canal and 95 miles of laterals. It took two decades and federal involvement to complete this system. (*See The Region, Agriculture and Irrigation, Bureau of Reclamation – Boise Project – Treasure Valley*.)

The Independent Order of Odd Fellows built a lodge in the new community in 1893. The chapter was named Meridian because it was on Meridian Road – so named because the surveyor's "prime meridian" line ran down the street.

That August C.G. Zenger filed a plat for the new town that he named "Meridian."

Incorporation

On August 2, 1903, Meridian became an incorporated village. The Boise Chamber of Commerce reported, "Citizens of the village are progressive and enterprising and need little encouragement in taking hold of any legitimate enterprise."

The Boise Chamber's evaluation proved accurate. By 1910 the village had a population of 619.

Headed to the creamery.

Turning Points

Irrigation Homesteaders looking to build their future in farming provided the economic foundation for Meridian. Diverting water from rivers and creeks onto their farms through a system of irrigation canals and ditches improved farm productivity and the new community's economy.

Irrigation started with small private diversions of water. Eventually, federal programs were needed to bring sufficient sustainable quantities of irrigation water to hydrate the high-desert lands surrounding Meridian.

Congress passed the Reclamation Act in 1902 creating the U. S. Reclamation Service – now Bureau of Reclamation (Reclamation). This law authorized federal construction and management of dams and irrigation systems needed to reclaim the arid West.

One of Reclamation's first endeavors was the "Boise Project" that eventually included an integrated system of hydroelectric dams on the Boise, Payette and Owyhee river drainages with thousands of miles of canals and ditches.

Reclamation also provided expertise and financial aid under a low-cost, long-term loan program. Within a few years, there was a complex system of canals and lateral ditches throughout the valley, transforming the high desert into an agricultural oasis. (*See The Region, Agriculture and Irrigation – Bureau of Reclamation – Boise Project – Treasure Valley.*)

Railroad The construction of the railroad spur from Nampa to Boise was a major step in the development of Meridian. It gave the community identity and a means for farmers to transport their agricultural commodities to market.

Meridian School District In 1950 patrons of 33 local school districts voted to consolidate into Joint School District No.2 – also known as the Meridian School District. The district includes the

Settlers Park.

cities of Meridian, Eagle and Star; west Boise; and parts of unincorporated Ada County and eastern Canyon County. It is Idaho's largest school district.

Meridian Creamery In 1897 the Meridian Creamery Association, Limited, was incorporated and built a creamery near the site of the present-day Zamzow's Feed Mill.

The Meridian Creamery Association closed after a few years, and Zamzow's predecessor used some of the facility for an elevator and feed business. Dairy farms sold their milk directly to their customers until the cheese factory on Meridian Road and the railroad tracks opened in 1913. For the next 15 years, the cheese factory was the principal purchaser of milk produced by local dairies. The

Meridian's New Senior Center.

Ada County Dairymen's Cooperative Creamery opened in 1929, establishing Meridian as a dairy center.

The creamery provided a steady year-round market for local milk production for 40 years until the facility was closed and the milk processing operations were moved to Caldwell. The creamery's 165-foot smokestack was a city landmark until it was razed in 2006 to make room for the new Meridian City Hall.

Orchards, Bees and Food Processing Many of the early settlers planted orchards. Fruit production, packing and shipping reached its apex during the 1940s before gradually phasing out.

As bees play a critical role in pollinating the fruit trees, local apiaries expanded to become some of the city's largest businesses. Through mid-century, producers shipped fresh-pack produce and honey, dried prunes and processed potatoes.

Interurban Electric Railway

El Dorado with towers.

The Interurban Electric Railway formed a loop connecting Meridian with Boise, Eagle, Star, Middleton and Caldwell in 1908. This convenient and affordable public transportation system carried passengers and freight – freight because it provided a means for outlying dairy farmers to ship milk to the Meridian Creamery as well as allowing Meridian producers to transport fruit, dairy products and honey to "loop" cities that also included Boise, Nampa, Caldwell, Eagle and Garden City.

With the advent of motor vehicles, the popularity of the electric railway declined and in 1928 it ceased operations.

Changing Economic Base For most of the last century, the agriculture industry underpinned the city's economy. In recent decades, urban growth, technological innovation and environmental regulations have led to the elimination of many small farming operations, although some multi-generational family farms still exist.

Downtown in autumn.

Meridian's population growth is largely a product of high-technology and other businesses developing in the Treasure Valley. These businesses provided thousands of high-paying jobs to a highly educated and skilled workforce. Many of these workers have chosen to live in Meridian's subdivisions.

This dramatic population growth, which began in the 1970s, is attracting an increasing number of businesses that, in turn, provide the jobs that further promote Meridian's economy and urban development.

Meridian Today

Amenities and Attractions Among Meridian's principal amenities and attractions are its municipal parks and the privately owned regional entertainment theme parks located in or near the city.

As of 2010 the city has 18 developed municipal parks on 186 acres, and a 60-acre memorial park under construction with plans for several more parks. Park amenities include playgrounds, a fishing pond, a public swimming pool, covered picnic areas, softball and baseball fields, open fields for soccer and football, a zero-depth splash pad, a skate park, basketball and tennis courts and restrooms. The City sponsors leagues and classes for youth and adult sports and recreational activities.

Paramount subdivision.

There are three golf courses in the city and several others nearby. The Homecourt YMCA offers four basketball courts, eight volleyball courts and a weight room. The Meridian Boys & Girls Club has announced plans to build a facility in the city.

Wahooz Family Fun Zone is a privately owned regional theme and water park with go-karts, bumper boats, miniature golf, batting cages, laser tag, a flight simulator and an arcade with more than 100 games.

The Meridian Speedway is a modified stock car racetrack that opened in 1951. It operates annually from April through September.

Meridian City Hall.

The Meridian Chamber of Commerce sponsors several family-oriented events. These include Dairy Days – a celebration of Meridian's early farming history each June that includes dairy exhibits, an arts and crafts show, a parade, a pancake feed, an outdoor concert and a carnival.

The Meridian Firefighters Association sponsors its annual chili cook-off in

February and salmon barbeque each August. In December, the town turns out for the annual Christmas Tree Lighting Celebration and Winterland Parade.

The Meridian Symphony Orchestra has a concert series that provides musical entertainment throughout the year with live summertime concerts held in City Hall's outdoor public plaza and amphitheatre.

The Idaho Peace Officers Memorial, located at the Idaho State Police headquarters in Meridian, commemorates Idaho peace officers who lost their lives in the line of duty.

Economy and Major Employers The Meridian School District is headquartered in the city. It has more than 3,800 employees and is Meridian's largest employer.

Meridian's other large employers include Crucial Technology, Bodybuilding.com, Complex Care Hospital, MWI Veterinary Supply, Scentsy, Power Engineers, United Heritage, St. Luke's Meridian Medical Center and Blue Cross of Idaho.

Meridian also has a strong entrepreneurial/small business community, some with over a hundred employees.

To promote economic development, Meridian has developed a "Business Enterprise Corridor" that encourages related business interests to cluster so companies with related business interests can thrive in an atmosphere conducive to attracting and retaining a highly qualified workforce.

The city's Health Sciences & Technology Corridor is the first area where Meridian's corridor concept is taking hold. This corridor is 1,800 acres on the east side of town. It presently has more than 40 new medical and technology businesses that include Idaho State University's (ISU) Meridian Health Science Center – Idaho State is Idaho's designated university for health sciences – and the business parks of Pinebridge, The Portico, Silverstone, El Dorado and Gramercy.

Education Joint School District No. 2 provides most of the city's primary and secondary education. The district has several elementary, middle and high schools distributed throughout its service area.

In addition, the district has magnet schools in the arts, mathematics and science. There are two charter high schools in the city which focus on technological training and medical vocations. In 2006 the Meridian School District reported a 93 percent graduation rate with 67 percent going on to college. There are more than 18 private schools in or near the city.

Several public and private universities, colleges and vocational and technical schools are located in or near Meridian. Those in Meridian include Idaho State University-Meridian Health Science Center, George Fox University and the University of Phoenix-Idaho. Boise State University is the largest of several institutions of higher learning in neighboring communities.

Health Care The 152-bed St. Luke's-Meridian Medical Center, several general clinics, nursing and assisted-living facilities and medical practitioner offices provide most of the medical care in the city. In addition, there are several regional medical centers and specialized clinics nearby.

Transportation Interstate 84 intersects the city. U.S. Highway 20-26 borders or intersects the city's northern boundary. State Highway 55, connecting the city with McCall and the Boise National Forest, is on the eastern edge of the city.

Airline and private jet service is available 10 miles east at Boise Municipal Airport. Railroad freight service is available in the city.

Utilities and Services Private companies provide electricity, telephone, gas, cable and satellite services. The City provides water, sewer and solid waste collection services and police and fire protection.

Vision for 2050

In recent decades, Meridian has experienced double-digit percentage population growth and a dramatic increase in new schools, churches and businesses. This growth will likely continue.

By 2050 Meridian's population will more than double with many of its boundaries abutting those of neighboring cities. Downtown areas will have several multi-storied buildings. Residential neighborhoods will provide a number of choices including patio homes, single-family houses, multi-family dwellings and estates of one or more acres.

Residents will have an increased number of choices in employment, dining, shopping and services. They will also have several options for spending their leisure time including walking or riding bikes on multi-pathway systems in the city and valley or in one of the city's many open space and special-use parks. They will be able to enjoy cultural and fine arts – listening to the symphony or viewing art gallery exhibits or visiting one of the city's Old Town pedestrian friendly caf's, shops or restaurants.

Meridian's city and community leaders have established a legacy of long-range strategic and comprehensive planning, building attractive infrastructure that will continue long into the future. This legacy includes ample recreation, parks and open space; continued improvement of Old Town as a commercial core and community center; supplying adequate public services, facilities and utilities to all residents; and working with neighboring cities and local and state transportation agencies to design and provide effective transportation infrastructure and public transportation systems for the city and the valley.

The core accomplishments, for which Meridian received regional and national recognition, are expected to continue and include an educated workforce, a business-friendly government that has developed streamlined regulatory processes, a central valley location that allows direct access to transportation for an expanding workforce and the relatively low cost of locating and running a business.

The successful management of Meridian's rapid growth and achievement of city goals is described by Mayor Tammy de Weerd as a "masterpiece in the making," a process wherein people work together towards the common goal of improving Meridian and providing amenities needed to insure Meridian remains a vibrant and caring family-oriented community; a premiere place to live, work and raise a family; a beautiful city of distinction.

Mayors

Rev. Harvey B. Powers **
1903 Samuel McClure Reynolds *
1903 Harvey B. Powers *
1904 Isaac N. Daley *
1905 James A. Fenton *
1907 George E. Atwater *
1909 James Madison Anderson *
1915 E.C. Pfaffle *
1916 Elmer E. Sharp *
1917 S.H. Griffith *
1920 A.W. Garrett *
1921 L.A. Songer *
1924 J.M. Dodds *
1925 W.R. Baird *

1926 W.S. Mateer *
1927 John B. Cato *
1931 E.H. Taylor *
1939 J.W. Rice *
1941 W.L. Lawson
1947 V.R. Botkiin
1949 A.G. Postlethwaite
1953 Don Storey
1980 Joseph L. Glansyer
1984 Grant Kiingsford
1996 Bob Corrie
2004 Tammy de Weerd
* Village Chairman
** Organizing Chairman

Star.

Star

Statistical Data

Population: 7,295 *
Elevation: 2,467 feet
Precipitation: 12 inches **
Average Snowfall: 22 inches **
County: Ada
Website: www.staridaho.org

Temperature Range – Fahrenheit: **
Spring: 31 to 73
Summer: 51 to 91
Fall: 28 to 79
Winter: 21 to 45
* U.S. Census Bureau Estimates July 2015

96

**Historical averages

Star is Idaho's newest city and one of its fastest growing. It lies on the western edge of northern Ada County. The Boise River flows through the southern edge of the city. The northern part of the city rises into the foothills.

Residents have impressive views of the 7,572-foot-high Shafer Butte, Bogus Basin Ski Resort and surrounding Boise National Forest mountains that lie about 20 miles directly northeast.

Pre-Incorporation Years

In 1812 European explorers/trappers came into the Boise River Valley. In 1813 one of these trappers, John Reed, attempted to establish trading posts in the area. He chose a location at the confluence of the Boise and Snake Rivers, 25 miles west of Star near what is now Parma. However, a band of American Indians killed Reed and the other eight men in his party. The wife and two children of one of the men, warned by a friendly Indian, escaped.

In 1834 Hudson's Bay Company representatives built an adobe fort near the site of Reed's old cabin. A French trapper, Francois Payette, who ran the fort for many years, named the river and the fort "Boise," the French name for "wooded."

In 1841 the first overland immigration of pioneers to Oregon took place. Within a few years, thousands more followed. The Oregon Trail passed on the south side of the Boise River near what is now U.S. Highway 20-26, about two miles south of Star. Fort Boise was a prominent Oregon Trail landmark until destroyed by the floods of 1856 and 1862.

On August 2, 1862, prospectors discovered large quantities of placer gold in the mountains near what is now Idaho City. In 1863 approximately 16,000 prospectors and miners converged on the area.

On July 4, 1863, the U.S. Army established a military post overlooking the Boise River 15 miles west of what is now Star. The military provided protection to the miners, settlers and Oregon Trail immigrants from hostile Indians.

Farmstead in Star.

They named their new post "Fort Boise," thus restoring the old Oregon Trail landmark – except the new fort was about 40 miles east of the original Fort Boise. Three days later, a group of local settlers platted a new town, which they named Boise City, next to the new fort.

The discovery of gold in the Boise Basin played an important role in the development of Star. Thousands of miners in the nearby mountains were paying premium prices for fresh food. Settlers began utilizing the newly enacted Homestead Act (1862), filed their 160-acre homestead claims along the Boise

River and began diverting irrigation water from the river onto their farms and ranches.

The stage line between Boise City and Umatilla, Oregon, passed near the future city of Star. This wagon road provided the transportation link needed to deliver farm production to the miners.

One of the first settlers in the area was M.B. Palmer. Palmer diverted water from the Boise River through an irrigation canal he named Pioneer Ditch. Several additional homesteaders settled between the future communities of Star and Middleton. They joined Palmer in improving Pioneer Ditch and extending it to the Middleton (flour) Mill.

Church groups were among the community's first public gatherings. In 1864 one of the settlers – a minister, David Fouch – held Church of Christ meetings in his home. In 1881 the congregation built a church that they would later move to Star. The Methodists also built a church.

Education was important to early settlers. In the case of Star, the schoolhouse provided the object that gave the city its name.

During the mid-1870s the settlers built their first schoolhouse just off, and facing, the stagecoach road. In an apparent attempt to underscore academic excellence, one of the settlers sawed a large five-pointed star and nailed it to the school's front door.

The school with the star door became an important landmark and frame of reference. For example, Western travelers seeking a nearby restaurant and lodging facility were often told that the facility was one mile east of the schoolhouse with a big star on the door. As the community grew into a farmer's market and trading center, it adopted the name "Star."

In 1880 postal authorities approved the Star Post office, housed in Shepp Grey's General Store. At that time, the community had two blacksmith shops, a schoolhouse, two churches and ten homes. The first hotel opened in 1888.

In 1890 the Fouch brothers built a ferry across the Boise River south of town. In 1904 the Star Bridge replaced the ferry.

In 1903 a new brick schoolhouse on River Street replaced the old frame school with the star on the door.

Interurban Railway station in Star.

During the early 1900s residents enjoyed a variety of activities. Main Street was a dirt road. They often held horse races down Main Street followed by a baseball game in the park. Some horse races were on-the-spot challenges, making it necessary for pedestrians to be alert.

Other community activities included a debating society that met weekly to discuss issues of the day such as railroads, Sunday laws and women's rights. In addition, there were literary society meetings, school sporting events and skating at the village rink. Star Trading Days were livestock sales held the third Saturday of each month.

In 1905 Star became an incorporated village. By 1907 Star's population exceeded 500. The Idaho Daily Statesman reported, "[Star had] five general merchandise stores; drug store; one hardware; one lumber and coal yard, carrying as complete a stock as is to be found in the state; two blacksmith shops; two first-class hotels; two livery stables; one real estate and land office; newspaper and printing plant; and the Farmers Bank of Star."

On August 7, 1907, the Interurban Trolley called the "Boise Valley Loop" was completed. This electric railroad carried passengers, freight and farm produce. It ran from Boise to Caldwell via Eagle, Star and Middleton and back through Nampa and Meridian to Boise – cost per passenger, 65 cents.

The Interurban Trolley also brought electricity to Star. In addition, Star received a handsome Interurban Depot with a freight office and passenger waiting room. The depot also served the stagecoach line to Emmett.

With the trolley came a surge of new businesses and residents. In 1909 residents and businesses built at least 30 new buildings including the two-story brick Odd Fellows Hall that also housed the Pinney Opera House. In 1911 the first issue of the weekly newspaper, the Star Courier, began publishing. In 1912 a new four-year high school started and the Friends Church constructed its building. A lumberyard came in 1917; and in 1919 W.T. Kirtley erected the Star Mercantile Co. building, a business that is still in operation.

The Interurban Trolley was a transitional mode of transportation used between the era of horse drawn carriages and motor vehicles. By 1928 demand for the trolley had dropped off so far that it ceased operations. The closure of the trolley had a significant adverse effect on Star's economy and the attitude of its residents.

In 1929 the Idaho Department of Transportation (ITD) paved the highway – now State Highway 44 – on the east and west sides of Star. ITD did not pave the road through the city because, under Idaho Law at the time, Star was an incorporated village and had its own highway jurisdiction. Thus, Star would have had to pay for the pavement laid through the village.

The residents wanted the paved road to bring in business lost due to closure of the trolley. However, they did not have the money to pay for it and raising taxes was out of the question. Accordingly, they opted for an expedient solution; they rescinded their village incorporation. Since Star was now legally a rural community, ITD had no option but to pave the road through town.

Queen Anne style house in Star.

The Great Depression took an added toll on the town. Perhaps the most significant was the 1934 failure of the Farmers Bank of Star. However, the bank's depositors ultimately recovered all of their money.

For about sixty years, Star's population stayed around 500. In 1955 area patrons formed the Star Fire District. In 1990 the town had a population of 648.

However, in the 1990s several high-tech and other businesses in the Treasure Valley began a period of rapid growth. The populations of Ada and Canyon Counties soared. This population growth spilled over into Star.

Incorporation

Ada County Commissioners were approving an increasing number of subdivisions in the Star area as families wanted more affordable housing on the one hand and large-lot subdivisions on the other. Many Star residents concluded that the growth was getting out of control. In order to manage the rapid growth, provide adequate services and preserve their quality of life, they needed to incorporate as a city.

On December 12, 1997, the Ada County Commissioners approved the incorporation of the City of Star. Star became Idaho's 200th city, the first since 1971. In addition, Star is the only city in Idaho that has been incorporated twice.

Turning Points

Post Office The 1880 decision by Shepp Grey to establish a post office named Star in his establishment brought immediate formal recognition of the community and fostered economic development.

Interurban Trolley The electrically-powered Interurban Trolley and Depot were of major importance to Star. It opened the town to travelers from throughout the Treasure Valley, brought electricity and opened the community for significant economic development. When the trolley closed in 1929, it had a devastating effect on the city and its residents.

One of Star's parks.

Rescinding Village Charter Rescinding the village charter in 1929 had a significant adverse effect on the economy and future of Star. By reverting to unincorporated county status, residents lost the benefits of central organization, structure and image. This lack of organization was likely a major factor in the community not growing for several decades.

In the 1990s the effects of inadequate municipal organization became apparent. With limited organization, residents were ill equipped to deal with the unexpectedly dramatic and sustained growth of the city. This rapid growth forced the residents to become an incorporated city.

Adapting to the New Economy Most residents of Star commute to other cities for employment and shopping. The city's commercial base lags behind residential development. Dealing with growth coming from this new urban economy is perhaps one of the greatest challenges facing the city.

Star Today

Amenities and Attractions
Blake Haven Park is located next to the elementary school.

The park has a playground, ball fields and picnic facilities.

Star's natural setting provides a variety of outdoor recreation opportunities. Many residents enjoy biking in the foothills on the north side of town. Others enjoy the Boise River that borders the town on the south. On almost any given day, people go to the river to float on

Westpointe Park.

tubes or rafts, fish, swim, bird watch or just walk along the banks.

The city has eleven historic buildings. Walking tour pamphlets are available at the City Hall. Many of these buildings date back to 1907, the time of the Interurban Trolley when Star had its last period of rapid growth.

Star Mercantile.

The Star cemetery has many historical markers including many who died along the Oregon Trail. The oldest are dated 1871. Some are obviously hand hewn.

One of the attractive aspects of living in Star is its proximity to Boise. Star residents live within 16 miles of the state capital and numerous Boise amenities including museums, parks, shopping, concerts, sporting events and the zoo.

Eagle Island State Park is five miles east. The state has recently completed a comprehensive plan for this 545-acre park. When complete, Eagle Island State Park will be a mixed-use facility with natural areas set aside for wild life, a wildlife interpretive center, lakes, many water features, areas for the performing arts and numerous walking paths connecting to the green belt that will extend through the Treasure Valley. Not only will Star residents enjoy this developing facility, but it will be a source for economic development for businesses in the city.

Downhill skiing is available at the 2,600-acre Bogus Basin Recreational Area in the Boise National Forest, 16 miles north of Boise. The resort has 7 chairlifts, 52 groomed ski runs and 165 acres of night skiing.

Many of Idaho's honored veterans are buried 14 miles east in Veterans Memorial State Park.

The four units of Lucky Peak State Park are located about 26 miles southeast in or near Lucky Peak Reservoir.

The four segments of the 16,944-acre Boise River Wildlife Management Area begins several miles west of Boise and crosses both sides of State Highway 21. This wildlife management area primarily provides winter habitat for deer and elk.

Economy and Major Employers Star Mercantile Co., the principal retail store in town, has fewer than 50 employees and is the city's largest private employer.

With just over 30 employees, the Meridian School District is the largest public employer.

Most of the city's residents commute to work outside the city. The farms that surround the city raise a variety of crops including alfalfa, sugar beets, wheat and oats.

Education Meridian Joint School District provides most of the elementary and secondary education in Star. Elementary students attend Star Elementary. Middle and high school students attend school six miles east in Eagle.

There are several institutions of higher learning within a 30-minute drive of Star. These include the College of Idaho in Caldwell, Northwest Nazarene University in Nampa and Boise State University in Boise.

Health Care Star has a medical clinic and several dental clinics. Four hospitals are within 14 miles of Star – St. Alphonsus Meridian Health and St. Luke's Meridian Medical Center, both in Meridian; Mercy Medical Center in Nampa; and West Valley Medical Center in Caldwell.

River Walk Park.

Transportation Idaho Highway 44 intersects the city. Interstate 84 can be accessed six miles south near Nampa or 10 miles west near Caldwell.

The nearest commercial airport is Boise Municipal.

Utilities and Services Private companies provide electricity, natural gas, telephone, cable, CATV and satellite services. The City provides water and sewer services. The Star Fire District and the Ada County Sheriff's Office provide fire and police protection, respectively.

Vision for 2050

The 2000 census reported Star's population at 1,795. By July 1, 2007, it reported a population of 4,754. Today, Star's growth is moderating. Barring any dramatic surge in Treasure Valley employment and a resulting need for housing, Star's population growth will likely continue to be moderate until it is a more sustainable 2 to 3 percent.

By that time, the Star business district will have changed dramatically. Most residents will be able to find many of the goods and services they desire in Star.

The Meridian School District will have built a middle and high school in or near Star. In 2008 the district acquired 116 acres as a future site for those schools and other facilities. In addition, the district will have added three more elementary schools in the city.

Parks and recreation are a top priority for the city. In the coming years, additional parks and facilities will compliment each major residential area.

City leaders will manage growth and work with other stakeholders, including developers, to provide land and resources for new parks, schools and other infrastructure paid through existing revenue streams, impact fees, grants or bonds approved by city voters.

Mayors

1997 Joseph E. Watson	2004 Nathan Mitchell
2000 Gussie O'Connor	2016 Chad Bell
2002 Gail R. Glasgow	

Cows grazing at Council.

ADAMS COUNTY

- Council (County Seat)
- New Meadows

Council in the fall.

Council

Statistical Data

Population: 812 *
Elevation: 2,940 feet
Precipitation: 27 inches **
Average Snowfall: 62 inches **
County: Adams
Website: www.councilidaho.com

Temperature Range – Fahrenheit: **
Spring: 29 to 72
Summer: 49 to 91
Fall: 27 to 80
Winter: 17 to 40
* U.S. Census Bureau Estimates July 2015
**Historical averages

Council, the Adams County seat, lies in a valley within the Payette National Forest. The West Mountains, forming the border between Adams and Valley Counties, lie about 13 miles due east. Council Mountain, rising to 8,126 feet, is about 5 miles east of town.

The Cuddy Mountains ascend to the west, with Pyramid Point – rising to 6,506 feet – lying 10 miles away. About 25 miles of improved roads lead northwest from the city to the famous Seven Devils Mountains in the Payette National Forest, bordering the Snake River and forming the deepest gorge in North America.

The city lies about 20 miles northeast of Cambridge on U.S. Highway 95 and 25 miles south of New Meadows.

Pre-Incorporation Years

The city of Council derives its name as the historic location where tribes of American Indians encamped to catch and dry salmon during the fish's annual migration up the Weiser River.

Perry Clark – a member of the Idaho Territorial Legislature that began its first session in Lewiston on December 7, 1863 – named the place Council Valley. Clark observed one of these Indian encampments from the top of a little hill north of what is now Council. He said he saw "...many hundreds of Indians and thousands of head of Indian horses at one site, literally covering the valley as a blanket."

In July 1862 gold prospectors, working the Snake River and its tributaries south of Lewiston in the Seven Devils Mountains, discovered about a 15-square-mile mineralized zone of highly colored blue rock that they later identified as high-grade copper. Years later, some of the ores were assessed as

Early Council.

containing 18 percent copper. They staked claims; however, commercial access to the ore deposits was virtually impossible. It would be decades before owners would attempt mine development.

The first white settlers in the valley, the George and Elizabeth Moser family came in 1876, one year before the U.S. Army defeated the Nez Perce Indians, suppressing what they deemed an uprising. (*See North Idaho, American Indians – Nez Perce War.*)

The Moser homestead was at the intersection of the two trails – the north-south trail through the valley and the trail to the Seven Devils Mountains. The area had an abundance of fish, game and timber. Moser used a plow that he borrowed from one of the settlers in nearby Indian Valley to fashion a wagon road down Mesa Hill, a summit located a few miles south. They built a log cabin and brought in a herd of hogs and 100 head of cattle. They built a second house that they used as a hotel and hauled or herded their livestock for sale to the miners working the Boise Basin and other mines.

In the early 1890s a grizzly bear killed some of Moser's hogs. George set off with his rifle and dog to kill the bear. However, the bear attacked George, badly injuring his legs and, eventually, leading to his death in 1896.

Council was becoming a bustling town. Mine owners in the Seven Devils and Black Lake were building a road from Council to the mines, and new settlers diverted water from the streams to irrigate their farms and

Early Council boardwalk.

bring water into the town that stood on the original Moser homestead.

The Pacific and Idaho Northern Railroad (P&IN) line from Weiser to New Meadows reached Council in 1901, and Council became the shipping point for copper ore hauled by wagon from the mines in the Seven Devils Mining District. At that time, a stagecoach ran daily from Council to the principal town in the mining district, Landore, a community with a population exceeding 1,000.

Incorporation

On January 20, 1903, Council became an incorporated village. It became an incorporated city in November 1967, as required by a change in state law.

Council was a booming community. By 1910 Colonel Edgar Heigho, the president of P&IN, built the Pomona Hotel at the corner of Main and Moser Avenue.

Street crowd in early Council.

The town also had a 400-seat opera house, several stores, shops and six saloons.

Fire was a constant concern to the residents of Council. The most devastating fire, occurring in 1915, began in a candy store and spread to the entire business community. Following the fire, the village board passed an ordinance requiring use of non-flammable construction materials.

Turning Points

Moser Family The decision by entrepreneurs George and Elizabeth Moser to establish their homestead, hotel and food production businesses on the critical wagon road intersection

Cars heading to Lewiston, May 15, 1924.

established the location of the future city of Council.

Seven Devils Mining District The discovery of copper in the Seven Devils Mountains was important to the city. Even though initial attempts were unsuccessful, the heroic efforts by mine owners to develop the mines underpinned the city's economy for decades.

Railroad The railroad, originally planned to serve the expanding mining activity in the region, had a major impact in establishing the viability of Council and allowing the city's timber and agriculture-based economy to offset the mining-based economy that never fully materialized.

Council Today

Amenities and Attractions Each June, the Council American Legion Post 72 sponsors the Council Mountain Flag Day Run with a motorcycle fun-run culminating at the elementary school.

The city celebrates Independence Day with a parade, car show, porcupine races, logging contests, lawnmower drag races and fireworks.

Adams County courthouse.

Near the end of July, the County sponsors its annual fair and rodeo.

Each August the chamber of commerce sponsors the Council Mountain Music Festival.

City residents enjoy their close proximity to the nearby national forest and mountains. Hunting, fishing, camping and ATV riding are popular in the warmer months and snowmobile riding and Nordic skiing are among favorite activities in the winter.

Economy and Major Employers With about 50 employees each, the Council Community Hospital, U.S. Forest Service, Adams County and the Council School District are the city's largest employers. Most of the remaining jobs are provided by the city's merchants and small businesses.

Education The Council School District provides most of the Council area's primary and secondary education. The school district operates an

Council City Hall.

elementary school for K-6 age students and a junior/senior high school for 7-12 age students within the city.

The closest institution for higher education is the College of Idaho, 100 miles south in Caldwell.

Health Care Council Community Hospital provides most of the medical services in the greater Council area.

Transportation U.S. Highway 95 intersects the city. Council Municipal Airport has a 3,600-foot runway that provides services for light private and charter aircraft.

Utilities and Services Private companies provide electricity, telephone and satellite services. The City provides water and sewer services. The city's volunteer fire department provides fire protection. The Adams County Sheriff's Office provides police protection under contract with the city.

Vision for 2050

For the past half century, Council's

Council street corner.

population has remained somewhat constant. Absent major changes in the use of the Seven Devils Mountains for recreation or mining, the city's population will likely remain somewhat constant.

By 2050 Council will still be a rural, peaceful hometown community set in the beautiful Payette National Forest, a beautiful place to live and raise a family.

New Meadows train depot today.

New Meadows

Statistical Data

Population: 475 *
Elevation: 3,868 feet
Precipitation: 26 inches **
Average Snowfall: 95 inches **
County: Adams
Website: www.newmeadowsidaho.org

Temperature Range – Fahrenheit: **
Spring: 20 to 64
Summer: 39 to 84
Fall: 20 to 73
Winter: 7 to 37
* U.S. Census Bureau Estimates July 2015
**Historical averages

The city of New Meadows lies near the center of the beautiful 16-mile-long and up to five-mile-wide Meadows Valley, which comprises over 30,000 acres. Flowing through the valley are the crystal-clear waters of the Little Salmon River. The Little Salmon joins the main Salmon River 34 miles to the north.

Pine and fir trees of the Payette National Forest surround most of the valley. Rolling foothills lie to the west and south; high mountains are to the north and east. About 10 miles northeast is the 8,478-foot-high Granite Mountain. The 8,048-foot-high Pollock Mountain lies about 15 miles northwest. The 7,803-foot-high Brundage Mountain, the home to Brundage Mountain Resort, is located about eight miles east.

Pre-Incorporation Years

Among the first settlers in Meadows Valley was the Calvin R. White family who arrived around 1878. One of the White children, Walter, said that when his parents moved into the valley the only settlers were three bachelors – Tom Cooper, Bill Jolly and Willis Williams – believed to have arrived a year earlier with around 60 head of horses.

In 1911 Meadows resident Katherine Kline Clay recounted her experiences during the Nez Perce War of 1877 where her first husband, Edward Osborn, and other early settlers lost their lives. (*See Northern Idaho, The Region, American Indians – Nez Perce War.*)

After living in the unincorporated gold mining boomtown of Warren, northeast of McCall, they traveled through Meadows Valley to French Bar – now White Bird – which, at the time, consisted of a few log cabins.

Although details of accounts vary, Katherine said that on June 13, 1877, the men were helping neighbors harvest hay when a messenger rode up with the news that a band of Indians had killed four men, apparently prospectors, working on nearby Slate Creek. Edward and those with him hurried to get to their families and move them to one of the cabins that had stronger fortifications. They no sooner arrived than a war party led by Chief White Bird – a Nez Perce leader – attacked the cabin, killing the men and one woman. The other women and children survived by lying flat on the floor as the bullets flew overhead. She said that Chief White Bird entered the cabin with some of his warriors. He told the women and children that he intended to spare them, but she said it was obvious he had great difficulty controlling his warriors who were drunk – apparently from drinking whisky discovered at an earlier raid.

She said that White Bird was able to get the women and children out of the cabin and saw them on their way to the home of a family member 12 miles away. The first to arrive at the destination were still in shock. The youngest of the Osburn children, a two-year-old daughter who traveled on the back of an adult, delivered the message of the tragedy. She said, "Pap shot dead, uncle dead, Indians shoot, Momma coming."

Early New Meadows.

Charlie and Caroline Campbell came in 1879. In 1884 they started a cattle ranch that they named the Circle C. When the Campbell descendents sold the ranch in 1973, it encompassed 29,000 acres of deeded land and 130,000 acres of leased grazing land. (*See Southwestern Idaho, The Region, Federal Lands – Private Ownership and Preservation Laws.*)

Around 1910 the Pacific and Idaho Northern Railroad began construction of a rail line from Weiser to Lewiston with a planned branch line to McCall. Railroad executives expected that mining and timber interests along the route would provide heavy demand for rail transportation – money that would help finance the undercapitalized enterprise. (*See Southwestern Idaho, The Region, Railroads.*)

Part of the railroad company's motivation was to provide service to the developing copper mine in Hells Canyon, the Seven Devils Mines, about 30 air miles west of Meadows. Mine owners were constructing a road between the railroad and the mine. During the period the mine operated, they used trucks to haul ore out of the mountains to the railroad at Weiser.

In 1911 the railroad reached the community of Meadows. However, rather than stopping as expected by the residents and business owners of Meadows, it proceeded two miles east. Several of the Meadows business owners and residents took the disappointment in stride and moved to New Meadows, the new railroad

Hotel Heigho.

terminus and railhead for the area settlements and cattle drives. Other Meadows residents were upset, feeling that the railroad representatives had lied to them.

The president and general manager of the railroad, Col. Edgar Heigho, was also the president of Cour'Or Company, a real estate development company that owned the land where the railroad stopped laying track.

Heigho's development company platted a town they named New Meadows. On one of the lots, Heigho built a two-and-a-half-story brick home for his family. In 1912 Heigho supervised completion of an elegant railroad depot on the west end of town with the palatial Heigho Hotel facing the depot about five blocks to the east. The hotel – containing mahogany

Hotel Heigho in winter.

furniture, 53 rooms, a lobby, a dining room and a kitchen – was a town landmark until it burned in 1929.

The December 28, 1911, edition of The Meadows Eagle reported, "...improvements in properties, business blocks, residences, hotels, schools ... the $25,000 P. & I.N. depot, practically the first building started in the new town, was put in only a little over a year ago. Most of the buildings were built this year ... (the) Hotel Heigho, when completed in January (will be) one of the finest in the state."

Because the Seven Devils Mines did not prove successful and with competition from another railroad running between Boise and McCall drawing away passengers, the Pacific and Idaho Northern Railroad shelved its plans to extend its rail line beyond New Meadows but kept the rail line open to serve the area's sawmill, logging, livestock and passenger business customers.

Each year local ranchers put together large cattle drives that brought thousands of cattle to the New Meadows railhead for shipment. The last of the great cattle drives occurred in 1979. Federal agencies also used the railroad around 1900 to transport elk from Yellowstone National Park for release in the nearby mountains to improve area elk populations.

In 1936 Union Pacific purchased the railroad for $60,000. In 1979 the company abandoned its rail line between the Tamarack sawmill and New Meadows and gave its New Meadows Train Depot to the city. The

Early New Meadows. Courtesy Idaho Historical Society.

Adams County Historical Society now owns and manages the historic depot. The railroad continues to serve the Tamarack sawmill.

Incorporation

On April 9, 1912, responding to a petition from New Meadows residents, Adams County Commissioners made New Meadows an incorporated village. The commissioners also appointed a five-member board of trustees to serve until the next election. The village became a city in 1967 in conformance with the change in Idaho municipal law.

Meadows stagecoach. Courtesy Idaho Historical Society.

Turning Points

Railroad The decision by Col. Edgar Heigho to build the train depot two miles west of Meadows was the basis for founding the city of New Meadows. However, with the declining demand for rail transportation, largely caused by competition from motor vehicles, the railroad ceased its service to New Meadows in 1979.

Agriculture and Wood Products For most of the past century, cattle ranches and timber underpinned the New Meadows economy. Beginning in 1924 and for two decades thereafter, several farmers went into fox farming, producing fox pelts for the distant furrier markets.

In the early 1990s the federal government began blocking access to federal lands for logging. This had the effect of restricting the growth of wood products businesses and cutting needed property taxes paid by those private businesses to the City and County.

Businesses underlying the city's economy changed. Real estate developers moved in, purchasing a large portion of the private land and built handsome developments, causing the economy to swell. The logging companies that survived have become construction companies that build roads, homes, subdivisions or other buildings. (*See Southwestern Idaho, The Region, Forest Products; and Mining and Forest Products – Leading Causes for Loss of Economic Dominance.*)

Beginning around 2007 the general economic recession led to a sharp decline in real estate prices and new construction, further adversely affecting the city's economy.

Adapting to the Changing Economy Over the past three decades, the hospitality industry has become a core industry for the city. This change is not due to a single event, but rather a process that is continuing in a dramatic way.

Harvesting timber near Meadows.

While logging, cattle ranching and mining were the economic drivers of the past, business that caters to tourism and serving the patrons of the nearby Meadow Creek Golf Resort and Village Estates and Brundage Mountain Resort are taking the economic lead today.

Many property owners are not full-time residents of this beautiful region. They own second homes or come for brief excursions to camp, hike, hunt, fish, ski, snowboard or ride snowmobiles or ATVs. These changes have promoted either new businesses or encouraged existing businesses to re-tool or adapt to serve this expanding market.

New Meadows Today

Amenities and Attractions The city's park, Dorsey Warr Memorial Park, is located on the west side of town. It has a covered picnic area and children's playgrounds.

Each Labor Day weekend, the community commemorates the region's logging heritage. The event starts with a parade of vintage automobiles, fire trucks, ambulances, logging trucks and dignitaries followed by activities at the park. Park activities include a BBQ; car show; craft fair; senior pie sale; and axe throwing, log tying, log running and log burling competitions. Over 2,000 people turn out each year to attend this event.

Next to the park is the historic Pacific and Idaho Northern Railroad Depot. This 1911 brick building is a community gathering place and conference center. The old freight room is restored and frequently used for conferences. The rest of the building will be restored as funds permit.

Two miles north of town is Meadow Creek Golf Resort and Village Estates. This resort is a master-planned community with private roads, underground utilities, an 18-hole golf course and several hundred single-family residential dwellings and building lots.

Thirteen miles southeast of the city on State Highway 55 is the resort city and regional shopping and medical center of McCall. This close proximity to McCall allows residents of New Meadows to enjoy a more affordable, quiet community and yet live close to the urban amenities of the much larger city.

Located just east of town and also in Adams County is Brundage Mountain Resort, a year-round resort primarily known for its winter sports. The resort has 1,500 skiable acres, 43 ski runs and an expanding number of ski lifts.

Zim's Hot Springs is a year-round swimming resort located north of town. In 1889 it was part of a homestead. The water was so hot that settlers used it to scald the hair off pigs that they had killed before the pigs were butchered. Today, the hot water flows through modern swimming pools at controlled temperatures.

Many campers, deer and elk hunters and anglers stop in New Meadows before heading into one of dozens of improved and unimproved campgrounds in the nearby mountains and national forests.

People outside a New Meadows store.

One of these campgrounds is Packer John's Cabin Park. The park is located three miles southeast of New Meadows and is operated by Adams County. Packer John, a late 1800s mail carrier, delivered mail to area settlements and Salmon River mining boomtowns such as the now historic ghost town of Warren located deep in the mountains 45 miles northeast of McCall. Packer John's restored historic cabin is in the park. The park was the site of the Idaho Territorial Democrat Convention of July 1864.

Many anglers hike in to one of the numerous high-mountain lakes to camp and fish. Others fish and recreate in rivers and streams in the area. In the summer, many anglers fish for steelhead trout and salmon in the Little Salmon River.

Economy and Major Employers Evergreen Forest Products, located just west of the city, has 80 employees. It is the city's largest private employer followed by

J.I. Morgan, Inc., a logging and trucking business, with 35 employees.

The city's largest public employers are the U.S. Forest Service Payette National Forest Ranger District Office with 35 permanent and 25 temporary seasonal employees and the Meadows Valley School District with approximately 30 faculty, support staff and administrators.

The local retail stores, restaurants, bars and service businesses employ many of the city's other residents. Several residents commute to Brundage Mountain Resort or to McCall for work.

In 2004 the city received an Idaho Rural Development Block Grant to build an industrial park. Businesses that have established operations in the industrial park include a custom meat packing plant, a pocket door factory and a high-tech metal machine shop.

In recent years, the increasing demand for second homes in the mountains or near resort areas has caused a sharp increase in the region's real estate values. Until recent years this real estate market boom had a major positive effect on the New Meadows economy. There were several real estate brokers, maintenance, housekeeping and related service businesses that added jobs to the city's economy. Today, the general economic collapse has caused jobs to dry up – most of the foreclosed homes are being purchased as second homes.

Federal laws and regulations have changed access to the natural resources and grazing on federal land. Cattle ranching and logging industries are but a shadow of what they were but continue to be important to the valley's economy.

Education The Meadows Valley School District provides most of the K-12 education. Meadows Valley Junior and Senior High Schools and Meadows Valley Elementary are all located on a single campus

United Methodist Church.

comprised of one building with a large attached gymnasium.

Health Care Medical care is available at a general clinic in the city. The closest hospital is the 25-bed St. Luke's McCall Hospital.

Transportation The city lies at the junction of U.S. Highway 95 and State Highway 55.

The city has free transit (bus) service from Mountain Community Transit, operated by Treasure Valley Transit in Nampa. The service is supported by Idaho and federal grants and connects with Riggins, McCall, Cascade, Grangeville and Lewiston.

The 2,400-foot runway of New Meadows Airport provides service for light private and charter aircraft. Larger aircraft use the 6,162-foot runway at McCall

Municipal Airport.

Utilities and Services Private companies provide electricity, telephone, propane, cable and satellite services. The City provides water and sewer as well as fire protection. The County provides police protection under a contract with the City and solid waste services.

Vision for 2050

For the past five decades, New Meadows population has remained somewhat constant at around 500 to 600.

However, historical trends will likely change to show moderate but sustained growth as several factors come into play. More families will choose to live in the smaller and more affordable community of New Meadows and commute to work at Brundage or McCall.

The city's industrial park is sufficiently successful to support development of the park's second phase. The city recently annexed 70 acres that developers plan for residential housing.

The capacity of existing municipal services is adequate to handle moderate growth for several years. The City will need to make improvements to certain systems to meet environmental requirements and citizens needs. The City will fund any major system expansions or improvements through existing revenue streams, growth impact fees or bonds approved by the voters.

Historic fire truck.

Mayors

1912	Lee Highly *	1968	Elmer Bouck
1917	A.L. Wiley *	1972	Daryl Dillon
1919	Geo. F. Brinson *	1984	Raymond Bennett
1921	C.C. Irwin *	1988	Jeff Luff
1937	J.D. Reeds *	1996	Nancy Welbaum
1946	Blake Hancock *	2000	Lloyd Perrin
1947	Carl Shaver *	2004	Sandy Schiffman
1955	Kenneth Johnson *	2006	Gale Stillman
?	Herb Fitz *	2012	Julie Spelman
1962	J.I. Morgan *	2014	Tony Koberstein
1968	Blake Hancock *		

* Village Chairman (Records not available from 1921-1937)

Big Wood River.

BLAINE COUNTY

- Bellevue
- Carey
- Hailey (*County Seat*)
- Ketchum
- Sun Valley

Bellevue City Hall.

Bellevue

Statistical Data

Population: 2,300 *
Elevation: 5,190 feet
Precipitation: 16 inches **
Average Snowfall: 78 inches **
County: Blaine
Website: www.bellevueidaho.us

Temperature Range – Fahrenheit: **
Spring: 20 to 64
Summer: 44 to 84
Fall: 22 to 73
Winter: 9 to 36
* U.S. Census Bureau Estimates July 2015
**Historical averages

Bellevue is the southern gateway city to the historic Wood River Valley – including the cities of Hailey and Ketchum, the famed Sun Valley Ski Resort, Redfish Lake and the rugged 756,000-acre Sawtooth National Recreation Area (SNRA).

The SNRA, with its pine and aspen forests, has over 300 alpine lakes, rivers and streams. Many species of wildlife – including pronghorn antelope, deer, elk, bear and wolves – inhabit the area.

The 116-mile-long Sawtooth Scenic Byway (Idaho Highway 75) intersects the city. The byway begins 40 miles south at the city of Shoshone and continues north through fertile farmland, prehistoric lava fields and sagebrush-covered terrain. It then continues through the Wood River Valley and the SNRA before ending at the city of Stanley and the Sawtooth Mountain Range.

Pre-Incorporation Years

In 1863 following the discovery of gold in the Boise Basin, 16,000 prospectors and fortune seekers descended upon the basin. Many prospectors began scouring the mountains and streams throughout the region in search of gold.

In 1864 Warren Callahan, a gold prospector, traveled from the mining boomtown of Rocky Bar, 60 miles northwest of Boise, to Montana. His route took him through the Wood River Valley. There he discovered galena outcroppings (lead and silver ore). However, at that time, development of hard rock mines in remote areas was problematic. Transportation alternatives and ore-refining technology were limited and there were still hostilities with American Indians.

Callahan returned to the Big Wood River ten years later; but, still finding no gold, he moved on.

By 1879 circumstances changed. There was general peace in the area as the military had suppressed incursions by members of the Shoshone and Bannock Tribes the year before. In addition, technology for refining lead-silver ore had improved and expectations were high that rail service would soon be available.

Large numbers of prospectors began coming into the mountains of the Wood River Valley where they found numerous deposits of galena ore, often lying in veins up to two feet thick. The veins contained 40 to 60 percent lead and up to 100 ounces of silver per ton. In 1880 lead sold for $.05 a pound and silver $1.50 an ounce. During this time, prospectors established the mining towns of Hailey and Ketchum.

The origin of Bellevue dates to the winter of 1879 to 1880 when a handful of determined prospectors built shelters where the Wood River Valley opens into a wide plain. At that time, thick stands of cottonwood and alder grew in the river's flood plain. The vegetation supported a variety of wild game and the river teemed with fish.

In the spring of 1880 prospectors working on the west side of what is now Bellevue and the Big Wood River made a major discovery – the lead-silver mine they subsequently named the Minnie Moore.

This discovery brought a rush of additional settlers to the little community. In 1880 they laid out the town streets and established a post office named Biddyville.

By the winter of 1880 to 1881, Biddyville had nearly 200 families and 1,000 single men. Temporary shelters of tents and shacks lined Main Street.

Obtaining food and other supplies to supplement the wild game bagged by the prospectors and miners was problematic. Supplies were shipped long distances by freight wagon or packhorse. The goods were expensive. A mineworker who earned $3 a day had to pay $1.50 a dozen for eggs; $8 and $7, respectively, for a hundred pounds of potatoes and flour. Cats used to control mice cost $5 each.

In the spring of 1880 one of the miners defied the conventional wisdom that asserted that the valley's elevation was too high for farming. He successfully planted a garden of mostly potatoes.

Many prospectors and miners filed homestead claims and planted wheat and other crops that grew well in the short growing season. Cattle and sheep ranchers brought in their herds to graze and sold meat and dairy products to the prospectors and miners. These agricultural businesses became important additions to the town's growing economy.

In 1881 Biddyville had 260 homes constructed with mostly cottonwood logs. Stores, restaurants, hotels and saloons soon replaced the tents and shacks on Main

Street. Merchants and the usual peripheral businesses of mining towns, notorious and otherwise, prospered.

Two daily stage lines connected the Wood River Valley towns. A racetrack built on the south edge of town was a major attraction. On race days, hundreds of people flocked to the track.

By 1881 the Wood River News began publishing and 13 students enrolled in the town's first school. The mining boomtowns of Hailey and Ketchum were also growing rapidly.

In 1881 the Oregon Short Line Railroad began building the segment of railroad between Granger, Wyoming, and

Bellevue in winter.

Huntington, Oregon. The railroad would cross Idaho in a northwesterly direction through Shoshone and Nampa before crossing into Oregon. When complete, the segment would provide a direct link between Omaha, Nebraska, and Portland, Oregon.

In 1882 the railroad reached Shoshone, Idaho. At that point, railroad officials stopped their westward construction temporarily to build a branch line to the mining towns of the Wood River Mining District to pick up the new business. The mines in the district were yielding prodigious quantities of gold, silver and lead and needed rail transportation to sustain their operations.

The railroad completed the branch line in 1883 and built a train depot on the south side of Biddyville. The railroad then returned to constructing the balance of the railroad to Huntington, which was completed in November 1884.

In 1882 the population center of Alturas County had shifted from the county seat at Rocky Bar to the Wood River Valley. The gold mines at Rocky Bar were playing out, the population was leaving and there was a growing sentiment that one of the rapidly growing towns of the Wood River Mining District should be the county seat.

Incorporation

The residents of Biddyville felt their city had superior qualifications for the county seat. However, they believed their town needed a more dignified name. They chose the name of Bellevue. The Idaho Territorial Legislature established Bellevue as Idaho's third chartered city on March 6, 1882.

Lewiston and Boise, the first two cities chartered by the Legislature, have since rescinded their charters.

Bellevue is the only remaining chartered city in Idaho. City residents cherish their unique status as it provides a degree of independence from county and state mandates. Bellevue's ruling body is officially termed mayor and aldermen.

In 1883 Alturas County residents voted on moving the county seat from Rocky Bar. Bellevue and Hailey were the principal options. Hailey won the vote; however, Bellevue residents claimed voter fraud, asserting, "Hailey has stolen the county seat."

In 1889 the Legislature created Logan County with Bellevue as the county seat. However, in 1895, the Legislature reorganized the boundaries of several counties and changed county names. The Logan and Alturas county names were retired and other counties created. The boundaries of one of these new counties – Blaine County, with Hailey designated as the county seat – encompassed all of the

Bellevue Library summer reading program.

Wood River Valley including Bellevue. Bellevue residents cried foul saying that Hailey "stole" the seat again. The rivalry between the two cities has continued, principally displayed in high school competitive sports.

In the late 1880s Bellevue and its two sister cities to the north, Hailey and Ketchum, constituted the core of the Wood River Mining District which yielded prodigious quantities of gold, silver and lead.

Turning Points

Lead-Silver Mines Bellevue owes its origins to the discovery of lead-silver ore in the surrounding mountains. The discoveries that began around 1879 brought boomtown prosperity to Bellevue. Periods of high metal prices and strong mine production brought economic prosperity. However, periods of sharp declines in metal prices, labor problems and mines playing out often followed.

This boom-bust economy continued until around 1970 when the largest mine, the Minnie Moore, shut down for the final time. From then on, mining ceased to be an important economic driver for the city.

Railroad The coming of the railroad in 1883 had a pivotal positive influence in the new community. It not only provided needed freight and passenger transportation for the emerging mining and agricultural industries, but it became another important industry that helped sustain the city's economy.

Agriculture Farming and cattle ranching were important industries during the city's early years. In the 1890s sheep ranching become the dominant agricultural industry.

The sheep ranching industry flourished because of Scottish and Basque emigrants. Many of these emigrants came to America and the Wood River Mining

District in search of gold and silver. However, they found their fortune by returning to their sheep ranching roots.

The railroad provided a major boost to the sheep industry as it provided the means of shipping fat lambs and wool to market.

By the early 1900s several hundred thousand head of sheep grazed in the Wood River area. Each spring and fall, sheepherders drove their herds through the towns of the Wood River Valley between the winter range on the southern plain south of Bellevue and the summer range in the mountains.

Today, no more than 25,000 head of sheep graze in the surrounding

New fire station, 2011.

mountains. Each October, the cities of the Wood River Valley commemorate their heritage of large sheep drives with the "Trailing of the Sheep Festival." The festival includes driving about 1,500 head of sheep from Bellevue through Hailey and Ketchum to Sun Valley plus three days of events and celebration.

Sun Valley Resort and Tourism In 1936 after extensive research, Union Pacific Railroad Chairman William Averell Harriman authorized construction of a grand ski resort on the west side of Ketchum that he called Sun Valley.

Harriman, who would later become governor of New York and a prominent national political figure, used his influence to promote Sun Valley to his many wealthy and celebrity friends and contacts.

In 1936 the mining businesses in the Wood River Valley were in sharp decline. However, the Sun Valley construction and service jobs revitalized the valley's economy. Today, many Bellevue residents still commute the 14 miles to Sun Valley and Ketchum for employment. Tourism, service and the hospitality industries now underpin Bellevue's economy.

Bellevue Today

Amenities and Attractions Bellevue has three city parks comprising 20 acres. City Park is located in the old section of town. It has old-growth trees, picnic and playground areas. O'Donnel Park has large fields for playing baseball, rugby, football and other field sports. The newest park is a nature preserve next to the Big Wood River. Five golf courses are also located in the city.

Since 1921 Bellevue has celebrated Labor Day weekend with a parade and a variety of activities at City Park. The 2007 celebration included a shootout, a series of performing arts entertainment, arts & crafts booths, kids' rides and games, a blue grass festival and lots of great food.

Each May, the City sponsors "Bellevue Clean Sweep Day," a volunteer effort to clean up the town. In addition, every August the Bellevue Fire Department holds a fundraiser to buy needed fire equipment.

Each year, thousands of people are attracted to the Wood River Valley's picturesque setting of high mountains, narrow valleys and mountain streams. They come to enjoy the beautiful scenery, crisp high-mountain air, variety of outdoor activities and the resort and convention amenities of Sun Valley. In the winter, there are downhill and cross-country skiing and other winter sports. The warmer season amenities include biking, horseback riding, hiking and fly-fishing. Many of the world's rich and famous have built spacious second homes in the valley.

There are many opportunities near Bellevue for outdoor enthusiasts to enjoy sports and nature. The visitor center for the Sawtooth National Recreation Area is 23 miles north of the city. The Craters of the Moon National Monument is 45 miles east. The Sawtooth National Forest lies northwest and the Challis National Forest lies northeast. In addition to Sun Valley, located 16 miles north, downhill skiing is also available at Soldier Mountain Ski Area, 35 miles west.

Economy and Major Employers The city's largest employers, with 35 employees each, are Blaine County School District and The Wood Connection (cabinetmakers).

There are also several small businesses and a robust downtown with several retail and service businesses.

Bellevue's population is growing about three percent annually. Many city residents choose to live in Bellevue, where housing is relatively more affordable, and commute to Hailey, Ketchum and Sun Valley for work.

Bellevue businesses.

Education Blaine County School District provides most of the K-12 education. Bellevue Elementary is located in the city. Middle and high school students attend Wood River Middle and Wood River High Schools in Hailey.

The nearest institution of higher learning is the College of Southern Idaho, 62 miles south in Twin Falls.

Health Care The nearest hospital is the 25-bed St. Luke's Wood River Medical Center in Ketchum. There are also medical clinics in Hailey.

Transportation State Highway 75, the Sawtooth Scenic Byway intersects the city. U.S. Highway 20 is 10 miles south. Interstate 84 lies 60 miles south near Twin Falls.

The closest commercial airport is Friedman Memorial Airport, five miles north in Hailey. It has a 7,550-foot runway and hosts ten flights a day. Charter flights are also available.

Today, tourism links the economies of the three cities. The Ketchum Area Rapid Transit system (KART) provides free public transportation on 20-minute schedules between the Wood River Valley cities and Sun Valley.

Utilities and Services Private companies provide natural gas, electricity, telephone, cable, CATV and satellite services. The City provides water and sewer services as well as police and fire protection.

Vision for 2050

Bellevue is a working community, supplying labor and services to the valley – once to the mines, later to the Union Pacific and, finally, to the Ketchum-Sun Valley resort economy. The city is characterized as small business owners, merchants and laborers serving the valley communities.

Over the past decade, the city has grown three percent annually. Those population growth trends will likely continue. By 2050 Bellevue's population will more than double.

Annexations of new subdivisions have and will continue to expand the city's boundaries. This growth is challenging the city's historic identity, infrastructure and government services. Real estate market values have skyrocketed.

As Sun Valley resort economy has grown, the cities of the Wood River Valley are becoming one community as homes fill the open spaces.

Managing growth is this land of beautiful scenery, rich history and tradition will require persistent and creative planning. Bellevue will grow and change to meet citizen needs with the same resilience that has kept it a proud community since 1880. In 2050 Bellevue's community spirit will continue strong.

Mayors

Unknown **   * Village Chairman
Jon Anderson 2012   ** Dates Unknown
Christopher (Chris) Koch

Welcome to Carey sign.

Carey

Statistical Data

Population: 603 *
Elevation: 4,790 feet
Precipitation: 16 inches **
Average Snowfall: 78 inches **
County: Blaine
Website: www.cityofcarey.org

Temperature Range – Fahrenheit: **
Spring: 20 to 66
Summer: 41 to 85
Fall: 18 to 73
Winter: 7 to 37
* U.S. Census Bureau Estimates July 2015
**Historical averages

Carey lies at the base of the sagebrush and grass-covered foothills and tree-filled ravines of the Salmon Challis National Forest and Pioneer Mountains where they abut the ancient lava flows on the Snake River Plain.

The Little Wood River flows through the city. In the foothills and mountains about 11 miles northwest of the city are the 129-foot-high Little Wood River Dam and 600-acre reservoir.

The visitor's center for the 750,000-acre Craters of the Moon National Monument and Preserve is located 25 miles northeast on the combined U.S. Highway 20, 26 and 93.

Arco is 45 miles northeast; Ketchum, 45 miles northwest; and Shoshone, 45 miles south.

Pre-Incorporation Years

The first settlers came in the early 1880s. The earliest water rights to meet the needs of early farmers bear a priority date of 1880.

In 1883 settlers joined forces to construct canals on both sides of the river to irrigate their farms and home gardens. Cattle and sheep were their most significant agricultural commodity and cash crop. They grazed the livestock on the open range that surrounded Carey and either wintered them on their farms or the warmer regions of the Snake River Plain.

It was around this time that the settlers applied to postal authorities for a post office. Postal authorities approved the request with the name of Carey – the name of the town's first postmaster.

In 1904 farmers persuaded the Bureau of Reclamation to look at building a flood control and irrigation dam in the foothills on the Little Wood River Canyon. While Reclamation performed site surveys, costs proved a limiting factor, and they put the project on hold.

In 1912 farmers formed the Carey Lake Company and obtained approvals to divert water into Carey Lake, located a few miles north of town. Their plan was to store sufficient water to irrigate 2,051 acres. However, the plan proved unsuccessful, and by about 1923 they abandoned the project.

In 1936 the Works Project Administration (WPA) – a federal agency assigned to build qualified public projects that put people to work following the Great Depression – built a dam. However, the height of the dam proved inadequate.

In 1940 the owner of the dam, the Little Wood Irrigation

Installation of the welcome sign.

District, hired a private engineering firm to evaluate raising the dam an additional 35 feet. Their attempts to get final approvals were unsuccessful until 1956 when the Bureau of Reclamation agreed to take on the project.

In 1960 Reclamation completed the revised project including raising the crest of the dam 39 feet and taking measures to preserve fish and wildlife. In 1985 the irrigation district built a 3,000-kilowatt hydroelectric power plant at the dam.

Incorporation

Carey became an incorporated city in November 1967.

Turning Points

Early Settlement The beauty of the Little Wood River's fertile alluvial flood plains formed by centuries of spring run-off water persuaded the early settlers to make the future city of Carey their home.

Little Wood River Dam Securing adequate irrigation water was critical to the successful settlement of Carey. Although it took several decades, the completion of the dam in 1960 now underpins the city's agricultural economy.

Carey City Council meeting.

Carey Today

Amenities and Attractions Each August Blaine County sponsors the county fair and rodeo at its fairgrounds in Carey.

The Craters of the Moon National Monument and Preserve begins about a mile west of town. The Preserve includes Idaho's Great Rift, the source of the lava flow that created this unique landscape. (*See Eastern Idaho – Craters of the Moon National Monument and Preserve and the Great Rift National Natural Landmark.*)

The internationally famous Silver Creek Trout Fly Fishery and Visitor's Center is located about 10 miles west near unincorporated Picabo.

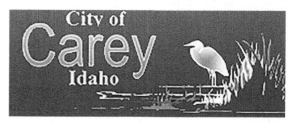

The Little Wood River Reservoir is an attractive boating, fishery and camp site. Recreationists throughout the region come to fish at this popular fishery as well as Carey Lake and the nearby smaller Fish Creek Reservoir. In 1949 the Idaho Department of Fish and Game purchased Carey Lake and now manages the 400-acre site as a wildlife management area.

Many of the early settlers and townspeople are members of the Church of Jesus Christ of Latter-day Saints. Their church building is one of the largest public buildings in the city.

Economy and Major Employers With about 35 employees, Blaine County School District is the city's largest employer. The city's merchants and small businesses provide most of the remaining jobs.

Education The Blaine County School District provides most of the K-12 education in the county. The district's Carey School is a single campus facility that houses elementary, middle and senior high schools.

The closest institution of higher learning is the College of Southern Idaho located about 70 miles south in Twin Falls.

Health Care Two hospitals are about 40 miles from the city and provide for most of the city's health care needs – St. Luke's Medical Center-Wood River in Ketchum and Lost Rivers District Hospital in Arco.

Transportation U.S. Highway 20 intersects the city from the west. U.S. Highways 26 and 93 intersect the city from the south before combining with Highway 20 and proceeding northeast.

The 2,650-foot runway at Carey airfield offers services for light private and charter aircraft. The closest commercial airport is in Twin Falls.

Leaving Carey sign (reverse of the welcome sign).

Utilities and Services Private companies provide electricity, telephone and satellite services. The City provides water. The homes and businesses have individual septic systems. The city's volunteer fire department provides fire protection. The Blaine County Sheriff's Office provides police protection under contract with the City.

Vision for 2050

The city's population has remained somewhat constant for over three decades. These historical trends will likely continue. By 2050 Carey will still be a peaceful rural community – a wonderful place to live and raise a family.

Mayors

Unknown
** Rick Baird
2010 Randall Patterson

* Village Chairman
** Dates Unknown

Hailey Visitors Center.

Hailey

Statistical Data

Population: 8,076 *
Elevation: 5,329 feet
Precipitation: 16 inches **
Average Snowfall: 78 inches **
County: Blaine
Website: www.haileycityhall.org
Temperature Range – Fahrenheit: **

Spring: 20 to 64
Summer: 44 to 84
Fall: 22 to 73
Winter: 9 to 36
* U.S. Census Bureau Estimates July 2015
**Historical averages

Hailey lies in the narrow Wood River Valley between its sister cities of Ketchum, 12 miles north, and Bellevue, four miles south. A mile northeast of Ketchum is the city of Sun Valley and the famed Sun Valley Ski Resort.

The Smoky Mountains in the Sawtooth National Forest border the city on the west and the Pioneer Mountains in the Salmon-Challis National Forest on the east. The rugged 756,000-acre Sawtooth National Recreation Area (SNRA) begins 19 miles north.

Pre-Incorporation Years

For millennia, nomadic American Indians – principally of the Shoshone and Bannock Tribes – had exclusive use of the Wood River Valley for their summer encampments. (*See Southwestern Idaho, The Region, American Indians.*) In the early 1800s trappers/explorers came into the area seeking beaver pelts and trading opportunities with the Indians. (*See Southwestern Idaho, The Region, Early Trappers/Explorers.*)

In 1862 prospectors discovered gold in the mountains 80 miles west. The ensuing gold rush attracted 16,000 prospectors and fortune seekers into what they would soon call the Boise Basin. These miners spread out, scouring the mountains and streams throughout the region in search of gold.

Hailey as seen from Carbonate Mountain looking east. Courtesy Hailey Public Library Mallory Collection.

The first recorded prospector coming into the Wood River Valley, then in Alturas County, was Warren Callahan. In 1864 when Callahan passed through the valley, he was en route to the gold fields in what is now Montana. Stopping to prospect, he discovered galena outcroppings (lead and silver ore). However, at that time, development of hard rock mines in remote areas was problematic and hostilities from the Indians, who resented the miners and settlers invading their historic domain, persuaded him to move on.

By 1879 circumstances had changed. The U.S. Army had compelled the Shoshone and Bannock Tribes to live on the Fort Hall Indian Reservation. Technology for refining lead-silver ore had improved and expectations were high that rail service was coming.

With the changed conditions, large numbers of prospectors began pouring into the Wood River Valley. John

Train arriving at Hailey Depot. Courtesy Hailey Public Library Mallory Collection.

Hailey (JH) – owner of the Utah, Idaho, Oregon Stage Company – immediately began providing stage service to the prospectors. In 1880 JH and three other investors – one of whom was E.S. Chase, the U.S. Marshall – acquired 440 acres and platted the townsite of what is now Hailey. They originally named the town "Marshall," then thought better of it and changed the town's name to Hailey.

Prospectors were finding deposits of galena ore, some of which were lying in veins up to two feet thick. The veins contained 40 to 60 percent lead and up to 100 ounces of silver per ton. In 1880 lead sold for $.05 a pound and silver $1.50 an ounce.

Hailey and Ketchum became some of the Wood River Valley's first mining boomtowns. Several other boomtowns – now ghost towns – built up near their respective mines. A short time later, prospectors found large ore deposits to the south and established the boomtown of what is now Bellevue. By the end of 1880 prospectors had filed approximately 2,000 mining claims in the Wood River Mining District. By April 1881 the town of Hailey had about 75 buildings, 100 tents and five saloons. (*See Southwestern Idaho, The Region, Mining – Wood River Valley-Silver and Lead.*)

In order to extract and separate the lead and silver from the galena ore, miners had to smelt it. In 1880 the closest smelters were in Salt Lake City, Utah, and Denver, Colorado.

To get their ore to the smelters, freight companies loaded the ore on wagons 16 feet long, 14 feet tall to the top of the canvas covering and four feet wide. The heavy wooden spoke wheels had a half-inch-thick and four-inch-wide iron band around the outside. From 14 to 24 mules pulled the heavy wagons whose pull-

At the intersection of Main and Croy Streets, looking south.
Courtesy Hailey Public Library Mallory Collection.

weight was generally equivalent to the aggregate weight of the mules – the origin of the axiom "pull your own weight." Initially, freighters moved the ore 170 miles to the railhead at Kelton, Utah. The ore was then loaded on railcars and shipped to the smelters. The freighters then loaded the wagon with food and supplies for the two-week trip back to the Wood River Valley.

In 1881 the Oregon Short Line (OSL) began construction of a railroad line between Granger, Wyoming, and Huntington, Oregon. The line, completed November 17, 1884, angled in a northwesterly direction through what are now Pocatello, Soda Springs, Caldwell and Weiser before crossing the Snake River for one final time near Huntington. The railroad connected the commercial centers of Omaha, Nebraska, and Portland, Oregon, and created another transcontinental railroad. Railroad interests completed the first transcontinental railroad in 1869 at Promontory Summit in northern Utah.

In 1882 the Philadelphia Mining and Smelting Company began the region's largest smelter operations on a high bluff on the west side of Ketchum. The site included construction of a hydroelectric power plant on the Wood River, producing the first electric lights in Idaho. Other mining interests were constructing smaller smelters near their mines.

As the Wood River Valley smelters became operational, the use of freight wagons for long hauls stopped except for hauling ore from outlying mines, such as from Challis.

In the spring of 1882 the gold mines at Rocky Bar, the county seat of Alturas County located 50 miles northwest of Hailey, were playing out, and the people began moving away. In 1883 Alturas County residents voted to move the county seat from Rocky Bar to either Hailey or Bellevue. Hailey won the majority vote, and residents of Bellevue

Main Street looking north past Croy Street. Aukema Drugstore and the Rialto were popular businesses. Courtesy Hailey Public Library Mallory Collection.

claimed voter fraud, asserting, "Hailey has stolen the county seat."

In February 1883 the OSL track reached Shoshone. There they suspended work on the main line long enough to build a branch line to Ketchum – reaching Hailey on May 23 and Ketchum soon thereafter. The railroad then resumed construction of its main line to Huntington. Telegraph service came to the Wood River Valley with the railroad. (*See Southwestern Idaho, The Region, Railroad.*)

In October 1883 community entrepreneurs built a telephone system in Hailey, the first telephone service in Idaho. Within a month, they had connected Hailey with Ketchum; Bellevue; and Bullion, a mining boomtown seven miles west of Hailey. In late 1884 Hailey's community leaders also constructed a

Jean Mallory on decorated bicycle for the 4th of July parade. Courtesy Hailey Public Library Mallory Collection.

water works, bringing clean water from higher elevations into the town's homes and businesses.

It was at this time that Homer and Isabel Pound came to Hailey. Homer was the presidential appointee to head the federal land office where all miners filed their claims. On October 30, 1885, Isabel gave birth to the legendary poet, Ezra Loomis Pound.

Concurrent with the discovery and development of the mines and smelters in the Wood River Valley, sheep owners began the cycle of grazing their sheep on the region's high brush and grass-covered mountain slopes in the spring and summer, then herding them south to the lower and warmer Snake River Plain for winter lambing and spring wool-shearing.

In 1893 a major economic depression and financial panic struck and the market price for silver and lead declined precipitously. By 1894 the price of silver had dropped 60 percent and lead 40 percent. Mine owners sought to reduce wages, labor conflicts ensued – albeit much less violent than that experienced in the Silver Valley. (*See Northern Idaho, Silver Valley Mines.*) Many of the Wood River Valley mines shut down causing some mining communities to become ghost towns. However, mines in certain areas, such as the Triumph Mine six miles due southeast of Ketchum, produced until the late 1950s. The Minnie Moore Mine near Bellevue was productive until 1970.

As the mining economy declined, the sheep industry continued to grow. When the nation pulled out of the depression, sheep ranching emerged as the Wood River Valley's dominant industry. By 1890 upwards of a million sheep were trailing through the valley each year. (See Southwestern Idaho, The Region, Livestock.)

Airplanes on display during the Friedman Airport dedication ceremony. Courtesy Hailey Public Library Mallory Collection.

As a result, the railroad shifted its primary emphasis from mining to providing the critical service of transporting sheep to their winter and summer ranges and fat lambs and wool to market.

In 1895 the Legislature reorganized the boundaries of several counties and changed county names. The names "Logan," a county created in 1889 with Bellevue as the county seat, and "Alturas" were retired and other county names approved. The boundaries of one of these new counties, Blaine County, encompassed all of the Wood River Valley including Bellevue. The voters approved Hailey as the county seat. Bellevue residents cried foul saying that Hailey "stole" the seat again. The rivalry between the two cities has continued, principally displayed in competitive sports.

Hailey City Hall.

Incorporation

On April 21, 1903, Hailey became an incorporated village. In 1911 with a population of around 1,200, village residents successfully petitioned the county commissioners to change the town's legal status to an incorporated city.

Turning Points

Mining Hailey owes its origins to the discovery of rich silver-lead ore in the mountains of the Wood River Valley. Those discoveries were the basis for John Hailey leading a small group of investors to establish the town of Hailey. Hailey then became a service and supply center and county seat.

Railroad The railroad played a critical role in underpinning the Wood River Valley's mining and livestock industries and was the catalyst that attracted investors to build the nearby Sun Valley Resort.

County Seat Voter approval, making Hailey the county seat of Alturas and, later, Blaine County, established the city as a business center for the valley and helped stabilize its economy in years of economic instability.

Airport The City of Hailey and Blaine County jointly own Friedman Memorial Airport located on land in part donated in the 1930s by the Friedman family. The airport serves the Wood River Region and the Sun Valley Resort. It plays a critical role in attracting visitors, second homeowners and commerce to this beautiful part of Idaho. The owners are planning to complete construction of a new larger airport in

2012.

Sun Valley Resort In 1936 after extensive research, Union Pacific Railroad Chairman William Averell Harriman authorized construction of a grand ski resort on the west side of Ketchum that he called Sun Valley.

Harriman, who would later become governor of New York and a prominent national political figure, used his influence to successfully promote Sun Valley to his many wealthy and celebrity friends and contacts.

Coming out of the Great Depression of the 1930s, construction of the Sun Valley Resort lifted the area's economy. Today, the tourism, service and hospitality industries underpin the valley's economy.

Hailey Today

Amenities and Attractions Hailey has an interconnected system of over a dozen neighborhood and other parks. The system includes trails, green spaces, natural places and recreational facilities. Three of the parks have play equipment, ball fields and soccer fields. The city's goals include providing diverse recreation opportunities within walking distance of most residents' homes.

The most prominent of these parks, Hailey Rodeo Park – formerly Wertheimer Park – has a multi-use event arena and grandstand used for the "4th of July Rodeo," equestrian, concerts and other special events. A key feature of the facility is its excellent skate park. The community is planning a complete renovation and upgrade of this historic event center.

Each year on Memorial Day weekend, the community sponsors Hailey Springfest, an art and crafts fair featuring displays, exhibits and performances by local artisans and musicians, vendor booths and family activities.

In addition to the rodeo, the 4th of July celebration includes a parade and fireworks.

The Northern Rockies Folk Festival, featuring national and local talent, takes place annually on the first weekend of August.

Located on Main Street, the Blaine County Historical Museum offers numerous artifacts and exhibits of Hailey's mining and agricultural heritage.

The city's most prominent attraction is its close proximity to the amenities of the Sun Valley Resort, including downhill skiing on 3,400-foot vertical drop ski runs, terrain for beginning

skiers and an open-air concert pavilion that can accommodate up to 4,000 patrons.
The resort area also has three golf courses – the 18-hole courses at Sun Valley
and Elkhorn and a 9-hole course at the Sun Valley Resort.

Hailey joins its sister cities in promoting and sponsoring the Trailing of the
Sheep Festival held each year in October to commemorate the area's sheep
ranching history and Wagon Days which occurs annually in July and features a
parade of historic freight and other wagons.

The 756,000-acre SNRA, including the spectacular Sawtooth Mountains,
begins 19 miles north. The SNRA has pine and aspen forests and over 300 alpine
lakes, rivers and streams. Many species of wildlife, including pronghorn antelope,
deer, elk, bear and wolves inhabit the area.

There are also excellent alpine and cross-country skiing and snowmobiling
trails in the area as well as 30 miles of paved bike trails and extensive mountain
bike and hiking trails available. Tennis, horseback riding, ice-skating and
swimming in natural hot springs are available in the valley.

Many anglers enjoy fly-fishing in the renowned Silver Creek Trout Fly Fishery.
The Nature Conservancy's Silver Creek Preserve and Visitor's Center is located
about 20 miles south near the unincorporated town of Picabo.

Economy and Major Employers With 360 employees, Power Engineers – an
employee-owned consulting engineering firm with offices across the nation and
abroad – is the city's largest private employer. Blaine County School District has
about 340 employees and is the city's largest public employer. Other residents have
jobs at a variety of small businesses, the downtown retail and service stores. Many
residents commute to Ketchum and Sun Valley for employment.

Education The Blaine County School District operates elementary, middle,
alternative and high schools in the city.

The closest institution of higher learning is the College of Southern Idaho, 76
miles south in Twin Falls.

Health Care The city has two general medical clinics. The closest hospital is
St. Luke's Wood River Medical Center in Ketchum.

Transportation The 116-mile-long Sawtooth Scenic Byway, Idaho Highway
75, intersects the city. The byway begins 45 miles south at the city of Shoshone and
continues north through fertile farmland, prehistoric lava fields and sagebrush-
covered terrain. It then continues through the Wood River Valley, the SNRA and
past Red Fish Lake before ending at the city of Stanley and the Sawtooth Mountain
Range.

U.S. Highway 20 intersects Highway 75 about 14 miles south. Interstate 84 is
accessible 64 miles southwest via Highway 20.

Friedman Memorial Airport has a 7,550 x 100-foot runway and serves
commercial commuter lines as well as private and charter aircraft.

The Ketchum Area Rapid Transit system (KART) provides free public
transportation on 20-minute schedules between the Wood River Valley cities and
Sun Valley.

Utilities and Services Private companies provide electricity, telephone, satellite and wireless services. The City provides water, sewer, solid waste and recycling services and fire and police protection.

Hailey in winter.

Vision for 2050

In 1960 Hailey had a population of 1,185. Over the succeeding 50 years, the population steadily increased seven fold. During the past decade, the city's average rate of growth has approximated three percent annually.

Through all of this growth, community leaders and residents have worked cooperatively to support building attractive infrastructure needed to sustain our safe, walkable and vibrant residential and commercial neighborhoods, with well-maintained streets, clean air and water, abundant open space and parks and strong education and social support networks.

Over the next 40 years, we believe this community will still have a strong community spirit. For example, in the near future, we anticipate our citizens will pass a bond to allow construction of Hailey Rodeo Park at the entrance to our city.

By 2050 Hailey will have a significantly larger population. However, we envision our city will continue to be a community in which families thrive; whose character of place is valued and defined as a community connected to and respectful of the natural assets surrounding us; a community that honors its history and embraces ethnic, cultural, generational and economic diversity.

We believe Hailey's future city governments will continue to be responsible stewards of public funds and resources and leaders in local and regional efforts toward increasing opportunities for resource and energy conservation and best development practices, a collaborator with local and state agencies as well as private landowners to achieve the community vision.

Mayors

1903	Dr. J.J. Plumer *	1953	Tony Croce
1905	Albert Wolters *	1957	John W. Davies
1907	Simon M. Friedman *	1964	George R. Allen
1911	Simon M. Friedman	1970	L.F. Heagle
1913	H.R. Plughoff	1978	Emory M. Dietrich
1915	J.C. Fox	1982	Wordell Rainey
1917	John R. Hart	1986	Paschal O'Drake
1919	Joseph Clayburgh	1990	R. Keith Roark
1921	W.P. Fowler	1994	Stephen T. Kearns
1923	John Cramer	1998	Brad Siemer
1925	W.P. Fowler	2002	Al Lindley
1927	H.C. Beamer	2002	Susan McBryant
1931	John M. Rutter	2008	Richard L. Davis
1935	John Cramer	2012	Fritz Haemmerle
1945	Robert R. Horne		* Village Chairman

Downtown Ketchum.

Ketchum

Statistical Data

Population: 2,720 *
Elevation: 5,845 feet
Precipitation: 24 inches **
Average Snowfall: 76 inches **
County: Blaine
Website: www.ketchumidaho.org

Temperature Range – Fahrenheit: **
Spring: 15 to 63
Summer: 38 to 81
Fall: 14 to 70
Winter: 4 to 37
* U.S. Census Bureau Estimates July 2015
**Historical average

Ketchum lies in the Sawtooth National Forest at the base of the beautiful and imposing 9,150-foot-high Mount Baldy. With its 3,400-foot vertical drop ski runs, Baldy is the principal attraction of the famed Sun Valley Ski Resort, located a mile northeast in the city of Sun Valley.

The Big Wood River flows through the city. The headwaters of the river are 15 miles north in the Boulder Mountains of the rugged 756,000-acre Sawtooth National Recreation Area (SNRA). The city of Hailey is 12 miles south.

Pre-Incorporation Years

The Wood River Valley is a historic summer encampment site of nomadic American Indians – principally of the Shoshone and Bannock Tribes. They had exclusive use of the valley until trappers/explorers came into the area to trap beaver and trade in the early 1800s.

The area was largely devoid of white settlers until prospectors discovered gold in the Boise Basin in the mountains 80 miles west in 1862. The ensuing gold rush attracted 16,000 prospectors and fortune seekers who spread out for hundreds of miles scouring the mountains and streams in search of gold.

In 1864 a prospector named Warren Callahan passed through the valley en route to the gold fields in what is now Montana. Callahan discovered deposits of galena, silver-lead ore. However, he had no means of processing the ore and the risk of hostilities with the Indians was high, so Callahan moved on.

By 1879 circumstances had changed. The U.S. Army had compelled the Shoshone and Bannock Tribes to live on the Fort Hall Indian Reservation, technology for processing lead-silver ore had improved and expectations were high that rail service was coming to the area.

Philadelphia smelter near Ketchum.

With those changed conditions, large numbers of prospectors and settlers began pouring into the Wood River Valley. They found galena deposits lying in veins up to two feet thick. The veins contained 40 to 60 percent lead and up to 100 ounces of silver per ton. In 1880 lead sold for $.05 a pound and silver for $1.50 an ounce.

One of these fortune seekers was David Ketchum. He built the first house in what is now Ketchum. Others followed and a new town named Leadville soon emerged. In 1880 community leaders unsuccessfully applied for a new post office with the name of Leadville – the name Leadville was already in use. However, postal authorities quickly approved the resubmitted application naming the post office Ketchum, in honor of the town's first settler.

By the end of 1880 prospectors had filed approximately 2,000 mining claims in the Wood River Mining District. Boomtowns soon dotted the valley and surrounding mountains. However, they all eventually become ghost towns except for Ketchum, Hailey and Bellevue.

Smelting was a critical process in extracting the silver and lead from the ore. In 1880 the closest smelters were in Salt Lake City, Utah, and Denver, Colorado.

In order to get the ore to the smelters, freight companies loaded the ore on wagons 16 feet long, 14 feet tall to the top of the canvas covering and four feet wide. The heavy wooden spoke wheels had a half-inch thick and four-inch wide iron band around each wheel. From 14 to 24 mules pulled the heavy wagons whose pull-weight was generally equivalent to the aggregate weight of the mules – origin of the axiom, "pull your own weight."

Freighters moved the ore 170 miles to the railhead at Kelton, Utah. The ore was then loaded on railcars and shipped to the smelters. The freighters then loaded the wagon with food and supplies for the two-week trip back to the Wood River Valley.

In 1881 the Oregon Short Line (OSL) Railroad began construction of a rail line between Granger, Wyoming, and Huntington, Oregon. The line – completed November 17, 1884 – angled in a northwesterly direction through what are now Pocatello, Soda Springs, Caldwell and Weiser before crossing the Snake River one final time near Huntington. The railroad connected the commercial centers of Omaha, Nebraska, and Portland, Oregon, and created another transcontinental railroad. Railroad interests completed the first transcontinental railroad in 1869 at Promontory Summit in northern Utah.

In 1882 the Philadelphia Mining and Smelting Company began the region's largest smelter operations on a high bluff on the west side of Ketchum. The site included construction of a hydroelectric power plant on the Wood River producing the first electric lights in Idaho.

As smelters in the Wood River Valley came on line, the use of freight wagons to Kelton stopped. However, mine owners still used the wagons for hauling ore from mines as far away as Challis.

In February 1883 the main OSL railroad track reached Shoshone. There they suspended work long enough to build a branch line to Ketchum. OSL then resumed construction of its main line to Huntington.

Telegraph service came to the Wood River Valley with the railroad. In 1883 community entrepreneurs also built a telephone system connecting the towns in the Wood River Valley.

Concurrent with the discovery of ore deposits and development of the mines and smelters, sheep owners began the cycle of grazing their sheep on the region's high brush and grass-covered mountain slopes in the spring and summer, then herding them south to the lower and warmer Snake River Plain pastures for winter lambing and wool-shearing.

In 1893 a major economic depression and financial panic struck. The market prices for silver and lead declined precipitously. By 1894 the price of silver had dropped 60 percent and lead 40 percent. Mine owners sought to reduce wages, labor conflicts ensued, albeit much less violent than that experienced in the Silver Valley. (*See Northern Idaho, Mining.*) Many of the mines shut down, and communities become ghost towns. However, when prices improved, certain mines resumed production. For example, the Triumph Mine, six miles due southeast of Ketchum, produced until the late 1950s. The Minnie Moore Mine near Bellevue was productive until 1970.

As the mining economy declined, the sheep industry continued to grow. By 1890 upwards of a million sheep were trailing through the valley each year.

As a result, the railroad shifted its primary emphasis from mining to providing the critical service of transporting sheep to their winter and summer ranges and fat lambs and wool to market.

In 1895 the Legislature created Blaine County with Hailey as the county seat.

Incorporation

On February 10, 1947, Ketchum became an incorporated village.

Turning Points

Mining Ketchum began as a mining town. Construction of the Philadelphia Mining and Smelting Company's smelter brought workers, tradesmen and merchants into Ketchum, making the town a regional center of commerce which lasted for decades.

Railroad The railroad played two critical roles in underpinning Ketchum's economy.

Beginning in 1883 it provided the transportation needed for the Wood River Valley's mining and livestock industries to flourish.

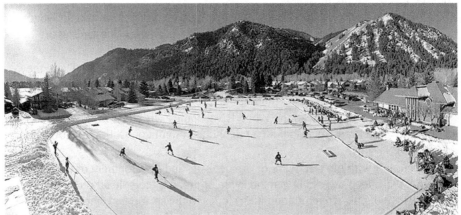

Christina Potters outdoor ice rink.

Around 1936 when Union Pacific Railroad Chairman William Averell Harriman sought the ideal site for a destination ski resort accessible by train, a Union Pacific employee told Harriman's representative that the rail line through the Wood River Valley to Ketchum cost the company more money for snow removal than any other stretch. That piece of railroad information led to the founding of the Sun Valley Resort and secured the future prosperity of Ketchum.

Sun Valley Resort Today, the Sun Valley Resort underpins Ketchum's economy. Tens of thousands of people come to town each year. Whether for skiing, conventions or mountain excursions, outdoor enthusiasts of all types come to enjoy the unparalleled year-round amenities and beauty of the area.

Austrian Count Felix Schaffgrotsch, William Averill Harriman's representative assigned to find the ideal site for a ski resort, described Ketchum and the surrounding area this way: "It contains more delightful features for a winter sports center than any other place I have seen in the United States, Switzerland or Austria."

Ketchum Today

Amenities and Attractions The city has 10 parks.

Ketchum's close proximity to the Sun Valley Resort and the Mt. Baldy downhill ski area that overlooks the city is perhaps its most prominent amenity. In addition to numerous ski runs, the mountain has 13 chairlifts'seven of which are high-speed quads – and three handsome day lodges. The resort offers year-round sporting activities as well as an open-air concert pavilion that can accommodate up to 4,000 patrons. There are two 18-hole golf courses nearby – one in Sun Valley and another at Elkhorn. There is also a 9-hole course at the Sun Valley Resort.

Each Labor Day weekend, the cities of Ketchum and Sun Valley host the historic "Wagon Days" celebration commemorating the bygone mining days when huge freight wagons carried ore to the smelters and supplies to the miners. The main event of the celebration is the "Big Hitch Parade," the largest non-motorized parade in the West.

Downtown Ketchum.

Parade entries feature a string of authentic freight wagons pulled by a 20-draft mule team jerkline with museum-quality buggies, carriages, tacks, carts, buckboards and wagons.

In October, the cities of Ketchum, Hailey and Sun Valley promote the annual three-day "Trailing of the Sheep Festival." The last major event of the Festival is driving a herd of over a thousand head of sheep down Ketchum's main street. This historic annual event commemorates the time when sheepherders moved their livestock from the summer pastures in the mountains to the warmer winter pastures on the Snake River Plain.

The SNRA has the rugged Sawtooth Mountain Range with over 20 peaks rising to between 10,000 and 10,751 feet. At the eastern base of these mountains is Red Fish Lake, the historic destination of spawning red Sockeye Salmon. The SNRA's pine and aspen forests have over 300 alpine lakes, rivers and streams. Many species of wildlife, including pronghorn antelope, deer, elk, bear and wolves inhabit the area.

Eidelweiss Park.

There are also excellent alpine and cross-country skiing and snowmobiling trails in the area as well as 30 miles of paved bike trails and extensive mountain bike and hiking trails. Tennis, horseback riding, ice-skating and swimming in natural hot springs are available in the valley.

Many anglers enjoy fly-fishing in the renowned Silver Creek Trout Fly Fishery. The Nature Conservancy's Silver Creek Preserve and Visitor's Center is located about 20 miles south near the unincorporated town of Picabo.

Economy and Major Employers Atkinson's Market has about 150 employees and is the city's largest employer. The U.S. Forest Service has about 50 employees and is the city's largest public employer. Several small businesses, hospitality establishments, retail shops, restaurants and service businesses provide most of the other jobs in the city.

Education Blaine County School District provides elementary and secondary education for Ketchum schoolchildren. Children in grades K-5 attend Ernest Hemingway Elementary in Ketchum. Junior and senior high school students attend school in Hailey. The closest institution of higher learning is the College of Southern Idaho, 87 miles south in Twin Falls.

Health Care St. Luke's Medical Center-Wood River is located in Ketchum and provides most of the city's health care.

Transportation The 116-mile-long Sawtooth Scenic Byway, Idaho Highway 75, intersects the city. The Byway begins 45 miles south at the city of Shoshone and continues north through fertile farmland, prehistoric

Trailing of the Sheep Festival. Sheep parade through Ketchum, 2014. Courtesy trailing of the sheep.org. Photo: Carol Waller.

lava fields and sagebrush-covered terrain, then through the Wood River Valley and the SNRA to the city of Stanley and the Sawtooth Mountains.

U.S. Highway 20 intersects Highway 75 about 26 miles south. Interstate 84 is accessible at Mountain Home 76 miles southwest via Highway 20 or at Twin Falls.

Hailey's Friedman Memorial Airport serves the cities of the Wood River Valley. It has a 7,550-by-100-foot runway and provides service to commercial commuter lines as well as private and charter aircraft.

The Ketchum Area Rapid Transit system (KART) provides free public transportation on 20-minute schedules between Wood River Valley cities and Sun Valley.

Utilities and Services Private companies provide electricity, telephone, satellite and wireless services. The City provides water and sewer services and fire and police protection.

Vision for 2050

In 1960 Ketchum had a population of 746. By 1970 the population nearly doubled to 1,454. By 2000, 30 years later, the population had grown to 3,011. Since 2000 the city's population growth has stabilized at less than one percent annually.

Recent population trends will likely continue. Should that occur, by 2050 Ketchum's population will approximate 4,500.

Single seat chairlift still hangs on Proctor Mountain and is listed on the National Register of Historic Places. Courtesy the Sun Valley Company.

Sun Valley

Statistical Data

Population: 1,412 *
Elevation: 5,940 feet
Precipitation: 15 inches **
Average Snowfall: 150 inches **
County: Blaine
Website: www.sunvalley.govoffice.com
Temperature Range – Fahrenheit: **

Spring: 15 to 63
Summer: 38 to 81
Fall: 14 to 70
Winter: 4 to 37
* U.S. Census Bureau Estimates July 2015
**Historical averages

The city of Sun Valley derives its character, economy and name from its principal commercial business – the internationally famous Sun Valley Resort.

Geographically, a small mountain saddle divides the city. To the north, the Sun

Valley Lodge, Sun Valley Inn, village shops, condominiums, single-family homes and an 18-hole golf course bordered by residential estates wind up Trail Creek Canyon. To the south lies Elkhorn Springs Village with shops, condominiums and an 18-hole golf course.

The city's western boundary borders the historic city of Ketchum. Both cities are in the Wood River Valley. The cities complement the ambiance of this laid-back, peaceful, and affluent resort community with its fresh mountain-desert climate, ski runs, golf courses, wilderness trails and the fast-running Big Wood River.

The Sawtooth National Forest is to the west and north of the city and the Salmon-Challis National Forest is to the east. The headwaters of the Salmon River are about 20 miles northwest in the Sawtooth National Recreation Area (SNRA). The SNRA includes the stunningly beautiful and jagged Sawtooth Mountain Range with over 20 peaks rising to between 10,000 and 10,751 feet. At the eastern base of the Sawtooth Mountains is Red Fish Lake, the historic destination of spawning red sockeye salmon.

Pre-Incorporation Years

The railroad, mining and sheep ranching preceded the founding of Sun Valley Resort by over 50 years. The first significant mining efforts in the Wood River Valley came in 1879 when prospectors discovered several deposits of silver-lead ore. By September 1879 they had filed 230 mining claims and organized the Wood River Mining District that included what are now the cities of Ketchum, Hailey and Bellevue. (*See The Region, Mining – Wood River Valley – Silver and Lead.*)

Ketchum/Sun Valley Train Depot.

Within two years, entrepreneurs had built a smelter at Ketchum to extract the metals from the ore. Heavy freight wagons hauled ore from the mines up Trail Creek Canyon and many other locations in the mountains to the smelter.

On February 3, 1883, the first railroad in the region reached Shoshone. At that time, the Oregon Short Line Railroad – in the process of building the line from Granger, Wyoming, to Huntington, Oregon, that created another transcontinental railroad – suspended work on its main rail line long enough to build a branch line north to the mines in the Wood River Valley and the Ketchum smelter. (*See The Region, Railroads.*)

The railroad was a boon to the smelter and mines until 1894 when silver prices and the Wood River mining industry collapsed. However, by that time the sheep and cattle ranching industries were flourishing. The city of Sun

Sun Valley Lodge circa 1938. Courtesy the Sun Valley Company.

Valley, founded over a decade after the resort began, features the heritage of the railroad and mine rail cars on its City Seal.

Sheep owners grazed their herds on the brush and grass-covered mountain slopes in the spring and summer and herded them to the warmer Snake River Plain in the fall and winter for lambing and shearing. The railroad was critical to transporting fat lambs and wool to market. By the early 1900s several hundred thousand sheep grazed in the foothills and mountains of the Wood River Valley. (*See The Region, Federal Lands – Private Ownership and Preservation Laws; and Livestock.*)

In 1936 life in the Wood River Valley changed when W. Averell Harriman, chairman of the board of the Union Pacific Railroad, conceived an idea to increase ridership on the train. Motivated by the success of the 1932 Winter Olympics in Lake Placid, New York, Harriman commissioned Austrian Count Felix Schaffgrotsch (the Count) to scour the Rocky Mountains for the ideal site for a destination ski resort accessible by train. The Count sought excellent snow and elevations, abundant sunshine, scenic mountain-protected valleys and little wind.

As the Count was concluding his search, a Union Pacific employee told him that the rail line through the Wood River Valley to Ketchum cost the company more money for snow removal than any other stretch. The Count immediately set out for the Ketchum area to investigate. He was so impressed that he wrote to Harriman, "It contains

Single seat chair lift. Courtesy the Sun Valley Company.

more delightful features for a winter sports center than any other place I have seen in the United States, Switzerland or Austria." Several weeks later, Harriman visited the Ketchum area. He agreed with the Count's findings.

Harriman directed Union Pacific Land Company to purchase the 3,888-acre Brass Ranch and develop a resort. To promote the resort, Harriman employed Steve

Hannigan, a New York public relations and marketing expert. Hannigan coined the name "Sun Valley."

Within the next several months, the company constructed a Swiss-style, four-story, 220-room lodge and inn with two circular shaped swimming pools and a ski complex that included ski runs and the world's first chairlifts on nearby Dollar and Proctor Mountains. The original Proctor Mountain Ski Lift and the Lodge built by Union Pacific are on the National Register of Historic Places.

Building ski runs on the towering Bald Mountain known as Baldy was more difficult. The mountain, leased from the federal government, has an elevation of 9,150 feet. The Resort opened its first ski runs on Baldy in December 1939.

Under Hannigan's skilled promotion plan, Union Pacific ran luxury trains to bring patrons from the east and west coasts. National magazines featured the new ski resort. Studios filmed movies on site, including the popular 1941 film "Sun Valley Serenade" starring Sonja Henie and the famous bandleader Glen Miller. Adding to the glamour and prestige of the Resort, its patrons included celebrities and movie stars such as Errol Flynn, Clark Gable, Ernest Hemmingway and Marilyn Monroe. Sun Valley soon became world famous for "amazing skiing."

All Sun Valley Resort operations closed in December 1942 due to World War II. On July 1, 1943, the military commissioned the Sun Valley Lodge as a Naval Convalescent Hospital. Averell Harriman explained, "I offered to do it. We'd have had to close it down anyway. It was the right thing to do, and it wouldn't have been possible to run this resort as a resort during the war." The last remaining bed from the time the Lodge was a hospital is on exhibit at the Blaine County Museum in Hailey.

Buses drop off skiers after a day of recreation. Challenger Inn and Sun Valley's outdoor swimming pool are in the background. Courtesy the Sun Valley Company.

Near the close of the war in 1945, patient occupation reached capacity at 1,603. During the two and a half years of occupation, almost 7,000 men received medical, surgical and neuropsychological treatment for combat fatigue, now known as post-traumatic stress disorder. That December, the Navy decommissioned the hospital.

Incorporation

On December 21, 1946, Sun Valley Resort reopened to the public, and on April

14, 1947, Sun Valley became an incorporated city.

Turning Points

Railroad The 1883 construction of the railroad line to the smelter and mines near Ketchum was the key event leading to opening the Wood River Valley for settlement. Promoting the business interests of the railroad is the underlying reason for establishing the Sun Valley Resort and, in turn, the basis for founding the city of Sun Valley.

W. Averell Harriman – 1936 The economy and culture of Sun Valley, as well as the entire Wood River Valley, was directly influenced by Harriman's decision to have Union Pacific develop a world-class ski resort in Sun Valley with the world's first chairlift.

Bill Janss Acquisition – 1964 In 1964 the railroad discontinued service to Ketchum. In November 1964 Bill Janss, the founder of the Snowmass Ski Resort in Utah, acquired the Sun Valley Resort. In 1968 he gained full control of Sun Valley and developed the north-facing Warm Springs and Seattle Ridge areas, and condominium and home construction increased significantly. He added seven chairlifts and increased the number of ski trails from 33 to 62. Janss installed the original Seattle Ridge double chairlift in 1976. However, a very poor snow year caused him to delay opening until December 20, 1977.

Earl Holding Acquisition – 1977 Oil magnate Earl Holding acquired the resort in 1977, and, under his ownership, there have been substantial improvements on both mountains. He brought snowmaking equipment to Baldy in the late 1980s and early 1990s. In 1988 he installed three high-speed quad chairlifts. Four years later, he opened an impressive day lodge at the base of Warm Springs, using the construction materials of logs, river rock and

Sun Valley Pavillion.

glass in an aesthetically pleasing design. He opened similar day lodges at the summit of Seattle Ridge in 1993 and at the base of River Run in 1995.

The new Dollar Mountain Lodge and headquarters for the Sun Valley Ski School opened in November 2004. Holding remodeled the interior of the original Sun Valley Lodge in 1985 and again in 2004 and the Sun Valley Inn in 2003.

In the summer of 2008 the Resort added a nine-hole golf course and the Sun Valley Club, a full service golf course club house built in the style of the resort's mountain day lodges.

150

In 2008 the Sun Valley Music Pavilion, which provides the Sun Valley Summer Symphony with a permanent home for the orchestra's annual two week series of free concerts, was built. The Pavilion is a one-of-a-kind state-of-the-art performing arts facility that hosts well-known performing and musical artists. Earl Holding and his family donated the lion's share of funds to bring this vision to fruition. Symphony supporters also helped fund the project.

Alexander Ebelof of Germany pulls a freestyle move at the end of his intermediate slalom snowboarding run at the 2009 Special Olympics World Winter Games in Sun Valley on February 11. Photo by Emma Patti.

In 2009 the Sun Valley Resort constructed the Roundhouse Express Gondola on Bald Mountain. The Gondola runs from the mountain's River Run Base to the Roundhouse Restaurant midway up the mountain, which was constructed in 1939 and remodeled in 2010. The Gondola carries patrons to the restaurant for lunch and dinner.

Elkhorn Springs Village Elkhorn Springs is a 280-acre resort complex developed by C.G. Elkhorn and situated along the base of Dollar Mountain in Sun Valley.

Robert Trent Jones and his son designed the championship golf course that originally opened in 1974. In 2001 new owners completely renovated the course including a new irrigation system, fairways, bunkers, greens, tee boxes and landscaping while retaining the integrity of the original design.

The resort includes condominiums, penthouses, golf lodges and a restaurant. In the summer, the resort offers tennis, swimming, hiking and biking. In the winter, Nordic and cross-country skiing are available. In the heart of the Village is the 16,000-square-foot

White Clouds Golf Course Club House.

Elkhorn Golf Club, a country club-type facility complete with a golf shop, dining room, locker rooms, administrative offices and a drive-up snack bar. Elkhorn Springs Village is a significant expansion of the city.

Sun Valley Today

Amenities and Attractions The city's most prominent attraction continues to be the Sun Valley Resort. The Resort includes beautiful Baldy and Dollar Mountains. Baldy with its 3,400-foot vertical drop ski runs overlooks the city and Ketchum. Dollar Mountain has an elevation of 6,638 feet. It is located across the street from Sun Valley City Hall and offers a more leisurely terrain for beginning skiers.

The Sun Valley Pavilion is an open-air concert pavilion with a 70-foot-high proscenium arch and a curved copper-shingled roof completed in 2008. The Pavilion seats 1,500 below a gently elevated terrain that creates an amphitheatre in full view of Trail Creek Canyon, Dollar Mountain and Baldy. The Pavilion can accommodate an additional 2,500 patrons on the grassy slopes. The guests can picnic and relax as they witness performances by the Sun Valley Summer Symphony and other performing artists and groups.

In addition to the 18-hole golf courses at the Sun Valley Resort and Elkhorn Springs Village, the Sun Valley Resort also has a 9-hole golf course.

In 2008 the Resort completed a 59,000-square-foot facility that serves as a Golf Clubhouse in the warmer months and a Nordic Center in the winter.

The city, Resort, community groups and the neighboring sister city of Ketchum produce or promote numerous special events and festivals throughout the year. The two most famous are the Trailing of the Sheep Festival each October and Wagon Days in July which features a parade of historic freight and other wagons.

The 756,000-acre Sawtooth National Recreation Area, including the spectacular Sawtooth Mountains, begins eight miles north.

In addition to the downhill skiing available at the Sun Valley Resort, there are excellent alpine and cross-country skiing and snowmobiling trails. There are also 30 miles of paved bike trails and extensive mountain bike and hiking trails.

Many anglers enjoy fly fishing in the renowned Silver Creek Trout Preserve. The Nature Conservancy's Silver Creek Preserve and Visitor's Center is about 33 miles south near the unincorporated town of Picabo.

Wild flowers in Sun Valley.

In addition, many tourists enjoy other recreational activities located in or near the city – including tennis, horseback riding, ice skating, swimming in natural hot springs and a skateboard park.

Wildlife seen in or near the city include mule deer, fox, bear, moose, coyotes, wolves, wolverines, mountain lions, raccoons, porcupines, squirrels, trout, eagles, hawks, sage grouse, blue grouse and a variety of waterfowl.

Economy and Major Employers With over 500 full-time employees, the Sun Valley Resort is the city's principal employer. St. Luke's Wood River Medical Center in Ketchum has 340 employees, many of whom are Sun Valley residents.

Education The Community School in Sun Valley is a private preparatory school serving children from pre-kindergarten through high school.

The Blaine County School District provides public education. Children from kindergarten through fifth grade attend school in nearby Ketchum. Older children travel to the district's middle and high schools in Hailey. Two private high schools also operate in Hailey.

The College of Southern Idaho, 82 miles south in Twin Falls, offers lower division college classes and community education programs at the Community Campus in Hailey.

Health Care St. Luke's Wood River Medical Center in Ketchum is a full-service medical facility that provides 24-hour emergency care.

Medical clinics, a nursing home, specialized private practice physicians as well as alternative medicine practitioners are available in or near the city.

The Sun Valley Wellness Institute provides education on health and wellness through programs and events including the Sun Valley Wellness Festival held each May.

Transportation Idaho Highway 75 intersects the city. Twenty-seven miles south, it intersects U.S. Highway 20, which in turn intersects Interstate 84 about 50 miles west at Mountain Home. Continuing south another 40 miles, it intersects Interstate 84 again at Twin Falls.

The Friedman Memorial Airport located in Hailey has a 6,602-foot runway. The FAA is evaluating three potential sites in south Blaine County for a larger airport.

The Mountain Rides Transportation Authority provides public transportation services to all of the cities of the Wood River Valley.

Utilities and Services Private companies provide electrical, telephone, gas, satellite and cable services. The City provides police and fire protection. The Sun Valley Water and Sewer District provides those municipal services.

Vision for 2050

The vibrancy of Sun Valley is inextricably linked to the Sun Valley Resort. The partnership has been a model of cooperation in advancing a peaceful yet dynamic community where people from around the world visit. In recent decades, many of these people stayed to build or buy second homes.

In 1960 Sun Valley had a population of 317. During the 1980s the population began to grow rapidly reaching 938 in 1990 and 1,427 in 2000 where it largely stabilized.

Over the next 40 years, the population will likely continue to grow at the slower rates experienced in the last decade. The citizens and public officials will continue to work together to preserve the qualities, environment, natural beauties and economy of Sun Valley. Visitors and residents will still enjoy a beautiful mountain setting and abundant outdoor recreational opportunities as well as world class performing and visual arts. The Sun Valley of the future is where residents and visitors agree, "This is where I want to be."

Mayors

1947	Winton S. Gray	2000	David Wilson
1980	Richard J. Heckman	2003	Jon Thorson
1981	Ruth Lieder	2008	Wayne Willich
1994	Joanne Levy	2012	Dewayne Briscoe
1995	Tom Praggatis	2016	Peter Hendricks

Central Crouch.

BOISE COUNTY

- Crouch
- Horseshoe Bend
- Idaho City (*County Seat*)
- Placerville

Crouch street.

Crouch

Statistical Data

Population: 156 *
Elevation: 3,021 feet
Precipitation: 23 inches **
Average Snowfall: 68 inches **
County: Boise
Temperature Range – Fahrenheit: **

Spring: 26 to 70
Summer: 43 to 88
Fall: 25 to 78
Winter: 17 to 42
* U.S. Census Bureau Estimates July 2015
**Historical averages

Crouch is 48 miles north of Boise in the Boise National Forest near the location where the North and South Forks of the Payette Rivers combine to form the Payette River.

The 33-mile Wildlife Canyon Scenic Byway, the state road paralleling the Payette River and its South Fork between the unincorporated communities of Banks on Idaho Highway 55 and Lowman on Idaho Highway 21, lies about a mile south of the city.

Pre-Incorporation Years

Circa 1900 Billy Crouch, a gold prospector and homesteader, filed his claims near what is now Crouch. Several other homesteaders joined him. During the 1920s Billy Crouch donated land for a hall and opened a general store.

In 1933 many of the federally employed Civilian Conservation Corps (CCC) workers working on the road between Banks and Lowman built temporary housing in Crouch and nearby Garden Valley. In 1934 community leaders applied for and received authorization for a post office they named Crouch.

156

Incorporation

The CCC workers caused the town's population to swell. In 1951 community leaders applied to county officials and became an incorporated village.

Turning Points

Civilian Conservation Corps The surge in CCC workers during the 1930s provided the rise in population – over 200 – sufficient for Crouch to become an incorporated village.

Vacation Homes In 1980 Crouch had a population of 69. Beginning in the late 1980s, developers and individuals, primarily from the Treasure Valley, began building and developing vacation homes – generally on private unincorporated land near Crouch and the unincorporated community of Garden Valley. By 2000 the city's population had more than doubled.

Crouch Merc.

Crouch Today

Amenities and Attractions Crouch's greatest attraction is its beautiful location in the Boise National Forest near the beautiful Payette River and its tributaries. Herds of elk and deer winter a few miles east of Crouch near the Danskin River access. Residents, outdoor enthusiasts, anglers and hunters also often observe wild turkey, chukers, eagles, osprey, cougars, bear and wolves.

Each summer, whitewater kayakers and rafters enjoy the nearby rapids on the forks of the Payette River – in some stretches rated Class III, IV and V.

Many Treasure Valley residents pass near Crouch as they take a recreational drive north from Boise on Highway 55; the Payette River Scenic Byway to Banks; then east on the Wildlife Canyon Scenic Byway; and then southwest back to Boise on Highway 21, the Ponderosa Pine Scenic Byway.

Economy and Major Employers The Crouch business community consists of a convenience store and several small retail shops. Most of the city's residents and vacation home owners do most of their shopping in nearby larger cities.

Education Horseshoe Bend School District provides K-12 education. Crouch students are bused 25 miles south to Horseshoe Bend to attend elementary, middle and senior high schools.

There are several institutions of higher learning in the Treasure Valley. The largest is Boise State University.

Health Care The Horseshoe Bend Clinic has a visiting doctor and nurse practitioner and dentist. Full ranges of hospital services are available in Boise.

Transportation Idaho Highway 55 south to Boise and north to McCall lies 10 miles west. Idaho Highway 52 begins in Horseshoe Bend and connects the city with Emmett.

Utilities and Services Private companies provide electricity, telephone and satellite services. The city's homes and businesses are on individual wells and septic systems. The Horseshoe Bend Volunteer Fire and EMT Department provides fire and emergency protection services. The Boise County Sheriff's Office provides police protection under contract with the City.

Vision for 2050

The city's population has remained stable for more than a decade. Historical trends will likely continue. By 2050 Crouch will continue as a community geared to serving tourists, outdoor recreationists and an increasing number of vacation home owners.

Welcome to Horseshoe Bend sign.

Horseshoe Bend

Statistical Data

Population: 669*
Elevation: 2,630 feet
Precipitation: 7.25 inches **
Average Snowfall: 12 inches **
County: Boise
Temperature Range – Fahrenheit: **

Spring: 26 to 72
Summer: 45 to 90
Fall: 24 to 79
Winter: 15 to 43
* U.S. Census Bureau Estimates July 2015
**Historical averages

Horseshoe Bend derives its name from its location. The lower part of the city lies on a fertile horseshoe shaped peninsula cut by the scenic Payette River.

The Boise National Forest and private rangeland surround the city. The city of Boise is about 21 miles south.

Pre-Incorporation Years

In 1862 prospectors discovered large quantities of placer gold in the Boise Basin. This led to a gold rush that, within the next year, brought 16,000 fortune seekers into the Basin. (*See Mining – Boise Basin.*)

Some of the prospectors came through what is now Horseshoe Bend en route to the Basin 20 miles east. At that time, the town was a way station between the Boise Basin mines and The Dalles, Oregon, a commercial supply center for goods shipped from Portland.

Some found that food prices paid by the miners were so high that there was more profit in producing and selling fresh food than in mining.

Log drive on the Payette.

Soon settlers began establishing homesteads in the arable parts of the region where they could divert streams for irrigation. They began raising farm animals and growing crops for sale to the miners.

Because of the Boise Basin's cold winters and deep snows, many miners came out of the mountains to winter in the Horseshoe Bend area where they could graze their livestock on the grass-covered foothills. Cattle and sheep ranching would later become a major industry in the low-lying western foothills of the Boise Basin.

During the gold rush, Benjamin J. Warriner built a sawmill in what is now Horseshoe Bend. They called the town that built up around the mill Warrinersville until 1867 when residents changed the name to Horseshoe Bend.

Other lumbermen built sawmills that they eventually consolidated into a single mill. Boise Cascade became the final owner of the mill. Most of the timber sawn at the mill came from the Smiths Ferry area in Long Valley. There, sawyers harvested logs and stored

Horsehose Bend Fire Department #1.

them in a large millpond constructed on the upper Payette. Each year during spring run-off, they released the logs to float to the mills in Horseshoe Bend and, further downriver, in Emmett.

Entrepreneurs constructed a small hydroelectric power plant in 1902 that produced power for the mill and community.

Ten years later, the Oregon Short Line Railroad built a line from Emmett through Horseshoe Bend up to Long Valley to transport logs to the mills.

Around this time, Horseshoe Bend residents began the first unsuccessful effort to move the county seat from Idaho City to the more populous Horseshoe Bend. The two cities are separated by a mountain range and directly connected by a 30-mile unimproved road. The distance between the cities on hard surface roads through Boise is about 70 miles.

In a 2004 organized attempt to change the seat of government, relocation supporters had to obtain 1,355 signatures to get the measure on the ballot and then receive a two-thirds majority in the election for passage. The attempt failed.

Incorporation

On April 14, 1947, Horseshoe Bend became an incorporated village.

Hotel and Smidt Store. Courtesy Shelly Family collection.

Turning Points

Boise Basin Gold Rush Fortune seekers heading for the Boise Basin gold fields were the impetus for founding the way station that became Horseshoe Bend.

Sawmill The vast forests north of Horseshoe Bend supplied the raw materials that established its sawmill-town reputation, which existed for most of the last century. Even though technological improvements gradually made the mill less labor intensive, in 1998 Boise Cascade closed the mill asserting that restricted access to timber in the federal forests was a major factor in that decision. The mill closure had

3,000 pound log on truck in front of Old Hotel, circa 1950. Courtesy Renfro Collection.

a significant adverse psychological and economic effect on the city.

Adapting to New Economic Realities With the decline of the natural resource-based economy, Horseshoe Bend is becoming an attractive community for people seeking small-town affordable housing within an easy commute to their jobs in Boise. In addition, the city benefits from its location as a gateway to the resort areas to the north, including McCall and Tamarack. Many tourist-based retail stores and shops are finding the city a good location.

Horseshoe Bend Today

Amenities and Attractions The city has a 2.5-acre park with picnic and children's play areas and restrooms.

The city's most significant asset is its proximity to Boise and the Treasure

Valley. Residents can live in a quiet rural community and still be close to shopping, health care, higher education and attractions available in a large urban community.

The Thunder Mountain Line Scenic Idaho Train Rides offers two and a half and five hour slow-paced trips in the backwoods along the beautiful Payette River between Horseshoe Bend and Cascade.

Zip Idaho is headquartered in Horseshoe Bend. It has a tour with seven ziplines carrying riders through the ponderosa pine of the Boise National Forest. The longest line is 1,800 feet, rising to over 100 feet.

Watching the horse races. Courtesy Sarah Deen collection.

The Payette River provides kayakers, tubers and anglers the exceptional recreational experiences they seek. Hunting, camping, snowmobile and ATV riding and fishing are available in the forest.

Economy and Major Employers The Horseshoe Bend School District is the city's largest employer. The business district consists of several restaurants and gasoline and convenience stores that serve the tourist traffic traveling Idaho Highway 55 through town.

Horseshoe Bend Park.

Education The Horseshoe Bend School District provides education to over 200 elementary, middle and senior high school students.

There are several institutions of higher learning in the Treasure Valley. The largest is Boise State University.

Health Care The Horseshoe Bend Clinic has a visiting doctor and nurse practitioner and dentist. Full ranges of hospital services are available in Boise.

Transportation Idaho Highway 55 south to Boise and north to McCall intersects the city. Idaho Highway 52 begins in Horseshoe Bend and connects the city with Emmett.

Utilities and Services Private companies provide electricity, telephone, cable, satellite and solid waste services. The City provides water and sewer. A volunteer fire and EMT department provides fire and emergency protection services.

Vision for 2050

Horseshoe Bend's population remained around 500 during the 1960s and 1970s. Subsequently, the population swelled to around 800 where it has remained for the past several years.

Looking to the future, we expect the city's population to grow moderately with spillover from Treasure Valley growth. Younger families with jobs in the valley will seek more affordable housing in our less crowded hometown community where they can raise their families.

Mustang Country building.

Existing city services are adequate to handle moderate growth. Community leaders will finance needed improvements to city services through existing revenue streams, voter approved initiatives or self-sustaining programs. In response to increasing demand, the city is evaluating vanpools to take residents to jobs in the Treasure Valley.

Mayors

1947	Frank W. Clarkson *
1947	John J. Quinn *
1949	Theodore Hoff, Jr. *
1953	James Draper *
1953	Harold Raper *
1961	Riger Charters *
1966	Steve Helm *
1967	Steve Helm

1972	Larry Roberts
1976	Steve Helm
1980	Lester Wallace
1982	Doyle Woods
2000	Brian Davies
2004	Doyle Woods
2008	Mary Hanson
* Village Chairman

163

Boise Basin Museum, Idaho City.

Idaho City

Statistical Data

Population: 461 *
Elevation: 3,906 feet
Precipitation: 23 inches **
Average Snowfall: 122 inches **
County: Boise
Website: www.idahocitychamber.com
(Chamber of Commerce)

Temperature Range – Fahrenheit: **
Spring: 22 to 67
Summer: 40 to 90
Fall: 20 to 75
Winter: 10 to 41
* U.S. Census Bureau Estimates July 2015
**Historical averages

Idaho City is nestled in a narrow mountain valley near the confluence of Elk and Mores Creeks in the Boise National Forest. It is 32 miles northeast of Boise. Rugged mountains, with some peaks rising over 6,000 feet, surround the city and the large timber-covered Boise Basin. The Sawtooth Wilderness and National Recreation Area, with its famous Sawtooth Mountain Range of jagged peaks rising over 10,000 feet, is about 45 miles northeast.

A year after the 1862 discovery of gold, 16,000 fortune seekers filled the Boise Basin searching for the precious metal. Idaho City – then called West Bannock – had the largest population in the Northwest – 6,167 – even larger than Portland.

The population persuaded the 1864 Territorial Legislature to make nearby Boise the territorial capital.

The gold mines played out long ago, but the history and many of the historic buildings remain, making Idaho City one of Idaho's most interesting communities and tourist attractions.

Pre-Incorporation Years

Long before whites came into the area and up until the 1860s, nomadic American Indians – principally of the Shoshone and Bannock Tribes – inhabited the region.

In 1811 European and American explorers and trappers began working the Snake River and its tributaries for pelts. Over the next 50 years, a seemingly unrelated series of events far removed from Idaho City played a role in its founding.

In 1834 the Hudson's Bay Company, a British enterprise, built a small trading post at the confluence of the Snake and Boise Rivers near what is now Parma. A Frenchman named Francois Payette later managed the remote post. Influenced by the heavily wooded river that flowed from the east, he named the post Fort Boise and the river "Boise," after the French word "bois" meaning "wooded."

Beginning in 1841 when the first immigrants began an overland migration to Oregon's Willamette Valley, Fort Boise became an Oregon Trail landmark.

In 1860 Elias Davidson Pierce discovered gold near what is now the city of Pierce – about 180 miles due north of Idaho City. The following year several thousand prospectors and miners rushed to Pierce and the surrounding mountains and streams where they made additional discoveries. One of these major discoveries was at Florence, near White Bird, located about 55 miles southwest of Pierce.

One of the miners was a man named Moses Splawn. While prospecting for placer gold at Florence, Splawn met an Indian named Bannock Louie who told him about a mountain basin to the south where the streams held large quantities of the yellow material he sought.

Splawn and fellow prospector George Grimes led a dozen other men south, and in June 1862 reached the west bank of the Snake River on the Oregon Trail. They

Pioneer Cemetery.

found the swollen river running about two miles wide due to the unusually high spring runoff. Across the river was the site of old Fort Boise – flooded in 1853, abandoned the next year and totally destroyed by the flood of 1862.

After several days of trying to cross the swollen river, three of the 14 men joined another group heading south to prospect in the Owyhee Mountains. After three weeks and numerous attempts, the 11 committed prospectors made it across the river and traveled 40 miles east to the mountains and the fabled basin and stream beds with gold-bearing gravels. They arrived in the Boise Basin on August 2, 1862.

On what is now Grimes Creek, they dug "prospect holes" and began panning for gold. Within a short time, they had $75 worth of the precious metal and excitedly began exploring other parts of the basin looking for the best spots to mark their claims.

A week later, Indians attacked the little band, killing George Grimes. The prospectors buried Grimes' body and quickly retreated to Fort Walla Walla, Washington, to get supplies and reinforcements.

A building with boardwalk.

They appealed to the U.S. Army to send troops for protection and proceeded to recruit other prospectors. Forty determined men reentered the Boise Basin a few weeks later prepared to spend the winter, stake their claims and fight the Indians if necessary.

The news of the gold discovery spread rapidly. The next year, 16,000 fortune hunters entered the Boise Basin. It was the biggest gold rush since California.

The prospectors established mining towns wherever they found large quantities of gold, including Placerville, Pioneerville and Centerville. Idaho City, then called West Bannock, was at the confluence of two streams – the most productive location in the basin.

Replica of water cannon.

When Oregon became a state in 1859, the part of Oregon Territory that included most of Idaho became part of Washington Territory, a territory that had not yet settled on its territorial capital. Three proposals were

166

being considered by Congress. A bill that passed the House on February 13, 1863, named Idaho City as Washington's territorial capital. However, the bill did not advance. On March 4, 1863, Congress created Idaho Territory and reduced the size of Washington Territory to what would become Washington State 26 years later.

Under the Organic Act that created Idaho Territory, the territorial governor was empowered only to select the provisional capital. However, it required an act of the Legislature to establish the permanent site. Idaho's new territorial governor, William H. Wallace, declared Lewiston the temporary capital.

In 1863 while embroiled in the Civil War, the U.S. Army sent a detachment of troops to establish a fort to protect the immigrants traveling the Oregon Trail, settlers along the Boise River and the miners working the gold fields in the Boise Basin and the Owyhee Mountains.

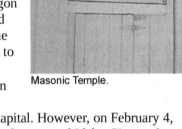

On July 4, 1863, U.S. Army Major Pickney Lugenbeel selected a location for the fort on a low foothill bench overlooking the Boise River. He named it Fort Boise, thereby retaining the Oregon Trail landmark name of the old flood-destroyed fort 40 miles to the west. A few days later, some of the area business people platted a town next to the fort and named it Boise City.

Masonic Temple.

The First Territorial Legislature convened in December 1863 in Lewiston. It took no action regarding the permanent site of the territorial capital. However, on February 4, 1864, it created Boise County with West Bannock, renamed Idaho City, as the county seat.

In 1864 Idaho City had two main streets next to the creeks, each a half mile long and lined with about 250 businesses – four sawmills, two dozen saloons, four breweries, 25 law offices, two bowling alleys, a mattress factory, a bookstore, a painters' shop, a photographer, two jewelry stores, a jail, 15 doctors, churches and theaters.

Boise Basin Merc.

The census listed 6,167 residents, including 360 women and 224 children.

When the Second Territorial Legislature convened on November 14, 1864, the gold mine claims that established the mining boomtowns closest to Lewiston had largely played out, and most of the miners had moved to more promising locations in the Boise Basin.

Influenced by the territory's population shift to the Boise Basin, the Second Territorial Legislature meeting in Lewiston, passed landmark legislation on December 12, 1864. It made Boise a chartered city, created Ada County with Boise as the county seat and established Boise as Idaho's permanent territorial capital.

Incorporation

In April 1864 Idaho City prospectors and business owners formed a village organization similar to many other boomtowns with a chairman, secretary and rules. However, it was not until October 17, 1895, that the community incorporated as a village.

Turning Points

Gold Idaho City owes its origins to the 1862 discovery of placer gold. By 1870 panning for gold gave way to the use of sluice boxes – diverting water over placer gold bearing soils shoveled into a sluice. The use of water cannon to wash mountainside soils into sluice boxes was another innovation. Later, heavy dredges scooped up the soils from the valley floor as areas prospectors had panned were reworked. Dredging continued until the 1950s.

The water cannon left huge scars on the mountainsides. Dredging turned level floodplains into thousands of four- to eight-foot-high piles of dredge tailings.

When the mining ended, the Boise Basin had yielded nearly 30 million troy ounces (tr. oz.) of gold.

Fires The threat of fire was a constant concern. The town's homes and businesses were built of wood, constructed close together, heated by wood-burning stoves and lit by oil lamps.

Major fires swept through the community in 1865, 1867, 1868 and 1871. Each fire caused extensive damage, but, each time, the town bounced back. The fire of 1865 was particularly devastating, wiping out 80 percent of the buildings.

When they rebuilt the town, they also re-platted the streets.

Chinese Settlement Beginning in the mid-1860s Chinese emigrants began arriving in Idaho City and the Boise Basin. By 1870 more than 45 percent of the area's population was Chinese, who were meticulous gold miners. They also developed businesses that provided food and clothes-cleaning services. However, many white residents looked down on the Chinese and treated them badly. Nearly all residents of Chinese descent eventually moved out of the area.

Idaho City Today

Amenities and Attractions Visiting Idaho City is like taking a nostalgic step back in time. Visitors walk on boardwalks as miners did more than a century ago.

The Boise Basin Museum, run by the local Historical Foundation, offers guided tours featuring buildings dating back over a hundred years and other landmarks that recapture the frontier character of a bygone era. The museum has an excellent collection of gold rush memorabilia.

Saint Joseph's Catholic Church, Idaho City.

Many downtown structures are on the National Register of Historic Places. At the old jail, visitors see where desperados carved their names on the thick wooden walls. They can also walk into the historic mercantile store where it once cost a pinch of gold dust to buy an apple. The Pioneer Cemetery, located not far from downtown, has many tombstones dating back to the mid-1800s.

The community holds most of its festivals and events in the 57-acre Municipal

Park, including the Chili Cook Off and Flea Market on the second weekend in February, Motorcycle Races on the last weekend in May and Mountain Bike Races in mid-June. The community celebrates the Fourth of July with a parade, an all-day flea market and night fireworks at the Idaho City High School football field. The Gold Dust Rodeo, including panning for gold, takes place the last week of June. The Idaho Shootists U.S. National Championships is a four-day event the last week in June. The Boise County Fun Run is the third Saturday in June. Halloween Night Children's Costume Party is on October 31. The Community Ladies Christmas Bazaar takes place on the first weekend in November. The Christmas Holiday with luminary and old-fashioned experience is held during the week of December 20. The Cowboy Poetry event is held every April and includes a melodrama, jug band and lots of laughs.

Local shootists have gun matches the first weekend of each month and gun fights the second Friday night of the month.

Throughout the summer, the Boise Basin Historical Museum opens to the public and conducts tours through the historic district.

The Ponderosa Pine Scenic Byway, State Highway 21, passes through the city. This 131-mile route starts in Boise and climbs over 3,500 feet to the city of Stanley. As the road winds through the mountains, it passes spectacularly beautiful forest and wilderness areas with vistas of largely pristine mountains, valleys, rivers, streams and meadows.

Twenty-six miles southwest is Lucky Peak Dam and State Park. This cold-water lake backs up to within 15 miles of the city. It is popular for fishing, boating and waterskiing.

The headquarters for the 33,540-acre Boise River Wildlife Management Area, managed by the Idaho Department of Fish and Game, is located on Highway 21 between Idaho City and Boise. This Management Area is prime winter range for mule deer with many segments open to the public.

In addition to experiencing the old town, Idaho City is a gateway to almost every type of outdoor activity. Visitors come to hunt, fish, camp, hike, ride horses, view the scenery and history or just enjoy the solitude that the area offers. Rainbow and brook trout are favorite game fish. Hunters find plentiful elk, deer and blue grouse.

Pioneer Cemetery grave.

Downhill snow skiing is available at Bogus Basin Ski Resort. The resort is located in Boise County and is visible from the tops of the Idaho City Mountains about 15 miles southwest. However, the only paved road to the ski area from Idaho City requires traveling to Boise and driving 16 miles up the mountain, a 55-mile trip.

Just north of the city are 15 maintained cross-country ski trails. They range in difficulty from beginner to advanced. Snowmobiles and ATVs can travel more than 150 miles of forest service roads. Yurts are available for reservation throughout the year. Contact the U.S. Forest Service office for permits and reservations.

Other attractions include side trips to other historic gold mining ghost towns of the Boise Basin including Placerville, Pioneerville and Centerville.

Economy and Major Employers The city's downtown includes several retail and service businesses. With fewer than 75 employees each, the U.S. Forest Service, Basin School District and Boise County government are the city's major employers.

Education Basin Public School District provides primary and secondary education. It has one high school and an elementary school.

The closest institution of higher learning is Boise State University. \

Health Care A general clinic offers medical care in the city. The closest hospital is St Luke's Regional Medical Center in Boise.

Transportation State Highway 21 intersects the city. It connects with Boise and Interstate 84 to the southwest and Stanley on the northeast.

The U.S. Forest Service maintains a 3,400-foot runway two miles outside the city. Commercial air service is available in Boise.

Utilities and Services Private companies provide electricity, telephone, cable, propane, satellite and wireless service. The City provides water, sewer, police and fire protection. The County provides solid waste services.

Vision for 2050

In 1960 Idaho City had a population of 188. The population has grown steadily since that time before stabilizing in recent years at around 500. With its mining town heritage, historic buildings and beautiful mountainous terrain, the city offers the visitor a nostalgic experience of living in an old-fashioned, historic mining community of bygone days.

In 2050 Idaho City's principal industries will still be tourism and recreation. The city's population will grow to accommodate the increasing numbers of tourists and families who come for interesting and fun historic day trips or family "mini-vacations."

The city's municipal systems are generally adequate to accommodate this modest to moderate growth.

Mayors

1947 ** Harry Penrod *	1956 Martina Nelson
1949 John Gorman *	1959 Clark Estell
1949 Harry Palmer *	1961 Ray Robison
1951 R.D. Ratican *	1965 Jim Bailey
1953 T.R. Adams *	1966 Donald Reed
1955 L.D. Jackson *	1966 Ray Robison

171

1969 Roger Jackson
1972 Charles Stevens
1973 John Brogan
1984 Larry Abbotnd
1986 Raymond Robison
1993 Frank Eno (acting mayor)
1993 Pat Campbell

1998 Tom Corum
2000 Phillip J. Canody
2008 James Obland
2010 Jackie Bridwell
2014 James Obland
* Village Chairman
** City records prior to 1947 destroyed by fire.

Placerville City Hall.

Placerville

Statistical Data

Population: 52 *
Elevation: 4,450 feet
Precipitation: 24 inches **
Average Snowfall: 81 inches **
County: Boise

Temperature Range – Fahrenheit: **
Spring: 28 to 77
Summer: 37 to 88
Fall: 15 to 64
Winter: 13 to 49
* U.S. Census Bureau Estimates July 2015
**Historical averages

Placerville is one of the historic gold mining boomtowns of the Boise Basin Mining District. It is in the heart of the beautiful Boise National Forest and is surrounded by a mixture of private, Forest Service and Bureau of Land Management lands. Rugged mountains, with some peaks rising over 7,000 feet, surround the city.

Today, the city is but a shadow of its boomtown period. However, many historic buildings remain. Many Treasure Valley residents have built second homes or purchased building lots in or near the city. Each summer the population swells with tourists, campers and part-time residents. They come to envision the events of a bygone era and enjoy the fabulous beauty of this high-mountain community.

Pre-Incorporation Years

The origin of Placerville followed the August 2, 1862, discovery of gold in the Boise Basin. At that time, a band of 11 prospectors came into the Boise Basin and made the first discovery of significant quantities of placer gold in what is now Grimes Creek. (*See Southwestern Idaho, Boise Basin Gold Mines and Idaho City.*)

Original Placerville school.

The news of the discovery spread rapidly. The next year, 16,000 miners and prospectors descended into the Boise Basin. It was the largest gold rush in the United States since California.

The prospectors established mining towns wherever they found large quantities of placer gold. The largest town was Idaho City, 14 miles southeast of Placerville.

By September 1863 about 3,200 miners and prospectors resided in Placerville. Tents, shacks, prospectors and mining claims lined the many creeks that run in or near the city.

Old Magnolia Saloon, now a museum.

Placerville was an unusual mining boomtown in that it had a street grid and a town square – known locally as the "plaza." Around the plaza was an Episcopal church; thirteen saloons; seven restaurants; five butcher shops; five blacksmith shops; hotels; druggists; express agents; bakeries; livery barns; carpenters; sawmills; and, attesting to the presence of women, a dressmaker and a millinery shop.

The miners first panned for gold. Then they used sluice boxes and, later, they brought in water cannon to wash mountainside soils into their sluice boxes.

By 1870 the mines had largely played out. By that time, the population had shrunk to 318. Many of those remaining were Chinese reworking the area's abandoned mining claims.

Incorporation

On February 4, 1864, the Idaho Territorial Legislature created Boise County with Idaho City as the county seat. On July 18, 1897, the Boise County commissioners made Placerville an incorporated city.

Turning Points

Gold Many of the prospectors and miners who came into the Boise Basin in 1863 founded the town of Placerville. For several years, Placerville was one of the most populous cities in Idaho.

Fire Around 1900 fire raged through the town destroying many of the buildings. Most of today's historic buildings were constructed following that tragic fire.

Emmanuel Episcopal Church.

The New Economy By the early 1900s the gold mines had played out and the miners moved on. Decades later, Placerville property owners determined that the best use of the land was for second homes and recreation.

The terrain around Placerville has a variety of elevations. In the late 1960s developers sold residential building lots on the higher elevations at auction creating what residents termed the "upper subdivision." The new property owners built both vacation and permanent homes. Then, as now, the Village Market is Placerville's only business.

Even though people must travel on gravel roads to access the city, increasing numbers of visitors come each year. For 20 days during July and August 2005, 5,920 vehicles were counted entering Placerville.

Placerville in winter.

Placerville Today

Amenities and Attractions

The former town square – "Plaza," dating back to 1863 – is still a historic community landmark. However, the historic plaza is now a park named Placerville City Square. It has a pavilion, picnic tables and electric power.

The city has two museums funded by public donations and manned by volunteers. These museums are open weekends from Memorial Day to Labor Day and by special request.

The entire old city of Placerville is on the National Historic Register. It has 31 historic buildings listed with the National Park Service. Many visitors visit the city cemetery and the many graves and markers that date back to gold rush days.

Numerous outdoor activities are available in the nearby mountains and streams. Many people, including families, come to hunt, fish, camp, hike, ride horses, cross-country ski, snowshoe, view the scenery, learn of the history or just enjoy the solitude that the area

Placerville Road.

offers. Rainbow and brook trout are favorite game fish. Hunters find plentiful elk, deer and blue grouse.

Snowmobiles and ATVs can travel for miles on forest service roads. Yurts are available for reservation throughout the year. Contact the U.S. Forest Service office for permits and reservations.

Other attractions include side trips to nearby historic Boise Basin boomtowns including Idaho City, Pioneerville and Centerville.

Economy and Major Employers The Village Market is the only private business in town. Most residents in the labor force commute to other cities for work.

Education Basin School District provides K-12 education. Students are bused 14 miles to the elementary and high schools in Idaho City.

The closest institution of higher learning is Boise State University.

Health Care The closest medical clinic is in Idaho City. The East Boise County Ambulance Service provides emergency medical services. Air ambulance is also available.

The closest hospital is St. Luke's Regional Medical Center 60 miles away in Boise.

Placerville cemetery.

Transportation Three graveled county roads intersect the city – Idaho City on the south; Crouch, 15 miles north; and a 19-mile-long graveled road to Horseshoe

Bend. The nearest paved highway is State Highway 21 in Idaho City.

Utilities and Services Private companies provide electricity, telephone and satellite TV service. Each residence and business has individual wells and septic systems.

The volunteer Placerville Fire Department provides fire protection. The Boise County Sheriff provides police protection.

The City provides snow removal services; maintains the community center, cemetery and the Placerville City Square; and provides irrigation water. The County contracts for solid waste service.

Vision for 2050

In 1960 Placerville had a population of 12. In the late 1990s the population increased to around 60, where it has remained. However, by 2050 the population will have more than trebled.

The lack of hard surface roads to the city is the primary growth-limiting factor. Better roads will encourage tourism and allow more residents to commute to work while living in

Placerville through the trees.

Placerville's quiet and beautiful mountain setting.

To allow this growth to happen, by 2050 the local highway jurisdictions will have consolidated into a countywide road district thereby improving efficiency and reducing redundant costs. The consolidated district will have paved the county roads to Placerville and other Boise County cities and historic places. As a result, the flow of tourists and outdoor recreationists will increase and new businesses will come to serve these visitors and an increasing number of residents.

By 2050 Placerville will have a restaurant, a hardware store, an antique shop, an RV park, a campground and a large recreation field.

Boise County will have designated and promoted the roads connecting the county's historic mining communities as county scenic byways.

Through public-private partnerships, the buildings listed on the National Register of Historic Places will be restored and in use. The original mile square of the Woof Creek area will be reacquired and set aside for hiking and fishing. New construction and landscaping will conform to the historic theme of the city. It will be aesthetically pleasing, environmentally responsive and energy efficient.

Mayors

1897 John H. Myer *
1899 Martin Cathcart *
1945 Penrod *
1960 Curtis X. Bacon *
1968 Mayors Albert Tillett
1973 Walter P. March
1986 Jack A. Craig

1993 Wilson L. Chesnut
1996 Gary L. Jones
2000 David Crowder
2004 Jessica Gasiorowski
2008 Brian J. Davies
* Village Chairman

CAMAS COUNTY

- Fairfield (*County Seat*)

Sheep grazing on the Camas Prairie.

Fairfield

Statistical Data

Population: 381 *
Elevation: 5,065 feet
Precipitation: 16 inches **
Average Snowfall: 80 inches **
County: Camas
Website: www.fairfieldidaho.us

Temperature Range – Fahrenheit: **
Spring: 19 to 67
Summer: 42 to 85
Fall: 18 to 76
Winter: 6 to 36
* U.S. Census Bureau Estimates July 2015
** Historical averages

Fairfield is the county seat and the only incorporated city in Camas County. The city lies near the center of over 125,000 acres of the Camas Prairie devoted to farming and ranching. The Camas Prairie comprises the southern third of the county. The Sawtooth National Forest, with mountain peaks rising to over 10,000 feet, comprises the northern two-thirds.

The city's natural setting largely characterizes its personality and economy. To the north, the city lies at the base of the Soldier Mountain Range and the Soldier Mountain Ski Resort. Nine miles west, near the historic ghost town of Corral, is the Soldier Mountain Ranch Country Club and Resort.

Several creeks and their tributaries flow down from the mountains into several small lakes and reservoirs on the Camas Prairie. The 3,700-acre five-mile-long

Magic Reservoir to the east, the smaller Mormon Reservoir to the south and the Camas Prairie Centennial Marsh to the southwest are the largest of these bodies of water.

Tourism, outdoor recreation, light manufacturing, farming and ranching are the principal industries that underlie the city's economy.

Pre-Incorporation Years

Prior to white settlement, Bannock and Shoshone Tribes of American Indians frequented the Camas Prairie each summer to hunt and harvest the Camas Lilly bulbs that grew profusely on the prairie. The lilies were a staple in their diet, sustaining them during the winter.

In 1862 Tim Goodale, a trader acquainted with the American Indian and fur trader trails north of the Snake River, led a group of

Train Caboose, now the Camas County Tourist Information Center.

Oregon Trail emigrants on a shortcut beginning at Fort Hall and rejoining the main trail east of Boise near Mayfield.

Goodale's Cutoff passed through the Camas Prairie a few miles north of what is now the city of Fairfield and became one of the more heavily traveled routes on the Oregon Trail.

In 1869 the U.S. military had largely subdued the Shoshone-Bannock Indians and assigned them to live on the Fort Hall Indian Reservation. However, the federal government failed to provide promised provisions. The Indians continued their summer migrations into the Camas Prairie to gather Camas Lilly bulbs and hunt wild game.

In the 1870s cattlemen began moving their herds onto the Camas Prairie to graze. Some brought hogs that foraged for food by digging up the bulbs with their snouts.

The Bannocks were incensed that the settlers were destroying their traditional food sources and the U.S. government was not fulfilling its promises. In May 1878 about 200 Bannock warriors began attacking white settlements – killing the settlers, taking provisions and destroying property. The U.S. Calvary and volunteer militia gradually tracked down the Indian warriors – killing them, scattering them or forcing them to return to the Fort Hall Reservation. The conflict – dubbed the Bannock War – was Idaho's last "Indian War."

With Indian hostilities suppressed, white settlement of the region surged. In early 1879 thousands of prospectors began flooding into the Wood River Valley where they discovered large lead-silver ore bodies. Homesteaders came into the Camas Prairie and the floodplain south of the future city of Bellevue to farm, ranch and sell their commodities to the miners.

Camas Prairie.

In 1881 the Oregon Short Line Railroad began building the segment of railroad between Granger, Wyoming, and Huntington, Oregon. The railroad crossed Idaho in a northwesterly direction through Shoshone and Nampa before crossing into Oregon. When complete, the segment would provide a direct link between Omaha, Nebraska, and Portland, Oregon.

In 1882 the railroad reached Shoshone, Idaho. At that point, railroad officials stopped their westward construction temporarily to build a branch line north to the mining towns of the Wood River Mining District. The railroad completed most of the branch line in 1883 then returned to constructing the balance of the railroad to Huntington, which they completed in November 1884.

By the early 1900s sheep ranching was a dominant industry in the region. Several hundred thousand sheep grazed on the Camas Prairie and in the mountains surrounding the Wood River Valley north of the future city of Fairfield.

In 1911 the railroad extended a branch line from its Wood River Valley line at Richfield, skirting the southwest side

Downtown Fairfield.

of Magic Reservoir, turning due west to Soldier Creek, continuing west to Corral before turning northwest to a terminus at a small ranching community named Hill City. Hill City became a prominent railhead for west Camas Prairie sheep ranchers shipping their fat lambs and wool to market.

When the railroad built its line through the Camas Prairie, it laid track about two miles south of the existing town of Soldier – the first town established on the

Camas Prairie. At the site south of Soldier, the railroad built a depot and named it Fairfield. Bypassed by the railroad, most of Soldier's residents moved to Fairfield along with other businesses attracted to the train depot.

Incorporation

On August 16, 1912, Fairfield became an incorporated village. On February 6, 1917, the town became the county seat of the newly created Camus County. At that time, the city's population approached 400.

Turning Points

Agriculture The railroad, brought to the Camas Prairie by agriculture, established Fairfield.

Cattle ranching and some homesteading started on the Camas Prairie in the 1870s. However, it grew dramatically following two events that occurred in 1879 – the end of the Bannock War and the discovery of lead-silver deposits in the Wood River Valley. At the end of the Bannock War, the U.S. Army forced the Bannock Indians back to the Fort Hall Indian Reservation.

In 1880 thousands of prospectors and miners, rushing to the mountains of the Wood River Valley, brought instant and significant demands for food commodities. That, in turn, encouraged the development of agriculture.

Several Scottish and Basque emigrants, who were among the Wood River Valley prospectors and miners, were impressed with the vast tracts of sagebrush and grassland for grazing sheep. They decided their fortune was not in mining but rather in returning to their sheep-raising roots. Cattle ranching continued; however, sheep ranching became dominant as hundreds of thousands of sheep grazed in the mountains and on the Camas Prairie.

In 1911 primarily to serve the sheep industry, the railroad built a branch line from Richfield northwest to the Camas Prairie then west to the sheep trailhead of Hill City. Fourteen miles before reaching Hill City, the railroad established a depot at a location it named Fairfield.

Sheep ranching generally prospered until the mid-1900s. The end of World War II and the Korean War brought a sharp falloff in demand for lamb and wool used by the military. In addition, consumer preference for lamb declined and new synthetic fibers became competitive alternatives to wool.

Downtown Fairfield at night.

Today, the sizes of Idaho's sheep herds are a small fraction of those of the mid-

1900s. The loss of the sheep industry had a significant adverse effect on Fairfield's economy.

Railroad The railroad was a key factor in the development of Fairfield and the growth of the sheep industry. It provided the means of shipping fat lambs and wool to market. However, as the mines of the Wood River Valley played out, motor vehicles became prevalent and the sheep industry declined, the railroad shut down. In the 1970s the railroad removed the tracks that ran through the Camas Prairie.

School Consolidation Education was important to the early settlers of the Camas Prairie. As communities developed, they started independent schools. The first of these schools started in 1883. Eventually, 27 small rural schools dotted the prairie. In order to reduce costs and improve school programs, the schools gradually consolidated with the schools in Fairfield. The last rural school closed in 1953.

Consolidation of the schools in Fairfield improved the quality of education delivered in the Camas Valley and had a stabilizing effect on the economy of the city.

The New Economy As mining, timber, sheep ranching and the railroad businesses declined, recreation, tourism and businesses attracted by the city's proximity to beautiful and vast natural resources have emerged to build the city's economy.

Fairfield Today

Amenities and Attractions The city has devoted four acres of land to two parks. Park amenities include picnic and children's playground areas and athletic fields. An 18-hole golf course is also located in the city.

The restored historic Fairfield Railroad Depot serves as a city museum. The museum has many exhibits relating to early settlers and the American Indians that once inhabited the area. The Fairfield Public Library attracts patrons throughout the Camas Prairie.

Soldier Mountain Ski Resort is 12 miles north of Fairfield. The 1,150-acre resort has 15 groomed downhill ski runs, two chairlifts and a rope tow for beginners. The ski runs have 1,425-feet of vertical drop from a top elevation of 7,177 feet.

Railroad Park.

In addition, the resort offers snowcat tours into the Sawtooth National Forest. The forest also has hundreds of miles of trails for snowmobiling and cross-country skiing.

The Soldier Mountain Ranch Country Club and Resort, located in the foothills nine miles west near Corral, offers an 18-hole golf course and conference center.

In the warmer months, many outdoor enthusiasts come to the Fairfield area to enjoy mountain biking, hiking, camping, fishing, horseback riding, bird and wildlife watching, and photography. Come autumn, hunting deer, elk, antelope and bear are popular sports.

The Camas Prairie Centennial Marsh Wildlife Management Area (WMA) lies 14 miles southwest of Fairfield. The total WMA covers over 3,100 acres. Each spring, runoff from the mountains covers about two-thirds of the WMA with about a foot of water. This annual springtime phenomenon attracts thousands of migratory waterfowl, shorebirds and a host of other wildlife.

For thirty days beginning in mid-May, the Camas Lilly bursts into bloom turning the Camas Prairie around the WMA into a carpet of cobalt-blue blossoms. In the fall and winter, the marshland dries and other wildlife inhabit the WMA.

Carey Lake Wildlife Management Area is 28 miles east of the city, just north of the city of Carey. This two-mile-long lake is both a fishery and a sanctuary for migratory waterfowl and other wildlife.

Economy and Major Employers High County Fusion Company is a niche business manufacturing high-density polyethylene pipes and fittings for a growing international clientele. The company has over 40 employees and is the city's largest employer.

Soldier Mountain Ski Resort has over 25 employees and is the city's second largest private employer. Other businesses include restaurants, a grocery store and a variety of other retail stores, specialty shops and service businesses. A grain mill and elevator business serves the outlying farms and ranches.

The largest public employer, with about 25 employees, is the Camas County School District. Camas County, the U.S. Forest Service and the City are also important public employers.

Education Camas County School District operates the Camas County Elementary/Junior High School, Grades PK-8, and the Camas County High School, Grades 9-12. Both schools are located in the city and serve students residing in the county.

The nearest institution of higher learning is the College of Southern Idaho, located 61 miles south in Twin Falls.

Health Care A physician and nurse practitioner, dentist and chiropractor visit Fairfield three days a week.

The nearest hospital is Gooding County Memorial Hospital, 29 miles south.

Transportation U.S. Highway 20 intersects the city. Highway 20 is a popular route connecting Boise and Mountain Home to Sun Valley, the cities of the Wood River Valley and the Sawtooth Scenic Byway – State Highway 75.

The junction of Highway 20 and State Highway 46 south to Gooding and I-84 is four miles east of the city. I-84 is 42 miles south of the city.

Camas County Airport in Fairfield has a 2,950-foot runway and serves light private and charter aircraft. The closest certified airport for carrier operations is Friedman Memorial Airport 40 miles northeast in Hailey.

Utilities and Services Private companies provide electricity, telephone, satellite and cable services. The City provides water and sewer services and fire protection. The County provides police protection and solid waste services.

Vision for 2050

Fairfield's population has remained somewhat flat at around 400 for over four decades. However, there are signs that this phenomena is beginning to change.

The popularity of downhill and backcountry skiing is bringing attention to further develop the amenities in the Soldier Mountains. For example, Smokey Dome – located just six miles west of Soldier Mountain Ski Resort – rises to 10,095 feet. Several other nearby peaks rise to over 9,000 feet.

As recognition and awareness of the area's unique year-round recreational opportunities grow, light manufacturing and service businesses will choose to expand in Fairfield.

Fairfield is a city in transition. Agriculture will continue to be an important element of the city's economy; however, existing businesses are growing and new businesses are coming. Necessary city services will grow to meet this growth as it develops.

185

Notus sunset.

CANYON COUNTY

- Caldwell (*County Seat*)
- Greenleaf
- Melba
- Middleton
- Nampa
- Notus
- Parma
- Wilder

Artist's sketch of Indian Creek project.

Caldwell

Statistical Data

Population: 50,224 *
Elevation: 2,385 feet
Precipitation: 10.9 inches **
Average Snowfall: 13.1 inches **
County: Canyon
Website: www.cityofcaldwell.com

Temperature Range – Fahrenheit: **
Spring: 37 to 65
Summer: 53 to 88
Fall: 36 to 65
Winter: 23 to 41
* U.S. Census Bureau Estimates July 2015
**Historical averages

Caldwell is one of Idaho's fastest growing cities. Located on the western edge of Idaho's Treasure Valley, it is about 30 miles west of the State Capitol.

The city is home to the College of Idaho, formerly Albertson College of Idaho, a private, residential liberal arts school. The 50-acre campus is located in the city and has an enrollment of about 800. National publications routinely rank the school as one of the top liberal arts colleges in the nation.

Fertile farms – producing alfalfa and corn seed, sugar beets, beans, onions, potatoes, wheat and hops – surround the city. These crops provide the basis for several food processing and fresh-pack businesses in the area.

The Boise River and Indian Creek run through Caldwell. The Snake River is less than 15 miles southwest.

Pre-Incorporation Years

Beginning in the early 1840s, Oregon Trail pioneers passed through the area as they followed the Boise River, crossed Canyon Hill and forded the Snake River on their way to Oregon's Willamette Valley. (*See Southwestern Idaho, The Region, Oregon and California Trails.*)

The discovery of placer gold in the Boise Basin on August 2, 1862, started another Idaho gold rush. Sixteen thousand prospectors and miners were scouring the basin searching for gold by 1863. Many of the fortune seekers were coming from the gold discoveries in Northern Idaho that were playing out and from Washington and Oregon. Those coming from the northwest passed through what is now Caldwell in a reverse direction from the Oregon Trail pioneers. During the same time, prospectors found gold 50 miles south of Caldwell in the Owyhee Mountains around Silver City. (*See Southwest Idaho, The Region, Mining, Boise Basin – Gold and Owyhee Mountains – Silver and Gold.*)

To support thousands of prospectors and miners, settlers set up along the Boise River raising beef, dairy and poultry; harvesting wild hay; and growing a variety of crops to sell to the miners. (*See Southwestern Idaho, The Region, Federal Land Use Laws – Reclaiming the West.*)

Two typical settlers, Fish and Rains, built a log cabin from the abundant stands of cottonwood trees and lava rock prevalent in the area and harvested a hay crop on the marshy south side of the Boise River near what is now Caldwell.

Gold mining processes in the Boise Basin moved from panning to sluice boxes then water cannon and, finally, in the 1950s dredging. However, the bloom of the gold rush had dissipated by the late 1860s. For the economy of Southwestern Idaho to continue to be robust, farmers and businesses would need railroad service, the kind that first came to the West with completion of the first transcontinental railroad in 1869 at Promontory Point in northern Utah.

Around 1881 area merchants and farmers looking for railroad service became excited when Robert E. Strahorn, an advance man representing railroad interests came into town ostensibly looking for a suitable place to site railroad facilities.

All eyes were on Strahorn when he appeared at the Boise City land office and bought the Haskell Ranch on the north side of the Boise River. Land speculators and farmers immediately began to bid up the price of land near the ranch.

Old Lincoln School, built in 1887, 524 Cleveland Blvd. Used from 1887 to 1943 when the new Lincoln Grade School was built.

However, while Strahorn distracted everybody with his land purchase, his confederate was buying tracts of land on the south side of the river near the future site of Caldwell. After they tied up the land, word got out that the railroad depot and future town site would be on the river's south side.

Before the Oregon Short Line Railroad reached the new townsite, Strahorn's employer, the Idaho & Oregon Land Improvement Co. (I&OLIC), platted the new town and began to sell lots.

The president of I&OLIC was Alexander Caldwell of Leavenworth, Kansas, a former U.S. senator and associated with Oregon Short Line officials in a number of other Idaho enterprises. Strahorn named the new town after Caldwell who visited the town but never lived there.

Strahorn then proceeded to encourage Middleton and Boise merchants to set up stores in his new railroad town that one early resident described as alkali and sagebrush "as far as the eye could see."

To facilitate the town's development, I&OLIC immediately established a lumberyard supplied with lumber from Boise

Trail depot and Pacific Hotel before 1906.

sawmills. Monte Gwinn, a Middleton merchant, set up Caldwell's first store, a general merchandise store, housed in a tent.

When the railroad reached Caldwell on September 6, 1883, it stopped to build a bridge across the Boise River Canyon before proceeding on to Huntington, Oregon. During the time the bridge was under construction, Caldwell was the railroad terminus and supply point for the region, described as a "town of tents."

Early residents on either side of the Boise River used a ferry to cross the river until entrepreneurs built a toll bridge that greatly facilitated the traffic that fueled Caldwell's growth. The town's first store owners built on a three-block stretch on the south side of Front Avenue facing the railroad tracks. They used a

Seventh Avenue.

"board and batten" construction technique where the exterior siding of the building was generally 1-by-12-inch boards set vertically with the joints covered by narrow boards or lath.

The first dwellings were located close to downtown. As the town grew, residences began spreading to upper Front Street which later became Main Street and across the railroad tracks along Kimball Street.

Strahorn and his wife and family were among the town's first residents. They cleared land on what are now Kimball and Fillmore Streets where they built a home and cultivated a small farm that was to serve as a model for other residents. They named their place "Sunnyside Ranch."

By January 1884 residents built the town's first school on Payette Avenue and a bandstand for the Caldwell Cornet Band. Church groups were also forming and holding services.

Incorporation

On January 15, 1890, less than six months before Idaho became the nation's 43rd state, Caldwell became an incorporated city.

Caldwell City Hall circa 1907. Designed by J.E. Toutillotte. Construction began 1907.

In a July 4, 1976, article "Caldwell Revisited," the local *News Tribune* reported on the incorporation of Caldwell: "The city was officially chartered by order of the Ada County commissioners on January 15, 1890. Its boundaries (six miles square) were set around the railroad. The first town officers appointed were Montie Gwinn, Chair; Frank Steunenberg, who seven years later would become

Canyon County Courthouse, circa 1892. Built by Lem Harding.

governor of Idaho (see Murder of Former Idaho Governor Frank Steunenberg, below); S.M. Coffin; A.F. Isham, and A.A. Hoover. They quickly appropriated monies for roads, crosswalks and culvert; purchased balls and chains in order to work prisoners; prohibited public amusements on Sundays; and passed a very controversial ordinance prohibiting cattle from running at large through the town. An early concern of the board was the condition of the railroad crossings. A letter was sent to the Oregon Short Line officials!"

Turning Points

Railroad Caldwell owes its origins to the railroad. The Oregon Short Line not only made Caldwell a station stop, but its agents platted the village and persuaded the town's first businesses and residents to locate there. (*See Southwestern Idaho, The Region, Railroads.*)

College of Idaho
The College of Idaho was founded in 1891 by the Presbyterian Church and their local leader, the Dr. Rev. William Judson Boone. Officials in the church's Wood River Presbytery were seeking to build a college in Idaho. Boone led a citizens

Saratoga Hotel, 7th and Main, circa 1904.

group that successfully persuaded church officials to build the school in Caldwell. He served as the school's president until his death in 1936. They held the first classes with 19 students in the Caldwell Presbyterian Church. The following year the school, placed in the hands of a self-perpetuating Board of Trustees, moved into a newly constructed building at a downtown location. Years later, the school received a donation of land at the site of its present campus and moved in 1910.

The school's strong reputation continues to provide recognition to the city. Its performing and fine arts programs add significantly to the city's culture and quality of life.

County Seat During the first Session of the Idaho Legislature following statehood on March 7, 1891, the legislature created Canyon County with Caldwell as the county seat. Shortly thereafter, the county built a brick and stone courthouse. Many businesses affected by county government opened offices in Caldwell. County employees and elected officials provided a stable, albeit small, employment base for the city.

Home of Gov. Frank Stuenenberg, at Sixteenth & Dearborn. Location of his assassination in 1905.

As the seat of county government, Caldwell was the dominant political and economic influence in the county for many years until the Idaho Central Railway Company completed its 20-mile branch line from Nampa to Boise in 1897 and

Nampa became the site of the Union Pacific terminal.

Murder of Former Governor Frank Steunenberg Idaho's most notorious murder occurred in Caldwell on the night of December 30, 1905, when former Idaho Governor Frank Steunenberg opened the picket gate to his Caldwell home and triggered a bomb that exploded in his face with enormous force. Caregivers carried the dying Steunenberg into his home. It had been just five years since he left the state's highest office.

Steunenberg was Idaho's fourth governor, serving from 1897 to 1900. At the beginning of his second two-year term in 1889, he found himself in the midst of a deadly conflict in Northern Idaho's Silver Valley between the Western Federation of Miners and the mine owners. The mine owners refused to accept the union demand of higher wages and exclusive bargaining rights for all mineworkers.

Outraged, union leaders organized over 1,000 miners to commandeer a Northern Pacific train parked at Burke, just north of Mullan; break into a mine powder house; and head down the valley to the Bunker Hill Mine complex with 3,000 pounds of explosives. There they assigned explosives experts to set charges at critical structure points. One of these experts, Harry Orchard, would later be convicted of the murder of Governor Steunenberg.

Following the destruction of the mill, union officials posted pickets around the mine. The pickets shot three mine employees who were coming to inspect the damage, killing one.

Indian Creek Flood. February 28, 1910. South Kimball & Arthur.

To quell the violence, Steunenberg declared marshal law and requested federal troops. Law enforcement personnel arrested a thousand miners and put them in a concentration camp to await trial.

According to testimony given at the murder trial, union leaders focused most of their distain and revenge on Steunenberg.

Following Steunenberg's death, the police apprehended Albert Horsley, who was using the name Harry Orchard. Orchard confessed to building and setting the bomb and conspiring with leaders of the Western Federation of Miners in the assassination.

The trial became nationally celebrated with the union hiring Clarence Darrow, the famous Chicago attorney, to lead the defense. W.E. Borah of Boise, later to become a U.S. senator, and James H. Hawley, later to become an Idaho governor, led the prosecution in a seemingly open and shut case.

The trial concluded with the court dismissing all charges against the union officials. Harry Orchard was found guilty and sentenced to life in prison. (See, Northern Idaho, The Region, Silver Valley Mines – Labor Union/Mine Owner Conflicts.)

Sterry Hall, College of Idaho, around 1893 to 1906.

Jack Simplot Caldwell is the birthplace of the frozen French fried potato and the first large commercial food processing facility in Idaho. It all started when city officials entered into a public-private partnership with Jack Simplot.

In the spring of 1940 the 31-year-old Jack Simplot, also called J.R., signed a contract on the back of an envelope to produce half a million pounds of onion powder and flakes for delivery to Berkley, California, that October. Prior to that time, Simplot had been shipping fresh onions to a California processor who chopped and dehydrated them and sold them to Simplot's new customer.

Simplot met the end user, saw a business opportunity to cut out the middleman and took it. He figured he could ship powder and flakes much cheaper than whole onions that are 89 percent water. "I had never made powder and I had never made flakes," he said. "I didn't know a dang thing about it. But I knew I could do it."

He discovered that his

Egg Day celebration circa 1926. J.H. Lowell, Wm Allison, H.R. Cleaver, Sec. of Commerce Herbert Hoover, Sen. Wm Borah.

former customer was drying onions using a commercial prune dryer. So Simplot ordered a prune dryer for a July delivery, went to work contracting with local farmers for large quantities of fresh onions and went looking for a suitable nearby location to build his dehydrating operation.

Caldwell city leaders learned of Simplot's enterprise and offered him five acres if he built the plant in their city. Simplot took their offer and became successful beyond his dreams.

A year later, several months before the Japanese attacked Pearl Harbor, U.S. Army Quartermasters Corps representatives called upon Simplot. They told him that he had one of a few vegetable drying operations in the nation and asked if he could dry large quantities of potatoes for the Army. When war broke out, Simplot became the leading supplier of dehydrated potatoes and onions to the military, a position that lasted through World War II and the Korean War.

In 1944 chemist Ray Dunlap, a Simplot employee working at the Caldwell plant, discovered the process of pre-frying raw potato strips to cook off the water and then freezing them. The potato strips, deep fried again for two minutes, had a golden brown crust with a chewy center. This patented process was the origin of the frozen French fried potato.

Simplot's subsequent sales contracts with McDonalds and other large retailers reinvigorated his business. He sold 5 million pounds the first year and 10 million pounds the next. The product is now a staple menu item in fast food restaurants throughout the world.

The city's decision to partner with Simplot not only produced hundreds of Caldwell jobs, but led to Simplot becoming one of the city's leading corporate citizens and benefactors.

Technological Innovation The Simplot story typifies the growth of agricultural-based businesses that underpinned the city's economy for more than half a century. Caldwell's influence as a regional agricultural center grew. By the 1960s subtle changes

Caldwell train depot, 2005.

were occurring that began reshaping the city's economic character. Within the last few decades, technological innovation and consolidation have eliminated hundreds of food processing and agricultural jobs and competition from businesses in the surrounding larger cities began attracting Caldwell workers and business. Caldwell residents started commuting to these other cities for work.

With the turn of the twenty-first century, however, conditions reversed. The city

194

is now experiencing a sharp increase in population and job growth.

Revitalizing the City Center In partnership with the Caldwell Urban Renewal Agency and several federal, state, county and regional agencies, the City has completed many of the principle components of its downtown revitalization plan.

Indian Creek project.

Caldwell Today

Amenities and Attractions Caldwell has two golf courses and seven parks with another park under construction. Park amenities include a public pool, tennis courts, playgrounds, soccer and softball fields and a rose garden.

The Oregon Trail Centennial Greenway offers jogging, bicycling, fishing and sightseeing opportunities.

The city's Caldwell Events Center that includes the fairgrounds, is the site of numerous events including the Caldwell Night Rodeo, the Simplot Stadium baseball games and the annual Canyon County Fair.

The College of Idaho adds an important cultural dimension to city life. Under its "Fine Arts Series," the school brings in performances of nationally recognized artists and theater companies. The series is open to the public and held at the school's Jewett Auditorium.

In May of each year the city celebrates the Cinco de Mayo Festival, a traditional Mexican celebration designed to enhance community relationships and celebrate Caldwell's different cultures. In addition each August, the community comes together for "Blues in the Park," a musical celebration with guest artists held at Memorial Park.

The Caldwell Historic Preservation Commission has created the Steunenberg Residential Historic District of 330 historic homes. Because of this effort, many Caldwell homes are on the National Register of Historic Places. The commission has also secured historic designations for two other districts – the Caldwell Historic District, the central business district that has some of the earliest brick buildings in the city, and the North Caldwell Historic District, which is the oldest residential district in Caldwell where many prominent citizens lived.

Visitors and residents may attend religious services at any of over 40 churches representing many Christian denominations.

Less than five miles south of the city is Lake Lowell and the Deer Flat National Wildlife Refuge. The lake is 10 miles long and one to two miles wide, covering a depression in the terrain once called Deer Flat. In 1909 the U.S. Reclamation Service, now the Bureau of Reclamation, built high earthen dykes around the depression making it into an irrigation reservoir fed by water from Lucky Peak Reservoir through the New York Canal. Irrigators deliver the water to their fields through a complex system of irrigation canals and ditches.

The lake's fishery includes large and small mouth bass. There are picnic facilities and boat ramps located around the lakeshore.

In 1909 the federal government designated the lake and 86 islands on 110 miles of the Snake River as the Deer Flat National Wildlife Refuge. Hundreds of thousands of migratory birds and 180 different bird species inhabit the refuge.

Fishing, boating and waterskiing are also available on other nearby lakes and reservoirs. Thirty miles northeast is the Payette River with whitewater rafting and kayaking.

Hunting, hiking and camping are within an hour's drive in the Boise National Forest to the northeast or the Owyhee Mountains to the south.

Economy and Major Employers Caldwell's business community is diverse. Several intermediate to small businesses comprise the city's employment base. The city's largest private employers include West Valley Medical Center, the College of Idaho, several food-processing and manufactured-housing plants, retailers and service businesses. Many residents commute to Nampa and cities in Ada County for employment.

Education Two public school districts provide most of the elementary and secondary education to Caldwell children. The Caldwell School District operates a high school, an alternative high school, two middle schools and six elementary schools in the city. Vallivue School District operates a high school, middle school, an intermediate school and four elementary schools.

The city's higher education students have many options. The College of Idaho, offers a 4-year liberal arts curriculum. Other nearby schools are Boise State University, the two-year College of Western Idaho and Northwest Nazarene University, both in Nampa and the Caldwell satellite campus of Treasure Valley Community College.

Health Care Caldwell's West Valley Medical Center is a 150-bed acute-care hospital with a Level III Trauma/Emergency Department. It is open 24 hours daily. Several clinics in the city and surrounding area serve the health care needs of the city's residents.

Transportation Interstate 84, U.S. Highways 20/26 and 95 and Idaho Highway 19 pass through or near the city. Union Pacific Railroad provides freight service at its terminal in Nampa.

Public transportation is available between Caldwell and Nampa. There is also a mid-day shuttle into Meridian, which connects with the Boise public transportation system.

Caldwell Industrial Airport, with its 5,500-foot runway, runs adjacent to the eastern edge of the city and Interstate 84. It is the designated reliever for the Boise Airport.

Utilities and Services Private companies provide electricity, telephone, natural gas, cable and satellite services. The City provides water, sewer and sanitation services as well as fire and police protection.

Vision for 2050

Over the past decade, Caldwell's population grew at over 6 percent annually. Those trends should moderate in the future. However, it is still likely that by 2050 Caldwell's population could exceed 100,000.

Within the next four decades, the city's and Caldwell Urban Renewal Agency's downtown revitalization efforts will be complete. Certain federal, state, county and regional agencies are already providing grants. The completed efforts will include restoration of Indian Creek to a beautiful free-flowing landscaped stream through town, restoration of the historic train depot, development of a public plaza and the addition of four blocks of landscaped parking to support the downtown and building a biking/walking trail system connecting the downtown with schools, parks and the new YMCA. The city's catalyst redevelopment project includes new housing, offices, restaurants, retail shops and a government center in the eight-block city center area along Indian Creek.

Surrounding the downtown core will be a growing commercial area with large retail stores and services. The residential areas will include a mix of multi-family and single-family dwellings.

There will be new development near the airport which is already in the midst of a $15 million expansion. When complete in 2012, the expansion will include a new executive terminal and extension of the runway to 7,700 feet.

By 2050 the Caldwell Airport will undergo further expansion. It will double in size with a new control tower, improved approach guidance system and a Boise State University operated maintenance training facility. New roads and utilities will have built up along the northeast side of the airport to provide airport access.

The airport will also be the focal point for a major commercial/industrial development. The majority of this development will be on approximately 400 acres to the west, east and north. This will include construction of a $110 million retail shopping complex, a new St. Luke's Regional Medical Center, an Idaho Department of Labor local office building and sports and physical fitness centers.

One or more of several initiatives to improve transportation in and near Caldwell will be completed and operating. These initiatives include expanded pedestrian and bicycling greenbelt paths and trails along the Boise River connecting Caldwell with other Treasure Valley communities. An improved bus system in Caldwell will link to other cities in the valley and the proposed rail system connecting Caldwell, Nampa and Boise will be a reality.

In 2050 the College of Idaho will also play a prominent role in advancing the economic and cultural interests of the city. Its professors and students will continue to bring national attention to the school and the city.

Mayors

1890	Montie Gwinn	1925	Dr. C.M. Kaley
1893	Howard Sebree	1927	S. Ben Dunlap
1894	M.B. Gwinn	1929	Fred McConnell
1895	Trobridge Egleston	1931	Fred Lilly
1896	M.B. Gwinn	1933	Emery Vassar
1897	George Alley	1937	W.R. Hottingsworth
1898	Charles Doan	1939	Edgar Oakes
1899	George Little	1941	Harry McCluskey
1900	A.F. Isham	1943	Thurlow Bryant
1901	Howard Sebree	1945	George Crookham, Jr.
1902	John Rice	1947	R.H. McNeill
1903	A.K. Steunenberg	1949	Leo Mason
1904	T.K. Little	1951	Jason Smith
1905	Ross Madden	1957	Ed Simmerman
1907	C.C. Smith	1962	Emery Vassar
1909	Justine Gowen	1964	N.E. Smith
1911	Walter Griffiths	1970	Charles Carpenter
1913	Charles Turner	1974	R.E. Pasley
1915	Fred Boyes	1980	A.H. McCluskey
1917	E.H. Plowhead	1986	Peter B. Cowles
1918	Fred Lilly	1990	James Dakan
1919	Grant Ward	1994	Dick Winder
1921	Amos Miller	1998	Garret Nancolas
1923	John Smeed		

Greenleaf Friends Church, corner of SH-19 & Friends Road, March 2012.

Greenleaf

Statistical Data

Population: 878 *

Elevation: 2,410 feet

Precipitation: 10 inches **

Average Snowfall: 13 inches **

County: Canyon

Website: www.greenleaf-idaho.us

Temperature Range – Fahrenheit: **

Spring: 35 to 73

Summer: 54 to 88

Fall: 32 to 79

Winter: 24 to 46

* U.S. Census Bureau Estimates July 2015

**Historical averages

Greenleaf is a quiet agricultural community in the western Treasure Valley about five miles west of Caldwell and five miles east of Wilder. Fields of onions, hops, seed corn, beans and alfalfa create the look of a tapestry around the city.

The Snake River flows about seven miles south and west of the city. The Boise River is four miles north.

Greenleaf is the only Idaho city founded by members of the Quaker faith. The city is home to a private, regionally-attended school, Greenleaf Friends Academy, which is associated with the faith.

Pre-Incorporation Years

Beginning in the early 1840s immigrants seeking to settle in Oregon's Willamette Valley began passing a few miles north of what is now Greenleaf on the Oregon Trail. (*See The Region, Oregon and California Trails.*)

In the decades that followed, the Treasure Valley experienced significant

199

development. In 1862 prospectors discovered gold in the Boise Basin and, a year later, in the Owyhee Mountains. These discoveries brought 16,000 fortune seekers into the Boise Basin – 2,500 later rushed to the Owyhee Mountains. The mining activity attracted farmers to the area to raise and sell fresh food to the miners. However, because these settlers established their homestead claims where they could divert irrigation water from streams onto their farmland, the sagebrush-covered high desert of southwestern Canyon County, including what is now Greenleaf, did not develop. (*See The Region, Mining, Boise Basin – Gold; and Owyhee Mountains – Silver and Gold*.)

The Oregon Short Line (OSL) began construction of a rail line between Granger, Wyoming, and Huntington, Oregon, in 1881. The line – completed on November 17, 1884 – angled in a northwesterly direction through what are now Pocatello, Mountain Home, Caldwell and Weiser before crossing the Snake River one last time to Huntington.

Church service at William Brown home, Greenleaf, 1905.

In September 1883 the railroad reached Caldwell, where workers stopped to build a bridge across the Boise River Canyon. While the bridge was under construction, Caldwell was a railroad terminus and supply point for the region. However, this growth still did not extend to the rest of southwestern Canyon County. (*See The Region, Railroads*.)

Congress established the U.S. Reclamation Service – now Bureau of Reclamation – in 1902. Reclamation almost immediately embarked on what would become the "Boise Project." Among other things, the Project provided federal funding and support to irrigators. When the project was completed decades later, Reclamation had successfully integrated or completed needed Treasure Valley

Greenleaf Friends Church and parsonage and Greenleaf Friends Academy, corner of Main Street & Academy Road, Circa 1918.

irrigation systems and added a system of dams and water storage reservoirs in the higher elevations of the Boise River, its principal tributaries and the Payette River. (*See The Region, Agriculture and Irrigation, Bureau of Reclamation – Boise Project – Treasure Valley*.)

Residents in southwestern Canyon County, led by J.H. Lowell, successfully petitioned the Reclamation Service to construct a reservoir and irrigation water system.

It was at this time that the first settlers began making their homestead claims in the Greenleaf area. Many planted orchards on their farms, irrigating the trees by hauling water from nearby rivers in horse-drawn water-tank wagons. (*See The Region, Federal Lands – Private Ownership and Preservation Laws.*)

In 1906 attracted by the high-quality soil and the potential for irrigation water, several members of the Quaker faith acquired land in and around what is now Greenleaf. They named their community after Quaker poet and abolitionist John Greenleaf Whittier and started the Greenleaf Friends Church. Two years later, they established the Greenleaf Friends Academy. The Quaker faith has since been associated with the city of Greenleaf.

In her 1984 book *From Sagebrush to Green Fields*, Dilla Tucker Winslow said of these Quaker settlers, "The founders of Greenleaf, Idaho, set about to build a

Fred L. Evans in his official Rural Delivery wagon, delivering mail on Route 1 in the Wilder-Greenleaf area. Photo courtesy of Edith Evans.

monument to their faith under the guidance of God. This monument was not to be carved from wood or chiseled from stone, or molded with cement, but was to be cast from their Quaker beliefs garnished from the Scripture into living flesh and blood and eternal souls, who would join them as sage brush acres blossomed into fertile fields. God honored and directed the plans of these courageous hard-working men and women of integrity."

It was during this time that Reclamation began construction of a reservoir at a natural depression in the earth's surface south of Caldwell called Deer Flat. They designed the reservoir to receive water diverted from the Boise River at Barber Dam, about 25 miles due east, and delivered through the New York Canal.

Greenleaf Store at original location near Peckham.

Reclamation named the 10-mile-long and up to two-mile – wide reservoir Lake Lowell. The reservoir has an earthen dam and a surrounding excavated dyke system that ranges from 46 to 74 feet high.

Reclamation also provided the expertise and financial aid – low-cost, long-term loans to farmers – needed to develop the irrigation canal systems.

The farmers organized the Water Users Association as the legal entity to work with Reclamation in providing labor to build the canal system and repay the loans.

By 1909 irrigation water began to fill Lake Lowell and, a year later, was released into canals, bringing water to Greenleaf. By then many settlers had cleared and leveled their land and were awaiting the water. Within a few years, southwestern Canyon County farmers transformed the newly irrigated high desert into an agricultural oasis.

Railroad interests built an 11-mile branch line through Greenleaf to Wilder in 1911. Businesses that used the railroad for passenger and freight transportation began to create a commercial center near the Greenleaf railroad siding.

Following World War I, motor vehicles became the desired mode of transportation. In 1929 the Idaho Transportation Department built Highway 19

Hull Homestead, 1924. Early settlers of Greenelaf: Calvin, Kenneth, and Hubert Hull with sagebrush collected to use for fuel.

through Greenleaf. With this change, the business district began moving from the railroad to the highway corridor. However, the residents placed a low priority on becoming an incorporated municipality because of "the fierce spirit of independence and close-knit culture of the community."

Incorporation

On June 8, 1973, Greenleaf became an incorporated city.

Turning Points

Railroad The Greenleaf and Wilder railroad spur connecting to the main line in Caldwell was a major boon to the town's residents and farmers, enhancing the community's identity. The railroad not only underpinned the success

This building was once Greenleaf's railroad station.

of farmers by providing rapid transportation for shipping their commodities to market, it facilitated development of small businesses including a lumberyard, a creamery and an ice cream factory.

The railroad also provided access to the electric trolley, the Boise Valley Loop, which connected cities throughout the Treasure Valley from 1907 to 1928.

Irrigation The fertile soil and prospects for irrigation water attracted the first settlers to Greenleaf. The reality of irrigation fulfilled their dreams and created a sustainable economy for the new community. In the 1980s the community formed a municipal irrigation system under city government.

City Government For over two decades following incorporation, City officials held business meetings in a cafe, maintained official records in a walk-in storage closet and City personnel were only available for limited hours.

As the community grew, it became increasingly clear that the city needed better facilities and improved service. During the 1990s, the community built a City Hall, hired a full-time City Clerk and paved all the city streets.

Discharge pipes: Lower left pipe is groundwater. Upper right pipeis wastewater treatment plant discharge into the West End Drain. Pictured: Mayor Brad Holton, Public Services Dir. Doug C. Amick, and Wastewater Treatment Plant Operator Jason Wereley.

Water and Sewer Infrastructure
Southwest District Health issued a Notice of Violation on February 21, 2001, declaring the Greenleaf sewer system, operated by the Greenleaf Water and Sewer Association, as failing and in need of interim corrective measures and ultimately replacement.

Voters approved the City acquiring the association's assets in 2001 and authorized a $1.6 million water and sewer improvement bond. The water system was soon completed but the new sewer facilities were not.

Under agreement with the Idaho Department of Environmental Quality, the City dug a 650-foot municipal drinking water well and added significant water delivery infrastructure. The new municipal wastewater system became operational in 2012.

Greenleaf Riding Club, 1923.

Greenleaf Today

Amenities and Attractions The city's only park is a small pocket park at the corner of Whittier Drive and Redwood. However, the Greenleaf Friends Academy allows public use of its football field, track and children's playground equipment area.

The Greenleaf Historical Society maintains a museum in the old Greenleaf High School building near the cemetery.

The Greenleaf Friends Academy sponsors public activities and fundraisers including the Home and Garden Fair each spring and the Greenleaf Friends Academy Benefit Auction in the fall. Each Independence Day, the academy hosts a pancake breakfast followed by a community parade and a patriotic program sponsored by Greenleaf Friends Church.

About 10 miles southeast is Lake Lowell and the Deer Flat National Wildlife Refuge. Lake Lowell is an excellent large and small mouth bass fishery. Picnic facilities and boat ramps are located around the lake. The Refuge includes the lake, 110 miles of the Snake River and 86 islands on the river. Hundreds of thousands of migratory birds and 180 different bird species inhabit the Refuge.

The 1,300-acre Old Fort Boise Wildlife Management Area at the confluence of the Snake, Boise and Owyhee Rivers is 15 miles northwest. The Roswell Marsh Wildlife Habitat Area is 10 miles northwest. Both are under the administration of the Idaho Department of Fish and Game. Many parts of the Management Areas are open for viewing wildlife, hunting and fishing.

Hunting, hiking and camping are available within an hour's drive of the city on nearby public lands in the Boise National Forest to the northeast or the Owyhee Mountains to the south. Whitewater rafting and kayaking are available on the Payette River north of Greenleaf.

The College of Idaho in Caldwell – known for several years as Albertson College of Idaho after grocery store chain magnate and school benefactor Joe Albertson, whose parents homesteaded about two and a half miles southeast of Greenleaf – adds an important cultural dimension to the city. Under its "Fine Arts Series," the college brings in performances of nationally recognized artists and theater companies. The series is open to the public and held at the school's Jewett Auditorium.

Many residents believe one of the city's most attractive amenities is its location – a small rural town close to the urban amenities of larger cities.

Economy and Major Employers The Greenleaf Friends Academy has over 40 employees and is the city's largest employer. Several small businesses and retailers provide most of the other jobs in the city. Many residents commute to nearby larger cities for employment.

The Greenleaf Air Ranch is a private residential airpark. Each lot has direct access to a 2,500-foot runway. The park is the recipient of a $500,000 Idaho Department of Commerce Community Development Block Grant for development of a commercial zone to support business relocation and job creation. To make this happen, in 2010 the city rezoned 22 of the park's 78 residential lots to commercial.

Education The Greenleaf Friends Academy provides private education to pre-kindergarten to 12th grade students. The school attracts students from throughout the Treasure Valley and the Northwest.

The Vallivue School District provides public education. Younger children attend West Canyon Elementary three miles south of Greenleaf. The district buses older children to the middle and high schools and an alternative high school south of Caldwell. There is also a charter school in the district.

There are several institutions of higher learning within an hour's drive of the city. The largest is Boise State University 40 miles west in Boise.

Health Care The closest hospital is West Valley Medical Center six miles away in Caldwell.

Transportation Idaho Highway 19 intersects the city. U.S. Highway 95 is four miles west. Interstate 84 is seven miles east in Caldwell.

Caldwell Industrial Airport, with its 5,500-foot runway, runs adjacent to the eastern edge of the city and Interstate 84. It is the designated reliever for the Boise Airport.

Utilities and Services Private companies provide electricity, telephone, natural gas, cable and satellite services. The City provides domestic and irrigation water and road maintenance services. The City constructed a sewer system which went into service in 2012. The City of Wilder provides police protection under contract with Greenleaf. The Caldwell Rural Fire Protection District provides fire protection.

Removal of unhealthy and damaged 100-year-old trees from the Greenleaf Friends Church.

The City contracts with a private company for solid waste services.

Vision for 2050

At the time of the city's first census in 1980, the town had a population of 663. By the late 1990s the population grew to nearly 900. Since 2000 the city's population has stabilized.

The principal factors affecting the city's population growth are the Greenleaf Friends Church, the Greenleaf Friends Academy and new residents seeking Greenleaf's affordable housing and quality of life while commuting to nearby cities for work.

If historical trends continue, by 2050 the city could have a population of around

1,000. However, regional trends indicate that the city could experience greater growth. With close proximity to transportation infrastructure and the population centers of the Treasure Valley, Greenleaf is an attractive location for future development.

Historically, the principal growth-limiting factor is the lack of an adequate municipal wastewater treatment infrastructure. In 2012 this was corrected when the City completed construction of a wastewater treatment facility including a sewer main that extends throughout Greenleaf.

Prior to 2009 private developers purchased approximately 1,500 acres in the city's area of impact. As the general economy improves, these developers will likely seek annexation into the city and proceed with their developments.

City officials have changed land use and development ordinances to simplify processes and facilitate development and coordination with the city.

In 2008 the Canyon County Commission worked cooperatively with Greenleaf and the neighboring cities of Wilder, Notus, Parma and Homedale in establishing each city's area of impact. Greenleaf's area of impact borders that of Notus to the north and Wilder to the west.

Ruben Flores, City of Greenleaf Public Services, with a carp pulled out of the city irrigation system. The city gets its irrigation water from the Wilder Irrigation System that distributes water from Lake Lowell, a man-made irrigation reservoir located about 8 miles from Greenleaf.

As the city prepares for future growth, the challenge becomes one of encouraging the rural small-town atmosphere while enhancing an already attractive quality of life and increasing public service levels.

Mayors

1973	Lloyd Puntenney	1991	Vernon Snyder
1974	Derrol Hockett	1994	Vance Taylor
1976	Dean Douty	1998	Don Cassity
1981	Myrtle Burton	2002	Victoria Kerns
1982	Bradley Holton	2004	Bradley Holton
1990	Richard Marcotte		

Aerial view of Melba for the community's 100 year celebration, August 2012.

Melba

Statistical Data

Population: 529 *
Elevation: 2,680 feet
Precipitation: 11 inches **
Average Snowfall: 14 inches **
County: Canyon
Website: www.cityofmelba.org

Temperature Range – Fahrenheit: **
Spring: 32 to 73
Summer: 50 to 89
Fall: 29 to 78
Winter: 22 to 46
* U.S. Census Bureau Estimates July 2015
**Historical averages

Melba is a small farming community located in the southernmost part of Canyon County. The Snake River flows about five miles to the south and west. Fertile farmland forms a buffer between Melba and Nampa – Idaho's second largest city that is 12 miles north. Melba area farmers are noted for their production of onion, carrot, pea, bean, sweet corn, alfalfa and clover seed.

Across the Snake River lies the historic South Alternate Route of the Oregon Trail and vast tracts of public lands managed by the BLM, including the Owyhee Mountains. The 590,000-acre Snake River Birds of Prey National Conservation Area (SRNCA), also managed by the BLM, begins about two miles east of town.

Pre-Incorporation Years

For centuries, the sagebrush-covered high desert of what is now Melba was the exclusive domain of nomadic American Indians, principally of the Shoshone and Bannock Tribes. Around 1810 the first explorers/trappers began passing through the area.

For the half century following the discovery of gold in the Boise Basin in 1862 and in the Owyhee Mountains in 1863, several events occurred that played important roles in the founding of Melba.

By 1863 the number of fortune seekers and miners searching for gold in the Boise Basin had risen to 16,000. In the same year, the U.S. Army established a new Fort Boise. Settlers around the fort established Boise City.

Mining activity encouraged settlers to divert irrigation water from nearby streams onto their homesteads to raise and sell fresh food to the miners.

Bird's eye view of Melba, circa 1920s.

Some of these settlers established farms south of what is now Melba near the Snake River.

In May 1863 Michael Jordon – the namesake of Jordon Valley, Oregon – led 29 men from the Boise Basin gold fields to the Owyhee Mountains. They found large quantities of gold at Jordon Creek and started a boomtown named Ruby City.

The Owyhee Mountains are named after three members of Donald Mackenzie's 1814 beaver-trapping party who were natives of the Hawaiian Islands. The name Hawaii was originally misspelled "Owyhee" in 1778 by Pacific Ocean explorer Captain James Cook. Mackenzie sent the three Hawaiians to assess the beaver-trapping potential of the mountain streams. They never returned. Mackenzie named the mountains in their honor.

In December 1863 the first Idaho Territorial Legislature, meeting in the temporary capital of Lewiston, created Owyhee County with the mining boomtown of Ruby City as the county seat. However, by 1867 with the Ruby City mines played out, prospectors

Todd Mercantile, circa 1920s.

found rich ore bodies of silver to the south. They named the new boomtown Silver City and voted to move the county seat and the buildings of Ruby City to Silver City.

In 1934 voters moved the county seat to the former railroad terminus town of Murphy. Today, Murphy is an unincorporated hamlet with a population of around 50. Murphy is still the Owyhee County seat, the smallest county seat in Idaho.

The Territorial Legislature granted mining entrepreneurs a 15-year franchise to build a toll road between Fort Boise and the Owyhee Mountain mines, which was later called the Silver Trail.

In 1863 entrepreneurs built a ferry across the Snake River about five miles southwest of what is now Melba. In 1886 following several changes in ownership, L.R. Walter became the sole owner of the newly named Walters Ferry.

In April 1867 the U.S. Geological Survey established "Initial Point," as the point of beginning of all land surveys in Idaho. It is located on a prominent 3,240-foot-high lava butte that protrudes out of the desert floor about eight miles west of

Clayton C. and Bessie Todd, founders of Melba, circa 1930s.

Melba. The Boise Survey Meridian runs north and south through the length of the state. The Idaho Base Line runs east and west through Initial Point. The city of Meridian derived its name from the meridian survey line that passes through the city. Base Line Road is a prominent road in Melba.

In 1881 the Oregon Short Line (OSL) began construction of the railroad line between Granger, Wyoming, and Huntington, Oregon. The rail line, completed on November 17, 1884, angled in a northwesterly direction through what are now Pocatello, Mountain Home, Caldwell and Weiser then crossed the Snake River one last time before reaching Huntington.

In 1883 the railroad intersected the Silver Trail. There, OSL officials converted a railroad caboose into a depot they named Kuna.

In 1898 in order to provide service to the Silver City mines, a new railroad company – the Boise, Nampa and Owyhee Railroad – completed a rail line from Nampa through Melba to a new terminal at Murphy. The railroad's signature accomplishment was a

Conyer's Store, the very first store in Melba - built 1913. Later McClain built the hardware store of brick in the front.

500-foot, two-span bridge across the Snake River south of Melba.

In the late 1800s several different Boise entrepreneurs attempted to build irrigation diversion dams on the Boise River with canals designed to deliver gravity flow water to thousands of acres downstream. Most of these ventures were undercapitalized and had limited success.

In 1902 Congress established the U.S. Reclamation Service – now Bureau of Reclamation. The Bureau of Reclamation almost immediately embarked on what would become the "Boise Project." The project provided federal funding and support that, when completed decades later, largely integrated or completed existing Treasure Valley irrigation systems and added a system of dams and water storage reservoirs in the higher elevations of the Boise River, its principal tributaries and the Payette River.

Around 1910 Boise Project construction workers building irrigation canals in south Canyon and Ada Counties established their headquarters in what is now Melba at a location named "Rock Spur."

By 1912 the decline in Silver City mining activity caused the railroad to close its Murphy terminal. However, with the freight demand coming from the development of hundreds

Melba's first polio auction, February 1950.

of new farms receiving irrigation water from the Boise Project, the railroad company built a new terminal 12 miles north at Rock Spur.

In 1912 Clayton C. Todd, a gold prospector on his way to Alaska, was staying with friends in Weiser. When informed of these events, he purchased 160 acres bordering the railroad siding, including the abandoned Rock Spur headquarters structures. There he platted a new town that he named Melba after his four-year-old daughter who was still in California with her mother.

Todd built the first store and applied to postal authorities for a post office to be operated out of his store. Within a short time, other commercial and residential buildings began to move onto their new city lots.

Incorporation

On August 30, 1935, Melba became an incorporated village.

Turning Points

Mines The 1863 discovery of gold then silver in the Owyhee Mountains initiated construction of a wagon road to Boise and a railroad line to Murphy. Both

210

roads passed near or through what is now Melba. These roads became catalysts leading to the founding of Melba.

Irrigation The availability of irrigation water made possible by the Bureau of Reclamation's Boise Project was the underlying basis for the development of Melba area farms and the city's economy.

Railroad In addition to providing the location for Clayton Todd to plat the town of Melba, the railroad provided critical transportation needed for the emerging agricultural community to grow and prosper.

Melba Today

Amenities and Attractions Melba City Park is a 16-acre facility featuring softball diamonds, children's playground equipment, a picnic area and restrooms.

The city celebrates Independence Day each July with a variety of events including a parade, arts and crafts fair, food concessions, antique tractor pull and fireworks.

Celebration Park, Idaho's only archaeological park, is managed by the BLM and located five miles due south of Melba off Idaho Highway 45 on the banks of the Snake River. The park is noted for its thousands of ancient American Indian petroglyphs, melon gravel dating back to Lake Bonneville times (see Eastern Idaho, Major

Tower Theater, Built in 1946-47 by Smith & Lindholm. Now the Walter's Butte Grange Hall.

Geologic Features – Prehistoric Lake Bonneville) and high-desert landscape and wildlife. Activities include hiking, fishing, boating, picnicking, camping, bird watching (birds of prey), BLM trails, tours and interpretive programs.

The Snake River Birds of Prey National Conservation Area includes federal, private and state land and 10,000 acres of surface water. Numerous species of small wildlife including rodents and rabbits inhabit the land covered with an abundance of desert brush and grasses growing from the deep silt-loam volcanic soils. These food sources along with the variety of fish in the Snake River and nearby reservoirs attract large numbers of falcons, eagles, hawks and owls as well as water fowl.

The SRNCA has the densest population of breeding raptors in North America. Many raptors nest along rock outcroppings and ledges along Snake River Canyon cliffs, rising to over 300 feet above the river below. SRNCA officials have identified up to 25 species of nesting, migrating or wintering birds of prey. In total, about 260 wildlife species inhabit the area, including one of the nation's largest concentrations of badgers.

Visitors, bird watchers and outdoor enthusiasts can easily access the SRNCA using the Western Heritage Historic Byway located six miles east of Melba and extending south of Kuna past Swan Falls Dam. The byway passes through diverse topography and ten points of historical interest, including old mining settlements and archaeological sites.

The World Center for Birds of Prey, famous for its conservation and recovery efforts of the Peregrine falcon and several species of rare and endangered birds of prey, is located in south Boise, about 34 miles northeast of Melba.

Kuna Cave, an underground lava tube often explored by Boy Scout troops and other amateur spelunkers, is located 14 miles northeast of Melba.

Deer Flat National Wildlife Refuge is located 10 miles north. The refuge encompasses 10,600 acres, including the 9,000-acre Lake Lowell and about 100 islands in the Snake River. The refuge provides habitat for wildlife including thousands of migratory and nesting ducks and geese.

The 107-foot-high hydroelectric Swan Falls Dam is located 18 miles southeast of Melba. It is the oldest hydroelectric dam on the Snake River and has 1,525 acres of reservoir surface area. The dam, built in 1901, initially provided electricity for the restored historic mining town of Silver City. The restored Silver City is about 41 miles south.

The historic Givens Hot Springs is a popular recreation facility about 15 miles northwest of Melba. Oregon Trail immigrants said the water was hot enough to boil an egg. They stopped to bath, wash their clothes and luxuriate in a pond they built. In 1881 Oregon Trail immigrants Milford and Martha Givens returned to settle and develop a resort. Their descendants now own and operate the property. Thousands of patrons come each year to enjoy the modern hot swimming pools and other resort amenities.

Cleo's Nature Trail at Historic Walters Ferry is open to the public year-round. The trail is a wonderland of displays, hundreds of birdhouses of intricate design and over 100 sculptures and statues that line a mile-long walking path, meandering in a loop through old growth Russian olive and other trees bordering the river. There is also a private museum which includes the historic adobe ferry master's building. The ferry master's building, built in 1863, is the oldest building on the property. It served as the ferry master's residence, a restaurant and a two-room hotel.

Economy and Major Employers With over 100 employees, Melba School District is the city's largest employer. Several small businesses and retail stores provide most other employment available in the city. Many residents commute to Nampa and other nearby cities for employment.

Education Melba School District operates elementary, middle and high schools in the city.

There are several institutions of higher learning within less than an hour's drive of the city. The largest of these schools is Boise State University, located about 34 miles northeast.

Health Care The closest hospital is Mercy Medical Center about 12 miles north in Nampa.

Transportation Idaho Highway 45 lies two miles west of town. Interstate 84 is accessed 16 miles north.

Utilities and Services Private companies provide electricity, gas, cable, satellite and wireless services. The City provides water and sewer services and police and fire protection.

Vision for 2050

In 1969 Melba had a population of 197. Since that time, the population has gown at about three percent annually. Most of this growth has been motivated by young families choosing to live in the more quiet and peaceful setting of Melba, where there is affordable housing, and to commute to work in nearby larger cities.

General economic changes will likely cause a reduction in current rates of growth from one to two percent annually. At these more moderate rates of growth, by 2050 Melba's population will still likely exceed 1,000.

City and community leaders will work together to see that growth pays for growth and to identify and deliver the municipal, recreational and cultural facilities and attractions needed to maintain Melba's peaceful lifestyle and enhance its quality of life.

Mayors

1966	Joe Amos, Jr.	2002	Sue Bock
1968	Elza Kellog	2003	Martin Luttrell
1977	Ron Wright	2012	Doug Sturges
1978	Charlotte Nelson	2013	Martin Luttrell
1986	Hal Forsgren		

City of Middleton.

Middleton

Statistical Data

Population: 6,420 *
Elevation: 2,398 feet
Precipitation: 12 inches **
Average Snowfall: 22 inches **
County: Canyon
Website: www.middletonidaho.us

Temperature Range – Fahrenheit: **
Spring: 33 to 75
Summer: 53 to 93
Fall: 28 to 81
Winter: 21 to 46
* U.S. Census Bureau Estimates July 2015
**Historical averages

Middleton is located in the north central part of the Treasure Valley. Fields of potatoes, sugar beets, grains, corn, mint, hops, beans and sod, trees and shrubs sold to retail nurseries surround the city, forming a checkerboard of color and texture.

The Boise River forms the southern boundary of the city. The mountain ranges that border the valley are in full view. The clouds that often drift over the mountains make for spectacular sunrises and sunsets.

The economic growth experienced in the Treasure Valley has spilled over to Middleton, making it one of Idaho's fastest growing cities. It is now Idaho's 30th largest city.

Pre-Incorporation Years

Several frontiersmen began traveling and trapping beaver on the Snake River and its tributaries in 1811. At that time, the nomadic Shoshone and Bannock Indian Tribes traversed the area. The prehistoric Boise River flood plain had an abundance of wild game. Salmon and steelhead trout filled the Boise River each year during their annual spawning migrations. (*See The Region, American Indians.*)

The British Hudson's Bay Company built a trading post in 1834 on the river floodplain at the confluence of the Snake and Boise Rivers about 17 miles northwest at what is now Parma. A French Canadian, Francois Payette, became the manager of the post. He named the river Boise and the trading post Fort Boise, the French term for wooded, because of the forests of cottonwood and willow trees bordering the river. (*See The Region, Early Trappers/Explorers.*)

Foote Flour Mill in Caldwell.

In 1841 the first wagon train of immigrants and explorers en route to Oregon traveled along the Boise River on what would become the southern border of Middleton.

Flour sack from Middleton Mill.

Two years later, Captain John C. Fremont, a topographical engineer, led a surveying expedition to the West and stopped at Fort Boise. He referenced the fort as a rest stop and landmark on his maps, which Congress would later publish. Oregon Trail immigrants used Fremont's maps extensively, finding rest at the fort until massive floods destroyed part of the fort, and it was abandoned in 1854. (*See The Region, Oregon and California Trails.*)

Prospectors discovered gold near Idaho City in 1862. In the following year, 16,000 prospectors and fortune seekers flooded into the mountains of the Boise Basin. Many of these prospectors and miners came from the Northwest, passing near Middleton in a reverse direction from the earlier Oregon Trail pioneers. (*See The Region, Mining – Boise Basin – Gold.*)

U.S. Army Major Pickney Lugenbeel led a detachment of troops in 1863 to construct a military fort to protect the miners and settlers from hostile Indians. On July 4, Lugenbeel selected a location on a sagebrush-covered foothill, several blocks north of the present-day State Capitol Building, and named it Fort Boise, the same name as the destroyed Oregon Trail landmark 40 miles west. Three days later, merchants and settlers living near the fort platted a new town they named Boise City.

The following year, the Territorial Legislature designated Boise as Idaho's permanent Territorial Capital. (*See The Region, Idaho Territory, Territorial Capitals – Lewiston and Boise.*)

Demise of the Boise River bridge.

The gold rush prompted an immediate demand for food and supplies. Initially, freighters hauled supplies for hundreds of miles on pack trains and wagons. In 1862 Congress passed the Homestead Act allowing citizens to convert 160 acres of public land to private ownership if they improved and lived on their claims for five years. Many homesteaders came into the Treasure Valley. They staked their claims on the fertile irrigable land in the river floodplain and tributaries and raised beef, dairy cattle and poultry; harvested wild hay; and planted a variety of agricultural crops for sale to the miners. (*See The Region, Federal Lands – Private Ownership and Preservation Laws.*)

The town dump in 1948. It was developed into the beautiful Middleton City Park.

One of the first homesteaders, William Montgomery, filed a plat for a new city he named Middleton on July 23, 1863. He named the town Middleton because it was midway between the old Fort Boise and new Fort Boise.

In surveying the townsite, Montgomery divided the town into eight city blocks, designating one lot as the town square. The lots were 136 feet square, and the streets 100 feet wide. He named the two principal streets Montgomery and Payette.

Homesteaders built small private diversions of water from the Boise River and its tributaries to irrigate their farms and ranches.

A local entrepreneur built the Middleton Flour Mill in 1871. Settlers throughout the region brought their wheat to the mill for sale or to exchange for flour.

The next year a heavy snowpack caused the Boise River to flood. Afterwards, residents literally moved the town about a quarter of a mile north to higher ground.

George Liggett, owner of the hotel and livery stable, gave a grand ball on

October 26, 1880, as a farewell to the old Middleton townsite.

In 1907 the Boise and Interurban Railway completed construction of an electric trolley connecting Eagle, Star, Middleton and Caldwell. At about the same time, the Boise Valley Railway built a line connecting Boise, Meridian and Nampa.

Five years later, investors acquired the two companies and completed the rail link

Middleton City Park, 1955.

between Caldwell and Nampa creating a passenger and freight service called the "Boise Valley Loop." The railroad built an electrical substation in Middleton called the Middleton Trolley Station to convert alternating current to direct current used to electrify the railcars. The City now owns the Trolley Station and rents it for non-City sponsored events.

Incorporation

On April 10, 1910, Middleton became an incorporated village. In 1967 it changed its legal status to that of a city as required by a change in state municipal law.

Turning Points

Gold The discovery of placer gold in the Boise Basin and the Owyhee Mountains was crucial to the founding of Middleton. It provided the impetus for homesteading in the Boise floodplain and William Montgomery's decision to plat the new town between the old and new Fort Boise.

Old Grange Hall. With the Interurban substation; Idaho Power substation to left. An entrance was built on the north side of the Interurban substation after the Grange bought the building. Courtesy Idaho State Historical Library.

Irrigation Irrigation was critical to the economic development of Middleton. It started with small private diversions of water from the Boise River and its tributaries. However, it would require federal programs and funding to build dams, reservoirs and canal systems to bring irrigation water to the sagebrush-covered high desert west of Boise. (*See The Region, Agriculture and Irrigation, Bureau of Reclamation – Boise Project – Treasure Valley.*)

Federal support began in 1902 when Congress passed the Reclamation Act creating the U.S. Reclamation Services – now Bureau of Reclamation – authorizing federal construction and management of the dams and irrigation systems needed to reclaim the arid West.

Interurban bridge above Caldwell. The pilings can still be seen in the river.

One of the Bureau of Reclamation's first endeavors which benefited Middleton farmers was the Boise Project, which eventually included an integrated system of hydroelectric dams on the Boise, Payette and Owyhee Rivers with thousands of miles of canals and ditches. The largest dams on the Boise River were Arrow Rock (1915), Anderson Ranch (1950) and Lucky Peak (1955). These dams provided storage capacity for release throughout the growing season.

Barber Dam, built a few miles east of Boise in 1908, diverted water into the New York Canal. This canal provided water for lower-elevation canals and emptied into the Lake Lowell Reservoir, completed by the Bureau of Reclamation in 1909. Lake Lowell was built around a natural depression in the earth's surface near Nampa called Deer Flat.

Idaho Power substation on East Main Street, circa 1917. Courtesy Idaho State Historical Library.

In addition to building the dams and integrating the canal systems, the Bureau of Reclamation provided expertise and financial aid under a low-cost, long-term loan program. Within a few years, it developed a complex system of canals and lateral ditches throughout the valley, and farmers transformed the dry high-desert landscape into an agricultural oasis.

Electric Trolley Construction of the Boise Valley Loop with an electrical substation in Middleton elevated the prestige of the town and provided jobs. Conversely, in the 1920s when ridership declined and the electric trolley finally closed in 1928, it had an adverse effect on Middleton's economy.

Middleton Today

Amenities and Attractions The City of Middleton has four parks. The largest, Middleton Place Park, is located on 12 acres. The park features a shelter, picnic facilities, two tennis courts, two basketball courts, a volleyball court, a baseball diamond, playground equipment and restrooms.

Roadside Park is in the heart of town along Idaho Highway 44. This park has three acres and features a creek, swings, picnic facilities, four horseshoe pits, restrooms and a walking bridge that leads to the City-owned and rentable Civic Center and Trolley Station.

Davis Park is a quarter-acre park next to the creek. It has picnic facilities and a shelter.

The Grove is a quarter-acre nature park bordering the city's west pathway greenbelt.

The Greater Middleton Park and Recreation District owns and maintains three additional parks in the city. Hawthorne Park has seven acres with four baseball diamonds, play equipment and restrooms. The Richard B. Foote Memorial Park is a 23-acre parcel of which five acres are developed with soccer fields and a sand volleyball court. The remaining 18 acres are undeveloped. Ed Payne Park sits on a three-acre site. It has a softball diamond that is also used by younger baseball players.

The Middleton Library is a focal point for learning. The library can

Middleton City Hall.

access books from other libraries and offers children's programs, a book club and personal computers with Internet access.

Each spring, Middleton Heights Elementary holds its annual Spring Carnival. This community event consists of carnival games, food, raffle items and auction baskets put together by each classroom. Local businesses contribute to the event, and the proceeds go to school projects and grants for classroom teachers.

In March each year, the Middleton Booster Club holds its annual

Dinner/Auction, and the Middleton Community Club sponsors an annual Chili Cook-Off.

The Saturday before Easter, the Greater Middleton Parks and Recreation District sponsors an Easter Egg Hunt at Foote Park for 5th grade children and younger.

Each April, the City sponsors Middleton Cleanup Day. This community-wide clean up brings everyone out to help get "our home" ready for summer activities.

Each May, seventh and eighth graders put on an "Evening of the Arts," where the children perform or display their talents.

The first Saturday in May is the annual Scout Plant Sale. Middleton Boy Scouts sell garden plants and flowers to raise funds for their camps and activities.

The May Day Fun Run, hosted by Middleton Elementary Schools, starts in the morning and ends with a bike fair. The bike fair raises bike safety awareness for community children and their parents.

The annual Middleton High School "Viking Homecoming" includes a community chili cook-off and fireworks.

The annual 4th of July Celebration includes a Fireman's Breakfast, a parade, a street fair, a horseshoe tournament, a street dance and a fireworks display.

The weekend before Labor Day is the annual Boy Scout Fair, which includes many activities and educational experiences for the youth.

September also brings the community's annual Dog Days of Summer K-9 Demo, sponsored by the Canyon County Sheriff's Department, with free hotdogs and corn on the cob.

Every Thursday from May to October from 4:30 to 7:30 p.m., local farmers and artisans bring their produce, plants, flowers, baked goods and handcrafted items to sell at the community's Farmers Market.

The Fall Harvest Carnival, hosted by the Purple Sage Elementary PTA, is held each fall.

A Community Craft Bazaar is held each October to help the Middleton Community Pantry and the Middleton Food Bank.

Each year after Thanksgiving, the Chamber of Commerce sponsors the Christmas Parade and Tree Lighting Festival.

In the fall and winter, the Greater Middleton Parks and Recreation District sponsors two train rides through the Thunder Mountain Line in Horseshoe Bend – the Pumpkin Liner in October and the North Pole Express in December.

Ten miles south of the city is the large and small mouth bass fishery, Lake Lowell and the Deer Flat National Wildlife Refuge. Picnic facilities and boat ramps are located around the lake.

The Deer Flat National Wildlife Refuge includes the lake, 110 miles of the Snake River and 86 islands on the river. Several hundred thousand migratory birds and 180 different bird species inhabit the refuge.

Fishing, boating and waterskiing are also available in other nearby lakes and reservoirs. Whitewater rafting and kayaking are available 20 miles northeast on the Payette River. Hunting, hiking and camping are within an hour's drive at the Boise

National Forest to the northeast or the Owyhee Mountains to the south.

The College of Idaho in Caldwell adds an important cultural dimension. Under its "Fine Arts Series," the College brings in performances of nationally recognized artists and theater companies. The Series is open to the public and held at the school's Jewett Auditorium.

Five miles south of Middleton is the Treasure Valley Marketplace, a newly constructed retail center including Costco, Target and many other large retailers and restaurants.

Residents generally say that the city's most attractive attribute is its rural location and home-town feel, yet it is within a short commute to nearby urban centers and employment.

Economy and Major Employers The Middleton School District has about 200 employees and is the city's largest employer. The Diamond Z, an industrial grinder and screen manufacturer, has approximately 100 employees and is the city's second largest employer. Rule Steel Tank, a steel fabricator, and Ridley's Food and Drug each have about 30 employees.

The city's downtown has a few retail establishments and two new business parks – Middleton Market Place and the Wellstone Business Park.

Most of the city's residents commute to nearby cities for employment and to shop.

Education The Middleton School District provides most of the city's elementary and secondary education. Within the city limits, the school district operates two elementary schools, a middle school, a high school and a transitional school.

There are several public and private universities, colleges and private vocational and technical schools located within a short commute of the city. The closest are the College of Idaho and Treasure Valley Community College in Caldwell and the College of Western Idaho in Nampa.

Health Care The closest hospital is the 150-bed West Valley Medical Center in Caldwell. Two assisted-living facilities operate in Middleton.

Transportation State Highway 44 passes through Middleton. Interstate 84 is located 3 miles west of downtown.

Commercial air service is available at the Boise Air Terminal. The 5,500-foot Caldwell Industrial Airport also provides services for certain commercial aircraft. The airport's lighted runway has 24-7 landing capability and is designated as a reliever to the Boise Airport. The Caldwell Airport also offers aircraft charter, rental, maintenance and flight instruction services.

Utilities and Services Private companies provide electricity, natural gas, telephone, cable and satellite services. The City provides water and sewer services. Middleton Rural Fire District provides fire protection. The County Sheriff's Office provides police protection under contract with the City. Canyon County provides solid waste services.

Vision for 2050

Over the past four decades, Middleton's population has grown more than seven fold. The city's strategic location of being within commuting distance to larger Treasure Valley cities is a major factor in prompting this growth. Families looking for affordable housing in a more rural setting with good schools have moved to Middleton in increasing numbers.

City and community leaders expect growth to continue but at slower rates. The City has strategic plans to accommodate this growth, including a Transportation Master Plan, and a Parks and Pathway Plan. The City and the Chamber of Commerce have formed the Middleton Economic Development Committee.

The City recently upgraded its wastewater treatment facilities and has capacity to accomodate a population of up to 30,000.

The City has recently established an urban renewal district and received an ICDBG grant for revitalization of the downtown area and is planning to build a community center.

Middleton School District leaders and patrons are proactive in providing facilities to accommodate a growing number of students. In September 2008 voters overwhelmingly approved a $51 million bond to build a new high school and other facilities. The district will convert the existing highschool into a middle school.

Mayors

1910 S.S. Foote *
1914 S.F. Chaney *
1917 A.J. Breshears *
1917 O.K. Nickerson *
1921 H.E. Foote *
1923 W.F. Bishop *
1925 William Lemon *
1927 F.C. Slotzenberg *
1931 Ralph Hadsall *
1933 C.J. Murphy *
1937 A.C. Zimmerman *
1939 W.S. Perkins *

1949 Earl Owen *
1957 Eldon Whitely *
1961 John Lanning *
1964 Lester A. Wallace *
1968 Milton Cram
1979 Alice A. Lanning
1992 L.D. Swigert
2000 Frank McKeever
2008 Vicki Thurber
2012 Darin Taylor
* Village Chairman

Nampa City Hall.

Nampa

Statistical Data

Population: 88,211 *
Elevation: 2,480 feet
Precipitation: 10.6 inches **
Average Snowfall: 9.6 inches **
County: Canyon
Website: www.cityofnampa.us

Temperature Range – Fahrenheit: **
Spring: 31 to 73
Summer: 51 to 91
Fall: 28 to 79
Winter: 21 to 45
* U.S. Census Bureau Estimates July 2015
**Historical averages

Nampa lies near the center of the Treasure Valley and is Idaho's second largest city. Just outside the city's downtown area, irrigated farms and open space interspersed by subdivisions and commercial development create a checkerboard of color and family and retail activity in this rapidly growing metropolis.

The 9,000-acre Lake Lowell, an irrigation reservoir and fishery, lies three miles southwest of the city.

Just outside the city and surrounding farmland to the west and south are vast tracts of public land. The majestic Owyhee Mountains – with peaks rising over 8,000 feet – punctuate the southwestern sky. About 15 miles to the southeast begins the 590,000-acre Snake River Birds of Prey National Conservation Area.

Idaho's capital city of Boise lies 16 miles east. Above Boise, the mountains of the Boise National Forest outline Nampa's eastern skyline.

Pre-Incorporation Years

In 1881 the Oregon Short Line (OSL) Railroad, an affiliate of Union Pacific Railroad, began construction of a rail line from the railhead at Granger, Wyoming, to the Huntington, Oregon, railhead just across the Snake River near Weiser. The rail line – completed November 17, 1884 – allowed the movement of passengers and freight between Omaha, Nebraska, and Portland, Oregon, at the then unheard of time of four and a half days.

The rail line crossed Southern Idaho in a northwesterly direction passing through what are now Pocatello, Mountain Home, Nampa and Caldwell. Much to the dismay of Boise residents, the effect of following this more direct and shorter route between railheads bypassed the capital city.

Upon reaching what is now Nampa, railroad workers constructed a steam engine water storage tank. They identified the site with a small white sign bearing the name "Nampa." The origin of the name is unknown. Many believe it is a derivation of a Shoshone Indian name for footprint or moccasin. However, Nampa is also the name of cities in Alberta, Canada; Finland; and Peru.

Greystone Hotel.

On September 6, 1883, the railroad stopped its rail line construction at Caldwell while crews built a bridge across the Boise River Canyon before proceeding to its destination at Huntington. As a railroad terminus, Caldwell quickly became a railhead supply point and boomtown. Settlers and businesses used so many tents for temporary shelter that they called Caldwell a "town of tents."

Early visitors to Caldwell were Alexander Duffes and his wife Hanna. Duffes – an entrepreneur and developer from Burlington, Canada, located 35 miles south of Toronto – had sold his merchandising and grain business. He had traveled to Caldwell searching for an investment opportunity in one of the developing railroad communities.

Duffes met James A. McGee, a resident of Caldwell. McGee was a speculator and promoter who moved from Pennsylvania also looking for an investment opportunity.

Most investors and developers focused on Caldwell, overlooking the Nampa train stop as a business

Nampa train station.

opportunity. This was understandable since at that time, Nampa was nothing more than a dry, sagebrush-covered plain with the Snake River 10 miles west.

McGee discussed the investment potential of Nampa with Duffes. Duffes agreed with McGee's assessment and immediately acquired 160 acres near the Nampa train stop and began building a four-room house for himself and Hanna.

In 1886 Duffes and McGee formed the Nampa Land and Improvement Company (NLIP) and platted the town of Nampa. Rather than aligning the streets on the typical north-south axis, they platted the streets in a northwest-southeast direction parallel to the railroad tracks. Duffes asserted it was a safety measure to give a better view of approaching trains. Within three months, the NLIP sold 92 lots.

Duffes tried to keep saloons out of town by refusing to sell commercial lots to anyone intending to build a saloon on the property. Duffes action led to the Nampa nickname of "New Jerusalem." However, Duffes restriction only delayed the inevitable. Those seeking to build saloons merely purchased lots offered for resale.

In 1885 Caldwell promoters began grading a 30-mile railroad line to Boise.

Duffes and McGee viewed this as a threat to their Nampa investment. They recognized that their investment hinged on where the railroad branch line to Boise connected to the OSL main line.

McGee traveled to Boston to convince railroad interests to support the shorter 20-mile Nampa to Boise alternative. McGee was successful and on June 26, 1886, McGee; Duffes; and James Stewart, another investor, incorporated the Idaho Central Railway Company (ICRC). On September

Old city hall.

5, 1897, the first train pulling a flatbed with 20 passengers and heavy stamp-mill machinery for the Boise Basin miners arrived in Boise. Boiseans celebrated the event with a picnic and speeches from dignitaries. They affectionately called the little railroad line, "The Stub."

On October 1, 1887, the OSL opened its Nampa Train Station and closed its Kuna facility. The following day, the mail route and stage line moved their headquarters to Nampa. On July 27, 1889, the OSL acquired the ICRC.

The future economic success of the western Treasure Valley and Nampa was dependent on bringing irrigation water to the several hundred thousand acres of sagebrush-covered land west of Boise. While homesteaders and settlers with farms near rivers and streams had irrigation water, most of the land was dry. Whoever could bring water to the parched land could reap handsome profits.

Nampa's elevation is about 360 feet below Boise. In 1882 investors from New York filed claims on 4,500 second feet of Boise River water – generally only available during spring runoff – and formed the Idaho Mining and Irrigation Company. The company engineer, A.D. Foote, surveyed a 75-mile-long main gravity-flow canal known as the New York Canal. His drawings included a system of canals and lateral ditches known as the New York Canal Tract. When complete, Foote and the investors expected the main canal would provide sufficient water to reclaim from 300,000 to 500,000 acres of the sagebrush-covered land.

However, the New York Canal project was plagued with financing and legal problems. It would take several years and intervention by the federal government to complete the project.

In 1886 McGee, Duffes and Stewart acquired the failed Phyllis Canal project, a diversion of Boise River water at a point about 14 miles west of Boise. Their efforts also failed. In 1902 following years of conflict, the Pioneer Irrigation Company, an entity formed by the water users, acquired the Phyllis Canal and brought the first irrigation water to some of the farms near Nampa.

First Street South.

Incorporation

In 1886 Nampa became an incorporated village. At that time, the business district consisted of a grocery store, a lumberyard, a hotel, two drug stores and three saloons. The U.S. Census reported Nampa's 1890 population at 799.

On April 17, 1901, the city's electorate voted to change the legal status of the village to an incorporated city of the second class. Following that change, city leaders proceeded to construct waterworks and sewer systems; make street improvements; and build an equipped fire station, city hall and library.

Turning Points

Railroad and Electric Trolley Nampa's origins date to 1883. At that time, it was an OSL Railroad stop where steam locomotives took on water. From those humble beginnings, it became an important railroad terminal. Branch lines went east from Nampa to Boise, another line went south to Murphy to serve the Silver City mines, and another went north to serve agricultural and timber businesses.

In 1905 construction began for the electric Interurban Trolley that formed a loop connecting most Treasure Valley communities. For more than a decade, the trolley was very popular. People used the low cost transportation for both business and pleasure. Farmers and merchants used it to transport produce and goods to sell in the larger cities. However, when motor vehicles became popular, ridership declined, and in 1928 the electric trolley closed.

Irrigation Development of the agricultural industry was critical to Nampa's early economic growth. However, the availability of an adequate supply of irrigation water was problematic. The water had to come through canals diverted from the Boise River several miles upriver. In 1882 private efforts to deliver irrigation water had limited success because of funding and other problems.

In 1902 Congress passed the Reclamation Act creating the U. S. Reclamation Service – now Bureau of Reclamation – allowing federal construction and management of dams and irrigation systems needed to reclaim the arid West.

Following passage of the Act, residents of southwest Canyon County – led by J.H. Lowell of Nampa – were instrumental in convincing the Reclamation Service to develop systems to irrigate the vast tracts of sagebrush-covered land west of Boise.

The Bureau of Reclamation developed its "Boise Project," which eventually included an integrated system of hydroelectric dams on the Boise, Payette and Owyhee River drainages with thousands of miles of canals and ditches. The dams on the Boise River drainage included Arrow Rock (1915), Anderson Ranch (1950) and Lucky Peak (1955). These hydroelectric dams provided storage capacity for release throughout the growing season.

Barber Dam (1908) located a few miles east of Boise diverted water into the New York Canal, which emptied into a reservoir completed in 1909 around a natural depression in the earth's surface near Nampa called Deer Flat – now named Lake Lowell.

The ten-mile-long and up to two-mile-wide Lake Lowell has an earthen dam and a surrounding excavated dyke system that ranges from 46 to 74 feet high.

In addition to constructing the dam and reservoir, the Reclamation Service provided the expertise and financial aid – a low-cost, long-term loan program – needed to develop a complex system of canals and lateral ditches

Dewey Palace Hotel.

throughout the valley. Within a few years, farmers transformed the dry high-desert landscape around Nampa into an agricultural oasis.

Public Schools Public schools started July 13, 1887, with the formation of the Nampa School District. On October 3, school began with 20 students taught on the second floor of the two-story building occupied by Mr. Bowman, the Justice of the Peace. Bowman also served as schoolteacher until school patrons hired a permanent instructor.

Northwest Nazarene University In September 1913 Eugene Emerson started the forerunner to Northwest Nazarene University. The school opened with 13 elementary students. From that modest beginning, the school grew to offer high school then college courses. In 1916 the school changed its name to Northwest Nazarene College. It became an accredited junior college in 1931. In 1937 the school offered a four-year college program. In 1999 it changed its name to Northwest Nazarene University (NNU).

Approximately 1,170 undergraduate students; 460 graduate students; and 8,236 continuing education students enrolled for the fall 2007 semester. NNU has a major impact on the educational, economic and social wellbeing of Nampa.

Dewey Family Investments In 1896 Colonel William Henry Dewey, one of the founders of the Silver City mines, purchased 2,000 of Nampa's unsold building lots.

In 1897 Dewey was influential in the formation of the Boise, Nampa and Owyhee Idaho Railroad that in 1902 constructed a rail line to Murphy, to serve the mines in Silver City. The railroad then extended a line from Nampa to Emmett and north to Smiths Ferry. In 1912 following financial problems, it sold to the OSL.

Sugar beet factory with sheep in the foreground.

In 1903 Dewey completed construction of a hotel he named the Dewey Palace. As an inducement for Dewey to build the hotel, the city put up $4,000 toward the purchase of a building lot. The hotel cost $250,000. It was a three-story, 43,000-square-foot structure with double balconies in the front. It had electric lights, a billiard room, bowling alley, barbershop, bar, dining room and ballroom. The facility served as a center for many of the city's social and business functions.

In 1901 investors built the Swan Falls Hydroelectric Dam on the Snake River to principally provide electrical power to the Silver City mines. Dewey acquired a 50-year franchise to bring electricity to Nampa. He brought the electricity into the city via power lines attached to Rocky Mountain Bell Telephone poles.

In spite of the magnificence of the Dewey Palace, it could not overcome broader adverse economic events. One of the more significant events affecting the Dewey Palace was Idaho law allowing local control over the sale or use of alcoholic beverages. In 1910 Canyon County citizens voted to make the county dry. This action gave competitive advantage to the hospitality businesses in Ada County.

The majority of Nampa residents were so upset with the Canyon County vote that they proposed legislation that essentially allowed Nampa to secede from Canyon County and join Ada. The State Legislature refused to take action on the legislation, thereby killing the bill.

The effect of the Canyon County vote on the Dewey Palace was devastating. Its business fell off so much that in 1912 it closed its doors. However, it opened again in 1916 when Idaho voters leveled the competitive playing field by approving an amendment to Idaho's Constitution prohibiting the sale or use of alcoholic beverages statewide – the Federal Prohibition law extended from 1920 to 1933.

The Dewey Palace continued to be a city landmark until it closed again in 1956. In 1963 following seven years of setting idle, the owners demolished the building.

Sugar Factory In 1906 the Western Idaho Sugar Company built a manufacturing plant in Nampa. During the first year of operation, the plant processed 48,000 tons of beets. The plant was an important economic stimulus for the city. However, infestations of white fly – an insect carrying a virus that causes a plant-killing blight – invaded the sugar beet crops with devastating effects. In 1911 crop yields were so poor the sugar factory closed.

Years later, effective insecticides and best practices aided farmers in controlling the white fly and other insect and disease problems. In 1942 Amalgamated Sugar Company built a new factory in Nampa. Today, this facility processes over a million tons of sugar beets a season and is one of the city's largest employers.

Fire On July 3, 1909, fire destroyed about half the downtown business district. The fire started when a stranger set off fireworks in Arnold's Cigar Store that ignited other fireworks. The fire quickly spread causing $350,000 of damage. The next day many of the business owners that sustained losses showed their pluck by marching in the Fourth of July Parade calling themselves the "Cinder Club." One carried a sign "Gone up in smoke, but have not lost hope."

Mercy Medical Center Mercy Medical Center is a Roman Catholic facility founded in 1917 by the Sisters of Mercy. The hospital has grown to a 152-bed acute care hospital and one of Nampa's largest employers. The hospital has had a major positive effect on the health, wellbeing and economy of the city.

Economic Development and Community Revitalization For over five decades, city and community leaders have aggressively pursued initiatives that have made Nampa a progressive, vibrant and fast-growing city.

On August 30, 1949, local business leaders formed the Nampa Industrial Corporation (NIC) as a business venture to promote economic growth. The NIC first platted and developed a 62-acre industrial park that by 1970 had largely sold out to several businesses that became major employers. In 1972 the NIC expanded the park by acquiring 92 more acres. Several more businesses came into the park. By 2007 the development sold out and the owners dissolved the NIC.

In 1965 developers built Karcher Mall – a shopping mall that, until completion of a larger regional mall in Boise in 1987, attracted shoppers from throughout the Treasure Valley. In 2007 a new interchange on Interstate 84 near Karcher Mall has encouraged restoration of Karcher Mall, as well as significant retail development on both sides of the freeway.

In 1982 with the support of the city's elected officials, business leaders formed a downtown Business Improvement District (BID). They raised over $2 million to improve infrastructure in the nine-square-block downtown redevelopment area.

In 1994 city and community leaders created the North Nampa Urban Renewal District (District). The District's principal success was the 1997 construction of the Idaho Center, a multiple-events center that could seat over 10,000. The Idaho Center has been a magnet for a broad range of commercial and residential development near the facility, including the 100-acre campus of Boise State University West and the College of Western Idaho. In 2005 the District concluded its work and closed its operation.

In 2005 the city created the Central Nampa Development Commission to oversee revitalization of the city and implementation of the Central Nampa Revitalization Blueprint commissioned by the City. In the same year, city leaders formed the Historic Preservation Commission to see that Nampa's history and historic structures are preserved. In 2008 the city formed the Nampa Arts Commission.

Nampa Public Library.

Nampa Today

Amenities and Attractions Nampa has 20 city parks and many walking trails covering more than 200 acres. In addition, it has Ridgecrest Golf Course, a course offering 45 holes. The city also has one private 9-hole golf course. Ridgecrest Golf Course consistently receives a four-star rating from Golf Digest.

The city also has a 140,000-square-foot Recreation Center. It has a large indoor climbing wall, three basketball courts, an indoor running track, five swimming pools, a spa and a senior center.

The 42,000-square-foot Nampa Civic Center has 14 separate meeting spaces including a 650-seat auditorium with a 3,500-square-foot stage floor and dressing rooms. The center's banquet facilities and culinary staff can accommodate up to

1,000 guests. The center is a community focal point for concerts, live theater and community events.

The Idaho Center includes an arena, horse park, outdoor amphitheater and sports complex. It is a regional attraction for concerts and events requiring seating where over 10,000 people can attend.

Nampa sponsors or supports several annual events. The most prominent of these events is the famous Snake River Stampede held for one week each July at the Idaho Center. The rodeo attracts about 45,000 patrons annually.

The city has an effective program for providing wholesome activities for high school youth. The Nampa Mayor's Teen Council teaches youth about the operation of local government and supports a variety of sports programs. Program efforts are coordinated with other youth groups such as Boys and Girls Clubs.

Lake View Park.

Lake Lowell is a popular bass fishery. The lake is part of the Deer Flat National Wildlife Refuge. The refuge includes two sectors. One sector includes Lake Lowell and about 1,600 acres of adjoining land. The other sector includes 101 islands on the Snake River stretching north 113 miles from the Canyon County/Ada County line. The refuge provides habitat for a variety of wildlife and thousands of migratory and nesting ducks and geese.

About 15 miles south of town, the Snake River winds through a dramatic desert canyon where rocks are painted with petroglyphs dating back 10,000 years. To the east of the canyon lies the Snake River Birds of Prey National Conservation Area.

A variety of outdoor activities including camping, hiking, ATV riding, boating, fishing and hunting are available in the public lands, lakes or streams located within a short drive of the city. Downhill skiing is available at Bogus Basin Ski Resort, in the mountains north of Boise.

Economy and Major Employers Nampa School District has over 1,300 employees and is the city's largest employer. Other large employers with 350 to 1,000 employees each include Mercy Medical Center; Armor Foods, a subsidiary of ConAgra Foods, Inc.; MPC Corporation, computers and electronics; Amalgamated Sugar Company; Woodgrain Millwork, Inc.; divisions of Plexus

Corp., a computer board manufacturing company; and Nestle USA, food processing.

Education Nampa and Vallivue School Districts provide most of the elementary and secondary education in the city. In addition, there are three public charter schools and four private Christian schools.

Nampa is home to Northwest Nazarene University, the College of Southwest Idaho, Boise State University-West (BSU) campus and the BSU Technology and Entrepreneurial Center.

Firehouse #5.

Health Care The 114-bed Mercy Medical Center and various doctors offices, clinics and retirement centers serve the health care needs of the community.

Transportation Interstate 84, U.S. Highway 30 and Idaho Highway 55 intersect the city. Idaho Highway 45 connects Nampa with the communities and public lands that lie to the south.

Public transportation is available from Valley Regional Transit, a public entity that administers a regional (Treasure Valley) transportation system.

The 5,000-foot runway at Nampa Municipal Airport provides service to private and charter aircraft. Heavier passenger and commercial service is available 20 miles east at the Boise Air Terminal, Gowen Field.

Nampa is one of two Union Pacific Railroad terminals in Idaho – freight only.

Utilities and Services Private companies provide electricity, telephone, gas, satellite and cable services. The City provides water and sewer services and police and fire protection.

Vision for 2050

Since 2000 Nampa's population has grown nearly 50 percent as an increasing number of families have found Nampa an attractive and affordable place to live and raise a family.

During the next four decades, the city's population will continue to grow but at a slower rate.

In 2009 as part of the downtown

Playground equipment.

revitalization plan, the City began construction of a four-story civic office building. The facility will house City offices including the Nampa Police Department and Fire Department Administration. A city-block sized park will be constructed nearby. These facilities will be an attraction for other mixed-use downtown development.

Other improvements will include street beautification, and venues for displaying public art. New bikeways and pathways extending 134 linear miles will meander through the city and connect with other greenbelts in the Treasure Valley.

Mayors

1886-1901 Unknown *	1933 Evert W. Rising
1901 W.J. McClelland	1935 George I. Van Name
1903 Frank Sutherland	1937 R. Lewis Ord
1904 Henry A. Partridge	1939 Ben H. Waigand
1905 R.W. Purdum	1943 Albert E. Lindsey
1907 Henry A. Partridge	1945 Sevren G. Honstead
1909 Edward H. Dewey	1947 Peter Johnson
1913 Henry A. Partridge	1951 Preston Capell
1915 Thomas Munhall	1957 Thomas A. Leupp
1917 Robert Davis, Jr.	1961 Ernest Starr
1919 Howard H. Keim	1982 Winston K. Goering
1921 J. Fremont Bow	1998 Maxine Horne
1923 Eugene Emerson	2002 Tom Dale
1925 George Meffan	2014 Bob Henry
1929 Eustace Smallwood	* Village Chairman
1930 Windsor Lloyd	

Notus City Hall.

Notus

Statistical Data

Population: 545 *
Elevation: 2,316 feet
Precipitation: 11 inches **
Average Snowfall: 15 inches **
County: Canyon

Temperature Range – Fahrenheit: **
Spring: 33 to 75
Summer: 53 to 93
Fall: 28 to 81
Winter: 21 to 46

* U.S. Census Bureau Estimates July 2015
**Historical averages

Notus is a quiet agricultural community located five miles northwest of Caldwell and eight miles southeast of Parma. It is one of the smallest cities in Canyon County.

For several miles in about every direction fields of alfalfa, corn seed, sugar beets, beans, onions, potatoes, wheat and hops form a checkerboard of color and texture around the city. Sheep and cattle dot the green pastures with occasional horses and haystacks. Small creeks and canals weave in and around the farmlands.

The town's southern border is nestled up against the Boise River. The terrain is slightly hilly with areas of flat lands, natural wetlands and marshes. About five miles north of the city is an approximate 30-square-mile tract of brush and grass-covered public foothill land managed by the BLM. (*See Southwestern Idaho, The Region, Distinctive Geographic and Geologic Features.*)

Pre-Incorporation Years

American Indians, principally of the Shoshone and Bannock Tribes who had seasonal encampments along the Snake River and were often called Snake Indians, were the principle inhabitants around what is now Notus until the early 1800s. (*See*

Southwestern Idaho, The Region, American Indians.)

In 1811 Wilson Price Hunt, an explorer/fur trapper for the North West Company, led an exploring expedition from St. Louis to the mouth of the Columbia River on the coast. Hunt hoped to identify locations to establish trading posts for the acquisition of beaver pelts whcih were in high demand in the European markets. En route, they passed near the confluence of the Boise and Snake Rivers and what is now Notus. (*See Southwestern Idaho, The Region, Early Trappers/Explorers.*)

Aerial view of Notus.

In July 1813 John Reed, a member of the Hunt expedition; Pierre Dorian; Dorian's Indian wife, Marie; and their two children enlisted seven men at the trading post at Walla Walla in what is now Washington to join them in setting up a trading post and trapping beaver near the confluence of the Boise and Snake Rivers near what is now Parma.

That winter a band of Indians attacked and killed the nine men as they were working their traps. It was the first massacre of whites by Indians in Idaho history. Notified by a friendly Indian, Marie Dorian hastily loaded dried meat and buffalo robes on a horse and set out for Walla Walla with her two children. After nine days of arduous travel, heavy snows in the Blue Mountains forced her to stop and build a horsehide – covered shelter where she and her children subsisted for nearly two months before the receding snow allowed them to walk out and tell their harrowing story. A statue of Mrs. Dorian stands in Parma's Old Fort Boise Park.

Notus School.

In 1834 the river flowing from the east and passing near what is now Notus was named "Boise," the French word for wooded, by French Canadian Francois Payette – the manager of the Hudson's Bay Company trading post, Fort Boise, built near the confluence of the Snake and Boise Rivers.

In 1841 the first of the immigrants en route to Oregon's Willamette Valley passed through what is now Notus and stopped at Fort Boise, a landmark shown on Oregon Trail immigrant maps. In 1854 floods destroyed the Fort Boise trading post. (*See Southwestern Idaho, The Region, Oregon and California Trails.*)

In 1862 and 1863 prospectors discovered gold in the Boise Basin and in the Owyhee Mountains, respectively. In the gold rushes that followed, 16,000 fortune seekers initially flooded into the Boise Basin and 2,500 scoured the Owyhee Mountains, mining and searching for the precious metal. (*See Southwestern Idaho, The Region, Mining – Boise Basin – Gold and Owyhee Mountains'silver and Gold.*)

The gold rush attracted a stream of farmers and ranchers to produce fresh food for sale at inflated prices, to the miners. Some of these homesteaders settled in what is now Notus. (*See Southwestern Idaho, The Region, Federal Land Use Laws*)

In the fall of 1864, emigrants from Missouri, Southern sympathizers fleeing the ravages of the Civil War, arrived near what is now Notus and homesteaded on the south side of the Boise River. They were impressed with the abundant water, grass, wild game and trees growing on the river's floodplain. They built cottonwood log cabins with bulrush-thatch roofs and called their settlement "Dixie Community."

Old Notus City Hall.

In the early 1880s German emigrants, Dr. Daniel and Mary Hartkopf (or Hartkoph), filed a homestead claim on the north side of the Boise River across from Dixie Community. The Oregon Trail and a stagecoach route crossed their property.

On November 17, 1884, the Oregon Short Line (OSL) completed construction of a railroad line between Granger, Wyoming, and Huntington, Oregon. This railroad link provided connection between the commercial centers of Omaha, Nebraska, and Portland,

Oregon. The railroad angled in a northwesterly direction across Southern Idaho passing through Pocatello, Caldwell, Notus and Weiser before crossing the Snake River near Huntington.

When the railroad crossed the Hartkoph homestead in 1883, OSL acquired some of the homestead land and built a siding platform, a lava rock-lined well, a water tank and a windmill. The railroad employed Daniel to keep the tank filled, which he did until his death in 1888.

In naming the siding, the railroad superintendent's daughter, who was studying

236

Greek mythology, suggested to her father that he name the siding "Notus" after the Greek God of the South Wind – which he did.

In 1887 Howard Sebree purchased a farmer-owned irrigation canal system – Johnson's Ditch-Sebree Canal – that diverted water from the Boise River. Sebree expanded the irrigation system to serve many Notus and Parma area farms. In 1902 Sebree sold the expanded system to the water users.

In 1890 railroad officials built a sectional house on their siding and transferred their employee, Thomas Burns, to manage the facility. Years later, Burns married the widow Mary Hartkoph. Following their marriage, Burns continued the work of improving the homestead. He leveled the land and planted alfalfa hay.

In 1902 Congress established the U.S. Reclamation Service – now Bureau of Reclamation. Reclamation almost immediately embarked on its "Boise Project." Among other things, the Project provided federal funding and support to irrigators. When completed decades later, Reclamation had successfully integrated or completed existing Treasure Valley irrigation systems and added a system of dams and water storage reservoirs in the higher elevations of the Boise River and its principal tributaries and the Payette River. (*See Southwestern Idaho, The Region, Federal Land Use Laws.*)

In 1904 Thomas and William Bridges purchased 26 acres from Thomas and Mary Burns for $7,982 and platted the townsite of Notus. That same year, Ida Mansell moved her store and post office three miles east into the new town, just east of the railway siding.

New homesteaders coming into the area were hopeful that water would soon be on the way. However, they were sadly

Notus fire truck.

disappointed. It would take two decades before irrigation water flowed from Black Canyon Reservoir on the Payette River east of Emmett. In the meantime, much of the community withered. "It was a ghost town," recalls R.C. Sleeper, a businessman and Village Clerk who came in 1916. "The only people who lived here were day laborers and a few businessmen. The railroad was the only steady work." Many homesteaders sold or abandoned their farms. Houses, outbuildings and fences fell into disrepair and were stripped of useful lumber and hardware.

In 1921 about 7,000 acres had been cleared of sagebrush and canals began carrying water from Black Canyon Reservoir to the parched land. "We really had a celebration," recalls settler and Village Chairman, L.E. Small. "People came from all over the country. The Governor from the State was present. There were speeches and a band playing and ball games, foot races, and barbecues to end all barbecues. That was a day to be remembered."

The Boise Project was a boon to area irrigators for another reason. The water storage reservoirs overcame late summer water shortages and provided water throughout the growing season.

In 1914 railroad officials built the Notus Depot. Two years later, the community had grown to include railroad facilities, several businesses, a church and over a dozen homes and tents.

Incorporation

On December 12, 1921, Notus became an incorporated village. In 1926 Idaho Power ran electrical lines to the village. Phone service soon followed.

In 1967 Notus became an incorporated city as required by the change in Idaho municipal law.

Turning Points

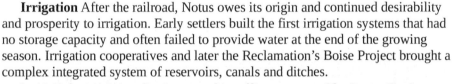

Notus water tower.

Railroad The availability of rail transportation provided employment for Notus residents and had a major effect in allowing Notus area farmers to move their commodities to distant markets. Many railroad workers built homes and raised their families in Notus.

Irrigation After the railroad, Notus owes its origin and continued desirability and prosperity to irrigation. Early settlers built the first irrigation systems that had no storage capacity and often failed to provide water at the end of the growing season. Irrigation cooperatives and later the Reclamation's Boise Project brought a complex integrated system of reservoirs, canals and ditches.

In 1940 the irrigation district moved its offices to town. The Parma Review writes, "A great boost to the village came in 1940 when work began on the second unit of the Black Canyon Irrigation District. Offices and shops were set up in Notus and employed 25 or more workers..."

Water and Sewer In 1937 the federal Works Projects Administration (WPA), the public works program that provided jobs across the nation during the Great Depression to build needed infrastructure, built the Notus water and sewer systems. In the 1950s the city drilled a second well and erected a tall silver-colored water tower to pressurize the domestic waterlines.

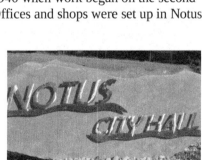

Notus rock.

Highway and Interstate Construction of U.S. Highway 20/26 attracted several retail and hospitality businesses'such as service stations, automobile repair shops and restaurants – to Notus.

However, during the 1960s federal and state transportation departments constructed Interstate 84 six miles east of Notus. The loss of traffic passing through town had a significant adverse effect on the city's economy. Only three Notus businesses have survived this loss.

Fire Late in the evening of March 14, 1944, residents saw flames, which would eventually engulf most of a city block, coming from a local lumberyard. Fire suppression equipment, primarily consisting of a pumper tank, was inadequate to contain the raging fire. Substantially all able-bodied residents turned out to fight the blaze. Working through the night, exhausted men would take refuge in a nearby home where women served food and drink. When they finally contained the fire, only three buildings in the city block survived unscathed. Many historical structures were lost.

Notus Today

Amenities and Attractions Notus has two city parks. The parks feature shaded rest areas and picnic tables. Tower Park is located under the water tower. Notus Park is in the business district next to the railroad and highway along the old Oregon Trail.

New Notus City Hall.

The Notus Museum is located downtown in the historic fire station. It has numerous artifacts and exhibits depicting early family and historical histories.

The Notus Library is a popular center for learning. In addition to normal activities, the library offers computers with Internet access and sponsors computer workshops, a book club and summer reading programs.

Each 4th of July, the city celebrates Independence Day with a flag raising ceremony, parade, breakfast and car exhibits at the city's Community Center.

The annual Community Spring Clean-Sweep is a time for residents to come together to clean and beautify their neighborhoods.

Community residents are big boosters of high school athletic events. Each fall, the community celebrates the Notus Pirates homecoming football game with a "Homecoming Parade" and a stadium packed with fans.

Each November the town sponsors a free "Thanksgiving Community Dinner" at the Community Center.

In December, the city ushers in the holiday season with Santa paying a visit to the children followed by refreshments, music and craft booths at the Community Center, lighting the downtown tree and Museum and touring the downtown displays.

One of the city's most attractive amenities is the ability of residents to live in a small rural setting, yet be close to a diversity of urban amenities available in nearby cities.

Boating, hunting, fishing, hiking, biking, jogging and camping are available along the Boise River and within an hour's drive of the city on nearby public lands, including the Boise National Forest to the northeast or the Owyhee Mountains to the south.

Economy and Major Employers Black Canyon Irrigation and Boise River Pack, a fresh packer of onions, are the city's largest employers. The Notus School District and agricultural businesses located outside the city limits provide significant employment for city residents. Several small businesses and retail establishments provide most of the other jobs available in town. Many residents commute to nearby larger cities for employment.

Education The Notus School District provides most of the city's K-12 education. The Notus elementary and junior-senior high schools are located on a hill a short distance north of the city limits. There are several institutions of higher learning within an hour's drive of the city. Boise State University is 38 miles southwest in Boise. Treasure Valley College and the College of Idaho are located six miles away in Caldwell. Northwest Nazarene University and the College of Western Idaho are 18 miles away in Nampa.

Health Care Residents travel to West Valley Medical Center in Caldwell, St. Luke's Meridian Medical Center in Meridian and Mercy Medical Center in Nampa for most of their health care needs.

Dental and medical clinics are available within 6 miles of the city.

Transportation U.S. Highway 20/26 borders the south side of the city. U.S. Highway 95 is six miles northwest. Interstate 84 is six miles southeast.

Railroad transportation is available at two sidings in the city for freight.

Utilities and Services Private companies provide electricity, gas, cable, satellite and wireless services. The City provides water, sewer and solid waste removal services. The Canyon County Sheriff's Department provides police protection. Caldwell Rural Fire Department provides fire protection, with a substation located in Notus.

Vision for 2050

Existing infrastructure will allow moderate growth. Improvements can be paid from normal revenue streams, grants or bonds as needed.

During the next 40 years, Notus will continue to have the peaceful, rural and attractive small-town attributes it has today – close to urban amenities, yet near public lands and streams that offer excellent outdoor experiences. Notus is a wonderful place for retirees to live or young families to raise their children.

Mayors

1921 L.E. Small *
1928 J.S. Babcock *
1935 S.O. Lewis *
1937 L.E. Small *
1938 Ray Lewis *
1938 L.E. Small *
1939 E.H. Millsap *
1940 C.L. Haines *
1943 O.P. Pennington *
1945 Wm Ross *
1947 A.W. Andrew *
1948 Ed Conway *
1949 C.D. Lewis *
1950 Ed Conway *
1951 Ted Wells *
1954 Kenneth C. Overman *
1955 O.H. Carlson *

1957 Howard Pennington *
1966 Carroll W. Dean *
1972 Gerlad Thomas
1973 Paul Jameson
1974 Donald Bittick
1976 James E. Martin
1980 Richard Lind
1982 Elizabeth Coulter
1986 E. Don Calkin
1990 Greg Kadel
1998 Paul Thomas
2002 Marjorie Ellemaker
2006 Anne Horn
2009 Chris Collins
2014 David Porterfield
* Village Chairman

Entering Parma from the east.

Parma

Statistical Data

Population: 2,066 *
Elevation: 2,240 feet
Precipitation: 11 inches **
Average Snowfall: 16 inches **
County: Canyon
Website: www.parmacity.net

Temperature Range – Fahrenheit: **
Spring: 30 to 73
Summer: 50 to 91
Fall: 27 to 80
Winter: 19 to 44

* U.S. Census Bureau Estimates July 2015
**Historical averages

Parma is the home of the original historic Fort Boise on the Oregon Trail. The city is in the western Treasure Valley about five miles southeast of the Idaho/Oregon border at the confluence of the Boise and Snake Rivers. The Boise River flows on the south edge of town.

Fertile irrigated farms of onions, potatoes, cereal grains, hops, corn, apples, grapes and hay form a mosaic of color and texture around the city. Parma area farmers ship between 22,000 and 24,000 train and truck carloads of onions each year.

About five miles northeast is a 30-square-mile tract of brush and grass-covered public foothills managed by the Bureau of Land Management (BLM). Caldwell is 14 miles southeast.

Pre-Incorporation Years

Wilson Price Hunt, an explorer and fur trapper employed by the Pacific Fur Company, led an expedition from St. Louis, Missouri, to the headwaters of the Snake River in Wyoming in 1811. They foolishly, as it turned out, abandoned their horses at Fort Henry and made canoes that they planned to use to float the Snake River to the mouth of the Columbia River on the coast. However, at a particularly treacherous section of the Snake River near what is now Twin Falls, they lost a canoe, supplies and a man. Concluding that the Snake River was not navigable, they cached their supplies and equipment and trekked overland on foot, passing through what is now Parma, as they continued to their destination. The purpose of this ill-fated expedition included finding optimum locations to establish trading posts for the acquisition of beaver pelts which were in high demand in the European markets. (*See The Region, Early Trappers/Explorers*.)

Hotel Shipley.

John Reed (sometimes Reid), one of the members of the Hunt expedition; along with Pierre Dorion (or Dorian); his Iowa Indian wife, Marie; and their two children enlisted seven men to set up a trading post and trap beaver at the confluence of the Boise and Snake Rivers. When they arrived in 1813, they built a log house and began their enterprise.

However, their trading and beaver trapping venture came to an abrupt end when a party of Indians – ostensibly angry at the trappers' intrusion into their fishing grounds and seeking the expedition's rifles, gun powder and goods – attacked and killed the nine men. It was the first massacre of white people by Indians in Idaho history.

Marie Dorion, who was at the cabin, received word of the massacre from a friendly Indian. She quickly loaded a packhorse with buffalo robes, dried meat and supplies and fled northwest with her children on the trail to the trading post, Fort Walla Walla, located several miles south of the confluence of the Snake and Columbia Rivers near what is now Wallula, Washington. The military Fort Walla Walla was built in 1856, 30 miles west of the old trading post at what is now Walla Walla, Washington.

Her harrowing, yet successful, 260-mile trip included trekking for nine days until exhaustion and heavy snows forced her to stop in the Blue Mountains. There she built a makeshift horsehide-covered shelter. Marie and her children subsisted for 53 days, primarily on dried buffalo and horse jerky, before the snows receded sufficiently for them to walk out and report the massacre.

Thomas McKay of the Hudson's Bay Company, a British enterprise, built a trading post in 1934 near the location of the massacre about three miles northwest of what is now Parma. A year later, McKay turned management of the outpost over to a French Canadian, Francois

Main Street, 1905.

Payette, who managed the fort until 1844.

Payette, obviously struck by the black cottonwood and willow forests that grew along the river flowing from the east, named the outpost Fort Boise and the river Boise, the French name meaning "woods" or "wooded." Settlers and governments would later give permanence to Payette's name, as well as the name of his outpost. "Payette" became the name of a city, a county, a river, a valley and a national forest. "Boise" would become the name of another fort, a city, a national forest, a valley, a county and a mining district and mountain basin that ultimately yielded 2.8 million tr. oz. of gold. (*See The Region, Mining – Boise Basin – Gold*.)

In 1841 thousands of immigrants en route to Oregon Country's Willamette Valley began passing through what is now the Treasure Valley on what became known as the Oregon Trail. Payette's original Fort Boise was a landmark

Hotel Illinois, the Pride of Parma.

and supply station on the trail. Captain John C. Fremont referenced Fort Boise on his 1843 military reconnaissance maps, later used routinely by Oregon Trail immigrants. The fort continued as a supply post until 1853 when massive snowmelts flooded and destroyed the outpost. (*See The Region, Oregon and California Trails; and Federal Lands*.)

Prospectors discovered gold about 50 miles east of what is now Parma in the mountains of the Boise Basin in 1862. The following year, 16,000 fortune seekers flooded the basin in search of the precious metal. Where settlers could easily divert irrigation water onto their homesteads, farms sprang up to provide food for the miners.

The U.S. Army established a military fort in 1863 on a foothill bench a mile north of the Boise River, 40 miles east of what is now Parma, to provide protection for immigrants, settlers and the miners. They named it Fort Boise, the same name as the destroyed trading post. A new town that settlers called Boise City immediately grew up around the fort. The military kept Fort Boise in operation until 1912. (*See The Region, Mining – Boise Basin – Gold; and Idaho Territory – Territorial Capitals – Lewiston and Boise.*)

The Oregon Short Line (OSL) began construction of the railroad line in 1881 between Granger, Wyoming, and Huntington, Oregon. This railroad connected the commercial centers of Omaha, Nebraska, and Portland, Oregon, and created another transcontinental railroad. Railroad interests had completed the first transcontinental railroad in 1869 at Promontory Summit in northern Utah.

Parma's first business center.

The rail line, completed on November 17, 1884, angled in a northwesterly direction through what are now Pocatello, Mountain Home, Caldwell and Parma before turning north to Payette and Weiser and crossing the Snake River one final time before entering Huntington.
(*See The Region, Railroads.*)

Upon entering what is now Parma, the railroad built a siding next to the tracks. Recognizing a business opportunity, two entrepreneurs Frank and Al Fouch, acquired land next to the railroad siding and began construction of a general mercantile store.

Railroad officials deferred naming their siding to the Fouch brothers because they were in the process of applying for a post office housed in their store.

Water lifter pumps.

Musing about a possible name, Al Fouch held up a book he was reading about the Duke of Parma, Italy, and asked, "How about Parma, Idaho?" "Not bad," said

Frank, "short enough to suit the railroad, too … Ever hear of Parma Purple? … There is a lot of that color around here summer evenings, hills and sunsets. Then there is [Parmesan] cheese. Plenty of cows here. Maybe someday Parma, Idaho, will make cheese as good as Parma, Italy. Who knows?" With the name settled, they completed their successful application for the Parma Post Office.

In 1887 Howard Sebree purchased a farmer-owned irrigation canal system, Johnson's Ditch, which diverted water from the Boise River. Sebree expanded the irrigation system to serve many Parma area farms and in 1902 sold the expanded system to the water users. (*See The Region, Federal Lands – Private Ownership and Preservation Laws.*)

The Fouch brothers filed a plat for the Parma townsite in 1890. The town – which at that time consisted of Fouch's store, a blacksmith shop, saloons and residences – grew slowly.

That all changed in 1902 when E.M. Kirkpatrick moved to Parma and purchased and completed the Riverside Canal located south of town on the Roswell Bench. Concurrently, he promoted the virtues of the area to potential settlers in the Midwest where he persuaded about 50 families to come, settle the land and purchase irrigation water rights.

Kirkpatrick also developed a commercial district of retail stores that sold dry goods, implements, drugs, furniture, groceries and hardware. He built a bank and hotel and was instrumental in bringing electricity and telephone service to the community. The Hotel Illinois, completed in 1906, became the town's focal point. It had a display room where traveling salesmen showed their wares, a popular dining room and a veranda for summer concerts.

Parma Company.

Kirkpatrick died March 24, 1916, at the age of 46. The newspaper paid uncommon respect to him for his contributions to the city and his accomplishments, naming him the "daddy" of Parma.

Incorporation

On February 2, 1904, the community received County approval to incorporate the Village of Parma. By 1910 the town had a population of 338. On June 30, 1940, the town completed construction of a bond-financed City Hall. Prior to that time, Village Trustee meetings were held in the offices of the village attorney and city clerk.

On March 11, 1957, the community received approval to become an Idaho city of the second class. Ten years later, the legislature passed law eliminating village and class designations for incorporated municipalities – all were designated cities.

Turning Points

Railroad The coming of the railroad in 1883 is the reason Frank Fouch chose the location for a new town. When extensive irrigation systems came, the railroad played the critical role of transporting the farm and ranch commodities that

AgriLines Irrigation.

underpinned the area's economy. Notably in 1913 and 1914 Parma exhibitors won first place for a carload of hogs at the Portland Livestock Show.

Irrigation. While the railroad provided the catalyst for founding Parma, the diversion of Boise River water for irrigation and extensive canal systems serving the area's agricultural community sustained it.

Parma Water Lifter. Parma is home to an irrigation water pumping system called the Parma Water Lifter.

The idea of the water lifter originated with F.A. Powers, a local apiarist (beekeeper). Powers had made improvements to the pumps then in use and had been selling a few models that he had assembled in his shop.

As demand for his pumps increased, Powers enlisted the help of L.G. Rose, an innovative blacksmith who came to Parma in 1907, to manufacture the pumps. Rose came up with a patentable idea that greatly improved the pump's performance. The improved pump was a hit with water users. The Parma Company began manufacturing and marketing his innovation as the Parma Water Lifter.

The company split in 1980. The Parma Company continued the manufacturing side of the business. AgriLines Irrigation, Inc., took the sales and service side.

Parma Today

Amenities and Attractions The city has five parks. City Park features picnic tables and a children's playground including a small stream of water that runs through the middle of the park where kids can float small boats. The park is also the location of the city swimming pool and kiddies' pool built in 1959 by the Parma Lions Club.

Grove Street.

America's Park includes picnic tables, basketball courts, a children's playground and skateboard ramps.

Railroad and Centennial Parks are quiet shady rest areas with trees and benches.

Old Fort Boise Park is near the replica of the 1834 trading post that post manager Francois Payette named Fort Boise. This park has a covered picnic area, children's swings and slides, restrooms, horseshoe pits and RV camping spots. Two statues stand in Old Fort Boise Park – one of

Parma City Hall.

the courageous Marie Dorion and the other of the infamous legendary character known as Bigfoot, an estimated seven-foot-tall leader of a band of renegade Indians that terrorized immigrants and settlers from what is now Twin Falls to the mouth of the Boise River. The fort is open for tours Friday, Saturday and Sunday afternoons from June through August.

The replica of the original Fort Boise has a museum featuring an old schoolroom, cabin, Indian relics, antique farm equipment and information showing early life in Parma.

Each June, the community celebrates Old Fort Boise Days. The event includes a parade, a Lion's Club breakfast, a carnival at Old Fort Boise Park, a beauty pageant, art exhibits and a vintage automobile 'show and shine' display.

Each summer, the Parma Rod and Gun Club holds its annual sharpshooting contest. Sharpshooters from all over the country participate.

The Parma Motor-Vu is one of the few open-air drive-in theaters still operating in Idaho.

The library is an important learning attraction. It not only provides books and periodicals, but computers and programs to promote learning.

Religion has always been an important part of Parma life. There are 11 religious denominations in the city.

Nearby rivers and public lands provide excellent opportunities for outdoor enthusiasts. Parma residents can enjoy fishing, hunting, boating, camping, hiking and ATV and snowmobile riding within a short distance from the city. There are at least five sportsmen's access locations to the Boise and Snake Rivers within five miles of the city.

Economy and Major Employers The Parma School District has 150 employees and is the city's largest employer. J.C. Watson Company, a food processor, has a seasonal employment base that ranges from 50 to 100. Riverside, Inc., an electric motor repair and rewinding business, employs 50 people. The Parma Company employs around 45. AgriLines Irrigation, Inc., has about 30 employees. Giant Onion Produce has seasonal employment ranging between 30 and 160. During the year, Champion Produce has from 40 to 70 employees. The University of Idaho operates a 45-employee agricultural research station outside the city – primarily working with onions, potatoes, cereal grains, hops, corn, apples, grapes and forage. The city's commercial district includes several retail stores, restaurants, gas stations, a regional furniture store, two banks, service businesses and several small agricultural-based companies.

Education Parma School District operates elementary, middle and high schools in the city. The district has broken ground for a new gymnasium next to the high school.

There are several institutions of higher learning within an hour's drive of the city. The largest, Boise State University, is 42 miles southeast. The College of Idaho is in Caldwell, and Treasure Valley Community College is 22 miles northwest in Ontario, Oregon. Northwest Nazarene University is located 25 miles southeast in Nampa.

Health Care The closest hospital is West Valley Medical Center 16 miles southeast in Caldwell. There is also a hospital in Ontario. Parma has an assisted-living and senior center.

Transportation U.S. Highways 95 and 20 intersect the city. Interstate 84 is 13 miles east and 13 miles north of Parma.

The 2,700-foot runway at Parma Airport provides service to light private and charter aircraft. Private and charter services for heavier aircraft are available at the Caldwell Industrial Airport. The closest full-service commercial airport is in Boise.

Utilities and Services Private companies provide electricity, gas, cable, satellite and wireless services. The City provides water and sewer services and police and fire protection.

Old Fort Boise replica.

Vision for 2050

We believe the recent past is a harbinger of the future. During the last few years, the City built an improved water system with new water meters, new streetlights, sections of new sidewalks with handicap access, new benches on the sidewalks and crosswalk lights. We have a new high school, new classrooms at the elementary school and a high school gymnasium under construction. Local medical practitioners have built a new pharmacy and dental office.

Looking toward the next 40 years, we expect the population growth of around one percent annually to continue. By 2050 the city's population will likely exceed 3,000.

During this time, Parma will continue to support a thriving agriculture community as well as continued development of high-quality residential subdivisions such as Trail Ridge, whose second phase is half sold out.

Parma Elementary School.

Parma's excellent quality of life, affordable housing and close proximity to larger urban areas will attract new small businesses. In 2050 Parma will remain a peaceful, friendly community – a wonderful place to live and raise a family.

Mayors

1904 Fred Fisk *	1946 Irvin Powers *
1911 Dr. R.J. Cluen *	1941 James Prichard *
1913 W.E. Fisk *	1951 Gordon Dickerson *
1915 D.O. Castater *	1953 Don Tolmie *
1916 F.J. Walmsley *	1957 James Watson
1919 J.H. Sloan *	1961 Preston Seely
1923 A.H. Lang *	1964 Clyde Hill
1926 Dr. DeBrett *	1966 Fred Newman
1931 John Kuehhorg *	1974 Patricia Romanko
1934 Don Tolmie *	1996 Bob Flowers
1935 Wm. Boehringer *	2006 Margaret Watson
1939 N.E. Leigh *	2010 Craig Telford
1942 Florie Martin *	2014 Bob Flowers
1944 James McCreight *	2015 Nathan Leigh
1945 Afton Welch *	* Village Chairman

Looking southeast from the new Wilder water tower.

Wilder

Statistical Data

Population: 1,597 *

Elevation: 2,424 feet

Precipitation: 9 inches **

Average Snowfall: 14 inches **

County: Canyon

Website: www.cityofwilder.org

Temperature Range – Fahrenheit: **

Spring: 30 to 73

Summer: 50 to 92

Fall: 27 to 80

Winter: 19 to 44

* U.S. Census Bureau Estimates July 2015

**Historical averages

Located on a fertile high-desert plain on the western edge of Canyon County and surrounded by fields of onions, hops, seed corn, beans and seed alfalfa is the peaceful community of Wilder.

The Snake River flows three miles to the southwest, and the Boise River is five miles north.

Pre-Incorporation Years

For millennia, Wilder area was part of a vast inhospitable sagebrush-covered plain. American Indians and, later, trappers, explorers and Oregon Trail immigrants merely passed through. In the early 1900s with the prospect of irrigation water coming to the arid but fertile land, that all changed. (*See The Region, American*

Indians; Early Trappers/Explorers; and Oregon and California Trails.)

Staking a homestead claim on land in a temperate climate with fertile soil and plenty of irrigation water excited the passion of settlers anxious to reclaim the land so they could have a good quality of life for themselves and their families and lay the foundation for a new community that became Wilder. It started when Congress established the U.S. Reclamation Service – now U.S. Bureau of Reclamation – in 1902. (*See The Region, Federal Lands, Private Ownership and Preservation Laws.*)

Led by J.H. Lowell, residents successfully petitioned the Reclamation Service to build a reservoir and irrigation water system that would reclaim parched land in western Canyon County.

The reservoir was to be built over a natural depression called Deer Flat, 12 miles southeast of Wilder. The

Some of Wilder's early settlers.

Reclamation Service designed the reservoir to receive water diverted into the New York Canal from the higher elevations of the Boise River at Barber Dam, about 25 miles east. Construction of an earthen dam and a system of 46-to-74-foot-high dykes that created a reservoir about 10 miles long and two miles wide named Lake Lowell began in 1906. (*See The Region, Agriculture and Irrigation, Bureau of Reclamation – Boise Project – Treasure Valley.*)

The Reclamation Service also provided expertise and low-cost, long-term loans to the water users to develop a complex system of irrigation canals and ditches.

The settlers organized the "Water Users Association," a co-op that would be the legal entity which was the debtor on the loans; worked with the Reclamation Service in the construction of the canal system; owned the system and would repay the loans. Many of the water users were employed in the construction of the irrigation systems.

Boise River water began filling Lake Lowell in 1909. A year later, Lake Lowell irrigation water finally reached Wilder through the Golden Gate Canal. By then, many settlers had cleared and leveled their land and dug ditches to flood irrigate their farms and were awaiting the arrival of the water. Within a few years, the farmers had transformed the high desert into an agricultural oasis.

The Water Users Association developed the town site and sold lots, but there was no agreement on what to name the town. One group preferred "Golden Gate," suggesting the town was a gateway to Southwestern Idaho farmlands, and they had already applied the Golden Gate name to a canal, a school, a church and one or two businesses.

Others supported the name of "Wilder," after Marshall P. Wilder, publisher of The Delineator, a popular women's magazine, and a man whom many believed had railroad connections. Wilder offered to print a favorable article in his magazine if they named the village after him. Some residents speculated that if they named the town Wilder, their benefactor would use his considerable influence and money to promote the town.

In 1911 the Water Users Association put the matter to a vote. They voted to name their town Wilder; however, there is no record that M.P. Wilder ever gave anything to the town.

The same year, the Oregon Short Line Railroad extended a branch line to Wilder, a long-awaited transportation service that allowed easier access to distant markets, faster communication and better transportation.

A general store and school were the first buildings erected in the new community. The school also served as a civic center and a place for church services.

Soon, the city had a drugstore, two churches, a barbershop, a farm implement store, a hotel, a hardware store, a lumberyard and an Odd Fellows Hall.

By 1918 the Wilder Herald newspaper was publishing and the town had a telephone company, fire department, Masonic Lodge, Ladies Service Club and a library.

Wilder High School.

Residents of that period liked to point out an apparent curiosity in the diversity that existed among Wilder area residents. The town had seven churches and seven bars, but churchgoers outnumbered bar patrons.

For a brief time, one entrepreneur named Mr. Small extracted gravel from a 20-foot-deep mine with lateral tunnels dug under parts of Wilder. One known use of the gravel was construction of the concrete walls in the now historic Methodist Church. Unable to stay ahead of the groundwater seeping into the mine, he filled the mineshaft and quit the gravel-mining business.

Incorporation

On May 15, 1919, Wilder was incorporated as a village. The Canyon County Commission appointed the first board of trustees, and, a week later, Wilder began operations. In accordance with a change in state law, Wilder became a city in 1967.

Turning Points

Irrigation Water truly was the lifeblood of Wilder's economy. When irrigation reached the town in 1910, it further opened the area to settlement that transformed the high desert into productive farmland.

Railroad In 1884 the Oregon Short Line completed its main rail line which passed through Caldwell and connected the railheads at Granger, Wyoming, and Huntington, Oregon, creating another transcontinental railroad. Twenty-seven years later, it built a branch line to Wilder from Caldwell. The railroad transformed the new community's commerce and transportation.

Agriculture, Crop Innovation
The temperate climate, fertile soil and irrigation systems encouraged farmers to innovate with a variety of crops. In addition to alfalfa for hay, wheat and barley, farmers diversified their crop rotation to include potatoes, onions, corn, beans and alfalfa seed. Corn seed would also soon become a major farm crop.

Wilder water tower.

In 1934 following the repeal of prohibition, the family of former Idaho Governor Phil Batt – 1995 to 1999 – experimented with raising hops, which are used in the production of beer. Their successes led to Wilder becoming noted for its hops production.

SSI Food Services, Inc. In 1985 the predecessor to SSI Food Services, Inc., opened a specialty meats processing plant in the city, creating hundreds of jobs that had a major stabilizing effect on the city's economy – and it is still the city's largest employer.

Wilder Today

Amenities and Attractions The city has two parks. The landscaped downtown two-acre City Park has a community bathroom, gazebo, children's playground, swings, merry-go-round, a brick fireplace and electrical hookups. The smaller landscaped Memorial Park is dedicated to our Armed Forces.

The City History Museum is located in the old city jail.

The city's premier annual event is the Independence Day celebration each July 4th. It begins with a parade that ends in City Park where there are food vendors and entertainment that includes games, contests, children's rides and even a dunk tank where the mayor is usually a target. A local band provides music for dancing on the gazebo floor. The Wilder Chamber of Commerce gives door prizes throughout the day.

Lake Lowell is an excellent large and small mouth bass fishery that offers boat ramps and picnic facilities. The lake is part of the Deer Flat National Wildlife Refuge that also includes 110 miles of the Snake River and 86 islands. Hundreds of thousands of migratory birds and 180 different bird species inhabit the refuge.

Twelve miles northwest is the 1,300-acre Old Fort Boise Wildlife Management Area at the confluence of the Snake, Boise and Owyhee Rivers. The Roswell

Marsh Wildlife Habitat Area is located another five miles northwest. Both are run by the Idaho Department of Fish and Game and provide opportunities for viewing wildlife, hunting and fishing.

Hunting, hiking and camping are available within an hour's drive northeast in the Boise National Forest or south in the Owyhee Mountains. Whitewater rafting and kayaking are available on the Payette River east of Emmett. Downhill skiing is available 54 miles northeast at Bogus Basin Ski Resort.

Economy and Major Employers The city's business district includes a variety of retail, financial and service businesses.

The city's largest employer is SSI Food Services, Inc., a subsidiary of the privately held CTI Foods. SSI produces specialty meat and other processed food products and employs approximately 400.

The largest public employer is the Wilder School District with 60 employees.

Education The Wilder School District operates Wilder High School and Holmes Elementary and Middle Schools in the same complex.

The closest institutions of higher learning are the College of Idaho, 11 miles away in Caldwell; Northwest Nazarene University, in Nampa 19 miles away; Treasure Valley Community College, in Ontario, Oregon, 28 miles away; and Boise State University, 41 miles away in Boise.

Health Care West Valley Medical Center has a clinic next to the Wilder City Hall. The closest hospital is West Valley Medical Center in Caldwell.

Transportation U.S. Highway 95 passes through the city. Interstate 84 is 11 miles east.

The nearest airstrip for private aircraft is five miles south – a 2,900-foot runway in Homedale. Private and charter aircraft services are available within a 30-minute drive at the Caldwell and Nampa airports. The Boise Air Terminal (BOI) is about 40 miles east.

Railroad freight service is available in the city.

Utilities and Services Private companies provide electricity, telephone, natural gas, cable and satellite services. The City provides water and sewer services and fire and police protection. The County provides solid waste services.

Vision for 2050

In 2050 the population of Wilder will exceed 15,000. Part of this growth will be due to the spillover effect from fast-growing western Ada and eastern and northern Canyon Counties. Many people looking for a quiet community with affordable housing and an easy commute to work or to use technology to work at home will choose to come to Wilder.

Gazebo at the city park.

Growth will also come from new industry. The SSI Food Services site on the north side of the city will be the hub for an industrial park. Light industrial and manufacturing facilities, many tied to the city's agricultural roots, will develop along the railroad spur between Wilder and Greenleaf.

The city limits will reach south to Upper Pleasant Ridge Road, to Jack's Road on the north, toward the Snake River on the west and abut the boundaries of Greenleaf on the east.

Cities and counties in the Treasure Valley will have developed mass transit systems that connect all the cities in the valley. Wilder will have a parking garage near the center of town for local citizens to leave their vehicles while accessing the less expensive mass transit system.

The city will have two new parks – one to the west bordering the Snake River and the other on the north toward the Boise River.

School district patrons will vote to replace the old schools with three new schools built on 36 acres northwest of Wilder's original townsite. There will be a multi-level elementary school, a middle school and a separate high school. Additionally, Boise State University will provide college-level coursework through a Wilder satellite school.

The city of Wilder will continue expanding to serve the cultural, educational, employment and business needs of this peaceful rural community.

Mayors

1919 B.G. Davies *	1955 John W. Batt, Jr. *
1921 C.W. Lindsey *	1956 John W. Batt, Jr.
1923 W.N. Rhoads *	1958 Bull Durham
1925 R.L. Griffin *	1964 Carl Mayes
1930 W.N. Rhoads *	1968 Cy Hoadley
1931 W.W. Kreider *	1972 Link Noe
1935 F.H. Saunders *	1976 John Bechtel
1938 J.L. Jewell *	1982 Joe Tabor
1941 C.L. Davenport *	1988 Doug Amick
1941 F.H. Saunders *	2000 Steve Rhodes
1943 Charles Farley *	2004 John Bechtel
1948 Boyd Shoffer *	2016 Alicia Almazan
1951 Tom Smith *	* Village Chairman
1953 K.J. Elliott *	

CASSIA COUNTY

Historic Oakley home.

- Albion
- Burley (*County Seat*)
- Declo
- Malta
- Oakley

Albion sign.

Albion

Statistical Data

Population: 272 *
Elevation: 4,725 feet
Precipitation: 11 inches **
Average Snowfall: 13 inches **
County: Cassia
Website: www.albionvalley.com

Temperature Range – Fahrenheit: **
Spring: 30 to 70
Summer: 50 to 89
Fall: 27 to 77
Winter: 20 to 44
* U.S. Census Bureau Estimates July 2015
**Historical averages

Albion lies in a mountain basin on the southern edge of the fertile Snake River Plain 20 miles southeast of Burley. Originally called Marsh Basin, the area has abundant ground water, springs and wetlands that extended out from Marsh Creek.

The Cotterel Mountains lie east of the city, the Jim Sage Mountains start on the south and the beginning of the Albion Mountain Range forms the natural basin as it wraps around south and southwest of the city. These mountain ranges are part of the Sawtooth National Forest. They contain remarkable rock formations, high-mountain lakes, streams and mountain vistas that provide excellent hiking, camping, rock and mountain climbing, hunting and fishing.

Pre-Incorporation Years

Beginning around 1846 pioneers on their way to California separated from the

Oregon Trail and began a trail to the southwest called the California Trail. The California Trail proceeded through Marsh Valley over the pass at Conner Creek and on through to the City of Rocks.

In 1864 trappers came into the valley followed by prospectors who unsuccessfully combed the mountains for gold and silver.

R.N. Howell and his family came into the valley in 1868, built their home three miles south of whar is now Albion and filed the first recorded water right in the area. Howell Canyon, Road and Creek bear the family name.

Hagar's Store.

Other settlers gradually moved into the valley. One of these settlers was Colonel Rice L. Wood. As a young man and member of a California wagon train, Colonel Wood had passed through the valley 19 years earlier. In 1870 Wood returned and built his home on Howell Creek, about two miles west of Albion. Wood would later organize a 70-man militia to defend the valley from a threatened Indian attack led by Bannock Chief Buffalo Horn. However, the attack never materialized at this location.

In 1875 several more families came into the valley. They came up from Utah and almost immediately began homesteading and constructing irrigation systems. In 1877 Congress passed the Desert Land Act, which allowed ownership of up to 640 acres of land for anyone who reclaimed the land by irrigating it for three years. Many settlers took advantage of this new law.

Following completion of the transcontinental railroad in 1869 at Promontory, Utah, Marsh Basin became a stagecoach and freight wagon stop along the heavily traveled stage line between Utah and Oregon.

By 1878 Marsh Basin was the most populous town in the region. It had grown to include a hotel, a general store and several other businesses.

Church of Christ & Masonic Lodge #14.

In 1878 Marsh Basin was part of Owyhee County. However, the county seat was 250 miles west at Silver City – too great a distance for conducting government business. Local residents petitioned the Legislature to create a new county with Marsh Basin as the county seat.

In making this petition, the citizens believed their town needed a more attractive name. They decided to change the name of their town from Marsh Basin to Albion. The name Albion means white land and is the ancient name the Romans gave to Britain and its white chalk cliffs at Dover. Presumably, the residents were attracted to the poetic meaning of the name and its consistency with the white, snow-covered mountains that bordered the town.

Miller Hall on Albion Normal School campus.

On February 20, 1879, the Legislature approved creation of Cassia County with Albion as the county seat. William Vaughn donated five acres for a county courthouse and other public buildings.

At the time Albion became the county seat, several other events brought a sense of community and permanence to the new town. The Methodists and the Church of Jesus Christ of Latter-day Saints established their congregations. The Masons organized Masonic Lodge #14.

When Idaho became a state in 1890, the federal government gave grants of land and money. Josiah Miller, a state senator and local resident, was instrumental in passing legislation to create Albion State Normal School and make it a grant recipient. He also donated five acres with permanent water rights for the campus.

Other local residents donated $3,000. In 1894 the school opened in a new rock building with 23 students. Subsequently, the Idaho State Legislature appropriated money for campus buildings.

Incorporation

On January 18, 1895, Albion became an incorporated village.

Turning Points

County Seat After 40 years, Cassia County voters approved moving the seat to Burley from Albion in 1919. Burley, established in 1905 because of irrigation and the railroad, had a population that was substantially larger than Albion.

The loss of the county seat designation had a major adverse effect on the economy and prestige of Albion. County employees and businesses linked to county government moved to Burley or closed.

Albion State Normal School

Establishing Albion State Normal School in 1879, added an important dimension to the city's economy and status as an educational center. However, attracting students to this rural teachers college was a lingering problem.

In 1946 the Legislature commissioned a study of Idaho's entire higher education system. One of the study's recommendations was closure of the Albion school unless, within five years, enrollment reached specified thresholds. Within the next five years actions to save the school included changing the name to Southern Idaho College of Education and accrediting it as a four-year school.

However, by 1951 state officials determined the school could not meet the state's enrollment standards. After that year's commencement exercise, Governor Len B. Jordon closed the school and transferred responsibility to Idaho State College – now Idaho State University – in Pocatello.

In the fall of 1951 private interests took over and operated the facilities as a liberal arts school named the Magic Valley Christian College. However, sustained enrollment did not meet expectations either, and in 1969 it closed its doors.

Beginning in 1951 the city's population began falling as businesses and professionals moved to other cities and Albion's position as a "college town" ended. Since 1969 the campus facilities have remained largely vacant.

It is noteworthy that 6,640 teachers graduated during the school's existence. One of these graduates was Lava Hot Springs native, Terrell H. Bell. After serving in the Marines in World War II, Bell graduated from the school in 1946. From 1981 to 1984 Bell was U.S. Secretary of Education in the Reagan administration.

New Direction for Growth The city has adopted the motto, "Linked to the Past, Committed to the Future" and has begun a long-range revitalization program. Present accomplishments include renovating the Normal School's original rock building for a museum and building a new fire station, children's playground and park pavilions. Improvements to the domestic water system and preservation of historic buildings and sites are progressing.

Albion Today

Amenities and Attractions City Park is a popular site for picnics, family reunions and children's playgrounds. Albion elementary school grounds have outdoor basketball courts and a large grass area for playgrounds and ball fields.

The local women's club sponsors the city library, which includes over 9,000 volumes. The city's events center can accommodate group meetings with seating for up to 200.

The Albion Valley Players, a local amateur theater group, brings in audiences from a wide area by putting on plays with a historical flavor.

Albion Street.

Albion has several buildings on the National Historic Register. They include the Masonic Lodge, built in 1885; the buildings on the Albion State Normal School campus, established in 1893; and the D.L. Evans Bank, constructed in 1904.

Albion is the northeast gateway to the 49-mile City of Rocks Back Country Byway. The byway follows Idaho Highway 77 south from Albion to other roads in a horseshoe arch around the southern Albion Mountains and through the City of Rocks National Reserve and Castle Rocks State Park. It then proceeds back northwest to the historic city of Oakley.

The City of Rocks National Reserve, located 27 miles south of the city, has unique rock formations that bring mountain climbers and visitors from around the globe. These high massive granite rock pillars and hills are eroded remnants of a large batholith that erupted millions of years ago. Castle Rocks State Park is a 1,240-acre historic ranch that offers excellent rock climbing, horseback riding, bird watching and hiking. California Trail pioneers used the City of Rocks as a rest stop. Their markings are still visible among these huge granite outcroppings.

Each August, bicyclists participate in the "Mount Harrison Hillclimb." The course starts in Albion and proceeds four miles south on Highway 77 before turning right on the steep Howell Canyon Road. It passes through scenic vistas as it climbs nearly 5,000 feet for over 16.9 miles to Lake Cleveland and on to the summit of the 9,265-foot-high Mount Harrison.

Diamondfield Jack Scenic Byway and park signs.

Near the top of Mount Harrison and south of Howell Canyon Road is the 8,000-foot Pomerelle Mountain Resort. In the winter, the resort has three ski lifts, Nordic loops and 24 groomed downhill slopes.

Wildlife often comes into town. They include Mule deer, squirrels, rock chucks, fox, skunks, coyotes, pheasants, partridge, quail, sage grouse, Canadian geese, ducks, hawks, eagles and owls. The dominant vegetation is sagebrush, fescue and wheat grass; trees include evergreens, birch, maple, poplar, Russian olive, willow and juniper.

D.L. Evans Bank.

Economy and Major Employers The city has no dominant employers. Several retail and service businesses are located in the downtown area and along highway 77. These companies cater primarily to the tourist trade and the agriculture businesses in the area. The closest regional shopping area is in Burley.

The city offers a quiet, safe place to raise a family. The public appeal of the area's natural outdoor attractions is causing the tourism industry to take a leading role in the future growth of the city's economy.

Education Cassia County School District provides most primary and secondary education. An elementary school is located in Albion. Junior and senior high school students travel nine miles north to Declo.

The closest institution of higher learning is the College of Southern Idaho, located 56 miles northwest in Twin Falls.

Albion Park.

Health Care The nearest hospital is located in Burley.

Senior citizens meet weekly for meals served in one of the Albion Normal School campus buildings.

Transportation Idaho Highway 77 intersects the city. Interstate 86 lies 14 miles northwest on Highway 77.

Utilities and Services Private utilities provide electricity, telephone and cable services. The City provides water and sewer services. Marsh Creek, which runs through the city, is the source of the city's domestic and irrigation water.

Cassia County provides emergency response services. A City officer and the County Sheriff's Office provide law enforcement. The city has a volunteer fire department that operates out of a fully equipped four-bay fire station.

Vision for 2050

For the past four decades, Albion's population has averaged around 270. However, in future years the growing interest in tourism and outdoor recreation will be principal factors in causing the city's population to increase.

The growing popularity of the year-round Pomerelle Ski Resort and Recreation Area, the Mount Harrison and Lake Cleveland Recreation Areas, the silent

Albion Campus Retreat.

City of Rocks National Reserve and Castle Rock State Park will bring more visitors and businesses to the city.

Many visitors will come to see "Historic Albion," including the Albion State Normal School campus buildings, Cassia County's first courthouse and the Masonic Lodge.

Family and business groups will find Historic Albion and the events center, which can accommodate up to 200 people at banquets and reunions, attractive.

Other new residents will include those who want to live in the peaceful and affordable rural community of Albion and commute to nearby larger cities for work. Still others will use technology to perform most of their business electronically at home.

Albion's agricultural base will continue to be important to the city's economy. However, technological innovation and consolidation will continue to improve agricultural productivity with less labor, thus reducing the city's workforce. At the same time, businesses that promote alternative energy such as geothermal, solar and wind could find opportunities on the farms and public lands near Albion.

City and community leaders are strategically planning for growth. Their plan is to encourage business and residential growth that builds on the city's family-oriented attributes.

Growth issues under consideration are planning and zoning, centralized vs. decentralized water and sewer facilities, an improved water system, annexation, school facilities, sidewalks, curbs and gutters and diversification of business interests affecting the city's economy.

By 2050 Albion will have a significantly larger population. However, it will retain its rural beauty and charm. It will have a peaceful hometown feeling, surrounded by natural scenic beauty.

Mayors

1897	John T. Hansen *	1976	H.W. "Chris" Cagle
1903	Andrew Lounsbury *	1982	John Kay Powell
1915-1933	Unknown **	1986	James D. Kelley
1933	Joe Simonsen *	1990	Donald B. Danner
1954	Marvin Tremayne *	1998	James D. Kelley
1955	Curtis Mahoney *	2002	Donald B. Danner
1967	Curtis Mahoney	2006	Don H. Bowden
1969	Marvin Tremayne	2014	Sharon Hardy-Mills
1970	O'Deen Redman		* Village Chairman
1974	Douglas Mahoney		** 1915 - 1933 Records Destroyed by Fire
1976	Robert Bouck		

Burley

Statistical Data

Population: 10,480 *
Elevation: 4,165 feet
Precipitation: 9.7 inches **
Average Snowfall: 23.4 inches **
County: Cassia/Minidoka
Website: www.burleyidaho.org

Temperature Range – Fahrenheit: **
Spring: 30 to 70
Summer: 50 to 89
Fall: 27 to 77
Winter: 20 to 44
* U.S. Census Bureau Estimates July 2015
**Historical averages

Burley lies on the fertile Snake River Plain 20 miles downriver from Minidoka Dam. The dam diverts Snake River water to irrigate over 100,000 acres of farmland around Burley and several other Magic Valley communities. Fields of potatoes, beans, corn, grain, alfalfa hay and sugar beets, many irrigated from deep wells, surround the city with a patchwork of color and open space.

The Snake River flows through the city. The Cotterel Mountains, rising to over 7,000 feet, and the Sawtooth National Forest begin about 15 miles southeast.

Burley's incorporated borders are in two counties. The Snake River forms the border between Cassia and Minidoka Counties. The original city of Burley is in Cassia County, where it is the county seat. The newer part of the city, North Burley, is a commercial area located immediately across the Snake River in Minidoka County.

Pre-Incorporation Years

The City of Burley owes its origins to the Minidoka Hydroelectric Dam and the railroad.

The Bureau of Reclamation, under the 1902 Newlands Act, constructed the dam on the Snake River 20 miles northeast of the city at a place called "Little Rapids" or "Minidoka Rapids."
(*See Southwest Idaho – Cities of the Magic Valley.*)

Construction of the dam started in 1904 and was completed in 1906. In 1905 the railroad completed a bridge over the Snake River Canyon from Heyburn. In 1909 the dam began to produce electrical power for the area.

Burley depot.

The dam diverted water through a system of gravity-flow irrigation canals on both sides of the river. The north side was gravity flow; however, on the south side, which included Burley, the land was too high for the water to flow directly into the canals. Electrical pumps lifted the water into the south side canals.

The public demand for homestead land in the Minidoka Project service area outstripped expectations. On April 23, 1904, the project received approval and homesteaders began filing on the land. The settlers filed to secure their farmland even though they knew there would be no water or power for a few years.

On December 23, 1904, the Twin Falls News reported, "Farm houses on the Minidoka tract ... are still going up like mushrooms, upwards of 300 already having been erected." By the spring of 1905 homesteaders had filed on most of the project land on both sides of the river.

The Reclamation Service had set aside land for three town sites on the north side of the river but had not provided for a town site on the south side.

Ira B. Perrine, the lead developer responsible for the Milner Dam Twin Falls Project, and four other investors filled the void. They formed a town site company to acquire the land, plat the village and sell lots. The townsite company purchased land owned by Josiah E. Miller and laid out a one-square-mile town site. They then surveyed and platted the town into business and residential districts with tracts set aside for schools and churches.

They named the new village after David E. Burley, an Oregon Short Line Railroad passenger agent who promoted the area.

An early resident, C.A. Johnson, recalled the layout of Overland Street as two parallel rows of stakes running north to south for one mile. Main Street had a similar thoroughfare. In the center of town, they cleared the streets of sagebrush. Johnson said that except for the cleared streets and the land around the lot sales office and the house used by the surveyors, "the town site was a sea of sagebrush."

The townsite company drilled a well near the intersection of Main and Overland Streets. A sign on the well tower proclaimed Burley would have 10,000 people in 1910. As it turned out, the prediction was excessively optimistic. The 1910 census recorded Burley's population at 900. However, by 1918 the city's population approximated 2,500.

Burley, 1908.

On May 23, 1905, with hundreds of railroad workers still laying ties and rails, the first train pulled into town.

Several weeks later, the editor of *The Nugget* in Silver City visited Burley. He wrote in his newspaper, "The first lot in town was sold May 1 (1904) and the construction of the first building begun the same day. Now, there is a hotel, several stores, three lumberyards, an established newspaper

Horse-drawn carts. Note water tower in background with "Burley 10,000 people in 1910" on it.

and several dwellings there, the number of structures counting at least 50. The newspaper, the *Burley Bulletin*, is still issued from a tent but has a large, two-story home nearly completed. The streets of the town are not yet well defined, only being partly cleared of their sagebrush."

Within eight months, Burley had a population approaching 400, over 100 buildings and nearly two miles of boardwalk. Ed F. Schroeder, an early resident, wrote that the boardwalks were a blessing as continuous travel of wagons, buggies and horses turned the streets into ankle deep dust – or mud when it rained.

On September 4, 1906, the opera house caught fire and spread to other buildings. Schroeder wrote, "This fire destroyed about 20 buildings – but they were soon rebuilt or replaced by others – and Burley continued to grow."

By the fall of 1905, townspeople had erected a three-room frame school building on the northwest corner of Normal Avenue and Main Street. It started with 96 students and three teachers. There were two classes for grades 1 through 4 and one class for grades 5 through 8.

Incorporation

On July 23, 1909, Burley became an incorporated village. The need for a municipal government became evident a few months earlier when a thief robbed one of the stores. Residents identified the thief, but when the citizens sought to bring the culprit to justice, it was not clear who could make the arrest. Burley had no police officer. They got the job done; but the experience exposed a weakness. The people had been so busy developing their

Southern Idaho Review Building.

businesses, homes and farms that they had neglected to establish a local government.

In 1915 three years before voters moved the county seat from Albion to Burley, the population increased sufficiently to become an incorporated city.

Turning Points

Minidoka Hydroelectric Dam and the Railroad
Two events – the construction of the Minidoka Hydroelectric Dam and the coming of the railroad – combined to make possible the founding of Burley. The dam provided the irrigation water and

Burley, 1950s.

electrical power needed to transform the desert into an economic oasis of fertile farms and ranches. The railroad provided the transportation system that allowed commerce to flourish.

Electricity The first priority for electrical energy produced by the Minidoka

Dam was to lift irrigation water into the southern canal systems. Excess electrical energy went to the cities, farms and ranches.

Electrical transmission lines reached Burley in the fall of 1910. Burley voters approved bond issues that financed its own electric distribution system and allowed the City to contract directly with the Reclamation Service for its electricity. In the winter, the irrigation pumps did not run. Then, the cost of electric heat was less than coal.

By 1913 Burley had electric streetlights. Homes and businesses were also purchasing electric heating and lighting systems as well as powering an increasing number of electric appliances coming on the market.

A 1915 issue of Harpers magazine featured the Burley and Rupert high schools in an article about the use of electric stoves in classroom science classes.

Street in Burley.

Water System In 1913 the city built a 100,000 gallon, 150-foot-high water tower to pressurize its municipal water system, which pumped water from a deep well. Irrigation water for lawns and gardens flowed through a system of ditches that paralleled the tree-lined streets and sidewalks.

Snake River Bridge The Snake River was a barrier to travel and commerce. In 1906 a Mr. Verburg sunk pilings into the river bottom upstream near Heyburn and constructed a toll bridge. Foot traffic often avoided the toll bridge and walked across the railroad bridge.

However, Burley leaders wanted a bridge that extended Overland Avenue north across the river, connecting with the road to Paul. Burley farmers and businesses pledged $6,500 toward construction costs if the State Legislature approved the bridge. This Burley-Paul bridge idea generated controversy between Heyburn and Burley. Heyburn residents feared road traffic would move from the Heyburn Toll Bridge to the free bridge at Burley and their economy would suffer.

The conflict was resolved when the Legislature appropriated sufficient money to build the new Burley Bridge, purchase the Heyburn Bridge and remove the toll.

Medical Care In 1907 Dr. Joseph Fremstad, a physician and surgeon who practiced in the Eastern United States, arrived in Burley. He was in failing health and told his Eastern friends that there was no cure for his ailment. He was going West to die. Instead of dying, he practiced medicine in Burley for decades. He started Burley's first drugstore, and in 1917 established the Fremstad Hospital, registered by the state and recognized nationally.

Agriculture A series of innovations and events had a gradual yet cumulatively profound effect on improving farm productivity with a fraction of the labor cost. The innovations included pumping water from deep wells, sprinkler irrigation, development of commercial fertilizers, certified seed, and development of more efficient farm equipment, improved farming practices, farm consolidation and bringing more land under private ownership and cultivation. In Cassia County, land under cultivation increased from 287,175 acres in 1940 to 645,568 acres in 1959.

These innovations and events had a direct effect on the city's economy. The loss of farm jobs reduced the customer base for the city's businesses. More land under cultivation had a positive effect on the city's economy.

Food Processing
Food processing businesses in Burley served as an economic stimulus to the city when they operated and had a depressive effect as equipment innovations eliminated jobs or the plants closed.

The Burley Flour Mill started in 1909 and later modified its milling equipment to produce refined flours.

Winter in Burley.

Until 1970 when it closed, the mill had sales contracts with national bakeries and groceries – including Procter and Gamble, Continental Baking, Keebler and Safeway.

U&I Sugar built a factory in Burley that operated for several years. Due to cost efficiency and competing cash crops grown by farmers, the factory closed.

Amalgamated Sugar continues to operate sugar factories in Paul and Twin Falls.

As World War II broke out, the military needed large quantities of dehydrated potatoes. J.R. Simplot received contracts from the military to process potatoes. In 1943 he purchased the Rogers Brothers Seed Company's potato flour plant in Burley and expanded its operation.

Potato processing expanded again when a Simplot employee invented the frozen French fry in Caldwell. Other companies began their own potato processing plants. Idaho Processing Company built a plant in Burley to produce frozen French fries and appetizers. In 1960 Ore-Ida Foods also built a potato processing plant and two warehouses in the city.

These businesses have experienced changes in ownership; however, most of these changes had little economic effect on the city. For example, Ore-Ida Foods purchased Idaho Processing Company; H.J. Heinz purchased Ore-Ida Foods; McCain Foods purchased Heinz's frozen foods division, which included the Burley facility. The McCain plant continues as Burley's largest private employer.

Annexation into Minidoka County Following completion of the Burley-Paul Road, the bridge across the Snake River Canyon and the I-84 interchange, retail business around the interchange grew rapidly and began to fill in along Highway 27 between the mile of land separating I-84, the river and the City of Burley.

About the same time, business interests representing the seven cities in Cassia County and the five cities in Minidoka County formed the Mini-Cassia Chamber of Commerce. With cooperation between the two counties and the cities, they formed the North Burley bi-county economic development zone. They determined that by working together, they would be a more effective force in promoting economic development.

As North Burley developed, the hospitality and retail businesses developing around the freeway interchange sought city services. Burley was the closest city to the interchange, and Minidoka County granted Burley authority to annex what is now North Burley.

Aerial view of Burley.

With the recent construction of the Burley Mall in the annexed area, North Burley now rivals downtown Burley as an important motel and retail shopping area.

Burley Today

Amenities and Attractions Burley has 19 city parks covering a total area of 190 acres. East, Freedom and West Parks are the most popular.

The Cassia County Historical Society and Museum offer exhibits that include a pioneer village, displays of vintage farm equipment and a stagecoach and railroad car.

The Snake River and the nearby Sawtooth National Forest offer boating, fishing, hunting, hiking and other amenities. Pomerelle Ski Resort is about 20 miles south of the city near Albion. Its 8,000 foot elevation has an average snowfall of 500 inches. The resort has 24 groomed trails and 3 chairlifts. The City of Rocks National Reserve, located 45 miles south of the city, has unique rock formations, some as tall as 60 stories. Mountain climbers and visitors from around the globe visit the reserve. These high massive granite rock pillars and hills are eroded remnants of a large batholith that erupted millions of years ago.

Near the National Reserve is Castle Rocks State Park, a 1,240-acre historic ranch offering excellent rock climbing, horseback riding, bird watching and hiking. California Trail pioneers used the City of Rocks as a rest stop. Their markings are still visible among these huge granite outcroppings. Oregon Trail wagon ruts are located 11 miles west.

Economy and Major Employers McCain Foods, a food processing company with operations across the U.S. and Canada, is the city's largest employer with over 1,050 employees. The company produces frozen French fries and appetizers at its Burley plant. Other large employers include the Cassia Regional Medical Center with 380 doctors, nurses and support personnel. The Boise Corporation, a manufacturer of cardboard boxes, employs 120. Gossner Foods, a Swiss cheese manufacturing plant located in the Mini-Cassia Industrial Park between Burley and the City of Heyburn, is another major employer. The largest public employers are the Cassia Public School District with 550 employees and Cassia County with 120.

In addition, the city's retail, financial, hospitality and service businesses collectively employ a large number of Burley citizens.

Education The Cassia County School District provides most of the city's elementary and secondary education. Within the city, the district operates three elementary schools, junior and senior high schools, an alternative high school, a regional professional/technical center and a newcomer center. Students in North Burley attend schools in the Minidoka School District. The city also has two private schools offering K-12 education. The closest institution of higher learning is the College of Southern Idaho, 40 miles west in Twin Falls.

Health Care Cassia Regional Medical Center has 25 beds and provides most of the medical care needed in the city. In addition, there are several private medical clinics and specialists.

Transportation U.S. Highway 30 and Idaho Highways 27 and 81, to Declo and Malta and connecting with Highway 77 to Albion, intersect the city. Interstate 84 lies on the city's northern edge.

Burley Municipal Airport provides service for light private and charter aircraft.

Joslin Field-Magic Valley Regional Airport in Twin Falls is the closest airport providing service for heavy aircraft. Railroad service is available for freight.

Utilities and Services Private companies provide electricity, telephone, gas, cable and satellite services. The City provides sewer and water services and fire and police protection.

Vision for 2050

Over the 30 year period from 1970 to 2000, Burley's population grew from 8,279 to 9,316 or 13 percent. Since 2000 the city's population has remained somewhat constant.

However, city and community leaders and investors are taking actions that will likely change the historical flat-line trends to that of one to two percent annual population growth. By 2050 the city's population will likely exceed 15,000.

The most prominent of these actions, annexation of the area north of the river, now known as North Burley is still developing. The annexation of North Burley established Burley as a gateway to the many outdoor amenities and tourist attractions in the Sawtooth National Forest, the City of Rocks National Reserve and Castle Rocks State Park. North Burley will continue to have most of the city's commercial growth. It will have a major economic impact on the economy of the city and the Mini-Cassia area.

Expansion and improvements to the city's municipal systems and services will be required over the next 40 years; however, city leaders will seek to allocate those costs proportionately to the residents and businesses.

Mayors

** Unknown
1998 Douglas Manning
2002 Jon Anderson

2010 Terry Greenman
2014 Merlin Smedley

Declo

Statistical Data

Population: 352 *
Elevation: 4,219 feet
Precipitation: 9.7 inches **
Average Snowfall: 23.4 inches **
County: Cassia

Temperature Range – Fahrenheit: **
Spring: 30 to 70
Summer: 50 to 89
Fall: 27 to 77
Winter: 20 to 44
* U.S. Census Bureau Estimates July 2015
**Historical averages

Declo lies on the fertile Snake River Plain 20 miles downriver from the Minidoka Dam. The dam diverts Snake River water to irrigate over 100,000 acres of farmland around Declo, Burley and several other Magic Valley communities. Fields of potatoes, beans, corn, grain, alfalfa and sugar beets – many irrigated from deep wells – surround the city with a patchwork of color and open space.

The Snake River flows near the city. The Albion Mountains, rising to over 7,000 feet, and the Sawtooth National Forest begin about eight miles south. Burley is eight miles west.

Pre-Incorporation Years

The community of Declo is a product of the agricultural development that followed construction of the Minidoka Hydroelectric Dam and the railroad.

The U.S. Reclamation Service – now the Bureau of Reclamation – built the Minidoka Dam under the 1902 Newlands Act. It constructed the dam on the Snake River 12 miles northeast of the city at a place called Little Rapids or Minidoka Rapids. (*See The Region, Agriculture and Irrigation – Bureau of Reclamation – Minidoka Project – Magic Valley.*)

Construction of the dam started in 1904 and was completed in 1906. In 1905 the Minidoka and Southwestern Railroad Company, later acquired by the Oregon Short Line Railroad (OSL), built a line between the OSL main line at Minidoka and Buhl. Their line included building the bridge over the Snake River Canyon 10 miles west of Declo near Heyburn. Four years later, the dam began to produce electrical power for the area.

The Minidoka and Southwestern Railroad Company, formed in 1904, built branch lines from the main Oregon Short Line railroad to several Magic Valley communities. The railroad sought to serve the huge agriculture market created by the availability of irrigation water. The railroad reached Heyburn in 1907 and played a critical role in the development of that city.

The dam diverted water through a system of irrigation canals on both sides of the river. On the south side, which included the future town of Declo, the land was too high for the water to flow directly into the canals. Electrical pumping stations lifted the water into an elevated part of the south-side gravity flow canal system.

The public demand for homestead land in the Minidoka Project area outstripped expectations. On April 23, 1904, the project was approved and homesteaders began filing on the land even though water and power would not be available for a few years.

The Twin Falls News reported on December 23, 1904, "Farm houses on the Minidoka tract...are still going up like mushrooms, upwards of 300 already having been erected." By the spring of 1905 homesteaders had filed on most of the project land on both sides of the river.

The Reclamation Service had set aside land for three town sites on the north side of the river but had not provided for a town site on the south side until, as part of the Minidoka Project in 1909 and 1910, they platted a town named Marshfield after nearby Marsh Creek.

The work of transforming the arid land into an agricultural oasis was arduous. In preparing for the life-giving irrigation water, the settlers cleared the sagebrush by dragging an iron railroad rail between two teams of horses. Then they had to level the land so it could be flood irrigated. They built and maintained irrigation ditches that moved the water from the canals to the fields which had to be plowed, harrowed, leveled, diked and planted. As soon as the plants emerged from the ground they had to shift their attention to protecting their crops from hoards of jackrabbits, grasshoppers, crickets and foraging wild game. (*See The Region, Agriculture and Irrigation – Fighting the Jackrabbit Menace.*)

The parents of two-year-old J.R. "Jack" Simplot, the future Idaho agricultural magnate, traded their home in Burley for an 80-acre farm in Marshfield in 1911. At that time, the farm had a one-room, dirt-roof cabin and was only partially cleared of sagebrush.

The Simplots built a home on the farm and purchased an adjoining 40-acre parcel that bordered Marsh Creek and included marshland that teamed with wildlife. That 40 acres would become the property on which young, eighth-grade educated Jack Simplot would launch a hog-raising business – the first in a long list of entrepreneurial ventures that would grow into a multi-billion-dollar empire and have a profound positive effect on the economy of Idaho and the world.

Three pelicans flying near Declo.

Incorporation

On January 12, 1920, Marshfield became an incorporated village. However, when the citizens applied for a post office, postal authorities denied their request. The Marshfield name was either too long or too common. If they wanted a post office, they would have to come up with a different name. Unable to reach agreement, the name-change committee decided to wait at the general store, take the first letter of the last name of the next five persons coming through the door and organize the letters into the town's new name. The first five people were Dethlefs, Engstrom, Cooley, Lewis and Olsen. They constructed and approved the name of "DECLO." It was truly a community name.

Turning Points

Minidoka Hydroelectric Dam and Railroad The dam provided the irrigation water that opened the arable land around Declo to development. The railroad came close enough to Declo to provide the transportation of freight, mail and passengers needed to support the growing community.

This almost magical transformation of the western Snake River Plain from a barren sagebrush-covered terrain to an agricultural oasis prompted R.S. Tofflemire, publisher of the Twin Falls News, to coin the term "Magic Valley" to describe the productive region.

Declo Today

Amenities and Attractions Declo has two city parks primarily used for picnics and family gatherings.

The city's most important attribute is a strong community spirit. When there is a need, the community pulls together to get the job done. After several years of needing a new fire station and better accommodations for the city hall and the city's public library which was housed in the front of a local butcher shop, the community came together to make the dream a reality. The city now has a new fire station which also houses the city hall. The old city hall building is now the public library.

Each year on the second Saturday in July the town celebrates Declo Days. Activities include an alumni breakfast, a parade, a flag-raising program, games, a barbeque lunch provided by the Lions Club and a gymkhana. The high school homecoming day becomes a community event in September with a parade and tailgate party before the football game. In December, it is "Christmas in the Declo Skies" including a chili supper and fireworks.

The Snake River and the nearby Sawtooth National Forest offer boating, fishing, hunting, hiking and other activities.

Pomerelle Ski Resort is about 20 miles south of the city near Albion. Its 8,000-foot elevation has an average snowfall of 500 inches, one of the heaviest in Idaho. The resort has 24 groomed trails and three chairlifts.

The City of Rocks National Reserve, 45 miles south of the city, has unique rock formations, some reaching 60 stories. Mountain climbers and visitors from around the globe visit the reserve. These high massive granite rock pillars are eroded remnants of a large batholith that erupted millions of years ago.

Near the national reserve is Castle Rocks State Park – a 1,240-acre historic ranch that offers excellent rock climbing, horseback riding, bird watching and hiking. California Trail pioneers used the City of Rocks as a rest stop. Their markings are still visible among these huge granite outcroppings. Oregon Trail wagon ruts can still be seen 11 miles west.

Economy and Major Employers The Cassia County School District employs about 80 people in its Declo schools and is the city's largest employer. The Declo business community consists of a convenience store and gas station. The majority of the city's residents do their shopping in Burley or 40 miles west in Twin Falls.

Education The Cassia County School District, headquartered in Burley, operates elementary, junior and senior high schools in the city. The closest institution of higher learning is the College of Southern Idaho in Twin Falls.

Health Care The Minidoka Memorial Hospital in Rupert and the Cassia Regional Medical Center in Burley provide for most of the city's medical care needs. There are also several private medical clinics and specialists in Burley.

Transportation Idaho Highway 77 intersects the city, connecting it with Interstate 84 four miles north and the City of Rocks 45 miles south.

The east-west segment of Idaho Highway 81 west to Burley and south to Malta and the Idaho/Utah border also intersects the city.

Utilities and Services Private companies provide electricity, telephone and satellite services. The City provides water, sewer and solid waste pick-up services. The Declo Volunteer Fire and EMT Department provides fire and emergency protection services. The Cassia County Sheriff's Office provides police protection under contract with the City.

Vision for 2050

In 2050 we envision Declo to still be a farming community. We do not see large industries and employers coming to the city. However, we do see an increase in population. Many families seeking a more rural atmosphere to raise their children and affordable housing will choose to live in Declo and commute to nearby cities for work. These families will live in a few new, small residential housing developments that will come. Schools will continue to grow in enrollment, necessitating new junior high and elementary schools.

The City will upgrade and continue to provide quality municipal services such as sewer and water. The new Free Public Library will have expanded into a viable and important community service. As the growth continues, a few small service businesses such as a grocery store; cafes; and, perhaps, a doctor's office – will come to Declo.

Declo will continue to be a safe, secure and singular place to live. Children will continue to thrive and the community will still be encouraging and nurturing all of its inhabitants.

Mayors

1920	Sam Gillette *	1962	George Shrenk *
1936	M.N. Gillette *	1976	Jones Leonard
1947	C.W. Vallette *	1988	Jay Darrington
1961	Thomas W. Matthews *		* Village Chairman

Site of pioneer water-powered flour mill. Established 1887 to 1907 by John and Jones Chatburn—the first roller mill in Southern Idaho.

Malta

Statistical Data

Population: 199 *
Elevation: 4,525 feet
Precipitation: 9.7 inches **
Average Snowfall: 23.4 inches **
County: Cassia

Temperature Range – Fahrenheit: **
Spring: 27 to 69
Summer: 44 to 88
Fall: 24 to 76
Winter: 17 to 42

* U.S. Census Bureau Estimates July 2015
**Historical averages

Malta is a small farming community on the western edge of the Raft River Valley, 25 miles north of the Idaho/Utah border. The Sawtooth National Forest borders the valley on both the east and west. On the west, mountain peaks rise to over 9,000 feet, punctuating the city's sunsets. About 12 miles across the valley to the east, the Sublett and Black Pine Mountain Ranges outline the eastern skyline.

Malta area.

About 25 miles southwest, beyond the Jim Sage Mountain Range, is the City of Rocks National Reserve and Castle Rocks State Park. Burley is situated 26 miles northwest.

Pre-Incorporation Years

In the years following the discovery of gold in California in 1847, a virtual thoroughfare of wagon trains left the Oregon Trail west of Soda Springs on two principal cutoffs to California. Both cutoffs – Lander Road from the northeast and Hudspeth from the east – converged to the southwest of what is now Malta before continuing southwest to the City of Rocks and then on through the northwestern corner of Nevada to California.

Both trails crossed the Raft River, which in those years was swift, muddy and deep, particularly during the time of early spring and summer snowmelt. Today, irrigation diversions have left a near-dry riverbed.

From 1847 to 1860 an estimated 200,000 people traveled the California Trail. (*See Oregon and California Trails.*)

Field near Malta.

Settlers first came to Malta in the late 1800s. Most of them were homesteaders seeking to establish ranching operations where there was plenty of open range and native grasses for their livestock to graze. The early farmers dry-farmed or irrigated their crops by diverting water from mountain streams and the Raft River.

The irrigation water from the Minidoka Hydroelectric Dam, constructed in 1906 by the Bureau of Reclamation, did not directly benefit Malta farmers and ranchers. However, the electricity produced by the dam and other sources eventually allowed Malta farmers to pump irrigation water from deep wells onto their crops.

Raft River geothermal project near Malta.

The Oregon Short Line Railroad, completing a bridge over the Snake River Canyon from Heyburn through Burley and cities to the west in 1905, was also important to Malta area farmers, ranchers, businesses and citizens because it brought them accessible transportation. (*See Southwestern Idaho – Cities of the Magic Valley.*)

The town gives credit to Julia Ada (Addie) Condit, its first postmistress for naming the city. In 1883 Addie successfully made application to postal authorities for a post office she named "Malta." As future mail addresses bore the name of Malta, the town took on the same name. There is no record of why Addie chose the name; however, those who knew her speculate that the high valley grasses waving in the wind were reminiscent of the waves of the Mediterranean Sea surrounding the island country of Malta.

Incorporation

On August 18, 1958, Malta became an incorporated village and then a city in 1967 in conformity with the new state law.

Turning Points

Minidoka Hydroelectric Dam. The Minidoka Dam did not provide water to Malta area farms but it did provide needed electricity.

Railroad The extensive farming activity in the Magic Valley that followed construction of Milner Dam in 1905 and Minidoka Dam in 1906 provided the economic base that attracted the railroad to the area. Even though the railroad did not reach Malta, it came close enough to make railroad transportation accessible to the city and the surrounding agricultural community.

Traffic jam, Malta style.

Malta Today

Amenities and Attractions Malta has a park with a covered eating area, a ball field and a playground.

Each July, Malta celebrates Independence Day with games and a meal followed by fireworks.

September marks the city's homecoming celebration.

Each March Malta hosts the Power Company's annual meeting.

The City of Rocks National Reserve and the 49-mile City of Rocks Back Country Byway are located several miles south of the city. The reserve has unique rock formations, some reaching 60 stories tall. Mountain climbers and tourists from around the globe visit the reserve. These high massive granite rock pillars and hills are eroded remnants of a large batholith that erupted millions of years ago.

Near the National Reserve, located 18 miles south, is Castle Rocks State Park. It is a 1,240-acre historic ranch that offers excellent rock climbing, horseback riding, bird watching and hiking. California Trail pioneers used the City of Rocks as a rest stop. Their markings are still visible among these huge granite outcroppings. Oregon Trail wagon ruts are still visible in the area.

The City of Rocks Back Country Byway can be accessed about seven miles west of Malta on Idaho Highway 77. This scenic byway parallels part of the California Trail as it passes through the unincorporated towns of Elba and Almo and wraps around the base of the Albion Mountain Range and the City of Rocks National Reserve.

Pomerelle Ski Resort is about 20 miles southwest of the city near Albion. Its 8,000-foot elevation has an average snowfall of 500 inches. The resort has 24 groomed trails and 3 chairlifts.

The Snake River and the nearby Sawtooth National Forest offer boating, fishing, hunting, hiking and other amenities.

Economy and Major Employers With 22 employees at its Raft River Elementary, Junior High and High Schools, the Cassia County School District is the city's largest employer. Raft River Electric Coop is the next largest employer.

Raft River High School.

The city's business community consists of gasoline stations, convenience and grocery stores and a cafe. City residents do most of their shopping in Burley.

Education The Cassia County School District, headquartered in Burley, operates elementary, junior and senior high schools in the city.

The closest institution of higher learning is the College of Southern Idaho 75 miles west in Twin Falls.

Health Care The closest hospital is the Cassia Regional Medical Center in Burley. There are also several private medical clinics and specialists in Burley.

Malta Fuel Depot.

Transportation Idaho Highway 81 intersects the city. About 35 miles north, it connects the city with Interstate 84.

Idaho Highway 77 extends west of the city to the City of Rocks National Reserve, Castle Rocks State Park and the City of Rocks Backcountry Byway.

Utilities and Services Private companies provide electricity, telephone and satellite services. The city's homes and businesses are on individual wells and septic systems. The Raft River Fire and EMT Department provides fire and emergency protection services. The Cassia County Sheriff's Office provides police protection under contract with the City.

Vision for 2050

Malta's population has remained somewhat constant for the past 50 years. Historical trends will likely continue.

However, U.S. Geothermal Inc is opening its Raft River Geothermal Project near Malta. This effort is follow-up on research performed by the U.S. Department of Energy wherein they drilled wells to depths from 4,500 to 6,000 feet and found large water reserves at temperatures ranging from 275 to 300 degrees Fahrenheit. This project has the potential of producing commercial amounts of electricity. Should this project prove successful, it could have a significant effect on the city's economy.

By 2050 absent any expansion of the Raft River Geothermal Project, Malta will continue to be a small agricultural community near the high mountains of the Sawtooth National Forest. Fertile fields of potatoes, sugar beets, wheat, alfalfa hay and pasture where dairy cows and other livestock graze will still surround the city. The planned improvements to the city – including a public library, a new children's playground at the park and sidewalks and curbs downtown – will be a reality. Malta will continue to be a wonderful place to live and raise a family.

Alpaca at the petting zoo.

Mayors

1958 A.E. Nicholsen *	2000 Randy Briggs
1961 Wayne Whitaker *	2003 Tina Loock
1966 Wallace Briggs	2016 Gary Bake
1980 Brent Udy	* Village Chairman
1985 Bud Tracy	

Oakley's historic Main Street.

Oakley

Statistical Data

Population: 790 *
Elevation: 4,584 feet
Precipitation: 12 inches **
Average Snowfall: 31 inches **
County: Cassia

Temperature Range – Fahrenheit: **
Spring: 28 to 67
Summer: 45 to 83
Fall: 27 to 74
Winter: 19 to 43
* U.S. Census Bureau Estimates July 2015
**Historical averages

Oakley is located in a beautiful high-desert valley named Goose Creek. Irrigated farms with lush fields of potatoes, wheat, barley and alfalfa surround the city. The Sawtooth National Forest borders the valley on the east and west.

The Albion Mountain Range, which rises to over 10,000 feet, is on the east. To the southwest, mountains rise to over 8,000 feet. Fifteen miles to the southeast are the City of Rocks National Reserve and Castle Rocks State Park. The city of Burley is 21 miles north.

Pre-Incorporation Years

For centuries, American Indians – primarily of the Shoshone and Bannock Tribes – migrated through what is now Oakley. In the early 1800s trappers/explorers traveled the land around the nearby Snake River and its tributaries in search of beaver pelts.

In 1834 the Hudson's Bay Company built Fort Hall, a trading post just north of what is now of Pocatello.

In 1841 the first overland immigrant wagon train to Oregon passed through Fort

Hall before turning northwest toward the original Fort Boise near what is now Parma. This was the beginning of the Oregon Trail.

In 1843 Joseph Walker led an immigrant wagon train to California. Walker's wagon train turned off the Oregon Trail at Fort Hall and traveled southwest to the City of Rocks before proceeding on to California. The trail that the Walker party blazed became the California Trail.

During the period of the California gold rush, 1849 to 1860, an estimated 200,000 immigrants passed through the City of Rocks on the California Trail – five times as many as traveled the Oregon Trail.

In 1862 prospectors discovered gold in the Boise Basin. The next year 16,000 people converged on the Boise Basin gold fields. For several years, the Malad Valley – 80 miles east of Oakley – became the principal corridor for freight and passenger wagons between Utah and Boise.

Old train depot, now a home.

In 1869 the Transcontinental Railroad connected at Promontory Point at the north end of the Great Salt Lake. The town of Kelton, Utah – now a ghost town located about 40 miles southeast of Oakley – became a train depot for transferring freight and passengers between the railroad and the freight wagons and stagecoaches headed north.

In the same year, John Halley opened a stagecoach route from Kelton to Boise and beyond. The road, called Kelton Road, passed to the west of the City of Rocks, north through what is now Oakley, then northwest to Rock Springs near what is now Twin Falls and on to Boise.

In 1870 Halley opened a stagecoach station near what is now

Old cheese factory, now a home.

Oakley and employed a man named William Oakley as station manager.

At the time Halley opened his station, ranchers from Texas and Colorado began bringing herds of cattle into the valley to graze in the meadows and foothills.

In April 1879 William C. Martindale led a group of men from Grantsville and Tooele, Utah, into Goose Creek Valley to assess the valley's suitability for homesteading. Settlers arriving the following year described the valley as covered with vegetation and teeming with wildlife. Antelope, deer, mountain sheep, moose, elk, bear and mountain cats were in abundance. The settlers filed their homestead and water right claims and immediately began building log homes and shelters as well as irrigation canals and ditches into which they diverted water from Goose

Creek.

The settlers were members of the Church of Jesus Christ of Latter-day Saints (Church of Jesus Christ or Church). They named their community Goose Creek Crossing and formed a branch of the church by the same name. They planted alfalfa, wheat and barley and ran herds of sheep and cattle. They held their first schools in private homes.

The freight wagon and stage line through the valley fueled the area's economy. Local farmers and ranchers used freight wagons to ship their commodities to the prospectors and miners in the Boise Basin and, later, to the miners working the silver and lead ore discovered in the Wood River Valley.

In 1882 the citizens of Goose Creek Crossing platted a town site and applied to postal authorities for a post office housed in the stagecoach station office. However, they submitted the name of the stage station manager and proposed postmaster, Oakley, as the name of the Post Office. As a practical matter, with all mail delivered to Oakley, that also became the name of the town.

Oakley historic home.

The next year, a group of citizens constructed the two-story Oakley Co-op building from stone.

In 1895 members of the Church began construction of the Oakley Tabernacle – completed in 1901. The tabernacle was the center of community activity. They not only used the building for church meetings, but musical programs, public meetings, funerals and graduations as well.

In February 1886 one of the first of a few deadly conflicts in Idaho between cattle and sheep ranchers happened near Oakley. A young sheep man named Gobo Fango was the first victim. In 1861 Fango, a black orphan child from South Africa, came to America with Mormon converts who befriended and educated him. At age 23 in 1879, he traveled with friends from Utah to

Oakley. There he became a partner in a small sheep-ranching enterprise.

Sheep ranching had become a major agricultural business in Southwestern Idaho. In those frontier days, federal and state grazing laws were largely non-existent. Grazing rights became a sharp point of contention between cattle and sheep ranchers. Cattle ranchers claimed that since they started grazing their animals first, they should receive preference to the public land. The sheep ranchers disagreed.

In the absence of federal law, the Idaho Territorial Legislature passed the "Two-mile Limit Law," that essentially supported the cattlemen's claim. The Act made it a misdemeanor to graze sheep within two miles of a cattleman's grazing claim. Federal law prohibited fencing public lands, making the Law impractical to interpret or enforce.

In early February 1886 Fango was with his sheep when two cattlemen approached and accused him of grazing his sheep within the two-mile limit. They pistol whipped Fango and shot him three times. They then rode to the sheriff in Albion to report the shooting, claiming self-defense.

Fango did not die immediately. He crawled four and a half miles to his former benefactor's house in Oakley with a terrible stomach wound where a bullet entered his back and came out through his intestines. He lived about five days, enough time to give his dying testimony of the shooting and prepare a will leaving his money and possessions to several of his friends and the Church.

Fango's murder trial ended in a hung jury. A second trial concluded with the same result. His grave marker in the Oakley Cemetery reads: "Gobo Fango, died February 10, 1886, 30 years old." Also buried in the Oakley Cemetery are two other sheepherders – Daniel Cummins and Don Wilson. In 1896 they were herding sheep in the area when they were shot and killed. The trial of their accused murderer – Jackson Lee "Diamondfield Jack" Davis – was one of Idaho's most famous murder trials. Davis, an employee of cattle ranching interests, had previous involvement in other hazing and shooting incidents involving sheepherders.

The jury found Davis guilty and sentenced him to hang. However, before authorities carried out the sentence, two men confessed to the crime and claimed self-defense – the story of one

Gobo Fango's headstone.

corroborating the other. Their trial ended in acquittal. Davis was eventually pardoned.

In 1905 Congress passed law establishing grazing permits as the means of allowing access to federal public lands for grazing. In 1934 Congress passed the Taylor Grazing Act that further clarified federal grazing law.

By the end of the 1890s, Oakley entrepreneurs had four brick kilns. George Bunn owned one of these brickyards. Bunn learned the brick making and brick mason trades before emigrating from England. However, in Oakley, Bunn did not have peat moss to fire his kiln. By experimenting, Bunn learned that quaking aspen wood burned at about the same temperature in the brick kilns as peat moss.

Joseph Beck, another early settler, was a mason's apprentice in Germany. He came to America at age 14 as a stowaway on a ship. He rode trains cross-country to Minidoka, Idaho. There he met an Oakley family who invited him to live with them. Beck developed his talents to design and built many Oakley buildings.

Bunn, Beck and other talented builders designed buildings using late Victorian architectural design. Many of these homes and business buildings still stand, making Oakley a historically distinctive community.

Incorporation

In 1896 Oakley became an incorporated village with an appointed board. The first election for village officers took place April 19, 1897.

At the time of incorporation, Oakley was the trading center for the greater Goose Creek Valley area. The town had hotels, general stores, drugstores, a furniture store, implement houses, a bank and numerous other buildings. Members of the Church of Jesus Christ had

Oakley public library.

also built a normal school – the Cassia Stake Academy – as well as a hall used for church meetings. By the 1910 census, the city had grown to 911.

Turning Points

Oakley Stage Station John Halley's 1870 selection of the Goose Creek Crossing site for his stage station with William Oakley as station manager was pivotal in establishing the future city of Oakley.

Immigrant Artisans The migration of settlers from Utah cities into Goose Creek Valley, beginning in 1879, turned a stage station and a valley used for cattle grazing into a vibrant frontier community.

Development and application of the immigrant's architectural and building skills resulted in the creation of many buildings of intricate Victorian design made of wood, brick and stone. These pioneer artisans built a village on the American Frontier with distinctive European and Eastern U.S. design and character at a time when homes in many frontier communities were earthen dugouts, tents and cabins.

Boom and Bust Ventures In 1919 the Vipont Silver Mine opened in the mountains south of Oakley. By August of that year, 100 men and 120 horses were working the mine and operating the ore-processing mill. In 1923 the bottom fell out of the silver market, and the mine closed. The closure was devastating to the town's economy. In 1925 silver prices improved, and the mine reopened with a small crew until 1927 when it closed permanently.

Early residents discovered deposits of a black-grey rock that some used as fuel. However, when burned, the rock did not reduce to ash. They discovered the rock was really oil shale.

In 1920 prospectors unsuccessfully drilled several oil wells. One well penetrated to 1,625 feet.

In 1923 local dairymen opened a cheese factory.

Oakley Reservoir In 1911 the Kuhn brothers from Pennsylvania – investors in the successful Milner Dam, a Carey Act irrigation project that led to creation of several Magic Valley cities and development of vast acreages of farmland – purchased water rights from Goose Creek Valley farmers. They began construction of another Carey Act project – the Oakley Dam on Goose Creek with an extensive

Oakley business.

system of gravity-flow canals and ditches. In 1913 the Kuhn brothers defaulted on their loans, and the settlers had to finish the project.

Originally, they expected to have enough water in the reservoir to irrigate 43,000 acres. Unfortunately, there was only enough water for 21,000 acres. Even so, the project had a profound positive impact on the local economy.

Railroad In 1911 the Idaho Southern Short Line Railroad built a line from Burley to Oakley. The railroad transported equipment and supplies used to construct the dam. It also stimulated further settlement and provided transportation needed to move agricultural commodities and livestock to market. Competition from motor vehicles eventually caused the railroad to stop providing service to Oakley.

The Great Depression In the early 1930s a drought exacerbated the economic problems brought on by the Great Depression. The two events had a devastating effect on the community. Many families lost their farms and moved away.

City of Rocks National Reserve, Castle Rocks State Park In 1988 Congress created the City of Rocks National

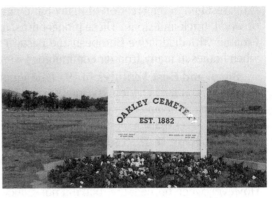

Reserve. In 2004 The Idaho Department of Parks and Recreation created Castle Rocks State Park. This natural amenity is bringing an increasing number of tourists, rock climbers and outdoor enthusiasts through Oakley.

Oakley city offices.

Oakley Today

Amenities and Attractions The Oakley City Park lies near the center of town. This two-acre park has several old-growth trees, a children's playground and a picnic area. A public swimming pool is adjacent to the park.

The city also has a public library, an RV park and a mineral Hot Springs resort located four miles outside of town. The Oakley Valley Historical Museum has exhibits and artifacts dating back to the time of the first settlers.

The Oakley Valley Arts Council sponsors theatrical productions and a Christmas concert at the historic Howells Opera House.

Each July, the city celebrates its pioneer heritage and the nation's independence with a parade, followed by a "Pony Express Race"; the Goose Creek Run-off; a rodeo; and, at City Park, a Dutch oven cook-off, deep pit barbecue, "gymkhana" for the kids and a spectacular fireworks display.

The city has many historic privately-owned late Victorian architecture homes made from brick and stone elaborately detailed with wood design and carvings. Some homes incorporate Queen Anne and Gothic styles. The oldest building is the two-story Oakley Co-op constructed in 1883. The City commemorates its building heritage each June by sponsoring the Historic Oakley Home Tour.

The first Sunday and Monday of December the city's Arts Council sponsors an annual Christmas Concert.

The city has over 100 historic buildings, a number so great the entire city is a historic district

Oakley city offices, and streetscape.

listed on the National Register of Historic Places.

The 14,440-acre City of Rocks National Reserve is 15 miles southeast of Oakley. The 1,440-acre Castle Rocks State Park is adjacent to the Reserve. The entire 25-square-mile site is the remains of a prehistoric batholith that eroded leaving massive granite rock outcroppings that resemble cathedrals, towers, domes, walls and weird shapes that stimulate the imagination. Two of the highest rock formations, the "Twin Sisters," are 600 feet high.

Historically, the site was a campground for thousands of California Trail immigrants who began traveling through the area in 1843. Pioneer immigrants used axel grease to paint names and messages on the smooth rock. Many of these markings are still visible.

Today, thousands of tourists and both amateur and professional rock climbers from around the world come to climb the many technically difficult granite outcroppings. In addition to rock climbing, the Reserve and Park amenities include hiking, picnicking, equestrian trails, wildlife viewing, Nordic skiing and photography. Wildlife includes mule deer, bighorn sheep, mountain lion, Sandhill crane, sage grouse and snipe.

Downhill skiing is available at the 8,700-foot Pomerelle Ski Area located 14 miles due east. The 7,200-foot-high Magic Mountain Ski Resort lies 20 miles due west. However, using hard surface roads, the two resorts are 44 and 63 miles distant, respectively.

The 814-acre Big Cottonwood Wildlife Management Area (WPA) is eight miles northwest of Oakley. The Big Cottonwood Creek intersects the property. The WPA provides habitat for over 95 species of upland birds.

Other outdoor amenities include camping, hunting, fishing, mountain biking, snowmobiling and ATV riding in the nearby forest and BLM lands as well as fishing and boating at Oakley Reservoir.

Economy and Major Employers Oakley Potato Pickers, a potato processor, has 45 employees and is the city's largest employer.

Cassia School District is the city's largest public employer.

Oakley Valley Stone has 17 employees and is the largest of several stone quarry businesses operating in the hills south of town. These companies mine quartzite stone – rock about the hardness of granite except it can be broken into sheets of uniform thickness – used by construction and landscape businesses. The stone comes in a variety of colors depending on the amount of mica and different minerals in the rock. Oakley has one of the largest deposits of quartzite in the nation. These quarry businesses ship stone both nationally and internationally.

The city's retail and service businesses provide additional jobs. Many residents also shop in Burley.

Education The Oakley Jr.-Sr. High School and Oakley Elementary School operate in the city and are part of the Cassia County School District. These schools provide most of the city's K-12 education.

The closest institution of higher learning is the College of Southern Idaho, 45 miles northwest in Twin Falls.

Health Care The nearest hospital is Cassia Regional Medical Center in Burley.

Transportation State Highway 27 links Oakley to Burley and Interstate 84.

The city is on the City of Rocks Back Country Byway – a local highway that makes a loop that proceeds south through the famous rock formations then turns northeast through Almo before connecting with Idaho Highway 77 to Albion.

The 3,800-foot runway at the Oakley Airport provides service for small private and charter aircraft. The closest airport with commercial airlines is Joslin Field-Magic Valley Regional Airport in Twin Falls.

Utilities and Services Private companies provide electricity, telephone and satellite services. The City provides water but does not have a municipal wastewater system. Residences and businesses have individual septic systems.

The city has a comprehensive plan and ordinances; however, Cassia County issues building permits. The city's volunteer "Quick Response Unit" provides fire protection and EMS services. The County Sheriff provides police protection under contract with the City. The County provides solid waste services.

Vision for 2050

For the past five decades, Oakley's population has generally ranged between 600 and 700. However, looking ahead to 2050 these historical trends are not likely to hold.

Existing businesses will likely grow their employment base – particularly as those associated with mining Oakley Stone identify new markets and products.

By 2050 federal, state and local transportation agencies will have reconstructed the City of Rocks Back Country Byway loop into a fully modern highway with connection to Interstate 84. The City of Rocks National Reserve and adjacent Castle Rocks State Park will be a must-experience tourist attraction and rock-climbing destination. As a result, Oakley, the Western Gateway to the Reserve and Park, will have numerous hospitality businesses serving the increased numbers of tourists and travelers.

As this growth occurs, the city will need to expand municipal services. These improvements will occur as needed – paid through existing funding streams, grants, impact fees or bonds approved by the voters.

While the city may grow significantly in the next four decades, city and community leaders will strive to manage the growth in a manner that preserves the city's heritage and uncharacteristic historic charm of homes built on the American frontier using the architectural design of the Victorian Era.

Mayors

1896	Dan P. Albee *	1940	W.J. Southworth *
1896	John L. Smith *	1945	W.B. Whiteley *
1904	Sol P. Worthington *	1949	H.C. Matthews
1909	John O. Lowe *	1957	J. Newell Dayley
1916	Joseph Y. Haight *	1959	C.Glen Elison
1918	W.C. Whittle *	1964	Unknown
1919	Georgge A. Day *	1967	Nathan A. Tanner
1921	C.A. Bauer *	1973	Thomas F. Miller
1923	Edward Warr *	1976	Jay Gorringe
1925	H.R. Matthews *	1980	Ray C. Bedke
1925	W.R. Gray *	1984	George F. Trombley
1929	S.P. Worthington *	1992	Dennis K. Smith
1931	Charles B. Payton *	2000	Garth Greenwell
1932	C.H. McMurray *	2008	Georgia Dimick
1933	Wm. G. Hardy *	2012	Larry Hinds
1934	J.A. Mercer *	2016	Robert Bell
1938	C.H. McMurray *	* Village Chairman	
1939	C.B. Payton *		

Glenns Ferry historic opera house.

ELMORE COUNTY

- Glenns Ferry
- Mountain Home (*County Seat*)

Glenns Ferry Chamber of Commerce and Visitor's Center.

Glenns Ferry

Statistical Data

Population: 1,341 *
Elevation: 2,560 feet
Precipitation: 9.5 inches **
Average Snowfall: 15.4 inches **
County: Elmore
Website: www.glennsferryidaho.org

Temperature Range – Fahrenheit: **
Spring: 29 to 75
Summer: 47 to 95
Fall: 26 to 83
Winter: 20 to 48
* U.S. Census Bureau Estimates July 2015
**Historical averages

Glenns Ferry lies on a fertile plain between high plateaus on the north side of the Snake River that forms a gentle crescent around the city and the adjoining Three Island Crossing State Park. Vast acreages of public lands interspersed by farmland extend beyond the city.

Oregon Trail pioneers found the least treacherous place to ford the Snake River where it divides to form three small islands. They used the river crossing until 1869. At that time, Gus Glenn constructed a ferry two miles upstream and started a small community, which later became a railroad town named Glenns Ferry.

Today, Interstate 84 borders the city, Boise is 70 miles northwest and Twin Falls 65 miles southeast.

Pre-Incorporation Years

Indians were the sole inhabitants of the land until around 1811 when trappers and explorers traveled the Snake River and its tributaries. (*See The Region, American Indians and Early Trappers/Explorers.*)

In 1841 the first overland migration of emigrants from Missouri and Iowa passed through the area headed for the Willamette Valley in Oregon Country – then claimed by both the U.S. and England, becoming part of the U.S. in 1846. Soon, many more

Three Island Crossing sign.

immigrant wagon trains headed for the free land and moderate climate of that lush valley. Many of them risked crossing the Snake River at what is now Three Island Crossing State Park to travel the less arduous route to the wooded and grassy valley of the Boise River and on to old Fort Boise, the trading post and rest stop near what is now Parma that was a landmark on many Oregon Trail maps.

Prospectors discovered large quantities of gold in the Boise Basin in 1862. The next year 16,000 fortune seekers came into the basin – many of whom used the Oregon Trail and new trails coming north from Utah to get to the gold fields.

The Idaho Territorial Legislature voted to make the 17-month-old Boise City the territorial capital in November 1864. This event encouraged even more traffic through Three Island Crossing.

A year earlier, Gustavus (Gus) F. Glenn, an entrepreneur who had come West to seek his fortune, acquired a

Kitty Wilkins, Idaho's Horse Queen, was born in the late 1850s. She was once engaged, but her fiancé was shot and killed in a range dispute and she never married. Her horse business peaked in 1900 with around 5,000 head. Kitty retired to Glenns Ferry. She passed away in 1935.

freight wagon pulled by 20 teams of oxen and began hauling freight between Fort

Hall – near what is now Pocatello – and Three Island Crossing.

The Union Pacific and Central Pacific Railroads met at Promontory, Utah, in 1869, completing the nation's first transcontinental railroad. At that time, former Civil War General Grenville Dodge, who was then the chief engineer for the Union Pacific, ordered a survey of a railroad line across Southern Idaho, essentially creating another transcontinental railroad. It would, however, take more than a decade before any tracks were laid.

In the same year, Glenn determined that there was sufficient wagon, stagecoach and horse traffic needing to cross the Snake River at Three Island Crossing that he could build and operate a successful ferry business – which he built and operated under his name, Glenns Ferry.

Glenn's wife was an Indian woman named Jennie. Some of Glenn's friends suggested he divorce her and marry a white woman. Glenn said that he would not, "she was good enough for me then (when they married), and she is good enough for me now."

Several settlers, including Harvey Glenn, Gus' father, had built a

Park on the Snake River.

fortified two-story rock house about 18 miles north of Glenns Ferry for protection should hostilities with the Indians break out.

In the spring of 1878 the Bannock Indians became angered over treaty violations, the increasing settlement of open lands and ranchers grazing livestock where the tribe previously hunted wild game and harvested camas roots. About 200 angry warriors left the Fort Hall Reservation and moved west, attacking and killing settlers, destroying property and stealing provisions.

One of the skirmishes took place at Glenns Ferry where the war party cut loose the ferryboat, burned freight wagons and stole goods. After leaving Glenns Ferry, the war party moved on to encounter the miners at Silver City and on into Oregon to pillage settlements and enlist support from other Indian tribes. These skirmishes – known as the Bannock War – concluded to a major extent several weeks later in northeastern Oregon where the U.S. Calvary defeated or dispersed the warriors. (*See The Region, American Indians – The Bannock War – Idaho's Last Indian War.*)

The Glenn family escaped the attack and after the danger passed, resumed their ferry business.

The community held its first school in an earthen dugout. Later, the Glenns Ferry, King Hill and Cold Springs communities combined to form a school district and soon moved the school to a tent. In 1886 a gentleman named Corker built a 16-

square-foot addition to his home to house the school district's 20 students. It was not until 1909 that the community quarried sandstone from across the river and carried it by wagon and barge to a site where they built a school, which they used until 1966 when patrons built a new school.

The Oregon Short Line, an affiliate of the Union Pacific Railroad, began construction of a rail line between the railheads at Granger, Wyoming, and Huntington, Oregon, in 1881. Two years later, the rail line reached Glenns Ferry. The railroad, completed in 1884, linked the commercial centers of Omaha, Nebraska, and Portland, Oregon, creating another transcontinental railroad. (*See The Region, Railroads.*)

At what is now Hammett, about eight miles west of Glenns Ferry, the railroad built a terminal, round house, depot, section houses and well. Unfortunately, in a few years the water supply proved inadequate to meet the needs of the steam-powered locomotives.

Glenns Ferry City Hall.

W.M. Stockton had acquired a large tract of "pre-empted land" in the area from the Federal Government. He offered part of his land to the railroad at no cost if the railroad moved its facilities onto the property. Jay Gould, a principal in the railroad, accepted the offer and in 1888 railroad personnel completed jacking up the Hammett buildings, putting them on rail cars and moving them to the new location. That move established Glenns Ferry as one of the railroad's major centers. (*See The Region, Federal Lands – Private Ownership and Preservation Laws' Preemption Act of 1841.*)

That same year, Stockton platted a townsite on his other land and named it Glenns Ferry. Stockton's historic farmhouse stood at the corner of Commercial and Garfield Streets until destroyed by fire in 2008.

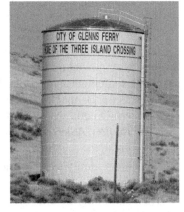

In 1893 two entrepreneurs built a second ferry across the river, but that year a fire broke out in town, destroying most of the business buildings. The property owners rebuilt only to see another fire break out in 1897, again devastating the business district.

During the next several years, the town experienced significant growth. The railroad, the dominant employer, had a payroll that reached $25,000 per month. A bank and several retail stores and shops opened. Ike Herron, an entrepreneur, built a waterworks and an electric plant that began providing electrical power in 1911. During that same period, a steamboat named Helen began operating on the Snake River; the city's first newspaper started; and other entrepreneurs started the King Hill Project under the Carey Act, which they expected would irrigate about 15,000 acres. (*See The Region, Agriculture and Irrigation.*)

Incorporation

On October 18, 1909, Glenns Ferry became an incorporated village. The 1910 census reported the village population at 800. In 1948 the village's legal status changed to an incorporated city.

Turning Points

Railroad The city of Glenns Ferry owes its name and origin to its favorable location on the Snake River – a location that allowed pioneers to ford the river and Gus Glenn to build his ferry. However, those pioneer attributes had a limited life. In 1883 when the railroad came, it provided the economic impetus to permanently establish the town and underpin its economy for decades.

The Glenns Ferry Historical Museum is located in the historic sandstone rock schoolhouse built in 1909. It has numerous displays and artifacts of area history. It is open during the summer.

With the advent of diesel locomotives in the 1970s trains could travel long distances without refueling. This technological innovation eliminated the need for the Glenns Ferry railroad fuel stop, and it was closed with significant adverse consequences to the city's economy.

Roadways In the mid-1950s the state bypassed the center of Glenns Ferry by diverting U.S. Highway 30 to the town's northern border. This was the beginning of the decline of Main Street. In later years, Interstate 84 bypassed the town, but left two highway interchanges on either end of town.

Irrigation Agriculture has been important to the city's economy from its inception, and irrigation is the industry's lifeblood.

The Reclamation Service – now the Bureau of Reclamation – completed two Carey Act projects in 1917 and turned them over to the King Hill Irrigation District.

Years later, sprinkler irrigation and large pump stations lifting water from the Snake River and deep wells allowed farmers to turn large tracts of arable high-desert land on the bluffs overlooking the Snake River into an expanse of beautiful farmland.

World War I In 1917 the United States entry into World War I galvanized considerable support for the war effort in Glenns Ferry. Although of lesser magnitude than other turning points, the level of patriotism engendered in the community and support for service men and women is striking and affected the attitude of town residents for many years. Mothers opened a chapter of "American War Mothers," an organization aiding the war effort by helping the men and women in uniform coming through on troop trains. They served dinner at the local opera house to all soldiers and their wives and sweethearts and the county commissioners awarded certificates of honor to all soldiers.

The Red Cross opened a chapter that started a Red Cross Canteen Station in Glenns Ferry. On March 26, 1918, local businesses and railroad employees donated enough refreshments to serve the first troop train that came through Glenns Ferry.

The project was so successful, the canteen stayed open continuously. When troop trains arrived, often at odd hours and numbering up to six per day, women volunteers came to serve free refreshments and provide necessary supplies to the troops. When the war ended 18 months later, the Glenns Ferry women had served 200,000 soldiers a variety of food, non-alcoholic beverages, tobacco, chewing gum, books, writing paper and pencils. The food items included 150,000 sandwiches; 35,000 donuts; 175,000 cookies; 15,000 chocolate bars; and thousands of pounds of bananas, oranges, grapes, apples and watermelon.

Carmella Winery features a restaurant, bar and golf course..

Glenns Ferry Today

Amenities and Attractions The city has two parks, a public library and a nine-hole golf course. Hull Memorial Park features a public swimming pool, children's playground, soccer and softball fields and picnic area. Railroad Park is a grass-covered area in the business district where people can stop and relax.

The city's most significant amenity is Three Island State Park located along the Snake River on the west side of the city. The state built the 613-acre park in 1971. It features RV parking, camping areas and the Oregon Trail History and Education Center. Area elementary schools often schedule field trips to the interpretative center to teach important elements of Idaho history.

In 1986 a group of local residents began what is now an annual reenactment of the Oregon Trail pioneers crossing the Snake River at Three Island Crossing. The memorial celebration takes place the second weekend of August and features horse and mule-drawn wagons and friends from the Duck Valley Indian Reservation dressed in native costume.

The Glenns Ferry Historical Museum is located in the historic sandstone rock schoolhouse built in 1909. It has numerous displays and artifacts of area history and is open during the summer. The City manages the Eddie Bostic Recreation Area on the Snake River which features boat docks and a picnic area. It is a family-friendly area used for boating, water and jet skiing and fishing.

The restored Gorby Opera House, built in 1914, is still in use for the performing arts, community events and private functions.

Seven Christian religions are represented in the city. Two are housed in historic facilities – Our Lady of Limerik Catholic Church, built in 1892, and the First Methodist Church, built in 1895.

The Elmore County Fairgrounds are located in the city. The county fair, held each July, features an array of events, exhibits and a rodeo.

Vast tracts of open public land outside the city offer residents a diversity of outdoor experiences and activities. Hiking, camping, horseback riding, hunting, fishing and ATV riding are common.

Economy and Major Employers The Glenns Ferry School District has about 85 employees and is the city's largest employer. Several small businesses and downtown establishments employ most of the balance of the city's workforce.

Farming – raising alfalfa, sugar beets, corn, beans, grain, potatoes and livestock – is important to the city's economy. However, in recent decades, technological innovation and consolidation have significantly improved productivity with considerably fewer workers. Fewer workers coming to town to shop has had an adverse effect on the city's economy.

Vineyards and wine production are relatively new agriculture-based industries that have come into the area. One has developed a golf course and restaurant on its premises.

Education The Glenns Ferry School District provides elementary and secondary education. The District operates three schools within the city – elementary, middle and high schools. Glenns Ferry also has a head start school for low-income families.

The closest institutions of higher learning are the College of Southern Idaho in Twin Falls and Boise State University.

Glenns Ferry is home to the Academy of Equine Dentistry. Students in groups of up to 60 from around the world come each quarter to receive specialized medical training in examining, treating, surgically correcting and caring for horses' teeth. Good dental hygiene and equilibration can extend a horse's life by several years.

Health Care A health clinic, dentist office, paramedics, senior center, meals on wheels and assisted-living center are located in the city.

The nearest hospital is Elmore Medical Center in Mountain Home.

Transportation Interstate 84 passes on the north side of the city with two freeway exits that serve east and west bound travelers.

The 3,050-foot-long runway at Glenns Ferry Airport is located at the city's southwest border. The closest commercial airfields are in Twin Falls and Boise.

Railroad service is available for freight.

Utilities and Services Private companies provide electricity, telephone, natural gas, cable and satellite services. The City provides water and sewer. The Elmore County Sheriff's Office has a substation in the city and provides law enforcement services. A volunteer fire department provides fire protection.

Vision for 2050

For nearly five decades, Glenns Ferry's core population has remained at around 1,400. The population spiked by about 200 between 1993 and 2005 when the need for farm workers expanded only to contract sharply due to changes in the use of the land, farming practices and equipment. If historical trends continue, in 2050 the city's core population will approximate 1,500.

There are several industrial buildings in the city. City and community leaders want to attract businesses that can use these attractively priced facilities. As this occurs, the city's core population will expand. Residential subdivisions will develop west of town. The city has prepared for this growth by recently constructing a new state-of-the-art water purification system that today has the capacity of producing a million gallons of water daily. In addition, the facility will allow for further expansion as needed.

The city's municipal wastewater systems are adequate for present needs. However, as part of the city's strategic planning efforts, city leaders are evaluating options to improve and expand wastewater systems.

Growth will also come as businesses develop near the two freeway interchanges that serve the city and as new residents come to enjoy the city's amenities of the river, state park and open space and development of new agriculture-based industries such as vineyards and wine production. The next four decades will resemble past years in that Glenns Ferry will continue to be a beautiful and peaceful place to live and raise a family.

Mayors

1909	Charles Skipper *	1957	C. Joseph Wells
1910	Ed M. Clark *	1959	Harry G. Bergstrom
1911	Joseph Rosevear *	1964	Herman G. Johnson
1913	Samuel B. Blackwell *	1966	Thomas L. Feeney
1915	J.W. Davis *	1970	E. Dayle Messerly
1920	Albert Stein *	1994	Leo E. McGhee
1921	E.W. Anrus *	1996	Sandra Cranor
1923	John Shrum *	1998	Glenn Thompson
1933	Sim Collins *	2006	JoAnne Coon-Lanham
1947	Clarence L. Moore	2014	Connie Wills
1953	Thomas L. Feeney		* Village Chairman

Mountain Home

Statistical Data

Population: 13,780 *
Elevation: 3,143 feet
Precipitation: 11 inches **
Average Snowfall: 14 inches **
County: Elmore
Website: www.mountain-home.us
Temperature Range – Fahrenheit: **

Spring: 30 to 72
Summer: 50 to 92
Fall: 27 to 80
Winter: 20 to 49
* U.S. Census Bureau Estimates July 2015
**Historical averages

Mountain Home is on the eastern edge of a broad high-desert valley surrounded by vast acreages of public land. The Boise National Forest and the Danskin and Bennett Mountain Ranges, with peaks rising to over 8,000 feet, lie a few miles east.

The Owyhee Mountains and the Silver City Mountain Range are across the valley 50 miles west. To the south, federal land managed by the Bureau of Land Management (BLM) stretches down the valley for over 100 miles. The city of Boise is 45 miles northwest.

Mountain Home is one of Idaho's "international" communities. The Mountain Home Air Force Base has squadrons of military aircraft and visitors and military personnel stationed on the Base from across the nation and many foreign countries.

Pre-Incorporation Years

In the early 1840s Oregon Trail immigrants began passing through the area around what is now Mountain Home. (*See The Region, Oregon and California Trails.*)

Following the discovery of gold in the Boise Basin in 1862 and the following year in the Owyhee Mountains, several thousand prospectors and miners began passing through the Mountain Home area en route to the gold fields. (*See The Region, Mining, Boise Basin – Gold; and Owyhee Mountains – Silver and Gold.*)

John Hailey started a stage line between Kelton, Utah – once a prominent railroad trailhead, now a ghost town located at the north end of the Great Salt Lake – and Boise in 1863.

One of the line's stagecoach stations was at Rattlesnake Springs, eight miles east of what is now Mountain Home. The Rattlesnake Springs Station housed a post office named Mountain Home. Jule M. Hager was the stage agent and postmaster.

In the early 1870s Commodore William Jackson, an intermittent miner and previous stagecoach station operator, purchased the Rattlesnake Springs Station. *The Idaho Statesman* reported on February 13, 1877, "The station...was called Rattlesnake...(and the) post office ... Mountain Home." Nineteen months later on

Oat field and residence of F.B. Daniels, April 25, 1907.

September 12, 1878, *The Idaho Statesman* reported, "Mountain Home is...a very pleasant home in the mountains."

The Oregon Short Line began construction of the railroad between Granger, Wyoming, and Huntington, Oregon, in 1881. The line, completed on November 17, 1884, angled in a northwesterly direction through Pocatello, Mountain Home and Caldwell. (*See The Region, Railroads.*)

In laying out the route for the railroad, the surveyors staked a line through the valley and what is now Mountain Home, eight miles west of Rattle Snake Station.

Seeing the railroad would bypass his station, Jackson laid claim to 320 acres parallel to the survey markers for the planned railroad tracks. Jackson then sold the land to other investors. In 1881 the Idaho and Oregon Land Improvement Company employed Robert Strahorn

Residence of Mrs. Longfellow.

and W.J. Turner to plat the new town. They sold corner lots for $50 and interior lots for $25. Turner built the first house and, later, a hotel and restaurant. Another entrepreneur, Roscoe Smith, built a drugstore.

Mountain Home Postmaster Jule Hager – recognizing that the train, not the stagecoach, would be transporting the mail in the future – purchased one of the residential lots, packed the Mountain Home Post Office letters and documents at Rattlesnake Station into a 50-pound soapbox, moved them to Roscoe Smith's drugstore and reopened the post office.

In July 1883 the first train rolled into town. Using the name of the post office where they delivered the mail, railroad authorities built a train depot that they named Mountain Home.

Nine years later, the Mountain Home Irrigation District completed the Camas, Long Tom and Mountain Home Reservoirs, providing irrigation water for several thousand acres. (*See The Region, Federal Lands – Private Ownership and Preservation Laws.*)

Wagon and team, 1884.

In the early years, livestock ranching was the dominant industry. The high desert was excellent winter range. The mild winter climate minimized animal health problems, particularly for sheep during the spring lambing and shearing season. Until the sheep industry began to decline in the mid-1900s, the Mountain Home Train Depot was a major railhead for shipping lambs and wool to market. (*See The Region, Livestock.*)

Incorporation

The Idaho Legislature established Elmore County on February 7, 1889, with the gold mining boomtown of Rocky Bar as the county seat. Rocky Bar was deep in the mountains but was the most populous community in the county. As the gold played out, most of the fortune seekers moved on. On February 4, 1891, Elmore County citizens voted to move the county seat 60 miles southwest to the more accessible community of Mountain Home.

The county commissioners approved incorporation of Mountain Home as a village in 1896.

The Mountain Home News reported on October 10, 1946, that the Village Council approved making Mountain Home a city of the second class, and their decision would be placed on the next year's ballot along with the election of a mayor and city council. The voters passed the initiative.

In accordance with a 1967 change in state municipal law that removed class designations, Mountain Home had its status as a city with the second class designation removed.

Turning Points

Railroad The coming of the Oregon Short Line Railroad in 1883 provided the basis for moving the Mountain Home Post Office from the Rattlesnake Stage Station in the mountains to the new railroad town that, in turn, was the basis for railroad officials naming their depot Mountain Home. In addition to confirming the name of the new town, the railroad provided the transportation needed for the emerging agriculture industry to flourish.

Agriculture Sheep and cattle ranching blossomed with access to the railroad. The vast open lands, mild climate and the demand for beef, wool fiber and lamb attracted many ranchers to the area.

Horse ranching also became an important agricultural business around 1917. The United States had entered World War I, and cavalry and draft horses were in great demand. Several ranchers began raising horses on the Bruneau Desert. Until displaced by motor vehicles, Mountain Home ranchers became important suppliers of horses to the military.

Jet in Mountain Home park.

Today, dairy farming has emerged along with cattle as the dominant agricultural businesses.

Mountain Home Air Force Base The city's most significant turning point came in 1942 with the creation of what is now Mountain Home Air Force Base.

On August 7, 1942, eight months after the U.S. entered World War II, construction started on the Mountain Home Army Air Field. The U.S. military approved the site for a new air base because of its ideal setting – the site was remote and on federal land. The vast tracts that surrounded the Base provided excellent training ranges. The weather was dry and conducive to year-round use. The valley was largely flat and there were large gravel deposits nearby for building base infrastructure.

The Air Field opened on August 7, 1943. During the war years, B-24 Liberator and, later, B-29 Superfortress crews used the Base for training.

When the U.S. Air Force became an independent branch of the military in December 1948, the Base was renamed the "Mountain Home Air Force Base." During the ensuing years, the commands assigned to the Base have changed. However, except for three brief periods of inactive status, the Base has been operational.

In 1996 the Air Force established a Composite Wing at the Base. This change increased the number of Base personnel from 2,500 to over 4,000. Today, the Base is home to the 366th Fighter Wing, hosting F15c and F15e jets.

Mountain Home Today

Amenities and Attractions The city has 11 parks on 101 acres, a golf course and a public library. The most prominent of the parks is Carl Miller Park, a memorial to a local son killed in World War I. Mounted in the park is a decommissioned F-111 fighter jet.

The park is the site of Air Force Appreciation Day where over 10,000 people turn out annually for a parade and barbeque held on the Sunday following Labor Day.

Desert Canyon Trail

The historic Andrew Carnegie Library, built in 1908 and listed on the National Register of Historic Places, houses the Mountain Home Historical Museum. The museum highlights the city's history and ethnic cultures and sponsors the "Self Guided Walking Tour of Historic Downtown Mountain Home" that includes the city's 33 historic buildings and the Basque Cultural District.

The Desert Mountain Visitor Center at the Junction of Interstate 84 and U.S. Highway 20 is an excellent source of other information about the area.

Mountain Home Reservoir, just east of town, is a small fishery that diverts water from Canyon and Rattlesnake Creeks for irrigation.

The 13,508-acre C.J. Strike Wildlife Management Area (WMA) that lies 15 miles south of the city includes 3,000 acres of streams, ponds and part of the C.J. Strike Reservoir. The Idaho Department of Fish and Game manages the Area to provide habitat for fish, waterfowl and upland game birds. The WMA is popular with birdwatchers, anglers and hunters.

Anderson Ranch Dam and Recreation Area are about 20 miles northeast of the city. The dam is 456 feet high and creates a 17-mile-long lake with 50 miles of shoreline. It is part of the U.S. Bureau of Reclamation's Boise Project which includes a complex system of dams and canals that primarily irrigate farms in the Treasure Valley. (*See The Region, Federal Lands – Private Ownership and Preservation Laws; Bureau of Reclamation – Boise Project – Treasure Valley.*)

The lake is popular for boating and fishing for trout; bass; and Kokanee, landlocked salmon that spawn in the creeks during late August and early September. The recreation area includes 380 miles of marked snowmobile trails. Some of the trails wind up to the Trinity Mountains and lakes eight miles above the north end of the lake and rising to 9,451 feet.

The 4,800-acre Bruneau Dunes State Park is 21 miles southwest of the city on State Highway 51. For thousands of years, blowing sand has settled in this natural basin, producing a landscape of sand dunes. One rises to 470 feet, the largest in North America. At the base of the dunes is a lake with bass and bluegill. To protect the serenity and ecology of this environmentally sensitive area, the Idaho Department of Parks and Recreation allows only non-motorized vehicles and boats on the dunes and lake.

Fifteen miles west, the Snake River Birds of Prey National Conservation Area managed by the BLM begins. The Area is mixed use; encompasses 485,000 acres of public land; and has high concentrations of falcons, hawks, eagles and owls.

Three Island Crossing State Park is 25 miles southeast near Glenns Ferry. This 613-acre park is the location where many Oregon Trail pioneers crossed the Snake River on the trek West.

Economy and Major Employers Mountain Home Air Force Base, nine miles southwest of the city, is the city's largest employer and underpins the local economy. Most of the Base's 4,000 active-duty and 900 civilian personnel live in the city with their families. They and most of those living on the Base shop in the city.

The city's largest private employers include the Walmart superstore with 300 employees; Simplot Livestock, a feedlot, with 150 employees; and the Marathon Cheese plant that presently has 400 employees but will grow to over 500.

Excluding the Air Force Base, the city's largest public employers are Mountain Home School District with 500 employees, Elmore Medical Center with 200 and Elmore County and the City of Mountain Home with approximately 120 employees each.

Education Mountain Home School District and three private schools provide most of the elementary and secondary education. The school district operates senior, virtual and alternative high schools; a high school; a junior high school; a middle school; and three elementary schools.

The closest institution of higher learning is Boise State University. College level courses are also available in the city through many other institutions and venues.

Health Care The 25-bed Elmore Medical Center with its attached nursing home, four assisted-care facilities and four general medical clinics provide non-Air Force Base medical care.

Transportation Interstate 84 is on the eastern edge of the city. State Highway 51 connects the city with Elko, Nevada, to the south, and State Highway 67 connects the city with Grand View to the west. U.S. Highway 20 connects with Anderson Ranch Dam and Recreation Area and cities in Eastern Idaho.

The Mountain Home Air Force Base terminal and runways are not available to the public. The city's Municipal Airport has a 5,000-foot runway and is available for private and charter aircraft services. The Boise Air Terminal is the closest commercial airport.

Utilities and Services Private companies provide electricity, natural gas, cable and satellite services. The City provides water and sewer services and police and fire protection. The County provides solid waste and jail services.

Vision for 2050

In 2050 Mountain Home Air Force Base will continue to be an important U.S. military base and the dominant factor in the city's economy. The City will continue to be one of Idaho's willing partners in helping Base personnel achieve their assigned missions.

The compliment of Air Force personnel assigned to the Base will remain somewhat constant. However, it is reasonable that U.S. military leaders or Congress may reassign greater responsibility and personnel as they did in 1996 to better utilize the Base's outstanding infrastructure, training resources and excellent relationship with the City and Idaho.

As this occurs, retail and other businesses that serve Base personnel and civilian employees and their families will also increase. To meet the higher education needs of Base personnel, there will be a community college.

There will be a continued increase in employment from food processing and light manufacturing businesses unrelated to the Air Force Base. The employment from these businesses will provide important diversification to the city's economy.

The City will continue to provide its residents with friendly, efficient and responsive government services and needed infrastructure at a reasonable cost.

The city will honor its pioneer and agricultural history and legacy while embracing the modern high-tech science taught in the schools and utilized on the Base and by its businesses and residents.

The city will have more community-wide cultural events, improved parks and activities that promote a sense of community and friendly hometown atmosphere.

Mayors

1896	A.B. Clark *	1934	R.P. Harmon *
1900	J.A. Purtill *	1935	Albert G. Nadler *
1901	F.W. Boyd *	1938	R.P. Harmon *
1902	John N. Brady *	1939	A.L. Gridley *
1903	George F. Mahoney *	1941	C.A. Carlson *
1907	W.L. Harley *	1945	H.K. Humphrey
1908	L.J. Wever *	1947	John V. Glasby
1909	J.A. Eyster *	1951	Raymond W. Harris
1910	C.W. Howeth *	1955	Willis M. Carrie
1910	J.H. Whitson *	1957	Charles Freeman
1910	J.B. Stanfield *	1961	Philip W. Gridley
1911	C.E. Corker *	1964	Frank A. Pearce
1911	F.G. Ticknor *	1973	Vern W. Everitt
1913	John F. Gaines *	1978	Nelson H. Olds
1915	Stanton Park *	1981	Roy A. Bledsoe
1917	R.P. Harmon *	1983	Stu Olbrich
1919	A.F. Anderson *	1983	Donald C. Etter
1922	R.R. Osborn *	2000	David A. Jett
1923	F.W. Bennett *	2004	Joe B. McNeal
1925	E.W. Latimore *	2008	Tom Rist
1929	J.A. Goodall *	2016	Rich Sykes
1931	R.P. Harmon *		* Village Chairman
1933	George E. Evans *		

GEM COUNTY

- Emmett (*County Seat*)

View of Emmett from Freezeout Hill.

Emmett

Statistical Data

Population: 6,599 *
Elevation: 2,375 feet
Precipitation: 13 inches **
Average Snowfall: 17 inches **
County: Gem
Website: www.emmettidaho.com
(Chamber of Commerce)

Temperature Range – Fahrenheit: **
Spring: 33 to 72
Summer: 52 to 90
Fall: 31 to 79
Winter: 23 to 45
* U.S. Census Bureau Estimates July 2015
**Historical averages

Emmett lies in a beautiful valley framed on three sides by high-desert foothills and buttes primarily managed by the U.S. Bureau of Land Management (BLM). Across five miles of foothills to the south are the populated areas of Ada and Canyon Counties. Boise is 25 miles southeast.

Five miles northeast is Black Canyon Dam. The dam creates a lake that is over a half-mile wide and extends back into the canyon for more than five miles.

To the west, the Payette River floodplain opens into a fertile valley two to seven miles wide. The river passes through Emmett before flowing into the Snake River 30 miles to the northwest.

Emmett citizens enjoy a quiet, affordable, quasi-rural community that, at the same time, is readily accessible to the jobs and urban services available in the much larger cities of Ada and Canyon Counties.

Pre-Incorporation Years

Prior to 1811 when explorers/trappers began traveling the Snake River and its tributaries, American Indian tribes camped in the Payette River Valley. The prehistoric flood plain had an abundance of wild game. Salmon and steelhead trout filled the Payette River each year during their annual spawning migrations. (*See The Region, American Indians*.)

In 1818 Alexander Ross led a band of beaver trappers who worked the Snake River and its tributaries. Many others followed.

In 1834 the Hudson's Bay Company, a British enterprise, built a small trading post at the confluence of the Snake and Boise Rivers near what is now the city of Parma. The remote trading post was managed by a French-Canadian named Francois Payette, the man who became the namesake for a city, a river and a national forest. Influenced by the black cottonwood and willow forests that lined the river flowing from the east and grew in the floodplain, he named the river Boise and the trading post, Fort Boise, the French word for "wooded." (*See The Region, Early Trappers/Explorers*.)

By 1841 the first migration from the East was making its way to Oregon's Willamette Valley. Fort Boise was a rest stop for the travelers and would later become a prominent Oregon Trail landmark.

In 1862 Tim Goodale, a wagon scout already recognized for making cutoffs that shortened travel time on the Oregon Trail, left a wagon train of 300 camped on the Boise River and struck out in a northwesterly direction with 60 wagons.

Goodale blazed this trail through what is now Emmett, partially to accommodate members of his group looking for a shorter route to the gold strikes in Oregon and central Idaho. Goodale's cutoff route to the north became popular even though travelers had to slide their wagons down the steep foothills into the Payette River Valley. (*See The Region, Oregon and California Trails*.)

In the same year, prospectors discovered gold in the Boise Basin that led to the gold rush of 1863 wherein 16,000 fortune seekers converged into the area. Jonathan Smith came to the Boise Basin gold fields in the spring of 1863 leading a group of miners from Oregon. (*See The Region, Mining – Boise Basin – Gold*.)

They traveled over Goodale's Cutoff but had to stop at the Payette River to wait for the spring runoff from the winter's mountain snows to recede. While they waited Smith and a member of the group, Nathaniel Martin, enlisted the miners to help build a ferry and a hotel where the Boise Basin Trail and the Overland Road met. They called the community Martinsville.

Martin, known as Squire Martin, became Justice of the Peace and ran the ferry. Smith and his wife ran the hotel that also housed the town post office in which Smith was the first postmaster. The Smiths raised produce to sell to the travelers and dug the first irrigation ditch.

In 1865 Thomas Cahalan started another town nearby, naming it Emmettville in honor of his son, Emmett. He was successful in moving the post office to Emmettville and changing its name, a factor in securing the town's future. Over the next several years, the Emmettville Post Office would change hands and locations, but postal authorities kept the post office name. The town of Emmettville built its first school in 1874.

The mid-1860s was a lawless period in many Idaho communities. The Payette River Valley was not immune to these criminal influences. A band of outlaws had a hideout about five miles east of what is now Emmett at a place called Picket's

Corral. The corral was a roadhouse overlooking the river. It sat below a cliff-like lava rock basin open on one end. Horse thieves placed a 10-foot-tall log picket fence across the opening making a corral to hold stolen horses until they could secret them out into the mountains to be sold in faraway locations.

The station quickly became the hangout for not only horse thieves but other criminals including bogus gold agents and highwaymen. The ringleader was ultimately identified as David Updyke, a man who led a double life as the Ada County Sheriff.

To confront this criminal menace, the citizens formed a band of vigilantes named the Payette Vigilance Committee. They elected William J. McConnell as their leader. McConnell would later become governor of Idaho and briefly serve as a U.S. senator.

Updyke resigned as sheriff and left Idaho. He was later lynched in Montana by unknown parties. Other accused criminals were summoned to appear before the committee. The summons assured them that they would receive a fair trial before a jury of seven citizens, and, if convicted, their punishments would fit their crimes. If they did not appear, they had 24 hours to leave the territory. If they were caught, they would be publicly whipped or hanged by the neck until dead. Many who received the letters of summons decided to just leave town and skip the trial.

At the end of three months, McConnell wrote, "...the committee transformed the Payette Valley, with its hitherto unsavory reputation, into a community of peaceful homes, where life and property were...safe..."

By 1870 the Jonathan Smith Company completed the area's first diversions of river water into irrigation ditches. With irrigation, farming, ranching and the fruit industry began to flourish and provide food to the miners working in the nearby gold fields.

In the winter of 1872 some freighters waited out a freezing night at the top of the steep hill on the southern rim of the Payette River Valley. They felt that it was not safe to make the steep descent in the dark. To make it down into the valley the next day, the freighters locked or froze their wagon wheels. Their oxen or mules slowly pulled the sliding wagons down the hill. When they got into Emmettville the next day, they recounted their harrowing experience by saying they were "froze out of the valley" and "nearly froze to death" when they spent that night on the hill. From then on the place has been called "Freezeout Hill."

In 1883 James Wardwell platted the Emmettville townsite. A year later, citizens built the first bridge across the Payette River to Ada and Canyon Counties and a year after that formed the Emmettville School District.

To eliminate confusion between Emmettville, Idaho, and Emmettsville, Iowa, in 1885 the U.S. Postal Service changed the name of Emmettville to Emmett.

Incorporation

In 1900 Emmett, with a population of over 200, became an incorporated village. On April 6, 1909, they changed Emmett's legal status to a city of the second class. The 1910 census reported the city had a population of 1,351.

Turning Points

Gold Discovered in the Boise Basin The discovery of gold in the Boise Basin in 1862

Emmett City Hall.

brought the first settlers and merchants to the Payette River Valley. They formed the nucleus that led to the founding of Emmett.

Railroad Forty years later in May 1902, the Idaho Northern Railroad Company completed its line from Murphy through Nampa to Emmett and the valley began to blossom. In 1910 the Payette Valley Extension Railway Company (PVR) built an 18-mile railroad from New Plymouth on the west to Emmett. In 1914 the Oregon Short Line acquired the PVR and extended the line to Cascade.

Rail transportation had a profound effect on the development of the valley's industries – particularly sawmills, the thousands of acres of orchards being planted, sheep and cattle ranching and mining. (*See The Region, Railroads.*)

Downtown Fire On April 26, 1908, a fire started in the Hotel Emmett. The fire was contained to a single block because of the resourceful intervention of the miners from the boomtown of Pear, located 11 miles away. They dynamited two structures on the east end of the block to check the spreading flames.

After the fire, several women spearheaded a drive to build a fire station. Their effort resulted in the town's first fire department with a station equipped with ladders and a hand-powered fire hose cart.

Irrigation and the Black Canyon Dam In 1905 farmers built a diversion dam on the Payette River about 15 miles north of the current Black Canyon Dam.

In 1924 the Bureau of Reclamation built a much larger, 183-foot-high hydroelectric dam up the river canyon about five miles east of town where the Payette River narrowed between black basalt walls; the new dam rendered the dam built two decades earlier obsolete. Reclamation also financed and built an extensive network of irrigation canals, laterals and sub-laterals. (*See The Region, Federal Land Use Laws – Bureau of Reclamation – Boise Project – Treasure Valley.*)

Orchards With the combination of the Black Canyon Dam increasing the supply of irrigation water throughout the growing season, moderate hillside temperatures and fertile soils ideal for producing high-quality fruit and the railroad ready to transport their production to market, Emmett's orchardists and fruit-packing industry prospered. In the early 1900s fruit packers adopted the "Valley of Plenty" label for their fresh-packed fruit.

One of the founding fruit farmers, Douglas Knox, planted his orchard in 1871. By 1909 there were orchards throughout the valley. In 1911 the Payette Valley Railroad shipped more than 1,000 railroad cars of fruit, over half of all the fruit shipped from the state of Idaho. In 1945 area growers shipped nearly 4,000 railroad cars of fruit to market.

Emmett's Cherry Festival is held annually in June.

Ranching The mild climate that favored growing fruit also made thousands of grass-covered foothills around Emmett excellent sheep and cattle ranching country. One of the more prominent sheep ranchers was Andrew Little. In 1894 the 24-year-old Andrew arrived in Emmett from his native Scotland. With $3 in his pocket and two sheepdogs at his side, he found employment with a local sheep rancher. By frugal living combined with taking part of his pay in sheep, he built a herd that three and a half decades later approached 100,000 head in number and yielded a million pounds of wool annually.

After World War II the demand for lamb and wool fell dramatically. The numbers of sheep in Emmett and Idaho declined until the numbers and size of today's sheep herds are but a small fraction of those of the past. (*See The Region, Livestock.*)

Sawmills Fueling Emmett's early development was its first significant sawmill constructed in 1905. Initially, it used logs floated down the Payette River and later hauled by truck and train. The mill changed hands multiple times, but with each change in ownership, the operation grew. Beginning in 1920 and for eight decades thereafter, the mill was Emmett's largest employer. In May 2001 Boise Cascade closed its Emmett Mill, and the following January fire destroyed the facility.

County Seat On March 19, 1915 the legislature created Gem County with Emmett as the county seat. That action established the city as an important center for government and business and provided a small but stable workforce.

Transformation of Emmett's Economic Base For decades, wood products, fresh-pack fruit, sheep and railroad businesses underpinned Emmett's economy. Market forces and the reduced access to federal forests and grazing lands brought a gradual decline or closure of those businesses. (*See The Region, Mining and Forest Products – Decline of Two of Idaho's Signature Industries*.)

Because of Emmett's close proximity to the rapidly growing cities in Ada and Canyon Counties, new residents with jobs in the larger cities began coming to live in Emmett. They were seeking a more rural lifestyle and affordable housing within commuting distance of their employment. Many parcels of land previously devoted to orchards and farming were converted to subdivision development. Emmett's last fruit packing shed closed in the fall of 2000.

Emmett Today

Amenities and Attractions The city has three municipal parks. The Emmett City Park has a swimming pool, tennis courts, playground and public band shell. The Gem Island Sports Complex, on a river island, is managed by Gem County and has lighted ball fields and other recreational activities and programs. Dirt bikers and cyclists have off-road fun at the Little Gem Cycle Park. The city celebrates Youth Appreciation Day on the last Saturday in April on the island.

The second full week in June marks the city's annual Cherry Festival, a commemoration of the valley's commercial cherry harvest. The festival started in 1923 when a packing shed employee suggested a dance would be a nice way to end the cherry harvest season. The idea caught on. Now upwards of 80,000 people come to Emmett each year to participate. The week of festivities includes Miss Gem County, Junior Miss Gem County, a carnival, food vendors, pie contests, a children's parade and a main parade.

The third Saturday in July is "Cruise Night." This annual "Back to the 50s" event features a hula hoop contest, jitterbug dancing and a 50s band. One of the featured Cruise Night events is a "Swap 'n Shine" where more than 500 classic cars are displayed at City Park. Informal cruising of Main Street and Washington Avenue goes on during the day and into the evening. Each August, Gem and Boise Counties combine efforts to produce the "Gem and Boise Counties Fair and Rodeo." In April, there is horse racing at the fairgrounds.

On the first full weekend in October, the Gem County Historical Society presents "The River Through Time" – a tribute to the people who settled the Payette River Valley. The fur trappers, settlers, miners, cowboys and sheepherders involve the public in their historical demonstrations. The Idaho Volunteers also skirmish with their Napoleon cannons. The two-day event is held at the Gem Island Sports Complex.

Many residents and visitors enjoy rafting or fishing on the stretch of the Payette River that passes through town. Black Canyon Reservoir is popular for water skiing, boating and fishing. The surrounding public lands, forests, lakes, rivers and streams provide many options for hunting, fishing, hiking, skiing and riding ATVs and snowmobiles.

Firebird Raceway, a National Hot Rod Association (NHRA) recognized drag racing track, is located seven miles south of the city. The track, which opened in 1968, draws car racing enthusiasts from throughout the region.

Ten miles north of Emmett is Roystone Hot Springs and swimming pool, a natural hot mineral spring developed in 1909. The facility is privately owned but open to the public by reservation.

The city has numerous churches representing several Christian denominations.

Emmett's Main Street includes several historic buildings converted to retail shops and offices. The Gem County Courthouse and several other buildings in the city are listed on the National Register of Historic Places.

The Gem County Historical Village Museum is a five-building complex that interprets the county's rich early history. A historical library and archive is under development. The city library has about 50,000 books.

At the summit of Freezeout Hill is a memorial to veterans and public servants. The memorial replaced a 1928 monument constructed by the Payette River Pioneer Society to honor the pioneers of 1862 to 1868 who traveled the original road and withstood its hardships. The original marker is now on display at the County Courthouse.

Economy and Major Employers The city has no dominant employer. Most of the city's workforce commutes to Ada and Canyon Counties.

With fewer than 100 employees each, Albertsons, Emmett Rehabilitation & Health and Walter Knox Hospital are the city's largest employers. Five businesses involving the light manufacturing of wood, sand products and axel systems each employ about 30 people.

Emmett has many retail businesses including boutique and gift shops, restaurants, antique shops, fitness centers, a bowling alley and a martial arts and recreation center.

Education Emmett School District provides most of the elementary and secondary education. Boise State University, the College of Western Idaho, the College of Idaho, Northwest Nazarene University and Treasure Valley Community College are each located within 30 miles of the city.

Health Care Walter Knox Memorial Hospital, a 24-bed facility, provides most of the city's medical services. In addition, several health clinics, assisted-living and nursing homes provide other medical care for area residents.

Transportation Idaho Highways 16 and 52 pass through the city. Interstate 84 is located about 20 miles west. Highway 16 is the primary road connecting Emmett with communities in Ada and Canyon Counties.

Private and charter air service is available at Emmett Municipal Airport's 3,250-foot-long runway. Large commercial air service is available in Boise. Rail service is available for freight.

Utilities and Services Private companies provide electricity, gas, cable, satellite and wireless services. The City provides water, sewer, police and fire protection. The City also manages the cemetery and runs the library. The County provides solid waste services.

Vision for 2050

In recent years, the city's population has grown just over two percent annually. If those trends continue, by 2050 the city's population will likely exceed 11,000.

City ordinances that require development to pay for public and private parks, open space, pathways and connectivity to schools and other developments will still be in effect and operating effectively. The small town ambience of beautiful landscaped public areas, open space and restored historic buildings designed for the enjoyment of all will be a city hallmark. Growth will pay an equitable share of the cost.

The 2008 improvements in city water and wastewater treatment systems have upgraded service for city residents and will handle growth for several years. By 2050 the Idaho Transportation Department will have made needed improvements to Highway 16, to State Highway 44 and to the planned Ten Mile Interchange at Interstate 84. The department will also have extended U. S. Highway 95 south from Council through Indian Valley, connecting with Highway 16 in Emmett.

The population will stretch the length of the valley from the eastern foothills south of the river at the base of the southern hills to about Bowman Road. It will likely cross the river and go up on to the fertile north bluff.

A light industrial business corridor will stretch from Airport Road to Toms Cabin or Bowman Roads. Farming and ranching will continue to locate along the river and up into the southern and northern foothills.

Mayors

1900-1908	Unknown *	1951	Wally Hart
1909	E.M. Reilly	1953	Lee Bolt
1911	W.R. Cartwright	1959	George Yost
1913	Dr. R. Cummings	1963	Lee Bolt
1915	D.M. Jones	1974	Rod Morgan
1917	R.E. Rose	1986	Marilyn Lorenzen
1919	J.C. Almon	1990	LeRoy Campbell
1921	Anthony Peterson	1994	John LaFordge
1923	Frank Knox	1998	Ron Morgan
1925	Charles L. Gamage	2004	Marilyn Lorenzen
1933	Claude Bucknam	2008	Bill Butticci
1939	Howard Eaton	2015	Gordon Petrie
1945	Emory Schoenwald	* Village Chairman	
1947	Dee Thurman		

City of Rocks near Gooding

GOODING COUNTY

- Bliss
- Gooding (*County Seat*)
- Hagerman
- Wendell

One of the Bliss dinosaurs.

Bliss

Statistical Data

Population: 302 *
Elevation: 3.262 feet
Precipitation: 10 inches **
Average Snowfall: 15 inches **
County: Gooding
Website: www.blissidaho.com

Temperature Range – Fahrenheit: **
Spring: 28 to 72
Summer: 49 to 90
Fall: 26 to 79
Winter: 18 to 43
* U.S. Census Bureau Estimates July 2015
**Historical averages

Bliss lies on a high-desert plateau at the northwestern edge of the Magic Valley. Vast tracts of public land covered with sagebrush, grass and prehistoric lava flows form an irregular crescent that wraps around the city and adjacent farms from the northeast, northwest and southwest.

The Snake River flows a mile west of the city before making a 90-degree turn to the west where it begins backing up to form Bliss Reservoir. The 615-foot-long and 70-foot-high hydroelectric Bliss Dam is located six miles due west of the city.

Pre-Incorporation Years

In the early 1800s trappers, explorers and other adventurers joined American Indians in traversing the area around Bliss. The Native Americans caught and dried salmon migrating up the Snake River and its tributaries and harvested camas bulbs from the prairie.

Some of the trappers were French. The trappers named the river that flows into the Snake River five miles south of Bliss "Rivere aux Malades," because they got ill from what they believed was bad river water. It was later determined that the water was good. The trappers likely became ill after eating the tail of beaver whose diet included plants poisonous to humans such as water hemlock. A similar event led to French trappers giving the same name to the river that runs through Malad City. Therefore, Idaho has two rivers named Malad.

The main Oregon Trail passed west of the Snake River about eight miles from what is now the city of Bliss. The Trail crossed the Snake River at Three Island Crossing before proceeding on to Fort Boise and Oregon.

Following completion of the transcontinental railroad in 1869 at Promontory, Utah, wagon freight and stagecoach service to Boise started from the railroad siding at Kelton, Utah, now a ghost town located 40 miles south of the City of Rocks. The wagon road called the Kelton Road crossed the Snake River north of what is now the city of Buhl, then crossed the Malad River and stopped at Malad Station where there were

Spring Cove Ranch.

stables, sleeping and eating accommodations. The road then proceeded through what is now the city of Bliss and on to the Clover Creek Station, located several miles north of town where teamsters could exchange for fresh horses.

In 1879 David and Lydia Bliss moved with their three children to the city's present location. They started a business on their homestead of supplying Kelton Road travelers with campsites and hay and pasture for their livestock. In 1880 they constructed a small store and saloon. In 1882 James L. Fuller, a son-in-law of David and Lydia, opened another saloon nearby.

Spring Cove Ranch.

On October 18, 1883, Fuller applied for a post office under the name of Bliss. Fuller's plan was to house the post office in his saloon. Postal authorities approved his application provided Fuller did not locate the post office in a saloon. Fuller complied and the community name of Bliss became a reality.

In 1883 the Oregon Short Line Railroad was in the process of building a railroad line from Granger, Wyoming, to Huntington, Oregon. Removing heavy deposits of lava rock from the rail bed was a frequent problem for railroad construction workers. Workers often used dynamite to break the lava rock up. During construction of the rail bed bear Bliss, 16 Chinese workers tragically lost their lives in one of the dynamite explosions. The railroad company placed their bodies in the village cemetery and marked it "Chinese Graveyard."

At Bliss, the railroad company built a depot with a rail siding consisting of docks, livestock pens and loading chutes. This new infrastructure established Bliss as a transportation hub for area railroad passengers and transporting the agricultural commodities produced by an increasing number of homesteaders and ranchers who were settling in the area. Soon other entrepreneurs came and built retail and service businesses at Bliss including a hotel, a bank and a drugstore.

Fruit train near Bliss.

In 1884 settlers built a school near the Malad River Railroad Bridge. In 1892 they built an additional school in Bliss, and Lydia Bliss was the teacher.

In 1892 Benjamin G. Mullins, who owned the land next to the railroad siding, surveyed and platted the city. He collected fees from those who had already built on his land. He later sold his property.

The early homesteaders were ranchers who grazed their livestock on public land. Later, with the coming of the railroad and the prospect of irrigation water, homesteaders began coming into the area. They first performed the arduous task of "grubbing" (removing) the sagebrush and leveling the land in preparation for the irrigation systems that would be critical to the development of area farms.

In 1897 Joel Sanders, one of the early settlers, constructed the Pioneer Reservoir located six miles northeast of town. In 1910 water from the Northside Canal system, part of the massive Minidoka hydroelectric and irrigation project that extends from Ashton to Bliss, reached the city.

Bob's Rock Museum.

With irrigation water, farmers were able to expand the type of commodities they grew from dry land wheat to such irrigated crops as alfalfa and potatoes.

In 1910 a railroad extension from Bliss to Rupert was completed. This additional line enhanced the city's status as a shipping point. During 22 months of the two-year period of 1911 to 1912, 109 rail cars – including 29 cars of wool, 23 cars of potatoes, 14 cars of sheep, 11 cars of horses, 10 cars of cattle and 10 cars of lumber – were shipped from Bliss loading docks.

In 1917 World War I brought an increased demand for agricultural products such as wool, beef, lamb and other commodities. Local ranchers even rounded up wild horses for sale to the military that needed riding and draft horses.

However, when the war ended, a national recession ensued. In Bliss, commodity prices collapsed and the local bank failed. Many ranchers again took to riding the range to round up wild horses. Except this time, they sold the horses to chicken feed manufacturers.

During succeeding years, the advent of the automobile and the construction of U.S. Highways 30 and 26 had a profound economic effect on the city. Bliss became a rest stop for the increasing number of cars and trucks traveling between Eastern Idaho and Boise and between highway 30 and Sun Valley.

Home and studio of Archie Teater, built by Frank Lloyd Wright in the 1950s.

The Federal New Deal programs that started in 1933 helped strengthen the economy of Bliss and the farming community. The program brought electricity to rural areas. The federal farm loan program made farm loans easier to obtain. Federal conservation practices changed to better managed grazing allotments as well as plant grasses that improved the range.

Incorporation

On May 20, 1947, Bliss became an incorporated village. In 1949 the village became an incorporated city.

Turning Points

Railroad The railroad's decision to build a depot at Bliss in 1883 was critical to the development of the city. That decision established Bliss as an important center for transporting agricultural commodities and a rest stop for travelers.

On the other hand, in the 1950s when the railroad ceased its Bliss operation, jobs were lost and the city's economy and population declined.

Highways By the mid-twentieth century, paved roads and motor vehicles were successfully competing with the railroad for passengers and freight. Construction of U.S. Highways 30 and 26 in Bliss brought increased traffic into the city and helped offset the loss of the railroad depot. The city's strategic location at the junction of these highways encouraged the development of retail businesses that serve truck freight carriers and the motoring public.

However, in 1975 when the federal government constructed U.S. Interstate 84 to the west of the city it dealt a serious blow to the city's economy. Prior to construction of the Interstate, an estimated 5,000 vehicles passed through the city daily. By 1982 the number of vehicles had declined to 1,400 cars a day.

Agriculture In the past century, the agricultural industry changed from a small-farm, labor-intensive industry to a larger-farm, technologically innovative and mechanized industry. The decline in the number of farm families and workers means fewer people coming into town to shop and do business. This has had a significant adverse effect on the city's economy.

Bliss School.

Bliss Today

Amenities and Attractions The two-acre Bliss Community Park is a gathering place for community events and family reunions. The park has facilities for picnics, a covered bowery, children's playgrounds and ball fields.

Over the years, the city has lost most of its historic buildings. The livery barn, built before 1901, is the oldest structure in Bliss.

Within a 35-mile radius of Bliss are numerous opportunities for hunting, fishing, boating, hiking, camping and other outdoor activities.

Five miles south is Malad Gorge State Park, one of the six units of the Thousand Springs State Park Complex. Up river from Malad Gorge, the Complex includes Billingsley Creek, The Earl M. Hardy Box Canyon Springs Nature Preserve (Box Canyon), Ritter Island, Niagara Springs and Crystal Springs. Each unit has distinguishing features and spectacular natural beauty. Fishing, camping, hiking or sightseeing are available throughout the Thousand Springs complex of state parks.

The units in the Complex are interspersed along a 30-mile stretch of the eastern side of the Snake River Canyon. For millennia, more than a thousand crystal-clear cold-water springs burst hundreds of feet high from the eastern walls of the canyon and cascade down the canyon walls into the Snake River. Other springs bubble up from the ground before flowing into the river.

Today, aquaculturists have captured many of the springs into raceways used in several public and private trout hatcheries and farms or channeled to produce electrical power.

Just outside of Bliss is the home and studio of Archie Teater, a renowned landscape artist. In the 1950s the world famous architect Frank Lloyd Wright, noted for his designs that blend with its natural surroundings, designed Teater's building on a high bluff overlooking the Snake River. Teater named the building "Teater's Knoll." It is the only building in Idaho designed by Wright.

Five miles to the south across the Snake River begins the 4,300-acre Hagerman Fossil Beds National Monument. Archeologists worldwide recognize the site for its prehistoric fossil and sediment deposits from the Pliocene Epoch. The National Monument's visitor center is eight

Bliss Post Office.

miles south of Bliss, in Hagerman. A segment of the Oregon National Historic Trail is on the southern end of the Monument. Ruts made by the Oregon Trail immigrant wagons are still visible from the parking lot that overlooks the Hagerman Fossil Beds.

The 613-acre Three Island Crossing State Park, the location where thousands of Oregon Trail pioneers forded the Snake River, is 20 miles west.

Thirty miles south of Bliss, in the Salmon Falls Creek Canyon, is the mushroom-shaped Balanced Rock. This wind-carved 48-foot-tall rock weighs 40 tons and is balanced on a (now reinforced) three-foot by 17-inch pedestal.

Economy and Major Employers The city's strategic setting at a freeway interchange and junction of two highways has caused several businesses that serve the motoring public to locate in Bliss. The largest of

these facilities, the Stinker Corporation, employees 50 people in its service station, store and restaurant.

The city's largest public employer, Bliss School District, has 25 employees.

Education The Bliss School District has a single facility that houses elementary, junior and senior high school programs. The school district provides most of the PK-12 education in the city.

The nearest institution of higher learning is the College of Southern Idaho, 34 miles southeast in Twin Fall.

Health Care The nearest hospital is Gooding County Memorial Hospital located 17 miles east in Gooding.

Transportation Bliss lies on the west side of the Interstate 84 interchange at the junctions of U.S. Highways 26 and 30. Highways 26 and 30 intersect the city.

Railroad service is available for freight.

Airport service for light private and charter aircraft is available at the 4,700-foot runway 14 miles east at the Gooding Municipal Airport in Gooding. The closest commercial air carrier is Joslin Field-Magic Valley Regional Airport in Twin Falls.

Utilities and Services Private companies provide electricity, telephone and satellite services. The City provides water services and fire protection. The city's homes and businesses have individual septic systems. The County provides police protection and solid waste services.

Vision for 2050

The population of Bliss has remained somewhat constant at around 250 for several decades. However, conditions are changing. By 2050 the population of Bliss will likely double.

Factors influencing this growth are the city's location as a transportation corridor and the transitioning of farmers into new aquaculture and vineyards.

The population growth in Twin Falls and Jerome will spill over to Bliss. More families will choose to live in Bliss because housing is more affordable and the environment more peaceful. Most of this new workforce will commute to larger cities. As evidence of this growth, developers are now planning a new subdivision in Bliss. The city has recently built a new water system and school and is working to build a new sewer system.

Mayors

Bef. 1949 J.C. Bronson *
1949 Frank D. Wright *
1970 Vernon Behrens
1972 Ray Armstrong
1977 Roland Zollinger

1991 Sam Bishop
1996 Jimmie J. Pruett
2012 Chris Pruett
* Village Chairman

Old TB Hospital in Gooding.

Gooding

Statistical Data

Population: 3,461 *
Elevation: 3,573 feet
Precipitation: 8 inches **
Average Snowfall: 28 inches **
County: Gooding
Website: www.goodingidaho.org

Temperature Range – Fahrenheit: **
Spring: 35 to 61
Summer: 53 to 86
Fall: 37 to 64
Winter: 21 to 38
* U.S. Census Bureau Estimates July 2015
**Historical averages

Surrounded by fertile farms inside vast tracts of prehistoric lava flows and public land, Gooding is about 33 miles north of Twin Falls. (*See Southwestern Idaho, TheRegion, Distinctive Geographic and Geological Features*.)

The Little Wood and Big Wood Rivers bracket the city and the Snake River comes within about 12 miles of the city on the west and southwest.

Pre-Incorporation Years

Fur trappers arrived in the area in the early 1800s and were the first newcomers to compete with the nomadic Indians for the natural resources of the Snake River Plain. The trappers primarily worked the tributaries draining into the Snake River. (*See Southwestern Idaho, The Region, American Indians and Early Trappers/Explorers*.)

Cattle and sheep ranchers began grazing their herds on the large expanse of rangeland near what is now Gooding in the 1870s. However, it was not until the railroad came that significant settlement began. (*See Southwestern Idaho, The*

Region, Livestock.)

In 1882 the Oregon Short Line Railroad built a rail line between Granger, Wyoming, and Huntington, Oregon. When the line reached Shoshone, the railroad stopped to build a branch line north to the mines in the Wood River Valley. A year later, the rail line passed through Gooding and on to Caldwell and Huntington, located just across the Snake River from Weiser. When completed on November 17, 1884, the line connected Portland with Omaha. (*See Southwestern Idaho, The Region, Railroads.*)

Some railroad workers and passengers returned to Gooding as homesteaders and settlers. They were attracted by the settlement potential of the large tracts of fertile land between lava-flow outcroppings and the prospect of using water from the Big Wood and Little Wood Rivers for irrigation. (*See Southwestern Idaho, The Region, Federal Land Use Laws.*)

The railroad's chief engineer, Jacob Blickensdorfer (or Blickensderfer, the exact spelling of his name cannot be confirmed) made a train stop he called Toponis, the site of what is now Gooding. Toponis is reportedly a Shoshone Indian word meaning "Black Cherries." The U.S. Postal Service opened the Toponis Post Office in 1887.

In 1876 the first registered settler in the area, Nathan R. Woodworth, homesteaded a site on the Little Wood River. He and his family built the first house, put in the first dam and dug the first ditch to divert water from the river.

One Toponis resident was prominent sheep man Frank R. Gooding. He came to the area in 1888 and homesteaded south of town. Over the next few years, he systematically increased his land holdings to several hundred acres.

Early city of Gooding. Courtesy Gooding Historical Society.

In 1893 the sheep ranchers formed the Idaho Wool Growers Association and named Gooding its first president.

During that time, Gooding became active in Idaho Republican politics. He served as an Idaho state senator and chairman of the Idaho Republican Central

Committee. He was elected governor in 1904 and re-elected for a two-year term in 1906. Gooding was elected to the United States Senate (six-year terms) in 1920 and again in 1926, dying in office in 1928.

Incorporation

Frank Gooding aggressively used his influence to develop his growing business interests. In 1907 while still governor of Idaho, he hired H.P. Blodgett to survey and plat 160 acres of his land near Toponis for a new townsite named after him.

He laid out the plat with Main Street running from south to north, ending at the railroad tracks. He divided the townsite with eighty acres on each side of Main Street. On Gooding's birthday, November 14, 1907, he began selling building lots.

Gooding and M. Mattson opened the first general store in the city under the name Gooding Mercantile Company.

Frank R. Gooding

On April 25, 1908, the new town of Gooding became an incorporated village with W.J. Gooding, Frank's brother as chairman. The 1910 census reported a population of 1,444. Six months later on November 21, Gooding became an incorporated city. With the economy of the area shifting to the city of Gooding, the adjoining town of Toponis lost its separate identity.

Turning Points

Railroad The railroad established the community of Toponis and laid the foundation for Frank R. Gooding to build the town that bears his name. The railroad made it possible for area farmers and ranchers to more easily ship their commodities and livestock to the market.

Frank R. Gooding Gooding not only founded the city, he was its greatest benefactor. He is the

Bank. Courtesy Gooding Historical Society.

primary reason the State built the Idaho School for the Deaf and the Blind (ISDB) in Gooding. The original school was located in Boise. However, after it burned down, the State accepted Gooding's offer of 20 acres of his property to rebuild the school in Gooding. The deed specifies that if the land is not used for the school or some other State purpose, the property reverts back to the Gooding heirs. The first campus building opened in 1910.

On January 28, 1913, the legislature formed Gooding County, with the city of Gooding as the county seat.

Four years later, Frank Gooding donated 70 acres to the Methodist Episcopal Church as the site for Gooding College, which the church planned to build and operate. The college operated until 1938 when it had to close because of declining enrollment, at which time the church gave the property to the State of Idaho for a tuberculosis hospital.

The Idaho Legislature established the Idaho State Tuberculosis Hospital on that site in 1941. The State moved the buildings used by the military in Rupert for housing World War II prisoners of war to the hospital property in 1947.

A decade later, the State built a new million-dollar hospital that for many years was in the forefront of tuberculosis and respiratory disease treatment. However, subsequent innovation in medical science essentially

Merchants Building. Courtesy Gooding Historical Society.

eradicated tuberculosis and the need for those hospital services. The hospital closed in the mid-1960s. All but one of the hospital buildings was razed. The remaining building, which was originally a dormitory at Gooding College, is now privately owned.

Gooding Today

Amenities and Attractions
A short drive from Gooding in almost any direction except the southwest puts you on public land. These open high-desert vistas and ancient volcanic flows provide a wide variety of year-round recreational opportunities. There is fishing, camping, hiking, skiing, horseback riding, boating, trap shooting and numerous

Gooding Hospital. Courtesy Gooding Historical Society.

opportunities for viewing wildlife in its natural habitat.

The city's amenities include a municipal golf course, swimming pool, county fairgrounds, baseball diamonds and tennis courts including some on public school grounds, a public gym located at the Idaho School for the Deaf and the Blind, two privately owned gyms that offer memberships, a bowling alley, library and four city parks including a skate park.

Many Gooding residents are of Basque heritage. Initially, they emigrated from

Spain to work in the area's sheep industry. They organized the Gooding Basque Association, which in 2003 built a new cultural center that is open to the public. The association seeks to preserve the Basque culture in Idaho by sponsoring an annual picnic the third Sunday of July and a dinner on the first Friday of each month. The picnic offers traditional Basque food accompanied by cultural dancing and weight carrying and lifting contests.

Gooding combines the friendly rural hometown atmosphere of a progressive Western farming community with the convenience of having easy access to the larger cities of Twin Falls and Boise.

Economy and Major Employers Gooding has a distinct agricultural character. Surrounding the city are crop and dairy farming and cattle and

Main Street, 1950. Courtesy Gooding Historical Society.

sheep ranching. Over 100,000 acres of rich irrigated land surround the city. The principal crops are potatoes, hay, grain, sugar beets and silage corn.

The city has a vibrant downtown district with a variety of retail, financial and service businesses.

It has created an urban renewal district and built an 80-acre industrial park along the Union Pacific Railroad mainline. Among the businesses coming to the park was Kiefer Built LLC, a horse and livestock trailer manufacturing company. It opened in 2004 with 43 employees.

Gambia Foods manufactures barrel cheese

Gooding High School. Courtesy Gooding Historical Society.

from milk produced at local dairy farms. It is the city's largest private employer with 200 employees. Three trucking companies also operate out of the city. D&D Transportation is the largest and employs 71.

The city's largest public employers include the ISDB and the Gooding School District, each employing about 130. Gooding County and the Gooding County Memorial Hospital each employ about 80.

Education The Gooding School District provides most of the elementary and secondary education. The school district operates a high school, accelerated learning center, middle and elementary schools in the city.

The campus for the ISDB is also located in the city. This century-old special needs school has a residency program for 35 to 40 students, serves a similar number of day-school students and oversees the education of about 700 deaf, hard – of-hearing, blind and visually impaired students in host public school districts across the state.

The College of Southern Idaho (CSI), 33 miles south in Twin Falls, is the closest institution of higher learning. Idaho's three universities also offer degree programs on its campus.

The University of Idaho operates an agricultural extension office in Gooding.

Health Care The 26-bed Gooding County Memorial Hospital serves the greater Gooding area and is the primary provider of medical care. Physicians representing a variety of specialized medical disciplines and living in other larger cities come to the hospital each week to serve their patients.

For the elderly, recovering and disabled, the city has a nursing home, rehabilitation center and two assisted-living facilities.

In 1976 the Walker Center, a nationally recognized alcohol and substance abuse treatment company, was founded in Gooding. The Center now has facilities in Gooding, Twin Falls, Boise, Hailey, Idaho Falls and Pocatello.

Historic Gooding Hotel.

Transportation U.S. Highway 26 and State Highway 46 intersect the city. Interstate 84 is located 12 miles west.

The Gooding Airport is three miles east of the city. It has a 4,736-foot runway and serves light private and charter aircraft. The closest commercial airport is Joslin Field in Twin Falls.

Rail transportation is available in the city for freight only.

Utilities and Services Private companies provide electricity, telephone, gas, cable and satellite services. The City provides water, municipal wastewater treatment services, police and fire protection. The County provides solid waste services.

Vision for 2050

For the past five decades, Gooding's population has ranged from about 2,600 to

3,400. By 2050 the city's population will likely more than double.

Factors influencing this growth include new and expanding private businesses in or near the city and in the industrial park, expansion of the Walker Center and Gooding Memorial Hospital, State agencies establishing or expanding offices on State-owned property and the spill-over effect of growth occurring in the Twin Falls area.

The city will have completed several important improvements to its park system, including a walking, biking, and riding path bordering the waterway running through the city; a skateboard park; and a park with a bandstand for concerts.

An active retail area will flourish at the south end of the city and an industrial area north of town. The current downtown area will consist of specialty shops, restaurants and a cultural center for the performing arts. Gooding Airport will have significant growth. There will be a depot at the north end of town as part of the region's mass transit system.

The city will enlist participation of residents in its strategic planning and decision making processes. In the next few decades, the city will need to make significant progress on a host of matters including economic development, water and energy management, residential development, historic preservation and road and street infrastructure.

By 2050 Gooding will stand as a community that honors its heritage and is noted for friendly people, safe streets, drug-free environment, low crime rate, educational opportunities, community events, numerous churches and ethnic and cultural diversity. It will be an attractive city to grow a business and raise a family.

Mayors

1908 W.J. Gooding *	1957 James Warrington
1909 I.C. Brubaker *	1959 Leo Rice
1911 E.J. Morrow	1966 R.W. Stuart
1911 Dr. J.L. Benson	1970 H.V. Crippen
1912 J.E. Palmer	1974 Leo Rice
1913 H.J. Leyson	1975 E.D. Gene Kelly
1917 John Thomas	1976 Don C. Morrow
1919 Anson E. Thompson	1980 Jasper "Gene" Heller
1925 A.F. James	1992 David J. Adair
1931 Harry Levy	1997 Ervin "George" Dains
1935 A.F. James	2002 Herb Stroud
1945 F.E. Barrett	2004 William Morton
1947 J. Wesley Miller	2014 Walter Nelson
1949 H.V. Crippen	* Village Chairman

Bank, Post Office, Museum - Hagerman.

Hagerman

Statistical Data

Population: 856 *
Elevation: 2,959 feet
Precipitation: 15 inches **
Average Snowfall: 15 inches **
County: Gooding
Website: www.hagermanidaho.org

Temperature Range – Fahrenheit: **
Spring: 29 to 76
Summer: 49 to 94
Fall: 27 to 83
Winter: 20 to 49
* U.S. Census Bureau Estimates July 2015
**Historical averages

The city of Hagerman lies in the fertile Hagerman Valley created 14,500 years ago when enormous Lake Bonneville breached its natural dam at Red Rock Pass near Downey and poured into the Snake River.

This mega flood cut deep gorges and left enormous sandbars as it followed the Snake River channel. One of these sandbars is now the Hagerman Valley. Smooth boulders, some the size of automobiles, were rolled by the flood for over a hundred miles before coming to rest in this now temperate valley. (*See Eastern Idaho, The Region, Distinctive Geographic and Geologic Features, Prehistoric Lake Bonneville.*)

Both hot and cold natural springs are common. Units of the Thousand Springs State Park Complex – with its stunningly beautiful, interesting and unique natural features and wonders – bracket the city on the north and south.

To the west across the Snake River is the 4,300-acre Hagerman Fossil Beds National Monument, a site recognized by archeologists worldwide for its prehistoric fossil and sediment deposits from the Pliocene Epoch.

The regional shopping and business center of Twin Falls lies 30 miles southeast.

Pre-Incorporation Years

At its peak discharge, the Lake Bonneville flood released 15,000 cubic feet of water per second through Red Rock Pass. The floodwaters not only shaped the Hagerman Valley but also changed the terrain all along the downstream Snake River before flowing into the Columbia River.

The elevation of the valley is much lower than the surrounding plain. The winters are generally mild. Shoshone, Paiute and Bannock Indians often wintered in the valley. When the salmon and steelhead were migrating up river to spawn, Upper and Lower Salmon Falls were major aboriginal fishing sites. (*See The Region, American Indians.*)

In 1811 Wilson Price Hunt led an expedition of fur trappers in a failed attempt to float the Snake River to the Columbia and the Pacific. In November of that year, part of the expedition camped one night in the Hagerman Valley. (*See The Region, Early Trappers/Explorers.*)

The first overland migration of pioneers to Oregon passed through Southern Idaho in the summer of 1841 when it was hot and dry. One wrote, "The country all the way down the Snake River is one of the most desolate and dreary wastes in the world ..."

However, when Oregon Trail immigrants reached the Thousand Springs area, they marveled at the contrast. Instead of dry desert, they traveled through miles of lush vegetation irrigated by springs bursting from the eastern walls of the Snake River Canyon. In addition, they were able to trade with Indians for fresh and dried salmon. (*See Turning Points and Amenities and Attractions below.*)

On August 20, 1845, Joel Palmer, an Oregon Trail immigrant, wrote: "We traveled about nine miles, reaching Salmon Falls. Here are eighteen or twenty Indian huts. Salmon came up to these falls; the Indians have an abundance of them, which they very readily dispose of for hocks, powder, balls, clothing, calico and knives, and in fact for almost anything we have at our disposal."

The Oregon Trail left the valley near Salmon Falls to ascend a long grade to the west in a direct approach to the Snake River crossing – Three Island Crossing State Park – near what is now Glenns Ferry. In 1852 a ferry crossing upstream of the Thousand Springs, Payne's Ferry, allowed immigrants to use a northern route through the Hagerman Valley. (*See The Region, Oregon and California Trails.*)

Prospectors discovered placer gold in the Boise Basin in 1862, and a gold rush ensued. By 1863 thousands of prospectors and miners were flooding into the basin. (*See The Region, Mining – Boise Basin – Gold.*)

The gold rush brought heavy freight wagons and fast stage lines from Utah to the Boise Basin. Some travelers used the Glenns Ferry - Salmon Falls route through the upper Hagerman Valley, while others came through Hagerman Valley by crossing at Payne's Ferry. The Overland Trail Stagecoach Station became the site of the city of Hagerman.

In 1870 prospectors discovered fine gold in the Snake River sand bars. For the next decade, prospectors worked the entire course of the river. The Salmon Falls region was designated as a mining district.

During this time, homesteaders and ranchers began settling in the Hagerman Valley. On January 8, 1879, a post office opened in Salmon Falls, a community located approximately 30 miles from what is now Hagerman. That year John Bell, one of the homesteaders, planted alfalfa. In 1880 he brought in grape vines and planted peach and poplar trees. The fast-growing poplar trees were a hit. Soon residents throughout the valley were planting the fast-growing shade trees. (*See The Region, Federal Lands – Private Ownership Laws and Preservation.*)

The Oregon Short Line Railroad completed its rail line from Granger, Wyoming, to Huntington, Oregon, in 1884, finishing the important link connecting Omaha, Nebraska, and Portland, Oregon, creating another intercontinental railroad. In 1883 the railroad reached Bliss where it built a depot. While the train depot was a boon to Bliss, it also was an important benefit to

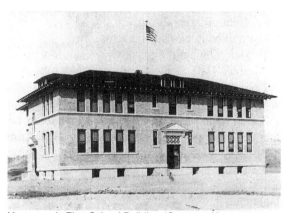

Hagerman's First School Building (Courtesy Hagerman Valley Historical Society)

Hagerman and the agriculture businesses in the Hagerman Valley. Within a few hours, the settlers could drive their livestock and haul their commodities to the Bliss railhead for shipment to market. (*See The Region, Railroads.*)

In 1894 A.D. Foote, a mining engineer searching for an electricity source for the Trade Dollar Mine at Silver City located 90 miles west, noted that the Thousand Springs area was a promising location for electrical power generation. However, it would take until 1903 before anyone tapped the area's electrical power generating potential. (*See The Region, Mining – Owyhee Mountains – Silver and Gold.*)

In that year, Thousand Springs Power Company of Arizona completed a dam and electrical power plant at lower Salmon Falls. The power company would later build a 400-foot flume along the face of the east rim that collected water from the springs pouring out of the Snake River Canyon Gorge. They dropped the channeled spring water 165 feet into electric turbines. In 1910 the electric company built another power plant on the Malad River. Idaho Power Company purchased the utility in 1917 and extended the flume another 250 feet.

Settlers built a school in 1892 and entrepreneurs Stanley Hageman and Jack Hess opened a general store. Hageman and Hess applied for a post office they named "Hageman" to be located in their store. Postal authorities approved the application; however, they spelled the name on their central registry as "Hagerman," thus establishing the name of the post office and, eventually, the city.

By 1893 the town had a new hotel. Another entrepreneur named Billy Coltharp built a structure that served as both a saloon and his residence. The saloon, initially consisting of a barrel of whiskey and a tin cup, was in front of the building. Coltharp lived in two small rooms at the back. The building is now the Masonic Hall.

Horse-drawn school buses at old grade school. This is the school that burned in 1925. (Courtesy Hagerman Valley Historical Society.)

Coltharp became one of the town's leading citizens. He built the original part of the Morris Roberts Store, now US Bank; established the city park, which today bears his name; and built the Park Opera House, now the American Legion Hall. Coltharp also helped organize the first bank in town, the Hagerman State Bank. Businesses that had grown up at Salmon Falls moved to Hagerman.

By 1900 several hundred settlers had come to the Hagerman area. They started a Sunday School and provided the economic basis for the new town. A decade later, Hagerman had three churches, two banks, three hotels, three

Looking west down Hagerman Avenue, once the main street in town. (Courtesy Hagerman Valley Historical Society.)

general stores, three real estate firms, a hardware store, a drug store, a meat market, a blacksmith shop, a harness shop, two livery barns, two restaurants and a pool hall. An opera house and three additional meeting halls also were available for public use. In 1909 the valley's first newspaper – The Hagerman Valley Sun, later the Herald – began publication.

Incorporation

On January 16, 1918, Hagerman became an incorporated village. Its status changed to a city with new law passed by the Idaho Legislature in 1967.

Turning Points

Railroad Unlike other communities bypassed by the railroad, Hagerman benefited from the railroad even though the depot was eight miles away in Bliss because the Hagerman agricultural economy was somewhat self-contained. It was only moderately inconvenient for the ranchers and farmers to drive their livestock and haul their farm commodities to Bliss for shipment to market and for the townspeople to do their business.

Thousand Springs Thousand Springs is an impressive unique natural feature in Idaho. It provides diverse employment opportunities and offers many types of outdoor recreation, including those available at Thousand Springs State Park. (*See Amenities and Attractions below.*)

These natural springs gush from the basalt canyon walls that are as high as 600 feet above the Snake River. At the bottom of the canyon, hundreds of underground springs percolate thousands of gallons of constant 58 degree Fahrenheit water into the river, a temperature that is ideal for raising commercial trout. This aquatic phenomenon stretches for over 20 miles

Billy Coltharp's Park Opera House. (Courtesy Hagerman Valley Historical Society.)

north of Hagerman to over 40 miles southeast toward Twin Falls, providing water for hydroelectric power plants and commercial and public fish hatcheries before flowing into the Snake River.

The commercial use of the spring water began in 1928 when Jack W. Tingey, a biologist, began a commercial fish operation. He discovered the springs offered exceptionally favorable conditions for large-scale rainbow trout production.

Hagerman Fossil Beds National Monument As Tingey began raising trout in 1928, Elmer Cook, a local rancher, discovered a bed of prehistoric fossils across the Snake River from Hagerman.

At the time, Harold T. Stearns, a prominent geologist and member of the United States Geological Survey team, was in the area working for the General Land Office studying irrigation projects. Stearns had already authored a report to the National Park Service recommending the Craters of the Moon as a national monument. So when Cook showed him the fossil bed discovery in 1929, Stearns contacted paleontologists from the Smithsonian Institution in Washington, D.C. The Smithsonian's expedition to the area determined that the discovery was a treasure trove of 3-million-year-old fossils from the Pliocene Epoch. The fossil beds included one they named the Hagerman Horse Quarry, a bed of fossils that yielded 120 horse skulls and 20 complete horse skeletons.

The Smithsonian named the horse skeletons the Hagerman Horse and shared the fossils with museums around the world. In 1988 Congress established the fossil beds as a national monument, and the Idaho Legislature declared the Hagerman Horse the state fossil.

The monument has given Hagerman international recognition. Today over 15,000 visitors come annually to visit this federally-managed monument and visitor's center.

Thousand Springs.

Hagerman Today

Amenities and Attractions The city has two city parks on 7.4 acres. Coltharp Park is located near the center of town and offers picnic areas and children's playgrounds. Pocket Park has picnic and RV facilities.

The Hagerman City Hall houses the Hagerman Valley Chamber of Commerce as well as city offices.

The city sponsors or supports several annual events that bring the community together. The St. Patrick's Day Fun Run/Walk takes place each March. It is a 5.5-mile run and 3.5-mile walk/run at the Malad Gorge State Park unit of Thousand Springs State Park north of Hagerman.

On Memorial Day weekend, the city and chamber of commerce sponsor the annual Fossil Days starting with a fundraiser breakfast followed by a parade and a variety of exhibits and events at Coltharp Park.

Each September, the Hagerman Improvement, Development, Education and Appreciation (IDEA) organization sponsors the Blues in the Park music festival a half mile north of the city at the Billingsley Creek unit of the Thousand Springs State Park.

The many units of Thousand Springs State Park are outstanding tourist attractions, adding an important economic base to the city's economy.

Prominent units of Thousand Springs State Park

Ferry near Thousand Springs (Courtesy Hagerman Valley Historical Society.)

are Malad Gorge, Billingsley Creek, the Earl M. Hardy Box Canyon Springs Nature Preserve, Ritter Island, Niagara Springs and Crystal Springs.

A few miles north of Hagerman is the 652-acre Malad Gorge State Park that includes a 250-foot-deep gorge cut prehistorically by the Malad River as it flows into the Snake River. The Malad River begins near Gooding where the Big and Little Wood Rivers combine and then flows west for nine miles where it cuts the two-mile gorge – the shortest river in Idaho. The park offers hiking, picnicking and day use. A steel viewing bridge crosses the gorge.

Billingsley Creek State Park covers 282 acres adjacent to the 284-acre Billingsley Creek Wildlife Management Area. The park is an outstanding trout fishery with large springs, a lake, hiking trails and areas for public events often used by the city of Hagerman. The park is also the historic home of the renowned author Vardis Fisher.

The Wildlife Management Area supports a trout fishery and habitat for migratory waterfowl, upland game birds and mule deer.

The 350-acre Earl M. Hardy Box Canyon Springs Nature Preserve features a crystal-clear cold-water spring at the back of the canyon that pours 180,000 gallons of water per minute into the Snake River. The spring is the eleventh largest in North America.

Ritter Island State Park on 300 acres has two miles of riverfront. The park lies about 10 miles south of Hagerman and sits between two large natural springs that burst from the canyon walls and flow into the Snake River.

Niagara Springs and Crystal Springs are also part of the state park system within a mile of each located several miles southeast of Hagerman. Niagara Springs is also a National Natural Landmark. Both of these parks are excellent fisheries.

The Hagerman Fossil Beds National Monument's visitor center is in Hagerman. A segment of the Oregon National Historic Trail is on the southern end of the monument. Ruts made by the Oregon Trail immigrant wagons are still visible from the parking lot overlooking the Hagerman Fossil Beds.

The defining feature of the Hagerman Valley is its plentiful water – a dramatic counterpoint in this arid Great Basin desert landscape.

The mild climate and abundance of year-round open water make the valley a preferred stop for migrating birds; offering superb waterfowl and upland bird hunting. This same abundance of water also provides numerous opportunities for water sports. Boating for sightseeing, water skiing and fishing on the river are common. Whitewater rafting, canoe and kayak adventures and year-round scenic river cruises and riverboat dining are available. The river's high palisade walls provide a majestic sight for boaters, rafters and kayakers at the bottom of the canyon as they navigate over tumbling, boiling rapids or drift lazily through the quiet stretches.

South of the city are several developed hot springs. These swimming pools and spas include Banbury Hot Springs, 1000 Springs Resort and Miracle Hot Springs.

The 68-mile Thousand Springs Scenic Byway follows U.S. Highway 30 near Bliss, south through Hagerman to Buhl, east on State Highway 50 in Twin Falls and on to Interstate 84.

Old Coltharp Saloon, now Masonic Hall.

Several private fish hatcheries and fish farms are located along the Snake River Canyon between Hagerman and Twin Falls. They are open to the public, and many have areas for public fishing. These Idaho commercial trout farms produced about 44 percent of the $80 million of fresh trout sold in the U.S. in 2008.

A state fish hatchery is on 35 acres about three miles south of Hagerman. It produces nearly 2 million trout annually for stocking Idaho lakes and streams. A national fish hatchery is located two miles southeast of the state hatchery and produces about 3 million trout annually for stocking waters in Idaho, Nevada and Oregon.

Hagerman has several historical buildings including the former home and studio of renowned artist Archie B. Teater – designed by the famous architect, Frank Lloyd Wright. The home is near Hagerman overlooking the Snake River and in 1983 was placed on the National Register of Historic Places. This private residence is not open to the public.

Economy and Major Employers Idaho Power Company is the city's largest employer with about 80 employees at its Hagerman Valley hydroelectric plant. The Hagerman School District has over 40 employees and is the city's second largest employer.

Many employees of agricultural businesses – including private trout farms, state and national fish hatcheries and fish research stations – reside in the city.

The city's retail district includes restaurants, motels and RV parks, bed and breakfasts, convenience stores and a variety of service businesses. Residents often shop in larger cities located nearby.

Hagerman General Store and US Bank.

Education The Hagerman School District provides most of the primary and secondary education. The Hagerman Junior/Senior High School and Hagerman Elementary School are located in the city.

The closest institution of higher learning is the College of Southern Idaho, 36 miles south in Twin Falls.

Health Care A general medical clinic is located in the city. The Gooding County Memorial Hospital, 16 miles northeast in Gooding, is the nearest hospital.

Transportation U.S. Highway 30 – the Thousand Springs Scenic Byway – intersects the city and is the city's main boulevard. Interstate 84 is eight miles northeast. Railroad service is available for freight. The Gooding Municipal Airport is available for light private and charter aircraft. The closest commercial airport is Magic Valley Regional Airport in Twin Falls.

Utilities and Services Private companies provide electricity, telephone and satellite services. The City provides water and sewer services and police protection. The Hagerman Fire District provides fire protection. The County provides solid waste services.

Vision for 2050

Since 1960 Hagerman's population has increased about 80 percent. If historical trends continue, by 2050 Hagerman will have a population approximating 1,400.

In 2050 the important attributes that define the city today will remain. The city's downtown will have wide sidewalks and landscaped features. Highway 30 will continue to be a boulevard through town providing a safe and efficient flow of traffic. Downtown Hagerman will still be pedestrian and bicycle friendly and have tree-lined streets and off-street parking designed to handle RVs.

City planning and zoning ordinances will continue to ensure that growth takes place in a logical and planned manner – that growth "pays its own way." The city water supply, wastewater treatment facilities and drainage systems will be adequate and operating effectively. City streets will still be well maintained and resurfaced on a planned schedule.

City offices, library, community center and a visitor center will be in an attractive building complex near the center of town. The city will continue to partner with state and federal agencies to insure the visitor center provides a one-stop opportunity for visitors to obtain complete information about the area. Tourist support facilities such as parking and restrooms, will be expanded as needed to meet the demand of the increasing numbers of tourists.

The city's per capita park acreage currently surpasses that found in most rural communities. By 2050 the city park system will continue to support active youth programs of soccer, baseball and softball while providing open space for other youth and family recreation opportunities.

Mayors

1909	W.H. Coltharp *	1982	Karen Yarbrough
1921	W.H. Dickenson *	1984	Merle E. Owsley
1923	R.S. Peterson *	1991	Gloria M. Jazwick
1929	J.S. Johnson *	1992	James G. Martin
1930	Edward Owsley *	1994	James Norwood
1955	Ralph Miller *	2004	Todd Bassett
1968	Frank West	2005	Noel E. Weir
1969	Marjorie West	2006	Robert J. Petronek
1970	Gene Overlie	2008	Jacob Rice, Jr.
1970	G.P. Russell	2012	Noel (Pete) Weir
1975	Dean Holt		* Village Chairman
1980	Bill Stinermates		

Wendell

Statistical Data

Population: 2,707 *
Elevation: 3,432 feet
Precipitation: 10.3 inches **
Average Snowfall: 27 inches **
County: Gooding

Temperature Range – Fahrenheit: **
Spring: 29 to 67
Summer: 50 to 86
Fall: 27 to 75
Winter: 19 to 40

* U.S. Census Bureau Estimates July 2015
** Historical averages

Wendell is one of several Magic Valley farming communities that were created following the 1905 completion of Milner Dam. The dam, located on the Snake River about 40 miles southeast of Jerome, produced sufficient water, fed through a complex system of irrigation canals, to irrigate and transform over 400,000 acres of fertile sagebrush-covered land into a farming oasis on, first, the south and, then, the north side of the river.

From its inception, agricultural-based businesses have dominated the city's economy. Today, lush fields of alfalfa hay, corn, wheat, barley, sugar beets, beans and potatoes form a beautiful patchwork of color and texture around the city.

Beginning about two decades ago, large dairy farms – attracted by its moderate high-desert climate, abundance of excellent quality cattle feed, water and open-space – began developing in the Magic Valley. Idaho is now one of the principal dairy producing states in the nation. Some of the state's largest dairy farms are located near Wendell.

Interstate 84 abuts the city's west and south boundaries. Twin Falls is 24 miles southeast and Gooding, the county seat, is 11 miles north.

Niagara Springs, one of nine units comprising Thousand Springs State Park on the Snake River, is located five miles south of the city.

The city's slogon is "Wendell, Hub City of the Magic Valley."

Pre-Incorporation Years

American Indians of the Bannock and Shoshone Tribes exclusively inhabited what is now the Magic Valley until around 1811 when the first explorers/trappers came into the area. They followed the Snake River and explored its tributaries in search of prime locations to trap beaver.

In 1841 the first overland migration of explorers and settlers destined for what is now western Oregon passed through the area. In 1842 Captain John C. Fremont, a military surveyor, led a 39-member exploration and survey detachment through Idaho and on to the Oregon coast. Future Oregon Trail immigrants benefited from Fremont's detail maps and descriptions of the terrain, including campsite locations.

The 1862 prospectors found gold in the Boise Basin. The following year, 16,000 people flooded into the mining district. In 1864 the U.S. military built Fort Boise 40 miles east of the original Fort Boise located near what is now Parma and destroyed several years earlier by flood. Residents living near the new Fort Boise almost immediately platted a town near the fort that they named Boise City. Mail, passenger and freight wagon services, coming up from Utah to the new fort and town, passed through the Magic Valley a few miles from what is now Wendell.

In November 1884 the Oregon Short Line (OSL) completed construction of a railroad line that began at Granger, Wyoming; angled in a northwesterly direction through what are now Pocatello, Shoshone and Nampa; until it connected with the railroad across the Snake River in Huntington, Oregon. With this rail line, trains could travel from Omaha, Nebraska, to Portland, Oregon, in less than four days.

Wendell, 1909.

In 1894 the U.S. Congress passed the Carey Act. Under the Act, the federal government ceded up to one million acres of arable federal land to any state that would bring the land under cultivation. Development of the land was a public-private partnership. Idaho would ultimately use 850,000 acres of its allotment.

Under the Carey Act Project, private interests financed and built dams and canals. The State sold 40 to 160 acre parcels of land to individuals. In Idaho, the Idaho State Land Board represented the State. The developers sold water rights, developed town sites and sold town site lots. (*See Southwestern Idaho, Cities of the Magic Valley.*)

Around 1900 Ira B. Perrine, a local farmer and entrepreneur who produced food for the miners in the Wood River district, sought to develop a "Carey Act" diversion dam – Milner Dam – across the Snake River at The Cedars.

In 1900 Perrine and several investors formed the Twin Falls Land and Water Company to build Milner Dam and a gravity-irrigation canal system on the south side of the river. In 1905 they completed the dam, and the first irrigation water reached farmland on the south side of the Snake River Canyon.

In 1907 Perrine and other investors – including William S. and James S. Kuhn from Pennsylvania and William's brother-in-law, Jerome Hill – formed the Twin Falls North Side Land and Water Company (North Side Project) to bring water to the north side of the Snake River. The North Side Project would include creation of Wendell as well as Jerome, Hazelton and Eden.

In July 1908 the company recorded the Wendell townsite plat – named Wendell after William Kuhn's 15-year-old son.

The company promised the settlers that the new community would have electricity, an electric railway and waterworks. A few months later, principals in the banks in neighboring towns opened Wendell State Bank.

In October 1908 Wendell constructed its own school,

Wendell Hub City sign at night, 1946.

which opened the following month with a single teacher and 12 students. In September 1909 the school opened with 117 students taught in four age groups and an elected board of trustees. The State provided $12 per student.

In December 1908 the Minidoka and Southwestern Railroad Company – building a 73-mile branch line from Rupert to Bliss, completed in 1910 – reached Wendell.

On April 15, 1909, the town's new newspaper, The Hub City Irrigationist, stated in its editorial, "...comfortable homes can be built here very reasonably...an energetic man with a drop of farming blood in his veins can establish a profitable horticultural dairy or general farm business under the substantial system of irrigation ditches through which water is secured..."

Incorporation

On September 21, 1909, 300 Wendell residents held a meeting to petition the Lincoln County Commissioners to become an incorporated village. Those who attended approved five men to be the village's first Board of Trustees. On October

12, 1909, the County Commissioners approved Wendell becoming an incorporated village.

The 1910 census reported the Wendell population at 482. The community continued to grow and, on February 14, 1947, was allowed to change its legal status to an incorporated city.

Turning Points

Irrigation. Wendell owes its origins to irrigation. The Carey Act, along with other federal reclamation laws allowed private investors, led by Ira B. Perrine, to build Milner Dam and construct the complex system of irrigation pumps, canals and ditches named the North Side Project that provided irrigation water to Wendell area farmers.

South Central Idaho Veterans Park.

Railroad The railroad was a lifeline to the community. It allowed farmers to ship their commodities to distant markets, merchants to bring in supplies and gave fast transportation to passengers and the mail.

Even though railroad service became available at Shoshone in 1883, it took the development of irrigation and farmland beginning in 1907 to bring the railroad to Wendell.

Motor Vehicles and Roads. In the early 1900s motor vehicles become popular. The construction of hard-surface roads soon followed. In 1963 Interstate 84 reached nearby Jerome and built two interchanges. With the completion of these roads, Jerome's retail business sector blossomed and trucks competed successfully against the railroad for freight business.

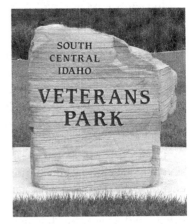

Agriculture. While agricultural-based businesses have underpinned Wendell's economy for the past century, the type of commodities produced and the labor-intensive nature of the industry have changed.

The first crops grown were primarily hay and grain, using flood irrigation. Today, alfalfa hay and corn are the largest acreages followed by potatoes and sugar beets. More efficient and water-conserving sprinkler irrigation systems have, in many cases, replaced flood irrigation methods.

In the early years, most farms had a variety of large animals and poultry. Some became involved in niche businesses. A major case in point happened in 1926. R.D. Bradshaw and Sons began a honey production and processing plant in Wendell that grew into one of the largest in the nation. In 1964 the company sold to Sue Bee Honey Company of Sioux City, Iowa.

In the latter part of the century, dairy farmers in other states discovered that the Magic Valley was a prime location for dairy farms. Now, dairies with several thousand milking cows each are common.

Over the past several decades, Wendell's smaller farms have either sold or leased to increasingly larger farm operators. Technological innovation, efficiencies of scale and the cost of environmental regulation are principal causes for this consolidation. Agriculture is now substantially less labor-intensive than just a few decades ago. This has had an adverse effect on the city's retail businesses that relied on the farm employment base for business.

Wendell Today

Amenities and Attractions Wendell has three parks. Their amenities include a swimming pool and tennis courts. Veterans Park is a memorial park recognizing men and women who served in the military.

Wendell's annual events include Dairy Days, held each June; Independence Day, held each Fourth of July with a fireworks finale; and each December Santa comes to kick off the Christmas season. Other city celebrations coincide with the holidays of Halloween, Spook House; Arbor Day; Veterans Day; and Memorial Day.

The 212-foot-high Shoshone Falls on the Snake River – higher than the famous Niagara Falls near Buffalo, New York – is 25 miles southeast.

All of the nine units of Thousand Springs State Park on the Snake River are within a short drive from the city. These parks, most of which are fisheries, have spectacularly beautiful spring-fed waterfalls and white-water rapids interspersed with crystal-clear pools of water that flow into the Snake River. Private trout hatcheries and commercial trout farms, as well as state and federal fish hatcheries open to the public, are located near many of these parks.

The 4,400-acre Hagerman Fossil Beds National Monument – the largest concentration of Pliocene epoch horse fossils in North America – is 10 miles northwest. The visitor center and fossil displays are in Hagerman.

The Sawtooth National Forest – with peaks rising over 8,000 feet – begins about 30 miles due southeast. Downhill skiing is available in the Sawtooth National Forest at Magic Mountain Ski Resort.

Three Island Crossing State Park, the location where Oregon Trail immigrants forded the Snake River, is 30 miles northwest at Glenns Ferry.

Many Wendell residents enjoy the hunting, fishing, hiking, camping, biking, swimming, boating and winter sports available in the nearby state parks, Snake River Canyon, reservoirs, national forest and open high-desert lands managed by the BLM.

Economy and Major Employers Wendell School District has about 170 employees and is the city's largest employer. Clear Springs Food Co., a commercial trout farm, and Magic Valley Growers, LTD, a wholesaler of pearl and boiler onions, are the city's largest private employers and have about 70 and 50 employees, respectively. The city's retail and service businesses and the many dairies, feedlots and other agricultural-based businesses located near the city employ most of the remaining workforce.

Education The Wendell School District provides most of the elementary and secondary education for the city and surrounding area. The district has around 1,100 students. School facilities include an elementary school, middle school, high school and gymnasium.

The closest institution of higher learning is the College of Southern Idaho in Twin Falls.

Health Care Two general medical clinics – St. Benedicts Family Clinic and the Associates in Family Practice – are in Wendell. The closest hospital is Gooding County Memorial Hospital in Gooding.

Transportation Wendell is situated on Interstate 84. State Highway 46 north to Gooding intersects the city.

Gooding Municipal Airport is available for light private and charter aircraft. The closest commercial airport is Joslin Field - Magic Valley Regional Airport in Twin Falls.

Railroad service is available for freight.

Utilities and Services Private companies provide electricity, gas, telephone, cable and satellite services. The City provides water, sanitation and sewer services as well as police and fire protection. Wendell also has a volunteer Quick Response Unit.

Vision for 2050

In recent years, Wendell's population has grown at less than one percent annually. If historical trends continue, by 2050 the city's population could exceed 3,400. In that case, the capacity of existing municipal services, except for periodic improvements to meet environmental regulations and community needs, will be adequate to handle the growth.

However, historical population trends may increase significantly. The population of two neighboring cities that have direct freeway access, Jerome and Twin Falls, are growing dramatically. It is but a matter of time before the growth from these cities will spill over to Wendell.

The dairy industry is continuing to grow. One of the large dairies near Wendell is participating in development of facilities that

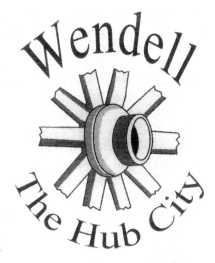

Incorporated October 12, 1909

will collect methane gas from animal waste and use the gas and residue for beneficial purposes. This will eliminate many environmental and air quality concerns. Broad application of this new technology will accelerate expansion of dairy and feedlot operations with Wendell being a direct beneficiary.

In order to meet the needs of existing residents and businesses and provide capacity for growth, the city constructed an improved sewage system that was completed in 2011.

While the future cannot be predicted with any degree of assurance, city and community leaders are strategically watching and planning the course of the city. Regardless of what happens, we will hold to our core principals. Wendell will continue to be a friendly, beautiful, peaceful and interesting place to live and raise a family.

Mayors

1909	B.M. Price *	1951	Les Lawton
1911	C.A. Miller *	1955	Carl Geissler
1913	F.J. Fussner *	1970	Eugene Soares
1915	E.J. Parr *	1974	Otto Lemke
1916	F.L. Dorman *	1990	George Benson
1917	William A. Pyne *	1994	Lynn Nelson
1920	H.D. Jackson *	1996	Gwen Rost
1921	Coe M. Price *	2002	Paul Isaacson
1923	Wilson Bowlby *	2006	Rex Strickland
1924	C.O. Davis *	2007	Ilene Rounsefell
1926	Robert P. Smith *	2007	Ricky Cowen
1927	L.A. Jones *	2010	Brad Christopherson
1935	R.D. Bradshaw *	2013	Ken Bates
1941	E.J. Parr *	2014	Lori Swainston
1945	M.L. Gates *		* Village Chairman
1947	Rex D. Bradshaw		

Playing basketball in Jerome.

JEROME COUNTY

- Eden
- Hazelton
- Jerome (*County Seat*)

Main Street, Eden.

Eden

Statistical Data

Population: 404 *
Elevation: 3,765 feet
Precipitation: 10 inches **
Average Snowfall: 26 inches **
County: Jerome

Temperature Range – Fahrenheit: **
Spring: 28 to 69
Summer: 49 to 88
Fall: 25 to 77
Winter: 18 to 42
* U.S. Census Bureau Estimates July 2015
**Historical averages

Eden is a quiet Magic Valley community surrounded by fertile farms interspersed by large tracts of public land and prehistoric lava flows. Twin Falls is 18 miles west.

The city received its name in recognition of the area's fertile volcanic soils. When given adequate water and care, the land produces heavy crops of commodities including wheat, potatoes, hay, corn and beans.

Pre-Incorporation Years

Until the first explorers/trappers began coming into the Snake River Plain around 1811, American Indians of the Bannock and Shoshone Tribes were the area's primary inhabitants.

On November 17, 1884, the Oregon Short Line (OSL) completed construction of a segment of railroad line that began at Granger, Wyoming; angled in a northwesterly direction through Shoshone and Nampa; and ended at the rail line in Huntington, Oregon. Upon completion, the rail line provided thru-traffic between Omaha, Nebraska, and Portland, Oregon. This railroad line passed about 40 miles north of what is now Eden.

As demand for railroad services grew, the railroad built an extensive system of branch lines throughout the Snake River Plain. In 1883 the OSL delayed construction of its main line long enough to build a branch line 50 miles north to the lead-silver and gold mines of the Wood River Valley. However, branch lines to the Magic Valley would have to wait until irrigated farmland replaced the sagebrush.

The groundwork for part of this land transformation came in 1894 with congressional passage of the Carey Act. The Act was one of several laws designed to encourage settlement of the West. (*See Southwest Idaho – Federal Land Reclamation Laws.*)

Under the Carey Act, the federal government ceded up to one million acres to any state that would bring the land under cultivation under a public-private partnership. Private interests financed and built dams and canals. The state sold parcels of land – 40 to 160 acres – to individuals. In Idaho, the Idaho State Land Board represented state interests. The developers sold water rights, platted towns and sold townsite lots. Idaho would ultimately use 850,000 acres of its allotment.

WWII Minidoka Japanese Relocation Camp.

Milner Dam, located about 12 miles southwest of Eden, was a Carey Act project. Milner Dam, a 73-foot-high 2,160-foot – long hydroelectric dam, creates a 4,000-acre reservoir. It provides irrigation water on the north and south sides of the Snake River. The south side is gravity flow; the north side requires pumping.

In 1905 irrigation water from Milner Dam reached the south side of the Snake River. It provided irrigation water for about 244,000 acres and led to creation of the farming communities of Hansen, Kimberly, Twin Falls, Filer and Buhl. In the same year, OSL built a branch line to those cities.

In 1907 investors formed the Twin Falls North Side Land and Water Company

– North Side Project – to build canals and pump irrigation water from Milner Reservoir to the farms on the north side of the Snake River.

The North Side Project would eventually irrigate 185,000 acres and lead to the establishment of Jerome, Hazelton, Eden and Wendell.

Within a few years, irrigation water from Milner Dam caused transformation of vast acreages of the sagebrush-covered Snake River Plain into a fertile oasis. This rapid transformation led to the designation of the area as Magic Valley.

In 1910 the OSL built a branch line from Rupert to Bliss. This railroad passed through Eden and Jerome.

While the railroad was critical to the transportation and communication needs of Eden and the other farming communities, it was not convenient for direct commerce between communities on opposite sides of the Snake River Canyon. The nearly 400-foot-deep canyon and the river posed major barriers. Travelers had to follow steep roads down either side of the canyon wall before crossing the river on a boat or barge.

The problem was overcome in 1919 with construction of a 900-foot-long two-lane suspension bridge near Eden. They called the bridge Hansen in honor of the city on the south side of the canyon. The state replaced Hansen Bridge in 1966.

In that same year, the Legislature created Jerome County from the older Minidoka County. Eden's county seat moved to the city of Jerome.

Incorporation

On October 20, 1916, Eden became an incorporated village. At that time, U.S. Highway 30 intersected the town. Eden's business district included a bank, a drugstore, three grocery stores, a hardware store, a hotel and two bars.

Turning Points

Eden Post Office.

Irrigation Eden owes its existence to Milner Dam and the complex irrigation canal and ditch systems of the Northside Project. These systems and farms still underpin Eden's agricultural commodity-based economy.

Railroad While Milner Dam and the Northside Project provided the economic basis for making the land around Eden productive, the railroad allowed the farms to prosper. Without the railroad, farmers could not readily ship their commodities to distant markets and their ability to import needed farm equipment and supplies would be frustrated.

Interstate 84 In 1966 Interstate 84 passed Eden about two miles to the south. At about that time, U.S. Highway 30 became State Highway 25. These events caused a major loss of traffic through the city and a sharp reduction in the city's business district. Eden's business community has still not recovered from that devastating loss of traffic and business.

Eden Today

Amenities and Attractions Eden has one city park. James Lulo Park occupies one city block near the center of town.

In 1941 the federal Works Progress Administration built Eden City Hall using volcanic rock prevalent in the nearby desert. The city hall is listed on the National Register of Historic Places.

Eden is the closest city to the Minidoka Internment National Monument, managed by the National Park Service. The monument is located about nine miles north of the city. It marks a national tragedy following the December 7, 1941, attack by the government of Japan on Pearl Harbor.

Following the attack, the federal government stripped the constitutional rights from all known Americans of Japanese ancestry. The military forced entire families – men women and children – to board trains and buses for transport to several internment, or prison, camps scattered primarily throughout the Intermountain West.

At its peak, the Minidoka Internment Camp – named "Hunt Camp" by postal authorities – held about 13,000 American citizens. The camp was in service from August 1942 to January 1945. The Hunt Camp land reserve consisted of about 33,000 acres – 1,000 of which were devoted to the developed camp.

The developed camp included about 600 barracks and other buildings, most of which were simple tarpaper-covered frame structures. Each residential barracks had six small one-room apartments and common dining, laundry, shower and toilet facilities. The military surrounded the compound with barbed wire fences, towers, armed guards and watchdogs.

About 1,000 internees at Hunt were of an age and physical condition to be eligible for military service. They volunteered for combat duty. Those who stayed behind worked as laborers on Magic Valley farms.

The military assigned the Japanese American volunteers into the 442nd Regimental Combat Unit. The unit fought against Nazi Germany in France and Italy. Many soldiers in the 442nd were highly decorated for valor. Two of the volunteers from Hunt received the Congressional Medal of Honor; 73 died. In 1946 President Harry S. Truman said of the 442nd, "You fought not only the enemy but you fought prejudice – and you won."

Today, little remains of the Minidoka Internment Camp. The Jerome County Museum in Jerome has a display honoring the camp's history. Within the next few years, the National Park Service will prepare a general management plan and environmental impact study for the Minidoka Internment National Monument.

Wilson Lake, a 600-acre fishery and reservoir used for water pumped from Milner Dam to the North Side Canal, is located about three miles east of Eden. In 1976 an angler caught the state's record size perch at the lake – 15.5 inches, weighing nearly two pounds ten ounces.

Shoshone Falls, often referred to as the Niagara of the West, is a Unique

Natural Feature on the Snake River. It is located 12 miles southwest of Eden. Shoshone Falls is 212 feet high – 36 feet higher than New York's Niagara Falls.

The six units of Thousand Springs State Park – Niagara Springs, Crystal Springs, Ritter Island, the Earl M. Hardy Box Canyon Springs Nature Preserve (Box Canyon), Billingsley Creek and the Malad Gorge – are interspersed along the Snake River between Twin Falls and Hagerman.

Eden's close proximity to vast acreages of public land, rivers and reservoirs makes available an attractive variety of outdoor sports including hunting, fishing, camping, hiking and ATV riding.

Garden of Eden Restaurant, Eden.

Economy and Major Employers Most city residents commute to the larger surrounding communities for shopping and employment. Some residents work on nearby farms.

The city's business district consists of a gas station, a post office, a senior center, a restaurant and a convenience store.

Education Valley School District, located five miles east in Hazelton, provides most of the elementary and high school education.

The nearest institution of higher learning is the College of Southern Idaho, 18 miles southwest in Twin Falls.

Health Care The closest hospital is Magic Valley Regional Medical Center in Twin Falls. Many residents also use St. Benedict's Family Medical Center, 23 miles northwest in Jerome.

Transportation State Highway 25 intersects the city. An I-84 interchange is within three miles of the city.

The closest full-service airport is Joslin Field-Magic Valley Regional Airport in Twin Falls.

Utilities and Services Private companies provide electricity, gas, cable and satellite services. The City provides water and sewer. The County provides police protection under a contract with the city. A rural all volunteer fire district that includes Eden provides fire protection. The district's fire station is located in the city.

Vision for 2050

Eden residents relish living in their small community. They are located close to the urban amenities of much larger cities, yet enjoy a slow-paced, friendly hometown environment.

The city's population of just over 400 has remained somewhat constant for several years. However, noticeable changes in the form of new residential construction are emerging.

Eden's population will continue to grow gradually. By 2050 there may be 50 percent more residents attracted by affordable housing and lifestyle.

When the National Park Service evaluation of the Minidoka Internment National Monument is complete, it may lead to federal development at the monument as a tourist attraction. Such action could lead to commercial growth in the city.

City leaders manage the city to meet the needs of its citizens plus a limited amount of growth. For example, the city is in the process of replacing its water tank and paying for it without incurring debt. The City's careful management of the people's money is another factor that pleases and attracts residents.

Main Street, Hazelton.

Hazelton

Statistical Data

Population: 747 *
Elevation: 3,955 feet
Precipitation: 10 inches **
Average Snowfall: 27 inches **
County: Jerome

Temperature Range – Fahrenheit: **
Spring: 28 to 69
Summer: 49 to 88
Fall: 25 to 77
Winter: 18 to 42
* U.S. Census Bureau Estimates July 2015
**Historical averages

Hazelton lies on the Snake River Plain and the north side of the fertile Magic Valley. Lush fields of potatoes, corn, beans, wheat, sugar beets and alfalfa hay surround the city.

Vast tracts of historic lava flows and public lands managed by the BLM, interspersed by large acreages of fertile volcanic soil farmland, begin a few miles north of the city. The Snake River flows about seven miles to the south. The Sawtooth National Forest, with peaks rising over 8,000 feet, begins 14 miles south of town. Twin Falls is 17 miles west.

Pre-Incorporation Years

American Indians – primarily of the nomadic Bannock and Shoshone Tribes – passed near what is now Hazelton on the way to their summer and winter encampments.

In the early 1840s Oregon Trail immigrants traveled the south side of the Snake River.

On November 17, 1884, the Oregon Short Line (OSL) Railroad completed construction of a segment of railroad line that began at Granger, Wyoming, angled in a northwesterly direction – about 21 miles due north of what is now the city of Hazelton – through Shoshone and Nampa and ended at the rail line in Huntington, Oregon.

Upon completion, the rail line connected the commercial centers of Omaha, Nebraska, and Portland, Oregon, creating another transcontinental railroad. Railroad interests completed the first transcontinental railroad in 1869 at Promontory Summit in northern Utah.

In 1894 Congress passed the Carey Act; one of several laws designed to encourage settlement of lands in the arid West. (*See Southwest Idaho – Federal Land Reclamation Laws.*)

Under the Carey Act, the federal government ceded up to one million acres to any state that would bring the land under cultivation under a public-private

Early Main Street in Hazelton.

partnership. Private interests financed and built dams and canals. The state sold parcels of land – 40 to 160 acres – to individuals. In Idaho, the Idaho State Land Board represented state interests. The developers sold water rights and often platted towns and sold townsite lots. Idaho would ultimately use 850,000 acres of its allotment.

Around 1900 Ira B. Perrine, a local farmer and entrepreneur who produced food for the miners in the Wood River Mining District, sought to develop a "Carey Act" diversion dam – Milner Dam – across the Snake River at The Cedars, a point about eight miles southeast of what is now Hazelton.

Perrine formed the Twin Falls Land and Water Company (TFL&W) and brought together several investors. When completed, the hydroelectric Milner Dam stood 73 feet high and 2,160 feet long and created a 4,000-acre reservoir. It provided irrigation water on both the north and south sides of the Snake River. They could use gravity flow on the south, but the north side required pumping.

Dunn Building.

In 1905 TFL&W delivered irrigation water to the farms south of the Snake

River Canyon, ultimately irrigating about 244,000 acres. The irrigation water led to the creation of the farming communities of Hansen, Kimberly, Twin Falls, Filer and Buhl. In the same year, the OSL built a branch line to those cities.

In order to bring water to the north side of the Snake River, Perrine assembled other investors to form the Twin Falls North Side Land and Water Company (North Side Project). They built canals and pumped irrigation water from Milner Reservoir into Wilson Lake Reservoir, which elevated the water to allow gravity flow through the Main North Side Canal to the farms on the north side of the Snake River.

The North Side Project would eventually irrigate 185,000 acres and led to the establishment of Hazelton, Eden, Jerome and Wendell.

In 1905 anticipating development of the North Side Project, Joe Barlow acquired land near the expected railroad siding. There he platted the town of Hazelton, named after his daughter, Hazel.

In 1907 water began flowing down the Main North Side Canal. By

Grace's Cafe.

September 30, 1907, North Side Project investors platted the new town of Jerome, named after one of the investors, and began selling lots.

In 1910 the OSL built a branch line from Rupert to Bliss. This railroad passed through Hazelton, Eden, Jerome and Wendell.

Incorporation

On December 28, 1916, Hazelton became an incorporated village.

Turning Points

Irrigation Milner Dam and the complex irrigation canal and ditch systems of the Northside Project are the basis for the founding of Hazelton. The success of the community's agricultural economy still relies on irrigation.

Railroad The railroad provided transportation critical to

City Hall, 1956.

the success of the city. It allowed convenient transportation of passengers and rapid movement of mail and freight, and farmers and ranchers could efficiently ship their commodities to market.

Interstate 84 In 1966 Interstate 84 bypassed Hazelton. Businesses that relied on the out-of-town business that used to pass through town on U.S. Highway 30 – now Idaho Highway 25 – either closed or moved out of the city.

Hazelton Today

Amenities and Attractions

Wilson Lake Reservoir is a recreational destination, with a 600-acre fishery and within a mile of the city. In 1976 the lake produced the largest perch caught in Idaho – 15.5 inches, two pounds, ten ounces.

Valley Service Station.

The Minidoka Internment National Monument, managed by the National Park Service, is located about 15 miles northwest of the city. It marks a national tragedy following the December 7, 1941, attack by Japan on Pearl Harbor and the subsequent stripping of constitutional rights from all known Americans of Japanese ancestry.

The military forced entire families – men, women and children – to board trains and buses for transport to several internment – prison – camps scattered primarily throughout the Intermountain West.

At its peak, the Minidoka Internment Camp – named "Hunt Camp" by postal authorities – held about 13,000 American citizens. The camp was in service from August 1942 to January 1945. The Hunt Camp land reserve consisted of about 33,000 acres – 1,000 of which were devoted to the developed camp.

About 1,000 internees at Hunt volunteered for combat duty and fought against Germany. Those who stayed behind worked as laborers on Magic Valley farms. The Jerome County Museum in Jerome has a display honoring the camp's history.

U.S. Bank.

The 212-foot-high Shoshone Falls on the Snake River – higher than the famous Niagara Falls near Buffalo, New York – is 14 miles west.

Thousand Springs State Park has several units located on the Snake River at various points between Twin Falls and five miles north of Hagerman. These park units and fisheries include spectacularly beautiful spring-fed waterfalls tumbling hundreds of feet from the north rim of the Snake River Canyon Gorge and white-water rapids interspersed with crystal-clear pools of water that restore the Snake River.

Downhill skiing is available at Magic Mountain Ski Resort in the Sawtooth National Forest about 30 miles south.

The southwest corner of the 750,000-acre Craters of the Moon National Monument and Preserve is a few miles north of the city. The Preserve includes Idaho's Great Rift, the source of the lava flow that created

City Hall and fire station, 1992.

the unique volcanic landscape. (*See Eastern Idaho – Craters of the Moon National Monument and Preserve and the Great Rift National Natural Landmark.*)

In addition to outdoor activities available in the Snake River Canyon, hunting, fishing, hiking, camping, biking, swimming, boating and winter sports are also available in nearby reservoirs, national forest and the Preserve.

Economy and Major Employers Valley School District is the city's largest public employer. Several small businesses, principally involved with the agricultural industry; a bank; and retail stores provide most of the other jobs available in the city.

Many in the workforce commute to other cities for employment. Most of the city's residents do their shopping in Twin Falls.

Chevron Station and Food Mart.

Education Valley School District has elementary, middle and high schools in Hazelton.

The nearest institution of higher learning is the College of Southern Idaho in Twin Falls.

Health Care The closest hospital is Magic Valley Regional Medical Center in Twin Falls. Many residents also use St. Benedict's Family Medical Center, 28 miles northwest in Jerome.

Transportation Idaho Highway 25 intersects the city. Interstate 84 is accessible about a mile from the city.

Hazelton Municipal Airport serves light private and charter aircraft on its

2,800-foot runway. The closest full-service airport is Joslin Field-Magic Valley Regional Airport in Twin Falls.

Railroad service is available for freight.

Utilities and Services Private companies provide electricity, telephone, satellite and wireless services. The City provides water and sewer services and fire protection. Police protection is provided by the County Sheriff under contract with the City.

Vision for 2050

In 1960 Hazelton had a population of 433. In 2000 the city had a population of 692. Since that time, the city has grown less than one percent annually.

Recent historical trends will likely continue. In which case, by 2050 the city's population will approximate 1,000.

Hazelton Cemetery entrance.

Mayors

1917 W.S. Dunn *	1967 Charles Webb
1917 H. Eyers *	1967 Joe Washer
1919 W.C. Abott *	1968 W.W. Presley
1919 H.K. Belmot *	1970 James Dryden
1925 E.L. Berry, M.D. *	1978 Kerm Douglas
1929 H Eyers *	1982 Robert L. Brutke
1932 W.A. Pyne *	1984 Louis Alastra
1939 H.E. Nye *	1986 Roy Crumrine
1943 Loster Saunders *	1990 Erve Van Sickle
1945 Paul E. Shider *	2002 Kerm Douglas
1947 Elmer E. Pyne *	2002 Wade Johnson
1949 Victor Kelly *	2004 Darrin Teener
1953 L.W. Wright *	2004 Ron Cline
1957 James Dryden *	2004 Darrell Dalrymple
1959 Grant Turner *	2010 Roy McDowell
1961 Leo Ross *	2014 Roy Crumrine
1961 Clint Watson *	2015 Jason Wethern
1966 Wallace Brag *	* Village Chairman

Jerome

Statistical Data

Population: 11,189 *
Elevation: 3,765 feet
Precipitation: 10 inches **
Average Snowfall: 26 inches **
County: Jerome
Website: www.ci.jerome.id.us

Temperature Range – Fahrenheit: **
Spring: 34 to 62
Summer: 53 to 87
Fall: 36 to 64
Winter: 20 to 39
* U.S. Census Bureau Estimates July 2015
**Historical averages

Jerome is a Magic Valley city located six miles north of the Snake River and 13 miles northwest of Twin Falls.

Beginning near the end of the twentieth century, Idaho became one of the largest dairy producing states in the nation. Some of the state's largest dairy farms are located near Jerome.

In 1907 investors in Milner Dam started the North Side Project and founded Jerome. The project's canal system brought irrigation water to 185,000 acres of arid land that lay on the north side of the Snake River.

Two of the investors, Ira Perrine and William Kuhn, selected a townsite on a sagebrush-covered rise where they had a clear view of distant mountains and hills. They named the townsite Jerome, the first name of one the project's investors and some of Kuhn's family.

Even though Jerome's roots are in agriculture, the city has a diversified economy. The city's major employers are a blend of manufacturing, food processing, health care, warehouse distribution and service businesses.

The nine park units comprising Thousand Springs State Park are located along the Snake River within a short drive from Jerome.

Pre-Incorporation Years

Around 1811 the first explorers/trappers came into what is now the Magic Valley. Prior to that time, American Indians of the Bannock and Shoshone Tribes inhabited the area.

In 1841 the first overland migration of explorers and settlers destined for what is now western Oregon passed through the area. In 1842 Captain John C. Fremont, a military surveyor, led a 39-

Drilling a well on the Northside Project. The vast underground aquifer made it possible for wells in the towns and in the construction camps.

member exploration and survey detachment through Idaho and on to the Oregon coast. Future Oregon Trail immigrants benefited from Fremont's detailed maps and descriptions of the terrain, including the locations of campsites.

The 1862 prospectors found gold in the Boise Basin. The following year, 16,000 people flooded into the mining district. In 1864 the U.S. military built Fort Boise 40 miles east of the original Fort Boise, which was located near what is now Parma and destroyed several

Tents, circa 1907.

years earlier by flood. Residents living near the new Fort Boise almost immediately platted a town near the fort that they named Boise City. Mail, passenger and freight wagon services coming up from Utah to the new fort and town passed through the Magic Valley several miles south of what is now Jerome.

In November 1884 the Oregon Short Line (OSL) completed construction of a railroad line that began at Granger, Wyoming, and angled in a northwesterly direction through what are now Pocatello, Shoshone and Nampa until it connected with the railroad across the Snake River in Huntington, Oregon. With this rail line, trains could travel from Omaha, Nebraska, to Portland, Oregon, in less than four days.

In 1894 the U.S. Congress passed the Carey Act. Under the Act, the federal government ceded up to one million acres to any state that would bring the land under cultivation. Development of the land was a public-private partnership. Idaho would ultimately use 850,000 acres of its allotment.

Under the Carey Act Project, private interests financed and built dams and canals. The state sold 40 to 160 acre parcels of land to individuals. In Idaho, the Idaho State Land Board represented State interests. The developers sold water rights, developed town

Jerome train depot.

sites and sold town site lots. Congress would later pass other land reclamation laws. For example, the U.S. Reclamation Service, created in 1902, built many other dams and irrigation systems in Idaho. (*See Southwestern Idaho, Cities of the Magic Valley*.)

Around 1900 Ira B. Perrine, a local farmer and entrepreneur who produced food for the miners in the Wood River district, sought to develop a "Carey Act" diversion dam – Milner Dam – across the Snake River at The Cedars, a point about 30 miles east of what is now Jerome.

Perrine formed the Twin Falls Land and Water Company and brought together several investors. In 1905 irrigation water from Milner Dam first reached farms south of the Snake River Canyon.

In order to bring water to the north side of the Snake River, Perrine organized other investors in 1907 to form the Twin Falls North Side Land and Water Company, North Side Project. The lead investors in the North Side Project were William S. and James S. Kuhn from Pittsburg and William's brother-in-law Jerome Hill.

On June 21, 1907, the North Side Project investors announced the "Big Sale" of platted lots and water rights would take place September 30, 1907. However, they would sell a limited number of commercial lots in advance.

The *Twin Falls News* reported on the announcement. The article said that the new township of Jerome would have a modern 50-room hotel; a two-story company building; a bank building; and would provide electricity, water works and a sewer system. A railroad to Jerome was already in progress.

In anticipation of the Big Sale, a flood of prospective land buyers joined construction workers living in tents. The number of tents was so great that the Jerome Townsite clerk set up a tent city headquarters so that he could manage the operation and monitor the construction projects.

Land lot drawing, the Big Sale, 1907.

Incorporation

On July 15, 1907, a month and a half prior to the Big Sale, Lincoln County Commissioners in Shoshone approved the application for Jerome to become an incorporated village. However, it took a year for many of the promised municipal services to be available.

In August 1908 the village dug a city well and installed a gas engine and pump. Anyone could get clean water free of charge. By that time, telephone lines came into town, sagebrush was cleared from the platted streets and new roads to Shoshone and Wendell were started. A six-day-a-week stagecoach run also began between Jerome and Shoshone.

First log cabin in Jerome.

On July 1, 1909, developers completed the Northside Inn, the first upscale hotel in the Magic Valley. In 1965 the building owners razed the facility. The 1910 census reported the city's population at 970.

On February 8, 1919, the Idaho Legislature divided Jerome County from

Lincoln County and designated the village of Jerome as the county seat. On March 24, 1919, the new Jerome County Commissioners made Jerome an incorporated city.

Turning Points

Irrigation Jerome is a product of irrigation water provided by investors in Milner Dam and the North Side Project, made available through passage of the federal Carey Act.

Railroad Even though railroad service began to be available in Shoshone in 1883, it took the development of irrigation and farmland beginning in 1907 to bring the railroad to Jerome.

In 1904 investors incorporated the Minidoka and Southwestern

Prescott Craig.

Railroad Company to construct branch lines into the newly opened farming communities. In 1910 they completed the 73-mile Rupert to Bliss branch line that passed through Jerome.

The railroad was a lifeline to the community as it allowed farmers and merchants to bring in supplies, gave fast transportation for passengers and mail and allowed farmers to ship their commodities to distant markets. In later years, it was an important factor in attracting manufacturing and food processing businesses.

Saint Benedict's Family Medical Center From 1918 to 1920 Jerome experienced flu epidemics. Sixteen people lost their lives. Each year, temporary emergency hospitals had to be set up. In 1923 the Benedictine Sisters purchased the Wendell Inn

and converted the facility into St. Valentines Hospital. On May 12, 1952, they replaced the old hospital with the new St. Benedict's Hospital. In 1961 the hospital opened a 40-bed long-term care unit. The hospital has had a major positive effect in attracting people and businesses to the city.

Motor Vehicles and Roads In the early 1900s motor vehicles began to become popular. The construction of hard-surface roads soon followed. The first road, State Highway 25 completed in 1932, connected Jerome with Eden and Hazelton. In 1951 the State completed U.S. Highway 93 connecting Idaho with Utah and Montana. In 1963 Interstate 84 reached Jerome and built two interchanges. With the completion of these roads, Jerome's retail business sector blossomed.

Building a Diversified Economy In the city's beginning, hundreds of family farms underpinned the economy. With technological innovation and consolidation, the agriculture industry has become much less labor intensive. For the city's economy to grow, leaders needed to find other sources of jobs.

Downtown Jerome.

A major breakthrough came when Tupperware built a manufacturing facility in Jerome. Within a short time, this company became the city's largest private employer and a major economic stimulus. However, on June 22, 1987, the company announced the plant's closure and the termination of 700 employees. Some described this event as Jerome's darkest hour.

Government and local business leaders began concentrated economic development efforts. In January 1989 Spears Manufacturing Company announced they had bought the Tupperware plant and would soon hire 400 employees.

Then Moore Wallis Business Forms built its facility in Jerome. However, in 2002 this plant closed with the loss of 130 jobs. Fortunately, in 2004 Hilex Poly Co. announced they were purchasing the Moore Wallis building and would employ 120.

These experiences have taught Jerome's leaders to be vigilant and proactive when it comes to keeping and attracting employers in today's dynamic economy.

Jerome Today

Amenities and Attractions Jerome has six city and three recreation district parks and three golf courses in the city.

The Jerome Recreation District Park offers such indoor sports as basketball and jujitsu. Their outdoor program offers swimming and white-water kayaking.

The 212-foot-high Shoshone Falls on the Snake River – higher than the famous Niagara Falls near Buffalo, New York – is 12 miles southeast.

Thousand Springs State Park has several units located near the Snake River at various points southwest of the city. Those closest to Jerome include Billingsley

Creek, the Earl M. Hardy Box Canyon Springs Nature Preserve, Malad Gorge and Niagara Springs. These fisheries have spectacularly beautiful spring-fed waterfalls and white-water rapids interspersed with crystal-clear pools of water that flow into the Snake River.

The 4,400-acre Hagerman Fossil Beds National Monument, the largest concentration of Pliocene epoch horse fossils in North America, is 22 miles northwest. The visitor center and fossil displays are in Hagerman.

The Sawtooth National Forest, with peaks rising over 8,000 feet, begins about 20 miles southwest of Jerome. Downhill skiing is available in the forest at Magic Mountain Ski Resort located 28 miles south of Hansen on Rock Creek Road.

Three Island Crossing State Park, the location where Oregon Trail immigrants forded the Snake River, is 42 miles northwest at Glenns Ferry.

The entrance to Craters of the Moon National Monument and Preserve is 75 miles northeast on U.S. Highway 93. However, the western edge of the 750,000-acre Preserve begins about 12 miles east of the city. The Preserve includes Idaho's Great Rift, the source of the lava flow that created the unique volcanic landscape. (*See Eastern Idaho – Craters of the Moon National Monument and Preserve and the Great Rift National Natural Landmark*.)

In addition to outdoor activities available in the Snake River Canyon, hunting, fishing, hiking, camping, biking, swimming, boating and winter sports are also available in nearby reservoirs, national forests and preserves.

Economy and Major Employers Spears Manufacturing Company – a pipe fittings manufacturer headquartered in Sylmar, California – has 380 employees in Jerome. Wal-Mart Stores, Inc employs 300. St. Benedict's Medical Center and Jerome Cheese Company – a division of Davisco Foods International, headquartered in Le Sueur, Minnesota – employ from 150 to 200 each. Two companies with over 100 employees each are Hilex Poly Co. – plastic bag and film manufacturer headquartered in Hartsville South Carolina – and Rite Stuff Foods – a local specialty frozen potato products manufacturer.

There are several other light manufacturing, retail, financial and service businesses operating in the city. The largest public employer is Jerome School District with 400 employees.

Education The Jerome School District is the largest provider of elementary and secondary education. About five percent of the K-12 students attend two private schools.

Jerome 1908.

The closest institution of higher learning is the College of Southern Idaho. The main campus is located 14 miles away in Twin Falls; however, the school has a second campus in Jerome.

Health Care The 25-bed St. Benedict's Family Medical Center, several clinics, assisted-living and nursing homes provide most of the city's medical care.

Transportation Interstate 84 passes on the southwestern side of the city. State Highways 79 and 25 intersect in the city's downtown. U.S. Highway 93 is three miles east.

The Jerome County Airport's 5,201-foot-long runway, located three miles east of town, provides air service for light private and charter aircraft. The closest commercial airfield is Joslin Field, 17 miles southeast near Twin Falls.

Railroad service is available for freight.

Utilities and Services Private companies provide electricity, telephone, satellite, natural gas and cable. The City provides water and sewer services as well as police and fire protection. The County provides solid waste services.

Vision for 2050

For the past several years, Jerome's population has grown about 2 percent annually. If these trends hold, by 2050 the city's population will more than double.

Over 43 percent of the Jerome County population resides in the city of Jerome. This urbanization of the county's population will continue.

Jerome 2007.

In 2050 Jerome will still be a major business center in the area. The infrastructure improvements east to Highway 93, along Highway 25 and the railroad will have significant commercial growth. Due to ease of access off I-84, there will be greater commercial growth along West Main Street towards the interstate. South Lincoln, Crossroads Development and areas in between will become important retail shopping centers for the area.

The Crossroads Development will include a state-of-the-art hospital, retail and commercial businesses. The Butte will host numerous technologically-based companies supplying bandwidth down Interstate 93 to the College of Southern Idaho. Downtown Jerome will take on a new look of specialty shops to attract the residents as major changes of the main transportation routes will avoid the main downtown areas.

The increased commercial base will attract residential subdivisions. To meet the recreation and open space needs and desires of the city's new residents, the city will place emphasis on creating additional parks, playgrounds and walking paths.

As part of this effort, the city will work with the owners of the undeveloped land along the canyon rim to make it into a large park with native plants. This park will not only preserve the natural beauty of the Snake River, but will allow visitors the opportunity to see the natural wonders Jerome has to offer.

The city's healthcare industry will attract development of residential areas suited for an aging population. This includes residential communities for seniors that provide a menu of assisted living services selected by the homeowner depending on their physical limitations and desires.

Mayors

1909 J.H. Josephson *
1911 E.G. Gauss *
1912 F.A. Busse *
1913 Wm. A. Peters *
1915 R.H. Traill *
1917 Anders Anderson *
1919 Anders Anderson
1921 Walter A. Heiss
1923 O.L. Thoreson
1925 Frank Daley
1931 A.L. Pyle
1933 P.H. Beveridge
1937 L.M. Zug
1942 George D. Petrie
1943 O.L. Thoreson
1943 George D. Petrie
1945 L.W. Greving

1947 John W. Hosman
1953 Theron W. Ward
1959 Wm. I. Spaeth
1959 Wm. A. Peters
1961 Paul Pratt
1964 Earl L. Greenawalt
1970 John (Jack) A. Russell
1974 Charles P. Hancock
1978 Marshall Everheart
1982 Ralph Peters
1990 Gerlad M. Ostler
1998 Dennis Moore
2002 Charles Correll
2010 John Shine
2014 David M. Davis
* Village Chairman

Train Town USA award in Shoshone.

LINCOLN COUNTY

- Dietrich
- Richfield
- Shoshone (*County Seat*)

Dietrich City Park.

Dietrich

Statistical Data

Population: 339 *
Elevation: 4,130 feet
Precipitation: 10 inches **
Average Snowfall: 35 inches **
County: Lincoln
Website: www.dietrichidaho.com

Temperature Range – Fahrenheit: **
Spring: 27 to 72
Summer: 49 to 91
Fall: 26 to 79
Winter: 17 to 46
* U.S. Census Bureau Estimates July 2015
**Historical averages

Dietrich lies in Lincoln County on the south slope of a sagebrush-covered extinct volcano called Crater Butte surrounded by fertile farms. With its high-desert climate; plenty of clean fresh air; and a vast blue sky, it is the perfect place to escape the noise and bustle of the modern world.

Entering the city from the south off Idaho Highway 24, eight miles east of Shoshone, the first building visitors see before crossing the Union Pacific railroad tracks is a church built in 1988 by The Church of Jesus Christ of Latter-day Saints and a new Highway District building built in 1999. The city's business district and private homes are generally on the north side of the tracks.

Pre-Incorporation Years

Dietrich's founding is directly related to the federal Carey Act and the railroad. The Idaho Irrigation Company received State approval in 1909 to build a dam on the Big Wood River 25 miles north of the city. The dam created Magic Reservoir, a

Carey Act irrigation dam that provided irrigation water for the "Dietrich Tract."

To promote buyers for the land and water rights, the company built a hotel and a prototype farm in the new town of Dietrich where the Oregon Short Line Railroad was also extending a rail line. They named the town after Frank S. Dietrich, a former attorney for Union Pacific Railroad and beginning in 1907 the U.S District Court Judge for Idaho.

The initial spurt of buying enthusiasm quickly faded when the water was turned into the canals. The developers apparently had not adequately evaluated the porous hydrology of the soils. As the water flowed from the newly constructed canals and ditches and flooded onto the fields, too much water seeped through the sandy soil making it difficult to sustain the head of water needed to get it to the end of the row or field. There was not enough water to flood irrigate all of the arable land in the district. Literally, the little town nearly dried up and blew away in the high-desert winds.

By 1960 farmers were changing from flood to more efficient sprinkler irrigation systems. These systems better utilized the water and opened the rolling hillside land to irrigation. These sprinkler systems converted marginal farming operations into instant successes.

The topography of the farmland was characterized by fields of hay, grain and potatoes often interspersed or bordered by outcroppings of rock and

Old Dietrich train station.

brush or grass-covered terrain not suitable for farming. Russian olive, locust and cottonwood groves lined fence lines, drainage ditches and swales. This vegetation next to farm crops created excellent habitat for pheasants and upland birds.

For many years, the area had a reputation for premier pheasant hunting. Nationally known dignitaries – such as Bing Crosby, Gary Cooper and Ernest Hemingway – came to Dietrich to hunt the birds.

Incorporation

Dietrich was incorporated as a village in 1913. However, subsequently identified "legal technicalities" led to the rescission of the incorporation. It was not until May 13, 1946, that Dietrich became an officially incorporated village.

Turning Points

Irrigation and the Railroad The city owes its existence to the federal Carey

Act that allowed private-public partnerships to reclaim the arid West through irrigation systems and the railroad that provided transportation to move farm and ranch commodities and livestock to distant markets. (*See The Region, Federal Land Use Laws – Carey Act Projects – Magic Valley.*)

The application of sprinkler irrigation technologies in 1960 dramatically improved water utilization and the resulting improvements to farm productivity and prosperity. Dietrich's economy benefited directly from this increasingly strong farm economy.

City Infrastructure The city began paving its streets in 1957. In 1993 it put in a community drinking water system and completed its municipal sewer system in 2002. The Dietrich School was the first sewer connection.

Dietrich's sewer project was a unifying effort among citizens to solve their common problem. The work qualified as a "Small Town Environment Project" (STEP), a federally sanctioned approach to constructing municipal sewer and water systems at affordable costs that, in this

Dietrich sewer lagoons excavated through layers of lava rock.

case, allowed volunteers to give time and equipment to help in the unusually hard work of excavating through layers of lava rock to construct a seven-acre sewer lagoon system.

In 2005 the school district remodeled the Dietrich School to enlarge classrooms and add a new gymnasium.

Annexation In 2004 the city doubled in size with the annexation of the Dietrich West Subdivision.

Dietrich Today

Amenities and Attractions The Dietrich City Park occupies a full city block with a log pavilion and open-air patio as the most prominent structure. Many town events, as well as family reunions and parties are held there. The park has many beautiful trees, grass, playground equipment and parking.

Located one mile north of

Aerial view of Dietrich School in the 1940s. Markings on the roof show directions to the Dietrich Airport.

Dietrich is the Dietrich Crater, a volcanic crater about a half mile wide and 100 feet deep.

The Sawtooth Scenic Byway starts eight miles west at Shoshone, passes near the Sun Valley Resort and ends 116 miles north at the nearly 11,000-foot-high Sawtooth Mountain Range in Stanley.

Economy and Major Employers The surrounding farms and feedlots provide most of the city's economic base. Dietrich School District employs 20 and is the city's largest employer. Most city residents are retired or commute to other locations in the Magic Valley for work.

There are two private businesses in town – The Dietrich Merc, a general store, and Eagles Nest, a combination bar and restaurant.

Education The Dietrich School provides elementary and secondary education. Children, including those from the outlying area, receive a very personalized education in low student-teacher ratio classes. Graduating classes of about 10 students are normal. The school is the focus of most community activities.

Old Dietrich Post Office.

The nearest institution of higher education is the College of Southern Idaho in Twin Falls, 30 miles south.

Health Care Medical care is available at a general medical clinic in Shoshone. The nearest hospitals are St. Benedicts, 25 miles away in Jerome, and St Luke's Magic Valley Regional Medical Center in Twin Falls.

Transportation Dietrich is a mile north of Idaho Highway 24, which connects with U.S. Highways 26 and 95 and Idaho Highway 75 in Shoshone. Interstate 84 can be accessed about 25 miles south or about 35 miles west.

Light private and charter aircraft use the 5,200-foot runway at Jerome County Airport in Jerome. The closest commercial airport is Joslin Field - Magic Valley Regional Airport in Twin Falls.

Utilities and Services Private companies provide electricity, telephone and satellite services. The City provides domestic water and sewer services. The volunteer Dietrich Fire District provides fire protection. The Lincoln County Sheriff's Department provides police protection under contract with the City.

Vision for 2050

Dietrich's population has been growing from 1 to 2 percent annually for several decades. This trend is expected to continue. By 2050 Dietrich's population will likely exceed 400.

The city will experience the spillover effect of industrial growth from Jerome, Gooding and Twin Falls as more citizens choose to live in Dietrich and commute to these larger cities for work.

Older people are also choosing to retire in Dietrich. It is quiet, peaceful and safe. Importantly, it is still near excellent medical facilities in Twin Falls and other nearby communities.

By 2050 Lincoln County's northern boundary will be the location of a new regional airport. This will be another factor causing the city's population to grow.

Other factors that will contribute to the city's growth are niche companies and families using communication technologies to work at home or take advantage of distant learning options.

Scores of wind turbines will whirl above the wind-blown highlands of the Dietrich Tract. These turbines will not only provide needed clean electricity but will also provide rental income to local landowners while not disrupting farming operations.

This growth will promote a variety of light retail businesses. The annexation of development property west of the city is indicative of this growth. Dietrich's next retail establishment will provide gas and diesel fuel.

Mayors

1946 Walter Fechner *	1982 Scott L. Bolton
1953 Ben Lauer *	1986 Willard Stevenson
1965 Dick N. Roice *	1986 Pete L. Gage
1967 DicK N. Roice	1988 Jeanetta R. Knowles
1969 Marvin Dean Durfee	2008 Don Heiken
1972 Homer Anderson	* Village Chairman
1973 Clifford L. Davis	

Aerial view of Richfield.

Richfield

Statistical Data

Population: 489*
Elevation: 4,310 feet
Precipitation: 10 inches**
Average Snowfall: 27 inches**
County: Lincoln

Temperature Range – Fahrenheit: **
Spring: 26 to 67
Summer: 46 to 85
Fall: 23 to 75
Winter: 14 to 36

*U.S. Census Bureau Estimates July 2015
**Historical averages

Surrounded by ancient lava flows and high-desert farmland, Richfield sits at the base of a seven-mile – wide, ten-mile-long irrigated agricultural oasis.

Richfield is one of several Idaho cities that owes its origins to federal Carey Act irrigation projects and the railroad.

The famous resort community of Sun Valley is 70 miles north and the regional shopping and health care center of Twin Falls 50 miles south. Shoshone, the seat of Lincoln County and its largest city, is 16 miles southwest.

Pre-Incorporation Years

In 1883 the Oregon Short Line Railroad built its line from Shoshone to

Ketchum through what is now Richfield. (*See Southwestern Idaho, The Region, Railroads.*)

Over two decades later, the Idaho Irrigation Company received state approval under the federal Carey Act to build a dam on the Big Wood River 30 miles northwest of the city. The dam created Magic Reservoir, which holds up to 190,000 acre feet of water. The reservoir fed a complex system of gravity-flow canals that served the farms in the Richfield, Shoshone, Dietrich and Gooding areas. (*See Southwestern Idaho, The Region, Federal Land Use Laws, Carey Act Projects – Magic Valley.*)

As part of the effort to sell the farmland, water rights and city lots, the Idaho Irrigation Company platted the town of Richfield and built the Richfield Hotel at the corner of Main and Lincoln Streets.

At first, company officers named the town Alberta after Alberta Strunk, the first child born in the community. However, they soon changed the name to Richfield, believing it better suited their marketing campaign to sell "rich fields" of land.

However, when water began flowing through the newly constructed canals and ditches and onto the fields, there was not as

Richfield street scene, circa 1910.

much water as projected. They had not taken adequate account of the porous nature of the soils. The water tended to seep into the sandy soil, reducing the efficiency of flood irrigation. The farms located furthest from the reservoir were most adversely affected.

In the 1960s farmers began changing from flood to sprinkler irrigation. Later, they also drilled irrigation wells. This more efficient irrigation method allowed more efficient utilization of water and opened the rolling hillsides to irrigated farming. Fields of potatoes, hay and grain used to support dairy and cattle operations are often interspersed or bordered by outcroppings of rock and brush.

Incorporation

After the Idaho Irrigation Company sold the arable land, city lots and water rights, it turned over its duties to the property owners. On April 15, 1909, the County approved the citizens' petition to make Richfield an incorporated village. At that time, the population was around 290 where it has essentially remained.

Turning Points

Federal Reclamation Law. Three events converged to lead to the founding of Richfield and its economy. The 1894 Carey Act encouraged private-public partnerships in reclaiming the high-desert lands of the West, application of the law in building Magic Reservoir with its irrigation canal systems and the railroad.

Although built for the principal purpose of serving the Wood River Valley mines, the railroad became important to the development of agriculture, particularly the sheep industry. (*See Southwestern Idaho, The Region, Railroads.*)

Sheep Industry. In the 1920s lamb and wool production became major agricultural commodities. The climate and the vast expanse of open grazing land on the Snake River Plain, including Richfield were ideal winter pastures for sheep. The industry flourished for several decades until competing

New $35,000 Idaho Irrigation Company Hotel, circa1921.

synthetic fibers and changes in consumer tastes and buying practices caused the market for wool and lamb to decline. (*See Southwestern Idaho, The Region, Livestock.*)

City Services. Availability of city services also made an important difference in the quality of life of Richfield residents. In the 1930s the city developed a waterworks system and, four decades later, a sewer system.

Paved Roads and Motor Vehicles. After construction of U.S. Highway 93-26 and the loss of competitive advantage to motorized vehicles in the 1980s, the railroad stopped passenger service. With better transportation options, residents began driving motor vehicles to the larger communities of Hailey, Jerome and Twin Falls to shop and do business.

Building a Diversified Economy. Technological innovation and economies of scale as well as market forces were transforming the agricultural industry, promoting consolidation of farms with increased productivity and fewer employees. With fewer shoppers coming to town, Richfield needed a more diversified economy.

Richfield Post Office.

Nelson-Ricks Creamery opened a small cheese factory in Richfield in 1907, and the area's dairy industry began to grow. Clifford Ward purchased the facility in the 1960s and built a substantially larger factory. In August 1990 Ward sold his company to Avonmore, and in 2000 Avonmore changed its name to Glanbia Foods.

Beginning in the 1980s residents started commuting 50 to 70 miles to Blaine County for work. Escalating real estate prices in Blaine County forced many workers to move to Richfield for affordable housing.

Richfield Today

Amenities and Attractions Richfield has two city parks and one RV Park. The main north park has tennis and basketball courts, children's play grounds and a picnic shelter. A nine-space RV Park is on the south side of town.

Reynolds Field has rodeo grounds and a racetrack. Every week during the summer there are rodeo events such as calf roping at the rodeo grounds. From November to February the track is used for chariot racing. On the second Saturday of June the city sponsors "Outlaw Day" to celebrate the founding of Richfield. The celebration is also a time for high school class reunions. On the Fourth of July, the town has a fireworks display put on by the local American Legion.

The city is near excellent trout fisheries. The Little Wood River runs near the city's southern border. Many creeks are within a two-hour drive. Magic Reservoir, a five-mile-long lake and fishery noted for its large rainbow trout, is located 30 miles northwest.

The lava flows northeast of the city are part of the 750,000 – acre Craters of the Moon National Monument and Preserve which includes Idaho's Great Rift, the source of the lava flows that created this unique landscape. The Monument entrance is 60 miles northeast on U.S. Highway 93-26. (*See Eastern Idaho – The Region, Distinctive Geological and Geographic Features – Craters of the Moon National Monument and Preserve.*)

The surrounding public land and forests are popular for a variety of outdoor sports including fishing; boating; hiking; and hunting deer, elk, pronghorn antelope, duck and geese.

Economy and Major Employers The city has no dominant employer. The majority of the workforce commutes to work in the resort cities of

Glanbia Foods whey processing facility in Richfield.

Blaine County where jobs are plentiful but affordable housing is limited. Glanbia Foods has about 60 employees. The Richfield School District is the city's next largest employer.

Farming and ranching are important to the local economy. However, the character of the agriculture industry is changing. Larger operators have acquired most of the smaller farms.

Downtown business establishments consist principally of a shopping center, a convenience store and an automotive repair shop. Most city residents commute to larger nearby cities for shopping and services.

Education The Richfield School District provides elementary and secondary education. The closest institution of higher learning is the College of Southern

Idaho in Twin Falls.

Health Care Shoshone Family Medical Center, 16 miles southwest in Shoshone, offers the nearest medical services. The closest dental is Sawtooth Dental in Shoshone. The closest hospital is in Jerome or Gooding.

Transportation Highway 93-26 intersects the city. The closest airport is Freidman Memorial, 40 miles north in Hailey.

Utilities and Services Private companies provide electric, telephone, cable and satellite services. The City provides water and sewer services. The Lincoln County Sheriff's Office provides police protection under a contract with the City. The Richfield Volunteer Fire Department, Quick Response Unit (EMS) and library and cemetery districts are independent service providers. The County provides solid waste services.

Vision for 2050

By 2050 the population of Richfield will likely exceed 500. Wireless communications and information systems will serve the city. These wireless systems will allow more city residents to work at home.

In the next several years, efforts by Blaine County to build a new airport just north of the Lincoln County line will be successful. The

Aerial view of Richfield.

employment base needed to build, operate and maintain the airport and the businesses that grow up around it will be significant. Many of those workers will choose to live in Richfield and commute to work.

This increased population will put pressure on the city's municipal systems. City and community leaders will carefully monitor events and adapt as necessary to insure that our citizens' quality of life is sustained or improved and new residents and businesses are welcomed.

Mayors

1909 Jas A. Green *	1945 George Coates *
1923 W.E. Emerson *	1947 Elmo Patterson *
1925 George Schwaner *	1951 Lon Woods *
1927 W. Hill *	1955 C.W. Ward *
1929 Floyd Stewart *	1957 Edgar Stubbs *
1931 T.B. Brush *	1959 Mont Johnson *
1935 A.M. Howard *	1965 Birk Albert *
1937 Elmer Swatman *	1967 C.W. Ward
1939 John Workman *	1979 Charles Buttcane
1943 Chas Smith *	* Village Chairman

Shoshone, a railroad town.

Shoshone

Statistical Data

Population: 1,493 *
Elevation: 3,965 feet
Precipitation: 10 inches **
Average Snowfall: 27 inches **
County: Lincoln
Website: www.shoshonecity.com

Temperature Range – Fahrenheit: **
Spring: 27 to 72
Summer: 49 to 92
Fall: 26 to 79
Winter: 16 to 40
* U.S. Census Bureau Estimates July 2015
**Historical averages

Shoshone is one of Idaho's historic railroad towns. The train still passes through town but no longer stops for passengers or freight. However, many historic buildings remain.

Vast acreages of prehistoric lava flows and public lands interspersed by fertile farmland surround the city. The Little Wood River flows through town. The distant Sawtooth Mountain Range presents a picturesque backdrop to the northern sky. Twin Falls lies 25 miles south.

Shoshone's population is growing at less than one percent annually; however, this trend is changing. An increasing number of people with jobs in Bellevue, Hailey, Ketchum and Sun Valley are buying more affordable housing in Shoshone and commuting to work.

Pre-Incorporation Years

The first settlers in the area were sheep and cattle ranchers who grazed their herds on the high-desert plains.

In 1881 the Oregon Short Line Railroad began construction of a rail line that began at Granger, Wyoming; angled in a northwesterly direction through Pocatello, Shoshone and Nampa; and connected with the rail line in Huntington, Oregon. The rail line, completed November 17, 1884, provided the necessary link to connect Omaha, Nebraska, with Portland, Oregon.

As soon as railroad surveyors staked the route, homesteaders began filing claims near the planned train stop at what is now Shoshone.

On February 3, 1883, the first train reached Shoshone. The railroad company suspended work on the main rail line, built a junction and depot that they named Shoshone after the Shoshone Indians and built a branch line north to the mines in the Wood

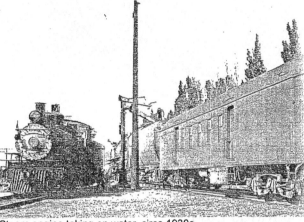
Steam engine taking on water, circa 1930s.

River Valley. Shoshone became a railhead and frontier supply center for both miners and settlers.

In the 1880s Shoshone was a wide-open frontier town. Carrie Strahorn, an early traveler to the town, wrote, "Ten and fifteen arrests per day were common and there was no other jail but a hole in the ground, with guards placed around the hole. There was a fight on the streets almost every hour of the day and night. Lot jumpers were numerous, bad whiskey was unlimited, dancehalls were on every corner, guns were fired at all

Shoshone train depot.

hours and the loud time from gambling dens was ever vibrating through the air."

Shoshone bars were renowned for their cold beer. Bar owners along with other local merchants and citizens routinely brought in ice from the Shoshone Indian Ice Caves – now Shoshone Ice Caves – located 19 miles north.

A diverse mix of nationalities settled in early Shoshone. Many were Chinese who had come to work in the Wood River Valley mines. Others were of Basque heritage that ran the area's vast herds of sheep. Many homesteaders had European, Scandinavian and Japanese backgrounds.

Train Town, USA.

At the turn of the century, Shoshone was a major railhead for transporting sheep and wool. The city's main street, named Rail Street, was a normal street except for its width. It had six sets of railroad tracks running through its center.

Sheep ranchers built boarding houses specifically to house the Basque families who immigrated to work on the ranches. One of these boarding houses – the historic Soloaga Basque Boarding House, built in 1907 – is on the National Historic Register.

In 1994 Christy Pyles, chairperson for the city's Gem Community Committee, summed up Shoshone's history as follows: "Since its wild beginnings, Shoshone has seen all the changes that created many ghost towns. Perhaps shaped and inspired by the surrounding desert, residents have always adapted and found new ways of life to keep the town alive."

United Methodist Church, constructed between the late 1890s and 1903.

Incorporation

The Legislature created Lincoln County on March 18, 1895, with the newly incorporated city of Shoshone as the county seat. The subsequent creation of Gooding, Minidoka and Jerome Counties reduced the size of the original Lincoln County; however, Shoshone remained the county seat.

Turning Points

Railroad Shoshone started as a railroad town located at the junction of the railroad's main line and the branch line to the Wood River Valley. The town's strategic location positioned it to become an important supply center and railhead for the mines and agricultural-based industries that developed in the area.

Cultural Transformation In the early days, Shoshone was a lawless frontier town. Bootlegging was prevalent in the 1920s and 1930s. At that time, the building now known as the Doncaster Building was a "Speak-Easy." When the voters repealed prohibition in 1933, bootlegging stopped.

Until the mid-1950s prostitution was legal. Rumor has it that while the mayor, Myrtle Burdett, and her husband, who frequented the establishment, were away on business, the city council, abolished this practice.

In an attempt to change the character of the town and attract families, the town site company gave two building lots to churches. The business community donated $75 toward a building fund for any church or school. The first church to take the offer was the Methodists, followed by the Roman Catholics and the Episcopalians.

In the 1940s Shoshone's stature increased as celebrities traveling north to Sun Valley often stopped in the Shoshone area to hunt pheasant.

Shoshone Today

Amenities and Attractions Shoshone's public library is an integral part of the community – offering Internet access, summer programs, reading to elementary classrooms and a growing selection of videos and DVDs.

The city's principal park, the Mary L. Gooding Memorial Park, is located on the banks of the Little Wood River near historic Oregon Trail

Shoshone City Hall.

campsites. The park has old-growth trees, a gazebo, picnic facilities, children's playground, a baseball diamond and the Lincoln County (outdoor) swimming pool (open May-August). On the second Sunday of each July, the park is the location of the Mannie Shaw's Old-Time Fiddlers' Jamboree. The park is popular for weddings, reunions and as a rest stop for travelers. The city also has a skateboard park and tennis courts.

The Lincoln County Fairgrounds are located in the city. Each August people from throughout the region come to enjoy the fair's exhibits, concessions and entertainment.

In 1994 the city's Gem Community Committee identified all of the historic and prominent buildings in the city and developed a history of each one. The committee published a Historical Walking Tour that features such buildings as the J. C. Penny Building, churches, boarding houses, hotels, mansions, show house and soda fountain, Manhattan Cafe, Lincoln County Court House and Bethany Lodge #21. Historical Walking Tour Brochures are available at the Lincoln County Court House and the Shoshone City Hall.

The Shoshone Senior Citizens Center is a popular amenity for seniors. At Thanksgiving and Christmas, the center delivers food baskets, clothing and toys for those less fortunate.

The Malad Gorge and Niagara Springs units of Thousand Springs State Park are 25 and 32 miles southwest, respectively. They offer camping and fishing in the cold-water springs that burst from the east rim of the Snake River Canyon.

Five miles southwest of Malad Gorge State Park and across the Snake River lies the Hagerman Fossil Beds National Monument.

The 212-foot-high Shoshone Falls on the Snake River lies 25 miles southwest of the city.

The Sawtooth Scenic Byway starts at Shoshone, passes near Sun Valley Resort and ends 116 miles north at the nearly 11,000-foot-high Sawtooth Mountain Range near Stanley.

Mammoth Cave, a one-and-a-quarter-mile-long lava tube, is located 10 miles north of the city. In the 1950s it served as a civil defense shelter.

Nineteen miles north of the city are the Shoshone Ice Caves. They are 1,700-foot-long, 40-foot-high ancient lava tubes that lie 110 feet underground. Water that seeps from the Big Wood River freezes in the tubes. Until 1900 the cave's 16-foot-thick glaciers provided ice for Shoshone residents.

Gazebo in park.

The six-mile-long Magic Reservoir lies 26 miles north of the city on the Big Wood River. The reservoir not only provides irrigation water for farmland near Shoshone but is also an excellent trout fishery and recreation area.

The U.S. Bureau of Land Management administers vast acreages to the west, north and east of the city. These public lands make Shoshone a gateway to a variety of outdoor recreational opportunities. Many residents hunt the deer, elk and pronghorn antelope that inhabit these lands. Pheasants and grouse flourish in the high-desert brush and grass as well as the habitat that edges the farms and canal banks. Hiking, biking, cross-country skiing, fishing, hunting and riding motorized vehicles are all available nearby.

Economy and Major Employers The District 4 office of the Idaho Department of Transportation is located in Shoshone. It has approximately 190 employees and is the city's largest employer.

The U.S. Bureau of Land Management employs about 100 at its Shoshone office and is the city's second largest employer. The Shoshone School District, the city's third largest employer, has about 50 employees.

The Shoshone business community consists of a variety of retail stores, restaurants and service businesses. Many residents also shop in Twin Falls.

Farming and ranching are important to the city's economy. In recent years, large dairy farms have become more prevalent than cattle and sheep ranching. Major farm crops include potatoes, beans, grain, alfalfa hay, corn, sugar beets and onions.

Shoshone business district by the railroad tracks.

Education The Shoshone School District provides most of the K-12 education and also offers adult education classes. The nearest institution of higher learning is the College of Southern Idaho in Twin Falls.

Health Care Shoshone has a medical clinic in the city. The nearest hospital is the 25-bed Jerome County Hospital, 16 miles south.

Transportation U.S. Highway 93 and State Highways 75, 26 and 24 intersect the city. Interstate 84 is 30 miles west.

The Gooding Municipal Airport is located 16 miles west. It has a 4,736-foot runway that primarily serves light charter and private aircraft. The closest commercial airport is Joslin Field in Twin Falls.

Utilities and Services Private companies provide natural gas, electricity, telephone, cable, CATV and satellite services. The City provides water and sewer services and police and fire protection.

Vision for 2050

From 1960 to today, Shoshone's population has increased about 11 percent. In the future, we expect these growth trends to increase as more people choose to live in the peaceful and affordable community of Shoshone and commute to work in either Twin Falls or the Wood River Valley.

City and community leaders are working cooperatively to insure the city's municipal systems are adequate to meet existing needs and future growth. The city's recently completed sewer and water systems have the capacity to meet the demands for many years. The city has recently annexed four new residential lot subdivisions on which homes will be constructed. This trend will continue as developers build to meet the increasing demand for affordable housing.

Through all of this growth, city leaders are committed to preserving the city's heritage and strategically planning the future so that Shoshone will always be a beautiful and peaceful community to live and raise a family.

Mayors

1902	J.F. White *	1953	Joe Pagoaga
1907	C.F. Borden *	1955	W.A. Hall
1909	Fred W. Gooding *	1957	Myrtle C. Burdett
1911	A.J. Newman *	1965	Victor Bozzuto
1913	A.I. McMahon *	1969	Ellwood Werry
1915	Frank E. Grosse *	1981	Reid J. Newby
1916	W.W. Custer *	1985	Tim Ridinger
1917	J.A. Keefer *	1997	Keith P. Haught
1919	J.A. McCallam *	2001	Richard Andreasen
1921	E.W. Sinclair *	2005	Wilson F (J.R.) Churchman
1921	Ben Darrah *	2013	David Wendell
1933	Chas. V. Pethick *	2016	Dan Pierson
1938	Ben Darrah *		* Village Chairman
1947	Myrtle C. Burdett *		

B canal where it passes under the railroad, in the Acequia area.

MINIDOKA COUNTY

- Acequia
- Heyburn
- Minidoka
- Paul
- Rupert (*County Seat*)

Acequia

Statistical Data

Population: 124 *
Elevation: 4,167 feet
Precipitation: 8 inches **
Average Snowfall: 27 inches **
County: Minidoka

Temperature Range – Fahrenheit: **
Spring: 28 to 69
Summer: 48 to 87
Fall: 25 to 76
Winter: 18 to 42
* U.S. Census Bureau Estimates July 2015
**Historical averages

The city of Acequia, a Spanish word for irrigation canal, is a peaceful high-desert farming community on Idaho Highway 24 and the Union Pacific rail line.

The fabulous public recreation and wildlife preserve of Lake Walcott, the reservoir created by Minidoka Dam; the dam itself; Lake Walcott State Park; and the Minidoka National Wildlife Refuge are about five miles east.

The North Side Canal runs near the city. This canal is the main feeder canal that delivers water from Lake Walcott to a complex system of subsidiary canals that ultimately irrigate 78,000 acres of farmland on the north side of the Snake River.

Pre-Incorporation Years

Acequia owes its origins to the railroad, but its growth and development followed construction of the Minidoka Dam and Lake Walcott.

When the Oregon Short Line Railroad completed its rail line from Granger, Wyoming, to Huntington, Oregon, on November 17, 1884, the line allowed through travel between Omaha, Nebraska, and Portland, Oregon. At that time, the closest railroad facility to what is now Acequia was a construction camp and post office eight miles northeast built by the railroad in 1882. The Oregon Short Line chief engineer named the camp Minidoka, a name believed to be of Shoshone

394

origin meaning "broad expanse."

At that time, the entire region was a dry high-desert plain covered with sagebrush. However, the volcanic ash-based soil was deep and fertile. Water was all it needed to become productive.

Twenty years later, Congress passed the Newlands Act that authorized the U.S. Reclamation Service – today, the Bureau of Reclamation – to construct facilities that would provide irrigation and electricity and promote conversion of arid public lands to private farms. (*See Cities of the Magic Valley.*)

Cheese factory, 1926.

In 1904 the Reclamation Service started building the hydroelectric Minidoka Dam and canal complex.

In the same year, the Minidoka and Southwestern Railroad Company, later acquired by the Oregon Short Line Railroad, started construction of a 75-mile rail line – completed in 1907 – from the main railroad line at Minidoka, southwest to Burley, then west to Buhl.

Frank Scherrer established a town site next to the railroad siding near what is now Acequia around 1904. Almost immediately, dam and canal workers began establishing homes around Scherrer and settlers began filing homestead claims.

Scherrer built a warehouse and small grocery store and was the town's first postmaster. The dam was completed two years later, and construction of the North Side Canal and subsidiary canal systems was well underway. It was at this time that town residents began reflecting on the importance of the North Side Canal, which ran near town, and circulated a petition calling for changing the name of the town to Acequia, a Spanish word for irrigation canal. Postal authorities were accommodating.

The *Rupert Pioneer-Record* reported on August 22, 1907, that the name of "Scherrer" was doomed because the U.S. Post Office had approved a petition to change its name to "Acequia."

By 1907 conversion of the arable sagebrush land into private farms was almost complete. Acequia, with its post office and rail stop, became a community center for goods and services needed not only by construction crews but for area farmers and ranchers as well. The early settlers

Jackrabbits by the millions were killed in rabbit drives—and still they were not eliminated.

obtained their drinking water from a central well and water tower in Acequia.

George Packham and his family – who came from Ogden, Utah – were one of the first farmers to settle in Acequia. After they secured their farmland and built lodgings and corrals, they shipped their household goods and livestock by train. Packham and his brother unloaded the livestock at the Acequia train stop and drove them through the sagebrush to their homestead.

The Comstock family came from Montana and operated a general store that eventually included a two-story icehouse where blocks of ice cut from Lake Walcott were stored in sawdust – ice blocks covered with straw or sawdust melted very slowly and could generally last through the summer. The store also had scales used to

Original Acequia LDS Church building.

weigh wagons and trucks. Comstock later replaced the older building with a larger brick structure, still standing but largely unused.

The early 1900s was a period of growth for the new community. In 1915 The Church of Jesus Christ of Latter-day Saints built a cooperative cheese factory near the town. A year later, church members built a hall used for community dances and other activities.

Subsequently, the Union Church built a facility to serve the needs of its members. Both churches held bazaars, dinners and other community activities.

The ongoing fight against the common peril of jackrabbits fostered other events that brought the entire community together. Periodically, jackrabbit populations reached epidemic proportions and threatened to devour entire fields of growing crops and stacks of harvested hay. Residents organized rabbit drives to destroy as many of the animals as they could. (*See Fighting the Jackrabbit Menace.*)

The railroad was important to Acequia businesses and residents. Through the 1930s it was the dominant means of transportation. Livestock shipments were so frequent that the railroad built a stockyard next to the tracks.

Train passengers would raise the flag and wait in a small

Sherrer warehouse.

yellow frame building called the station house for the train to stop.

The railroad also delivered the mail. If there were no passengers or freight, a train employee threw out a mail pouch to the Acequia Postmaster as the train went past the station house. For outgoing mail, the postmaster put the mail in a pouch and hung it from a pole. As the train passed, a railroad employee extended a metal arm with a hook on the end and snagged the pouch. The first schools were two adjacent one-room buildings with one teacher manning each. In 1908 Acequia voters approved a $2,940 school bond to construct a new high school.

During the Great Depression of the 1930s, the federal Works Progress Administration constructed a new high school and gymnasium. High school students moved onto the new facilities during their 1936 Christmas vacation. Elementary grade students

High School building, circa 1930, facing North.

moved from their one-room buildings into the old high school.

Incorporation

In January 1952 the Minidoka County Commission approved the incorporation of Acequia as a village. Acequia's status changed to a city in 1967 in conformity with a change in state municipal law.

Turning Points

Railroad Acequia owes its origins to the railroad. The prospect of the railroad led Frank Scherrer to build his commercial facilities and post office near the tracks. By constructing its rail stop and stockyard facilities in town, the railroad set the stage for the city to benefit from the construction of Minidoka Dam and reclamation of the surrounding sagebrush-covered land.

However, in the mid-1900s as trucks became the dominant freight carriers, the railroad ceased serving Acequia, and many of the city's businesses closed or moved five miles southwest to Jerome.

Minidoka Dam The railroad established critical transportation services. But the availability of irrigation water is what allowed agriculture and the city's economy to flourish. The construction of the Minidoka

The last customer in the Acequia Post Office before it closed: Irel Kent being helped by postmistress Nina Stephenson.

Dam and irrigation systems by the U.S. Reclamation Service transformed the entire region from an arid wasteland to a fertile agricultural oasis.

Adapting to the New Economy Agriculture-based businesses continue to underpin the city's economy. However, for the city's economy to grow, it needs business diversification.

While it has not yet happened, the city's proximity to Lake Walcott State Park and the Minidoka National Wildlife Refuge complex provides opportunity. The city could extend its boundaries to the complex entrance, and tourism and outdoor recreation businesses could develop.

Acequia Today

Amenities and Attractions Perhaps the city's most significant attribute is its location next to a fabulous public recreation complex that includes Lake Walcott, the reservoir created by the Minidoka Dam; the dam itself; Lake Walcott State Park; and the Minidoka National Wildlife Refuge.

Present Acequia Elementary School.

Minidoka Dam Road, less than a mile northeast of the city off Idaho Highway 24, is the primary access into the complex.

Lake Walcott State Park offers water skiing, power boating, windsurfing, sailing, bird watching, camping, fishing and picnicking under old-growth hardwood trees. One popular feature of the park is an 18-hole "Disc Golf Course" with metal baskets for holes.

The Minidoka National Wildlife Refuge extends 25 miles east and upriver from the dam. It encompasses nearly 21,000 acres – over half is open water and marshes.

Economy and Major Employers The agriculture industry underpins the city's economy. The principal businesses in or near the city include Land View Fertilizer, a wholesale and retail distributor of

Clinton Ranch Office, now part of Nature's Best Produce Company.

commercial fertilizer; Teton Trees, a tree farm; Jentzsch Kearl Farms; and Acequia Automotive, a car, truck and farm equipment repair shop with three employees.

Most Acequia residents travel five miles southwest to Rupert for employment and to do their shopping.

Education Minidoka School District provides most of the primary and secondary education services. Acequia students attend schools located in Rupert.

The closest institution of higher learning is the College of Southern Idaho in Twin Falls, 40 miles west.

Health Care The nearest hospital is Minidoka Memorial Hospital in Rupert.

Transportation Idaho Highway 24 passes through the city. Ten miles to the southwest, it connects with Interstate 84. Private and small charter airline services are available 12 miles southwest in Burley. Commercial airline service is available at Twin Falls and Pocatello.

Newcomb grain facility.

Utilities and Services Private companies provide electric, telephone and satellite services. The city's homes and businesses have individual wells and septic systems. The County Sheriff's Office provides police protection, and the Jerome Fire Department provides fire protection.

Vision for 2050

The population of Acequia, which was 107 in 1960, has remained somewhat constant for decades. However, historical trends may not be indicative of the future. The city is located less than a mile northeast of the Highway 24 exit into the Minidoka Recreation and Wildlife Preserve complex. The complex is one of Idaho's outstanding family and sportsman recreation areas. As the populations of Twin Falls and other area cities grow, public and commercial interests may promote greater public use of the complex. Should that occur, the city's proximity to the complex entrance off Highway 24 could have a positive effect on its growth.

Downstream division of A and B Canals.

Mayors

1952 Vernard Comstock *
1967 Vernard Comstock
1976 Margaret Comstock

1980 Larry Wall
* Village Chairman

Heyburn Police Department.

Heyburn

Statistical Data

Population: 3,183 *
Elevation: 4,152 feet
Precipitation: 10 inches **
Average Snowfall: 23 inches **
County: Minidoka
Website: www.heyburnidaho.org

Temperature Range – Fahrenheit: **
Spring: 36 to 61
Summer: 53 to 86
Fall: 36 to 63
Winter: 21 to 40
* U.S. Census Bureau Estimates July 2015
**Historical averages

Heyburn is located on the fertile Snake River Plain just south of Interstate 84 and two miles northeast of Burley.

Fields of potatoes, beans, corn, grain, alfalfa hay and sugar beets surround the city. The Snake River flows about a mile southwest. The mountains of the Sawtooth National Forest outline the city's southeastern sky.

Pre-Incorporation Years

Heyburn owes its origins to the 1906 completion of the Minidoka Dam on the Snake River by the U.S. Reclamation Service – now the Bureau of Reclamation (Reclamation) – operating under the authority of the 1902 Newlands Act. In addition to the dam, Reclamation built a complex system of irrigation canals and ditches to irrigate 116,000 acres. (*See The Region, Federal Lands – Private Ownership and Preservation Laws and, Agriculture and Irrigation – Bureau of Reclamation – Minidoka Project.*)

As the dam neared completion, Reclamation surveyed three town sites below the dam. One of the sites was Heyburn, which they called Riverton. Building lots for the new community began selling on October 20, 1906.

Prior to completion of the dam, homesteaders began filing their claims and clearing sagebrush off their land. Many also worked for Reclamation building irrigation canals and ditches.

The fertile soil, irrigation, the town's proximity to the Snake River and the railroad line that was expected to arrive a year later made the new town and surrounding land particularly attractive.

Senator Weldon
Brinton Heyburn.

Word of the new town attracted a variety of merchants, craftsman and professionals. Within a year, there was a downtown business community that included a bank, a newspaper, three lumber yards, a brick yard, a doctor's office, a railroad depot, a general store, two grocery stores, a meat market, a millinery store, a hardware and seed store, a harness shop, rooming houses, a restaurant, a barber shop, a cream station, a livery board, a saloon, churches and a school. A movie theater and telephone exchange soon followed.

At the time lots were sold, the city applied with postal authorities for the "Riverton Post Office." Postal authorities denied the application because the Riverton name was already in use.

Town leaders successfully resubmitted the application with the name of Heyburn in honor of Idaho's then U.S. Senator Weldon Brinton Heyburn.

Train depot.

From the beginning, settlers wanted their children educated. The first school was a two-room building on a hill north of the railroad tracks. In 1906 a three-room schoolhouse was built just south of the present grade school. In 1908 a four-room brick building was completed with 168 students enrolled.

Most of the settlers were Christians, but of different denominations. As a nucleus of similar believers developed, they built new church buildings. The Presbyterians were first. In 1910 the Church of Jesus Christ of Latter-day Saints organized a ward and completed a white frame chapel.

Incorporation

On January 18, 1911, Heyburn became an incorporated village. Its legal status changed to a city in 1967 as required by the change in state municipal law.

Turning Points

Irrigation Congressional passage of the Newlands Act and creation of the Reclamation Service led to construction of the hydroelectric Minidoka Dam, its complex irrigation system and the formation of Heyburn in 1906.

J.R. Simplot plant, circa 1961.

Railroad A year later, the Minidoka and Southwestern Railroad Company, which was formed in 1904, built branch lines from the main Oregon Short Line railroad to several Magic Valley communities including Heyburn. The railroad sought to serve the huge agriculture market created by the availability of irrigation water and played a critical role in the development of the city.

Great Depression The Great Depression of the 1930s dealt a devastating blow to Heyburn. The bank closed and many businesses failed. The owners of failed businesses either tore down their buildings or moved them to other communities – leaving only one grocery store.

Heyburn State Banks, located at 18th Street and J Street.

World War II When America entered World War II in 1941, prices for agricultural products increased; however, good labor was in short supply. Most of the able-bodied men were called uto fight in the war. Many men and women traveled to other cities for high-paying jobs building goods and weapons for the military.

Japanese-American citizens held in Camp Hunt internment camp near Minidoka and German prisoners of war held at Camp Rupert near Paul helped overcome the farm labor shortage. (*See The Region, World War II – Hunt Camp, Imprisonment of American Citizens of Japanese Descent.*)

Food Processing In 1956 the J.R. Simplot Company built a potato processing and starch plant in Heyburn with frozen French fries and frozen and dehydrated potatoes as the plant's principal products. The complex, which included huge cellars for storing raw potatoes, employed several hundred people and was a tremendous boost to the city's economy. Hundreds of people moved to Heyburn and the surrounding area to work at the plant. However, as time progressed, technological improvements allowed the company to increase productivity with fewer and fewer workers. By the 1990s the aging facility had become outdated. Cost factors and market forces had also changed.

In 2003 Simplot announced that rather than incur the high cost of rebuilding the plant with new technology, it was closing the facility and moving the operation to Canada to be closer to its Midwestern markets and where greater cost efficiencies were available. The loss of over 650 jobs was a heavy blow to Heyburn and the surrounding communities.

The Riverton Hardware Store during the flood of 1907.

On March 12, 2004, in an effort to ameliorate problems caused by the closure of its plant, the J.R. Simplot Company gave the 276-acre, 20 building complex with 1.1 million feet of floor space to the city of Burley. The facility straddles the border between Minidoka and Cassia Counties. It is now the Burley Industrial Park.

Economic Development In 1993 the Rupert and Burley Chambers of Commerce merged into the Mini-Cassia Chamber of Commerce with general offices in Heyburn. The Chamber serves 12 towns in Minidoka and Cassia Counties and has more than 400 members.

The city built a municipal park, boat dock and RV park along the Snake River in 2000 that attract many tourists.

Heyburn Today

Amenities and Attractions The Mini-Cassia In-Line Hockey Association – consisting of parents, kids and volunteers

Heyburn School, built in 1908.

– raised the money to build the Heyburn In-line Hockey Rink, which is open to the public.

Heyburn is undergoing revitalization. Postal authorities have recently remodeled the post office, and the City has remodeled city hall and the police department.

The City has expanded development of the Snake River shoreline to include a one-mile nature path, a day camp, three picnic areas and grills, a city park, boat dock, overnight RV park and the Mini-Cassia Chamber of Commerce office and visitor's center.

Particularly inviting to RV travelers is the city's "Riverside RV Park that offers full-service parking, restroom and shower facilities for 29 units. It is also home to the Heyburn Amphitheater.

An interesting city attribute is the display of 46 privately owned oil paintings in Heyburn Elementary School. The collection belongs to the estate of J.M. Whiting, a former school district superintendent from 1932 to 1940 who sought to instill a love for fine arts in the students. During his tenure, he held annual art exhibits in the schools, attracting exhibitors and patrons throughout the region.

The fabulous public recreation and wildlife preserve of Lake Walcott, the reservoir created by Minidoka Dam; the dam itself; Lake Walcott State Park; and the Minidoka National Wildlife Refuge lie about 20 miles northeast of Heyburn.

The city's close proximity to the state park, the Snake River and the Sawtooth National Forest provides city residents with a broad variety of outdoor activities. Camping, fishing, boating, water skiing, hunting, hiking and ATV riding are popular.

Economy and Major Employers The city's largest employer at 50 is Gossner Foods of Magic Valley, a cheese processing plant and retail store owned by Gossner Foods of Logan, Utah. Other significant Heyburn employers include two restaurants, light manufacturing and service businesses.

Education Minidoka County School District provides most of the primary and secondary education for Heyburn's children. The city's K-6 age children attend Heyburn Elementary, soon to be replaced with a new facility. Older children attend school in Rupert.

The closest institution of higher learning is the College of Southern Idaho

about 60 miles west in Twin Falls.

Health Care Minidoka Memorial Hospital in Rupert and Cassia Regional Medical Center in Burley provide most of the health care needs for city residents.

Transportation U.S. Highway 30 intersects the city. Interstate 84 is a mile north. Railroad service is available for freight.

Airport service for light private and charter aircraft is available at the 4,094-foot runway at J.R. Simplot Airport, three miles southwest. Joslin Field-Magic Valley Regional Airport is in Twin Falls.

Utilities and Services Private companies provide natural gas, cable, telephone and satellite services. The City provides electricity, water and sewer services and police protection. The Minidoka Fire Protection District provides fire protection.

Vision for 2050

The 1960 U.S. Census reported Heyburn's population at 829. By 1980 the population reached 2,889 where it has essentially remained. Changes to the city's population are primarily  a function of the economic growth of the region. If recent population trends hold, by 2050 Heyburn's population will approximate 3,500.

Should that occur, routine maintenance and improvements of existing municipal systems will be adequate to meet citizen needs.

However, that could change dramatically as it did in the 1960s and 1970s. It is a reasonable expectation that Heyburn's mild climate, rich agricultural heritage and small town atmosphere will attract new businesses with employees who want a good place to live and raise a family. The city has designed many of its amenities for children and families.

Mayors

1911 T.J. Smith *	1952 Roy Skinner *
1914 W.W. Brim *	1952 W.P. Boyd *
1915 H.C. Phelan *	1953 Leo Handy *
1917 V.C. Pullman *	1959 Harold Hurst *
1919 N.W. Wilson *	1968 Harold R. Hurst
1921 W.F. Mainfold *	1992 Glen J. Loveland
1935 W.B. Christenson *	1997 George M. Froom
1939 Kenneth King *	2000 Cleo K. Cheney
1947 Keith Mourtison *	2004 George A. Anderson
1947 Golden Moffett *	2016 Cleo Fay Gallegos
1948 William Hellewell *	* Village Chairman

Minidoka Town Hall.

Minidoka

Statistical Data

Population: 112 *
Elevation: 4,281 feet
Precipitation: 9 inches **
Average Snowfall: 28 inches **
County: Minidoka

Temperature Range – Fahrenheit: **
Spring: 26 to 69
Summer: 49 to 88
Fall: 25 to 78
Winter: 15 to 42
* U.S. Census Bureau Estimates July 2015
**Historical averages

Minidoka lies on the Snake River Plain about five miles due north of the hydroelectric Minidoka Dam on the Snake River and Lake Wolcott, created by the dam.

A few miles to the north begin vast tracts of public lands and the prehistoric lava flows of the Craters of the Moon National Monument. Rupert is about 13 miles southwest.

Pre-Incorporation Years

Until the early 1900s travelers through the area generally considered the region around what is now Minidoka as a sagebrush wasteland.

In 1843 Captain John C. Fremont, a topographical engineer, led a military surveying expedition that mapped much of the West. His party stopped at two Idaho trading posts – Fort Hall near what is now Pocatello and Fort Boise near what is now Parma. Both forts started in 1834. Oregon Trail pioneers used Fremont's Congress-published maps extensively.

Fremont, who had little experience with irrigation and understanding of the high fertility of Snake River Plain soils, spoke dismissively of the land between the two forts. He said, "There does not occur for a distance of 300 miles to the westward a fertile spot of ground sufficiently large to produce the necessary quantity of grain or pasturage enough to allow even a temporary repose to the emigrants."

For decades, Oregon Trail pioneers and others shared Fremont's view. American Indians may have passed near what is now Minidoka en route to their summer and winter encampments where fresh water was abundant, but they did not stay.

However, in the late 1800s attitudes began to change. Pioneers from northern Utah began settling in the Upper Snake River Plain. They successfully applied their irrigation techniques and experience gained from three decades of desert reclamation in the Great Basin. In 1881 the Utah &

City of Minidoka.

Northern Railway Company completed its railroad line from the railhead at Franklin, Idaho, to the Montana gold fields and the boomtowns of Virginia City, Butte and Garrison. This railroad greatly accelerated the settlement of Eastern Idaho.

In 1881 the Oregon Short Line Railroad (OSL) began building a railroad connection between the railheads at Granger, Wyoming, and Huntington, Oregon – a distance of 472 miles. The rail line angled from Granger in a northwesterly direction through Pocatello and Caldwell before connecting with the rail

Minidoka, looking north toward the depot.

line in Huntington. In 1882 when the construction crews reached what is now Minidoka, the railroad built a railroad construction camp and post office. The OSL chief engineer named the camp Minidoka.

The origin of the word. "Minidoka" is not known. Local legend has it that the name is of Shoshone origin, meaning "broad expanse." However, regional historians and educators familiar with area Shoshone and Bannock languages discredit that notion, asserting that the word has no resemblance to any word sounds used by those tribes – American Indians generally did not have written languages. Some scholars have pointed out similarities with the "mini" and "doka" sounds of words used in one or more of the dialects of the Lakota Sioux Indians whose historic tribal areas included parts of what is now Minnesota and North and South Dakota – "mini" meaning "water" and "doka" probably meaning "without any, gone or not there." How those Lakota Sioux language terms were transported to Idaho – either by railroad officials or Sioux Indian scouts – is open to speculation.

When completed at Huntington on November 17, 1884, it created another continental railroad. Railroad interests completed the first continental railroad in 1869 at Promontory Point near Corinne, Utah. The OSL line opened Southern Idaho to the commerce centers of Omaha, Nebraska, and Portland, Oregon.

Center Street after the fire of 1906.

In 1902 Congress passed the Newlands Act. The Act authorized the U.S. Reclamation Service, later renamed the Bureau of Reclamation, to construct facilities that would provide irrigation and electricity and promote conversion of arid public lands to private productive farms.

In 1904 the Reclamation Service started construction of the hydroelectric Minidoka Dam on the Snake River and a complex system of canals and ditches. In

City of Minidoka viewed from the coal chute. Courtesy Gary Schorzman.

1906 they completed construction of the Dam. In addition, construction of the North Side Canal and subsidiary canal systems were well underway.

In contemplation of irrigation water becoming available, farmers began settling

the land. Those who settled around what is now Minidoka cleared the land and used dry-land farming techniques to plant winter wheat. (*See Southwest Idaho, Cities of the Magic Valley and Federal Land Use Laws.*)

Unfortunately for settlers around Minidoka, their farms were too far north to receive water from Minidoka Dam. They had to continue dry farming. While dry-farm production was acceptable for a few years, the weather turned dry and the perpetual problems of hoards of jackrabbits and insects became insurmountable. Many farmers had to sell or abandon their farms. (*See Southwestern Idaho – The Jackrabbit Menace.*)

However, in 1946 conditions changed. Innovation in irrigation equipment and drilling deep wells allowed farmers to tap into the massive Snake River Aquifer for the irrigation water needed to produce higher-value crops. Minidoka farmland was now valuable as deep wells and sprinkler irrigation turned the high desert into an oasis of potatoes, sugar beets, wheat and feed crops of barley, corn and alfalfa hay. The community's population grew rapidly. In a few years, the town had the number of people – 200 – needed to qualify for incorporation as a village.

Higgins house and drug store. Courtesy Gary Schorzman.

Incorporation

On October 10, 1904, the Minidoka County Commissioners approved incorporation of the village of Minidoka. In 1967 Minidoka's legal status changed from a village to a city as required by the new state law.

Turning Points

Railroad From its humble beginnings as a railroad work camp and for decades later as a struggling farm community, the Legislature elevated recognition of the town when on February 18, 1913, it gave the town's name to the newly created Minidoka County with the county seat at Rupert. That action was the catalyst that

Sears Hotel, 1904. Courtesy Gary Schorzman.

essentially gave regional prominence to the Minidoka name far beyond the obscure railroad location where it started. "Minidoka" not only became the name of a city and county, it also became the name of a national wildlife refuge and the World War II Japanese-American relocation center, located near Eden – also known as Hunt Camp. Many institutions, government agencies and businesses also included "Minidoka" as part of their formal name.

Irrigation Even though the area around Minidoka missed receiving water from Lake Walcott, use of technological innovation in deep-well drilling, electrical pumps and sprinkler irrigation systems ultimately turned the land around Minidoka into an agricultural oasis, just as water did decades earlier on Magic Valley farms irrigated from Minidoka Dam.

Minidoka Today

Amenities and Attractions Perhaps the most significant attribute for the city is its location next to a fabulous public recreation complex that includes Minidoka Dam, Lake Walcott, Lake Walcott State Park and the Minidoka National Wildlife Refuge. Lake Walcott State Park offers water skiing, power boating, windsurfing, sailing, bird

Woods Hotel. Courtesy Gary Schorzman.

watching, camping and fishing, as well as picnicking under old-growth hardwood trees. One popular feature of the park is an 18-hole "Disc Golf Course" with metal baskets for holes.

The Wildlife Refuge extends 25 miles east and upriver from the dam. It encompasses nearly 21,000 acres of which over half is open water and marshes.

Camping, hiking, hunting and ATV riding are also available on thousands of acres of public land located just north of the city.

Economy and Major Employers The agriculture industry underpins the city's economy. Minidoka residents travel to Rupert to do most of their shopping.

Education Minidoka School District provides most of the K-12 education. Minidoka students attend schools in Rupert.

The closest institution of higher learning is the College of Southern Idaho located 70 miles southwest in Twin Falls.

Health Care The closest medical care is the Minidoka Memorial Hospital and clinics in Rupert.

Transportation Minidoka sets at the point of an elbow turn made by Idaho Highway 24 as it moves northeast from Rupert and abruptly turns northwest paralleling the railroad track into Shoshone. Interstate 84 is accessible 18 miles southwest on Highway 24.

The closest commercial airline service is Joslin Field in Twin Falls.

Utilities and Services Private companies provide electric, telephone and satellite services. The city's homes and businesses have individual wells and septic systems. The County Sheriff provides police protection, and the Jerome Fire

Department provides fire protection under contract with the City.

Vision for 2050

In 1990 the city's population hit a low of 67. By 2000 it had grown to 129. Since that time it has held at around 120. Historical trends should continue for the next few decades. By 2050 Minidoka's population will likely not exceed 200.

Looking east on Idaho Street in Paul.

Paul

Statistical Data

Population: 1,188 *	Spring: 26 to 68
Elevation: 4,147 feet	Summer: 46 to 86
Precipitation: 9.4 inches **	Fall: 23 to 76
Average Snowfall: 23 inches **	Winter: 15 to 41
County: Minidoka	* U.S. Census Bureau Estimates July 2015
Temperature Range – Fahrenheit: **	**Historical averages

Paul lies on the fertile Snake River Plain about 2.5 miles north of Burley and five miles east of Rupert. Lush irrigated fields of sugar beets, wheat, potatoes, alfalfa hay and beans surround the city.

The hydroelectric Minidoka Dam and Lake Walcott, created by the dam on the Snake River, are about 18 miles east.

About 25 miles north begin vast tracts of public lands and the prehistoric lava flows of the Craters of the Moon National Monument. Approximately 20 miles southeast of the city is the Sawtooth National Forest, with mountain peaks rising to over 9,000 feet.

Paul, 1919.

Pre-Incorporation Years

The Southern Idaho travelers of the early 1800s – including explorers/trappers, Oregon/California Trail pioneers and the prospectors of the 1860s and 1870s – almost uniformly considered the Snake River Plain a sagebrush wasteland. There was nothing but desert and wide expanses of sagebrush for miles.

In 1843 Captain John C. Fremont, a topographical engineer, led a military surveying expedition, mapping much of the West. He wrote of the Snake River Plain: "There does not occur for a distance of 300 miles to the westward, a fertile spot of ground sufficiently large to produce the necessary quantity of grain or pasturage enough to allow even a temporary repose to the emigrants."

However, in the late 1800s attitudes began to change. Around 1880 pioneers from northern Utah began settling in the Upper Shake River Plain. Over the next several years, they successfully applied irrigation techniques and experience gained from three decades of desert reclamation in the Great Basin and transformed fields of sagebrush into an agricultural oasis.

In 1884 twenty-two-year-old Ira B. Perrine, who a decade and a half later would become the driving force behind construction of the Carey Act project Milner Dam, also successfully demonstrated that irrigation could transform desert land.

Perrine sold dairy products and meat to the Wood River Valley miners. Looking for a more favorable climate to winter his cows, Perrine moved his herd of 40 dairy cows from the Wood River Valley to the Blue Lakes in the Snake River Canyon near what is now Twin Falls. Perrine built a flood irrigation system; planted fruit trees; and grew berries, wheat and vegetables which he sold to Wood River Valley miners. Perrine's Blue Lakes Fruit Ranch ultimately comprised 1,000 acres.

In 1881 the Oregon Short Line Railroad (OSL) began building a railroad connection between the railheads at Granger, Wyoming, and Huntington, Oregon – a distance of 472 miles. The rail line angled from Granger in a northwesterly direction through Pocatello, Shoshone and Caldwell before connecting with the rail line in Huntington.

When completed at Huntington on November 17, 1884, it created another continental railroad. Railroad interests completed the first continental railroad in 1869 at Promontory Point near Corinne,

Paul State Bank.

Utah. The OSL line opened Southern Idaho to the commerce centers of Omaha, Nebraska, and Portland, Oregon.

In 1902 Congress passed the Newlands Act. The Act authorized the U.S. Reclamation Service, later renamed the Bureau of Reclamation (Reclamation), to construct dams and canal systems in the Western U.S., sell arable land and water rights to settlers, periodically plat townsites needed to serve each farming community and provide irrigation water and electricity to promote conversion of arid public lands to productive privately-owned farms.

One of the first irrigation projects completed under the Act was the 82-foot-high, one-mile-long Minidoka Dam located near the Minidoka Rapids on the Snake River. Reclamation started the dam in 1904 and completed it in 1906. The 7000-killowatt hydroelectric power plant built at the dam began delivering electrical power in 1909. The water impounded by the dam created Lake Walcott and provided irrigation water on the north and south sides of the river, a total of 116,000 acres. (*See Southwestern Idaho, Cities of the Magic Valley and Federal Land Use Laws.*)

In contemplation of receiving irrigation water from Minidoka Dam, settlers immediately began buying land and water rights. Within a year, hundreds of settlers had moved onto their property and commenced clearing their land of sagebrush and preparing the soil for planting. The first years were harsh living in tents and hauling water from the Snake River as far as four miles away. Pioneers somehow managed to hang on for three years until the water arrived, and then their dreams began to come true.

In 1905 Reclamation platted the town of Paul – named after Reclamation's chief engineer, C. H. Paul.

No sooner did the settler's crops emerge from the ground, than hoards of jackrabbits and insects converged on the fields, devouring the tender crops and threatening the settlers' livelihood. As one settler wrote, "Jackrabbits came to the green wheat fields about sundown. They came from the lavas [lava beds] and the uncleared sagebrush fields where they shaded-up during the daytime. They came in hoards so thick that it looked as though the ground was moving..." The settlers fought the menace with every tool available. (*See Southwestern Idaho – The Jackrabbit Menace.*)

In 1907 the Minidoka and Southwestern Railroad Company – acquired by the Oregon Short Line Railroad in 1910 – completed the 75-mile railroad spur that started at Minidoka, passed through Rupert and Paul and ended at Buhl. In 1910 the railroad came to Paul, crossing land owned by James Ellis.

After the railroad arrived, the first building was constructed, a large two-story wood frame structure known as the Woodman Hall. It contained a lodge upstairs and J.J. Smoot's general store on the ground floor. Then two acres were purchased from Mr. Ellis and the first schoolhouse went up. M.E. Watson built an elevator and flour mill, R.H. Adams constructed a warehouse and a bank was then built, which still stands today. Then a $70,000 hotel was built by the Grimm brothers. Later, the community got together on a $30,000 water system. The old school, with its 16 students, was getting over filled. A $250,000 brick structured school was built. Some of the land was owned by T.E. Clark. They came up with several names for the town – Clarksville, Clarkston, and Clarkopolis to name a few. They finally decided it would be called Paul – getting the name from the supervisory engineer, Charles H. Paul, in his honor for the Minidoka Project.

Incorporation

On May 7, 1917, Paul became an incorporated village. Its status changed to a city with the passage of a new Idaho law in 1967.

Turning Points

Minidoka Dam

Three general events combined to make the existence and

Basalt quarry near Paul.

prosperity of the Paul possible – congressional passage of the Newlands Act, construction of Minidoka Dam and its system of irrigation canals and the production of electricity which began in 1909.

Railroad The railroad was as important to the economic development and prosperity of Paul and the Magic Valley as irrigation. The railroad transported farm commodities to market as well as transporting equipment, supplies, passengers and mail needed by the growing agricultural industry and community.

Amalgamated Sugar Company The Amalgamated Sugar Company was built in the 1920s and is still running today.

World War II One of the tragedies of World War II, which began in 1941 following the Japanese attack on Pearl Harbor, was the action taken by the federal government to strip Japanese-American citizens of their constitutional rights and place them into concentration camps called "relocation centers."

One of the "relocation centers," the Minidoka Relocation Center – which postal authorities called Hunt – was built on 68,000 acres of sagebrush land located between the cities of Rupert and Jerome.

In May of 1944 Italian prisoners of war were sent to a 300-acre camp just five miles west of Paul. The prison camp was called Camp Rupert. The Italians were only there for a few short months before German prisoners were brought in to take their place in the fall of 1944.

During the war years, most able-bodied men had been called up to fight in the war. In addition, other Magic Valley men and women moved to other cities for high-paying jobs building goods and weapons for the military. Consequently, there was a shortage of laborers to work on the farms.

Hunt Camp prisoners and German POWs filled part of this labor shortage. The U.S. Government contracted them out as farm hands to the local farmers. Still today, the area is made up largely of Knopps, Kraus, Martsch, Schorzman and Schenks. (*See Southwestern Idaho – Hunt Camp – WWII Imprisonment of American Citizens of Japanese Descent.*)

Paul Today

Amenities and Attractions A 11.5-acre city park is being constructed with walking paths, an 800-foot spray park, a sled hill for the children in the winter time, two soccer fields, picnic areas, Frisbee golf and workout areas.

The city of Paul has easy access to everywhere. If you go five miles east, you're in Rupert; 2.5 miles south and you're in Burley or Heyburn; or west and you hit the Interstate to Twin Falls and beyond. State Highway 24 is 15 miles north, and you have a shortcut to Magic Reservoir, Stanley, Ketchum, Hailey and Sun Valley.

One of the more significant city attractions is its location near the fabulous public recreation complex that includes Minidoka Dam, Lake Walcott, Lake Walcott State Park and the Minidoka National Wildlife Refuge.

Lake Walcott State Park offers boating, windsurfing, sailing, water skiing, bird watching, camping and fishing, as well as picnicking under old-growth hardwood trees. One popular feature of the park is an 18-hole "Disc Golf Course" with metal baskets for holes.

The Wildlife Refuge extends 25 miles east and upriver from the dam. It encompasses nearly 21,000 acres of which over half are open water and marshes.

Downhill skiing is available at Pomerelle Ski Resort, 38 miles south of the city. Its 8,000-foot elevation has an average snowfall of 500 inches. The resort has 24 groomed trails and 3 chairlifts.

Many residents take advantage of the national forest and the vast open ranges managed by the BLM for hunting, fishing, hiking, biking, snowmobiling and ATV riding.

Economy and Major Employers
The city of Paul has approximately 60 businesses within the city limits, as well as several businesses on the outskirts of town.

With about 250 full and part-time employees, Amalgamated Sugar Company is the city's largest employer. Magic Valley Produce and Kodiak Northwest, a manufacturer of heavy snow removal equipment, have 75 and 60 employees, respectively. Other major businesses include Kloepfer Concrete, Merrill's Poultry, Butte Irrigation and Rain for Rent. Small businesses and downtown retail stores and shops provide most of the remainder of the city's employment base.

The surrounding area is still a large farming community which produces grain, potatoes, beets, hay, beans and corn.

Water tower at Paul.

Most of the city's residents do their shopping in Rupert and Burley.

Education The Minidoka County School District provides most of the primary and secondary education for Paul children. Students attend Paul Elementary, approximately 450 students, and West Minico Jr. High, about 450 students, in Paul. High school students attend school in Rupert.

The closest institution of higher learning is 45 miles west at the College of Southern Idaho in Twin Falls.

Health Care The closest hospital is the 25-bed Minidoka Memorial Hospital in Rupert.

Transportation State Highway 27 intersects the city. Interstate 84 is two miles south. Private and light charter air service is available at the 4,094-foot runway at Burley Municipal Airport, five miles south. The closest commercial airport is Joslin Field in Twin Falls. Rail service is available in the city for freight.

Utilities and Services Private companies provide electric, telephone, natural gas, cable and satellite services. The City provides water and sewer service and fire protection. The County Sheriff provides police protection under contract with the City.

Vision for 2050

In the year 2050 we envision the city of Paul as a quiet bedroom community to the surrounding larger cities. Parks, green belts and walking paths will add to a comfortable lifestyle.

Mayors

1917 Frank Manning *	1947 Samuel E. Packer *
1920 L.G. Taylor *	1947 K.K. Maier *
1921 H.N. Yerkes *	1948 Wayne S. Drake *
1922 W.L. Johnson *	1949 San Sprier *
1923 E.N. Smith *	1952 Harvey Jensen *
1923 Davis Green *	1953 Marvin Looslie *
1926 Samuel W. Osgood *	1957 C.W. Platts *
1927 H.A. Whitton *	1961 Tom Felton *
1930 Charles B. Wiley*	1966 Harold Wilson *
1930 Fred J. Johns *	1967 Harold Wilson
1931 Oscar Nelson *	1972 Robert K. Larson
1931 S.W. Osgood *	1986 Gene Hanson
1933 F.J. Johns *	1995 Randy Jones
1939 J.H. Widdison *	2016 Bruce Hossfeld
1941 J.B. Fridley *	* Village Chairman
1944 U.U. Locander *	

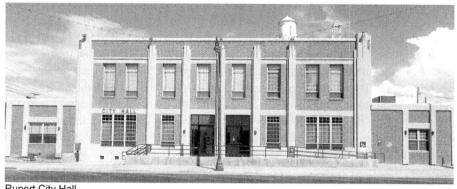

Rupert City Hall.

Rupert

Statistical Data

Population: 5,673 *
Elevation: 4,206 feet
Precipitation: 8 inches **
Average Snowfall: 27 inches **
County: Minidoka
Website: www.rupert-idaho.com

Temperature Range – Fahrenheit: **
Spring: 28 to 69
Summer: 48 to 87
Fall: 25 to 76
Winter: 15 to 42
* U.S. Census Bureau Estimates July 2015
**Historical averages

Rupert is located in the fertile Snake River Plain on State Highway 24. Beautiful irrigated fields of sugar beets, wheat, potatoes, hay and beans surround the city. The Snake River flows four miles to the east. Ten miles southeast, the Albion Mountains of the Sawtooth National Forest rise to over 9,000 feet.

Rupert is one of the towns platted in 1904 by the U.S. Reclamation Service – now the Bureau of Reclamation – following construction of Minidoka Dam and the system of irrigation canals and laterals of the "North Side Minidoka Tract.

Pre-Incorporation Years

In 1884 the Oregon Short Line Railroad – now Union Pacific – completed its rail line connecting the railhead at Granger, Wyoming, to the railhead at Huntington, Oregon. Completion of this critical link of railroad reduced travel time between Omaha, Nebraska, and Portland, Oregon, to three and a half days. The rail line passed 14 miles northeast of what is now Rupert.

From 1904 to 1910 the Minidoka and Southwestern Railroad Company, acquired by the Oregon Short Line in 1910, built 200 miles of branch lines connecting several Magic Valley communities. They completed the 75-mile spur line from Minidoka to Buhl in 1907. This line passed through Rupert. In October

1910 the railroad completed a 73-mile branch line from Rupert to the main line at Bliss.

In 1902 Congress passed the Newlands Act. The Act authorized the federal government to construct dams and canals in the Western United States, sell arable land and water rights to settlers and periodically plat townsites needed to serve each farming community.

One of the first irrigation projects completed under the Act was the 82-foot-high, one-mile-long Minidoka Dam located near the Minidoka Rapids on the Snake River. The U.S. Reclamation Service started the dam in 1904 and completed it in 1906. The 7000-killowatt hydroelectric power plant built at the dam began delivering electrical power in 1909.

Rupert, 1911.

The water impounded by the dam created Lake Walcott. It provided irrigation water on the north and south sides of the river, a total of 116,000 acres.

In 1904 the Reclamation Service platted the village of Rupert, one of the "Northside" communities, with a town square and community well in the center of the village. For several months, the well was the city's most prominent feature. Many local residents took to calling the community "Wellfirst" because the town had the only well within miles. Many settlers drove their wagons into town to shop and fill their water barrels. Today, the Town Square, now named Historic Square Park, has a fountain over the original well.

Settlers began acquiring and clearing the land well in advance of the irrigation water becoming available. These early settlers first cleared their land of sagebrush, roots, rocks and native grasses. In the fall they planted hard winter wheat for harvest the next summer. One woman described her first look at the land when she got off the train as, "...nothing but a wide expanse of greenish-grey sagebrush. Not a building, nor a tree, not a living thing was in sight."

As soon as the wheat began to grow, jackrabbits and insects moved in to devour the tender crops, destroying the settlers' livelihood. One homesteader recorded, "Jackrabbits came to the green wheat fields about sundown. They came from the lavas (lava beds) and the uncleared sagebrush fields where they shaded-up during the daytime. They came in hoards so thick that it looked as though the ground was moving..." (*See Southwestern Idaho, Fighting the Jackrabbit Menace.*)

The railroad had the contract with the postal authorities to transport the mail. John Henry Rupert was the local railroad employee designated to receive the mail. The railroad painted "Rupert" on the mailbag. Addressing incoming mail with the name Rupert assured the sender their mail would get to the right place. To avoid confusion, the Reclamation Service filed the official plat of the new village with the name "Rupert."

On July 17, 1905, W.N. Shilling, the city's first postmaster, established the Rupert Post Office in his store, the Rupert Mercantile Company. In addition, in 1905 patrons opened the town's first school and the Rupert Opera House produced its first play.

Incorporation

On April 12, 1906, the Lincoln County Commissioners approved incorporation of the village of Rupert and appointed the first officers.

In April 1909 the village held its first municipal election. Elected officials included Trustee Chairman, trustees, clerk, treasurer, marshal, street superintendent, dog catcher, park keeper and pump master. In 1910 the city had a population of 297.

On January 28, 1913, the Legislature created Minidoka County with Rupert designated as the temporary county seat. At the next election, county voters ratified the Legislature's action.

Historic Wilson Theater, 1920s.

In February 1917 with a population approaching 1,500, Rupert became an incorporated city. The period from 1915 through 1920 was a time of significant growth. During that period, the county held its first fair. In addition, the Minidoka County Courthouse; Caledonian Hotel, razed in 1970; Pershing Elementary School; and the Wilson Theatre, a city landmark, were built.

Turning Points

Railroad The railroad came into the Magic Valley long before construction of the Minidoka Dam. When federal public land became available for farming, the railroad built spur lines to transport agricultural goods and commodities to market. The railroad was as important as irrigation to the economic development and prosperity of Rupert and the Magic Valley.

Minidoka Dam Three general events combined to make possible the existence and prosperity of Rupert. These events were the federal laws, authorizing conversion of federal land to private farm ownership; the construction of the Minidoka Dam and irrigation canals in 1906; and the production of electricity in 1909.

County Seat The creation of Minidoka County in 1913 with Rupert as the county seat gave the city a stable labor base of county employees and elevated the

420

prestige of the city as the center of county government.

World War II For the United States, World War II broke out in 1941 following the Japanese attack on Pearl Harbor. At that time, prices for agricultural products increased; however, good labor was now in short supply. Most of the able-bodied men had been called up to fight in the war. In addition, many men and women traveled to other cities for high-paying jobs building goods and weapons for the military.

One of the tragedies of the war came because the federal government made the ridiculous assertion that all citizens of Japanese descent were a potential threat to the United States. Consequently, the U.S. military essentially stripped all Japanese-American Citizens of their constitutional rights and placed them into concentration camps called "relocation centers."

One of the "relocation centers" was the Minidoka Relocation Center called Hunt Camp. It was built on 68,000 acres of sagebrush land located between the cities of Rupert and Jerome.

Hunt Camp prisoners and German POWs filled part of the farm labor shortage caused by the loss of local younger men called up to fight in the war. (*See Southwestern Idaho – Hunt Camp – WWII Imprisonment of American Citizens of Japanese Descent.*)

Building a Diversified Economy Technological innovation, economy of size and other market forces have caused significant consolidation of farming operations and in many food-processing businesses. Productivity has increased with a much smaller workforce.

Rupert has been able to offset the loss of agricultural industry jobs by encouraging food-processing and other companies to build in the city.

Three of the women who guarded the Minidoka Power Plant at the Minidoka Dam during World War I and World War II.

In 1993 in an effort to retain and attract business, the Rupert and Burley Chambers of Commerce merged to create the Mini-Cassia Chamber of Commerce. The Chamber includes 12 communities in Minidoka and Cassia Counties and has over 400 members with headquarters in Heyburn.

Rupert Today

Amenities and Attractions Rupert has nine municipal parks. Historic Square Park is the centerpiece of the city and the location of many city celebrations and functions.

In the summer, several flowerbeds are interspersed among Square Park's tall stately trees. Old-fashioned looking lampposts light the park at night. The park has a fountain, gazebo, wisteria-covered arbor and two carved bears.

Christmas is an exciting time in Rupert. Using proceeds from the annual "Christmas in July" breakfast, held as a kick-off to the Fourth of July Celebration, city leaders and residents decorate Historic Square Park, the city streets, businesses and residences with an array of lights and ornaments. Christmas decorations begin going up on the Friday following Thanksgiving.

In addition to the Christmas in July breakfast, the city's annual Fourth of July Celebration includes food booths, a parade, a Dutch oven cook-off, a rodeo, carnival and horse races.

Other annual celebrations and events include the Boat Regatta Fish Fry, Heritage Day, Farm Worker Appreciation Day and the Potato Fest.

The other eight city parks encompass a total of 40 acres and include such amenities as a skateboard park, ball fields, a bike path, picnic areas and children's playground equipment.

Two golf courses are within two miles of the city. DeMary Memorial Public Library, with its 44,000 books; Neptune Park; and Minidoka County Museum are important community attractions.

Hunt Camp near Rupert.

Fifteen miles northeast lies the large and spectacular recreation complex that includes Lake Walcott, the reservoir created by Minidoka Dam; Lake Walcott State Park; and the Minidoka National Wildlife Refuge.

Lake Walcott State Park offers water skiing, power boating, windsurfing, sailing, bird watching, camping, fishing and picnicking under old-growth hardwood trees. One popular feature of the park is an 18-hole "Disc Golf Course" with metal baskets for holes.

The Wildlife Refuge extends 25 miles east and upriver from the dam. It encompasses nearly 21,000 acres – of which over half are open water and marshes.

Rupert train depot.

Downhill skiing is available at Pomerelle Ski Resort, 30 miles south of the city. Its 8,000 foot elevation has an average snowfall of 500 inches. The resort has 24 groomed trails and 3 chairlifts.

Many residents take advantage of the national forest and the vast open ranges managed by the BLM for hunting, fishing, hiking, biking, snowmobiling and ATV riding.

Economy and Major Employers The city's largest private employers are two food processing companies. Magic Valley Foods employs 250, produces dried potato products and ships fresh whole potatoes. Kraft Foods, Inc., employs about 100 at its Rupert cheese plant.

With 660 employees, the Minidoka County School District is the city's largest employer. The city's two other large public employers are the City of Rupert and Minidoka County. Many of the employees of Amalgamated Sugar Factory located four miles west in Paul live in Rupert.

The city's downtown business district – including Minidoka Memorial

The Gathering Place.

Hospital, the post office, several retail shops, stores, restaurants, professional and other service businesses – make up the balance of the city's employment base.

Education The Minidoka County School District and its schools located in Rupert provide most of the primary and secondary education in the city and county.

The closest institution of higher learning is 56 miles west at the College of Southern Idaho in Twin Falls.

Historic Wilson Theater today.

Health Care The 25-bed Minidoka Memorial Hospital and several medical and dental clinics and offices provide most of the medical care needed in the city.

Transportation State Highway 24 intersects the city. Interstate 84 lies four miles southwest.

Private and light charter air service is available at the 4,094-foot runway at Burley Municipal Airport, seven miles southwest. The closest commercial airport is Joslin Field in Twin Falls.

Rail service is available in the city for freight.

Utilities and Services Private companies provide electric, telephone, natural gas, cable and satellite services. The City provides water and sewer services and police and fire protection. The County provides solid waste services.

Vision for 2050

In 1960 Rupert's population was 4,200. In 1994 it reached a high of about 5,900. Subsequently, the city's population has declined at an average rate of about one-percent a year. Those trends have recently reversed. The city has returned to a moderate rate of growth at around one percent a year. By 2050 Rupert's population should approximate 7,000.

Existing infrastructure is adequate with normal maintenance and improvements to meet changing environmental standards to handle the moderate growth of one percent a year.

When 2050 arrives, Rupert will retain its friendly home-town charm – a progressive community where people will want to come to work and rear their children.

Mayors

1906	M.M. Mackey *	1937	E.E. Fisher
1909	F.N. Victor *	1945	Henry T. Breazeal
1911	E.R. Eauphier *	1949	Clark Cameron
1912	William Lyman *	1949	A.C. Duffin
1913	Cal Masterson *	1949	A.F. Beymer
1914	Carl Titus *	1951	Glover Acock
1915	John Tollefson *	1964	Wendell Johnson
1917	William Lyman	1978	W.F. "Bill" Whittom
1919	J.W. Murphy	1994	Dwinelle Allred
1921	I.W. Creasey	2000	Audrey R. Neiwerth
1925	A.F. Beymer	2008	Paul Fries, Sr.
1929	B.B. Titus	2012	Michael Brown
1931	R.B. Titus		* Village Chairman
1932	R.B. Turner		

Families on the river.

OWYHEE COUNTY

- Grand View
- Homedale
- Marsing

County Seat: unincorporated hamlet of Murphy

Grand View wildlife.

Grand View

Statistical Data

Population: 444 *
Elevation: 2,459 feet
Precipitation: 7 inches **
Average Snowfall: 1 inch **
County: Owyhee
Website: www.grandview.id.gov

Temperature Range – Fahrenheit: **
Spring: 31 to 75
Summer: 52 to 91
Fall: 28 to 79
Winter: 21 to 47
* U.S. Census Bureau Estimates July 2015
**Historical averages

Grand View lies on the south side of the Snake River about 25 miles southwest of Mountain Home and about eight miles downriver from the hydroelectric C.J. Strike Dam and Reservoir. The Owyhee Mountain Range and the restored mining town of Silver City are about 45 road miles west. Homedale, the largest of Owyhee County's three incorporated cities, is 65 miles northwest of Grand View.

The city sits among irrigated fertile farms and fields of alfalfa hay, corn, sugar beets, wheat and barley that extend along both sides of the river.

Beyond the farmland are vast tracts of public land. To the north is the Snake River Birds of Prey National Conservation Area, which includes the Ada County National Guard Maneuver Area. East and northeast is the Mountain Home Air Force Base and Gunnery Range. To the west and south is a broad expanse of high-desert land, managed by the Bureau of Land Management, and interspersed with private farms and ranches and six national wilderness areas that comprise 517,000 acres. This type of landscape encompasses most of Idaho's second largest county, the 4.9 million-acre Owyhee County, and adjoining lands in the neighboring states of Oregon, Nevada and Utah. (*See The Region, National Wilderness Areas.*)

Pre-Incorporation Years

Until the first explorers and trappers began passing through the area in 1810, the grass and sagebrush-covered high desert that is now Grand View was once the exclusive domain of nomadic American Indians – principally of the Shoshone and Bannock Tribes.

In the early 1840s emigrants from the East began an overland migration on a route that would soon be known as the Oregon Trail to what was then a disputed land called Oregon Country. After the Treaty of 1848 with England that established the boundary between the two countries at the 49th parallel, England released its claim to Oregon Country and Congress established it as Oregon Territory. (*See The Region, Federal Lands – Private Ownership and Preservation Laws.*)

The Old West at Grand View.

Oregon Trail pioneers, who were fearful of crossing the Snake River at what is now Three Island Crossing State Park and Glenns Ferry, took the South Alternate of the Oregon Trail. The South Alternate passed through what is now Grand View and proceeded in a northwesterly direction along the south and west side of the Snake River before rejoining the main trail northwest of Parma. (*See The Region, Oregon and California Trails.*)

In 1862 prospectors found gold in the Boise Basin. A year later, 16,000 fortune seekers were scouring the region in search of the precious metal. The U.S. Army also established a new Fort Boise – the original Fort Boise near what is now Parma having been destroyed by flood – and settlers platted a new town around the fort that they named Boise City. (*See The Region, Mining, Boise Basin – Gold.*)

Historic ferry. Courtesy Dale Gray.

That same year, Michael Jordon – the namesake of Jordon Valley, Oregon – led 29 men from the Boise Basin gold fields to the Owyhee Mountains. They found large quantities of gold at Jordon Creek and started a boomtown they named Ruby City. (*See Mining, Owyhee Mountains – Silver and Gold.*)

The Owyhee Mountains are named after three natives of the Hawaiian Islands, who were members of Donald Mackenzie's 1818 Snake River exploring and beaver-trapping party. The name Hawaii was originally phonetically spelled and recorded by 1778 Pacific Ocean explorer Captain James Cook as "Owyhee." Mackenzie sent the three men to assess the beaver-trapping potential of the mountains west of the Snake River. They never returned. Mackenzie named the mountains in their honor and the name and spelling stuck. (*See The Region – Early Trappers/Explorers.*)

Mining activity encouraged settlers to divert irrigation water from nearby streams onto their homesteads to raise and sell fresh food to the miners. Some of these settlers established farms and ranches near what is now Grand View.

The first Idaho Territorial Legislature, meeting in the temporary capital of Lewiston, created Owyhee County in December 1863 and made the mining boomtown of Ruby City its county seat. By 1867 the Ruby City mines had played out. However, prospectors found rich silver ore bodies to the south. They named the new boomtown

Square Deal Store, circa 1924. Courtesy Dale Gray.

Silver City and voted to move the county seat to the new town. In 1934 voters moved the county seat again – this time to the former railroad terminus town of Murphy, 30 miles northwest of Grand View. Today, Murphy is an unincorporated hamlet with a population of fewer than 100, but it is still the Owyhee County seat – the smallest county seat in Idaho.

In 1887 the Snake River Land Irrigation Company of Rhode Island (SRLIC) began construction of an earthen dam on the Bruneau River about 10 miles southeast of Grand View. They planned to sell gravity-flow irrigation water to the farmers settling the area.

A Mr. Hall established a ferry across the Snake River several miles above the mouth of the Bruneau River in the late 1880s. To meet his competition, another man named Dorsey moved the ferry he was operating on the Bruneau River to the Snake River several miles downriver from Hall's Ferry. A small community began to grow up around the Dorsey Ferry landing on the south side of the Snake River. Those promoting the

Grand View in days gone by.

irrigation project established a townsite at Dorsey's Ferry and successfully applied for a post office that they named Grand View.

Grand View is to be the name of the town situated at Dorsey Ferry on the Snake River in this (Owyhee) county," the Owyhee Avalanche newspaper reported in 1887. "We suppose it is so named by the reason of the view that can be had from that point of Old War Eagle and Quick Silver Mountain (location of the Silver City mines in the Owyhee Mountains) to say nothing of the serpentine Snake River flowing near the hotel now being built."

Three years later, the Bruneau River flooded again, washing out the dam. Undeterred, leaders in the SRLIC began rebuilding but were unable to complete the irrigation system until the turn of the century.

Prospectors found gold in the Snake River gravels in 1892 and filed 26 placer mining claims near Grand View.

The irrigation dam on the Bruneau River broke for the last time in 1910. At

Fall in Grand View.

that time, water users created the Grand View Irrigation District, rebuilt the dam and completed the system of irrigation canals and ditches. In addition to producing livestock feed, many farmers planted orchards and began raising commercial quantities of fruit, berries and melons.

Sheep ranchers found the mild temperatures of the Grand View area attractive to winter their lambing ewes. Local farmers raised alfalfa hay for the large herds of sheep. In 1915 the Elmore Times newspaper estimated that 150,000 head of sheep wintered in the area. In the mid-1900s the demand for lambs and wool declined, and the sheep industry ceased to be an important contributor to the Grand View economy. However, in 1945 the J.R. Simplot

Courtesy Dale Gray.

Company built a cattle feedlot four miles north of Grand View that had the capacity of fattening up to 150,000 head.

The Idaho Bureau of Highways – now known as the Idaho Department of Transportation – built a bridge across the Snake River at Grand View in 1921. At that time the community's downtown consisted of a four-room brick schoolhouse, a two-story brick band building, a dance hall, an ice cream parlor, two general stores, a saloon and a pool hall.

Idaho Power completed the C.J. Strike Hydroelectric Dam on the Snake River in 1952. The earthen dam is 3,220 feet long and 115 feet high. The reservoir extends 36 miles up the Snake River and 12 miles up the Bruneau River. The backwater from the dam covered the original Bruneau River dam and several of the early farms and ranches. As a condition for licensing the dam, Idaho Power has made many significant improvements to enhance camping, fishing and recreation facilities and wildlife habitat.

Grand View at play.

Incorporation

On October 27, 1971, Grand View became an incorporated city.

Turning Points

Irrigation Facilitated by ferries that transported agricultural commodities and supplies across the Snake River in the early years, the agriculture industry has underpinned Grand View's economy from the beginning. Pumping water from the Snake River and from deep wells accompanied by the advent of

Fishing at Grand View.

pressurized sprinkler system technologies has transformed Grand View into the agricultural oasis that exists today.

Gold The discovery of placer gold and subsequent filing of mining claims had a significant, albeit short-term, effect on Grand View's early economy.

Grand View Today

Amenities and Attractions In 2014 Grand View dedicated Riverside Park, a new day-use park located at the intersection of Main and Riverside Avenue on the Snake River.

The city's Centennial Park features a children's playground and covered picnic areas. The Bruneau-Grand View School District also has, for public use, an athletic field for baseball, softball and soccer.

Other amenities include the Rio Lindo Boat Launching Ramp on the Snake River. The Lawson's Emu-Z-Um is a private museum with exhibits of early settlement artifacts dating back to the late 1800s – the name of the museum is reminiscent of the time the Lawson's raised emu on their ranch.

Many tourists drive through Grand View on their way to Silver City, the one-time county seat of Owyhee County and now a mining ghost town with many restored buildings.

Each year on the last week of June, the city celebrates Grand View Days. The celebration includes a parade, carnival, crafts, rubber duck race, softball tournament, pit barbeque, "adopt-a-pole contest" and fireworks.

The Bureau of Land Management operates 26 camp units around the 7,500-acre C.J. Strike Reservoir. Free restrooms and drinkable water are available. There are also private camping facilities near the reservoir. The Idaho Department of Fish and Game manages a 10,664-acre Wildlife Management Area (WMA) on the Bruneau River side of the reservoir. The WMA provides habitat for 240 species of nesting and migrating birds and is popular with birdwatchers, anglers and hunters.

Each Sunday following Labor Day, about 10,000 people come to Carl Miller Park in Mountain Home to celebrate Air Force Appreciation Day with a parade and barbeque.

The Desert Mountain Visitor Center at the Junction of Interstate 84 and U.S. Highway 20 is another excellent source of information about the area.

Knight Community Church.

Anderson Ranch Dam and Recreation Area is about 45 miles northeast of the city. The dam is 456 feet high and creates a 17-mile-long lake with 50 miles of shoreline. It is part of the U.S. Bureau of Reclamation's Boise Project, a complex system of dams and canals that primarily irrigates farms in the Treasure Valley.

Anderson Reservoir is popular for boating and fishing for trout, bass and Kokanee – landlocked salmon that spawn in the creeks during late August and early September. The recreation area includes 380 miles of marked snowmobile trails. Some of the trails wind up to the Trinity Mountains and lakes eight miles above the north end of the lake and rising to 9,451 feet.

The 4,800-acre Bruneau Dunes State Park and Observatory is 30 miles southwest of the city on State Highway 78-51. For thousands of years blowing sand has settled in this natural basin producing a landscape of sand dunes. One of the dunes rises to 470 feet, the highest in North America. At the base of the dunes is a lake with bass and bluegill.

Rimrock Senior Center, courtesy of Dale Gray.

The observatory is the largest public observatory in Idaho. Generally, its telescopes are open for public use on Friday and Saturday evenings.

To protect the serenity and ecology of this environmentally sensitive area, the Idaho Department of Parks and Recreation restrict use of the dunes and lake to non-motorized vehicles.

Five miles north begins the Snake River Birds of Prey National Conservation Area managed by the Bureau of Land Management. The half-million-acre area has high concentrations of falcons, hawks, eagles and owls.

The 103-mile Owyhee Uplands Back Country Byway – a gravel and paved road that runs from Grand View to Jordon Valley, Oregon – offers a view of the sagebrush-steppe ecosystem and habitat for more than 180 bird and mammal species.

Valley Health Care, courtesy Dale Gray.

Economy and Major Employers The Bruneau-Grand View School District appears to be the city's largest employer, though the majority of its 80 employees commute to work from outside the city. If asked, Grand View residents would say that agriculture industries, primarily cattle and farming, are the city's largest employers. Simplot Livestock's feedlot, at one time one of the largest in the world, is only three miles from town. The city's business district consists principally of retail shops, stores, service businesses, restaurants, a bank, a senior center, a bar and businesses serving the agricultural community.

Education The Bruneau-Grand View School District provides public education for Grand View; Bruneau, an unincorporated town about 18 miles southeast; and Oreana, an unincorporated town 20 miles west. Younger children attend school at Grand View or Bruneau Elementary. Junior and senior high school students attend Rimrock Junior and Senior High School, half way between Grand View and Bruneau on State Highway 78.

The closest institution of higher learning is Boise State University, about 55 miles north in Boise.

Health Care Valley Health Care, a private general clinic, provides most of the city's medical services. The closest hospital is Elmore Medical Center in Mountain Home.

Transportation Idaho Highway 78 intersects the city. Interstate 84 is accessible on the eastern side of Mountain Home.

The Mountain Home Air Force Base terminal and runways are not available to the public. Mountain Home Municipal Airport has a 5,000-foot runway and is available for private and charter aircraft. The Boise Air Terminal is the closest commercial airport.

Utilities and Services Private companies provide electricity, telephone,

Welcome to Grand View.

satellite and wireless services. The City provides water and sewer services. The Grand View Rural Fire Protection District provides fire protection. The Owyhee County Sheriff's Office provides police protection.

Vision for 2050

Since 1980 Grand View's population has fluctuated between 330 and 476. Since 2000 the population has stabilized at around 450. Historical trends will likely continue for several years before returning to a growth rate of less than 1 percent annually. By 2050 Grand View's population will likely be around 600.

Mayors

1971	Ben Johnson	1994	Richard Rector
1981	Leroy Beaman	1998	J. Allen Long
1986	Pat Cooper	2004	Paul R. Spang
1986	Allie Pennington	2011	Tammy Payne
1988	Gus Gustavson	2013	Opal Ward
1994	Richard Coop	2014	Franklin Hart

Bette Uda City Park dedication.

Homedale

Statistical Data

Population: 2,582*
Elevation: 2,237 feet
Precipitation: 9 inches **
Average Snowfall: 14 inches **
County: Owyhee
Website: www.cityofhomedale.com

Temperature Range – Fahrenheit: **
Spring: 30 to 73
Summer: 50 to 91
Fall: 27 to 80
Winter: 19 to 44
* U.S. Census Bureau Estimates July 2015
**Historical averages

Homedale lies on the western edge of the Treasure Valley, five miles east of the Idaho/Oregon border. The Snake River forms the city's eastern boundary. Vineyards and fields of alfalfa seed, sugar beets, corn, onions, potatoes, wheat and barley lie just outside the city limits. Caldwell is 12 miles east, and Nampa is 18 miles southeast.

Past the fertile irrigated farms, the Owyhee Mountain Range – with peaks rising up to 8,386 feet – outlines the city's southern and western skies.

Pre-Incorporation Years

The nomadic American Indians – principally of the Shoshone and Bannock Tribes – were the exclusive inhabitants of southern Idaho until around 1810 when the first explorers/trappers began passing through the area.

In 1814 the explorer/trapper Donald Mackenzie led a beaver-trapping party up the Snake River. Three members of his expedition were natives of the Hawaiian

Islands. At that time, the Hawaiians spelled their homeland "Owyhee," the same as the 1778 Pacific Ocean explorer Captain James Cook had phonetically spelled and recorded it. Mackenzie sent the three men to assess the beaver-trapping potential of the mountains west of the Snake River. They never returned and were assumed killed by Indians. Mackenzie named the Owyhee River in their honor. Later, others applied the same name and spelling to the mountains and county.

In the early 1840s emigrants began an overland wagon migration from the Midwest to Oregon's Willamette Valley on the Oregon Trail. Those who were fearful of crossing the Snake River at what is now Three Island Crossing State Park and

Langford-Forney Feed Barn, 1913.

Glenn's Ferry took the South Alternate of the Oregon Trail. The South Alternate passed through what are now Grand View, Marsing and Homedale along the south and west side of the Snake River before rejoining the main trail northwest of Parma.

In 1862 prospectors found gold in the Boise Basin. Sixteen thousand fortune seekers were scouring the region in search of the precious metal by 1863. The U.S. Army established Fort Boise at the base of the Boise Basin foothills. The original Fort Boise, a former Hudson's Bay Company fur-trading outpost near what is now Parma, had been destroyed by floods. Francois Payette, a French Canadian who managed the

Homedale school bus.

outpost from 1835 until 1844 had named it Fort "Boise," a French word meaning "woods or wooded," after the heavily wooded river from the east [Boise River]. Settlers seeking safety and commerce opportunity platted a town, named "Boise City," next to the new fort.

In May 1863 Michael Jordon – the namesake of Jordon Valley, Oregon – led 29 men from the Boise Basin gold fields to the Owyhee Mountains. They found large quantities of gold at Jordon Creek. This started a gold rush, and a boomtown named Ruby City was soon established.

In December 1863 the first Idaho Territorial Legislature, meeting in the temporary capitol of Lewiston, created the 4.9-million-acre Owyhee County with Ruby City as the county seat. Owyhee County is second in size only to the 5.4-million-acre Idaho County.

Prospectors found rich silver ore bodies a few miles south of Ruby City. In 1867 as the Ruby City mines played

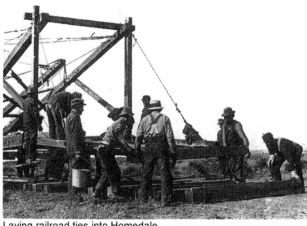

Laying railroad ties into Homedale.

out, the miners literally put Ruby City buildings on horse-drawn skids and moved them south to the new boomtown named Silver City. They then made Silver City the Owyhee County seat. In 1934 voters moved the county seat again – this time to the former railroad terminus town of Murphy, 30 miles southeast of Homedale. Today, Murphy is an unincorporated hamlet with a population of around 50 and is still the Owyhee County seat – the smallest county seat in Idaho.

In 1881 the Oregon Short Line (OSL) began construction of a railroad line between Granger, Wyoming, and Huntington, Oregon. The line angled in a northwesterly direction through what are now Pocatello, Mountain

Roy King service station.

Home, Caldwell and Parma; then turned north to Payette and Weiser before crossing the Snake River for one final time near Huntington. Completed November 17, 1884, it connected the commercial centers of Omaha, Nebraska, and Portland, Oregon, and created another transcontinental railroad. Railroad interests completed the first transcontinental railroad in 1869 at Promontory Summit in northern Utah.

With the railroad, the town of Caldwell grew rapidly. Some pioneers began to settle on the west side of the Snake River. In 1898 Jacob and Ada Mussel built a ferry across the river at what is now Homedale. Construction of the ferry was a major event for the settlers. The Mussels planned a new town next to the ferry landing on the west side of the river. They asked local people to write down their suggested name and place it in a hat. Then Jacob reached his hand into the hat and pulled out one ballot. With the suspense likely building, he read the ballot and announced that the name of the new town was "Homedale."

To increase traffic flow, Mussel blazed a wagon road about eight miles north to the settlement of Roswell and sought to extend the road another five miles from Roswell across the Snake River to Parma.

In 1902 Congress established the U.S. Reclamation Service – now Bureau of Reclamation (Reclamation). Reclamation almost immediately embarked on what would become the "Boise Project." Among other things, the Project provided federal funding and support to irrigators. When completed decades later, Reclamation had successfully integrated or completed existing Treasure Valley irrigation systems on the east side of the Snake River and added a system of dams and water storage reservoirs in the higher elevations of the Boise River, its principal tributaries and the Payette River.

Ethel Hayes Shea and son Brian in front of Homedale Meat Co.

In 1910 as part of the project, Reclamation constructed a reservoir, Lake Lowell, at a natural depression in the earth's surface south of Nampa named Deer Flat. They designed the reservoir to receive water diverted from the Boise River at Barber Dam, about 25 miles due east, and delivered through the New York Canal. Reclamation also provided the expertise and financial aid – low-cost, long-term loans to farmers – needed to develop the irrigation canal systems.

Water users organized a legal entity that worked with Reclamation in providing labor to build the canal system and repay the loans. Within a few years, southwest Canyon County farmers transformed the newly irrigated dry high-desert landscape into an agricultural oasis.

However, the land on the south and west sides of the Snake River largely remained sagebrush-covered desert and dry-farms. However, settlers took heart in what they saw on the east side of the river. They were encouraged because Reclamation was considering the "Owyhee Project" to reclaim arable land on the west side of the Snake River.

In 1913 railroad interests built a spur line from Caldwell through Homedale to Nyssa, Oregon. With the railroad and the prospect of irrigation water, settlers began staking homestead claims in the Homedale area.

It was during this period of exuberance that scam artists took advantage of Austrian emigrants working in the Wyoming coalfields. Because of the emigrants' inability to write and speak English and their desire to get a fresh start farming in the new land opening up around Homedale, the scam artists conned the emigrants into buying property that the scammers did not own. The emigrants thought they were buying land with a home and planted fields. However, in February 1914 when their train arrived in the Homedale area, they found only sagebrush-covered desert land that they did not own.

As a testimony of the character and resilience of these emigrants, they shrugged off their loss and disappointment, acquired or homesteaded land and became an important part of the Homedale community.

In 1920 the Idaho Department of Transportation (ITD) erected a steel bridge over the Snake River, and the ferry ceased operating. In 1970 ITD replaced the steel bridge with one of reinforced concrete.

Basque dancers.

Incorporation

On September 15, 1920, the Village of Homedale was incorporated. On January 7, 1947, Homedale became a 2nd Class City.

Turning Points

Railroad Even though it would take irrigation to make the farmland west of the Snake River fully productive, the railroad paved the way for the agricultural community to market its commodities and allow the farmers and town to prosper.

Irrigation In 1932 the U.S. Bureau of Reclamation completed construction of the hydroelectric Owyhee Dam on the Owyhee River in Oregon, 12 miles northwest of Homedale. The dam, 417 feet high and 833 feet long, was part of Reclamation's "Owyhee Project" which provided irrigation water to Oregon and Idaho farms on the west side of the Snake River. Water flows from the dam through tunnels cut into the mountains into a complex system of irrigation canals. The project included irrigation water from the dam as well as water pumped from the Snake River. The Homedale/Marsing area received their distribution of water via the South Canal, managed by the Gem Irrigation District.

With the availability of irrigation water, settlers reclaimed large tracts of sagebrush-covered land and irrigated farms that were previously dry. Within a few years, the arid Homedale/Marsing area became an agricultural oasis.

Homedale Today

Amenities and Attractions The city has two city parks that comprise six acres.

The city's most attractive characteristics are its location near Idaho's largest cities and convenient access to a wide variety of urban amenities, while at the same time being able to live in a peaceful rural environment.

About 10 miles southeast is Lake Lowell and the Deer Flat National Wildlife Refuge. Lake Lowell is an excellent large and small mouth bass fishery. Picnic facilities and boat ramps are located around the lake. The Refuge includes the lake, 110 miles of the Snake River and 86 islands on the river. Hundreds of thousands of migratory birds and 180 different bird species inhabit the Refuge.

The 1,300-acre Old Fort Boise Wildlife Management Area – located at the confluence of the Snake, Boise and Owyhee Rivers – lies about 15 miles north. The Roswell Marsh Wildlife Habitat Area is located 10 miles north. Both of these wildlife preserves are under the administration of the Idaho Department of Fish and Game. Many parts of the Management Areas are open for viewing wildlife, hunting and fishing.

Hunting, hiking and camping are available within an hour's drive of the city on nearby public lands, in the Boise National Forest to the northeast or the Owyhee Mountains to the south. Whitewater rafting and kayaking are available on the Payette River east of Emmett.

Angel walk.

Economy and Major Employers The Homedale School District has about 135 employees and is the city's largest employer. Several small businesses, retail stores and service businesses – many of which support the agricultural economy – employ a high percentage of the city's remaining workforce. Many residents have jobs in other cities and commute to work.

Education The Homedale School District operates an elementary school, a middle school and a high school in the city. There is also a private school offering primary and secondary education.

There are several institutions of higher learning within an hour's drive of the city. The largest of these is Boise State University 37 miles west in Boise.

Health Care There is a general medical clinic in the city. The closest hospital is West Valley Medical Center in Caldwell.

Transportation US Highway 95 and Idaho Highway 19 intersect the city. Interstate 84 can be accessed in Caldwell.

Homedale Municipal Airport has a 2,900-foot runway that provides service for light private and charter aircraft. Caldwell Industrial Airport, with its 5,500-foot runway, runs adjacent to the eastern edge of the city and I-84. It is the designated reliever for the Boise Airport.

Railroad service is available in the city for freight.

Utilities and Services Private companies provide electricity, telephone, satellite and wireless services. The City provides water and sewer services and fire and police protection.

Vision for 2050

The population growth of nearby cities has had a spillover effect on Homedale's population. In 1960 Homedale's population was 1,381. By 1980 the population had increased to 2,048. However, during the past decade the population has stabilized at around 2,500.

Recent historical trends will likely continue for several years before the city's population resumes a moderate rate of growth of around one percent annually. By 2050 Homedale's population will likely be less than 3,500.

Mayors

1947 James Hays	2000 Ervin Gifford
1954 Harry Frye	2000 Harold Puri
1955 Lester E. Carter	2003 Hap Duryee
1957 Joe Eiguren	2004 Paul F. Fink
1959 Orville Soper	2008 Harold Wilson
1966 Lester E. Carter	2012 Paul F. Fink
1971 George T. Murray	2014 Gheen Christoffersen
1984 Paul F. Fink	

Lizard rock at Marsing.

Marsing

Statistical Data

Population: 1,316 *

Elevation: 2,280 feet

Precipitation: 11 inches **

Average Snowfall: 14 inches **

County: Owyhee

Website: www.marsingcity.com

Temperature Range – Fahrenheit: **

Spring: 35 to 73

Summer: 54 to 88

Fall: 32 to 79

Winter: 24 to 46

* U.S. Census Bureau Estimates July 2013

**Historical averages

Marsing is a small farming community that borders the west bank of the Snake River 17 miles west of Nampa. The city lies under the watchful eye of the 2,602-foot-high Lizard Butte – a jutting prehistoric basalt rock formation across the river that resembles a giant lizard sunning on the east side of a huge pile of black rock.

The Oregon border is 11 miles due west. The Owyhee Mountains begin several miles west and southwest.

Pre-Incorporation Years

Until the early 1800s American Indians were the exclusive inhabitants of what is now Marsing. One cave near the city has artifacts dating back about 4,000 years.

The South Alternate cutoff of the Oregon Trail passed through what is now Marsing. This cutoff separated from the main Oregon Trail – principally used from 1841 to 1869 – where it crossed the Snake River at Three Island Crossing near what is now Glenns Ferry. After crossing the river, the main trail proceeded northwest through what is now Boise before continuing on to Oregon's Willamette Valley.

Those taking the South Alternate were fearful of crossing the treacherous Snake River, preferring the more difficult trail on the south and west side of the river. South Alternate travelers also proceeded in a northwesterly direction. These pioneers found respite at the geothermal hot springs – now Givens Hot Springs – about 12 miles south of what is now Marsing. The South Alternate rejoined the main trail near what is now Parma.

Following the 1863 discovery of gold and, later, silver in the Owyhee Mountains, miners built roads to transport passengers and supplies to the mines. One road connecting the mines with Boise used a ferry to cross the river at what is now Marsing. A business began to grow up around the ferry to serve the freight wagon and stagecoach traffic.

The miners and prospectors were paying premium prices for fresh food. Homesteaders responded to this demand by filing homestead claims and developing farms and ranches on the best arable land. They particularly looked for claims where they could divert irrigation water from nearby streams.

In November 1884 the Oregon Short Line Railroad completed the critical railroad link between Granger, Wyoming, and Huntington, Oregon. It allowed trains to move between Omaha, Nebraska, and Portland, Oregon, in less than four days. The link passed through Nampa and Caldwell but bypassed Boise. In 1887 railroad interests completed a branch line from Nampa to Boise.

Several years later, entrepreneurs began plans to connect cities in the Treasure Valley via electric trolleys. By 1912 the Interurban "Loop" started in Boise and connected Meridian, Nampa, Caldwell, Marsing and Eagle before ending back in Boise. In 1907

Peach orchard near Marsing.

entrepreneurs extended an electric trolley line the few miles to the south to carry freight and workers constructing the dam and dykes creating Lake Lowell. In 1915 they extended the trolley through the orchards of Sunnyslope to Marsing's Ferry. Primarily due to competition from the increasingly popular motor vehicles, the electric trolley lines began shutting down. The Marsing line shut down in 1922. By 1928 the entire Interurban Loop had largely closed.

In 1913 the Gem Irrigation District built a pump plant near what is now Marsing and began pumping water from the Snake River. Availability of this irrigation water further encouraged settlement.

In the same year, two brothers – Earl Q. and Mark Marsing – settled in the area. They joined with C.A. Johnson to purchase 44 acres on which to plat a townsite. They platted the town and named it "Butte" in recognition of Lizard Butte.

In 1913 the railroad completed a branch line from Nyssa, Oregon, to Homedale. In 1922 they extended the line to Butte where they built a depot. However, the railroad named its depot Erb, after the former Idaho Public Utilities Commissioner George Erb.

In 1920 the Idaho Transportation Department connected State Highway 55 across the Snake River by building a bridge near the town of Butte. The bridge attracted further settlement to the town.

In 1922 one of the new residents, Walter Volkmer, applied for a post office in Butte. However, postal authorities rejected the name of Butte because it was already in use. Volkmer resubmitted his application with the name of Marsing after the Marsing brothers who first settled in the area. His revised application was accepted. With everyone's mail delivered to Marsing, the confusion as to the town's name was finally resolved.

However, the railroad was the last holdout. It was not until 1937 that the railroad changed the name of its depot from Erb to Marsing.

In 1932 the U.S. Bureau of Reclamation completed construction of the hydroelectric Owyhee Dam on the Owyhee River in Oregon, 20 miles northwest of Marsing. The dam, 417 feet high and 833 feet long, was part of Reclamation's "Owyhee Project" that provided irrigation water to Oregon and Idaho farms, including farms in Homedale and Marsing. Water flows from the dam through tunnels cut into the mountains into a complex system of irrigation canals. The project included irrigation water from the dam as well as water pumped from the Snake River. The Marsing area received its distribution of water via the South Canal managed by the Gem Irrigation District.

With the availability of irrigation water, settlers reclaimed large tracts of sagebrush and irrigated their farms, which were previously dry. Within a few years, the arid Marsing and Homedale area became an agricultural oasis.

Incorporation

On January 13, 1941, Marsing became an incorporated village.

Turning Points

River Crossing The city owes its origins to the location of the ferry and, later, the bridge that crossed the Snake River. The ferry, established in the 1860s to connect the gold and silver mines in the Owyhee Mountains with Boise, established the new community. The 1920 construction of highway 50 and the bridge underpinned its continuance.

Irrigation Agriculture underpins the prosperity of the greater Marsing area. Initially, homesteaders cleared the land and established their farms. However, major agriculture production did not come until irrigation water became available. The federal 1932 Owyhee Project made the most profound difference in making the land on the west side of the Snake River productive.

Railroad The availability of railroad transportation went hand-in-hand with irrigation in making the farmlands on the west side of the Snake River profitable. Irrigation sharply improved commodity production while the railroad delivered the commodities to market.

Marsing Today

Amenities and Attractions Marsing has a library and two city parks.

Annual community events include Independence Day, celebrated each year with a barbeque and fireworks. Each Easter, a local church sponsors a sunrise service on Lizard Butte and the City sponsors an Easter Egg Hunt for the children in the City Park. Sprint boat races on the Snake River are popular events on many summer weekends.

On the first Saturday in February, the City holds the Marsing Disaster Auction to raise funds for local special-needs families.

Each May, the city celebrates "The Leroy Breshears Memorial Fishing Day" in honor of this late Fish and Game instructor. Hundreds of children come each year to Marsing Island Park Pond to catch trout.

The R-Lucky Star Ranch owns and operates the Farm Museum. This museum, located two miles southwest of town on W. Pershall Road, features over 3,500 historic and modern wrenches alphabetized by manufacturer and a large collection of historic sugar sacks made from cloth.

A few miles northwest across the river are several thousands of acres of commercial fruit farms and vineyards lining the western slope of land bordering the Snake River. The area, named Sunnyslope, is a favorable location where the sun warms the soil and extends the growing season. Many vineyardists consider the soil and climate of Sunnyslope ideal for wine grapes.

The historic Givens Hot Springs is a popular recreation facility south of Marsing. Oregon Trail immigrants said that the water was hot enough to boil an egg. They stopped to bath, wash their clothes and luxuriate in a pond they built. In 1881 Oregon Trail immigrants Milford and Martha Givens returned to settle and develop a resort. Their decendents now own and operate the property. Thousands of patrons come each year to enjoy the modern hot swimming pools and other resort amenities.

Eight miles south of Givens Hot Springs across the Snake River from Historic Walter's Ferry is Cleo's Nature Trail. Open to the public year round, the trail is a wonderland of displays, hundreds of birdhouses of intricate design and over 100 sculptures and statues that line a mile-long walking path, meandering in a loop through old growth Russian olive and other trees that border the river. There is also a private museum. The museum includes the historic adobe ferry master's building.

The ferry master's building, built in 1863, is the oldest building on the property. It served as the ferry master's residence, a restaurant and a two-room hotel.

The Owyhee County Historical Museum is located 30 miles south at the Owyhee County Seat in Murphy. Owyhee County has 4.9 million acres and is the second largest county in Idaho – Idaho County, with 5.4 million acres is the largest. Marsing is one of three cities in the county and the closest city to Murphy – Grand View and Homedale being the other two cities. Murphy is unincorporated and has a population of about 50. It is the only unincorporated county seat in Idaho and has the smallest population of any county seat in the state and, perhaps, the nation. Homedale, the largest city in Owyhee County and located about 42 miles northwest, has a population of about 2,500.

About 20 miles southwest of Murphy on unimproved roads is the partially restored mining ghost town of Silver City and its sister town – the abandoned Ruby City. Ruby City was the Owyhee County seat for over three years before moving to Silver City in 1867 and then to Murphy in 1934. The silver and gold mines around Silver City rivaled those of the Comstock Lode in Nevada. Silver mining activity continues in the area at De Lamar, five miles west of Silver City, and at War Eagle Mountain.

The 590,000-acre Snake River Birds of Prey National Conservation Area (SRNCA) lies about 22 miles southeast of the city. Numerous species of small wildlife – including rodents, rabbits, and birds –  inhabit the SRNCA, which has the densest population of breeding raptors in North America. A variety of fish in the nearby Snake River and reservoirs add to the diversity of wildlife.

The World Center for Birds of Prey, famous for its conservation and recovery efforts for the Peregrine falcon and several species of rare and endangered birds of prey, is located south of Boise, about 35 miles due east of Marsing.

Deer Flat National Wildlife Refuge lies a few miles to the east. The refuge encompasses 10,600 acres, including the 9,000-acre Lake Lowell and about 100 islands in the Snake River. The refuge provides habitat for wildlife including thousands of migratory and nesting ducks and geese.

The 107-foot-high hydroelectric Swan Falls Dam is located 30 miles south of Marsing. The dam is the oldest hydroelectric dam on the Snake River and has 1,525 acres of reservoir surface area. Built in 1901, the dam initially provided electricity for the Silver City mines.

The Roswell Marsh and Fort Boise Wildlife Management Areas provide habitat for waterfowl and upland game. These wildlife management areas are located 30 and 25 miles north of Marsing, respectively. Eagle Island State Park is about 30 miles northeast of the city in Eagle.

Economy and Major Employers The Marsing School District has over 100 employees and is the city's largest employer. In addition to downtown retail shops and service businesses, four small businesses with fewer than 40 employees each – an onion packing plant, grocery store, lodge pole furniture manufacturer and an agricultural chemical company – round out the city's employment base.

Education Marsing School District crosses into Canyon County as it provides elementary and secondary education for over 800 students in the greater Marsing area.

Several institutions of higher learning are within an hour's drive of the city. The closest, The College of Idaho, is 12 miles north in Caldwell. The University of Idaho's Owyhee County Extension Office is located in Marsing.

Health Care A medical clinic is located in the city. The nearest hospital is West Valley Medical Center in Caldwell.

Transportation Idaho Highways 55 and 78 intersect the city. U.S. Highway 95 lies two miles east. Interstate 84 is 17 miles east on Highway 55.

Commercial air service is available at Caldwell Industrial Airport or Boise Municipal Airport.

Utilities and Services Private companies provide electricity, telephone, cable, CATV and satellite. The City provides water and sewer services and fire protection. The County provides police protection.

Vision for 2050

Over the past several years, Marsing's population has grown over one percent annually. This growth will likely continue as more families come to Marsing for affordable housing on the banks of the beautiful Snake River within commuting distance of the job markets of Nampa and Caldwell.

If historical trends continue, by 2050 Marsing's population could nearly double. This growth will require expansion of city services. However, the city will manage the cost of these services within existing revenue sources and impact fees assessed on new development.

A winter night in Fruitland.

PAYETTE COUNTY

- Fruitland
- New Plymouth
- Payette (*County Seat*)

Fruitland City Hall.

Fruitland

Statistical Data

Population: 4,949 *
Elevation: 2,228 feet
Precipitation: 11 inches **
Average Snowfall: 21 inches **
County: Payette
Website: www.fruitland.org

Temperature Range – Fahrenheit: **
Spring: 31 to 74
Summer: 51 to 93
Fall: 27 to 81
Winter: 18 to 43
* U.S. Census Bureau Estimates July 2015
**Historical averages

Fruitland lies at the north end of the Treasure Valley on the eastern shore of the Snake River, where the river forms the boundary between Idaho and Oregon, immediately across the river from Ontario, Oregon.

The Payette River is on Fruitland's northern border. The city of Payette is one mile north.

Fruit orchards and fertile fields of alfalfa hay, sugar beets, onions, potatoes, corn, mint and wheat surround the city, forming a mosaic of color and texture.

Pre-Incorporation Years

In 1862 prospectors discovered gold about 50 miles due east of Fruitland in the Boise Basin. The following year, 16,000 fortune seekers flooded the basin in search of the precious metal. Settlers established homesteads along streams where they could divert water to irrigate their low-lying farmland to provide food for the miners. (*See The Region, Mining.*)

The Oregon Short Line (OSL) launched construction of the railroad between Granger, Wyoming, and Huntington, Oregon, in 1881. This rail link would complete another transcontinental railroad and connect the commercial centers of Omaha, Nebraska, and Portland, Oregon. (*See The Region – Railroads.*)

448

The rail line – completed on November 17, 1884 – angled in a northwesterly direction through what are now Pocatello, Mountain Home, Caldwell and Parma, then north to Payette and finally Weiser before crossing the Snake River a final time to Huntington.

The founding of Payette coincided with the coming of the railroad in 1883. Later, settlers formed irrigation districts made up of water users who filed for rights to Payette River water and built small diversion dams upstream to feed gravity-flow canals and ditches that delivered water to their fields. With irrigation, farmers transformed their

Fruitland State Bank.

sagebrush-covered high-desert homesteads into agricultural oases. (*See The Region, Agriculture and Irrigation.*)

John Hall filed a homestead claim in the Fruitland area in 1887. He and the homesteaders who followed found the land and climate favorable for raising apples, prunes, plums and other fruits. Hall sold half his acreage to Anthony and Amelia Zeller in 1902. (*See The Region, Federal Lands – Private Ownership and Preservation Laws.*)

Four years later, the Payette Valley Railroad Company – later acquired by OSL – constructed a branch line from Payette through Fruitland to New Plymouth.

Anthony Zeller platted the future town of Fruitland in 1908 on his land that bordered the railroad siding and a crossroad on the property. He named the town "Zeller's Crossing," a name that only lasted a few years.

B.F. Tussing, who owned an apple orchard south of town, started a fresh pack shipping operation. He shipped his fruit by rail to distant markets under the name "Tussing Apples." Several other agricultural entrepreneurs were also developing or expanding orchards and fruit packing businesses. Responding to the marketing desire of orchardists to promote their products on their printed shipping cartons and characterize the community with its dominant industry, Tussing led the effort to change the name of the town to Fruitland after the "luscious fruit grown in the area." He also received credit for naming the north-south avenues after different states.

Fruitland's first school opened in 1903. It had one teacher who taught all of the children in one room. Five years later, school patrons moved the school to a retail store that provided two rooms for the school's use. The children were separated into two groups with four grades meeting in each room. A year later, the community completed construction of an elementary school and in 1916 a high school.

School patrons approved money to hire vehicles to transport the children to and from school. In the warmer months, six canvas-covered wagons traveled routes to the outlying areas. In the winter, wagon owners replaced the wheels with runners. As motor vehicles became available, trucks replaced the wagons. One driver pulled a trailer behind his Denby truck

Universal Motor Company.

for overflow students. Due to the exhaust fumes, the students riding in the trailer named it the "gas chamber."

Telephone service started in 1925 with 12-phone party lines that were eventually converted to private lines. In order to have a telephone, a person had to purchase stock in the company – the Farmers Mutual Telephone Company.

Incorporation

On March 29, 1948, with a population of 573, Fruitland became an incorporated village. Initially, volunteers provided fire protection. When a fire started in town, fire fighters formed a bucket brigade – fire fighters standing in a line between the burning building and the water in one of two irrigation ditches running through town, handing buckets of water from one man to another with one of the strongest men at the end of the line to throw the water as far as possible onto the fire. In 1948 the town purchased a used fire truck and installed 12 fire hydrants on street corners.

In 1967 the community changed its legal status to a city in compliance with a change in state municipal law.

Turning Points

Railroad Even though the railroad preceded agricultural development of the Fruitland area, it was instrumental in making the town's agricultural businesses successful. In the early 1900s six fruit packing plants operated along the railroad line.

Irrigation Irrigation systems were critical to the development of the agricultural industry in the Fruitland area.

The Bureau of Reclamation completed construction of the Black Canyon Dam with a complex system of canals and ditches in 1924. That system was integrated with existing canal systems including those serving Fruitland area farms – the most notable being Farmers Cooperative Irrigation Company, Noble Ditch Company and Washoe Irrigation and Power Company.

The 183-foot-high Black Canyon Dam is five miles east of Emmett, where the Payette River narrows between black basalt walls. The dam significantly improved the availability of irrigation water throughout the growing season as well as producing electrical power. (*See The Region, Agriculture and Irrigation – Bureau of Reclamation – Boise Project – Treasure Valley.*)

Orchards The prevalence of fruit orchards gave the community its name and economy. In the early years, growers used cool dirt-covered cellars to store their fruit until it could be loaded on trains for shipment. By 1916 growers were shipping several train carloads of fresh fruit across the nation each season. Today, they use climate control technology that holds the freshness of the fruit for several months.

Economic Development During the economic recession of the early 1980s, community leaders took action to diversify their economy beyond agriculture. (*See Economy and Major Employers below.*)

Fruitland Today

Amenities and Attractions The city has four parks on 12 acres. The principal park, Fruitland Community Park, is downtown next to the post office. It has winding sidewalks, park benches, flower gardens and a tall information kiosk modeled after the original bell tower that served the city's first school building. In addition, the park has covered and lighted picnic areas with city water, tables, horseshoe pits, a volleyball court, public restrooms and a telephone. Families frequently celebrate birthdays, receptions, reunions and even weddings in this lovely park. The park is also the location of the annual Payette County Fair and Rodeo kick-off breakfast each August, the Fruitland Family Fun Days in September and December's Christmas in the Park sponsored by the Chamber of Commerce with the annual peace candle lighting ceremony sponsored by the

Fruitland Lions Club.

Swire Park offers an inviting grass-covered half-acre with picnic tables at the intersection of NW 4th Street and N. Kansas Avenue.

The two other parks, Crestview and Mesa, are next to subdivisions of the same names. Crestview is on SW 8th Street just west of U.S. Highway 95 about half a mile west of the Snake River. When fully developed, this park will include a trail that passes through an intersecting gully to the Snake River.

Mesa Park is part of the Payette County Recreation District (PCRD). It is primarily a sports facility featuring four lighted softball/athletic fields, four lighted tennis courts, a basketball court, a large tot lot, a picnic shelter, a concession stand and restrooms.

On the Saturday preceding Mothers' Day, the community celebrates the Fruitland Spring Fair. Activities include the Lions Club Chicken Barbecue and a parade featuring school bands and floats. The fair concludes with the Fruitland Fire Department Bull Riding Burnout fundraiser for the Fire Victims Burnout Fund.

Clay Peak Recreation Area – a regionally popular 750-acre Payette County-managed facility about three miles north of Fruitland – has sanctioned motocross races and off-road activities for motorcycle/ATV riding enthusiasts.

Nearby rivers and vast tracts of public land provide diverse opportunities for outdoor enthusiasts. Fruitland residents can enjoy fishing, hunting, boating, camping, hiking, ATV riding and snowmobile riding within a short distance from the city. There are at least five sportsmen accesses to the Payette River within five miles of the city.

Economy and Major Employers Woodgrain Millwork, Inc., a manufacturer of wood moldings, windows and doors has about 550 employees and is the city's largest employer. Dickinson Frozen Foods, a processor of onions and other vegetables, employs 250. Swire Coca-Cola Bottling Co., Henggeler Packing Co., D&S Factors and the Fruitland School District round out the largest employers in the Fruitland area. Several smaller businesses in the city's downtown area, U.S. 95 corridor and north business district provide other employment opportunities.

Education The Fruitland School District operates an elementary school, an intermediate school, a middle school and a high school.

There are several institutions of higher learning within an hour's drive of the city. The largest is Boise State University, 50 miles southeast in Boise.

Health Care The closest hospital is Holy Rosary Medical Center, three miles away in Ontario, Oregon. Saint Alphonsus Dominican Health Services, St. Luke's Clinic - Fruitland and St. Luke's Mountain States Tumor Institute are the larger medical providers. Other private practices provide vision, dental, general medical services and hospice care. Payette County Paramedics ambulance service is operated by the City and serves all of Payette County.

Transportation U.S. Highways 95 and 30 intersect the city. Two access points to Interstate 84 are available a half mile west and two miles south of the city.

Ontario Municipal Airport and Payette Municipal Airport are within three miles of Fruitland and provide service for small aircraft. The closest full service airport is in Boise.

Railroad freight service is available in the city.

Snake River Transit provides weekday bus service between Ontario, Fruitland and Payette.

Utilities and Services Private companies provide electricity, telephone, natural gas, solid waste disposal, cable, satellite and wireless services. The City provides water and sewer services as well as police and fire protection.

Vision for 2050

In 1960 the city had a population of 804. In 1967 following annexation of adjacent developments to the north, Fruitland's population ballooned to 1,543. By 1980 the population had increased to 2,559. In subsequent years, Fruitland's population has grown generally commensurate with the growth in industrial development. Since 2000 the city's population has grown at nearly 3 percent annually. City officials expect this industrial growth to continue. In preparation for this growth, the city has approved residential developments with hundreds of residential lots.

In 2010 the City completed a new $15 million water treatment plant on the Payette River. Studies are underway to combine the city's two wastewater plants into one state-of-the-art treatment facility. These facilities will have sufficient capacity to accommodate current needs and many years of growth.

Over the past 10 years, the City has acquired land adjacent to City Hall for a public safety building to accommodate the growing law enforcement and ambulance service needs. The facility will be built once funding becomes available.

City officials have given top priority to improving Pennsylvania Avenue, NW 7th Street and N. Arizona Avenue to accommodate growing traffic needs.

Funding for required improvements will come from normal revenue streams, user fees, voter-approved bonds and grant opportunities.

Mayors

1948	T.H. Beckwith *	1976	L.L. Bishop
1951	A.R. Heap *	1977	Ralph L. Barker
1953	H.E. Dressen *	1978	Lloyd R. Puntenney
1955	N.W. "Tex" Nelson *	1982	John H. Shelden
1957	Dorell E. Trussell *	1984	Joseph P. Wozniak
1958	J.A. Beckwith *	1994	Thomas E. Limbaugh
1959	Harold L. Merritt *	2010	Ken Bishop
1966	Floyd J. Holton		* Village Chairman
1971	C.L. "Andy" Anderson		

New Plymouth

Statistical Data

Population: 1,510 *
Elevation: 2,250 feet
Precipitation: 11 inches **
Average Snowfall: 21 inches **
County: Payette
Website: www.npidaho.com

Temperature Range – Fahrenheit: **
Spring: 32 to 74
Summer: 53 to 91
Fall: 29 to 80
Winter: 20 to 46
* U.S. Census Bureau Estimates July 2015
**Historical averages

The historic 1897 planned community of New Plymouth lies at the north end of the Treasure Valley. Midwestern promoters, seeking to demonstrate the use of irrigation in reclaiming the arid West, designed the horseshoe shaped townsite to achieve their idyllic concept of a model farming community.

The Payette River flows about two miles east of the city. The city of Payette is 10 miles northwest. The Snake River, separating Idaho and Oregon, is about five miles west.

Fruit orchards and fertile fields of alfalfa hay, sugar beets, onions, potatoes, corn and wheat surround the city, forming a checkerboard of color.

Brush and grass-covered mountains and foothills, mostly public lands managed by the Bureau of Land Management (BLM), lie five miles west. An approximate 30-square-mile tract of public foothill land, also managed by the BLM, begins about two miles south of the city.

Pre-Incorporation Years

In 1881 the Oregon Short Line (OSL) began construction of a railroad line between Granger, Wyoming, and Huntington, Oregon. This railroad link would complete another transcontinental railroad, connecting the commercial centers of Omaha, Nebraska, and Portland, Oregon. Railroad interests completed the first transcontinental railroad in 1869 at Promontory Summit in northern Utah.

The rail line, completed on November 17, 1884, angled in a northwesterly direction through what are now Pocatello, Mountain Home, Caldwell and Parma then headed north to Payette and Weiser then crossed the Snake River one last time before reaching Huntington.

Most of the early settlers in what is now Payette County established homesteads along streams where they could more easily divert water to irrigate their low-lying farmland. However, the arable land around what is now New Plymouth had a higher elevation and remained covered with sagebrush until the 1890s. Unique among Idaho cities, New Plymouth began as a planned agricultural community.

July 1, 1896, first celebration of Plymouth Colony. Courtesy the brother of Fred Naher.

Around 1884 William E. Smythe, Chairman of the Executive Committee of the Northern Irrigation Congress, led a group of like-minded individuals to form "The Plymouth Society of Chicago" (Society). The Society sought to find an ideal location in the West where they could divert water for irrigation and build a self-reliant agricultural community where farmers had homes at the center of the community with farmland located around the city. Smythe lectured throughout the East encouraging settlers to go West in colonies to build irrigation systems and reclaim the West.

The Society identified several potential reclamation sites in the Western U.S. where they could build their model colony. They chose the Southwest Idaho location and acquired about 325 acres near the Payette River and the railroad. They named their community New Plymouth Farm Village after one of the first colonies in America – Plymouth, Massachusetts.

The Society platted the town in the shape of an arch or horseshoe with the open end facing north. The area at the mouth of the horseshoe was the industrial part of town. Around and within the horseshoe they platted two semi-concentric streets fronted by one-acre lots with parks and public areas in the center. A main thoroughfare bisected the city.

A.R. Ingalls, Village Chairman, 1921-25.

In February 1896 the Society offered the platted lots for sale. Generally, colonists purchased a one-acre lot in town and a 20-acre farm lot outside of town. Colonists cleared the sagebrush off their property and planted their fields. Most of them planted apple trees.

They formed an irrigation district and diverted Payette River water to their colony. To get adequate elevation to the water so that crops could be irrigated using gravity flow, the irrigation district placed a series of water wheels in the fast flowing canals to lift the water into the lateral irrigation ditches or pipes – five of these water wheels are still in use.

The coming of the railroad in 1883 provided the impetus that led to the founding of Payette and the underlying basis for its subsequent economic success as an agricultural community.

Aerial views of New Plymouth. Both pictures were presented to the City of New Plymouth on August 7, 1961, by Chest Council, departing City Council member.

In 1906 the Payette Valley Railroad Company, later acquired by OSL, constructed a branch line from Payette through Fruitland to New Plymouth. In 1910 the Payette Valley Extension Railroad Company, later acquired by OSL, extended railroad service from New Plymouth to Emmett.

Incorporation

On October 19, 1908, with a population of over 200 – the 1910 U.S. Census reported a population of 274 – and using the shortened name of New Plymouth, the community successfully applied to the Canyon County Commissioners to become an incorporated village. On February 14, 1917, the Idaho Legislature divided Canyon County, creating Payette County. Forty years after the town's incorporation, the Payette County Commissioners approved changing its legal status to a city.

Turning Points

The Plymouth Society of Chicago The Society is responsible for the founding of New Plymouth. In creating the community, they fulfilled their objective to plat and attract settlers to their idyllic planned agricultural community, hoping to inspire settlers to reclaim the arid Western U.S.

Railroad Even though the railroad followed the development of New Plymouth, it played a major role in the development of the agricultural community and the economy of the community.

With irrigation and the railroad, the colonists achieved their dreams of converting the sagebrush-covered high-desert land into a model town and an agricultural oasis.

Irrigation A key criterion for the Society to select its New Plymouth location was the availability of irrigation water from the Payette River. However, the uncontrolled river did not always provide an adequate supply of water through the entire growing season.

In 1924 the Federal Bureau of Reclamation completed construction of the hydroelectric Black Canyon Dam about five miles east of Emmett where the Payette River narrows between black basalt walls. They also built or integrated the new source of irrigation water into new or existing canal systems including those serving New Plymouth farms. The 183-foot-high Black Canyon Dam had a profound effect in improving the availability of irrigation water throughout the growing season.

Idaho Sales Tax In 1965 Idaho adopted a 3% sales tax (currently 6%). This had a significant adverse effect on New Plymouth retail businesses as well as those in other cities near Ontario, Oregon. Oregon voters have rejected multiple attempts to implement a sales tax. As a result, many Idaho residents near the Idaho/Oregon border drive across the state line to buy retail goods with no sales tax added.

New Plymouth Today

Amenities and Attractions The city has two parks that comprise 13 acres.

Clay Peak County Park and Recreation Area is a regionally popular 750-acre facility owned and operated by Payette County. The park's principal attractions are motocross races and mud drag races for pick-ups and quads. The facility is located about nine miles northwest of the city.

Economy and Major Employers With about 120 employees, the New Plymouth School District is the city's largest employer. Several small businesses, with fewer than 25 employees each, provide most of the city's remaining employment.

Education The New Plymouth School District operates elementary, middle and high schools in the city.

There are several institutions of higher learning within an hour's drive of the city. The largest of these is Boise State University, 50 miles southeast in Boise.

Health Care The closest hospital is Holy Rosary Medical Center, located about eleven miles west in Ontario, Oregon.

Transportation US Highway 30 intersects the city. Interstate 84 and US Highway 95 are about five miles west. Idaho Highway 72, south of town, connects the city with Idaho Highway 52 which extends to Emmett on the east and Payette to the northwest. The closest full service airport is in Boise. Railroad freight service is available in the city.

Utilities and Services Private companies provide electricity, gas, cable, satellite and wireless services. The City provides water and sewer services and police and fire protection.

Internet Truckstop, a new three-story building being constructed in New Plymouth, is owned by Scott Moscrip, a former Mayor of New Plymouth.

Vision for 2050

Since its early development, the city's population grew at a moderate pace of over one percent annually until around 2000 when the city's rate of growth stabilized. Recent historical trends will likely continue for several years. By 2050 New Plymouth will likely have a population in excess of 1,600.

Mayors

1908	Arthur Meyer *	1964	James Tipton
1913	J.F. LaCrone *	1966	Lowell Simonson
1915	H.F. Kinight *	1969	Frank Robertson
1919	Geo. Ackerman *	1970	Paul Gilmore
1921	A.R. Ingalls *	1974	Lowell Simonson
1925	W.P. Ackerman *	1978	Dick Platz
1933	C.F. Eder *	1990	Gordon Collinsworth
1943	Clyde Makinson *	1994	James Peart
1947	Phil Roney *	1995	Dale Williamson
1949	Ned Gard	2004	Scott Moscrip
1951	C.H. Galvin	2008	Joe Cook
1953	Phil Roney	2016	Elizabeth Earles
1955	John Stafford		* Village Chairman
1957	E.A. Harvey		

Payette

Statistical Data

Population: 7,422 *
Elevation: 2,150 feet
Precipitation: 11 inches **
Average Snowfall: 20 inches **
County: Payette
Website: www.cityofpayette.com

Temperature Range – Fahrenheit: **
Spring: 32 to 74
Summer: 53 to 91
Fall: 29 to 80
Winter: 20 to 46
* U.S. Census Bureau Estimates July 2015
**Historical averages

Payette lies on the eastern banks of the Payette River where it converges with the Snake River. The Snake River forms the city's northernmost boundary. The state of Oregon is on the opposite side of the Snake River.

Fertile farmland surrounds the city except to the east across the Payette River where there are vast tracts of brush-covered foothills, primarily public lands managed by the Bureau of Land Management. Boise is 60 miles southeast.

Pre-Incorporation Years

Explorers/fur trappers began traveling the Snake River and its tributaries in 1811 to principally trap beaver and establish trading posts with American Indians. (*See The Region, American Indians.*)

In 1834 after previous failures by others to develop a permanent trading post at the confluence of the Boise and Snake Rivers, the Hudson's Bay Company, a British enterprise, built a trading post near what is now Parma, 20 miles south of Payette. For several years a Frenchman named Francois Payette managed the remote outpost.

Payette, obviously struck by the black cottonwood and willow forests that grew along the river flowing from the east, named the river Boise, the French name meaning "woods" or "wooded," and the trading post "Fort Boise." (*See The Region, Early Trappers/Explorers.*)

The "Boise" name Francois Payette gave to the trading post and river also became the name of a mining district and mountain basin, another Fort Boise located about 40 miles southeast, a city, a national forest, tributaries to the Boise River, a valley and a county. Settlers and governments also gave permanence to Payette's name. In addition to the city of Payette, a county, a river with three forks, two lakes, a valley and a national forest also bear his name. Francois Payette is likely responsible for or is the object of naming more Idaho places and natural features than any other person in Idaho history.

In 1841 thousands of immigrants en route to the "Oregon Country" began passing through what is now the Treasure Valley on a trail used by explorers and trappers. It became the Oregon Trail, and Payette's Fort Boise was a landmark and supply station on the trail. The fort continued as a supply post until 1854 when river flooding and Indian hostilities resulted in

Payette train depot.

its abandonment. (*See The Region, Oregon and California Trails.*)

Prospectors discovered gold in 1862 about 75 miles southeast of what is now Payette in the Boise Basin. The following year, 16,000 fortune seekers flooded the basin in search of the precious metal. Where settlers could divert irrigation water onto their homesteads, farms sprang up to provide food for the miners.

A year later, the U.S. Army established a military fort near the Oregon Trail about 45 miles west of the destroyed trading post and named it "Fort Boise." A new town called Boise City immediately grew up around the new fort. Oregon Trail immigrants still had a Fort Boise where they could rest and resupply.

The Oregon Short Line (OSL) began building a rail line in 1881 between Granger,

Doughboy Statue inits original location.

Wyoming, and Huntington, Oregon. This line connected the commercial centers of Omaha, Nebraska, and Portland, Oregon, creating another transcontinental railroad. Railroad interests completed the first transcontinental railroad in 1869 at Promontory Summit in northern Utah.

The rail line – completed on November 17, 1884 – angled northwesterly through Pocatello, Mountain Home, Caldwell and Parma then turned north to Payette and, finally, Weiser before crossing the Snake River a last time before reaching Huntington.

About this time, brothers N.A. and August Jacobsen came to the Payette area. Impressed by the excellent soil and abundance of water, they determined this would be the place where they would settle, grow fruit trees and start a new town.

Settlers William F. Masters and Bill Case, who came at about the same time, had similar opinions. In the spring of 1884 the four men founded the town they named "Payette" after the river. Masters filed on 200 acres of land near the Payette River, which he platted into lots. Payette has wide streets today because N.A. Jacobsen interceded when the townsite was surveyed and suggested they make the streets wider.

Another entrepreneur, David S. Lamme, saw where the railroad survey crews marked the path of the rail line and

Old courthouse and city hall.

purchased land where it crossed the river. A few months later, A.B. and Frank C. Moss, who had a contract to deliver 250,000 ties to the railroad, built a base camp at the mouth of the river near Lamme's property.

When the railroad construction crews began arriving in 1883, they built a tent city they called "Boomerang" because of the log boom the Moss brothers put across the river to catch the logs coming from the timberlands further upstream to their railroad tie sawmill.

The railroad completed its bridge across the Payette River and built the Payette Train Depot.

Other entrepreneurs started the Payette Brick Factory, which supplied the large quantities of brick needed for the many new business buildings and homes that ushered in what became known as the brick age of Payette. For many years, the brick factory was one of the town's largest employers.

The Moss brothers built a brick mercantile store a few blocks from the train depot, and Lamme built a small retail store on his property and stocked it with goods he shipped in from Chicago. Others built two hotels, a bank and an Odd Fellows Hall. One of the hotels, the Coughanour, was built by William A. Coughanour, who was a community leader and major developer of downtown properties. The 1890 census reported the town's population at 396.

The day after Idaho became a state – July 3, 1890 – trains sounded their whistles as they passed the Payette depot, which was flying from its roof a newly hand-made American flag with 43 stars sewn by the wife of the railroad agent David Carl Chase.

Incorporation

On July 16, 1891, Payette became an incorporated village, the first community founded in what is now Payette County.

On March 5, 1903, Payette had grown sufficiently to change its legal status to a city of the second class. The 1910 census reported its population at 1,948.

Turning Points

Railroads. The railroad was the basis for the founding of Payette and provided the foundation for the town's subsequent economic success as an agricultural community. Railroad spurs were extended to fruit storage warehouses, where fresh fruit was packaged and loaded on rail cars for shipment to distant markets.

The Payette Valley Railroad Company built a branch line from Payette through Fruitland to New Plymouth in 1906, and four years later the Payette Valley Extension Railroad Company began service to Emmett. Both of these railroads were later acquired by the Oregon Short Line which reported that Payette area farmers shipped more fruit and poultry than any other city it served

Fruit Orchards. After seeing Payette apples at the 1896 World's Fair in Omaha, Nebraska, Leroy Vernon Patch was so impressed that he visited Payette and bought 1,000 acres – which he planted with apple trees – and hired workers to care for his orchard while he was away. Each summer he returned, bought more land and planted more apple trees. He fell in love and married

Chase House.

his wife, Ernestine, in 1901, and they moved to Payette.

Patch teamed up with the Moss and the Jacobsen brothers and opened the Idaho Canning Company. The business became a major employer and buyer of local produce, giving incentive for orchardists to raise all types of fruit. Patch also had military interests. He started the Second Regiment of the Idaho National Guard and became a brigadier general. In 1920 he donated the "Doughboy Statue" that still stands in downtown Payette.

Fruit packers built cold storage warehouses and produce packing sheds along the rail line and spurs, adding significantly to Payette's economic base. During the hard times of the Great Depression of the 1930s, fresh fruit generally continued in demand, staving off many of the problems experienced in other parts of the country.

County Seat. The Idaho Legislature created Payette County on February 14, 1917. The city of Payette became the county seat, adding to its prestige and providing a stable source of employment.

Interstate and Highway Bypasses. In 1960 federal transportation authorities announced that the route of Interstate 84 would be through nearby Ontario, Oregon, as opposed to Payette, significantly reducing tourist traffic through the city. Three years later, transportation authorities built the U.S. Highway 95 bypass around the downtown area, further taking business away from Payette retailers.

Idaho Sales Tax. The Idaho Legislature adopted the state's first sales tax of 3 percent in 1965 and, over the

Central Park.

years, has incrementally increased the tax to its current rate of 6 percent, adopted in 2006. For Idaho merchants bordering Oregon, such as those in the city of Payette, the tax creates a significant disadvantage. Since Oregon has no sales tax, Idaho residents often find they can save money by driving across the state line to buy retail consumer goods such as food, clothing and appliances, with no 6 percent Idaho sales tax added.

Payette Today

Amenities and Attractions Payette has nine parks that comprise 47 acres. The largest, Kiwanis Park, features a historic band shell, tennis courts,

New fire station.

picnic areas, children's playground equipment, a skate park and the city's indoor/outdoor swimming pool, which is open 11 months of the year.

The Payette Greenway is a paved path along the beautiful Payette River. It is presently two miles long with significant extensions planned.

The Payette County Historical Museum is open Wednesday through Saturday and is free to the public.

The city celebrates Harmon Killebrew Day each April. This native son and Payette High School and Minnesota Twins star athlete was inducted into the National Baseball Hall of Fame in 1984. The city has named a major thoroughfare and the high school's athletic complex in his honor.

Each May the community sponsors Apple Blossom Days with a week of events that feature a parade, food vendors and a carnival.

The annual Payette County Fair and Rodeo takes place each August at the county fairgrounds.

Every September A&W Restaurant and the community sponsor the A&W Car Show, a display of vintage motor vehicles in over 60 categories, and a nostalgic "Cruise Night," where streets are blocked off for the vehicles "cruise." It includes a chili cook-off, live music, dancing in the street and vendors in Bancroft Park.

About three miles outside the city is the County-owned Clay Peak Recreation Area that comprises over a thousand acres and includes a privately operated motorcycle raceway, which draws racing enthusiasts from throughout the region.

Nearby rivers and vast tracts of public lands provide excellent opportunities for outdoor enthusiasts. Payette residents can enjoy fishing, hunting, boating, camping, hiking, ATV riding and snowmobiling within a short distance of the city. There are at least five sportsmen's access locations to the Payette River within five miles of the city and one to the Snake River. In its June/July 2009 issue, Outdoor Life magazine ranked Payette as number 67 among the nation's top cities for outdoorsmen.

Economy and Major Employers The city's largest employer is Seneca Foods Corporation, a food processing plant that began as the Idaho Canning Company. Even though it has changed ownership over the years, it remains a vital economic part of the city.

The Payette School District has the second most employees. Several small businesses and divisions of large businesses employ fewer than 100 each. Downtown retail and service businesses provide most of the other jobs in the city.

Education The Payette School District provides most of the elementary and secondary education in the city. The district operates a primary school, elementary school, middle school, high school and an alternative high school. There are also two private schools in the city.

Several institutions of higher learning are within an hour's drive of the city. The largest is Boise State University, 56 miles southeast in Boise.

Health Care The Valley Family Health Care Clinic provides most of the general medical services needed by city residents. The closest hospital, the 49-bed Saint Alphonsus Medical Center in Ontario, Oregon, is five miles away. Payette Care and Rehabilitation Center provides physical therapy and nursing home care.

Transportation U.S. Highway 95 intersects the city in a north-south direction. Idaho Highway 52 intersects the city before turning west across the Snake River bridge into Oregon. Interstate 84 is five miles west.

Payette Municipal Airport, two miles northeast, provides air service for small private and charter aircraft. The closest full service airport is in Boise.

Railroad freight service is available in the city.

Snake River Transit provides public bus transportation in Payette County in Idaho and Malheur County in Oregon.

Utilities and Services Private companies provide electricity, gas, cable, satellite and wireless services. The City provides water and sewer services and police and fire protection.

Payette High School and Killebrew Field.

Vision for 2050

Payette's population remained relatively stable at around 4,000 to 4,500 until the 1970s, when it began growing over 2 percent annually. Since 2000 the city has grown at about 1 percent a year. This trend will likely continue into the foreseeable future. By 2050 Payette's population could approximate 20,000. At that time, the commercial and residential development between Payette, Fruitland and New Plymouth will blend in a manner that obscures the legal boundaries except to the trained observer.

City leaders will manage this growth in accordance with their comprehensive plan. Most of this growth will be to the north and east. Any construction of buildings in flood plain areas to the west and south of the city and along the rim of the valley will be limited in accordance with the City's comprehensive plan and standards.

City leaders will make every effort to retain the city's rural character. Many homes will be on large lots, allowing room for gardens and small animals that can contribute to the seasonal Farmer's Market, which is held weekly at the Bancroft Town Square. The city will encourage apartment building developers to provide space for garden plots and underground parking facilities.

By 2050 the Little Willow Creek Nuclear Power Plant, located 15 miles away, should be approved and operational. The Payette River Green Way will extend from the Payette River bridges along Highway 95 to the North 6th Street Bridge over the Snake River then to the NW 19th Avenue intersection. It will then connect with side trails to several of the river islands using hand-cranked 4-person ferries to islands that don't have bridges. Trail enthusiasts will be able to continue on to meet up with Weiser's Rails to Trails heading north to McCall then looping back to Horseshoe Bend, through Emmett and back to Payette.

The "Pumpkin Vine Dinner Train" will be operational, taking visitors from Payette to Emmett with catered meals and local actors entertaining the passengers with tales of the area's history.

There will be riverboat tours on the Payette and Snake Rivers to historic places and harvest tours through orchards, vineyards and gardens – with carts provided for carrying the harvest and preparation areas where produce can be immediately washed and eaten.

Commemorating the 10 current and former National Hockey League players living in the city, the indoor ice-skating rink on the south side of Payette will be completed to help area youth develop their hockey talents.

With strategic planning and adherence to the City's comprehensive plan, periodically updated for current conditions, 40 years from now Payette will still be a warm, friendly and safe community in which to live and raise a family.

Mayors

1891	A.B. Moss *	1936	I.R. Woodward
1892	J.H. Richards *	1941	J.A. McMillan
1894	Travis Brown *	1953	Ursus Dalton
1895	A.B. Moss *	1955	J.A. McMillan
1897	W.A. Coughanour *	1956	A.V. Kinney
1899	David Lamme *	1959	C.T. Clauser
1900	W.A. Coughanour *	1961	L.J. Josephson
1901	F.M. Satoris *	1969	Wesley Roehr
1903	F.M. Satoris	1978	Dick Butcher
1904	Frank Crighton	1990	Floyd Moyer
1905	R.E. Haynes	1994	James E. McCue
1907	W.A. Coughanour	1998	Ann Crosby
1911	H.P. Brannock	2002	Mark Heleker
1913	C.B. Compton	2006	Doug Henderson
1915	Burt Venable	2010	Jeff Williams
1917	I.R. Woodward		* Village Chairman
1933	J.J. Wood		

Trout scramble at Buhl.

TWIN FALLS COUNTY

- Buhl
- Castleford
- Filer
- Hansen
- Hollister
- Kimberly
- Murtaugh
- Twin Falls (*County Seat*)

Trout sculpture, Buhl.

Buhl

Statistical Data

Population: 4,231 *
Elevation: 3,763 feet
Precipitation: 13.5 inches **
Average Snowfall: 19 inches **
County: Twin Falls
Website: www.buhl.govoffice2.com

Temperature Range – Fahrenheit: **
Spring: 29 to 67
Summer: 50 to 86
Fall: 27 to 75
Winter: 19 to 40
* U.S. Census Bureau Estimates July 2015
**Historical averages

Buhl is the southern gateway to the 30-mile-long geologic wonder that includes the Thousand Springs State Park complex.

Every minute, millions of gallons of crystal-clear cold water burst from the north and east side of the 350-foot-high basalt walls of the Snake River Canyon a few miles north of the city.

This phenomenon largely occurs across the Snake River between the Niagara Springs unit of Thousand Springs State Park located about six miles northeast of Buhl and the Malad Gorge unit, located about 20 miles almost due north of the city.

The water comes from the massive Snake River Plain Aquifer, perhaps the largest aquifer in the nation. It covers several thousand square miles and, in many places, is more than a thousand feet deep.

The aquifer begins in eastern Idaho over 200 miles east near Yellowstone National Park. The Big Lost River near Arco and other mountain streams and irrigation waters flow or seep into the deep, porous volcanic rock. It takes more than a century for the water to complete its journey from the eastern edge of the aquifer before it gushes out of the canyon walls into the Snake River below. Privately-owned aquaculture and hydroelectric businesses own most of the water. However, many of the springs are publicly owned and used for fish hatcheries and parks.

Pre-Incorporation Years

In 1904 the region that includes Buhl was largely a vast sagebrush-covered desert plain under control of federal agencies.

In 1905 private investors built Milner Dam – located 40 miles upriver from the city – and an irrigation canal complex, selling arable land under the provisions of the Carey Act. Under the Carey

Buhl Hotel.

Act, the federal government granted each Western state up to one million acres of arid land for reclamation purposes. The Act, among other things, provided the state could sell land and authorize private interests to finance and construct diversion dams and canal systems and sell water rights to the individual farmers.

Ira B. Perrine, one of the first entrepreneurs in the region, was the primary force behind construction of Milner Dam.

Frank H. Buhl and Peter Kimberley – iron and steel manufacturers of Sharon, Pennsylvania

– were investors in the project. Perrine created the Twin Falls Land and Water Company to oversee construction of the dam, develop the irrigation canal system, negotiate with the railroad to provide service and establish new towns served by

the irrigation canals.

Ultimately, water from the dam would irrigate over 244,000 acres. Buhl was one of the farming communities created when ownership of the land moved to private hands.

The Twin Falls Land and Water Company acquired land and created a town site company to survey, plat and sell lots for the project. In 1905 the surveying and platting began for the future community. They named the new town Buhl, after Frank H. Buhl. Frank Buhl would later contribute money to the community's first school, named the F. H. Buhl School.

In November 1905 the Buhl Stage Line was opened, charging $3.00 for about a 30-mile round trip from Twin Falls to Buhl and $1.75 for a one-way trip to Buhl via Filer.

Bird's eye view of Buhl, looking from OSL Depot, 1907.

By the end of 1905 the investment company began advertising that on April 17, 1906, platted lots would become available for sale.

In January 1906 F. William Eickhoff, of Twin Falls, speculated that the new community of Buhl would boom, the same as the other Carey Act towns had done.

Eickhoff purchased the rooming house built near the town site, likely built by the townsite company for the surveyors who platted the city. He added additional floor space and called it a hotel. He then hired John Hinkley and his sister Mary from Steamboat Springs, Colorado, to manage it.

Eickhoff then built a general store and a warehouse for hay, grain

Eastman's Store.

and feed. He said that by spring he was expecting "lively times" as irrigation water should arrive by June.

As part of its promotion, the Buhl Town Site Company announced that it would develop an experimental farm in Buhl and build a block of model homes. Eickhoff advertised that he would have 160 acres in crops that year.

The Oregon Short Line Railroad publicized its rail line from Twin Falls to Buhl. The Twin Falls Land & Water Company said that bridges across Cedar Draw and Rock Creek and telephone and electric power would be coming soon. In 1909 Minidoka Hydroelectric Dam produced the first electricity in the region.

Incorporation

In February 1906 the Buhl Town Site Company filed with the county to incorporate. At the same time, the Buhl Post Office was opened. Meanwhile, the Land and Water Company announced the purchase of 5,000 shade trees for the Buhl and Twin Falls townsites.

Even though platted lots would not be available for sale until April, prospective buyers were already arriving. The Twin Falls Weekly newspaper published the plat and ran stories on the

Lee family Belgians in a parade.

progress of events. In March it reported that prospective buyers were building temporary living structures and biding their time.

On April 17, 1906, the townsite company drew names of land subscribers to determine the order for purchasing lots. The first lot was sold to Clarence S. Peck for $1,750 and the second to R. C. Beach for $1,600.

The Weekly News reported that Buhl property values doubled in three days. Buhl merchant and postmaster, F. William Eickhoff, reported his general store was experiencing robust sales.

April brought a flurry of other activity. The town streets and common areas were cleared and grass planted awaiting the shade tree saplings that were on their way to town. A new hotel was under construction near the intersection of Main and Broadway. A livery stable was running daily stagecoach mail and passenger service from Twin Falls. Construction of a farmers' meeting hall was announced and a U. S. weather station established.

Domestic water was another matter. In the absence of wells, residents followed the common practice of using canal water for both irrigation and domestic purposes.

Turning Points

Founding Buhl owes its existence to three key events: the Carey Act, the resulting availability of irrigation water and the railroad. (*See Southwest Idaho, Cities of the Magic Valley.*)

Agriculture Initially, basic production agriculture underpinned the city's economy. However, over the years that has changed. Technological innovations, including pumping water from deep wells, sprinkler irrigation, development of commercial fertilizers, certified seed, better farm practices, weed control mechanization and automation have dramatically increased farm and food processing productivity with a much smaller but better skilled and educated labor pool.

These changes have encouraged farm consolidation that further reduced the number of farm families that sustain the city's economy. In response, the city began seeking a more diverse employment base.

Aquaculture An innovation in the agriculture community is aquaculture. In 1948 Earl Hardy and Alfred Iverson began the first commercial trout farms and processing business using the natural spring waters that flowed into the

Christmas lights.

Snake River north of Buhl. They found that the pure, clean, oxygenated water from the Snake River Plain Aquifer maintains a constant temperature of 58 degrees Fahrenheit, ideal conditions for fish hatcheries and the commercial production of rainbow trout.

From modest beginnings, trout farming and processing in the Thousand Springs area have developed into major businesses in Idaho. Commercial hatcheries and processors in this area produce over 70 percent of the trout sold in the United States. The largest of these facilities, Clear Springs Foods, is located near Buhl. The continued expansion of this industry will only add to the city's economic stability.

Buhl Today

Amenities and Attractions Buhl has three city parks that include a heated swimming pool, soccer fields and softball and baseball diamonds. The community also uses track and other facilities developed in conjunction with the new Buhl High School. There is also an 18-hole private golf course in the city that is open to the public.

The city has constructed a skateboard park with an exceptionally large cradle. Skateboard Magazine rated Buhl's park as having the largest "cradle" and second best skateboard park in the nation.

For outdoor enthusiasts, there are numerous amenities within an hour's drive of the city. The Snake River with its thousand springs and the many lakes, ponds and parks along the river provide excellent opportunities to camp, fish and hike.

Across the river from Buhl are the nine units of Thousand Springs State Park. They include properties of several cold crystal springs and fisheries. Among the individual units of the park is the 652-acre Malad Gorge Park. Billingsley Creek offers fishing and horseback riding. Bird watching opportunities and the annual Thousand Springs Art Festival are at Ritter Island. Around 180,000 gallons of cold spring water tumble over waterfalls and bubble up from the crystal-clear pools at Earl M. Hardy Box Canyon Springs Nature Preserve. Niagara and Crystal Springs are at the base of the Snake River Canyon where large springs burst from the canyon walls. At Niagara Springs, water flows through the traces of state and national fish hatcheries and a beautiful public fishery near an old-growth tree covered park.

Balanced Rock, a unique natural feature, lies 10 miles west of the city.

About 20 miles northwest is the 4,300-acre Hagerman Fossil Beds National Monument. Archeologists worldwide recognize the site for its prehistoric fossil and sediment deposits from the Pliocene Epoch. The National Monument's visitor center is in Hagerman. A segment of the Oregon National Historic Trail is on the southern end of the Monument. Ruts made by the Oregon Trail immigrant wagons are still visible from the parking lot that overlooks the Hagerman Fossil Beds.

The Sawtooth National Forest – located 32 miles south of the city – offers camping, hiking, fishing and hunting.

Buhl is a haven for those looking for a beautiful and progressive place in which to live.

Economy and Major Employers Clear Springs Foods, with approximately 300 employees, is the city's largest year-round employer. It performs research and grows and sells millions of fresh trout and trout related specialty products for markets around the world. The fry that are grown in Buhl are produced from propriety brood stock at the company's Soda Springs, Idaho, facility. Over 80 million Rainbow Trout eggs a year can be produced at that facility.

At its Buhl facility, the company also maintains a landscaped park where visitors can picnic, as well as view large trout and sturgeon swimming in a natural setting either in a crystal-clear pond or through an underground viewing window.

The city illustrates the importance of aquaculture on its economy by its slogan,

"City of Buhl, Trout Capital of America."

However, trout is not the only aquaculture product produced. Some businesses are producing caviar from sturgeon native to the Snake River.

There are also numerous hot springs in this formerly volcanic region. Hot spring water warms cold water to temperatures ideal for more tropical aquatic life. Aquaculture entrepreneurs are also growing alligator, tilapia and other species.

Aquaculture-based business is a more recent innovation; however, water has always been the underlying basis of Buhl's economic lifeblood.

Agriculture and food processing in Buhl date back to 1906 when Milner Dam and extensive irrigation systems were constructed. Production from these farms and the food processing businesses they fostered are still an economic mainstay for Buhl.

Seneca Foods averages 125 full-time employees at the company's Buhl facility. This food processing company produces canned and frozen peas, asparagus and corn at its Buhl facility. During packing season, the number of employees swells to more than 800.

Rangen Feeds has 115 full-time employees. It manufacturers formulated fish and animal food and supplements and warehouses farm commodities such as grain and beans.

Buhl School District has about 150 employees and is the city's largest public employer.

Buhl's commercial district includes a broad range of retail businesses. Many residents also travel 17 miles east to the large shopping malls and regional hospital services in Twin Falls.

Education Buhl School District provides pre-kindergarten through grade five at Popplewell Elementary, grades six through eight at Buhl Middle School and grades nine through twelve at the new Buhl High School.

The school district encompasses 140 square miles and has an average annual enrollment of approximately 1,500 students. Three private K-12 schools with a total enrollment of 140 students also serve families in the area.

Higher education is available at the College of Southern Idaho in Twin Falls.

Health Care Regional hospital services are located in Twin Falls.

Transportation U.S. Highway 30 intersects the city. Interstate 84 is about four miles north at Twin Falls.

The 3,900-foot-long runway at Buhl Municipal Airport provides service for small private and charter aircraft. Commercial air service is available at Magic Valley Regional Airport at Joslin Field about four miles south of Twin Falls.

Railroad service is available in the city for freight.

Utilities and Services Private companies provide electricity, telephone, natural gas, cable and satellite services. The City provides water and sewer services and fire and police protection.

Vision for 2050

Over the past several years, Buhl's population has remained somewhat constant at around 4,000. However, the population outside the incorporated city but within the city's area of impact is growing. This growth is coming from the expansion of the businesses in and around Buhl and the spillover effect of being located near the faster growing city of Twin Falls, which is growing over three percent annually.

Over the next four decades, Buhl's average rate of growth could approach one percent annually. Should that occur, by 2050 Buhl's population could approximate 6,000.

The city's strategic plan anticipates this moderate rate of growth. City leaders will routinely upgrade existing systems and infrastructure to meet the needs and desires of the citizens as well as accommodate growth.

By 2050 the community will be more diverse in age, ethnicity and religious groups. It will be a haven for those looking for a beautiful and progressive place in which to retire. The businesses in and around the city will provide interesting jobs for young people to work, recreate and raise their families. Youth involvement will continue to be an important part of the community, together with preservation of the city's heritage and quality of life.

Mayors

1911	Charles Wetherbee	1953	James W. Hart
1913	E.W. Byrne	1955	M.J. Ambrose
1915	H.W. Herman	1957	Frank N. Squires
1917	E.B. Johnson	1959	William Aldrich
1917	W.A. Amos	1963	Reed P. Mayghan
1919	Charles H. McQuown	1967	Dr. M.W. Thompson
1920	N.O. Thompson	1971	Theo R. Pence
1921	A.F. McClusky	1975	Dale I. Christensen
1927	J.A. Howard	1979	Kelly Houk
1929	L.J. Johnson	1980	Dale I. Christensen
1931	E.M. Thomlinson	1981	Jim Barker
1935	H.A. Deneal	1985	Claude McKercher
1937	Gan L. Thompson	1988	Tom Tappen
1939	C.C. Voeller	1989	Theo R. Pence
1946	C.D. Boring	1997	Barbara A. Gietzen
1947	Leonard Ahmquist	2006	Charles Sheridan
1949	Dr. Fred A. Kallusky	2010	Tom McCauley
1951	J. Ray Rugg		* Village Chairman
1951	Thomas L. Smith		

Castleford City Hall and Community Center.

Castleford

Statistical Data

Population: 234 *
Elevation: 3,660 feet
Precipitation: 13.5 inches **
Average Snowfall: 19 inches **
County: Twin Falls

Temperature Range – Fahrenheit: **
Spring: 30 to 71
Summer: 48 to 87
Fall: 27 to 76
Winter: 20 to 43

* U.S. Census Bureau Estimates July 2015
**Historical averages

Castleford lies on the southwestern edge of the fertile Magic Valley about nine miles southwest of Buhl. A patchwork of farm fields irrigated from wells and water from Milner Dam delivered by the High-Line Canal surround the city.

Salmon Falls Creek and vast tracts of Bureau of Land Management (BLM) lands are four miles west of the city.

Pre-Incorporation Years

In 1904 the region now known as the Magic Valley was a vast sagebrush-covered desert under control of federal agencies.

In 1905 private investors built Milner Dam on the Snake River, located about 45 miles due west of the city. (*See Southwest Idaho, Cities of the Magic Valley.*)

They built the dam and irrigation canal complex and sold arable land under the provisions of the Carey Act. Under that act, the federal government granted each Western state up to one million acres of arid land for reclamation purposes. The Act authorized the state to sell land and authorize private interests to finance and construct diversion dams and canal systems and sell water rights to individual farmers.

Ira B. Perrine, one of the first entrepreneurs in the region, was the primary force behind the construction of Milner Dam.

Perrine secured Eastern investors. Then he created the Twin Falls Land and Water Company to oversee construction of the dam, develop the irrigation canal system, negotiate with the railroad to provide service and establish new towns served by the irrigation canals. In 1907 the railroad completed its line from Minidoka to Buhl. In 1909 the Minidoka Hydroelectric Dam built by the federal Bureau of Reclamation produced the first electricity in the region.

Ultimately, water from Milner Dam would irrigate over 244,000 acres. Castleford was one of the farming communities created when ownership of the land moved to private hands. However, rather than being named after investors in the Milner Dam project, as was the case in several other Magic Valley communities, Castleford was named after an early wagon crossing of the nearby Salmon Falls Creek.

Balanced Rock.

Incorporation

Castleford was incorporated as a village in 1941. On September 5, 1967, Castleford became an incorporated city.

Turning Points

Irrigation and Agriculture Castleford owes its existence to the Carey Act, the resulting availability of irrigation water and the railroad.

Castleford Today

Amenities and Attractions The regionally famous Balanced Rock – a wind-carved monolithic rock weighing 40 tons, standing over 48 feet high and resting on a 3 foot by 17.5 inch pedestal in Salmon Falls Creek Canyon – lies six miles northwest of Castleford in Balanced Rock State Park.

Several miles north are the nine units of Thousand Springs State Park, which include properties of several cold crystal springs and fisheries. Among the individual units of the park is the 652-acre Malad Gorge Park. Billingsley Creek offers fishing and horseback riding. Bird watching and the annual Thousand Springs Art Festival are at Ritter Island. Around 180,000 gallons of cold spring water tumble over waterfalls and bubble up from the crystal-clear pools at Earl M. Hardy Box Canyon Springs Nature Preserve. Niagara and Crystal Springs are at the base of the Snake River Canyon where large springs burst from the canyon walls. At Niagara Springs, water flows through the traces of state and national fish hatcheries and a beautiful public fishery near an old-growth tree covered park.

About 20 miles north is the 4,300-acre Hagerman Fossil Beds National Monument. Archeologists worldwide recognize the site for its prehistoric fossil and sediment deposits from the Pliocene Epoch. The National Monument's visitor center is in Hagerman. A segment of the Oregon National Historic Trail is on the southern end of the Monument. Ruts made by the Oregon Trail immigrant wagons are still visible from the parking lot that overlooks the Hagerman Fossil Beds.

The Sawtooth National Forest, located about 30 miles east of the city, offers camping, hiking, fishing and hunting.

Economy and Major Employers With about 40 employees, Castleford School District is the city's largest employer. An increasing number of the city's residents commute to other cities for employment.

Education Castleford School District provides pre-kindergarten through high school education to most of the children in the city and surrounding area.

Castleford Post Office.

The closest institution for higher learning is the College of Southern Idaho, located about 20 miles east in Twin Falls.

Health Care Saint Luke's Magic Valley Medical Center in Twin Falls provides for most of the city's health care needs.

Transportation Hard-surface county roads intersect U.S. Highway 30 about seven miles north. Highway 30 intersects Interstate 84 on the northern edge of Twin Falls.

The closest air service is Magic Valley Regional Airport in Twin Falls.

Utilities and Services Private companies provide electricity, gas and satellite services. The City provides water. The Twin Falls Sheriff's Office provides police protection under contract with the City. The city's volunteer fire department provides fire protection. The city's homes and businesses have individual septic systems.

Vision for 2050

Castleford's 1960 population was about the same as it is now. However, most of its work force now commutes to other cities for employment.

During the next four decades, the city's population will grow moderately as the nearby cities of Buhl and Twin Falls grow and more young families move to Castleford to find more affordable housing. By 2050 Castleford will still be a quiet peaceful hometown – a pleasant place for young parents to come and raise their families.

Mayors

1941	William Rosencrantz *	1976	W. Alexander
1944	Emory Bryant *	1978	Robert Sample
1946	F.E. Bybee *	1987	Richard Schlund
1950	Daniel Philips *	1992	Mary Pinkston
1955	Henry Todd *	2001	Rita Ruffing
1958	Gerald Bybee *	2009	Richard Schlund
1967	Richard Featherston	2010	Jeremy Reeves
1969	Carl H. Peterson	2010	Ryan Black
1970	Willis Owen	2012	Twila Crawford
1972	Virgil Reeves		* Village Chairman
1973	E.F. Pinkston		

Filer city offices.

Filer

Statistical Data

Population: 2,655 *
Elevation: 3,765 feet
Precipitation: 9 inches **
Average Snowfall: 19 inches **
County: Twin Falls
Website: www.cityoffiler.com

Temperature Range – Fahrenheit: **
Spring: 29 to 70
Summer: 51 to 88
Fall: 27 to 77
Winter: 20 to 43
* U.S. Census Estimates July 2013
**Historical averages

The city of Filer is located in the heartland of the Magic Valley about 10 miles west of Twin Falls.

New residents are attracted to Filer because it offers affordable housing near the urban amenities of Twin Falls where many commute to work.

Pre-Incorporation Years

Prior to 1811 when the first Euro-American explorers/trappers came, American Indians of the Bannock and Shoshone Tribes inhabited the vast sagebrush-covered lands now known as the Magic Valley. Beginning in the 1870s cattle ranchers used the land as winter range for their livestock.

Twenty-two-year-old Ira B. Perrine moved his herd of 40 dairy cows from the

Wood River Valley to Blue Lakes in the Snake River Canyon in 1884. He had a business providing dairy products and meat to the Wood River miners. However, with winter approaching, he needed a place with abundant grass to winter his livestock.

Perrine built a flood-irrigation system and grew fruit, berries, wheat and vegetables, which he sold to the Wood River Valley miners along with dairy products and meat.

In 1894 the U.S. Congress passed the Carey Act. Under the Act, the federal government ceded up to one million acres to any state that would bring the land under cultivation. Development of the land was a public-private partnership. Idaho would ultimately use 850,000 acres of its allotment.

Filer train depot.

Under the Act, private interests financed and built dams and canals. The State, represented by the Idaho State Land Board, sold 40- to 160-acre parcels of land to individuals, and the developers sold water rights and town site lots. Congress would later pass other land reclamation laws. For example, the U.S. Reclamation Service – created in 1902 – built many other dams and irrigation systems in Idaho. (*See Southwest Idaho, Cities of the Magic Valley.*)

Around 1900 Perrine sought to develop a "Carey Act" diversion dam – Milner Dam – across the Snake River at a point above Shoshone and Twin Falls known as The Cedars. Ultimately, water from the dam would irrigate over 244,000 acres.

Perrine formed the Twin Falls Land and Water Company (TFLWC) and brought together investors in the project. Several Magic Valley communities and places bear the names of TFLWC investors and officers.

One of the company's principles, Walter J. Filer, was an engineer born in Sharon, Pennsylvania. He became the company's vice president and general manager for dam and canal construction.

Walter Filer.

On January 2, 1903, the State Land Board approved the TFLWC dam and irrigation plan and signed the contract. TFLWC formed a townsite and an investment company, platted the new town of Twin Falls and filed the plats with the county.

On August 7, 1905, the Oregon Short Line railroad reached Twin Falls. However, connecting branch lines west to Filer and Buhl would not come until 1907.

Achille Duquesne filed the first homestead claim in the area that became Filer. Two other homesteading families, Rettig and Lorain, pooled their resources with Duquesne and formed the Filer Townsite Company (FTC) in 1905. The FTC named its new town Filer after Walter J. Filer, platted the town and formed the Filer Investment Company, Ltd. The Investment Company opened the town for the sale of lots on April 14, 1906 – the same day Buhl opened its lots for auction.

On November 18, 1905, the Idaho Superintendent of Public Instruction came to Filer to appoint a School Board. The school was established and opened January 15, 1906, with 18 pupils.

Finalizing the site for the business section of town, however, proved problematic. After the plat was completed, a representative of the Oregon Short Line Railroad indicated that the railroad planned to build a rail siding northeast of what is now the fairgrounds.

Achille Duquesne with a team of horses.

Several businesses actually put their buildings on skids, hooked them up to teams of horses and moved them to where they believed the railroad siding would be constructed.

However, a couple of entrepreneurs, the Coffin Brothers, saw an opportunity and bought the entire proposed railroad siding site. The businesses that had moved their buildings had to move them again. They moved them to lots they

Lookimg south from tracks.

acquired near what is the city's present business center on Main and Yakima. John Sommer, a child of one of the proprietors, said that with all the moving of buildings, he did not know where to find his school the next morning.

Incorporation

Filer became an incorporated village on November 11, 1909. On July 30, 1926, Filer became an incorporated city, effective after the election in May 1927.

Turning Points

Irrigation and the Railroad Passage of the Carey Act and subsequent construction of Milner Dam and the irrigation canal systems were instrumental in the formation of Filer.

The railroad was also a critical development. It provided the transportation needed to move farm commodities to market as well as to open the area for further investment and growth.

County Fairgrounds The 1915 decision of Filer city and business leaders to acquire 40 acres of land and then deed it to Twin Falls County for the construction of the county fairgrounds was an important turning point for the city. It made a significant contribution to the city's economic base and prestige.

Twin Falls County Fair.

On September 21, 1916, the County Fair – then called the "Harvest Festival" – opened with a grandstand, horse race track and a few buildings to house animals.

From 1942 to 1944, the U.S. military used the fairgrounds to hold German prisoners captured in World War II. This resulted in the cancellation of county fairs during that period.

Filer Today

Amenities and Attractions The city has two parks built on a total of 15 acres. The parks

Main Street looking east from Union with Munyon House on right.

have picnic and playground facilities and ball fields.

The Twin Falls County Fairgrounds are located in Filer. The county fair is held annually in September and has grown to be one of the largest fairs in Idaho. The fairgrounds are also the center of activities almost every weekend, especially in the summer months.

The historic Union School, constructed in 1900, houses the County Historical Museum, which features a large collection of early artifacts. A blacksmith shop, pioneer house and craft house are available on the grounds for viewing during the summer months. In addition, two ice wagons, a steam tractor, a 1940 Twin Falls Fire Engine, and numerous other pieces of old farm equipment and other items of interest are displayed outside.

Bank building on right, first brick building in Filer, now home to Filer City offices.

The Snake River and the deep canyon that it cut is six miles north of the city and extends several miles in an east-west direction.

On the western stretch of the river and canyon are four separate units of Thousand Springs State Park. These four park units are Billingsley Creek, the Earl M. Hardy Box Canyon Springs Nature Preserve, Malad Gorge and Niagara Springs. The units are excellent fisheries and have spectacularly beautiful crystal-clear cold water bursting out of the canyon walls and flowing into the Snake River.

The city of Twin Falls is on the southern edge of the eastern stretch of the canyon. Two miles further upstream are the spectacular Shoshone Falls – the "Niagara Falls of the West."

The Sawtooth National Forest starts 20 miles southeast of Filer. Downhill skiing is available at Magic Mountain Ski Resort, which rises to over 8,000 feet. The resort is located in the forest about 40 miles from the city on Rock Creek Road.

Several state and federal reserves, monuments, wildlife management areas and attractions are located within an

Homes on Yakima Street.

hour's drive from the city. Balanced Rock, a Unique Natural Feature, is located 20 miles west of the city. The 49-mile-long City of Rocks Back County Byway to the City of Rocks National Reserve and Castle Rocks State Park starts 30 miles southeast in the city of Oakley.

Starting to the west of Balanced Rock are vast acreages of U.S. Bureau of Land Management (BLM) public lands. These lands extend well into the neighboring states of Oregon and Nevada.

The nearby public lands offer a variety of hunting, fishing, hiking, camping, biking, swimming, boating, rock climbing and winter sports adventures to both the casual and experienced outdoor enthusiast.

Economy and Major Employers

Filer is home to several small businesses that either serve the local farm economy or process farm production. The largest of these businesses – with 33 to 50 employees each – are Acme Manufacturing, a manufacturer of farm harvesting equipment; SeaPac of Idaho, a processor of trout fillets; and Apex Container, a trucking and storage business.

Looking west on Main Street in days of yore.

During the past few decades, three factors have contributed toward changing Filer's economy. Technological innovation and farm consolidation have improved farm productivity with significantly fewer workers. Many of these displaced workers resided in the city.

In addition, many farmers owning property close to urban populations are selling their land for residential development.

These events are causing a shift in the businesses that underpin the city's economy. On the one hand, local bean

Filer Elementary School.

warehouses have closed and their buildings have been remodeled for non-agricultural purposes. Retail businesses that compete with large retail stores in Twin Falls are struggling and some have closed.

On the other hand, Filer's downtown business area is showing signs of revitalization. The city has recently become home to a number of specialty and boutique shops including an art gallery, ceramic shop, gift shop, wedding chapel/ballroom, antique store and an internet cafe.

Education The Filer School District provides most of the city's K-12 education. It operates a high school, middle school and two elementary schools.

2nd school building in Filer District, erected 1907. Destroyed by fire July 3, 1909.

The closest institution of higher learning is the 350-acre campus of the College of Southern Idaho (CSI) in Twin Falls. The Herrett Center for Arts and Sciences, a non-profit museum, is located on the CSI campus. Thousands of visitors, including elementary and secondary students, come on campus annually to enjoy and study at the Center's Faulkner Planetarium and observatory, the anthropological artifacts and natural history museum and the Jean King Gallery of Contemporary Art.

Health Care Filer residents travel to Twin Falls for most of their health care needs. Twin Falls has three hospitals, several medical clinics and nursing and assisted-living homes. The three hospitals, the largest of which is St. Luke's Magic Valley Regional Medical Center, have an aggregate of 213 beds.

Transportation U.S. Highway 30 intersects the city and connects it with Buhl on the west and Twin Falls on the east. The north-south U.S. Highway 93 passes two miles east. Federal Interstate 84 lies 12 miles east of the city.

Railroad service is available for freight. The closest airport is Twin Falls Joslin Field, located seven miles southeast of town. The airfield is named after

Filer First Baptist Church.

Sergeant Raymond R. Joslin of Filer, who lost his life in World War II.

Utilities and Services Private companies provide electricity, telephone, gas, cable and satellite services. The City provides sewer and water services and fire and police protection. Solid waste services are provided by the County.

Vision for 2050

The population of Filer is growing at about three percent annually. If historical trends continue, by 2050 Filer's population will approximate 5,000.

During the past several years, new subdivisions have developed, greatly affecting the city's infrastructure including streets, water and sewer systems, parks, schools and fire and police protection.

The city is currently making upgrades and expansions to its potable water and wastewater systems to meet the needs of growth and governmental regulations. These and other upgrades to the city's infrastructure will continue as necessary.

By 2050 the long hoped for event center at the fairgrounds will be a reality. The center will bring visitors year round. The event center will also promote new motels and service businesses needed to accommodate these tourists.

Mayors

1907	W.P. Shinn *	1946	Cecil Macaw
1911	J.W. Tammer *	1947	Earl Ramsey
1911	W.T. Higgenbotham *	1949	R.L. Williamson
1913	R.A. Reynolds *	1951	F.C. Anderson
1915	C.C. Stevens *	1953	Robert G. Brackett
1915	J.L. Edwards *	1955	John B. Storrs
1917	D.H. Davis *	1957	Shelby P. Dukes
1919	Charles McCleary *	1959	Henry Westendorf
1921	Guy H. Shearer *	1961	Walter Schenkel
1923	G.C. Davis *	1966	Ralph W. Pitts
1925	R.K. Dillingham *	1970	Dan Kauffman
1927	W.P. Shinn	1974	Paul Shover
1928	H.G. Munyon	1976	John Glandon
1932	Frank E. Anderson	1978	Elden Ryals
1935	R.K. Dillingham	1982	Perry F. Dyke
1937	Harry E. Hammerquist	1986	Robert Fort
1939	J.C. Musgrave	1992	Russell Sheridan, Jr.
1941	W.R. Higgenbotham	2002	Jay Fort
1944	F.M. Hudson	2006	Bob Templeman
1944	George H. Truitt	2014	Rick Dunn
1945	Lee R. Jordan		* Village Chairman

Hansen City Hall.

Hansen

Statistical Data

Population: 1,226 *
Elevation: 4,025 feet
Precipitation: 9 inches **
Average Snowfall: 20 inches **
County: Twin Falls
Website: www.cityofhansen.org

Temperature Range – Fahrenheit: **
Spring: 34 to 60
Summer: 53 to 85
Fall: 34 to 63
Winter: 19 to 35
* U.S. Census Bureau Estimates July 2015
**Historical averages

Hansen is a quintessential southern Idaho farming community. Its roots go back more than 100 years to when settlers began clearing the land of sagebrush and delivering Snake River water to the deep rich soil. Fertile farmland surrounded the city. A major part of the business community is still tied to agriculture.

However, Hansen's demographic character is changing. Located just nine miles northwest of Twin Falls, it is a growing bedroom community. As the prices for building lots increase in Twin Falls, more families choose to build homes in Hansen and commute to Twin Falls for work.

Pre-Incorporation Years

Before the Milner Dam was completed on the Snake River in 1905 about 20 miles above what is now the city of Hansen, the region was largely federal land covered with sagebrush.

Ira B. Perrine, one of the regions first entrepreneurs, put together a group of investors to build Milner Dam under the provisions of the Carey Act, passed by

Congress in 1894 to transfer federal land to private ownership in a manner that encouraged settlement and made the land productive. (*See Southwestern Idaho, The Region, Federal Land Use Laws.*)

Perrine and his investors applied to the State to build the dam and develop the land. Ultimately, 244,000 acres were irrigated. Hansen was one of the farming communities created when the land moved into private hands.

Land and water rights were being sold a year before the dam was completed. The land around Hansen was among the most desirable because of its deep fertile soil and more senior water right due to its close proximity to the dam.

Supply wagons.

The mild winter temperatures let farmers get a head start on clearing the sagebrush from off the land. By late January 1905 settlers were already planting grain.

Seven miles south was the stage-stop community of Rock Creek. John F. Hansen, a merchant and associate of Perrine in developing the dam, began making scheduled wagon deliveries of goods to the new settlement. He transported the goods from his "John F. Hansen and Co" store in Rock Creek and when Perrine and his associates platted the new community, they named it "Hansen."

In June 1905 another associate in the development, Thomas J. Rauch, filed on 160 acres of land that would become Hansen's original plat. John Hansen acquired the first commercial lot and began building a 24-by-40-foot general store and post office. Rauch was the first postmaster.

Rock Creek Store, 1890s.

The Oregon Short Line Railroad reached Twin Falls on August 7, 1905. Residents throughout the region celebrated the arrival as "Railroad Day." Hansen was a designated train stop on the route.

By January 1906 John Nichols had built a merchandise store, Charles Upton a restaurant and W.N. Rose another general merchandise store that included a post office. By that time, there were also two hotels, a lumberyard and a new brick factory.

The Hansen public school district was also formed in 1906, and held a successful school bond election to build a schoolhouse from brick produced at the local factory.

Since it would take several months to complete the schoolhouse, they erected a large tent. The school opened on schedule in September with Ms. Stella Mores the first teacher of 25 students grades one through eight.

Each Sunday they used the tent for a Bible school that started with 42 members.

Around 1908 Rauch sold the remaining townsite property to a group of Chicago capitalists whose agent, S.T. Hamilton, became the townsite manager. Hamilton ordered construction of two city parks and directed the planting of shade trees along each street. He opened the town site for lot sales on August 5, 1908. The railroad depot opened a year later.

Original Hansen suspension bridge.

By 1910 a new bank opened, and local Methodists built their church. The imposing Overland Hotel, a community focal point, was also built. Entrepreneurs financed a telephone system with telephone lines connecting city residents and businesses as well as outlying farms and ranches. School patrons added an annex and furnace to the school. A second school wagon extended transportation services to the rising number of students in the outlying areas.

On September 5, 1912, John Hansen completed construction of a new grain elevator next to the railroad tracks. At 105 feet, the reinforced concrete structure was the tallest elevator in the region. The Shoshone and Twin Falls Power Company brought in electrical power in time for the elevator's opening. With the elevator, Hansen became a center for the shipment of locally produced grain to distant markets.

A sugar beet factory was constructed in Twin Falls in 1916, opening the door to greater farm profitability and better crop rotation. Rail access facilitated the factory's success.

When the United States entered World War I in 1917, 164 men from the greater Hansen area enlisted in the military. To compensate for this loss of their younger men, women and children worked in the fields beside men too old to enlist.

Incorporation

In 1919 the Hansen Improvement League won approval from Twin Falls County to incorporate the village of Hansen. The petition stated that the population exceeded the required 200 residents. Laverne Hansen became the village's first Chairman. The legal status of the village changed to a city in 1967 in accordance with a new state law.

Turning Points

Carey Act, Milner Dam and the Railroad Following passage of the Carey Act, two events occurred in 1905 that largely underpinned the establishment of Hansen – the construction of Milner Dam and the advent of the railroad.

While the Carey Act inspired Milner Dam is still critical to Hansen's economy, the railroad's influence has diminished. Sixty-five years of passenger service ended on January 4, 1970, the victim of motor vehicles and good roads, albeit freight service continues.

Hansen Bridge The opening of Hansen Bridge across the Snake River Canyon on July 17, 1919, provided a major economic benefit to the region. The suspension bridge, paid with county bonds and an appropriation from the State was 688.5 feet long, 333 feet above the canyon floor and had a load capacity of 106 tons.

A few decades later, the size and volume of motor vehicles crossing the bridge forced the State to restrict traffic to a single lane before it was replaced with a stronger arch bridge, also called Hansen Bridge and completed on September 22, 1966. With the new bridge in operation, they dropped the old bridge into the Snake River Canyon where it was burned.

World Wars I and II and the Great Depression World War I brought sharp demand and inflated prices for farm crops and a period of painful deflation when it ended. Lower farm prices were a major factor in the December 1922 closure of the Bank of Hansen.

The economy gradually recovered over the next decade only to later collapse with the Great Depression of the 1930s. At that time, area banks closed, citizens protested the hiring of foreign farm workers and scores of homeless men were living in a "jungle town" along Rock Creek Canyon.

The federal Civilian Conservation Corps (CCC) provided work replanting forests, building park campsites and improving roads. However, many people still could not find jobs. To top it off, 1934 was one of the worst drought years on record.

When the United States entered World War II in 1940, the Hansen economy again recovered, but at great cost. Many of the area's young men and some women volunteered or were drafted into the armed forces. Others moved to work in cities where there were high-paying jobs producing goods for the war effort.

As in World War I, the shrinking farm labor pool became a problem. Older men, women and youth helped fill the void augmented by German prisoners of war and U.S. citizens of Japanese descent, who had been denied their civil rights and imprisoned by the federal government because of their race.

The military imprisoned about 10,000 innocent U.S. citizens without trial in a hastily constructed internment camp near Jerome. About 2,000 of these internees worked on nearby farms. Many others volunteered to fight in the war against Germany and served with distinction. (*See Southwestern Idaho – Hunt Camp – Imprisonment of American Citizens of Japanese Descent.*)

City Services In the decades that followed, Hansen made several municipal improvements – completing domestic water, septic and fire protection services; park improvements; a library; and new public school buildings – which positioned the city for the population growth that was to come.

Changing Economy Technological innovation and farm consolidation are significantly reducing the demand for labor and changing Hansen's traditional agricultural-based economy. Agricultural and food processing industries are more productive with a fraction of the employees that used to come to town to shop. Today, an increasing number of Hansen's residents commute to Twin Falls and other cities for work.

Hansen Community Library.

Hansen Today

Amenities and Attractions Hansen has 15 acres devoted to three municipal parks. City Park and Rolling Hills Park have ball fields, playground equipment and picnic areas. Dixon Park has a rose garden for more quiet enjoyment.

The city is close to a variety of outdoor activities. Hunting, fishing, hiking, camping, biking, swimming, boating and winter sports are available within a short drive. Several lakes, reservoirs, streams and the Snake River are within 30 minutes. The Sawtooth National Forest begins 10 miles south. The Niagara Springs and Malad Gorge units and fisheries of Thousand Springs State Park are 28 and 43 miles northwest, respectively.

Downhill skiing is available at Magic Mountain Ski Resort in the Sawtooth

National Forest, 28 miles south on Rock Creek Road. Mountain peaks in the area rise to over 8,000 feet.

Several state and federal reserves, monuments, wildlife management areas and attractions are located within an hour's drive. The 2,120-foot-high Shoshone Falls on the Snake River is 10 miles northwest. Balanced Rock is 40 miles west. The City of Rocks National Reserve and State Park is 45 miles southeast. The Minidoka recreation and wildlife preserve that includes Lake Walcott State Park and a 21,000-acre national wildlife refuge is 40 miles northeast.

Economy and Major Employers The city has no single dominant employer. Agriculture-based businesses include bean warehouses, a grain elevator, seed companies and farming and excavation equipment companies.

Other businesses include a grocery and convenience market, cafe, two bars, home storage units and a nearby truck stop and motel. Residents generally drive to Twin Falls to do their retail shopping.

Education Hansen School District provides elemenetary and secondary education. Higher education is available at the College of Southern Idaho in Twin Falls.

Health Care Medical care is available at St. Luke's Magic Valley Regional Medical Center and other medical clinics and practitioners in Twin Falls.

Transportation U.S. Highway 30 intersects the city. Interstate 84 is three miles north.

Joslin Field, the Magic Valley Regional Airport located 14 miles southwest, provides commercial air service. Railroad service is available for freight only. Commercial bus service is available in Twin Falls.

Utilities and Services Private companies provide electric, natural gas, telephone, cable and satellite services. The City provides water, sewer and solid waste services.

Hansen contracts with the City of Kimberly for police protection. The City has made available its fire station and three trucks to the Rock Creek Fire District which provides fire protection.

Vision for 2050

Hansen's population has remained around 1,000 for the past several years. An increasing number of residents commute to Twin Falls for their employment and shopping. This trend will continue. However, as Twin Falls residential lot prices increase, more people will choose to live in the more rural, peaceful and affordable environment Hansen provides.

By 2050 annexation of new subdivisions will cause the incorporated boundaries of the two cities to grow closer together. Vacant lots within the city limits will be developed. Small service businesses, such as grocery and auto supply stores, will locate in the city. Schools and city services will expand to meet growing demand.

A public transit system will connect Twin Falls, Hansen and other cities around the valley. Some industrial and manufacturing businesses will likely develop in the city along corridors that are close to the railroad and I-84.

By 2050 the city limits and population will more than double. Controlling factors of this growth will be the availability of good water and adequate waste treatment facilities. As annexation occurs, ordinances, policies and fees will need to be established to ensure that adequate schools, parks, fire, law enforcement, recreation and municipal services are provided.

Mayors

1919	Laverne Hansen *	1949	Robert Day *
1920	S.M. McCoy *	1952	Norville Reynolds *
1921	J.E. Schaefer *	1956	Robert Perkins *
1923	C.E. Clavert *	1966	Virgil Ball *
1926	John Rigney *	1967	Virgil Ball
1928	M.L. Hill *	1970	Allen Bourn
1929	C.F. Romig *	1972	Harold Miller Jr.
1932	E.G. Marlin *	1976	Galen Stimpson
1933	W.B. Chastain *	1984	Tom Butler
1933	M.P. Kenworthy *	1988	George Uri
1934	Howard Walker *	1996	Joseph Ratto
1935	C.E. Bedow *	2000	George Uri
1939	M.P. Kenworthy *	2008	Chad Urie
1943	L.J. Prior *	2012	Joseph Ratto
1944	J.E. Coleman *		* Village Chairman
1947	W.R. Mushlitz *		

Hollister City Hall.

Hollister

Statistical Data

Population: 274 *
Elevation: 4,524 feet
Precipitation: 10 inches **
Average Snowfall: 20 inches **
County: Twin Falls

Temperature Range – Fahrenheit: **
Spring: 29 to 70
Summer: 51 to 87
Fall: 27 to 77
Winter: 20 to 43
* U.S. Census Bureau Estimates July 2015
**Historical averages

Hollister is a Magic Valley farming community located about 16 miles south of Twin Falls. Thousands of acres of BLM public land begin several miles west. A few miles to the east and southeast is the Sawtooth National Forest with mountain peaks rising to over 8,000 feet.

Pre-Incorporation Years

For millennia, the now fertile Magic Valley was a vast dry desert plain covered with sagebrush. American Indians passed through the plains to get to their fishing and hunting encampments on the Snake River and its tributaries. Early explorers and Oregon Trail pioneers described the plain as a desolate wasteland.

In 1884 Ira B. Perrine, one of the Magic Valley's first entrepreneurs, established irrigated farming and ranching operations in the bottom of the Snake River Canyon near what is now Twin Falls. He had dairy and beef cattle, raised grain, fruits and vegetables and sold his agricultural commodities to the miners in the Wood River

Valley. (*See Western Idaho, Mining – Wood River Valley.*)

In 1894 Congress passed the Carey Act. The Act granted up to one million acres of federal land to each Western state that brought arid land under irrigation. Under the Act, each state was required to create a regulatory commission. In Idaho, this was the State Land Board. Under this law, private investors built dams and canals. The investors also platted townsites and sold water rights; the State sold the land. The law allowed farmers to purchase parcels of up to 160 acres. (*See Western Idaho, Cities of the Magic Valley – Carey Act Projects.*)

Perrine saw an opportunity to irrigate the desert by building a dam on the Snake River. In 1895 he explored the river and selected the site of the Cedars as the location for the dam – now Milner Dam.

John T. Bressler homestead, 1911.

In 1900 Perrine, along with several investors, incorporated the Twin Falls Land and Water Company (TFLWC), filed a claim for Snake River water and applied to the Idaho Land Board for 270,000 acres under the Carey Act. Ultimately, water from the dam would irrigate over 244,000 acres.

By 1905 the dam was complete and the first water was flowing into the new irrigation canals and ditches near Twin Falls.

Heading to Idaho Falls from Hollister, June 1911.

On April 1, 1907, Perrine formed the Twin Falls North Side Land and Water Company (TFNSLWC) to extend irrigation water to land further south of Twin Falls. One of the investors was H.L. Hollister, a mining entrepreneur. In the fall of 1907, following the practice of naming new towns after investors, the TFNSLWC platted the new townsite and named it Hollister.

The Oregon Short Line Railroad (OSL) completed its line across southern Idaho in 1884. This line ran on the north side of the Snake River. On August 7, 1905, Twin Falls celebrated "Railroad Day" when the OSL train pulled into town on a branch line that crossed the river at Milner Dam. October 2, 1909, the OSL extended a line through Hollister to Rogerson.

With the railroad in place, TFNSLWC opened the land for sale. Two special trains ran to Hollister, with over 1,000 people for the sale of lots and land on the Salmon Tract.

Using wooden pipe they piped water for the town from an artesian well five miles away. Property owners gave easements for the water line. The pipe was made of wood cut in wedges with metal strapping holding it together. When wet, the wood

Century-old Hollister Elementary School.

swelled making a watertight seal. In 1978 a well was drilled and the old system replaced, except for the wooden tank which was replaced in 1988.

Five electric arc lights with electricity coming from the hydroelectric plant at Milner Dam lighted the town.

The first building on the new townsite was a bunkhouse shack on the corner of Main and Purdy.

One of the town lots was devoted to a two-story school building that still stands. The first graduating class was in 1912.

The downtown soon had two churches, a hotel, a bank, a telephone office, a drug store, gas stations, lumberyards and several small shops and offices.

Incorporation

On March 9, 1917, Hollister became an incorporated village.

On March 17, 1917, the Twin Falls North Side Investment Company, LTD – a corporation and the owner of the described land of section 28 of Twin Falls County, State of Idaho – granted

Home of Boy Scout Troop 62.

and donated the town site to the use of the public including all the streets and alleys as shown on the plat of Hollister.

Turning Points

Irrigation The availability of irrigation water made it possible for Ira Perrine and his investor group to induce farmers to come to this agricultural-based town. Later, when low water years caused a reduction in irrigation water to Hollister, many farm families gave up and moved away.

Railroad While motor vehicles have now replaced train service, the early development of the community was dependent on train transportation.

Silo on Highway 93 near Hollister.

Hollister Today

Amenities and Attractions Hollister has a city park with picnic areas and a gazebo.

The city is close to a variety of outdoor activities. Hunting, fishing, hiking, camping, biking, swimming, boating and winter sports are available within a short drive from the city. Several lakes, reservoirs, streams and the Snake River are within a thirty-minute drive from the city.

Downhill skiing is available at Magic Mountain Ski Resort in the Sawtooth National Forest about 20 miles due southeast of the city or 33 miles on a hard-surface road.

Several state and federal reserves, monuments, wildlife management areas and attractions are located within an hour's drive from the city. The 2,120-foot-high Shoshone Falls on the Snake River are located about 20 miles northeast. Balanced rock is located 32 miles northwest of the city.

Economy and Major Employers Most of the city's residents commute to Twin Falls and Jackpot, Nevada, for work. Residents travel to Twin Falls to do most of their shopping.

The Hollister commercial businesses and public facilities consist of a gas station and convenience store, two churches and a general store.

Education Twin Falls School District provides K-12 education. The district provides Hollister's elementary, middle and high school students" bus transportation to Twin Falls schools. The closest institution of higher learning is the College of Southern Idaho in Twin Falls.

Health Care The nearest hospital is Magic Valley Regional Medical Center in Twin Falls. Residents travel to Twin Falls for most of their health care needs.

Transportation U.S. Highway 93 connecting Twin Falls and Wells, Nevada, intersects the city.

Utilities and Services Private companies provide electricity, telephone and satellite services. The City provides water and sewer. The County Sheriff provides police protection.

Vision for 2050

In 1960 Hollister had a population of 60. In the 1980s it grew rapidly and leveled off several years ago at fewer than 240. We expect that recent historical trends will continue for many years.

However, these trends could change as the Twin Falls economy grows and younger families with jobs in Twin Falls choose to commute to work while enjoying the affordable housing and quiet rural atmosphere available in Hollister.

The city has plenty of room to grow. Hollister covers one square mile. Most of the homes are in the center of the section.

Mayors

1917	W.A.F. Klusmeyer *	1993	James R. Carmichael
1926	A.F. Craven *	1993	Ed Pagett
1935	J.G. Schwing *	1994	Karla Edwards
1961	M.P. Corak *	2004	Dixie Choate
1968	Charles R. Shepard	2014	Richard Self
1981	Delbert Whitney		* Village Chairman
1985	Steve H. Taylor		

Kimberly City Hall.

Kimberly

Statistical Data

Population: 3,510 *
Elevation: 3,921 feet
Precipitation: 9 inches **
Average Snowfall: 19 inches **
County: Twin Falls
Website: www.cityofkimberly.org

Temperature Range – Fahrenheit: **
Spring: 29 to 68
Summer: 48 to 85
Fall: 26 to 74
Winter: 19 to 42
* U.S. Census Bureau Estimates July 2015
**Historical average

Kimberly is near the center of the Magic Valley about four miles east of Twin Falls.

The Snake River flows about three miles north of the city. The Sawtooth National Forest, with peaks rising over 8,000 feet, begins at the Forest Service Headquarters about four miles south of town.

Pre-Incorporation Years

For millennia, the land around what is now Kimberly was an arid sagebrush-covered desert. American Indians – primarily the nomadic Bannock and Shoshone Tribes – passed through the area on their way to their summer and winter encampments. (*See The Region – American Indians.*)

In 1810 trappers began exploring the Snake River and its tributaries seeking to trap and trade for beaver pelts and map the land. (*See The Region – Early Trappers/Explorers.*)

Beginning in the early 1840s Oregon Trail immigrants traveled along the south bank of the Snake River near what is now Kimberly. (*See The Region – Oregon and California Trails.*)

On November 17, 1884, the Oregon Short Line Railroad (OSL) completed construction of a line that began at Granger, Wyoming; angled in a northwesterly direction through Shoshone, about 27 miles due north of what is now Kimberly; then through Caldwell to the railhead at Huntington, Oregon.

On completion, the rail line connected the commercial centers of Omaha, Nebraska, and Portland, Oregon, creating another transcontinental railroad. Railroad interests had completed the first transcontinental railroad in 1869 at Promontory Summit in northern Utah. (*See The Region – Railroads.*)

In 1894 Congress passed the Carey Act, one of several laws designed to encourage settlement of lands in the arid West. (*See The Region, Federal Lands – Private Ownership and Preservation Laws.*)

Train at Kimberly depot.

Under the Carey Act, the federal government ceded up to a million acres to any state that would cultivate the land under a public-private partnership. Private interests financed and built dams and canals. The State sold parcels of land – from 40 to 160 acres – to individuals. In Idaho, the Idaho State Land Board represented State interests. The developers sold water rights and often platted towns and sold townsite lots. Idaho would ultimately disperse 850,000 acres of its allotment. (*See The Region, Agriculture and Irrigation – Carey Act Projects – Magic Valley.*)

Ira B. Perrine, a local farmer and entrepreneur who produced food for the miners in the Wood River Mining District, sought to bring water to the fertile soils of the valley at the turn of the twentieth century. (*See The Region – Mining, Wood River Valley – Silver and Gold.*)

Perrine attracted several investors –

Old school buses lined up ready to transport students.

including Frank Buhl and Peter Kimberly, iron and steel manufacturers from Sharon Pennsylvania, and Stanley Milner, a Salt Lake City banker – who raised $3.5 million. They built the dam across the Snake River at The Cedars, a point about 18 miles due east of what is now Kimberly. They formed the Twin Falls Land and Water Company (TFL&W) to build the dam and a system of irrigation canals for hundreds of new farms owned by agricultural entrepreneurs who had purchased land and water rights.

When completed, the hydroelectric Milner Dam stood 73 feet high and 2,160 feet long and created a 4,000-acre reservoir. The dam provided irrigation water on both the north and south sides of the Snake River. It utilized gravity flow on the south, but electric pumps were required on the north side. Several new towns and the dam itself were named after some of the major investors.

Downtown Kimberly in the early days.

The TFL&W delivered irrigation water to the farms south of the Snake River Canyon in 1905, ultimately irrigating about 244,000 acres. The irrigation water led to the creation of the farming communities of Kimberly, named after Peter Kimberly; Hansen; Twin Falls; Filer; and Buhl.

Attuned to the freight demands for the new farms and communities that were opening up, OSL completed a branch line to each of those cities. The first train entered Kimberly in 1905. The next year, the OSL completed the Kimberly Train Depot.

In order to bring water to the north side of the Snake River, Perrine assembled other investors and formed the Twin Falls North Side Land and Water Company, known as the North Side Project. They built canals and pumped irrigation water from Milner Reservoir into Wilson Lake Reservoir which fed the Main North Side Canal.

The North Side Project would eventually irrigate 185,000 acres and lead to the establishment of Hazelton, Eden, Jerome and Wendell.

The TFL&W platted the town of Kimberly in 1905 and began selling building lots. The village soon took shape with a general store, a bank, a livery stable, a blacksmith, a meat market, a pool hall and

Kimberly, 1908.

a post office.

Turning sagebrush lands into productive farms was particularly arduous. After families labored by hand and horse-drawn conveyances to clear the sagebrush, they had to plow and level the land sufficiently to allow flood irrigation. After they planted their fields, thousands of jack rabbits spread across the land, devouring the crops as they emerged from the soil. (*See The Region, Agriculture and Irrigation – Fighting the Jack Rabbit Menace.*)

Incorporation

In 1905 Kimberly became an incorporated village. On August 8, 1967, Kimberly became an incorporated city in conformance with the new Idaho municipal law.

Idaho Veterans Memorial, Kimberly.

Turning Points

Irrigation Milner Dam and the complex irrigation system of canals and ditches provided the basis for the founding of Kimberly. The success of Kimberly's agricultural economy still relies on irrigation.

Railroad The railroad provided transportation critical to the success of the city. It not only allowed convenient transportation of passengers and rapid movement of mail and freight, but area farmers and ranchers could then efficiently ship their commodities to distant markets.

Kimberly Today

Amenities and Attractions Kimberly has three parks. City Park has two baseball fields, a tennis court, basketball hoops, a playground, three horseshoe pits, a pavilion, a picnic area and a covered stage. Kimberly Meadows has a playground for kids.

Stricker Ranch, a museum with many artifacts and exhibits of the Oregon Trail and the area's early settlement, is just outside of town. Also known as the Rock Creek Store and Stage Station established in 1865 as a stage stop on the Kelton Road – a wagon road that generally ran between Salt Lake City, Utah, and Boise, and also, after the first intercontinental railroad was completed in 1869, from the railhead at Kelton, Utah, on the north end of the Great Salt Lake to Boise – it is now owned and managed by the Idaho State Historical Society with assistance from the Friends of Stricker, Inc.

The Kimberly Public Library is located in the historic train depot. The library provides an After School Program once a week and a four-week summer program for grade school children as well as a "Mommy and Me" program for toddlers. High school students volunteer in this program as do members of the Kiwanis

Club. The library also offers after school and evening hours and safe Internet accessibility.

Each year at the end of April, the city celebrates the Day of the Child – a day filled with children's activities including a special lunch and book reads. At that time, school children also learn about and plant trees, celebrating Arbor Day and the city's heritage as a "Tree City."

Each June, the Kimberly Business Owner's Association (KBOA) sponsors Kimberly Cruise, an antique car show.

On the second weekend in July, the city celebrates Kimberly Good Neighbor Days at City Park. The celebration includes a parade, dinner in the park, family activities and vendor booths.

KBOA hosts a Halloween Trunk-or-Treat event in City Park for a safe environment for the youth in the community. They serve hotdogs and give out bags of candy to every participant. All of the vehicles pull in with their trunks facing inward toward the park. The kids are able to visit each decorated car "trunk" and receive candy. The association hands out nearly 1,000 bags of candy each year.

On the first weekend in December, the community ushers in the holiday season with the Christmas Tree Lighting celebration. Residents gather in downtown Kimberly for an evening of festivities including the lighting of the tree and the arrival of St. Nicholas on his horse, bringing gifts to the children. The streets are closed

Kimberly downtown revitalization.

to traffic and burn barrels are placed in the streets for heat. The stores remain open, and the Senior Citizens serve meals.

Wilson Lake Reservoir, 15 miles northeast, is a 600-acre fishery that, in 1976, produced the largest perch caught in Idaho – 15 inches, two pounds 10 ounces.

The Minidoka Internment National Monument, managed by the National Park Service, is about 13 miles northwest of town. It marks a national tragedy following the December 7, 1941, surprise attack by the Empire of Japan on the United States at Pearl Harbor when all known Americans of Japanese ancestry living in West Coast communities were stripped of their constitutional rights and imprisoned. The Jerome County Museum in Jerome has exhibits and artifacts commemorating the camp's history. (*See The Region, World War II – Hunt Camp, Imprisonment of American Citizens of Japanese Descent.*)

The 212-foot-high Shoshone Falls on the Snake River – higher than the famous Niagara Falls near Buffalo, New York – and park are three miles north.

Thousand Springs State Park has several units located on the Snake River at various points between Twin Falls and five miles north of Hagerman. These park units and fisheries include spectacularly beautiful spring-fed waterfalls tumbling hundreds of feet from the north rim of the Snake River Canyon and white-water rapids interspersed with crystal-clear pools of water and springs that restore the Snake River. (*See The Region, Distinctive Geographic and Geologic Features.*)

Downhill skiing is available at Magic Mountain Ski Resort in the Sawtooth National Forest about 28 miles south of the city and Pomerelle Resort a similar distance to the southwest.

The 750,000-acre Craters of the Moon National Monument and Preserve begins about 14 miles to the north. There is no road access on this side of the preserve. The preserve includes Idaho's Great Rift, the source of the lava flow that created the unique volcanic landscape. (*See Eastern Idaho, The Region – Distinctive Geographic and Geologic Features.*)

In addition to outdoor activities available in the Snake River Canyon, hunting, fishing, hiking, camping, biking, swimming, boating and winter sports are also available in nearby reservoirs, the national forest and the preserve.

Perhaps the most significant amenity that Kimberly residents enjoy is living in a quiet rural environment while being within a few miles of Twin Falls with its regional shopping mall, hospital, airport and community college.

Economy and Major Employers Kimberly School District has over 150 employees and is the city's largest employer. The University of Idaho Research Center has about 30 employees and is the next largest employer. Several small businesses involved with the agricultural industry and downtown retail stores provide most of the city's other jobs.

Many family breadwinners commute to Twin Falls for employment.

Education The Kimberly School District provides most of the city's primary and secondary education. The district operates two elementary schools, a middle school, a high school and the district offices in Kimberly.

The mayor has formed the Mayor's Youth Advisory Council to inform, teach and train high school students in an interactive way about current issues and the workings of municipal government. The nearest institution of higher learning is the College of Southern Idaho in Twin Falls.

Health Care The closest hospital is Magic Valley Regional Medical Center in Twin Falls. Kimberly has a physical therapy clinic, a dentist office, a nursing home and a senior center.

Transportation U.S. Highway 30 intersects Kimberly. The closest access to Interstate 84 is the interchange located on Idaho Highway 50 about six miles northeast of the city. The closest full-service airport is Joslin Field-Magic Valley Regional Airport in Twin Falls. Railroad service is available for freight a few miles from town.

Utilities and Services Private companies provide electricity, telephone, satellite, cable, natural gas and wireless services. The City provides water, sewer, and solid waste removal services and police protection. The Rock Creek Fire Department provides fire protection.

Vision for 2050

In 1960 Kimberly had a population of 1,298. By 2000 the population doubled to 2,629. Since 2000 the city's population has grown at about 2.5 percent annually. For the next several years,

Downtown Kimberly.

these growth trends will likely slow, as a result of the decline in the general economy, before resuming historic trends. Over the next 40 years the city's population will likely double to around 6,000.

Within the next few years, the City will have completed construction of curb, gutter and sidewalks along Center Street East using a $400,000 grant that it received. In addition, the City has begun a $6.6 million project to replace many of the underground water mains, drilling a new well, replacing an existing redwood tank and installing the city's first electronically read residential water meters.

The City's excellent management of its water system has earned it statewide recognition for the quality of its drinking water and the City's Public Works Superintendent, Rob Wright, the 2009 Idaho Rural Water's Administrator of the Year award.

The City will continue to pay for infrastructure improvements needed to accommodate this growth from existing revenue sources, grants or bonds approved by the citizens. Over the next several years, people will continue to choose Kimberly as their new home for the same reasons as those of the past – they want to live in a quiet, peaceful community where they can find affordable housing near the urban amenities of larger cities.

Mayors

1917	R.G. Wilson *	1958	Willard M. Rees *
1920	J.M. Steelsmith *	1959	M.L. Ledbetter *
1921	W.F. Breckon *	1967	Walter Slaughter Jr.
1927	W.M. Arnold *	1971	Von Nebeker
1929	L.H. Walden *	1979	RosaLea Whitehead
1930	H.V. Newkirk *	1983	Ron Jones
1933	Mervin B. Gill *	1986	Jesse Posey
1939	R.H. Denton *	1994	George McAdams
1947	Lloyd K. Wright *	1995	Jim Sorensen
1947	J.h. Henry *	2008	David Overacre
1949	Frank H. Horsh *	2012	Tracy Armstrong
1953	Audrey F. Graham *	2016	Burke Davidson
1955	Willard M. Rees *		* Village Chairman
1957	Frand H. Horsh *		

Boat docks at Murtaugh Lake Park.

Murtaugh

Statistical Data

Population: 120 *
Elevation: 4,085 feet
Precipitation: 10 inches **
Average Snowfall: 22 inches **
County: Twin Falls

Temperature Range – Fahrenheit: **
Spring: 28 to 69
Summer: 49 to 88
Fall: 25 to 77
Winter: 18 to 42

* U.S. Census Bureau Estimates July 2015
**Historical averages

Murtaugh is a farming community around which, except for the Snake River, lay fields of potatoes, corn, alfalfa hay, sugar beets, wheat and beans.

The city lies near the southern shore of the southernmost point of the Snake River, where the river abruptly changes its southwesterly course and heads northwest toward Twin Falls about 20 miles away.

Murtaugh Lake and Twin Falls County's Murtaugh Lake Park are three miles south of the city. The Sawtooth National Forest, with peaks rising over 8,000 feet, begins about six miles south of town.

Pre-Incorporation Years

For millennia, the land around what is now Murtaugh was but an arid sagebrush-covered desert. Nomadic American Indians – primarily of the Bannock and Shoshone Tribes – passed through the area on their way to their summer and winter encampments. (*See Southwestern Idaho – American Indians.*)

Around 1810 trappers/explorers began traveling along the Snake River and its tributaries, seeking to map the land and trap and trade for beaver pelts that were bringing premium prices in the European markets.

Beginning in the early 1840s Oregon Trail immigrants traveled along the south border of the Snake River through what is now Murtaugh.

In 1862 prospectors discovered gold in the Boise Basin. The following year, 16,000 fortune hunters poured into the basin and then spread out for hundreds of miles searching for the precious metal. Some of these prospectors discovered

Working on the Milner Canal near Murtaugh. Courtesy of www.waterarchives.org.

deposits of placer gold along the Snake River near what is now Murtaugh. At the same time, entrepreneurs began building ferries across the river. One of these river crossings was Starrhs Ferry. The ferry's southern landing was near the mouth of Dry Creek. There a small settlement named Drytown developed.

On November 17, 1884, the Oregon Short Line Railroad (OSL) completed construction of a segment of railroad line that began at Granger, Wyoming; angled in a northwesterly direction through Shoshone, 35 miles north of what is now Murtaugh, and Caldwell; before ending in Huntington, Oregon.

Upon completion, the rail line connected the commercial centers of Omaha, Nebraska, and Portland, Oregon, creating another transcontinental railroad. Railroad interests completed the first transcontinental railroad in 1869 at Promontory Summit in northern Utah.

In 1894 Congress passed the Carey Act, one

Hall's Market, General Merchandise Store, circa 1944.

of several laws designed to encourage settlement of lands in the arid West. (*See Southwestern Idaho – Federal Land Reclamation Laws and Cities of the Magic Valley – Carey Act Projects.*)

Under the Carey Act, the federal government ceded up to one million acres to any state that would bring the land under cultivation under a public-private partnership. Private interests financed and built dams and canals. The State sold parcels of land, 40 to 160 acres, to individuals. In Idaho, the Idaho State Land Board represented State interests. The developers sold water rights and often platted towns and sold townsite lots. Idaho would ultimately use 850,000 acres of its allotment.

Around 1900 Ira B. Perrine, a local farmer and entrepreneur who produced food for the miners in the Wood River Mining District, sought to develop a "Carey Act" diversion dam – Milner Dam – across the Snake River at The Cedars, a point about eight miles northeast of what is now Murtaugh.

Perrine formed the Twin Falls Land and Water Company (TFL&W) and brought together several investors – including Peter Kimberly, a steel manufacturer from Sharon, Pennsylvania – to construct the dam and build a system of irrigation canals to the new farms. When completed in 1905 the hydroelectric Milner Dam stood 73 feet high and 2,160 feet long and created a 4,000-acre reservoir. It provided irrigation water on both the north and south sides of the Snake River.

TFL&W managed construction of the irrigation systems on the south side of the river. Later, Perrine assembled other investors to form the Twin Falls North Side Land and Water Company, called the North Side Project, to handle construction of the irrigation systems on the north side of the river. Mark M. Murtaugh was the assistant manager for TFL&W for dam and canal construction on the south side. They were able to use gravity flow on the south side while the North Side Project required pumps. For water flowing south from the dam, they constructed a canal 10 feet deep, 80 feet wide at the bottom and 120 feet wide at the top.

About seven miles from the dam they built a reservoir they named Murtaugh Lake. The reservoir raised the elevation of the water before it continued into the complex system of irrigation canals and ditches, ultimately irrigating about 244,000 acres. The TFL&W irrigation system led to the platting of Kimberly, Hansen, Twin Falls, Filer and Buhl. It was also about this time that the residents of Drytown changed the name of their village to Murtaugh.

In 1907 the Minidoka and Southwestern Railroad Company, later acquired by OSL, completed a rail line from Minidoka to Buhl. The line passed through Burley, Murtaugh and Twin Falls. In 1908 the railroad company built a depot at Murtaugh.

Incorporation

On January 1, 1932, Murtaugh became an incorporated village.

Turning Points

Irrigation Milner Dam and TFL&W's complex irrigation system of canals and ditches on the south side of the Snake River provided the basis for giving the city of Murtaugh its name and establishing the long-term viability of the city's agricultural economy.

Railroad The railroad provided transportation critical to the success of the city. It not only allowed convenient transportation of passengers and rapid movement of mail and freight, but area farmers and ranchers could efficiently ship their commodities to market.

Murtaugh Today

Amenities and Attractions Murtaugh Lake and Twin Falls County's Murtaugh Lake Park are a popular fishery and recreation area.

Ranch near Murtaugh.

Perhaps the most significant amenity Murtaugh residents enjoy is living in a quiet rural environment while being within a half hour drive from the regional commerce center of Twin Falls with its shopping malls, hospital, airport and community college.

The 212-foot-high Shoshone Falls on the Snake River – higher than the famous Niagara Falls near Buffalo, New York – and park are 18 miles northwest.

Downhill skiing is available at Magic Mountain Ski Resort in the Sawtooth National Forest about 25 miles south.

Economy and Major Employers The city's commerce district consists of a few small businesses and a convenience store. Many residents commute to Twin Falls to work, shop and do business.

Education Hansen School District provides K-12 education for the city's children. Higher education is available at the College of Southern Idaho in Twin Falls.

Health Care The closest hospital is Magic Valley Regional Medical Center in Twin Falls.

Transportation U.S. Highway 30 passes two miles south of the city. The closest Interstate 84 interchange is about 15 miles northwest, three miles north of Hansen. The closest full-service airport is Joslin Field-Magic Valley Regional Airport in Twin Falls.

Utilities and Services Private companies provide electricity, telephone, satellite and wireless services. The City provides water and sewer services and fire and police protection.

Vision for 2050

In 1960 Murtaugh had a population of 214. By 1970 the population had fallen to 124. Since 1990 the city's population has held somewhat steady at between 134 and 150. Historical trends will likely continue. In 2050 Murtaugh's population will likely not exceed 200.

Aerial view of Twin Falls.

Twin Falls

Statistical Data

Population: 46,528 *
Elevation: 3,729 feet
Precipitation: 9 inches **
Average Snowfall: 19 inches **
County: Twin Falls
Website: www.tfid.org

Temperature Range – Fahrenheit: **
Spring: 29 to 70
Summer: 51 to 88
Fall: 27 to 77
Winter: 20 to 43
* U.S. Census Bureau Estimates July 2015
**Historical averages

The city of Twin Falls is in the heart of Idaho's Magic Valley on the southern rim of the Snake River Canyon. Shoshone Falls, the "Niagara of the West," is five miles east of the city. The City owns the beautiful park overlooking the 212-foot-high, 900-foot-wide falls. Upstream from Shoshone Falls is the 180-foot-high Twin Falls, from which the city derived its name.

Thousands of acres of farmland interspersed occasionally with open high desert terrain form a patchwork of color and texture around the city.

The Perrine Memorial Bridge is the northern gateway into the city from Interstate 84. The 1,500-foot-long bridge crosses the Snake River Canyon with its basalt rock cliffs that drop sharply then grade out to the Snake River, flowing 486 feet below. A visitors center and parking area at the south end of the bridge are an access point to a system of canyon trails with spectacular overlooks.

Across the Snake River about 10 miles west begin the nine units of the fabulous Thousand Springs State Park. For over 30 miles, several million gallons of cold crystal-clear water of the giant Snake River Aquifer burst from springs and the high walls of the canyon into the Snake River.

Twin Falls is a regional center for commerce and home to the College of Southern Idaho.

Pre-Incorporation Years

Prior to 1811 when the first explorers and trappers came into the region, bands of Bannock and Shoshone Indians wintered in the Snake River Canyon. During the annual salmon migrations, they came to the Snake River below Shoshone Falls to catch and dry the big fish. (*See The Region, American Indians.*)

In 1811 Wilson Price Hunt, in the employ of the American Fur Company, led a party of 62 men, one woman and two

View of Twin Falls from Bickel School, looking west.

children up the Missouri River, across what is now Wyoming and Jackson Hole and into Idaho's Teton Basin. Believing they could float the Snake River to the Columbia River and the Pacific Ocean, they built 15 large canoes from cottonwood trees; left their horses, a decision they would later regret; and set off downriver.

They portaged around what is now Idaho Falls and American Falls, but then encountered the treacherous rapids and waterfalls west of what is now Twin Falls. There, they lost one man and a canoe loaded with supplies. They scouted the river ahead for over 35 miles and saw so many waterfalls and rapids that they abandoned their canoes and set out on foot to the Columbia River. Their description of the land as a place to settle was not favorable. (*See The Region, Early Trappers/Explorers.*)

Three decades later, Captain John C. Fremont, a trained surveyor for the military, led a 39-member exploration and survey detachment to Oregon. Their route took them through Idaho. On

Main Avenue looking southeast from Shoshone Street.

September 28, 1843, Fremont's party camped at Rock Creek, about six miles south of what is now Twin Falls.

Future Oregon Trail immigrants benefited greatly from Fremont's detailed maps – published by Congress with descriptions of the terrain, including landmarks and the locations of good campsites. (*See The Region, Oregon and California Trails.*)

Major Osborne Cross, a veteran of the Mexican War, led a military exploration party along the Oregon Trail five years later. On August 15, 1849, two members of Cross' party, Lieutenant Lindsay and George Gibbs, went with the party's guide to explore the great waterfalls. Lindsay named the waterfalls Shoshone Falls and Gibbs made a pencil sketch – the first known picture of Shoshone Falls.

Wagon and stagecoach traffic through the Twin Falls area increased dramatically following the discovery of gold in the Boise Basin in 1862. Sixteen thousand people flooded into the basin the following year, with many spreading out and making additional discoveries throughout the region. (*See The Region, Mining.*)

Responding to pleas for protection four months after the creation of Idaho Territory on March 4, 1863, the U.S. Army established Fort Boise on a bench overlooking the Boise River. The original Fort Boise,

Hogt High School, 1922.

a trading post and Oregon Trail landmark 40 miles west near what is now Parma, had been destroyed by flood a few years earlier. Three days after the fort was founded, merchants and settlers platted a town nearby and named it Boise City. The Territorial Legislature made Boise City the permanent territorial capital on December 7, 1864. (*See The Region, Idaho Territory – Territorial Capitals – Lewiston and Boise.*)

In March 1864 Ben Holladay obtained a contract to deliver mail three times a week between Salt Lake City, Utah Territory, through Boise to Fort Walla Walla in Washington Territory. One of his stage stops was at Rock Creek, about six miles southeast of the future site of Twin Falls.

James Bascom built the Rock Creek Store and Stage Station in 1865. In 1877 he sold the property to Herman Stricker and his partner, and the station became known as the Stricker Store and Homesite.

The Rock Creek Stage Station is the oldest building in Twin Falls County and is now managed by the Idaho State Historical Society and the Friends of Stricker volunteers.

The Oregon Short Line (OSL) began constructing a rail line in 1881 from the Granger, Wyoming, railhead. The line angled across Idaho in a northwesterly direction through Pocatello, Shoshone and Caldwell to the western rail head just across the Snake River at Huntington, Oregon. The rail line was completed on November 17, 1884. Trains could now travel from Omaha, Nebraska, to Portland, Oregon, in less than four days. (*See The Region, Railroads.*)

In 1883 the OSL interrupted construction of its main line to extend a 50-mile spur from Shoshone to the 3,000 miners working the silver-lead mines and smelters in the Wood River Valley cities of Bellevue, Hailey and Ketchum. (*See The Region, Mining – Wood River Valley – Silver and Lead.*)

To encourage passenger traffic, the OSL promoted Shoshone Falls as a tourist attraction. Tourists would get off the train at the Shoshone Depot and travel 26 miles by stagecoach to Shoshone Falls. Entrepreneurs built a ferry and hotel on the south side of the falls where the view was more spectacular. They also built an eight-mile toll road to the growing community of Rock Creek.

Ira B. Perrine, a 22-year-old entrepreneur, sold dairy products and meat to the Wood River Valley miners. With winter approaching, he moved his herd of 40 dairy cows from the Wood River area to Blue Lakes in the Snake River Canyon in the fall of 1884. He needed a warmer place with abundant grass for his livestock.

Perrine Memorial Bridge.

The land he settled had two crystal-clear lakes fed by underground springs – the present site of Blue Lakes Country Club on the west side of Perrine Bridge. Perrine built a gravity-flow irrigation system; planted fruit trees; and grew fruit, berries, wheat and vegetables for sale in the Wood River Valley. Perrine's Blue Lakes Fruit Ranch ultimately covered 1,000 acres.

The U.S. Congress passed the Carey Act in 1894, ceding up to a million acres to any state that would bring arid public land under cultivation. Development of the land was a public-private partnership. Idaho would ultimately use 850,000 acres of its allotment.

Upon approval of a Carey Act Project, private developers financed and built dams and canals. The State, represented by the Idaho State Land Board, sold up to 160-acre parcels of land to the settlers. The developers sold water rights and town site lots. Congress would later pass other land reclamation laws including the establishment of the U.S. Reclamation Service in 1902, which built many other dams and irrigation systems in Idaho. (*See The Region, Federal Lands – Private*

Ownership and Preservation Laws.)

At the turn of the century, Perrine prepared to develop a Carey Act diversion dam – Milner Dam – on the Snake River at a place known as The Cedars 35 miles upriver from his Blue Lakes farm.

Perrine formed the Twin Falls Land and Water Company (TFLWC) and brought together investors who included men whose names were Buhl, Hansen, Kimberly and Milner after whom certain cities and prominent places in the Magic Valley were named. Ultimately, water from the dam would provide gravity-flow water to irrigate over 244,000 acres on the south side of the river and, later, pump water to irrigate an additional 185,000 acres on the north side where other cities such as Jerome, Hazelton, Eden and Wendell were founded. (*See The Region, Agriculture and Irrigation – Carey Act Projects.*)

The State Land Board approved the TFLWC dam and irrigation plan and signed the contract on January 2, 1903. Among other things, TFLWC acquired a 640-acre section allowed under the Act; formed a townsite and an investment company; platted the new town of Twin Falls; and, in October 1904, filed the plat with the County – at that time, Twin Falls was in Cassia County. The county seat was in Albion.

John Hays, the man who surveyed the Twin Falls town site, did not design the streets on a north/south axis. He angled the streets so they followed the gradient of the land to facilitate irrigation, drainage and sewer construction. The street alignment also allowed the sun to shine on all four sides of a house over the course of a day.

By the end of 1904 there were about 75 buildings in the town including the Perrine and Burton General Merchandise Company on the corner of Main and Shoshone Streets. As the Milner Dam and canal system neared its completion in 1905, building lots sold rapidly. For example, during a 10-day period in February 1905, the townsite company sold 165 lots.

James H. Hawley, in his 1920 book History of Idaho, *The Gem of the Mountains,* referenced an unnamed newspaper article and photograph of Twin Falls in 1904 compared to 1912. He said in 1904 the city "consisted of one large, ornate shanty with porch attached and a tent in the rear." By 1912 a person could 'stand on the cement sidewalk in front of his residence on Seventh Avenue North and look down Shoshone Street for over a mile, and...see a...paved street lined with magnificent shade trees. A city park two blocks distant fronted by the finest courthouse in Idaho, a $250,000 high school building and prosperous homes....[a block away from the residence he could] hold up two fingers and flag an electric car to take him out to Shoshone Falls, the greatest scenic wonder of the West."

CITY OF
TWIN FALLS
PEOPLE SERVING PEOPLE

Incorporation

On April 13, 1905, Twin Falls became an incorporated village with over 2,000 people living in the town, including some 500 in tent houses at the bottom of Rock Creek Canyon.

Above the canyon, hotels and boarding houses provided lodging. On March 18, 1907, the Village of Twin Falls became a city of the second class, and on January 1, 1952, its legal status changed to a city of the first class.

Farmers seemed to work around the clock clearing the land and planting their crops. During that time, merchants remained open until 10 p.m. seven days a week to accommodate the settlers.

The Oregon Short Line Railroad's branch rail line from Minidoka reached Twin Falls on August 7, 1905. People came from all around for the great celebration called Railroad Day.

Turning Points

Milner Dam and the Railroad Twin Falls owes its origins to two important factors that occurred at about the same time – the railroad and the construction of the hydroelectric Milner Dam and its complex system of irrigation canals and ditches. In addition to providing electrical power, the dam allowed farmers to convert vast acreages of sagebrush desert into an agricultural oasis.

Due to the almost magical transformation of the land from sagebrush to a fertile plain plus his desire to strike a unified concept for the area, R. S. Tofflemire – publisher of the Twin Falls News and the Idaho Evening Times – coined the term "Magic Valley" to describe the productive region.

The railroad provided the transportation system that allowed commerce to flourish. In September 1905 sheep ranchers shipped 4,000 head of sheep to Chicago – the first major shipment of livestock from Twin Falls.

The railroad coupled with the production of agricultural commodities fostered construction of elevators and warehouses near the railroad for the storage and shipment of commodities.

County Seat The Idaho Legislature split off Twin Falls County from Cassia County on February 21, 1907, and named Twin Falls as the county seat. This provided the city with a relatively small but stable employment base and increased its prestige as a regional center for government and commerce.

Electricity The Great Shoshone & Twin Falls Power Company, with Ira B. Perrine as vice president, brought electricity to the city from Shoshone Falls in 1907. With this critical improvement, Twin Falls was able to became a modern city. The Great Shoshone & Twin Falls Power Company later merged into Idaho Power Company.

Bridges and Roads One of Twin Falls' major barriers to commerce was the difficulty in crossing the Snake River and Rock Creek Canyon. In 1919 the bridge over the Snake River near Hansen was completed, but it was 10 miles east and not convenient.

A year later, the bridge over Rock Creek opened. In September 1927 a toll bridge, named after Ira B. Perrine, crossed the Snake River Canyon leading into Twin Falls. The bridge was 27 feet wide, 502 feet high and 1,400 feet long.

Downtown Twin Falls.

Interstate 84 was under construction on the north side of the Snake River Canyon in 1966. It was important that Twin Falls have truck access to the freeway. However, inspections of the Perrine Bridge disclosed structural deficiencies requiring truck weight restrictions. A decade later, the matter was resolved when the new four-lane Perrine Memorial Bridge replaced the old one.

The Great Depression and World War II After the Great Depression hit Twin Falls in 1931, the community's struggle to maintain a viable economy was compounded by extreme drought. However, within a few years the weather had improved and new jobs helped reinvigorate the city's economy. In 1935 Idaho Power Company built a power plant upriver from Shoshone Falls at Twin Falls. The next year Amalgamated Sugar reopened its Twin Falls factory, which had been closed for three years.

World War II caused a major change in the farm and business labor pool. Most of the male workforce left to fight in the war, creating a labor shortage which required women and older men to work the fields.

In February 1942 the U.S. military issued a proclamation requiring all persons of Japanese ancestry living in Western Coastal states to immediately dispose of their property and report to authorities. Nearly 10,000 of the 110,000 displaced Japanese-Americans were sent to the Minidoka Relocation Center, known as Hunt Camp, about 12 miles northeast of Twin Falls off State Highway 25.

Many of these disenfranchised citizens initially worked on nearby farms. However, many of the Japanese-American men, despite the terrible treatment they and their families received at the hands of their government, enlisted in the U.S. military, and many lost their lives fighting in Europe for their country. (*See The*

517

Region, World War II, Hunt Camp – Imprisonment of American Citizens of Japanese Descent.)

The College of Southern Idaho In 1965 the voters in Twin Falls and Jerome Counties established the College of Southern Idaho (CSI) in the city of Twin Falls. The college has had a profound positive effect on the economy, quality of life and culture of Magic Valley citizens.

Twin Falls Today

Amenities and Attractions The city of Twin Falls has over 14 parks on 650 acres. Park facilities include flower gardens, athletic fields, a skate park, a swimming pool, wildlife habitat, locations for picnicking and children's play equipment areas.

In 2003 the city purchased over 500 acres of Snake River Canyon land

Chobani groundbreaking.

along the 30-foot-high Augur Falls at the end of Canyon Springs Road west of the city's wastewater treatment plant. The Auger Falls Heritage Park serves recreational and wetland purposes and is a demonstration project for reusing municipal wastewater.

The city has five golf courses including Blue Lakes Country Club in the Snake River Canyon at the northern entrance to the city on the west side of Perrine Memorial Bridge. The county's Centennial Waterfront Park, the home of the annual "Jazz in the Canyon" concert series, is near the Blue Lakes Country Club.

The Perrine Memorial Bridge is an attraction for BASE (Bridges, Antennae, Spans and Earth) jumpers. These bungee-cord jumpers use the bridge as a launch point for their "Xtreme" sport. Their use of the bridge has brought international recognition to the city as the jumpers set world records in their sport.

The city and the Snake River Canyon also received international recognition in 1974 when Evel Knievel attempted to jump the canyon on his rocket-modified motorcycle. He came close, but high winds and premature deployment of his parachute caused him to fall short of landing on the opposite canyon rim. Knievel was injured but survived.

Tourist and recreation travel on the Snake River is also gaining in popularity. Tour boats transport people upstream from Centennial Park to a series of rapids called Pillar Falls. Some of the more adventuresome individuals portage around the falls and kayak or canoe the remaining distance to the base of Shoshone Falls.

The College of Southern Idaho has a 350-acre campus in the city. The college has strong academic and professional/technical programs for 4,300 students. A paved fitness trail passes through the campus.

The Herrett Center for Arts and Sciences is a non-profit museum located on the CSI campus. Thousands of visitors including elementary and secondary school students come on campus annually to enjoy the center and study at its Faulkner Planetarium and Observatory, the Anthropological Artifacts and Natural History Museum and the Jean King Gallery of Contemporary Art.

The Magic Valley Arts Council promotes performing, visual and literary arts.

The Twin Falls County Historical Museum is west of town on U.S. Highway 30. The Twin Falls Public Library and Senior Center have new facilities that add to the cultural and educational resources of the city.

In addition to outdoor activities available in the Snake River Canyon, hunting, fishing, hiking, camping, biking, swimming, boating and winter sports are also available in the Sawtooth National Forest starting 20 miles south of the city. In addition, the nine units of Thousand Springs State Park are all located northwest and within 40 miles of the city.

Downhill skiing is available at Magic Mountain Ski Resort in the Sawtooth National Forest on Rock Creek Road. Mountain peaks in that area rise over 8,000 feet.

Glanbia groundbreaking.

Several state and federal reserves, monuments, wildlife management areas and attractions are within an hour's drive from the city. Balanced Rock is located 40 miles west of the city. The City of Rocks National Reserve and Castle Rocks State Park are 55 miles southeast. The 49-mile-long City of Rocks Back County Byway starts 40 miles southeast in the city of Oakley. The Minidoka Recreation and Wildlife Preserve – including Lake Walcott State Park and a 21,000-acre National Wildlife Refuge – is 40 miles northeast near the city of Acequia.

The downtown area is a historic district listed on the national register. The city's historic or prominent structures include the Twin Falls County Historical Museum, formerly the old Union School; St Edwards Catholic Church built in 1921; the Methodist Church built in 1909; the First Christian Church completed in 1929; and the recently completed landmark, the Twin Falls Idaho Temple of The Church of Jesus Christ of Latter-day Saints.

One unusual historic attraction is the giant white sturgeons that inhabit the Snake River drainage below Shoshone Falls. Today, the Idaho Department of Fish and Game have specific regulations regarding the fish.

Economy and Major Employers The city has a dynamic business district with numerous retail, service and hospitality businesses and financial institutions. People throughout the greater Magic Valley come to Twin Falls to shop and do business.

The city's largest employers, with over 800 employees each, are St. Luke's Magic Valley Regional Medical Center, food processor Lamb Weston and the College of Southern Idaho. The next tier of major employers, with over 300 employees each, is Amalgamated Sugar and Twin Falls Clinic Physicians.

Twin Falls has established an Urban Renewal Agency that is successfully attracting new service and light manufacturing businesses to the city.

Education The Twin Falls School District provides most of the primary and secondary education. Several private schools also provide kindergarten through 12th grade education.

The College of Southern Idaho is a community college. It provides university parallel curriculum accepted by Idaho's other institutions of higher learning. It also offers professional/technical programs that prepare students for immediate gainful employment. Idaho's universities offer programs on the CSI campus where students who successfully complete two years of college can enroll in one of those universities and earn certain bachelor degrees without leaving the Magic Valley. CSI has four off-campus centers in Burley, Gooding and Hailey and at the Micron Technology facility in Boise.

Health Care The city has three hospitals, several medical clinics, nursing homes and assisted-living centers. The largest of these facilities is St. Luke's Magic Valley Regional Medical Center.

Transportation U.S. Highways 93 and 30 and State Highway 74 intersect the city. Interstate 84 is located three miles north across the Snake River Canyon.

Commercial air service is available three miles south at the 8,700-foot-long runway at Joslin Field-Magic Valley Regional Airport. Railroad service is available in the city for freight.

Utilities and Services Private companies provide electricity, natural gas, telephone, cable and satellite services. The City provides water and sewer services as well as police and fire protection. The County provides solid waste services.

Vision for 2050

Between 1960 and 2000 Twin Falls' population grew from 20,126 to 34,469. Subsequently, the city has grown around 3 percent annually. If historical growth rates continue, by 2050 the city's population will exceed 80,000.

By 2050 the city's boundaries will likely extend from Rock Creek Canyon on the west to Kimberly on the east. The Snake River Canyon will continue to be a natural barrier on the north. The city will preserve North Rim Park, which lies between the North Rim and I-84, for recreational use. The city's southern boundary will extend to the airport.

The College of Southern Idaho will continue to have the attributes of a community college. However, the courses and degrees offered by Idaho's universities at CSI will broaden to meet the needs of Magic Valley residents.

New infrastructures that will be in place by 2050 include the new Snake River Canyon Crossing between Filer and Jerome County, the Centennial Canyon Rim Trail connecting Shoshone Falls Park with Rock Creek Park and trails from Rock Creek at the South Entrance of downtown through Rock Creek Park and on to

Auger Falls.

In addition, major investment by the professional and financial services businesses will revitalize Historic Downtown. The St. Luke's Magic Valley Regional Medical Center will offer expanded services. Other parties will acquire, remodel and use the old medical facility.

The Twin Falls Canal Company and state and federal agencies will participate in diverting water to a storage facility south of Twin Falls. Through a system of pumps, siphons and canals, the water will serve the new Twin Falls/Salmon Tract Irrigation District, thus preserving some of the city's agricultural heritage and providing a recreational lake and a source for aquifer recharge. Hydro and wind power will be an integral part of the project.

As the city grows, leaders will require that developers incorporate water conservation, open space, storm water management, traffic management, walking & bike trails and other amenities and infrastructure including schools that will maintain the character, culture and quality of life presently enjoyed by Twin Falls residents. In preserving one aspect of the city's culture, before 2050 the city and patrons of the arts will have restored the Twin Falls City Band Shell to its original design. It will have a retractable soft canopy used to shade audiences attending live performances by the city orchestra or other performing artists and speakers.

Mayors

1905	S.A. Bickel *	1968	Egon H. Kroll
1906	S.T. Hamilton *	1969	Frank H. Feldtman
1907	Fred A. Boight *	1972	John F. Christoffersen
1908	C.J. Hahn	1974	Col. Winston I. Jones
1911	Geo. S. Aldrich	1976	Paul E. Ostyn
1911	C.O. Meigs	1978	Leon E. Smith, Jr.
1915	E.M. Sweeley	1980	Henry Woodall
1916	F.F. Bracken	1982	Chris Talkington
1917	A.L. Swim	1984	Emery Petersen
1918	W.H. Eldridge	1986	Doug Vollmer
1919	A.L. Swim	1990	Tom Condie
1921	P.W. McRoberts	1992	Howard L. Allen
1922	J.D. Tucker	1994	Gale Kleinkopf
1923	Shad L. Hidgin	1996	Jeff Gooding
1925	L. Ashton	1998	Gale Kleinkopf
1927	R.E. Bobier	2000	Elaine Steele
1929	E. Bobier	2002	Lance Clow
1931	R.E. Bobier	2004	Glenda Thompson
1933	Duncan McD Johnston	2006	Lance Clow
1937	Lem A. Chapin	2009	Don Hall
1939	Joe K.E.R. Koehler	2012	Greg Lanting
1943	Bert A. Sweet	2014	Don Hall
1947	H.G. Lauterbach	2016	Shawn Barigar
1949	R.J. Schwendiman		* Village Chairman

Old barn near Donelly in winter.

VALLEY COUNTY

- Cascade (*County Seat*)
- Donnelly
- McCall

Aerial view of Cascade.

Cascade

Statistical Data

Population: 919 *
Elevation: 4,760 feet
Precipitation: 22 inches **
Average Snowfall: 103 inches **
County: Valley
Website: www.cascadeid.us

Temperature Range – Fahrenheit: **
Spring: 19 to 61
Summer: 39 to 79
Fall: 20 to 69
Winter: 10 to 35
* *U.S. Census Bureau Estimates July 2015*
***Historical averages*

The city of Cascade lies on the southeastern shores of Lake Cascade. The city and lake are at the southern end of Long Valley, a 35-mile-long and up to eight-mile-wide high-mountain meadow that extends north to McCall. Several creeks and two rivers, the North Fork of the Payette and Lake Fork, flow through the valley.

The Boise National Forest lies within a few miles of the city. The ridgelines of the West Mountains rise to nearly 8,000 feet and border the lake's western shoreline.

Even though presently shuttered due to financial problems, the development in recent years of Tamarack Resort across the lake from Cascade and west of Donnelly has advanced Cascade as a resort community.

Boise is 73 miles south and McCall is 29 miles north of Cascade.

Pre-Incorporation Years

For centuries, Long Valley and Payette Lake near McCall were the summer hunting and fishing grounds of American Indians.

Around 1824 European fur trappers and trading companies began working the area.

In 1834 the British Hudson's Bay Company built Fort Boise about 70 miles southwest at the confluence of the Boise and Snake Rivers. A manager of the fort was Francois Payette, a person whose name settlers gave to several of Long Valley's natural features.

In 1888 Tom McCall and his son Homer arrived in Boise. They had left the rest of the family in Missouri and had come west to find opportunity. Their plan was for Tom's wife, Louisa, and the rest of the children to join them when they found the right place to settle.

Tom and Homer were in Boise at the Overland Hotel when they heard a trapper give the following description of the land to the north:

"I think the Long Valley country is the

Cascade, July 1941.

future cattle country. You just otta see the grass and the fine range up there. Bunch grass belly deep to a horse. And talk about hunting and fishing – why a man can just naturally live off the country if he has some bacon, flour and a few beans. Then there are simply miles and miles of the finest timber that I ever saw – huge yellow pines and firs – acres and acres of them...Payette Lake at the head of Long Valley (is) the prettiest lake I ever saw in all my life – and just chuck full of big fish. Great big lake trout – and are they gamey. Simply aching to get caught. It's a region of mountain lakes – just hundreds of them, and all of them great fishing. I never saw so many deer and other game. And the red fish and white fish run every fall – just millions and millions of them."

By early 1889 the family had gathered in Boise. With two wagons, two teams and harnesses, 25 head of cattle, chickens and household goods, they set out for Long Valley and Payette Lake.

Ten other families came at the same time, but most staked their homesteads south of Payette Lake.

Incorporation

On July 20, 1917, Cascade became an incorporated village.

Turning Points

Sawmills Boise Cascade built a sawmill in Cascade that brought many jobs to the small agricultural community. In May 2001 Boise Cascade closed the sawmill. The closure had a major adverse effect on the city's economy.

State Highway 55 The coming of the automobile and completion of paved State Highway 55 opened the city to increased tourist traffic and investment in second homes by affluent people whose primary residences were in the Treasure Valley.

Railroad In 1914 the Oregon Short Line Railroad extended a branch line from Nampa through Emmett and Cascade to McCall. A principal reason the railroad constructed the line was to meet the freight needs of the developing lumber industry. However, it also had a profound effect in other ways. It opened Long Valley communities to more rapid passenger transportation, freight and mail services needed for the city's future growth and prosperity.

County Seat On February 26, 1917, the State Legislature created Valley County with Cascade as the county seat. This event had a major effect in increasing the prestige of the community and in providing stable employment for many residents.

Lake Cascade As part of a complex of six dams in western Idaho known as the Boise Project, the U.S. Bureau of Reclamation issued specifications in 1941 to build Cascade Dam and relocate the Oregon Short Line Railroad track around the reservoir. However, because of World War II, the construction contracts were withdrawn. In 1946 Reclamation reissued  the contracts and the contractor, Morrison-Knudsen Company, completed the project in 1948. The 107-foot-high and 785-foot-long dam is located on the northern edge of the city and creates a reservoir that is about 16 miles long and up to five miles wide.

Cascade Reservoir, renamed Lake Cascade in 2004, changed the principal economic base of the city from agriculture to recreation and tourism.

Lake Cascade State Park The 4,450-acre Lake Cascade State Park was created by Idaho Parks and Recreation on the southwest side of the lake. The park – including camping and restroom facilities, hard paths and boat docks – further added to the city's reputation as a recreation center.

Tamarack Resort Tamarack Resort, a four-season mountain resort located on the west side of Lake Cascade across from Donnelly, began operations in 2003. The complex is still under construction and includes ski runs on West Mountain, a clubhouse, a golf course, condominiums and executive homes. The resort had a profound effect on tourist traffic and raising property values. However, the economic downturn of 2008 and the inability of the developers to service their debt brought completion of the complex to a halt, causing the development to file for bankruptcy. The failure of the development had a significant adverse effect on Cascade's economy.

Cascade Today

Amenities and Attractions Lake Cascade State Park is a major attraction bringing thousands of visitors from the Treasure Valley each year. They come to go boating, sailing, windsurfing, and fishing.

Although presently shuttered, Tamarack Resort still has certain venues open for business. When open, skiers enjoy the 7,700-foot summit with 2,800-foot vertical drop, seven lifts, 1,100 skiable acres and 300 inches of annual snowfall.

The Payette River is a popular river for kayakers seeking adventure shooting the river's complex rapids. The Thunder Mountain Line offers Scenic Idaho Train Rides. The more prominent of the rides is along the Payette River between Horseshoe Bend and Cascade.

Economy and Major Employers Valley County is the city's largest employer, followed by the Boise National Forest and the Cascade School District. Several downtown retail businesses, the medical center and the City provide most of the other jobs.

Education The Cascade School District provides most of the K-12 education offered in the city. Cascade Elementary and Cascade Junior and Senior High Schools are located within the city. The closest institution of higher learning is Boise State University, located 74 miles south.

Health Care Cascade Medical Center, a critical access hospital, and a general medical clinic provide for most of the city's health care needs.

Transportation The Payette River Scenic Byway, Idaho Highway 55, intersects the city. The 4,300-foot-long runway of Cascade Municipal Airport provides service for light private and charter aircraft.

Utilities and Services Private companies provide electricity, telephone and satellite services. The City provides water and sewer services as well as police and fire protection. The County provides solid waste and EMS services.

Vision for 2050

For the last several decades, the city's population has fluctuated in a narrow range. For example, in 1940 the city's population was 1,029. Historical population trends will likely continue. In 2050 Cascade will continue to be a quiet community providing services to second homeowners and Treasure Valley residents coming to enjoy the beautiful amenities of Lake Cascade, the Boise National Forest or traveling through town en route to McCall.

Mayors

Unknown	2014 Robert Terry
** Larry J. Walters	* Village Chairman
2006 Richard W. Carter	** Dates Unknown

Aerial view of Donnelly.

Donnelly

Statistical Data

Population: 144 *
Elevation: 4,864 feet
Precipitation: 25 inches **
Average Snowfall: 120 inches **
County: Valley
Website: www.cityofdonnelly.org

Temperature Range – Fahrenheit: **
Spring: 21 to 61
Summer: 39 to 80
Fall: 22 to 70
Winter: 13 to 37
* U.S. Census Bureau Estimates July 2015
**Historical averages

Donnelly is located near the northeastern shoreline of the 30,000-acre Lake Cascade, Idaho's fourth largest lake. It is also near the heart of Long Valley, the 35-mile-long six- to eight-mile-wide Payette River valley meadow that runs from about seven miles south of Cascade north to McCall.

The city is near some of Idaho's most prominent ski resort communities. Twelve miles north, near the southern shoreline of Lake Payette, is the historic resort city of McCall. Brundage Mountain Resort is a few miles west of McCall.

Tamarack Resort and Village is located eight miles west of Donnelly. Tamarack is a four-season resort located on the northwestern shoreline of Lake Cascade in the Payette River Mountains. The popularity of Tamarack has brought a surge in upscale home construction on resort property as well as a boom in real estate valuations elsewhere in the county.

Fourteen miles south, on the southeast shoreline of Lake Cascade, is the resort city of Cascade.

Pre-Incorporation Years

In 1828 European fur trappers and traders came into the region. At that time, the upper Long Valley was the summer hunting and fishing grounds of American Indians.

Beginning in the mid-1880s cattle ranchers, who grazed their animals in the valley during the warmer months, and farmers began coming into the valley. Many of those who settled around what is now the City of Donnelly were Finnish emigrants whose country at that time was under the control of Russia.

Old barn near Donnelly in winter.

They liked Long Valley because the open fields and distant mountains were reminiscent of their former agricultural way of life.

Even though Congress passed the Homestead Act in 1862, land surveys were not complete. The first settlers in Long Valley occupied their land as "squatters." Around 1890 the federal government surveyed the valley and the settlers filed homestead claims.

The winter of 1887 to 1888 was mild and animals could forage in the tall bunch grass that grew in the meadows. However, the winter of 1888 to 1889 had exceptionally heavy snowfall. Snow covered the meadow grasses. Many settlers were caught by surprise. Those who had not stored an adequate supply of grass hay lost animals to starvation. Some of them became so discouraged they moved to milder climates.

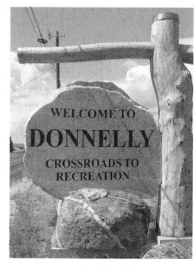

However, as some left the valley others started arriving. In the spring of 1889 eleven families came into the valley. One of these families was Tom and Louisa McCall, founders of the City of McCall. They, along with their four sons and daughter, settled at the north end of the valley at Payette Lake.

They came with two wagons, two teams and harnesses, 25 head of cattle, chickens and household goods.

When they arrived, they met Mr. Devers, a settler who had come several years earlier. There they bartered a team of horses, harnesses and a wagon for Dever's cabin and property. The other families that came with McCall settled elsewhere in the valley.

Tom McCall came to the valley because he was impressed with the report he had heard the previous year while in Boise. At that time, he was looking for a place in the West to bring his family to settle. He and his son Homer were in the Overland Hotel where they heard a trapper give a bit exaggerated but colorful description of Long Valley. McCall related the trapper's description as follows:

"I think the Long Valley country is the future cattle country. You just otta see the grass and the fine range up there. Bunch grass belly deep to a horse.

"And talk about hunting and fishing – why a man can just naturally live off the country if he has some bacon, flour and a few beans. Then there are simply miles and miles of the finest timber that I ever saw – huge yellow pines and firs – acres and acres of them...

"Payette Lake at the head of Long Valley (is) the prettiest lake I ever saw in all my life – and just chuck full of big fish. Great big lake trout – and are they gamey. Simply aching to get caught.

"It's a region of mountain lakes – just hundreds of them, and all of them great fishing. I never saw so many deer and other game. And the red fish and white fish run every fall – just millions and millions of them."

Each summer, cattlemen brought their herds into the valley to graze. However, they resented the influx of settlers and their fences. On the other hand, the settlers resented the range cattle destroying their fences and eating their crops.

"Range-wars" were common throughout the West. Some even turned deadly. In 1905 the federal government established a system of polices and permits governing livestock grazing on federal lands. In 1934 Congress passed the Taylor Grazing Act that further strengthened federal grazing laws.

In 1892 a few settlers started a community about a mile and a half east of what is now the City of Donnelly. They named the town Roseberry after Lewis Roseberry who applied to postal authorities for a post office naming himself as postmaster. In the same year, two other residents, J.W. Pottenger and W. B. Boydsten, built a general store. Pottenger provided lumber from a small sawmill he and Mrs. Sult built a few miles south on the Gold Fork River. Another source of lumber was from a sawmill located about 30 miles south on Clear Creek.

Supplies came in by freight wagon. It took a minimum of five days for a freight wagon to make the trip from Boise.

Strategically located near the center of Long Valley, Roseberry became the largest town in the valley. Within a few years, it had a hotel, a bank, a drug store, a flour mill, a harness shop, a general merchandise store, a hardware store, a restaurant, a soda fountain, a creamery, a brick kiln, a two-room school house, a church and a regional newspaper named The Advocate.

However, Roseberry had no bars. The town was dry because the townsite deed had a restriction forbidding the sale of alcohol on townsite land.

In 1914 the Oregon Short Line Railroad built a line from Emmett to McCall. They built depots along the line, one of which was at what is now Donnelly. Colonel W.H. Dewey, a wealthy mining entrepreneur and one of the founders of the mother lode at the Owyhee mining town of Silver City, acquired land next to the train depot and donated sufficient land for a new town. He named the town Donnelly after his long-time friend and employee, Patrick Donnelly.

The railroad carried the mail and established a post office at Donnelly, which became the local center for commerce. Many Roseberry settlers and merchants put their buildings on log skids and pulled them with horses or steam-driven tractors to the new town of Donnelly. Roseberry became a ghost town.

The railroad provided the transportation services needed for the agriculture and timber industries to grow. The cool weather was excellent for growing peas. The Richmond and Samuel Pea Company used migrant workers in their packing and shipping sheds.

The Boise-Payette Lumber Company operated a logging camp two miles south of town. The loggers brought logs to the railroad siding for shipment. In remote backcountry areas, lumber companies used greased chutes to slide logs to the collection points.

In addition to the pea sheds, Donnelly soon had a three-story hotel, a livery stable, blacksmith shops and two creameries. The town soon had dance and pool halls and bars.

During the Depression years of 1933 to 1940, Donnelly was a popular recreation destination for men working on the federal work projects under the Civilian Conservation Corps and the Public Works Administration (WPA). Construction of State Highway 55 and the historic Rainbow Bridge, which crosses the North Fork of the Payette River 15 miles south of Cascade, were WPA funded construction projects.

Historically, about a third of Long Valley was a shallow depression in the earth's surface created anciently by the North Fork of the Payette River and smaller streams. In 1948 the U.S. Department of Reclamation built an earthen hydroelectric irrigation dam near the city of Cascade. The dam, 785 feet long and 107 feet high, impounded water creating the 16-mile-long and up to five-mile-wide Lake Cascade. The north end of the reservoir backed up to within a mile of Donnelly.

Incorporation

On June 10, 1952, Donnelly became an incorporated village.

Turning Points

Railroad The railroad not only created Donnelly, but for nearly five decades it was the basis for the community's economic growth and vitality. In 1949 the railroad ceased operations and some sections of track were abandoned, including the track between Cascade and McCall. However, passenger excursions between Cascade and Smith's Ferry, called the Thunder Mountain Line still operate.

The gradual loss of railroad traffic leading up to the closure of the railroad had a significant adverse effect on Donnelly's economy. Concurrent with the decline of the railroad, market forces changed the economies of wood products and agriculture businesses. By 1970 Donnelly's population declined from over 200 to 114.

State Highway 55 With the decline in railroad service, completion of Highway 55 became the only effective land-based transportation alternative for commerce. However, even though the highway is beautiful as it borders the North Fork of the Payette River, the road's narrowness and winding curves through the canyons impose practical limitations on commerce.

Lake Cascade and Tamarack Resort Construction of Cascade Dam and the creation of Lake Cascade set the stage for increased tourism in Donnelly and the valley. Development of Tamarack Resort and Village has added to the attraction of the lake and the growth of recreation and tourist industries.

Donnelly Today

Amenities and Attractions
Donnelly has two city parks comprising 15 acres.

Tamarack Resort and Village is the first newly permitted four-season resort in North America in more than two decades. The resort provides opportunities for

mountain biking, hiking, picnicking, fishing, sailing, kayaking, waterskiing, wakeboarding, snow skiing, snowmobiling and cross-country skiing. A zipline, an extreme sport of riding a pulley harnessed to a steel cable across an open expanse, is also available. The resort includes a professional golf course, tennis courts and walking paths from the Village to the shores of Lake Cascade.

The resort's Tamarack Village has numerous up-scale homes, condominiums and building lots in its planned unit development.

The nearby historic town of Roseberry has several restored buildings preserved as an outdoor museum commemorating the lives of the valley's early Finnish emigrants. Each September, an ice cream social raises money to help preserve Roseberry.

The museum complex includes a replica of a fully stocked general store, turn-of-the-century church, school, city hall, residence, farm machinery and museum building. The general store still sells souvenirs, apple mint and other herbs used during that time.

The indoor museum has photos of early Finnish emigrants, farm equipment, logging and woodworking tools, a spinning wheel and a loom used by the Finnish pioneers.

The business office of the 4,450-acre Lake Cascade State Park is in Cascade; however, the park's campgrounds and six boat launch ramps are dispersed around the lake's shoreline. Certain of these facilities are within a mile of Donnelly. Park amenities include camping, biking, boating, sailing, windsurfing and fishing. In the winter, anglers ice fish for the trout, Coho salmon, small mouth bass and perch that fill the lake.

The North Fork of the Payette River below Lake Cascade has over 2,100 feet of fall over the 50 miles to Horseshoe Bend and the main Payette River. Several segments of the river attract kayakers from throughout the region.

The 1,515-acre Ponderosa State Park on Payette Lake is 19 miles north of town near McCall.

The northern boundaries of the Boise National Forest borders private land on the east and west of the city. The Payette National Forest and the Frank Church-River of No Return Wilderness Area lie several miles to the north and east. Hundreds of miles of hiking and snowmobile trails are located in the surrounding national forests.

Economy and Major Employers Donnelly's business district consists largely of small retail, restaurant and convenience stores serving the tourist trade largely attracted by Tamarack Resort and the other resort communities in the region.

Education McCall-Donnelly Joint School District provides public schooling for elementary and secondary students in Donnelly. Donnelly Elementary is located within the city and serves K-5. Students in grades 6-12 attend Payette Lakes Middle School and McCall Donnelly High School in McCall.

The nearest institution of higher learning is Boise State University, 100 miles south.

Health Care The nearest hospital is McCall Memorial Hospital. Tamarack Resort also has a medical clinic.

Transportation Idaho Highway 55, the Payette River Scenic Byway, intersects the city. The highway joins U.S. Highway 95 twenty-five miles northwest at New Meadows.

Light private and charter aircraft use the 2,500-foot runway at Donnelly. Cascade Municipal's 4,300-foot runway and McCall's 6,162-foot runway accommodate larger aircraft.

Utilities and Services Private companies provide electricity, telephone, cable, CATV and satellite services. The City provides water and sewer services and fire protection. The County provides police protection.

Vision for 2050

The recent growth of resort areas near Donnelly has brought a significant increase in city traffic. For the five and a half years ended July 1, 2006, the population of Donnelly, and its sister cities of McCall and Cascade, grew two to three percent annually. However, for the comparable period, the population of unincorporated Valley County grew 15 percent annually. Much of this increased population in the unincorporated parts of the county are due to the development of Tamarack.

Donnelly is eight miles east of Tamarack. Some of Tamarack's employees are building their homes in Donnelly and commuting to work. In 2007 the city annexed a new subdivision, doubling the city's size.

Tamarack Resort and Village is becoming a destination resort rivaling Sun Valley. As it develops, Donnelly officials will evaluate how the cities of Ketchum, Hailey and Bellevue dealt with their growth issues and learn from their experiences.

Currently, the City operates with essentially a volunteer mayor, city council and planning and zoning commission. The City has two full-time employees – a clerk and a maintenance technician.

Since the continued growth of Donnelly is largely a function of rapidly changing events occurring outside the city, projection of what the city will look like in 2050 is excessively hazardous. However, City officials are committed to periodically evaluating infrastructure and service needs and making improvements when the means for paying the costs are clear.

Payette Lake and May Marina, McCall.

McCall

Statistical Data

Population: 3,006 *
Elevation: 5,031 feet
Precipitation: 28 inches **
Average Snowfall: 173 inches **
County: Valley
Website: www.mccall.id.us

Temperature Range – Fahrenheit: **
Spring: 21 to 61
Summer: 39 to 81
Fall: 22 to 70
Winter: 13 to 37
* U.S. Census Bureau Estimates July 2015
**Historical averages

McCall is one of Idaho's premier resort cities. It lies at the base of the crystal-clear Payette Lake. The heavily wooded Payette National Forest borders the city and valley on the north, east and west. To the south are the high-mountain meadows and cattle ranches of Long Valley, which is 35 miles long and up to eight miles wide.

Many Boise residents routinely travel 100 miles to McCall to vacation or spend a weekend enjoying the city's numerous outdoor amenities and attractions.

Pre-Incorporation Years

For centuries, Payette Lake and Long Valley were the summer hunting and fishing grounds of the Shoshone and Nez Perce Indian Tribes. (*See The Region, American Indians.*)

From 1818 to 1835 Hudson's Bay Company fur trapping brigades that included French Canadian, Francois Payette explored and trapped in the Snake River tributaries, including what later would be called the Payette River drainages.

The Hudson's Bay Company built a trading post in 1834 that they named Fort Boise about 70 miles southwest of McCall at the confluence of the Boise and Snake Rivers. The commander of the fort, Francois Payette, named the fort and river Boise after the French word "bois" meaning "wooded." Three lakes near McCall, a river and certain of its tributaries, a national

Early McCall.

forest and a city now bear the name Payette. (*See The Region, Early Trappers/Explorers.*)

James Warren, a gold miner who had been prospecting to the north at Florence, found gold in July 1862 near what is now the ghost town of Warren, 50 miles northeast of McCall and accessed on Forest Road 21. At its peak, the boomtown had a population of 2,000. (*See The Region, Mining – Boise Basin – Gold.*)

Fred Burgdorf, who had mined gold at Warren, acquired the curative hot springs 20 miles southwest of Warren and in 1865 built a ranch with a lodge for travelers making the trip from McCall to Warren.

Sam Deavers, the first settler in the area, acquired 160 acres on the south shore of Payette Lake where he

Tom and Louisa McCall (seated) with their daughter and three of their sons.

built a cabin in the early 1880s. (*See The Region, Federal Lands – Private Ownership and Preservation Laws.*)

Tom McCall and his son, Homer, arrived in Boise in 1888. They had left the rest of their family in Missouri and came West seeking good land for ranching and farming. Tom's wife, Louisa, and the rest of the children stayed in Missouri until McCall and his son found the right place and sent for them.

Tom McCall and his son were in Boise at the Overland Hotel when they heard a trapper describe the land to the north:

"I think the Long Valley country is the future cattle country. You just otta see the grass and the fine range up there. Bunch grass belly deep to a horse. And talk about hunting and fishing – why a man can just naturally live off the country if he has some bacon, flour and a few beans. Then there are simply miles and miles of the finest timber that I ever saw – huge yellow pines and firs – acres and acres of them...Payette Lake at the head of Long Valley [is] the prettiest lake I ever saw in all my life – and just chuck full of big fish. Great big lake trout – and are they gamey. Simply aching to get caught. It's a region of mountain lakes – just hundreds of them, and all of them great fishing. I never saw so many deer and other game. And the red fish and white fish run every fall – just millions and millions of them."

The trapper's description sold the McCall's, and by early 1889 the family was together in Boise. They then worked on the Marsh-Ireton Ranch near Montour – an agricultural community eight miles east of Emmett – through the summer, autumn and winter to prepare for their journey into the high country. When the snow had sufficiently melted, Tom McCall and his wife, Louisa, took their four sons and

Downtown McCall, circa 1914. Courtesy McCall Public Library Collection.

daughter to Payette Lake. They made the 100-mile trip with 25 head of cattle and two wagons pulled by teams of horses and loaded with chickens and household goods.

Ten other families joined them, some stopping to settle in Long Valley. When they arrived at their destination, Tom McCall met Deavers and traded a wagon and the best team of horses with harnesses for the Deavers' property and cabin.

In the first year in their new home, the McCall family planted a garden and expanded the size of their cabin. However, they did not put up enough grass hay for the unusually severe and long winter. By March of the following year, they watched most of their cattle die of starvation.

Undeterred by their setback, McCall purchased a small sawmill, and he and his sons began producing lumber. They built the McCall House Hotel for the increasing number of visitors. As other settlers arrived, they sold lumber and started other businesses. In 1896 Tom McCall's sawmill burned down, but he immediately rebuilt. His property was recorded as a homestead in 1896.

Three years later, McCall platted the four block McCall townsite on part of his 160-acre homestead. By 1900 the town had two general stores, a blacksmith shop, a butcher shop and a hotel.

Tom unsuccessfully petitioned postal authorities for a post office that he wanted to name McCall. He was denied because there was already a post office in the region. The settlements of Lardo, two miles west, and Elo, six miles southeast, took turns as home to the regional post office until 1909 when it moved to McCall.

Incorporation

On July 19, 1911, the Boise County Commission approved McCall as an incorporated village. In 1917 Valley County was created by the Legislature from portions of Boise and Idaho Counties with its county seat at Cascade. In accordance with the change in municipal law enacted by the 1967 Idaho Legislature, McCall became a city.

Turning Points

Sawmills. For decades the wood products industry dominated by the Hoff and Brown Lumber Company, successor owners of Tom McCall's sawmill, underpinned McCall's economy. In 1929 after 16 years in the sawmill business, Hoff left the partnership. Carl Brown continued the McCall business under the name Brown Tie and Lumber Company. One of Hoff and Brown's largest accounts was producing railroad ties which were sold to the railroad.

Brown Tie and Lumber Company. It burned down July 16, 1940.

The Hoff and the Brown families were pillars of the community. Brown's company continued to operate during the Great Depression, providing a stabilizing influence on the city's economy. The mill burned in 1940 but was rebuilt and opened in 1942. It was later sold to the Boise Cascade Lumber Company.

Market forces and the reduced availability of timber caused Boise Cascade to close its McCall mill in 1977. The closure dealt a major blow to both the social and economic wellbeing of McCall.

Little Ski Hill Jump was the training site for McCall's Winter Olympians.

(*See Southwestern Idaho, The Region, Forest Products.*)

Payette National Forest. In 1905 President Theodore Roosevelt created the Forest Reserve, headquartered 15 miles west of McCall in Meadows. However, Tom McCall wanted the headquarters in McCall. In 1908 he offered the Forest

Service supervisor low cost office space in the McCall Lake Street Station plus $80 for the supervisor to pay the cost of moving his family to McCall. The supervisor accepted, the U.S. Forest Service moved the headquarters of what later became the Payette National Forest to McCall.

Railroad The Oregon Short Line Railroad extended its line in 1914 from Emmett to McCall for the purpose of hauling logs from the mountains near McCall to the Boise-Payette Lumber Company sawmill in Emmett. Emmett was already connected to the main rail line in Nampa. (*See The Region, Railroads.*)

Rather than naming the depot McCall, the railroad executives called it Lakeport. However, the citizens refused to change the name of their town. They wanted to continue honoring the name of Tom and Louisa McCall – sawmill owners, postmaster and the driving force behind the early development of the city.

McCall residents celebrated the beginning of train service on July 19, 1914. The train virtually opened the city to the regional markets necessary for its future growth and prosperity.

North Fork of the Payette River.

The Hoff and Brown Lumber Company sold 250,000 railroad ties for construction of the rail line from Emmett to McCall.

State Highway 55. The Payette River Wagon Road connecting Boise with the old State Wagon Road from Meadows to Payette Lake was completed through Long Valley to McCall in 1911. This became Idaho Highway 55 and the first motor car arrived in McCall the same year. McCall was now opened

Hotel McCall and holiday lights in winter. Courtesy Gary Ertter.

to outdoor enthusiasts and tourists, generally traveling up from the Treasure Valley for recreation and to build second homes.

Airport – Forest and Smokejumpers Austin Goodman built the McCall airport for his barnstorming airplane in 1926. He gave the land to the city of McCall, which doubled its size, and contracted with Johnson Flying Service to fly backcountry supply missions for the Forest Service and to begin smoke jumping in 1943. The Forest Service and its smokejumper base are a major part of McCall life. The airport continues to serve the Forest Service and the public as a base from which to fly forest fire fighting missions and to access backcountry landing strips. Today, the airport occupies about 175 acres. It is considered a general aviation facility and is the fifth busiest airport in the state, providing air service to many other cities in Idaho and surrounding states.

Conversion From a Sawmill Town to a Resort Community. For decades, natural resource-based industries had access to federal public lands for grazing livestock, mining, harvesting timber and providing railroad corridors or roads. Around 1970 federal law began to limit access to federal land. (*See The Region, Mining and Forest Products – Leading Causes for Loss of Economic Dominance.*)

However, long before then, other entrepreneurs were using public lands for recreation and tourism. One of the first was "Jews Harp" Jack Wyatt, who had built a house and inn on the lake edge where the road to Meadows began. In 1888 he built a sailboat and then the 30-foot wooden steamboat, Lyda. Until his death in 1907, he crisscrossed Payette Lake hauling supplies for loggers and miners as well as selling sightseeing excursions.

While sawmills were still an economic mainstay of the community, Judge Samuel H. Hays of Boise built the Payette Lakes Inn and Clubhouse. The facility became a community social center with dining, dancing and games. Carl Brown was a popular caller for square dances there and at Charles Nelson's Sylvan Beach Resort.

The Little Ski Hill west of the city opened in 1937 and was the training ground for several future Olympic skiers. It continues to serve as the home of the McCall ski teams. The larger Brundage Mountain Ski Resort opened in 1961.

In 1937 further notoriety came to the city when MGM filmed its blockbuster movie "Northwest Passage" at the lake with the cast and crew staying at Sylvan Beach. The McCall Winter Carnival began in 1924 with ski racing, skijoring, ski jumping and, in more recent years, its famous ice sculptures. Several youth and church groups purchased or were given large tracts of land in the area. Each year, thousands of their members come to enjoy group camping and water sports.

Today, McCall is a first-class resort community with excellent hotels and amenities that attract visitors from around the world. (*See The Region, The Region's Economic Base – Historically and Today.*)

McCall Today

Amenities and Attractions Payette Lake, three miles long and a mile and a half wide, is the city's centerpiece. The lake is up to 392 feet deep, covers 5,330 acres and has a summer temperature of around 56 degrees. Two other nearby lakes also bear the Payette name. Little Payette Lake, a 1,500-acre irrigation reservoir built in 1926, is a mile southeast of Payette Lake. Upper Payette Lake is about nine miles north of the larger lake. All afford opportunities for boating, fishing, hiking and photographing the alpine scenery.

Payette Lake is the remains of a deep depression carved into the earth's surface over 10,000 years ago by a series of massive glaciers. Timber-covered moraines ring the lake with trails leading to many smaller lakes and camping areas. The village resort hotels and a marina border the lake on the south. Hundreds of homes, about 60 percent of which are second homes, line the privately owned part of the shoreline.

The city has six parks on a total of 15 acres and an exceptionally scenic 27-hole golf course. Its Harshman Skateboard Park is one of the largest in the state. The Manchester Ice and Event Centre includes an NHL-sized hockey rink, ice skating, curling and ice shows.

Legacy Park.

Over the past eight decades, the McCall Winter Carnival has evolved into a festival featuring large ice sculptures and other winter events that attract visitors from throughout the Northwest.

Ponderosa State Park, a 1,000-acre peninsula that juts into the lake has some of the oldest pine and fir trees in Idaho, multiple campgrounds and cottages and miles of hiking trails. In the winter, these become a network of Nordic skiing and snowshoe trails.

Ten miles northwest of the city is Brundage Mountain Resort. This ski resort has multiple lifts and an average annual snowfall of 300 inches. The lifts serve 1,340 acres of downhill ski runs that rise to 7,640 feet with a 1,800-foot vertical drop. There is an additional 19,000 acres of backcountry terrain for cross-country skiing, snowshoeing and transporting passengers on snowcats for alpine skiing and snowboarding. Many groomed trails accommodate snowmobiles, including the Warren Wagon Road with its 45-mile trip between McCall and Warren.

Little Ski Hill is two miles northwest of town on Highway 55. This public facility has a 405-foot vertical drop and 18.6 miles of groomed Nordic trails.

Thirty miles south is Tamarack Resort, another prominent area destination ski and year-round resort. It is 7,700 feet high at the summit with a 2,800-foot vertical drop, seven lifts, 1,100 skiable acres and 300 inches of annual snowfall.

The 4,450-acre Lake Cascade State Park is located on the northwestern shore of Lake Cascade, which begins 10 miles south of McCall. The park has RV parking and boat docking facilities. The lake – popular for boating, sailing, windsurfing and fishing – is a 14-mile-long, 4-mile-wide reservoir fed by the North Fork of the Payette River, the outlet from Payette Lake.

In the 1930s the Southern Idaho Timber Protective Association (SITPA), a public-private organization formed to protect forests from fire and disease, set up its headquarters in McCall. The Civilian Conservation Corps, the federal work program instituted during the Great Depression, employed Finnish emigrants to build the SITPA headquarters compound using Finnish construction methods. These buildings are now on the National Register of Historic Places and currently house the Central Idaho Historical Museum.

Economy and Major Employers The U.S. Forest Service with its smokejumper base has 275 employees and is the city's largest employer. The McCall-Donnelly School District employs 180 and is the next largest employer. The largest private employers, with fewer than 170 employees each, are the Shore Lodge, a resort hotel; Brundage Mountain Resort; and St. Luke's McCall Hospital. The city has numerous retail and service businesses that provide a

Aerial view of McCall, 2015.

substantial number of jobs serving thousands of tourists and sports enthusiasts visiting the city.

Education The McCall-Donnelly School District provides most of the city's primary and secondary education. The school district's high school, middle school and one elementary school are located in McCall. These are all recently constructed or remodeled with state-of-the-art computer and science facilities.

The closest institution of higher learning is Boise State University. The University of Idaho maintains the Field Campus in McCall. The McCall Outdoor Science School is an environmental education program for grade school through high school students.

Health Care The 25-bed St. Luke's McCall Hospital, four general medical clinics and several dentists and eye care professionals provide most of the city's health care services.

Transportation Idaho Highway 55 is routed from the south to the west through the town. U.S. Highway 95 is 12 miles northwest at New Meadows.

The McCall Airport is on the southern edge of the town. The Forest Service smokejumper school and private and charter aircraft are the principal users of the airport's 6,162-foot runway.

Utilities and Services Private companies provide electricity, telephone, propane, cable, satellite and wireless services. The City provides water and sewer services and police protection. Fire protection is provided by a regional fire district for structure fires and by the Southern Idaho Timber Protection Agency and the U.S. Forest Service for wildland fires. Ambulance service is provided by a regional emergency medical services district.

Vision for 2050

For the past three decades, McCall's population has ranged between 2,000 and 3,000. However, those numbers do not portray the city's actual population. There are an increasing number of vacation homes, townhouses and condominiums owned by non-residents. The ratio of resident to nonresident ownership is now 40 percent to 60 percent.

These mixed-growth phenomena add complexity and pressure for sound planning and zoning to protect the city and lake environment and provide appropriate municipal services and infrastructure.

In addition to protecting the lake, the declining availability of affordable housing and an overwhelming need to attract lower-paid workers needed to provide services to the community, schools and businesses are challenging growth management problems. A planned community of managed low-income apartments has been added to the housing inventory. A free regional bus service has been enlarged to include neighboring towns.

The city's affirmative actions to address these problems were preceded by consultation with professional planners and leaders in other resort communities who have dealt with similar issues. During a one-year building moratorium, community leaders re-evaluated and updated the city's zoning ordinances and comprehensive plan, developing policies governing water and sewer capacity and instituting standards needed to protect the city and lake environment.

McCall was one of five communities nationwide to receive a Smart Growth Implementation Assistance Grant, which helped in the comprehensive planning of two new areas. The City invested in a Global Imaging System (GIS) for land use and infrastructure analysis. In addition, the City's comprehensive plan now includes smart growth principles that will benefit the city long into the future.

Everyone in McCall, whether raised here or visiting for the day, gains respect and the desire to protect the blue, crystal-clear lake surrounded by forested hills and a beautiful mountain village. McCall and Payette Lake lie in an outdoor amphitheatre from which everyone can enjoy the ever-changing drama of the alpine lake and mountains. Indeed, as N.B. Willey wrote, "This piece of country is worth looking after."

Mayors

1911-1916 Unknown *	1966 Ed Sizemore *
1917 John R. Berry *	1968 Don Boos
1919 A.H. Lang *	1976 Bill Evans
1920 W.A. Bates *	1982 James R. Lyons
1921 W.W. Williams *	1982 Clifford Lutes
1923 Ed J. Peabody *	1982 William L. Crowley
1925 Summer W. Dee *	1984 Clyde L. Archer
1929 Phelps E. Whitney *	1988 John J. Allen
1930 William Bothwell *	1992 Larry Smith
1931 John R. Berry *	1994 Dean Martens
1931 N.A. Carr *	1996 William M. Killen
1932 J.D. McCall *	1998 Kirk L. Eimers
1933 N.A. Carr *	2000 Allan Muller
1935 W.C. Peer *	2002 Ralph Colton
1937 W.P. Gillespie *	2004 Kirk L. Eimers
1941 W.E. Jordan *	2006 Bill Robertson
1948 Ralph Paris *	2008 Bert Kulesza
1948 Glenn Howell *	2010 Donald C. Bailey
1949 Arthur Roberts *	2014 Jackie Aymon
1963 Bob H. Fogg *	* Village Chairman
1964 Arthur Roberts *	

Ranch near Midvale.

WASHINGTON COUNTY

- Cambridge
- Midvale
- Weiser (*County Seat*)

What's at the end of the rainbow? Cambridge Middle School!

Cambridge

Statistical Data

Population: 314 *

Elevation: 2,651 feet

Precipitation: 21 inches **

Average Snowfall: 47 inches **

County: Washington

Temperature Range – Fahrenheit: **

Spring: 29 to 72

Summer: 49 to 91

Fall: 27 to 80

Winter: 15 to 38

* U.S. Census Bureau Estimates July 2015

**Historical averages

Cambridge is a small farming community located in the upper Weiser Valley. The Weiser River flows about a mile east of the city. The Payette National Forest and BLM public lands, with mountains rising to over 7,500 feet, border the valley on the west, north and east. The city of Weiser is 31 miles southwest on U.S. Highway 95.

Hells Canyon and three hydroelectric dams and reservoirs on the Snake River – Brownlee, Oxbow and Hells Canyon – lie about 25 miles northwest on State Highway 71.

Pre-Incorporation Years

In 1899 the Pacific and Idaho Northern Railroad (P&IN), an independent railroad, began constructing a 90-mile rail line from the Oregon Short Line Railroad main line at Weiser to New Meadows. At that time, there was a small town named Salubria located two miles east and across the Weiser River from what is now Cambridge. Salubria was then a thriving community, started in the early 1880s. It had several stores, several shops, a newspaper, a hotel and a saloon.

The P&IN originally planned its rail line north from Weiser with a train stop in Salubria. However, one Salubria resident, who owned acreage that lay in the railroad's path, raised the asking price for the land well in excess of what P&IN was paying.

Another area resident, Mose Hopper, owned acreage on the west side of the river. He contacted P&IN and offered to plat a

Bird's eye view of early Cambridge.

new town with every other lot deeded to the railroad if they built their rail line and depot in the new town. The P&IN accepted Hopper's offer. They named the new town Lewisville, after the railroad's president, Lewis Hall. However, when they applied for a post office, postal authorities rejected the use of the name, probably because it could cause confusion with other communities with Lewis in their names. They resubmitted the application with the name of Cambridge – the city in Massachusetts where Harvard, Lewis Hall's alma mater, was located.

Cambridge, 1925.

With the train depot established in Cambridge, the Salubria business community moved to the new railroad town causing the town of Salubria to dry up.

In addition to serving timber and agricultural businesses, the railroad anticipated significant business coming from mining interests that were attempting to develop mines in the Seven Devils region of Hells Canyon – a development that never materialized.

However, in the 1950s Idaho Power Company began construction of three large hydroelectric dams – Brownlee, Oxbow and Hells Canyon – on the Snake River. The State and Idaho Power constructed Highway 71 between U.S. Highway 95 and Hells Canyon to provide access to the dams, making Cambridge the eastern gateway to the canyon and the reservoirs and recreational areas created by the dams.

Incorporation

On April 22, 1902, Cambridge became an incorporated village. It became an incorporated city in November 1967, as required by a change in state law.

Turning Points

Railroad Cambridge owes its existence to the railroad. The city stands as a testament to the entrepreneurial spirit of Mose Hopper, who offered incentives to build the rail line through his

Cambridge water tower.

property, and the lack of vision of the Salubria property owner who put at risk long-term prosperity for the chance of short-term gain.

Idaho Power Company's Hydroelectric Dams Thousands of recreationists and tourists pass through Cambridge each year because of Brownlee, Oxbow and Hells Canyon Dams with their reservoirs parks and connecting paved roads. This traffic is a benefit to Cambridge businesses and gives the city recognition as the eastern gateway to Hells Canyon. The canyon is also accessible from the Oregon side of the Snake River.

Cambridge Today

Amenities and Attractions The city has a small park under the water tower, Tower Park.

The city sponsors or supports several annual community events. Each August the County puts on the Washington County Fair and Rodeo at the fairgrounds located in Cambridge.

On the first Mondays of June, July, August and September, the

City sponsors "Music in the Park" with an ice cream social at Tower Park.

The first weekend in June, the City puts on Hells Canyon Days with a bull-a-rama bull riding rodeo and antique power show, a farm toy show, a library book sale and yard sales all over town.

The Harvest Festival is held the beginning of October with the whole downtown putting out harvest decorations.

Cambridge has a small museum on the corner of Highway 95 and Hopper Avenue that has artifacts and exhibits displaying the history of the upper valley. The museum is open in the summer and staffed by volunteers.

The 84-mile-long Weiser River Trail – a "Rails to Trails" project that converted the abandoned Pacific and Northern Railroad bed from Weiser, through Cambridge to a point about eight miles south of New Meadows – passes through the city. With city support, in 1997 the Union Pacific Railroad donated the entire right-of-way to the Friends of the Weiser River Trail. The largely unimproved public trail is open to non-motorized traffic – including equestrian – and passes through a variety of terrain and wildlife habitat that borders the river – including desert hills, rocky cliffs and forested mountains. Deer, elk, bear, waterfowl, birds of prey, turkey and upland game birds are common sightings.

The city's most prominent attraction is its location as the eastern gateway to Hells Canyon and the fishing, boating and camping facilities at Brownlee, Oxbow and Hells Canyon Reservoirs. Each reservoir impounds Snake River water for several miles. The largest reservoir, Brownlee, extends upriver for over 30 miles.

Economy and Major Employers The Cambridge School District has about 45 employees and is the city's largest employer. Hughes River Expeditions, a whitewater rafting outfitter and guide service provider, is the city's largest private employer. The city's downtown businesses provide most of the remaining employment.

Cambridge parade, 2008.

Education The Cambridge School District provides most of the area's K-12 education. Cambridge Elementary School and Cambridge Jr./Sr. High School are located in the city.

The closest institution for higher education is Treasure Valley Community College, 54 miles away in Ontario, Oregon.

Health Care Weiser Memorial Hospital, located in Weiser, provides for most of the city's health care needs.

Transportation U.S Highway 95 intersects the city. Idaho Highway 71 begins in Cambridge, intersecting Highway 95 and proceeding northwest to connect with

Hells Canyon, the Idaho Power Company dams on the Snake River and across Oxbow Dam to Oregon Highway 86.

Lee Williams Airport, located nine miles south in Midvale, has a 3,250-foot runway and provides service for light private and commercial aircraft.

Utilities and Services
Private companies provide electricity, telephone and satellite services. The City provides water and sewer. The city's volunteer fire department provides fire protection. Police protection is provided under contract by the Washington County Sheriff's Office.

Cambridge Harvest Festival.

Vision for 2050

In 1960 the population of Cambridge was 473. Since 1990 it has remained relatively constant at around 350.

Unless tourism to Hells Canyon increases thereby causing the city to experience increased business activity, recent historical population trends will likely continue.

Mayors

1902 Moses H. Hopper *	1951 Richard Corriell *
1903 E.V. Johnson *	1953 George Danielson *
1904 Archibald B. Hudleson *	1955 John Harm *
1905 Francis A. Barber *	1956 H.B. Clure *
1907 J.H. Anderson *	1959 Clyde Snell *
1909 E.V. Milligan *	1961 Warren Avery *
1910 Harry T. Brown *	1964 Grant Williamson *
1911 H.J. Devaney *	1968 Jack Gardner
1913 Thomas A. Bell *	1980 Robert D. Wood
1915 James A. Hudelson *	1981 Ezma Pearson
1917 Daniel O. Danielson *	1982 George Wheelock
1919 Thomas A. Bell *	1984 Clyde Snell
1921 A.W. Gipson *	1988 Harvey Braun
1923 Dr. R.T. Whiteman *	1993 Jo Soules
1925 John P. Welker *	1994 Bob Wood
1927 John G. York *	1995 Larry Keller
1931 Dr. R.T. Whiteman *	2004 Mike Campbell
1941 Daniel O. Danielson *	2010 Nanette Rhodes
1947 Ellis C. Peterson *	* Village Chairman
1949 Floyd A. Burgess *	

Midvale City Hall.

Midvale

Statistical Data

Population: 165 *
Elevation: 2,545 feet
Precipitation: 21 inches **
Average Snowfall: 47 inches **
County: Washington

Temperature Range – Fahrenheit: *
Spring: 29 to 72
Summer: 49 to 91
Fall: 27 to 80
Winter: 15 to 38
* U.S. Census Bureau Estimates July 2015
**Historical averages

Midvale is located in a fertile valley that lies between high-desert mountain ranges and foothills. The Payette National Forest and BLM lands are about 15 miles west. About 20 miles northeast is the Payette National Forest. The Boise National Forest lies about 20 miles west. The city of Weiser lies 15 miles southwest. Cambridge is 10 miles north.

Pre-Incorporation Years

For millennia, American Indians frequented the north slope of what is now Midvale, making stone tools. In 1963 archeologists excavated numerous artifacts left by the Indians in their seasonal encampments at the site.

The first white settlers, the John Reed family, arrived in 1868. Reed built a cabin and sawmill and sold lumber to the homesteaders coming to settle in the valley. A community that settlers called Middle Valley began to develop.

In 1881 a wagon train of 40 settlers arrived and filed homestead claims.

In 1883 the settlers joined together to build a bridge across the Weiser River near Middle Valley. While the wooden bridge could withstand spring flooding, the dirt approach to the bridge was susceptible to washout. In 1896 such a washout separated a young couple seeking to be married from the town and the minister. The ceremony went ahead anyway with the minister standing on the river's west bank and the bride and groom standing on the east side of the river. In 1911 they replaced the wooden bridge with a steel structure.

In 1899 the Pacific and Idaho Northern Railroad began constructing a rail line between Weiser and New Meadows. The railroad was a boon to the emerging sheep industry as it provided ranchers rapid transportation

Ranch near Midvale.

of their fat lambs and wool to distant markets.

Incorporation

On July 10, 1910, Midvale became an incorporated village. It became an incorporated city in November 1967, as required by a change in state law.

Turning Points

Railroad The railroad was of major importance to Midvale. It not only provided transportation for shipping agricultural commodities to market, it opened the town to much more rapid mail delivery, transportation of goods and passengers and

Midvale Community Library.

communication with the outside world.

Midvale Today

Amenities and Attractions The city's most prominent attractions are the hunting, fishing, camping and other outdoor activities available in the nearby national forests. Located on Idaho Highway 71, which begins at Cambridge, is Hells Canyon with fishing, boating and camping facilities at Brownlee, Oxbow and Hells Canyon Reservoirs. Each reservoir impounds Snake River water for several miles. The largest reservoir, Brownlee, extends upriver for over 30 miles.

Economy and Major Employers Midvale School District has about 30 employees and is the city's largest employer. The city's few downtown businesses that principally include two small businesses – a restaurant and a grocery store – provide most of the city's remaining jobs.

Education The Midvale School District provides most of the area's K-12 education. The district has Midvale Elementary School, Midvale Jr./Sr. High School and Midvale Alternative School in the city.

The closest institution for higher education is the College of Idaho, 65 miles south in Caldwell.

Health Care Weiser Memorial Hospital, located in Weiser, provides for most of the city's healthcare needs.

Transportation U.S. Highway 95 intersects the city.

Utilities and Services Private companies provide electricity, telephone and satellite services. The City provides water. Homes and businesses have individual septic systems. The volunteer fire department, also serving the city of Cambridge, provides fire protection. The Washington County Sheriff's Office, under contract with the City, provides police protection.

Roads near Midvale.

Vision for 2050

Midvale's population has remained somewhat stable at around 200 for the past 50 years. Historical trends will likely continue for many years.

Economic development efforts to promote additional small businesses and the continued success of small businesses that operate in the city will have a moderate effect on the city's growth.

Weiser train station.

Weiser

Statistical Data

Population: 5,356 *
Elevation: 2,130 feet
Precipitation: 12 inches **
Average Snowfall: 21 inches **
County: Washington
Website: www.cityofweiser.net

Temperature Range – Fahrenheit: **
Spring: 34 to 73
Summer: 55 to 90
Fall: 30 to 80
Winter: 21 to 44
* U.S. Census Bureau Estimates July 2015
**Historical averages

Weiser is located at the northwest end of the Treasure Valley near the confluence of the Snake and Weiser Rivers. It is the county seat and largest city in Washington County. Fertile farmland and orchards surround most of the city and the Weiser River runs through it.

The Snake River forms the city's western boundary and marks the state line between Idaho and Oregon. At Weiser, the Snake River turns sharply west for about 15 miles before turning north again.

The Payette National Forest lies 25 miles north and the Boise National Forest is 36 miles east.

Pre-Incorporation Years

For millennia, American Indians frequented the Southwestern Idaho area around Weiser. Archaeologists have excavated numerous prehistoric Indian artifacts a few miles west of town, 10 feet deep along Monroe Creek. (*See Southwestern Idaho, The Region, American Indians*.)

Thomas Galloway, Jacob Weiser and William Logan settled in what is now Weiser in 1863. Galloway operated a mail station from his small willow-log, dirt-floor cabin. Mail riders stopped for food and a place to stay the night, but they had to use their own blankets.

In the same year, Ruben Olds and two partners received a franchise from the first Idaho Territorial Legislature to build and operate a ferry across the Snake River on the Oregon Trail

Early Weiser.

at Farewell Bend about 12 miles west of Galloway's mail station. The law allowed them to charge $3 for a team and wagon, $1 for an extra team, 75 cents for a loaded pack animal, 50 cents for a returning pack animal, 75 cents for a horse and rider and 25 cents for each person on foot and each loose animal.

The origin of the name "Weiser" – which was first applied to the name of the river, then the bridge that spanned it and the valley – is not known. Some say the river was named after Jacob Weiser, a local settler who came in 1863. However, "Wisers" was also the name of a band of Indians and the name of a river shown on an 1818 map. As immigrants named Weiser came to America, their name was spelled in a variety of ways. It is

Galloway Inn.

more likely that the river was named after Peter M. Weiser, a member of the Lewis and Clark Expedition who, later, under employment with Manual Lisa's Missouri Fur Company returned to Southwestern Idaho to trap and trade for beaver pelts. (*See Southwestern Idaho, The Region, Early Trappers/Explorers*.)

Weiser Valley settlers divided the valley into two parts. The land between the

554

Weiser and Snake Rivers, the location that included the site of what is now Weiser, was called "Lower Weiser." They designated the northern end of the valley that included the small community of "Salubria," meaning a favorable or healthy place and located just west of what is now Cambridge, as "Upper Weiser."

Galloway successfully applied to postal authorities to convert his small mail station to a post office with the name "Weiser Bridge" and himself as postmaster. Residents dropped "Bridge" from the name of their community in 1887.

The town's strategic location on a transportation corridor surrounded by a growing agribusiness community attracted a variety of lodging, retail and service businesses.

The Oregon Short Line Railroad began surveying a 424-mile route angling northeasterly across Southern Idaho from Granger, Wyoming, to Huntington, Oregon, around 1878.

Huntington was only two miles away on the

Downtown Weiser.

western side of the Snake River and railroad surveyors were marking the exact route straight through Weiser Valley. The expectation of the railroad made Weiser an even more attractive location for new settlers who began buying and developing land in Weiser.

When the Idaho Territorial Legislature created Washington County on February 20, 1879, the voters picked Weiser over Salubria for the county seat. Two years later, taxpayers built the county courthouse and a one-room schoolhouse.

The anticipation of the railroad turned Weiser into a frontier boomtown. Railroad camp followers sat up their nefarious businesses in Weiser. In 1882 following two shootouts, Thomas Galloway wrote in the Idaho Statesman, "All the assaults, drag-outs, knock-downs, dirk carving and pistol practice of which we have heard so much has been

St. Agnes Catholic Church.

intimately connected with one or the other of the whiskey mills in Weiser City."

In 1883 as construction of the railroad neared Weiser it stopped south of town while the railroad bridge across the Snake River was completed.

At this time W.E. Strahorn, a land speculator and townsite promoter who developed Caldwell, began buying land along the surveyed rail line east of the present depot in the name of his company, the Idaho and Oregon Land Improvement Company. There he platted a town – which he named New Weiser – and started a marketing campaign to sell lots. Strahorn apparently had an agreement or understanding with the railroad that it would build its depot in New Weiser.

However, when Weiser residents discovered what was happening, they instigated a storm of protest, as they had major investments in the existing town. The railroad relented and in 1885 built its permanent depot in Weiser where the present depot now stands. Located too far from the train depot, Strahorn's New Weiser development withered until, several years later, when it gradually became part of Weiser.

National Old Time Fiddlers' Contest and Festival. Courtesy Shamont Photography.

The advent of motor vehicles spelled an end of Olds Ferry at Farewell Bend. In 1904 federal and state governments financed construction of a motor vehicle bridge over the Snake River that linked up with Highway 201 in Oregon. They named the road U.S. Highway 95 Spur.

Incorporation

Weiser became incorporated as a village on October 12, 1887. Two years later, the town changed its legal status to an incorporated city.

Turning Points

County Seat The voters' decision to make Weiser the county seat after the Territorial Legislature created Washington County in 1879 provided the community with both political recognition and a stable, albeit relatively small, employment base.

Fire The fledging city had a brush with near disaster in 1890 when fire swept through, burning most of the old part of town to the ground. It devastated the business community, but only for a short time as most businessmen quickly rebuilt with brick exteriors. Their show of commitment attracted more businesses. These resilient people turned disaster into economic opportunity.

Railroad The community's economy was further solidified with the decision by the Oregon Short Line Railroad to build its train depot there, ensuring Weiser's importance as a regional economic center.

Weiser got an unexpected boost in 1899 when the small independent Pacific and Northern Railroad Company built a 90-mile line from Weiser to serve the mines in the Seven Devils on the Snake River west of the line's terminus at New Meadows. The mines never materialized; however, the railroad found many other customers who needed it to transport wood products and agricultural commodities.

Irrigation Agriculture was a major component of Weiser's economic foundation. Obtaining an adequate and stable supply of irrigation water was problematic. Developers and farmers made repeated attempts to divert water from the Weiser River. Where one company or irrigation district failed, another was formed to pick up the pieces. In 1886 entrepreneurs were finally successful in diverting

Out for a buggy ride.

Weiser River water into the Galloway Canal, irrigating thousands of acres through a complex system of ditches.

Intermountain Institute Founded in 1899 as the Idaho Industrial Institute to provide children who lived too far out in the country to attend high school with the opportunity to obtain an education, it changed its name to Intermountain Institute in 1915. Over the years, its students came from eight states and one foreign country. In addition to attending classes, all students worked five hours per day to pay for part of their tuition, room and board. The school educated more than 2,000 students during its 34-year existence. The institute closed in 1933 and in 1939 deeded the property for use by the public school district. When a new high school was built in 1967, the Institute property was vacated. Today, the property is home to the Old Time Fiddlers Festival and the Snake River Heritage Center.

Weiser Today

Amenities and Attractions Weiser is known far and wide for the annual National Oldtime Fiddlers' Contest and Festival held the third week of June. It attracts hundreds of contestants from across the nation. Thousands of spectators join each year's celebration, which includes wonderful foot-stomping music and a carnival.

Another major event is the Weiser Valley Round-Up & Rodeo on the second weekend of June.

The city has a golf course and seven municipal parks, one of which is the historic Oregon Short Line Railroad Depot.

The Snake River Heritage Center displays artifacts and exhibits about the social and economic history of the region. The museum is in H.M. Hooker Memorial Hall on the grounds of the historic Intermountain Institute. The Intermountain Institute was a private boarding high school from 1899 to 1933. The museum is open from Memorial Day through Labor Day. Private tours are available by appointment.

In the wake of the 1890 fire, many building owners rebuilt with brick. Several of these brick buildings still stand and are listed on the National Register of Historic Places.

Economy and Major Employers Weiser has many retail and service businesses. Its largest private employers include food processor Appleton Produce and Champion Home Builders, each with from 225 to 250 employees. Weiser Care Center and Weiser Memorial Hospital each have around 75 employees. Consumers Co-op, McDonalds and Idaho Timber Corporation each employ around 55.

The largest public employer, with a payroll of 220, is the Weiser School District.

Education Weiser School District provides most of the elementary and secondary education. The district operates a high school, intermediate, middle and primary schools in the city.

The closest institutions of higher learning are Treasure Valley Community College, 20 miles away in Ontario, Oregon; the College of Idaho, 47 miles away in Caldwell; and Northwest Nazarene University and the new College of Western Idaho, both in Nampa, about 55 miles away.

Triangle Park

Health Care The 27-bed Weiser Memorial Hospital and a health clinic provide most of the medical care. Weiser Care Center provides nursing home and assisted-living services.

Transportation U.S. Highway 95 passes through the city. Interstate 84 is in Oregon, 15 miles west on Highway 201.

The Weiser Municipal Airport provides private and charter air service on its 4,000-foot runway. The closest all-purpose airport is in Boise.

Railroad service is available for freight only.

Utilities and Services Private companies provide natural gas, cable and satellite services. The City has an electric department that purchases electricity under contract from Idaho Power Company at wholesale and distributes it throughout the city with any savings passed on to customers. The City also provides water, sewer, police and fire protection. The County provides solid waste services.

Vision for 2050

For the past three decades, Weiser's population has grown about a third of a percent annually. This slow growth trend will likely continue. By 2050 the city's population will be between 5,500 and 7,000, and the city will retain its present-day charm and vitality.

Weiser's infrastructure and road systems are adequate to handle moderate growth. That infrastructure, including the city parks, will be carefully maintained but will not likely require significant improvements.

Mayors

1900	A.B. Anderson	1964	Ray R. Jackson
1904	E.A. Van Sicklin	1966	William Brummett
1907	J.R. Numbers	1970	B.R. Westberg
1911	Raymond B. Ayers	1978	Seth Dunn
1919	Woodson Jefferies	1982	Clark Syme
1920	J.B. Lloyd	1986	R.Dale Thomason
1925	W.C. Van Sice	1990	J.K. "Cherokee" Jones
1927	Theo J. Fisher	1994	Terry L. McDaniel
1929	F.S. Gwilliam	1995	Marshall Dickerson
1947	Robertson Smith	1996	Don Stephens
1951	John Mason	2003	Steve Patterson
1955	F.S. Gwilliam	2008	John Walker, Jr.
1957	John Lloyd	2012	Diana Thomas

BIBLIOGRAPHY

The 2000 Comprehensive Plan: City of Eagle, Idaho. Eagle: Eagle City Council, 1999.

2005-2006 Teton Valley Visitors Guide. Idaho Falls: Canyon Media for the Teton Valley Chamber of Commerce, 2004.

The 2007-2008 Teton Valley Activity Guide. Idaho Falls: Canyon Media for the Teton Valley Chamber of Commerce, 2006.

2009 and 2010 Answer Book. Coeur d'Alene: Coeur d'Alene Press (supplemental publication), March 31, 2009, and April 28, 2010.

Abramson, Ruby. Spanning the Century: The Life of W. Averell Harriman, 1891-1986. New York: William Morrow & Co., 1992.

Aiken, Katherine G. Idaho's Bunker Hill: The Rise and Fall of a Great Mining Company, 18851981. Norman: University of Oklahoma Press, 2005.

Alt, David, and Donald W. Hyndman. Roadside Geology of Idaho. Missoula: Mountain Press Publishing Company, 1989.

---Roadside Geology of the Northern Rockies. Missoula: Mountain Press, 1972.

Anderson, Abraham C. Trails of Early Idaho. Caldwell: Caxton Printers, Ltd., 1940.

Anderson, Alfred Leonard. Detailed Geology of the Minnie Moor and Queen of the Hills Mining Property. Moscow: University of Idaho, 1950.

---, et al. Detailed Geology of Certain Areas in the Mineral Hills and Warm Springs Mining District. Moscow: University of Idaho, 1950.

---, and Warren Richard Wagner. A Geological Reconnaissance of the Hailey Gold Belt (Camas District) Blaine County, Idaho. Moscow: University of Idaho, 1946.

Arrington, Leonard J. History of Idaho. Moscow: University of Idaho Press, 1994.

Atteberry, Jennifer. "Domestic and Commercial Architecture in Caldwell." Idaho Yesterdays, Winter 1980, pp. 2-17.

Baker, Bessie's Meadows Valley High School English Class. History of Meadows Valley. 1945.

Basalt Centennial Committee, Verlyn Dye Outcelt, Chairman. Basalt Idaho Centennial. Idaho Falls, Idaho: Valley Litho., 1985.

Beal, Merrill D., and Merle W. Wells. History of Idaho. New York: Lewis Historical Publishing Company, 1959.

Beierle, Amber. "Boise's Birthday." Office of the City Historian <http://www.boisehistory.com> 2004.

Benedict, Hope A. "A Common Heritage: A Promise of Abundance: Cow Camps, Mining, and Timber Operations of Lemhi County." Salmon: Salmon National Forest, 1994.

Bingham County History. Written and compiled by the people of Bingham County, Idaho. Blackfoot: Bingham County Centennial Book Committee, 1985.

Bingham, Randy E. Burley Irrigation District History: The First 100 Years. Burley: Burley Irrigation District, nd.

Bird, Annie Laurie. Boise, the Peace Valley. Caldwell: Canyon County Historical Society, 1975, c1934.

---My Home Town. Caldwell: Caxton Printers, 1968.

---Old Fort Boise. Parma: Old Fort Boise Historical Society, 1971.

Blase, Fred W. "Political History of Idaho Territory 1863-1890." Master's Thesis, University of California, 1924.

Boone, Lalia Phipps. From A to Z in Latah County, Idaho: A Place Name Dictionary. Moscow: Latah County Historical Society, 1983.

Bottolfsen, C.A. Author and editor. Articles about the early history of the Lost River from the files of the South Custer County Historical Society.

Bourasaw, Noel V. "James Frederick Wardner Series." Skagit River Journal of History and Folklore. <http://www.skagitriverjournal.com/WA/Whatcom/FairhavenSth/Pioneers/Pre1900/Wardner/Wardner01-JamesBioPortal.html> August 2010.

Bowen, A.W. Progressive Men of Southern Idaho. Chicago: A.W. Bowen & Co., 1904.

Brainard, Wendell. Golden History Tales from Idaho's Coeur d'Alene Mining District. Ray Chapman, ed. Kellogg: Wendell Brainard, 1990.

Brock, Eugene Linda, et al. Pioneer Settlers and Pioneer Ranches of Valley County. A Valley County History Project. Grand Junction: Action Services, 2002.

Brosnan, Cornelius James. History of the State of Idaho. Idaho: Charles Scribner's Sons, 1918.

Buckway, JaNene Johnson. Wendell: Hub City of Magic Valley. Shoshone: Wendell 75th Anniversary Committee, 1984.

Burg, Thomas E. White Pine Route: The History of the Washington, Idaho and Montana Railway Company. Coeur d'Alene: Museum of North Idaho Publications, 2003.

Caldwell Centennial Calendar 1883-1983: 100 Years of Documentary in Words and Pictures. Caldwell: Caldwell Historic Preservation Commission, 1982.

Each day of this 1983 calendar contains an historic note. It is indexed.

Caldwell Public Library. Oral History Committee. Voices from the Past. Caldwell: Caldwell Public Library.

A series of slide-tape programs about early Caldwell including businesses, music, women, architecture and irrigation.

"Caldwell Revisited 1883-1923." News Tribune. July 4, 1976. A special edition printed during the U.S. bicentennial year.

Carlson, Jimmie I. "Remaking Idaho's Capitol City: A Case Study in Urban Renewal." Masters' Thesis, Boise State University, 1996.

Carney, Ellen. Historic Soda Springs: Oasis on the Oregon Trail. Wayan: Traildust Publishing, 1998.

Carns, Iva Hollingsworth. Steamboats and Memories. Coeur d'Alene: Iva Carns, 1990.

Casner, Nick, and Valerie Kiesig. Trolley: Boise Valley's Electric Road, 1891-1928. Boise: Black Canyon Communications, 2002.

"Cavalcade Issues." Idaho Press Tribune. The Idaho Press Tribune publishes a special series in the spring of each year, which often includes historical articles. Some have been indexed.

Chapman, Ray. Uncle Bunker. Kellogg: Chapman Publishing, 1994.

---. History of Idaho's Silver Valley: 1878-2000. Kellogg: Chapman Publishing, 2000.

---. History of Kellogg, Idaho, 1885-2002. Kellogg: Chapman Publishing, 2002.

Chedsey, Zona, and Carolyn Frei, eds. Idaho County Voices: A People's History From the Pioneers to the Present. Grangeville: Idaho County Centennial Committee, 1990.

Clanton, Dorothy M. The Georgie Oakes: The Lady of the Lake.

---Bringing the Iron Horse to the Coeur d'Alenes.

Clark, Lynda Campbell. Nampa, Idaho, 1885-1985: A Journey of Discovery. Nampa: Pacific Press, 1985.

Clements, Louis J., and Harold S. Forbush. Pioneering the Snake River Fork Country.

Rexburg: Eastern Idaho Publishers, 1972.

A Completed Century 1888-1988. Caldwell: Centennial Committee Boone Presbyterian Church, 1987.

Conley, Cort. Idaho for the Curious: A Guide. Cambridge: Beckeddy Books, 1982.

Cox, Cheryl A., and Lexie Ann French. Second Stories: Historical Narratives of Idaho Falls Women. Idaho Falls: The Graphic Experience, 1986.

Crosby, Mike. "A Common Heritage: Lemhi County, the Salmon National Forest, and the Civilian Conservation Corps." Salmon: Salmon National Forest, 1994.

Crow, Donna Fletcher. Kathryn: Days of Struggle and Triumph. Chicago: Moody Press, 1992.

---Elizabeth: Days of Loss and Hope. Chicago: Moody Press, 1993.

---Stephanie: Days of Turmoil and Victory. Chicago: Moody Press, 1993.

Crowder, David Lester. Rexburg, Idaho: The First One Hundred Years 1883-1983. Rexburg: D.L. Crowder, 1983.

Culdesac Idaho Centennial 1903-2003: 100 Years of Memories. Culdesac: Culdesac Gem Committee, 2003.

Davis, Belinda. A Study of Irrigation and the Development of Ada County. Boise: Ada County Historical Preservation Council, 1990.

Davis, L.J. "Tearing Down Boise." Harpers. November 1974.

Declo History Committee and Declo Alumni Association, contributors. Declo, My Town, My People. Burley: Burley Reminder, Incorporated, 1974.

DeVoto, Bernard, ed. The Journals of Lewis and Clark. Boston: Houghton Mifflin Company, 1953.

Dillion, Wilda Collier. Deaths and Burials: Boise Barracks Military Reserve, Idaho, 1863-1913.

Boise: W.C. Dillion, 2003.

Downing, James L. History of Teton City, Idaho: 1833-1900. Rexburg: Ricks College, 1971.

Driggs, B.W. History of Teton Valley, Idaho. Louis J. Clements and Harold S. Forbush, ed.
Rexburg: Arnold Agency, 1926, revised 1970, copyright 1970 by Louis J. Clements, Rexburg: Eastern Idaho Publishing Company.

Driggs Idaho Stake: Diamond Jubilee 1901-1981. Rexburg: Ricks College Press, 1982.

Driscoll, Ann Nilsson. They Came to a Ridge. Moscow: News Review Pub. Co., 1970.

Druss, Claudia, et al, eds. Patterns of the Past: The Ada County Historic Sites Inventory. Boise: The Arrowrock Group, 2001.

Eagle Island State Park Master Plan. Boise: Beck & Baird, 2000.

Elsensohn, Sister M. Alfreda. Pioneer Days in Idaho County, Volume 2. Cottonwood: Caxton Printers, 1971.

Etulain, Richard W., and Bert W. Marley, eds. The Idaho Heritage: A Collection of Historical Essays. Pocatello: Idaho State University Press, 1974.

Fanselow, Julie. "Idaho Off the Beaten Path: A Guide to Unique Places." Guilford: Globe Pequot Press, 2010.

---"What a Democracy Looks Like – Kuna, Idaho: Where a Community Pulls Together to Face Growth." Study Circle Resource Center, 2004.

Feser, Bonnie Jean Bacon. Georgetown, ID (Twin Creeks), 1869-1950. Georgetown: Bonnie Jean Bacon Feser, 2006.

Fick, Bob. "Idaho Governor Awards $2.1 Million in Community Grants." Gem County Chamber of Commerce. OpenPotion. 7 July 2006. <www.emmettidaho.com> August 2010.

Fisher, Vardis. Idaho Encyclopedia. Federal Writers Project. Caldwell: Caxton Printers, Ltd. 1938.

Fisk, Dale, and Don Dopf. The P&IN to the Golden Heart of Idaho: The Story of the Pacific

& Idaho Northern Railway. Boise: Writers Press, 2001.

Flanders, Robert Bruce. Nauvoo: Kingdom on the Mississippi. Urbana: University of Illinois Press, 1965.

Fogg, P.M. A History of the Minidoka Project, Idaho, to 1912 Inclusive. Boise: Bureau of Reclamation, 1915.

Frandsen, Rebecca, and Ruth Ann Olson. The Best Trader on the Emigrant Road: The Life and Adventures of Bob Dempsey, Mountaineer. Lava Hot Springs: Greater Lava Hot Springs Chamber of Commerce, 1979.

---Lava Hot Springs. For City of Lava Hot Springs Tourist Information Center

Franzen, John G. Southeastern Idaho Cultural Resources Overview, Burley and Idaho Falls Districts: Final Report R-2196. Jackson: Commonwealth Associates, 1981. Pp 115-191.

French, Hiram T. History of Idaho: a narrative account of its historical progress, its people and its principal interests. Chicago: Lewis Publishing Co., 1914.

Fritzen, Mary Jane, ed. Idaho Falls, City of Destiny. Idaho Falls: Bonneville County Historical Society, 1991.

---Bonneville County: Its Formation and Description. Idaho Falls: Bonneville County Heritage Association, 2006.

Gentry, James R., et al. A Centennial History of Bliss, Idaho: 1883-1983. Gooding: Pilot Press, 1983.

---In the Middle and on the Edge: The Twin Falls Region of Idaho. Twin Falls: College of Southern Idaho, 2003.

Gidley, J.W. Hunting Fossils on the Old Oregon Trail. Smithsonian Institution, 1930.

Gilbert, Millie. "Emmett: Spotlight City." Idaho Magazine. March 2005. 33-40.

Gittins, H. Leigh. Pocatello Portrait: the early years, 1878 to 1928. Moscow: The University Press of Idaho, 1983.

Gooding County History Book Committee. Gooding County Roots and Branches, 1989. Gooding: Taylor Publishing Company, 1989.

Graff, Leo W. Jr. "Fred T. Dubois-Biographical Sketch." Idaho State University: Eli M. Oboler Library. Idaho State University. n.d. <http://www2.isu.edu/library/special/mc004b.htm> 12 Jan 2007.

Gray, Dale M. "Moved Properties in American Falls, Idaho." National Register of Historic Places. Nomination 2005.

Groefsema, Olive. Elmore County: Its Historical Gleanings " A collection of pioneer narratives, treasured family pictures, and early clippings about the settling of Elmore County, Idaho. Caldwell: Caxton Printers, Ltd., 1949.

Hafen, LeRoy R., ed. Trappers of the Far West: Sixteen Biographical Sketches. Lincoln: University of Nebraska Press, 1965.

Hailey, Leona Cartee. "Boise in the Seventies." Cartee Collection, Idaho State Historical Society MS 376.

Haines, Aubrey L. Historic Resource Study: Historic Sites Along the Oregon Trail. Denver: Denver Service Center, Historic Preservation Team, National Park Service, 1973.

Haines, Jr., Francis D., ed. The Snake Country Expedition 1830-1831: John Work's Field Journal. Norman: University of Oklahoma Press, 1971.

Hall, Jory. Kuna Civil War to Chauatuqua: Thumbprints Across the Pages of History. Kuna: Thumbprints, 1997.

Hart, Alfred B. "History of Bloomington, Idaho." compiled May 12, 1933.

Hart, Arthur A. Wings over Idaho: An Aviation History. Caldwell: Caxton Press, 1991.

Hartkopf, Frank. History of Bingham County, Idaho. Laramie: University of Wyoming, 1942.

Hartman, Hugh H. The Founding Fathers of Boise. Boise: Hugh H. Hartman, 1989.

Hawkes, Blaine. (Uncopyrighted local history book, used with permission of the author.)

Hawley, James H. History of Idaho, the Gem of the Mountains. Chicago: The S.J. Clarke Publishing Co., 1920.

Hay, O.P. "The Pleistocene of the Western Region of North America and Its Vertebrate Animals." Washington: Carnegie Institution of Washington Publication N. 322B:1-346, 1927.

Hine, Robert. Community on the American Frontier. Norman: University of Oklahoma Press, 1980.

History of Arimo: Including Arkansas, Hawkins Basin, Marsh Center, and Robin. Compiled by the Arimo Centennial History Committee for the Idaho Centennial. Arimo: Arimo Centennial History Committee, 1991.

History of the Brick Plant at Troy, Idaho. Troy: Troy Historical Society.

History of Cassia County and Burley Idaho. 1952.

History of North Idaho. or An Illustrated History of North Idaho: Embracing Nez Perce, Idaho, Kootenai and Shoshone Counties, State of Idaho. Spokane: Western Historical Publishing Company, 1903.

Holladay Engineering Company. "Wastewater System Preliminary Engineering Report " 6/1/051-12.

Holland, Wendolyn. Sun Valley: An Extraordinary History. Ketchum: The Idaho Press, 1998.

Holm, Debra Nelson, et al. Nampa's People, 1886-1986: Discovering Our Heritage. Nampa: Nampa Centennial Committee, 1986.

Horton, Alice, et al., eds. Beautiful Bonneville. Logan: Herff Jones, 1989.

House, Connie. Firestorm! Big Blowup II in North Idaho. Coeur d'Alene: Listos Publications, 1992.

Hult, Ruby El. Steamboats in the Timber. Coeur d'Alene: Caxton Printers, 1952.

---Northwest Disaster: Avalanche and Fire. Portland: Binford & Mort, 1960.

Idaho Poets and Writers Guild. These to Remember. S.L.: The Guild, 1962.

Idaho Power Company. "Early History of the Idaho Power Company." 1929.

Idaho State Historical Society. Emigrant Trails of Southern Idaho. (Idaho Cultural Resource Series Number 1). Boise: U.S. Bureau of Land Management, 1993.

---. "Goodale's Cutoff from Boise Valley to Powder River." (Reference Series Number 1048). Boise: Idaho State Historical Society, 1994.

---"Massacre Rocks." (Reference Series Number 234). Boise: Idaho State Historical Society, 1971.

---"Route of Alexander Ross, 1824." Idaho State Historical Society Reference Series, Number 86. July 1990. <http://history.idaho.gov/sites/default/files/uploads/reference-series/0086.pdf> April 2016.

---Postmarked Idaho: A List of Idaho Post Offices. Boise: Idaho State Historical Society, 1975.

---"Weldon Brinton Heyburn: May 25, 1852 " October 18, 1912. (Reference Series Number 544). Boise: Idaho State Historical Society, 1971.

---"The Beginning of the New York Canal." Idaho State Historical Society Reference Series, Number 190. March 1972.

---"Packer John's Cabin." Idaho State Historical Society Reference Series, Number 292. 1996.

---"Seven Devils." Idaho State Historical Society Reference Series, Number 116. 1981.

---"Gilmore and Pittsburgh Railroad." Idaho State Historical Society Reference Series, Number 215. 1976.

---"Salmon Falls and Thousand Springs." Idaho State Historical Society Reference Series, Number 184. 1987.

---"Oregon Trail Routes in and around Boise." Idaho State Historical Society Reference Series, Number 921. 1989.

564

Idaho State Transportation Department. Idaho Highway Historical Marker Guide. Boise: Idaho State Transportation Department, 2010.

Idaho Travel Council. Idaho: Official State Travel Guide. Boise: Idaho Department of Commerce, nd.

Idaho: Where the Past Comes Alive. Idaho City: Idaho City Chamber of Commerce.

Inman, Mary J. Twin Falls Centurybook: 1904-2004. Twin Falls: Hosteler Press, 2003.

International Daughters of the Utah Pioneers. Pioneer Women of Faith & Fortitude. Salt Lake City: Daughters of the Utah Pioneers, 1998.

Iona Centennial History Book 1883-1983: A Centennial History Book, Containing Historical Material and Personal Histories, Submitted by the Residents and Previous Residents of Iona, Bonneville County, Idaho. Rexburg: Ricks College Press, 1983.

Irving, Washington. Astoria or Anecdotes of an Enterprise Beyond the Rocky Mountains. Philadelphia: Carey, Lea & Blanchard, 1836.

Johnson, Stella E. History of Troy 1892-1992. Troy: Stella E. Johnson, 1992.

Jordan, Grace Edgington. The King's Pines of Idaho: A Story of the Browns of McCall. Pontiac: Kirkwood Pub. Co., 1998.

Klenck, Dee. A Jewel Between Two Rivers: the History of Fruitland, Idaho. Fruitland: Gem Publishing Company, 1990.

Kunkler, Lois Roark. "A Brief History of the Eagle High School Broncs." The Eagle Express, Jan. 13, 1995, p. 1.

Kuna Chamber of Commerce. Gateway to the Birds of Prey: Kuna, Idaho. Kuna: Economic Development Committee, Kuna Chamber of Commerce, 1999.

Layton, Stanford J., ed. Utah's Lawless Fringe: Stories of True Crime. Salt Lake City: Signature Books, 2001.

Lee, William H. "A History of Phosphate Mining in Southeast Idaho." U.S. Geological Survey, U.S. Department of Interior, Open File Report #00-425, Version 1.0. <http://geopubs.wr.usgs.gov/open-file/of))-425> September 2010.

Lemhi County History Book Committee. Centennial History of Lemhi County, Vol. I. Salmon: Lemhi County History Book Committee, 1992.

Leppert, Elaine and Lorene Thurston. Early Caldwell Through Photographs. Caldwell, Idaho: Caldwell Committee for the Idaho State Centennial, 1990.

Link, Paul Karl, and E. Chilton Phoenix. Rocks, Rails & Trails, 2nd Edition. Pocatello: Idaho Museum of Natural History, 1996.

Lohrey, Dana, et al. The Elk City Wagon Road. Centennial Edition. Grangeville: Dana Lohrey, 1995.

Longley, C.L. "Assay Office in Boise Holds Venerable Place in Story of Yellow Dust." Boise: Idaho Statesman, January 19, 1930.

Longteig, Margaret Nell, and Rheba Miller. Remember When. 1976.

Lorenzen, Marilyn. Personal knowledge and writings.

Lovell, Edith Haroldsen. Captain Bonneville's County. Idaho Falls: The Eastern Idaho Farmer, 1963.

Lowell, Helen, and Lucile Peterson. Our First Hundred Years: A Biography of Lower Boise Valley 1814-1914. Caldwell: Caxton Printers, 1976.

Lucas, F.A. The Fossil Bison of North America. Washington: Smithson.Proceed.v.21, 1899.

Lukas, J. Anthony. Big Trouble. New York: Simon and Schuster, 1997.

Lyon, Ruth B. The Village that Grew: Emmettsville, Martinsville, Emmett. Lithocraft for R.B. Lyon, 1979

MacGregor, Carol. "The Founding Community in Boise Idaho: 1882-1910. Ph.D. Diss., University of New Mexico, 1999.

Madsen, Brigham D. The Shoshoni Frontier and the Bear River Massacre. Salt Lake City,

Utah: University of Utah Press, 1985.

"Magic Valley Region Wildlife Management Areas." Idaho Fish and Game. <www.fishandgame.idaho.gov/cms/wildlife/wma/carey> April 2016.

Marker, Joe L. Eagle Rock, U.S.A. (now Idaho Falls, Idaho). Idaho Falls: Roboco Printing, 1980.

Market Lake Centennial Committee, ed. Market Lake Centennial (1867-1967). Roberts: Market Lake Centennial Committee, 1967.

McConnell, W.J. Early History of Idaho. Glendale: The Arthur H. Clark Company, 1913.

McDevitt, Thomas. Idaho's Malad Valley: A History. Pocatello: Little Red Hen, Incorporated, 2001.

McGonigal, Mary Brown. Spring of Gladness: Reminiscences of Pioneer Life in the Wood River Valley. Ketchum: McGonigal, 1976.

McLeod, Geo A. History of Alturas and Blaine Counties Idaho. Hailey: The Hailey Times, 1930.

Mendiola, Judy. "A History of Eagle, Idaho." Eagle: The Author, 1998.

Meyers, Rex. "The Implausible Gilmore and Pittsburgh." The Colorado Rail Annual, No. 15. Golden: Colorado Railroad Museum, 1981.

Miller, John B. The Trees Grew Tall. Moscow: The News Review Publishing Company, 1972.

Mills, Nellie Ireton. All Along the River: Territorial and Pioneer Days on the Payette. Montreal: Payette Radio Limited, 1963

Mini-Cassia Chamber of Commerce & Visitor Center. <http://www.minicassiachamber.com/> April 2016.

Mitchell, Victoria E. History of Selected Mines in the Alder Creek Mining District, Custer County Idaho. Special Staff Report. Moscow: Idaho Geological Survey, University of Idaho, 1997.

Monroe, Julie R. Moscow: Living and Learning on the Palouse. Charleston: Arcadia Publishing, 2003.

---et al. Rekindled Spirit. Moscow: Idaho State Historical Society, 2009

Neilsen, Judith. "A Brief History of the Washington, Idaho & Montana Railway Company." University of Idaho Special Collections & Archives, Manuscript Group 139, 1982.

Okelberry-Jones, Sharon. History of Oakley, Idaho. Unspecified Publisher, 1990.

Oppenheimer, Doug. Sun Valley: A Biography. Boise: Beatty Books, 1976.

Otness, Lillian Woodworth. A Great Good Country: A Guide to Historic Moscow and Latah County, Idaho. Moscow: Latah County Historical Society, 1983.

Parker, Karen, et al. Teton Centennial: 100 Years of Progress, 1883-1983. Teton: Teton Centennial Committee, 1983.

Petersen, Keith. Company Town: Potlatch, Idaho, and the Potlatch Lumber Company. Pullman: Washington State University Press, 1987.

Pettite, William Stibal. Memories of Market Lake, Vol. II. Roberts: William Pettite, 1977.

Pfeifer, Friedl. The Sun Valley Ski Book. New York: A.S. Barnes & Company, 1939.

Plastino, Ben J. Coming of Age: Idaho Falls and the Idaho National Engineering Laboratory 1949-1990. Ed. Diane Plastino Graves. Chelsea: Bookcrafters, 1998.

"Portrait of a Small City: Eagle, Idaho." Boise: Journal of Commerce, 1979, no paging.

Postmarked Idaho: List of Idaho Post Offices. Boise: Idaho State Historical Society, 1975.

Quinn, Larry. A History of Magic Valley. Twin Falls: Publishing West Associates, 1996.

Ransel, Sandra, and Charles Durand. Crossroads: A History of the Elmore County Area. Mountain Home: Elmore County Historical Research Team, 1985

Rasker, Ray, and Ben Alexander. Working Around the White Clouds. Bozeman: Sonoran

Institute, 2003.

Records and minutes of the various cities in Idaho.

Reed, Mary. "Latah Legacy" articles published by Latah County Historical Society

Reid, Wallace and Bates. Blackfoot Historic Homes and Buildings. 1996.

The Renaissance: a Book of Historical Nature and Especially a Record of Past Year's Events at the College of Idaho. Caldwell: Associated Body of the College of Idaho, 1908.

Rexburg Community Review. Boise: Idaho Rural Partnership, 2004.

Ricketts, Virginia. Then and Now in Southern Idaho. Jerome: Falls City Publishing, 1998.

Roberts, Edwards. Shoshone and Other Western Wonders. New York: Harper & Brothers, 1888.

Robertson, Donald B. Encyclopedia of Western Railroad History; Volume II: The Mountain States. Dallas: Taylor Publishing Co., 1991.

Rockwood, Craig, et al. Iona History Book, Vol. II. Iona: Iona Historical Committee, 2005.

Ronda, James P. Lewis and Clark among the Indians. Lincoln: University of Nebraska Press, 1984.

Route of the Oregon Trail in Idaho. Boise: Idaho Department of Highways, 1963.

Rowland, Frank P. Founding of McCall, Idaho. Caldwell: Caxton Printers, 1960.

Russell, Osborne. Journal of a Trapper: Nine Years in the Rocky Mountains, 1834-1843. Edited from original manuscript by L.A. York. Boise: Syms-York, 1914.

Salant, Priscilla, et al. Profile of Rural Idaho. Boise: Idaho Commerce & Labor, nd.
Scharnhorst, Marie H. "Genesee, 100 Years." Latah Legacy (Spring, 1989, V. 18 No. 1). Moscow: Latah County Historical Society, 1989. Pp 3-36.

Scott, Donna. A ribute to the Past, a Legacy for the Future. Miriam Booth Breckenridge, et al, eds. Twin Falls: Twin Falls County Business History, 1990.

Scott, Orland A. Pioneer Days on the Shadowy St. Joe. Coeur d'Alene: Caxton Printers Ltd, 1968.

The Settlement of the Kuna Region, 1900-1925. Caldwell, Caxton Printers, 1983.

"Seventieth Anniversary and 'Days of '83' edition." Caldwell News Tribune. May 6, 1953. An excellent special edition of the newspaper describing Caldwell's early days; the advertisements are histories of many local businesses.

Shadduck, Marvin E. The Dalton Story. Coeur d'Alene: Museum of North Idaho, 2003.

Shallat, Todd, and Johnny Hester. "Trails and Rails: Boise as a Transportation Hub." Office of the Boise City Historian. <http://www.boisehistory.com/> 2005.

Shoup, George E. History of Lemhi County. Reprint. Salmon: Salmon Public Library Association, 1992.

Sims, Robert C., and Hope Ann Benedict, eds. Idaho Governors: Historical Essays on Their Administrations. Boise: Boise State University Press, 1992.

Singletary, Robert. Kootenai Chronicles. Coeur d'Alene: Century Publishing, 1995.

Slavik, Walter K.M. "Pioneering Public Power: Minidoka Project, Idaho." The Reclamation Era. Boise: Bureau of Reclamation, 1941.

Smith, Evelyn L. A Century of Progress, Evolution to Excellence, 1889-1989: A History of the Schools of Mullan, Idaho. Mullan: Mullan Education Foundation, 1989.

Smith, Robert Wayne. The Coeur d'Alene Mining War of 1892: A Case Study of an Industrial Dispute. Corvallis: Oregon State University Press, 1961.

Smythe, Rachel. Entertaining Strangers. Salt Lake City: Amber Pen, 2005.

Solum, Romola Hansen. History of Georgetown. Lola Hoskins, researcher.

South Custer County Historical Society, Inc. photograph collection.

Spence, Clark C. For Wood River or Bust: Idaho's Silver Boom of the 1880s. Moscow: University of Idaho Press, 1999.

Stacy, Susan M. Proving the Principle: A History of the Idaho National Engineering and Environmental Laboratory, 1949-1999. Washington: United States Government Printing, 2000.

---Legacy of Light: A History of the Idaho Power Company. Boise: Idaho Power Company, 1991.

Stapilus, Randy. It Happened in Idaho. Guilford: Globe Pequot Press, 2002.

Stearns, H.T., Lynn Crandall, and Willard G. Steward. Geology and Ground-water Resources of the Snake River Plain in Southeastern Idaho: Water Supply Paper 774. Boise: U.S. Government Print Office, 1938.

Stene, Eric A. The Minidoka Project. Denver: Bureau of Reclamation History Program, 1993.

Stoll, William T., and H.W. Whicker. Silver Strike: the True Story of Silver Mining in the Coeur d'Alenes. Boston: Little, Brown, and Co., 1932.

Stoddard, Bonnie J., researcher and compiler. History of Dubois.

Strahorn, Carrie Adell. Fifteen Thousand Miles by Stage. New York: Putnam's, 1911. Two chapters tell of the establishment of Caldwell, "City Building-Caldwell, and other Towns on the Frontier" and "Pot-Pourii." The University of Nebraska published a twovolume edition in 1988.

Tacke, Kathryn. Regional Economist. "Idaho County Workforce Trends." Boise: Idaho Department of Labor, January 2010

Taking the Scenic Route: A Guide to Idaho Scenic Byways. Boise: Idaho Transportation Department, 2000.

Taylor, Dorice. Sun Valley. Sun Valley: Ex Libris Press, 1980.

Tollefson, Gene. BPA and the Struggle for Power at Cost. Portland: Bonneville Power Administration, 1987.

Toponce, Alexander. Reminiscences of Alexander Toponce. Norman: University of Oklahoma Press, 1971.

Travel the Oregon Trail in Caribou County: A Self-guided Tour of Sites Documented in Emigrant Diaries & Journals of Early Explorers. Soda Springs: Soda Springs Chamber of Commerce, 2004.

Trego, Byrd. Author, editor, and newspaper publisher. Articles about the history of the Lost River from the files of the South Custer County Historical Society.

Trent, Geneva. History of Eagle Fire Department. Eagle: Eagle Historic Preservation Commission, 1997.

Tweedy, Doug. Clearwater County Profile. Orofino: Idaho Department of Commerce and Labor, 2006.

Twin Falls Historical Society. Twin Falls County Territorial Centennial 1863-1963: A Folk History of Twin Falls County, Idaho. Twin Falls: Standard Printing Company, 1963.

Walgamott, Charles S. Reminiscences of Early Days: a Series of Historical Sketches and Happenings in the Early Days of Snake River Valley. Twin Falls: Idaho Citizen, 1926.

---Six Decades Back. Moscow: University of Idaho Press, 1936

Walker, Deward E., Jr. Indians of Idaho. Moscow: University of Idaho Press, 1978.

Walker, Lola, Lula Barnard, and Faunda Bybee. Tosoiba: Sparkling Waters. Soda Springs: Daughters of the Utah Pioneers, 1958.

Wells, Merle. Gold Camps and Silver Cities: Nineteenth Century Mining in Central and Southern Idaho, 2nd edition. Moscow: Idaho Department of Lands, Bureau of Mines and Geology, 1983.

Wells, Merle, and Arthur Hart. Boise: An Illustrated History. Sun Valley: American Historical Press, 2000.

Whitlock, Flint, and Bob Bishop. Soldiers on Skis: A Pictorial Memoir of the 10th Mountain Division. Boulder: Paladin Press, 1992.

Whitman, Narcissa Prentiss. My Journal 1836. Edited and with introduction by Lawrence L.

Dodd. Fairfield: Ye Galleon Press, 1994.

Winslow, Dilla Tucker. From Sagebrush to Green Fields: A History of Greenleaf Idaho. Private Printing, 1984. (Permission to re-publish granted to the City of Greenleaf by the heirs of Dilla Tucker Winslow.)

Witherell, Jim. "History Along the Greenbelt." Boise: Ada County Centennial Committee, 1990.

Woods, Shelton, ed. Valley County Idaho Prehistory to 1920. A Valley County History Project. Grand Junction: Action Publishing, 2002.

Wright, Patricia, and Lisa B. Reitzes. Tourtellotte & Hummel of Idaho: The Standard Practice of Architecture. Logan: Utah State University Press, 1987.

Young, Virgil M. The Story of Idaho. Moscow: University of Idaho Press, 1990.

Yorgason, Blaine and Brenton. Roger and Sybil Ferguson History. Unknown.

Unpublished works:

Adkinson, Virginia, local White Bird resident and historian. Research and writings.

Asker, Bonita, local White Bird resident and historian. Research and writings.

Baker, Ronald J. "Chronology of Eagle, Idaho" Unpublished manuscript on file at Eagle Public Library Reference Dept., 2005.

Benedict, Hope Ann. "Place and Community in the Mining West: Lemhi County, Idaho, 1866-1929" Ph.D. diss., University of Oregon, 1996.

Bennett, E.H. "Genesee Timeline." Unpublished history and notes about Genesee, Idaho.

Benton, Jon. "Thirsty for a Water System."

Benton, Josh. "Telephone Troubles."

Brown, Kimberly Rice, unpublished files.

Burtenshaw, Frances D. Compiled writings of George F. Shelley, Theodocia M. Dana, and Mary S. Davis. "Eagle Public Library History." Unpublished manuscript on file at Eagle Public Library Reference Dept., 1984.

Hale, Kent. "Oakley Has Magnificent Homes." (Information sheet provided by the City.)

Hansen, Hortense. History of the City of Shelley."

Kreiman, Marilyn. "Biography of Pear Lucile Small Lewis."

"A history of the Kuna Grange," unpublished manuscript, 2005. Compiled by Sharon Fisher, Lecturer, Kuna Grange, 2005, from information originally written by Mrs. Laura Rea (originally made available by Mrs. Ben Aylsworth of Nampa, and compiled from old record books and data collected by E. G. May and B. Mathews), Lois Dustman, and Ruth Burningham. Help also provided by Wayne and Blanche Kuhlman and Florence Chaney.

Miller, John B. Unpublished articles.

Peterson, Lynn. Research paper: History of St. Charles, Idaho.

Sleeper, Richard. "Biography of Richard Crampton Sleeper."

Smith, Elizabeth. "History of the Salmon National Forest," ca. 1970.

Strong, Sam. Unpublished recollections.

Thomason, William J. "Reubens History." 1990.

Wilde, J.P., Journal Correspondent. "Story of Georgetown."

Newspapers and Magazines:

American Falls Press. "Tragedy Brought Moral Uplift, Recollections of W.T. Oliver." February 25, 1915.

---"American Falls Townsite Jumped, Recollections of W.T. Oliver." March 11, 1915.

---"Untold Wealth Within Reach, Recollections of W.T. Oliver." March 18, 1915.

American Whitewater Journal. Issue 4, July/August 1997.

The Arco Advertiser. Bound files.

Better Roads Magazine. November 1952.

Blackfoot Magazine. By the Greater Blackfoot Area Chamber of Commerce, 2005-2006.

The Blackfoot News.

Bonner County Daily Bee. <www.bonnercountydailybee.com>

Bovill Herald. 1911-1912.

Bovill Record. 1913.

Buhl Herald. April 1941.

Burley Bulletin.

Burley Herald.

Burley Herald-Bulletin.

Caldwell Daily News.

Caldwell News.

Caldwell News Weekly.

Caldwell News Tribune.

Caldwell Press Tribune.

Caldwell Progress Bulletin.

Caldwell Times.

Caldwell Tribune.

Daily Idahonian.

Family Circle Magazine. August 2010.

Forbes Magazine. March 2008.

Gem State Rural. Sept 15, 1895-May, 1916.

Genesee News. 1888-1968.

The Harrison Searchlight. June 2005 and June 2006 issues.

Hoot Owl. On microfilm at the Salmon Public Library.

Hub City Irrigationist.

Idaho County Voices.

The Idaho Enterprise.

Idaho Farm Journal. Black Canyon Edition, September 29, 1949.

The Idaho News.

Idaho Press-Tribune.

Idaho Recorder. On microfilm at the Salmon Public Library.

Idaho State Journal. "Malad's Early History Was Replete with Color." By Mary Matthews, November 25, 1982.

Idaho Statesman.

Idaho's Yesterdays. Vol. 7 No. 4.

Inc. Magazine. 2008.

Independent Enterprise.

Irrigation Age. September 1980.

Kiplinger. 2008.

The Kooskia Mountaineer. 1927.

Latah County Press. 1944-46.

Lemhi Herald. On microfilm at the Salmon Public Library.

Lewiston Morning Tribune. "Town sprouts out of nowhere." By Jodi Walker, April 27, 2006.

Mackay Miner Newspaper. Microfilm and hard copy newspaper issues 1907-1975.

McCall Magazine.

Money Magazine. June 2010.

The Morning News.

Moscow Mirror. January 1, 1892. (Article on Vollmer first published in the Alliance Ledger.)

Mountain Home News.

Mullan News Bulletin. Summer Edition.

Mullan Progress. 1912-1918.

Mullan Tribune.

News Review. 1934.

News Tribune. Nov 16, 1966 " June 30, 1981.

North Side News. Bicentennial Edition, July 1, 1976.

---October 22, 1981.

North Side News: 75th Anniversary Edition. August 5, 1982.

Northern Idaho News. September 22, 1908.

---1908-1910.

Outdoor Life Magazine. June/July 2009.

Parma Review. "Our Yesterdays from 1910 to 1980, a historical record published December 1980 in celebration of its 70th anniversary.

Pierce city ordinances.

The Recorder Herald. July 2010.

Rupert Pioneer Record. August 22, 1907.

Sandpoint Online. <www.sandpointonline.com>

Semi-Weekly Mining News. On microfilm at the Salmon Public Library.

Snake River Echoes.

South Idaho Press. July 6, 1970. (Article by Al Dawson)

---March 11, 2004. (Article by Renee Wells)

Spokesman Review.

Star Mirror. 1934.

The Star-News.

The Times News. June 24, 1987.

Twin Falls News.

Twin Falls Weekly. 1904-1906.

United States Department of Agriculture, Issue 12-06. "Agriculture In Idaho." June 28, 2006.

US News and World Report. November 29, 2007.

The Warren Times.

Wendell Irrigationist.

Documents and Records:

1888 Polk Directory for Shoshone County.

1981-92 Polk Directory.

2000, 2008 and 2010 Census.

2005-06 Emmett Area Telephone Book.

2005-2006 Idaho Blue Book.

2006-2020 City of Driggs Comprehensive Plan. Adopted November 2, 2006, by the Driggs City Council.

A Pause for Reflection. Estes.

Ada County Historic Preservation Council 2006 Preservation Plan for Cultural and Historic Resources.

Adams County historical records.

Bloomington Comprehensive Plan. November 2008.

Boise Basin Museum.

Bonner County Historical Society.

Books of Deeds filed in Valley County Courthouse, Cascade, Idaho.

Boundary County Museum.

Bruneau-Grand View School District Records.

"Cassia County Agent Annual Report for 1923."

City of Dubois records.

City of Mountain Home records.

City of Orofino records.

City of Post Falls records.

City of Roberts Comprehensive Plan Revised. 2007.

City of Stites archives of meeting minutes and published ordinances.

City of Teton Comprehensive Plan, 2004.

City of Wendell Gem Community Update. "A Peek Into the Past." 2003-2008.

Clark County Historical Society.

Clearwater County Guide for Newcomers brochure.

Clearwater Historical Museum.

Coeur d'Alene Tribe official website. <http://www.cdatribe-nsn.gov/> 2016.

Comprehensive Plan for the cities of Juliaetta and Kendrick.

Craig Mountain Lumber Company papers, University of Idaho, September 1980.

Downtown Rexburg Revitalization Blueprint.

Elmore County Historical Foundation.

Excerpts taken from paper written by JaNene Buckway, chair, Lincoln County Centennial Committee, 1995.

Excerpts taken from Shoshone Historic Walking Tour, written by Christy Pyles, chair, Gem Community Committee and the residents of Shoshone, 1995.

Explorations and Fieldwork of the Smithsonian Institution in 1929, Publication 3060:31-36.

"Final Environmental Impact Statement." U.S.D.A. Forest Service, Salmon National Forest, June 1991.

Fremont and Clark County courthouse records.

Grand View City records.

Grand View Water and Sewer Association, Inc., records.

Historic Opera Theatre brochure, Glenns Ferry Opera Theatre.

Historic Oakley brochure.

Idaho Atlas and Gazetteer. DeLorme, 2002.

Idaho Historical Society archives and public records.

Idaho Parks and Recreation records.

Idaho State Archives/Historic Records. Collection AR202: "Bridge and Highway Contracts."

Idaho State Mining Records.

Idaho State Veterans" Cemetery: Cultural Resource "Inventory and Assessment, Ada County, Idaho." Grand View: Frontier Historical Consultants, 2002.

J.R. Simplot Company records.

Jerome Jt. School District No. 261 Physical Plant Inventory.

Jerome School District records.

Jobs Plus records.

Johnson Flying Service records, Missoula, MT.

Larsen Farms.

Latah County Courthouse Records and Documents.

Latah County Historical Society Archives.

Latah County Historical Society Research Library. Moscow, Idaho.

Lemhi County Commissioners Records.

Madison Economic Partners. 2008-2009 Community Profile. "Sugar City: Sweetest Town Around."

---Sugar City Business Park: a Great Place to Build a Business. 2009.

McCall Area Comprehensive Plan.

Meadows Valley School District records.

Minutes and Ordinances from the City of Bovill Archives.

Minute books for the City of Cambridge.

Minutes of past meetings of the Horseshoe Bend City Council.

Minutes of stockholders of Georgetown Reservoir Company held April 27, 1903.

Minutes of the Salmon City Council.

Mountain Home Economic Development records.

Mountain Home Historical Museum pamphlet.

National Weather Service.

New Meadows City and Village records.

New Meadows Master Plan & Revitalization.

North Central Idaho Travel Association. Discover North Central Idaho. 2004-2006.

Personal records and pictures of Iona Residents.

Post Falls Chamber of Commerce.

Post Falls High School documents and records.

Post Falls Historical Society files.

Post Falls School District records.

Recreation Features Report.

The Rexburg Civic Life and Community Involvement Focus Team.

Richards, Bob, Economic Development, History of Spears Mfg. Jerome Idaho: Historical timeline from Spears purchase of Tupperware Plant to 2003.

Riverbed Commerce Park records.

Salmon Historical Society records.

Sanborn Fire Insurance Maps: Caldwell. New York: Sanborn Map Company. The Caldwell Public Library has mounted photocopies of the maps for 1888, 1890, 1892, 1900, 1908, 1911 and 1921.

Sandpoint Experiment Station 1910-2004.

Scenic Payette River Historical Society records.

Sugar City 2008 Comprehensive Plan.

Teton Scenic Byway Corridor Management Plan. Teton Scenic Byway Committee, Planmakers Planning & Urban Design, 2008.

The Twin Falls North Side Land and Water Company records. August 31, 1909.

University of Idaho Library Archives.

Upper Snake River Historical Society records and archives.

U.S. Forest Service records.

Valley County Comprehensive Plan.

Village of Notus Ordinance book dated 1921-1988.
Wastewater Status Update for the City of Greenleaf. April 28, 2009.
Wikipedia. "Skaggs Family."
Welcome to Oakley brochure.

Websites:

About the University of Idaho. <http://www.ucm.uidaho.edu/default.aspx?pid=86023> November 2005.

Ada County Development Services. "A Brief History of the Kuna Area." (PowerPoint Presentation.) <https://adacounty.id.gov/Portals/0/HisPreServ/Doc/ABriefHistoryoftheKunaAreaforweb.pdf> May 2016.

---"Ada County Chronicles: An Overview of the Development of Ada County." (PowerPoint Presentation.) <https://adacounty.id.gov/Portals/0/HisPreServ/Doc/AdaCountyChroniclesHandout6perpage.pdf> May 2016.

Ada County Historic Preservation Council. "A Walking Tour of Kuna's Beginnings." <https://adacounty.id.gov/Portals/0/HisPreServ/Doc/kuna_Walking_Tour_Brochure201 2.pdf> May 2016.

AirNav.com <http://www.airnav.com> 2005.

America's Promise Alliance for Youth. "100 Best Communities for Youth: Meridian, Idaho." May 2016.

Bannock Development Corporation. <www.bannockdevelopment.org> July 2010.

Bonner County History Museum. <http://www.bonnercountyhistory.org> August 2010.

Cassia County. "Cassia County History." <http://www.cassiacounty.org/about-cassiacounty/history.htm> 2005.

Cinema Treasurers "Howells Opera House." <http://cinematreasurers.org/theaters/4167>

City Data. <www.citydata.com>

City of Ashton. "Whistles and Smoke: Ashton's Railroad Legacy." <www.cityofashton.com/whistles-and-smoke> April 2016.

City of Dalton Gardens. <www.daltongardens.govoffice.com> 2005.

City of Dover. <www.doveridaho.org> 2016.

City of Eagle. "Official web site of the City of Eagle, Idaho." <http://www.cityofeagle.org> September 2010.

City of Fairfield, Idaho. <www.fairfieldidaho.us> 2016.

City of Hayden. <www.cityofhaydenid.us> 2005.

City of Heyburn. <www.heyburnidaho.org> May 2016.

City of Kooskia. <www.kooskia.com> 2016.

The City of Lewiston: Idaho's Only Seaport. <http://www.cityoflewiston.org/> May 2016.

City of Moscow. <http://www.ci.moscow.id.us> 2005.

---Peterson, Jon R., et al. "Growth in Moscow: A Study of Modest Population Growth and Rising Economic Prosperity." <http://www.ci.moscow.id.us/records/City20Reports/Why_is20_Moscow_Growing_06.pdf#search=Growth%20in%20moscow%3A%20a%20study%20of%20modest%20population%20growth%20and%20rising%20economic%20prosperity> 2006.

The City of Mountain Home. <www.mountain-home.us> May 2016.

City of Pocatello. <www.pocatello.us> August 2010.

City of Rigby. <www.cityofrigby.com> 2016.

574

CityTownInfo.com. <http://www.citytowninfo.com> May 2016.

Community Library. <http://leadore.lili.org> May 2016.

"Dam Details: Little Wood River Dam." Bureau of Reclamation. <http://www.usbr.gov/projects/Facility.jsp?fac_Name=Little+Wood+River+Dam&groupName=General> April 2016.

Drive the Top Ten. <www.drivethetop10.com> 2005. (May 2016, no longer a viable site.)

Elk River Lodge & General Store. <www.elkriverlodge.net> 2006.

Ellersick, Steven Donald. White Pine Savages: Ellersicks in the Lumber Industry. <http://myplace.frontier.com/~sde22ssw/Eller5-sde.html> May 2016.

Epodunk. <http://epodunk.com> 2005.

Farnovision. <http://www.farnovision.com/> 2016.

Felton, Ann. "Airport Expansion, 1929." Office of the Boise City Historian. <http://www.boisestate.edu/history/cityhistorian/3workpapers_pdf/airport_expands.pdf> 2004.

Fremont County Idaho. <www.co.fremont.id/us> 2016.

Full text of History of Custer County, Idaho. <http://www.archive.org/stream/historyofcusterc00blac/historyofcusterc00blac_djvu.txt> 2016

Gem County Historical Society and Village Museum. <www.gemcountymuseum.org> August 2010.

Grand Targhee Resort. <www.grandtarghee.com> 2016.

Greater American Falls Area Chamber of Commerce <http://www.amfallschamber.com/> May 2016.

Greater Newport Area Chamber of Commerce. <http://newportareachamber.com/> 2016.

Greater Pocatello Chamber of Commerce. <www.pocatelloidaho.com> July 2010.

Greater Yellowstone Resource Guide. <http://www.free-press.biz/> 2005.

Handy, J.A. Heyburn " Its Origin and Early History. 1959. <http://heyburn.id.gov/index.asp?SEC=59AED487-1297-4A0D-B5FB6B8A80C30AB0&DE=8A62CC31-8BB8-4F3C-9E05D99AB627AC01&Type=B_PR> May 2016.

Hayden Chamber of Commerce. <www.haydenchamber.org> 2016.

Hester, Johnny. "Subdivisions of Boise." Office of the Boise City Historian. <http://www.boisestate.edu/history/cityhistorian/2atlas_subdivisions/index_subdivisions.html> 2005.

History of Kootenai County. <www.kcgov.us/community/history>

History of Latah County: Moscow. <http://users.moscow.com/lchs/history.html#moscow> November 2005.

Howell, Thomas. Snake River 4x4. "History of Warm River, Idaho." <http://www.snakeriver4x4.com/warmriver.php> 2005.

Idaho Chapter Oregon California Trail Association. <www.idahoocta.org> August 2010.

Idaho City Chamber of Commerce. <www.idahocitychamber.org> May 2016.

Idaho Community Profiles. <http://www.epodunk.com/communities_id.html> May 2016.

Idaho Department of Commerce. <http://commerce.idaho.gov/> 2016.

Idaho Fish and Game. <http://www.fishandgame.idaho.gov> 2005.

Idaho Fish and Wildlife Service. <www.fws.gov> 2016.

Idaho Rural Partnership. March 2005 Community Review. Kuna: A World of Potential. <http://www.irp.idaho.gov/Documents20and20Settings/14/Site20Documents/Site20Media/Community20Review/Kuna20Community20Review%20Report.pdf> May 2016.

Idaho State Parks. <http://www.stateparks.com/idaho_parks_and_recreation_destinations.html> May 2016.

Idaho State University. <http://www.isu.edu> 2005.

Idaho Wool Growers Association. <http://www.idahowool.org/> August 2010.

inidaho.com. "Plan Your Trip to Donnelly Idaho." <http://www.inidaho.com/City.asp? City=Donnelly> 2016.

Jackson Hole. <http://www.jacksonhole.com/> 2006.

Kiplinger. <http://www.kiplinger.com> September 2010.

"Lake Pend Oreille History." Sandpoint Online.com: Lake Guide. <http://www.sandpointonline.com/rec/lakeguide/history.html> August 2010.

Lava Hot Springs Area History. <http://lavahotsprings.com/info/history.html> May 2016.

Los Angeles Times. "Regional Report: Vanishing Railroads." <http://articles.latimes.com/1990-06-20/news/mn-226_1_union-pacific> 2005.

Miners Inch. <http://sizes.com/units/miners_inch.htm> August 2010.

Minidoka County Idaho. "Minidoka County History." <http://www.minidoka.id.us/general/history.htm> May 2016.

Moscow Chamber of Commerce. <http://www.moscowchamber.com> March 2007.

National Park Service. <https://www.nps.gov> May 2016.

---National Register of Historic Places. <https://www.nps.gov/nr> May 2016.

National Weather Service. <www.weather.gov> 2016.

Nez Perce Tribal Web Site. <www.nezperce.org> 2016.

Northwest Nazarene University. <www.nnu.edu> 2016.

OVAC Oakley Valley Arts Council. <http://oakleyvalleyartscouncil.org/>

Palouse Country. "Moscow's Unique Beginning." <http://the.palouse.net/Moscow/history/history_beginnings.htm> November 10, 2005. (No longer a viable site in May 2016.)

Pocatello Marathon. <www.Pocatellomarathon.com> August 2010.

Portneuf Greenway Foundation. <www.pgfweb.com> August 2010.

Portneuf Medical Center. <www.portmed.org> August 2010.

Roots Web. "Coeur d'Alene Tribe History." <http://www.rootsweb.ancestry.com/~idreserv/cdhist.html> 2016

Rupert's Wilson Theatre. www.ruperttheatre.com

Rural Northwest.com. "Kootenai History: Hayden was booming at turn of century." <http://www.ruralnorthwest.com/artman/publish/printer_4478.shtml> 2005.

Sangres. <http://www.sangres.com> August 2016.

School District #25. <www.d25.k12.id.us> August 2010.

Schwantes, Carlos. "A Brief History of the University of Idaho." <www.ucm.uidaho.edu/default.aspx?pid=86022> November 2005.

"Silver Creek Preserve." The Nature Conservancy in Idaho. <http://www.nature.org/ourinitiatives/regions/northamerica/unitedstates/idaho/placesweprotect/silver-creek-preserve.xml> April 2016.

Smith, Jerry E. A History of "Rancharrah". <http://www.jerryesmith.com/index.php/42> 2016.

Snake River Stampede. <www.snakeriverstampede.com> 2016.

Southeast Idaho: Be Here! <www.seidaho.org/grace.htm> April 2016.

South Lemhi School District. <www.leadoreschool.org> May 2016.

St. Luke's Jerome Medical Center. <https://www.stlukesonline.org/communities-andlocations/facilities/hospitals-and-medical-centers/st-lukes-jerome-medical-center> 2016.

Stanley: Trailhead to Idaho Adventure. <http://stanleycc.org/> 2016.

Star Idaho. <http://staridaho.us/> 2016.

Steppe, Kali. "Clang, Clang, Clang Went the Trollies." Office of the Boise City Historian, <http://www.boisehistory.com/> 2004.

Swan Valley Elementary School. <http://sd92.k12.id.us> 2006.

Tamarack Resort. <http://www.tamarackidaho.com> 2005.

Teton Valley Trails and Pathways. <http://tvtap.org> 2016.

Three Rivers Ranch: for the discriminating flyfisher. <http://www.threeriversranch.com> May 2016.

Time. "Electrical Engineer Philo Farnsworth." <http://content.time.com/time/magazine/article/0,9171,990620,00.html> 2016.

Topozone. <www.topozone.com> 2016.

Troy, Idaho USA. <http://www.troyidaho.net> May 2016.

Twin Lakes Canal Company history <http://www.twinlakescanalcompany.com/history.html> 2006.

Uhlenkott, Dale "Popeye." "Ferdinand, Idaho: Memoirs of Frank M. Bieker." <http://idaho.idgenweb.org/PDF/Ferdinand%20Story%20Aug%2013%202004.pdf> April 2016.

Ultimate Idaho.com. <www.ultimateidaho.com> 2016.

United States Census Bureau. <http://www.census.gov/> 2016.

United States Geological Survey. <https://www.usgs.gov> 2016.

Upper Lemhi Valley Chamber of Commerce. <www.leadorechamber.com> May 2016.

U.S. Bureau of Reclamation. <www.usbr.gov> May 2016.

U.S. Forest Service. <www.fs.fed.us> May 2016.

U.S. Parks. <http://www.us-parks.com/> 2016.

Utah Power in the Gem Valley and Grace. <http://www.graceidaho.com/html/utahpower.html> April 2016.

Visit Idaho. <https://visitidaho.org/> 2016.

"The War Mothers" Organization in Elmore County." Elmore County, Idaho: a proud part of the ID GenWeb Project. <http://elmore.idgenweb.org/Military/Mothers.html> April 2016.

Warner, Eva. Historical Sketch of Heyburn, Idaho: The Town that Refused to Die. Written March 1970. <http://heyburn.id.gov/index.asp?SEC=59AED487-1297-4A0D-B5FB6B8A80C30AB0&DE=5E77EFFE-88FA-4D41-AD99034E9E5D0C36&Type=B_PR> May 2016.

Washington County: The Heart of Idaho. "History of the County." <http://co.washington.id.us/about-washington-county/> May 2016.

Water Archives. <http://www.waterarchives.org> August 2016.

The Weather Channel. <https://weather.com/> May 2016.

Weather Today. <www.weathertoday.net> July 2010.

Welcome to Glenns Ferry, Idaho: A Community of Opportunity! <http://glennsferryidaho.org> April 2016.

Welcome to Grace & Gem Valley: Grace Chamber of Commerce. <http://www.graceidaho.com> April 2016.

Wendell Chamber of Commerce: Hub City of Magic Valley. <http://www.wendellchamberofcommerce.org/> May 2016.

Western Regional Climate Center data <http://www.wrcc.dri.edu/> 2016.

Wheels That Won the West. <www.wheelsthatwonthewest.com> April 2016.

Wikipedia: the Free Encyclopedia. "Teton Dam." <http://en.wikipedia.org/wiki/Teton_Dam> December 12, 2005.

---"Fort Hall" <https://en.wikipedia.org/wiki/Fort_Hall,_Idaho> 2005.

---"Notus, Idaho." <https://en.wikipedia.org/wiki/Notus,_Idaho> 2016.

---"Oregon Shortline Railroad." <https://en.wikipedia.org/wiki/Oregon_Short_Line_Railroad> 2016.

---"Pend Oreille County, Washington." <https://en.wikipedia.org/wiki/Pend_Oreille_County%2C_Washington> August 2010.

577

Wolf Education & Research Center. <http://wolfcenter.org/> 2016.

Interviews:

Baker, Laurie, Eagle Historical Museum.
Bath, Teri, Eagle Chamber of Commerce.
Banner, Kent.
Bentz, Laurice.
Bergmann, Sharon, City of Eagle City Clerk.
Blanchard, Tom.
Brown, David.
Buster, Dick, Environmental Protection Specialist. September 2005.
Cada, Dave.
Carnegie, Amy.
Clark, Walter E., history of Georgetown, Idaho.
Collard, Mark.
Coyner, Barbara.
Crosby, Wayne.
Dahl, Melanie.
Everett, Kelly.
Fiori, Frank A.
Fisher, Betty.
Friend Dan, City of Eagle Fire Chief.
Gibson, Mike, Business Manager, Jerome School District.
Gillerman, Dr. Virginia, Economic Geologist/Associate Research Geologist, Idaho Geological Survey.
Good, Austin. Oral History.
Goodman, Don. Oral History.
Guerber, Steve, Former Eagle City Councilmember.
Hart, Arthur A., historian.
Hatzenbuhler, Ron, ISU Professor.
Hays, Sam H. Oral History.
Henderson, Ray, Minerals Specialist, U.S. Forest Service. September 2005.
Hiller, John.
Hopkins, Terry, First American Title.
House, Rod, Idaho State Archives/Historic Records Center.
Hatzenbuhler, Ron, ISU Professor.
Jackson, Kathy, Reubens City Clerk.
Jatkevicius, Jim. Boise Public Library.
Kenyon, Dale.
Kesler, Kelly.
Kunau, Lex.
Lierman, Amy. Public Relations, Idaho Transportation Dept. "History of I-84 US93 and Hwy 25." April 26, 2006.
Marshall, Ron.
Matheson, John.
Mendiola, Judy.

Merrill, Nancy, Former Eagle Mayor.

Miller, Amy.

Miller, Wendy.

Moldenhauer, Rocky and Dawn.

Moser, Lynn, Eagle Sewer District.

Ogden, Jerry.

Parrish-Manwaring, Angelyn.

Peak, Clifford.

Porath, Mrs.

Pruett, Jimmy J.

Richardson, Greg.

Rupe, Kevin.

Sales, Dorothy.

Scott, Diane, Eagle Historical Preservation Commission.

Sims, Larry, Hauser Fire Chief.

Standley, Carla, a historian writing a book about the PI&N Railroad and a genral historian and researcher of Meadows Valley.

Stephens, Dick, 1964.

Stevens, Louise Powers, September 29, 1994.

Thomasen, Everta. February 26, 2007.

Trent, Geneva, Eagle Historical Museum.

Urquidi, Richard.

Utt, Edith.

Valantine, Virgil.

Wallace, Doris, EISF Manager, 2005.

Ward, Opal.

Wiggers, Gene, Chief Pocatello Project. 2008.

Made in the USA
Middletown, DE
19 February 2021